Holding up a Mirror

Holding up a Mirror

How Civilizations Decline

Anne Glyn-Jones

CENTURY · LONDON

This edition published by Century Books Limited 1996

1 3 5 7 9 10 8 6 4 2

Century
Random House UK Ltd, 20 Vauxhall Bridge Road, London SW1V 2SA

Arrow Books Ltd
Random House UK Ltd, 20 Vauxhall Bridge Road, London SW1V 2SA

Random House Australia (Pty) Limited
20 Alfred Street, Milsons Point, Sydney,
New South Wales 2061, Australia

Random House New Zealand Limited
18 Poland Road, Glenfield
Auckland 10, New Zealand

Random House South Africa (Pty) Limited
PO Box 337, Bergvlei, South Africa

Random House UK Limited Reg No 954009

A CIP catalogue record for this book
is available from the British Library

Papers used by Random House UK Limited are natural, recyclable products made from wood
grown in sustainable forests. The manufacturing processes conform to the environmental
regulations of the country of origin.

ISBN 0 7126 7633 3

Typeset by Deltatype Ltd, Ellesmere Port, Cheshire

Printed and bound in the United Kingdom by
Mackays of Chatham plc, Chatham, Kent

Preface

During the evening of 7 November 1917 Bolshevik rebels in Petrograd stormed through the gilded façade of the Winter Palace, where, in a gold and malachite chamber hung with crimson brocade, Kerensky's provisional government sat, fearful and indecisive. Pitirim Sorokin, a twenty-seven-year-old lecturer at the university and a leading activist in the Socialist Revolutionary Party, whose members formed the bulk of the provisional government, heard from his home the mounting furore in the streets and went, in an impotent little procession of local political representatives, through the unlit streets towards the Palace, hoping to negotiate for the safety of the ministers, the cadets and the regiment of women soldiers, all that was left of the guards. They failed to reach the Palace. The ministers were arrested and removed to prison, the cadets murdered and the women raped.

That is the story as told by Sorokin in his *Leaves from a Russian Diary*. He had been born north of St Petersburg in 1889, the child of illiterate peasants. His mother died, the children were frightened of their drunken father, and by the age of ten Pitirim and his fourteen-year-old brother had left home and were earning a living of sorts gilding icons and church domes in north-west Russia. Rescued and educated by the Orthodox Church, Pitirim proved an outstanding scholar, achieving high academic honours and a teaching post at St Petersburg University. He had also become an active revolutionary, which resulted in his serving a prison sentence under the Tsarist government. By the spring of 1917 he was acting as personal assistant to Prime Minister Kerensky.

After the Bolshevik revolution he was again arrested, and this time he was condemned to death. Thanks to the influence of old comrades in the revolutionary movement, he was released – to a life in which someone else was living in his flat, and the new occupant had burnt all his books and papers for fuel. Following the introduction of Trotsky's policy of permitting recalcitrant intellectuals to go into exile, Sorokin left his homeland in 1922 and after a brief sojourn in Czechoslovakia spent the remainder of his life in the United States, first at the University of Minnesota, and later at Harvard, where he established, and became head of, the Department of Sociology. He died in 1968.

He had experienced, at first hand, social theory in action. For most of the two decades after he arrived in America he was working out his own interpretation of why societies change. Founding fathers of sociology such as Max Weber had urged that if it was to qualify as a science, sociology must strictly avoid value judgements. Sorokin, on the contrary, considered that an understanding of human societies could not begin without an assessment of what people cared about, and how that influenced their activities. He sought to analyse the dominant temper of the age across many different civilizations, from ancient Babylon to twentieth-century America.

The great problem, of course, is that research into what makes a society tick cannot take place in a laboratory, as can investigations in the physical sciences. Instead, hypotheses have to be tested through the process of statistical correlation. This requires the amassing of a vast quantity of factual data. Sorokin recruited an army of collaborators and research teams based in Prague and in Cambridge, Massachusetts. With their help he analysed the manifestations of the human spirit in different periods and among different peoples, as revealed in painting, sculpture, literature, architecture and music – not in aesthetic terms but in terms of social content. For instance: were the subjects religious or secular? Aristocratic or common people? How was nudity portrayed – erotically or ascetically? What social priorities did literature express – e.g. duty or comfort? He worked through developments in philosophy and politics, in science and technology, and he looked at the way changing attitudes were reflected in changes in the law and in the delineation of crime. He examined too the scale and intensity of wars and civil commotion.

These vast labours provided the material for his *Social and Cultural Dynamics*, the first volume of which was published in 1937. The whole work runs to some three thousand pages, many of them packed with statistics and written in language which employs more sociological jargon than most non-specialists find palatable.

Before publication was complete, the Second World War broke out, and by the time it was over there was not much interest in sweeping analyses of society at large other than Marxism, a creed for which Sorokin foresaw only a limited future but which had the fashionable advantage of immediate pragmatic application.* Sorokin was forgotten. But he does not deserve to be. In the fifty years since his theories were first published, events have justified his predictions at every level.

I have written this book, which incorporates much research not available at the time he wrote, in the hope of bringing his ideas to a new generation of readers. Understanding what Sorokin called the social and cultural dynamics operating within society can help us to assess where our own society stands, and enable us to form our judgements and choose our courses of action with greater insight into what we are doing. In order to enliven the picture of the societies under examination, I have used anecdote and example rather than statistics. Those who seek a firmer foundation for scientific persuasiveness must return to the original sources in *Social and Cultural Dynamics*.[†]

Sorokin's vast canvas stretched far more widely, geographically, chronologically and in terms of subject matter, than I can attempt to do, and in the light of current debates on multiculturalism, I must record my admission that my own researches are limited to aspects of only four civilizations, all of them European, namely ancient Greece, ancient Rome, medieval Christendom, and England since the Reformation. This book traces four main strands in the development of these four civilizations: the process of change in philosophy and theology; the impact of these changes both on our ideas of right and wrong, and on knowledge about the physical world (and hence on our capacity to manipulate it, particularly in relation to economic and medical development); and finally how these developments interact with and are manifested in creative art as represented by the theatre.

In his search for what the arts can tell us about the temper of the societies in which they flourished, Sorokin mentions, but gives only cursory attention to, drama and the theatre. Shakespeare's Hamlet says of the theatre that it is 'to hold, as t'were, the mirror up to nature; to show . . . the very age and body of the time . . .'. The reflections in that mirror are a major constituent of this book, but there are other mirror-images included within its pages, images where different civilizations or centuries mirror one another (as Barbara Tuchmann noted when she

---

* Sponsorship, and hence career prospects, in sociology departments favoured studies restricted in scope to topics relevant to practical application, such as research into crime, drugs or violence; into the needs of special groups in society, the elderly, the disabled, racial or religious minorities; into town planning and its relevance to the life of the neighbourhood; into transport and the impact of the motor car.
† For those who find that prospect too daunting, I recommend *History, Civilisation and Culture*, a trenchant exegesis by F.R. Cowell.

called her analysis of the fourteenth century *A Distant Mirror*); and in its final chapters, the book seeks to capture unadorned an image of the society of our own time and place, and present it – for reflection of quite another kind.

I owe a great debt of gratitude to the Western European Studies Centre (now the European Studies Centre) at the University of Exeter, whose award to me in the years 1985 to 1991 of an Honorary Research Fellowship gave me access to invaluable expertise as well as space and the use of university facilities. In a work so extensively dependent on the scholarly researches of others, librarians have been of inestimable value in my pursuit of texts, and I record my especial gratitude to Sue Parr and her colleagues of Devon Library Services (Topsham branch), Jane Lashbrook of Devon and Cornwall Constabulary Force Library, Peter Thomas of Exeter Cathedral Library, and, among the university librarians, Virginia Newton of the Postgraduate Medical School Library, Paul Kershaw of the Law Library, and subject librarians Susanna Guy and Stuart Macwilliam, on whose special expertise in classics, social studies and history I extensively relied. I am also much indebted to the librarians of the British Theatre Association and of the Theatre Museum, London, which inherited the Association's collection following its sad demise. John Alderson, former Chief Constable of Devon and Cornwall, spared time to acquaint me with aspects of modern policing, and draw appropriate texts to my attention. My school Latin and Greek and rudimentary German proving quite unequal to the task of comprehending documents of which no English or French translations existed, I owe a great deal to Frank Pollock for helping me with German texts; Professor Wiseman of the University of Exeter Classics Department, both for help with Latin and for cogent advice; and Hugh Stubbs for Greek, and in particular for translating for me, annotated with his own frequently ribald witticisms, the whole of Chorikios's lengthy 'Defence of the Mime'. Professor Emeritus Duncan Mitchell, formerly of Exeter's Sociology Department, and James Smeall, formerly Principal of St Luke's College (now the University of Exeter School of Education), read and advised on the text as it progressed, and I owe more than I can say to their unstinted encouragement and support.

There is no tribute to diligent typists; the wonders of the modern word-processor enabled me to do all that for myself, thanks to boundless help and advice from Neil Brooks and his colleagues of the University Information Technology Services.

Finally, the whole undertaking would have been very difficult, perhaps impossible, without Sheila Gardner of Devon County Home

Preface

Help Service and, later, Jan Robshaw, Jackie Cuthbert and the staff of Courtlands, Exmouth, whose devoted and kindly care of my mother in her ninth and tenth decades freed me to pursue the lengthy researches on which this work is based. My grateful thanks to them all.

Anne Glyn-Jones
Topsham, November 1995

Chapter 1

Illusion and Reality: Does It Matter Which Is Which?

Is there any reality other than the one we can hear and see and smell and touch? If so, is it in the end the only reality that matters, when all the material world of our experience, including ourselves, has been absorbed into Nature's unending process of recycling?

No one knows. But human beings hold, and have always held, strong opinions on the subject, and have sought to fashion their societies according to these beliefs.

In communities dominated by belief in some other, non-material world, the purpose of life on earth is to obey the Unseen Powers, either in the hope of personal salvation in an afterlife or at least to be worthy of protection or favour in this; at its most extreme, a life of anxious supplication and propitiation. Whether the dominant emotion in the devotee is fear or adoration, the morality is strict; and since deviation may result in disaster for the whole community, it will be firmly enforced by law. Sorokin identified Greek society prior to the fifth century BC, and European civilization from about the fifth to the twelfth centuries AD, as being predominantly of this type. Khomeini's Iran is an obvious contemporary example.[1]

Such a society, which Sorokin calls 'ideational', distrusts the experience of the senses as illusory, believing that reality is immaterial, transcendental, eternal and unchanging. It is to be experienced by looking inwards into the soul, not outwards at the world around us. Truth is attained through revelation, its interpreters are the priests and prophets. Proposed changes to the existing way of doing things are tested by reference to sacred books and traditions. Men and women do not feel restricted by supposed biological limits, for there is a strong belief in the power of mind over matter. Fire-walking or yogic demonstrations such as remaining alive without food or air are products of this point of view. Miracles are taken for granted – they are a logical outcome of prevailing attitudes; and when in sickness or distress, believers will place much

7

more faith in miracles than in medicine. Where the other world counts for so much, frugality in daily life, even asceticism, is admired and emulated.

A society less worried by a sense of impotence in the face of occult forces, more confident about its ability to control its environment, can dare to relax in its enjoyment of the material world. Attitudes towards human aspirations become more gentle. The Unseen Powers are envisaged as positively benign and understanding of human beings, whose happiness is now a legitimate objective, though only achievable within the moral framework established by the transcendent world. The material world begins to be valued for its own sake, for its beauty and bounteousness, and its potential begins to be explored. But while the material world is now accepted as real and important, it is not seen as having any authority in the realm of values, either moral or aesthetic. Sorokin calls such societies 'idealist'. Greece in the fifth and fourth centuries BC he views as conforming predominantly to this approach to truth, which in Europe was ending by the fourteenth century.

In a society in which materialism is the only reality recognized, the purpose of life is fulfilment in the here and now, the pursuit of happiness, which is increasingly interpreted in material terms. (This does not exclude, at least in theory, an altruistic preference for someone else's fulfilment rather than one's own, as in the self-sacrifice of the committed Marxist on behalf of some other generation.) Europe and America since the eighteenth century clearly exemplify this trend,* as did Greece of the third and subsequent centuries BC. Roman writers themselves identified the second century BC as the period when the values of their own society began to shift towards what we would now call consumerism.

The pursuit of happiness is worthless unless each individual can pursue his own definition of what for him constitutes happiness; thus individualism is a marked characteristic of hedonistic societies. In the early phases of the evolution from a society based on otherworldly tenets, a vestigial absolute moral order may remain, but absolutes give way to relatives. Law is brought into conformity with the demand for maximum choice in the pursuit of personal fulfilment, subject only to constraints where conduct might lead to unhappiness for others; thus in our own society the law has been amended to decriminalize abortion and homosexual practices between consenting adults, and to abolish such

---

* Sorokin pushed the dating back to the sixteenth century, but there is room for continuing dispute about the depth and direction of the impact of the Reformation and Counter-Reformation.

impediments to personal self-expression as the censorship of literature or the theatre.

In this system of thought, 'true reality and true value is sensory . . . beyond the reality and value perceived by our sense organs there is no other reality and no value.'[2] When Sorokin called such societies 'sensate', he chose a word implying not only the pursuit of sensual satisfaction, but also the instruments by which truth was to be apprehended. Knowledge must be tested by practical experiments. The importance of the senses for the collection of evidence is enhanced by every available and inventable way of extending sensory perception, such as microscopes and telescopes. The interpreters of this version of truth, the validity of which permeates almost all assumptions, are the scientists.

Of course no society of any size or complexity is a pure manifestation of any of these world views. Exponents of all three, and variants of them, exist in all societies, though unevenly distributed among different social groups and different historical epochs. In some ages philosophic confusion is such that no world-view is dominant, and such transitional periods, when there are no accepted criteria of conduct or belief, may be very uncomfortable for those – in government or in the family, for instance – in positions of responsibility for others. At the other extreme are societies that are clearly dominated by a *Weltanschauung* that is widely shared; but even so it will contain maverick individuals, and whether they are tolerated as eccentrics, imprisoned as dissidents or expunged as heretics, their attitudes are the germ from which will spring the orthodoxy of a different generation.

These three different views of the world and our place in it can be traced in the evolution of law and custom; in the relationship between religion and science; in attitudes to technology, and to the exploitation of the material world; in the dominant philosophies, political, moral and metaphysical; and in the way in which different societies behave. Above all, they are made manifest in the arts.[*]

Sorokin's analysis paid particular attention to painting. The purpose of the analysis is *not* to establish some sort of hierarchy of aesthetic

---

[*] To use any one field of human endeavour in isolation from others as the basis for a contention about the values dominant at a particular time and place is a form of circular reasoning, since the evidence available is precisely what has been used to establish the criteria on which judgement is based. Only when the criteria are applied across several fields does the argument have cogency. Bearing that caveat in mind, the arts are the clearest window through which to view the culture of an age and assess its standing on the religious/materialist spectrum, or 'ideational/sensate', to use Sorokin's more specialized though rather ponderous vocabulary.

excellence (an ambition which in any case would be hard put to escape the accusation of being purely subjective), but to illustrate through its art what mattered most to the society under scrutiny.

Sorokin's conclusion, based on the massive collection of data provided by his teams of collaborators, was that ideational art is largely abstract or symbolic. He maintains that the seemingly crude art of primitive peoples is not the result of lack of skill; some simply chose to be non-naturalistic. Female figurines all bust and belly are not failed attempts to depict twentieth-century sex goddesses, they are saying something symbolic about fertility. Evidence abounds among the cave paintings of early times to show that primitive peoples did not lack talent for representational art. The style derives not from the degree of creative ability, but from the viewpoint being expressed.

Others have pointed out how reluctant deeply religious societies are to represent the Unseen Powers except symbolically. Islam was not alone in forbidding representations of the Deity; and Joseph Vogt, in *The Decline of Rome*, remarks on the Old Testament prohibition of images which the early Christians inherited from the synagogue. The gravestones in the catacombs, he notes, depict fish, bread and wine; the earliest pictorial representation of Christ, a fresco in the baptistry of a house-church, probably dates from the third century. As more naturalistic depictions occur they take symbolic form – such as Christ the Good Shepherd.[*3]

Sorokin's 'idealist' art registers the natural world, but uses it to depict religious topics. Serenity, permanence, beauty and imperturbability are the hallmarks. The icons of Byzantium typify this phase. As Marina Warner has said, 'Icons get under the skin of reality[†] and convince us that they are showing the supernatural from the inside, precisely because they are so indifferent to the look, scale and colour of reality.'[4] 'Worldly'

---

[*] Robin Lane Fox, in *Pagans and Christians* (pp.393–4), makes a similar point. 'However much we search for this ''early Christian art'' and ponder the meanings of the crude paintings in the Roman catacombs, we cannot bridge the gap between its schematized, symbolic style and the artistic patronage of the upper classes in the pagan cities . . . Only one group of early Christians, the heretical Carpocratians, are known to have owned portraits of Christ . . . In a famous scene, the ''Acts of John'', (*c*.300) told how a pagan convert had attempted to paint John's portrait in Ephesus, but the Apostle had denounced him for daring to perpetuate his form in the material world . . . The exceptions are very modest . . . By the mid-third century variable figures of Christ . . . could be seen in wall paintings of the house-church in Dura . . . Early Christian art was based firmly on Scripture and used a densely compressed symbolism which expressed much more than it represented. In the Book of Revelation . . . God appears in the abstract, like a precious stone, blazing in brilliant red and white . . .'

[†] Quite what constitutes 'reality' is, of course, precisely what is at issue between the three differing cultures.

10

pagan art had disappeared by the sixth century. In Western art, the Madonna is a beautiful but entirely non-erotic young woman, Christ is a child, but the symbolic strand is still there, and the child is often portrayed as a small-scale adult, wise, suffering or regal. Scenes of the Crucifixion portray a dying king, any element of common humanity is absent. Not until the end of the first millennium does any suggestion of the sensuous enter the art of Christian nations.

Gradually the natural world impinges on the world of art. Landscapes begin to fill the background of religous paintings, at first as elements in a biblical story, then as celebrations of nature in its own right. Francis A. Schaeffer, in *Escape from Reason*, calls attention to a Van Eyck miniature of 1410.

> It measures only about five inches by three inches. But it is a painting with tremendous significance ... the theme is Jesus' baptism, but this takes up only a small section of the area. There is a river in the background, a very real castle, houses, hills and so on – this is a real landscape; nature has become important.

He traces further steps in the progression by which, to use his words, 'nature' becomes autonomous and then proceeds first to challenge and finally to eliminate 'grace'. In 1435 Van Eyck paints a picture in which the donor is portrayed the same size as the Madonna instead of smaller. Towards the end of the same century a more startling change occurs, when Filippo Lippi not only depicts the Madonna as a pretty girl rather than an otherworldly symbol, but his model is widely known to be his mistress.[5]

Traditional Christians opposed this laxity. 'You have given the Virgin the dresses of courtesans ... That is how the divine cult is profaned,' thundered Savonarola in Tuscany.[6] Infrared photographs taken in 1987 of Stefan Lochner's Altar der Stadtpatrone in Cologne Cathedral 'show beneath the head of the Madonna another, sketched, head which is remarkably different. The sketch is of a pretty, smiling girl with large eyes and long wavy hair. The final version, which was done in 1445, is of a much primmer, more serious-looking Madonna, with her hair brushed severely back. In the sketch St Ursula wears a low neckline and an enormous brooch on her dress. In the picture the dress is closed to the neck and without the brooch.'[7] Clearly Lochner had moved too fast for his patrons.

Meanwhile, early in the fourteenth century, what claims to be the first pure landscape of the Christian era was painted – *A Castle by a Lake*, by

Ambrogio Lorenzetti. It can be seen today in the Pinacoteca Nazionale in Siena. Similar claims to be the first secular paintings are made for the wall frescos with which the papal palace in Avignon is decorated. The papal bedchamber has walls and ceilings covered with depictions of hundreds of birds perched on trailing vines; the beautiful *chambre du cerf*, painted in 1343, is filled with lively accounts of hunting, fishing and other country pursuits. By the fifteenth century secular illuminated manuscripts are appearing, inspired by hunting and falconry. Lavishly illustrated copies of Gaston Phébus's *Livre de chasse*, for instance, are extant, allowing full scope to depictions of horse and hound, stags and boars, lords and ladies, their castles and retainers.

Sorokin classifies only the late twelfth, the thirteenth and part of the fourteenth centuries as idealistic, after which religious symbolism is largely superseded by naturalistic, visual art. The Child is a genuine baby, not a symbol of majesty. From the period of the Renaissance it is the humanity rather than the spirituality of Christ that is being stressed. *Et incarnatus est.* As Leo Steinberg explains in his *The Sexuality of Christ in Renaissance Art and in Modern Oblivion*, 'In many hundreds of pious, religious works, from before 1400 to past the mid sixteenth century, the ostensive unveiling of the Child's sex or the touching, protecting or presentations of it, is the main action. And the emphasis recurs in images of the dead Christ . . . proving nothing less than what the Creed itself puts at the center: God's descent into manhood.'[8]

The Reformation and the Counter-Reformation marked a temporary ebb in the sensate tide, as the Church, both Protestant and Catholic, fought a rearguard action against the rising tide of humanism. In the Vatican, following the Council of Trent, de Voleterra was commissioned to clothe St Blaise and St Catherine of Alexandria, shown nude in the Sistine Chapel. Puritanism painted out the wall frescos, tore down the statues and smashed the stained-glass windows.

The recoil did not last. Religious art begins to lose its serenity, concerning itself with torment, both in this world and in the world to come. Satan, who, until about the twelfth century, had been a fallen angel, becomes more demonic. Sorokin considers that by the end of the fifteenth century religious art has entirely ceased to be, in his sense of the word, idealist.[9] The dead Christ is a corpse. The tortures of the damned become increasingly prominent, and by the sixteenth and seventeenth centuries have reached sadistic proportions. But alongside it a sensate art is developing, celebrating humanity and its preoccupations in this world. The Renaissance rediscovery of classicism chose the Roman and Hellenistic world in its full sensate phase; and when biblical subjects were portrayed, interest centred on those with the greatest erotic or voluptuous possibilities (Susanna bathing, for instance).

Ideational art was often an object of veneration in itself, carrying a message beyond itself. Sensate art is art for art's sake, and it is intended to entertain. Baroque develops into rococo, which Fowler's *Modern English Usage* delightfully defines as 'a form taken by baroque when it aimed no longer at astounding the spectator with the marvellous, but rather at amusing him with the ingenious'.[10] After 1767 a new phrase, 'fine arts', gains currency, implying, according to the *Oxford Dictionary*, the arts which are concerned with 'the beautiful' or which appeal to taste.

The subject matter glorifies the material world. 'Turner relocates divinity, hitherto the prerogative of religious painting . . . in the secular tradition of landscape,' says the art critic Andrew Graham-Dixon. 'Whether he actually said so or not, in his art the sun *is* God.'[11] No longer enmeshed in the portrayal of eternal verities, the world of Being, sensate art explores the changing surfaces of the world of Becoming. The Impressionists could return over and over again to the same subject, painting it in new colours each time according to how the light fell or the seasons advanced. Michael Brenson, discussing Monet's work, says, 'since light in nature is constantly changing, painting the movement of light was a form of realism'[12] – again, a reminder that it is the exploration of phenomena rather than the search after metaphysical essences that now constitutes 'reality'.

The Impressionists, remarks Christopher Lloyd, Surveyor of the Queen's Pictures, 'record the pleasures and disappointments of every-day life, as opposed to the religious, historical or mythological themes that preoccupied their predecessors'.[13] Nicholas Wadley, assessing the nineteenth-century art critic Edmond Duranty, quotes his insistence that the credibility of 'the new painting' depended 'on truth to the reality of daily life in the modern world'.[14] The high life of the nobility yields pride of place to middle-class solidity before interest switches to the low life of the prostitute and the pimp. Graham-Dixon's insights into Degas provide an apt commentary:

Degas painted laundresses, aching, stretching and drinking their way through days of unrelieved tedium; alcoholics (as in the famous *L'Absinthe*); and, above all, prostitutes . . . Prostitutes sprawl or lie carelessly across sofas in dim, seedy interiors; their clients are sheepish, guilt-ridden gents in suits, or brutish gawpers, like the fatuously beaming chap who leers up at the nude taking a bath in *L'Admiration*. The brothel is more than a topical milieu, for

Degas. A place of sad, transitory couplings, it comes to stand for the modern world itself: as soon forgotten as experienced, emptied of moral significance.

And he goes on to say: 'They are modern pictures, in that Degas's nudes take their place in no discernible narrative, express no high ideals, embody no moral philosophy. They simply exist.'[15]

The willingness to explore simple existence, unconstrained by taste or illusion, is exemplified in the same critic's assessment of Lucien Freud's mid-twentieth-century nudes, his 'undoubted masterpieces'.

Breasts are rarely pert, self-sustaining, in these pictures; they droop and sag, veinously overabundant, from bodies marked by the dimples and creases and stretchmarks of time. Pubic hair is disobedient to bikini-line convention. Vaginas are unconcealed – there is no sense, in Freud, of genteel propriety. These bodies are rendered with a mature, open-eyed awareness of physical realities – modern *vanitas* paintings, Freud's nudes are ripe with mortality ... analogies for his glum, lonely sense of himself and others ...[16]

Loneliness, that ultimate perquisite of untrammelled individualism, is a quality that distinguishes the work of another highly praised twentieth-century painter – Francis Bacon.

In almost all Bacon's paintings man is displayed in absolute solitude, and deliberately severed from his fellows by a suffering which no pity can allay ... the solitude in Bacon's paintings is not simply the loneliness of consciousness: it is a solitude of flesh and is revealed precisely by the torturing of the flesh, which has nothing to give, nothing at all, save the solitary 'I', fought out, in a glare of electric light, and usually in some highly focused raised area such as a podium or cage. It is this 'I' which is projected by Bacon's screaming mouths ... Bacon gives us no simple or dogmatic answers to the question of our nature: he tells us only that we are *here* and *now*; this is the source of our solitude, and the occasion of our responsibility for a life that we alone can live ...[17]

'Ebullient despair' is Bacon's own description of his work.[18] Bernard Levin has commented that Bacon's version of the Crucifixion is a story of shame, degradation, failure and death, lacking all those intimations of triumph, incorruptibility and eternal life with which earlier artists had managed to invest their paintings of the Passion.[19] His subject matter has included *Paralytic Child on All Fours*, two pictures of a friend dying on the lavatory of a haemorrhage, and assorted pictures of homosexual activities, including 'his most important work in the permanent collection . . . his central panel of buggers'.[20]

Obsessive representational authenticity is not, however, the only influence at work. The human psyche is easily bored. Writing in the second century BC, the Greek historian Polybius remarked, 'I would appeal to the testimony of Nature herself, who in the case of any of the senses never elects to go on persistently with the same allurements, but is ever fond of change . . .', and he goes on to illustrate how ear, palate, eye and even intellect require variety.[21] The more 'sensate' the content of the art, the more rapidly novelty is sought, and 'innovative' becomes the highest accolade.[*] Sorokin emphasizes that, as the palate becomes jaded, the appetite must be stimulated by stronger fare.

> The basic sensory values, through constant repetition, come to lose the fascination of novelty – to become hackneyed and boring. Without novelty, the entertainment value begins to evaporate . . . The art is forced, under these circumstances, to pass rapidly from one object, event, style and pattern to another, at an ever increasing tempo . . . [hence] . . . the morbid concentration of sensate art on pathological types of persons and events.[22]

For the best part of a century we have seen a challenge to the boredom of representational, naturalistic art from a changing spectrum of modern artists – the Cubists, Dadaists, futurists, surrealists. Although Sorokin recognized that they constituted a revolt against the sensate art of surface appearances, he saw them as an artistic cul-de-sac rather than as harbingers of a new ideational art, since they remain, in his opinion, rooted in the exploration of the material world; not least when the use of three dimensions (sculpture) introduces an additional sense – that of touch.[†23]

So far as popular art and entertainment are concerned, the result of this tendency to boredom is a search for an increasingly provocative appeal to increasingly anaesthetized emotions, with ever-cruder depictions of

---

[*] A trait well explored by Christopher Booker in his 1969 publication, *The Neophiliacs* (London: Collins).

[†] By the same token, nor does a political revolution changing the beneficiaries of the economic system but not the materialist assumptions on which it operates constitute a change on the ideational-sensate spectrum.

violence, and a progressively more explicit treatment of sex, until sex and violence coalesce in the amalgam of pornography.

Traditionalists may find such an art distasteful. But it may well co-exist with – indeed, as this book seeks to show, it is implicit in Sorokin's analysis of the values inherent in sensate societies that it is *likely* to co-exist with – increasingly successful manipulation of the material world, and thus rising living standards. Christopher Booker, using architecture as his medium of interpretation, illustrates the point.

> Architecture is ultimately about human identity – it is one of the most important external things which help to tell us who we are. There is no clearer book in which to read changes in the prevailing view of who we are and what is most important to us than in the kinds of building which our civilization has raised over the past 800 years.
>
> In the soaring verticals of the great Gothic cathedrals we see the reflection of a society ultimately centred on its sense of the transcendent. In the harmoniously proportioned horizontals of the Renaissance or the 18th-century terraces of Bath, we see a society becoming more materialistic and 'man-centred', but for which the highest values were still aesthetic and intellectual.
>
> In the hideous sprawl of the 19th-century factories, railways and slums, we see a society for which the highest value was becoming man's material power to transform nature. In the suburban semis of the first half of the 20th century, we see the true architecture of democracy, everyone an individual in his own individual (though almost identical) box.
>
> Finally, in the neogargantuan architecture of the past 30 years, the great office blocks and housing estates, shopping centres and multi-storey car parks, we see the full visible reflection of a society whose highest values are material comfort for the greatest number, and the re-submergence of the individual in a new kind of collectivism, based on subservience to the all-providing machine.'[24]

The emotions of awe and sublimity inspired by a Gothic cathedral may be absent from the multi-storey car park, but the latter represents a society in which a far higher proportion of people are warm, well fed, well sheltered, well clothed, and, if not 'well' read, at least literate. Who is to say that the one civilization is somehow less 'great' than the other?

Yet a sense of unease persists in our Western society, and seems to be deeper than the simple recognition that new contenders like Japan are achieving levels of wealth comparable to, or even in excess of, those we have enjoyed. We know that past civilizations with notable achievements to their credit have not reached some plateau and remained there. They have 'fallen'. Subsequent generations look back on ruined cities where diminished populations live in squalor and wretchedness, where the struggle for bare existence leaves no place for either the creation or the enjoyment of any but the most minimum level of artistic endeavour, and where, if conquest or infiltration by outsiders has accompanied the decline, as it all too often has, even the language and place names of the people may have been wiped out. The uneasy are uncomfortably aware that what Sorokin calls the sensate phase, others have called decadent, effete or 'aged'.

Are we trapped in some ineluctable process which it is beyond our power to influence? When, in 146 BC, the victorious Roman general Scipio stood watching flames consume the Carthage he had been sent to destroy, there were tears in his eyes, and his *aide-de-camp* heard him murmuring lines from Homer's *Iliad*, foretelling the destruction of Troy. When questioned, he said that his tears were for Rome, for his own nation, which must share the fate of all things human. 'All cities, nations, and authorities must, like men, meet their doom.'[25]

His fears were a little premature. The Roman Republic had another century to run, the Empire had yet to come into being. But in the long run, of course, the intuition was to prove correct.

Hindu and Buddhist philosophies take a cyclical view of events, in which similar sequences recur across the aeons of eternity. Christians, Marxists and humanists share the assumption that history is linear; not only are events moving in one direction, the journey is from worse to better, notwithstanding digressions, deviations and temporary breakdowns on the way. Medieval Christians admittedly were not sanguine about the direction of change; for them history was moving towards the final apocalypse, but this pessimistic assessment came to be superseded by the optimism of the Enlightenment. The linear viewpoint, however, can still accommodate a belief that so far as particular cultures or civilizations are concerned, Scipio's pessimism is well founded. But founded on what?

In his *Civilisation*, Kenneth Clark says, 'if one asks why the civilization of Greece and Rome collapsed, the real answer is that it was exhausted'.[26] Material resources can be exhausted, but to suggest that the well-springs of creativity have run dry raises more questions than it answers. Biological organisms can become exhausted; indeed the analogy of an organism, progressing from birth to death, is often used as if it explains the rise and fall of civilizations. The Romans themselves did so. The elder Seneca, writing his history in the early Empire, placed Rome's childhood in the time of the ancient kings and her youth during the conquest of Italy; maturity he identified as the period of overseas expansion beginning in 146 BC; and his own era he believed to be senescent, with the emperors the prop of an exhausted old age.[27]

But the concepts of youth, maturity and senility are not helpful when applied to structures that are not in themselves biological – however firmly grounded in the physical world their manifestations may be. The human beings of whom a culture is composed are renewed in each generation, and to say of a culture brimming with creative ideas that it is 'young' while a century later, in a period of artistic or innovative inertia, it is 'old' is to use labels, not to provide explanations. As Sorokin remarks, what does 'Gothic' mean in relation to childhood or adolescence?[28] The most comprehensive *tour d'horizon* along these lines is probably Spengler's *Decline of the West*, but fascinating though its mass of detail is, it remains a catalogue, it explains nothing, and is without predictive value.

For Toynbee civilization is not an organism of which human beings

---

* An example of the difficulties involved in the youth-maturity analogy may be found in the epilogue to Jean Gimpel's *The Medieval Machine*. Seeking to compare the growth and decline of medieval France with that of twentieth-century America, Gimpel says, 'I placed the beginning of France's mature age in 1254 when St Louis returned from the Crusades and stamped the age with his own decisive maturity, and its end in 1277 when mysticism gained ascendancy over reason.' He goes on, 'I chose 1850 as the year the United States entered her era of growth, and I tentatively considered 1953 to be the year she entered her era of maturity because that was the year in which the celebrated Lever House Building was constructed on New York's Park Avenue. A glass structure only 30 stories high and built primarily for aesthetic reasons rather than with a view to commercial profit, it symbolized a turning point in American psychology . . . Eventually I came to believe that 1947 might better be considered the point when the United States became ''mature'', for that was the year of the Truman Doctrine when the United States took upon herself the responsiblity for all the ''free world''.'

No unifying criteria underpin these judgements. They range from the personality of the head of state through varying priorities in philosophy and enterprise to power politics. Gimpel's analysis of an ageing civilization fares no better. Visiting America in 1956, he notices that people no longer hustle, they walk slowly and take long lunch breaks. They are no longer fascinated by gadgets, the evidence of a society's inventiveness – yet this very fascination for gadgets is advanced in the same chapter as one of the hallmarks of an outworn technology, as typified by the late Hellenistic period. To be fair, Gimpel does list twenty-one factors which he considers indicative of the 'age' of a society, almost all of them aspects of the economy, for the crucial measure of success or failure in his eyes is the extent of applied technology. But he takes a highly determinist attitude, remarking of the USA, for instance, 'When would the United States move out of her era of maturity into her ageing era? I forecast that this could happen as early as the 1970s, since the absolute preeminence of a nation often lasts only some twenty-five years.'

are the prisoners, but is a product of human choices. For Sorokin it is the changing convictions about what constitutes ultimate reality that fashion the choices made, and explain the rise and fall of civilizations. It is the culture of the people that determines whether their society will survive or perish. Thus, he dismissed all accounts of human societies which seek to explain change in terms of neurological or physiological psychology, or in environmental, racial, climatic, biological and economic theories: in Cowell's words, 'all mechanisms external to the character, personality and creative power of individuals'.[29]

A wholly sensate, materialist society, in Sorokin's opinion, ultimately loses all moral restraint to the point at which crime and lawlessness make the pursuit of happiness a hollow goal. Competition for goods becomes increasingly vicious as greed, untrammelled by other values, outstrips the speed at which resources can be induced to match demand. The resulting loss of social cohesion leaves the community defenceless; revulsion against moral anarchy and the sordidness of sensate arts invites belief in a new and more challenging philosophy of life, thus further disrupting traditional loyalties. In the end, the sensate society commits suicide.

All this the theatre faithfully reflects. Beginning as a form of worship; continuing with human protagonists wrestling with the commands, complexities and incomprehensibility of moral order; switching its focus from the heroic to the common man, its language from poetry to prose, its milieu from cloud-capped towers to kitchens, it seeks for attention through increasingly opulent spectacle and display, before conspiring with the prevailing ethos of late sensate society in an orgy of explicit violence and sex.

Chapter 2

From Metaphysics to Physics: the Sixth to Fourth Centuries in Greece

Drama begins as worship. It has its origins in the rituals of deeply religious societies. Margot Berthold, in *A History of World Theatre*, is describing the evolution of Sorokin's ideational society when she writes:

> In the second millennium BC . . . the people of Mesopotamia found that the contours of their harsh, despotic gods were growing milder. Men were beginning to credit them with justice and themselves with the capacity to obtain the god's benevolence. The gods were coming down to earth, becoming partners in the rituals. And with the descent of the god comes the beginning of theatre.[*][1]

'The art form begins with the god's epiphany and, in quite utilitarian terms, with man's effort to enlist the god's favour and help.'[2] Central to the god's epiphany are myths of a god or hero who dies annually and is reborn – myths which can be traced back at least six thousand years.[3] In ancient Greece that god was Dionysus, god of wine and of revelry, of fertility, exuberant life and the bounty of nature. To him were sacred the December village festivals and the Athenian floral festivals in February and March, when the people processed to the temples singing choral hymns in his honour.

These celebrations involve two deeply different emotional responses – jubilation at the joy of life; awe, even horror, at the mystery of death. Dionysus's traditional devotees, the prancing satyrs celebrating the vintage, their faces daubed with wine-dark mulberry juice, huge artificial phalluses symbolizing fertility and fecundity, are the originators, according to Aristotle, of comedy (from the Greek *komos*, a band of

[*] Fragments of tablets of *The Epic of Gilgamesh*, found recently in Soviet Armenia, are written in script form, with elements suggesting the presence of a chorus, an indication that this ancient epic may have been a drama some two thousand years before the first known Greek dramatic texts (Robert Temple, *The Times*, 15 October 1991).

20

revellers). Comedy stems, he holds, from 'the prelude to the phallic songs which still survive as institutions in many cities'.[4] Tragedy he traces to improvised elaborations explaining the content of the ensuing choral passage. Berthold believes that the choral hymns were not originally Dionysiac, but were amalgamated with the Dionysiac revelry during the sixth century BC.

'Tragedy' comes from the Greek for 'the song of the goat'. Already in classical times this puzzled people. The Roman poet Horace, writing in the first century BC, seems to have thought goats were involved because they were awarded as prizes, his translator correcting this misapprehension with the reminder that the frolicking chorus of satyrs forming part of the primitive procession were dressed in goat skins.[5] Virgil, Horace's contemporary, was nearer the truth when, in the *Georgics*, his panegyric to rural life, he spoke of the necessity to weave hedges to keep cattle from the vineyards because of the terrible damage they did.

> For no other crime is it that a goat is slain to Bacchus at every altar,
> and the olden plays enter on the stage; for this the sons of Theseus
> set up prizes for wit in their villages and at the crossways, and gaily
> danced in the soft meadows on oiled goat-skins.[6]

Martial, Roman poet of the late first century AD, followed Virgil, 'guilty of having gnawed a vine, a he-goat, doomed to die, stood at the altar, a victim, Bacchus, welcome to thy rites'.[7] But there may be a deeper symbolism involved in this rite of sacrifice – not just a punishment for wayward trespass, but the ritual dying of the ancient horned god.

About the middle of the sixth century BC a leading singer and dancer named Thespis introduced the idea of a soloist interacting with the chorus. This was followed by the use of male and female masks, and – in a development which shocked the older generation of Athenians – direct impersonation of the gods.[8]

Worship was taking dramatic form. During the last half of the sixth century the ruler of Athens enlarged the Festival of Dionysus and 'for the first time gave public status to a new art – tragic drama'.[9] Human beings as well as gods were now to figure in the rituals – though the human protagonists were limited to the high-born. In about 535 BC the first tragic contest was staged; and the winner was Thespis.

In 484 BC the prize for tragedy was won by a soldier poet who had fought at Marathon in 490 BC and was to serve again ten years later at the naval battle of Salamis, where the defeat of the enemy came only after Athens had been attacked and burnt, the temples of the Acropolis destroyed. His name was Aeschylus, and when he died in 456 BC it was not his plays that his epitaph recorded, but his service with the Athenian armed forces and the battles in which he had fought. He had first entered the contest in 499, at the age of twenty-five, but was forty by the time success at last came his way. The winning play is no longer extant; his earliest extant winning entry dates from 472, and is a reflection on the great war in which he was personally involved. It is called *The Persians.*

Eight years had passed since Salamis and the burning of Athens – almost as long as the decade which separates the end of World War I from R.C. Sherriff's agonized epic of the trenches, *Journey's End.* Aeschylus, however, is not concerned to explore the effect of war on human relations – indeed, as H.D.F. Kitto points out in *Greek Tragedy*,[10] his characters are not well rounded, their relationships shown as necessary to the theme rather than to other characters in the drama. And that theme is profoundly religious. Is there a supreme power guaranteeing 'a unity in things, some direction in events'? Aeschylus answers in the affirmative, and he identifies that power with Zeus. In Kitto's words, Aeschylus in *Persae* was

> constructing a religious drama out of the Persian War, in just the same spirit that he constructed another out of the Trojan War. Xerxes's hubris led him to break a divine law. He sinned as Paris sinned, and Agamemnon, and like those sinners he was punished by Zeus through instruments chosen by Zeus, Paris through the two sons of Atreus, Agamemnon through Clytemnestra, Xerxes through the Greeks and Greece.[11]

Victims, in Aeschylus, have fallen foul of some god as well as of a human being, and when the aggrieved human being wreaks vengeance, the god also is being avenged. The transcendental and the material worlds, the sacred and the profane, interpenetrate. Zeus engineers the Trojan War to avenge the wronged Menelaus, sending the army of the House of Atreus to fight it. Artemis, appalled at the slaughter, or (as a later version has it) angered at Agamemnon's wanton killing of one of her stags, requires him to sacrifice his daughter Iphigenia in order to obtain the winds needed for the ships to sail to Troy, trapping him in an action that seals his doom at the hands of his wife Clytemnestra – who has her own adulterous reasons for wishing him out of the way. Orestes, seeking vengeance for Agamemnon's death, confronts Clytemnestra in *Choephori* only to be told that if he kills her he will never escape pursuit by her Furies, to which his reply is that if he does not, he will be pursued by his father's Furies. Implacably, inescapably, outrage begets outrage.

In *Eumenides* Aeschylus is seeking a path out of this impasse. The Erinyes, the Furies, are the incarnation of blind, automatic vengeance. The dramatist shows the goddess Athena involving men as a jury rationally to determine degrees of guilt and punishment, with the Furies exacting measured retribution on behalf of society. The chorus of black-robed Erinyes reappear clothed now in purple, transformed into the Eumenides, Zeus's stern but merciful agents.

Throughout his work Aeschylus is absorbed by the question of man's relation to God, Fate, the Universe, rather than his relationship to his fellow man. In 466 BC, eighteen years after Aeschylus's first dramatic prize, and six years after *The Persians*, a new dramatist defeated Aeschylus to win first prize. Sophocles, who as a fifteen-year-old adolescent had led the chorus of triumph round the trophy raised at Salamis,[12] explored human character more profoundly than Aeschylus had done, but he shared Aeschylus's bleak appraisal of the impotence and vulnerability of human beings.

In Sophocles's treatment of the Trojan War and its aftermath, the same inexorable sequence of crime, revenge and retribution is manifested, but there is another element, an idea that is implicit in earlier treatments of the old legends but is perhaps never more explicit than in Sophocles's portrayal of the Oedipus story. Those who rescue the abandoned infant Oedipus and ensure his survival and adoption are acting morally, for the best. Yet their action makes possible the whole succession of horrors that results from his later unwitting incest with his mother. He is the victim of accursed behaviour in an earlier generation of his family, which is bringing its nemesis even unto the third and fourth generations.

Doctrines of the ineluctable working out of cause and effect in the moral sphere are familiar under the name of karma to today's adherents of Buddhist and Hindu philosophies, but belief in reincarnation provides a moral nexus between victim and perpetrator. No such cosy equation was open to Sophocles. The pain and bewilderment echo down the centuries, to today's child trapped in the black waters off Zeebrugge as the *Herald of Free Enterprise* foundered – 'But I've always been good, I've never told lies.' The naked injustice of suffering had to be confronted head on. For Sophoclean man, Margot Berthold points out, suffering is the hard but ennobling school of self-knowledge. The meaning of suffering lies in its apparent meaninglessness. For, 'in all this there is nothing that does not come from Zeus,' he says at the end of the *Trachinian Maidens*.[13]

His response is not the despair of Thomas Hardy – that we are sport for the gods. Divine caprice is not the explanation. There is a moral order in the universe to which even the gods themselves are ultimately subject. To believe that we control our own destiny, that intelligent calculation can enable us to evade the mystery of injustice, therein lies the ultimate pride, the sin of hubris. Beyond our understanding though it may be, if we reverence the gods, are humble in the face of our own ignorance, and strive to do the best we can in the circumstances, we have at least the option of living with dignity and self-respect.

What price, then, being alive at all? Nietzsche, in *The Birth of Tragedy*, on which he embarked in 1870, sought to explore the 'great note of interrogation concerning the value of existence' in the light of the work of the Greek tragedians.[14] 'Greek tragedy in its earliest form,' he says, 'had for its theme only the sufferings of Dionysos and . . . for some time the only stage hero therein was simply Dionysos himself.'[15] Dionysus stands for the basic creative urge, the will to live, the principle not of Being but of Becoming, primordial, remorseless, amoral, inexhaustible, irrevocable. But this very process of producing life, this Will to Become, results in separation, in individuation, in the vulnerability of individual consciousness. Nietzsche makes Apollo the god of this phase of 'shaping energies', of 'measured limitation'.

With consciousness comes the capacity to recognize the awfulness and absurdity of the human condition, the pain of existence, the inevitability of death. 'Apollo seeks to pacify individual beings precisely by drawing boundary lines between them and by again and again calling attention thereto, with his requirements of self-knowledge and due proportion, as the holiest laws of the Universe.'[16] Apollo represents the material world which we perceive with our senses, in contrast to the invisible creative energies represented by Dionysus. Nietzsche sides with those who entirely distrust sense perceptions as a gateway to apprehending reality. They can apprehend only 'phenomena', illusions, and thus Apollo's function fails to offer consolation to humanity. '. . . Only as an *aesthetic phenomenon* is existence and the world eternally *justified*.'[17] Art alone

> is able to transform these nauseating reflections on the awfulness or
> absurdity of existence into representations wherewith it is possible
> to live: these are the representations of the *sublime* as the artistic

subjugation of the awful, and the comic as the artistic delivery from the nausea of the absurd.[*18]

Dionysian art ... seeks to convince us of the eternal joy of existence ... joy not in phenomena but behind phenomena ... All that comes into being must be ready for a sorrowful end. We are compelled to look into the terrors of individual existence ... we are pierced by the maddening sting of those pains at the very moment when we have become, as it were, one with the immeasurable primordial joy in existence ... in spite of fear and pity, we are the happy living beings, not as individuals, but as the one living being, with whose procreative joy we are blended.[19]

There is a problem here, however, for 'all our knowledge of art is at bottom quite illusory because as knowing persons we are not one and identical with the Being who, as the sole author and spectator of this comedy of art, prepares a perpetual entertainment for himself'.[20] In the escape from this impasse lies a crucial aspect of Nietzsche's attitude to Greek tragedy, as well as an explanation of his tremendous influence on Wagner. 'Music stands in symbolic relation to the primordial contradiction and primordial pain in the heart of the Primordial Unity, and therefore symbolizes a sphere which is above all appearance and before all phenomena.'[21] Music, he says, drawing on Schopenhauer, is not a copy of a phenomenon (as are all other arts) but a direct copy of the will (the urge to creation) itself, and so represents the metaphysical essence of everything physical in the world. The comfort of the old tragedy was in the music – the full title of Nietzsche's essay is *The Birth of Tragedy from the Spirit of Music*.

Because the music has not survived we too easily forget that the Greek tragedies were nearer to oratorios than to plays. Actors were judged by their voices in language now used for opera singers.[22] The chorus is just that – a choir, albeit a mobile, dancing, gesturing choir; and the lyric poetry in which at moments of high emotion the characters express themselves is arias intended to be sung. The choirs were initially composed of local free citizens, amateurs; perhaps one should say worshippers. They performed with paid professionals, just as professional soloists perform with amateur choirs today – though all Greek performers were male, no women took part. The costs of the production

---

[*] The twentieth century, with its Theatre of Cruelty and its Theatre of the Absurd, was to reveal how late sensate art performed that transformation – see Chapter 18.

were borne by a wealthy local citizen appointed by the city-state, and as time went on the choir also came to consist of paid professionals. In Aeschylus's time the choir probably numbered about fifty, but the half-century after his death witnessed the stringencies of the Peloponnesian War, and possibly for economic reasons the chorus in Euripides's time is thought to have numbered only about fifteen. Though the chorus are dramatis personae, representing in different plays the peoples of Thebes, for instance, or a group of sailors, their dramatic role varies. Sometimes, as in the chorales of Bach's St John and St Matthew Passions, they stand outside the action, brooding on the unfolding saga; sometimes they are participants, as in the Passion music when the chorus represents the crowd baying, 'Crucify him! Crucify him!'

With Euripides comes a change. Born on the day of the battle of Salamis, while Aeschylus fought and the teenage Sophocles prepared to dance at the victory celebrations, his first play appeared in 455 BC, when he was twenty-five. Aeschylus had died the previous year, creative almost to the last, with his masterpiece of the Trojan War, the *Oresteia* trilogy, produced in 458. Sophocles and Euripides were to contest the remaining decades of the century between them, both dying in 406 BC, one aged nearly ninety, the other seventy-four.

Symbolic of Euripides's new approach was his choice of music. 'His music, according to Aristophanes, who burlesqued it, was adapted from popular sources.'[23] Nietzsche called this new kind of music 'tone-painting', a reflection of the natural world and thus no longer the direct manifestation of the creative ultimate reality, but only of phenomena, of appearances. Among the elements of the new music, Sorokin pinpoints an increasing secular component whose main aim is to give pleasure, and a rising appeal to individual emotions rather than sacerdotal serenity, coupled with enhanced technical complexities designed to impress. He identifies it as 'sensate' music, and quotes Plato for the view that Euripides was at the boundary line of decadence.[24]

Deprived of metaphysical comfort through the sublimity of the music, the austere vision of the world presented by Aeschylus and Sophocles becomes unbearable. It must be made more palatable to human self-respect. Plato, in *The Republic*, says:

Nor must we allow our young people to be told by Aeschylus that 'Heaven implants guilt in man, when his will is to destroy a house utterly.' If a poet writes of the sorrows of Niobe or the calamities of the house of Pelops or of the Trojan War, either he must not speak of them as the work of a god, or, if he does so, he must devise some such explanation as we are now requiring: he must say that what the god did was just and good, and the sufferers were the better for being chastized. One who pays a just penalty must not be called miserable, and his misery then laid at heaven's door. The poet will only be allowed to say that the wicked were miserable because they needed chastisement, and the punishment of heaven did them good.[25]

A century after Aeschylus, Aristotle would refuse to allow a blameless character to meet with disaster: 'it is obvious to begin with that one should not show worthy men passing from good fortune to bad. That does not arouse fear or pity but shocks our feelings.' It contravenes natural justice. '[The] change . . . from good to bad fortune . . . must not be due to villainy but to some great flaw in [the protagonist].'[26]

Kitto, in his surveys of Greek tragedy, holds that it is the loss of a religious frame of reference that accounts for the repugnance felt by the moral philosophers like Plato and Aristotle when faced with the tragic poets' willingness to show innocence and minor faults requited with total destruction. Faith in a universe that is coherent, even though we may not fully understand it, is being replaced by a creed that looks no further than the individual human being. 'We are now dealing only with the character, motives, actions, of an individual, and their logical results, not with anything greater than the individual.'[27]

Instead of the inexorable working out of a destiny transcendentally prefigured, Euripides probes his characters for the inner drives that motivate their disastrous conduct, exploring the dynamics of the natural, non-moral forces which they ignore at their peril. (It is of course to Euripides that Freud turns for his vocabulary of human psychological drives.) 'Euripides . . . will show us that there are laws of nature that demand obedience as well as laws of morality.' Aphrodite, in *Hyppoly-tus*, goading the would-be virtuous Phaedra with forbidden passion for her stepson, is an internal tyrant not an external force, 'a potentially disastrous element in our nature'.[28] Where Aeschylus is preoccupied with metaphysical problems, and Sophocles with portraying men and women of heroic stature confronting their supernaturally ordained destiny, the focus for Euripides switches to humanity in all its natural frailty. 'I represent men as they should be,' said Sophocles, 'Euripides represents them as they are.'[29] For Nietzsche, 'while Sophocles still delineates complete characters and employs myth for their refined development, Euripides already delineates only prominent individual traits of character'; thus, 'Here also we observe the victory of the phenomenon over the Universal'[30] – of this world, in other words, over any transcendental reality. To quote Peter Arnott:

> His intent, as Aristophanes shows in parodic form, was to humanise tragedy, to abandon Aeschylean metaphysics . . . and to force his audience, by reinterpreting the stock situations of myth, to a new evaluation of the stock situations of life . . . He created characters more human than those of Aeschylus and Sophocles . . . revealing the pettiness as well as the dignity of the human condition. The personages of his dramas are no longer drawn chiefly from kings, queens and supermen, but embrace the lowest levels of society.[31]

What is more, as Kitto points out, whereas Aeschylus and Sophocles are both in their different ways exploring moral order, Euripides in *Orestes* is presenting

> the picture of three aristocratic degenerates who, completely lost to reason and devoid of any moral responsibility . . . fly in the face of an ordered society. Electra . . . is an entirely private and personal assemblage of faults with no universal significance. She is a Medea without the tragedy – but with all Medea's Grand Guignol effects; in other words, a heroine of melodrama.[32]

Medea herself is not a noble but flawed character; she is a villainess. In the original legend it is not she who murders her children, but the people of Corinth. Euripides embroiders on tradition to emphasize the depth of her abandonment to jealousy and revenge.

An appeal to sensationalism becomes apparent. Grand Guignol effects are not imposed directly on the audience; Euripides remains true to the taboo – perhaps merely the convention – on on-stage violence. But *descriptions* of violence become increasingly graphic. In *Electra* Aegisthus is described as lying on the ground with his back split, screaming and dying in convulsions following Orestes's attack on him. In *Phoenissae*, the tale of a battle is embellished with 'an account of limbs cart-wheeling in all directions, hair reaching Olympos while blood reached the earth'. This may be a later interpolation, but if so the scribe was progressing in a direction Euripides himself had indicated.[33]

Sensation is sought, too, in spectacle and ingenuity. The gods who walked and talked with the protagonists of earlier dramas now make their entry literally from the skies, arriving in flying machines – probably contraptions suspended from cranes. It is Euripides who introduces this *deus ex machina.*[*] Nietzsche read a deeper significance into this, seeing in it a method of escape from the harsh logic of the true tragedies, allowing characters to be rescued by arbitrary interventions, such as Medea's departure in the chariot of her grandfather the sun god. 'The force . . . of Greek tragedy,' says Robin Lane Fox in *Pagans and Christians*,

> was bound intimately with interventions of the gods, and they lie at the heart of Sophocles's tragic art, in Athena's visible presence to the deluded Ajax, Oedipus's farewell in the sacred grove at Colonus and above all in the *Antigone*, where the chorus summon the gods to Creon's city in a moment of distress, only to receive the 'arrival' of a human messenger instead. The gods, as in Homer, are known more by their power than by their discrete personalities . . . When these interventions became trite, tragedy tended to melo-drama, an effect which has often been found in Euripides.[34]

For Euripides, the traditional myths are raw material, unworthy of inherent respect. He 'makes fun of legend, exposes divination, attacks Delphi, ridicules Heracles, the Dioscori and Hermes . . .'.[35] One scholar believes that great resentment was caused when Euripides opened his tragedy *Melanippe* with the words 'Zeus, whoever Zeus may be, for I do not know it, except from rumour',[36] but Kitto inclines to the view that the audience, too, were abandoning any strict adherence to the old myths, and that 'the conviction that these things are false was held so widely in Athens that there was no point in insisting that they are false, but great amusement in pretending that they are true'.[37] In 404 BC, just after Euripides's death, Critias, one of the Thirty Tyrants, wrote a satyr play[†] in which one of the characters describes religion as 'the invention of a pedagogic smart-aleck'.[38] Man, not the gods, not even superman, is the measure. 'A legend in which tragedy has found some of the noblest of its material is, for this new age, passed in review, with every attention paid to the possibilities of dramatic situation and narrative, but with no trace of tragic thought.'[39]

This departure from the 'solemn religious stamp' of the earlier drama,

---

[*] Mary Renault's *Mask of Apollo*, though set in the next century, includes an imaginative and plausible picture of the use of these machines – and of the qualms of the actors compelled to use them.
[†] Satyr plays were episodes of buffoonery with which the day-long performances were concluded.

which began only after Aeschylus's death, distressed the older generation. It greatly grieved one of Aeschylus's principal actors, Mynnisius, who long survived his old actor-manager.[40] The very language was changing. As Arnott elaborates, Euripides puts into his characters' mouths 'language that increasingly through his career broke down the standard rhythms of Greek tragic verse and approximated the vernacular more closely, in both vocabulary and speech patterns. Euripides has been accused of writing barely versified prose.' It was exactly this naturalism that commended Euripides to the Roman advocate Quintilian some five centuries later. Discussing the relative merits of the great Greek dramatists, he remarked:

> Euripides will be found of far greater service to those who are training themselves for pleasing in court. For his language, although actually censured by those who regard the dignity, the stately stride and sonorous utterance of Sophocles as being more sublime, has a closer affinity to that of oratory, while he is full of striking reflexions, in which indeed, in their special sphere, he rivals the philosophers themselves, and for defence and attack may be compared with any orator that has won renown in the courts.[41]

The reference to the philosophers is significant. Euripides grew up a free-thinker and a sophist. Socrates, born in 469 BC, was eleven years his junior. The Greek mind, says Kitto, was shifting

> from intuitive intelligence, based on a generalized reflection about human experience and expressing itself through art and the traditional imagery of mythology, to a conscious analysis of experience which made use of new intellectual techniques and was expressed, inevitably, in prose . . . [I]n Greece, big-scale poetry of importance dies with Euripides and Sophocles. Exquisite poetry was still to come, but no longer did it even pretend to grapple with what matters most; that became the province of the philosophers.[42]

He remarks on

> the extent and swiftness of the change which came over the intellectual temper of Greece between say 450 and 400 . . . Within the space of one generation the Greeks, always intelligent, became intellectualist . . . the old intuitive approach to the truth no longer served . . . In all the arts, not in drama only, the current was setting

30

strongly away from the old seriousness towards elegance or prettiness, and individualism or even sensationalism . . .

Succeeding centuries did not produce poets, they produced 'Plato and Aristotle and Zeno and Epicurus and a long line of mathematicians and scientists'.[43]

Many scholars see the insistence of the tragedians that, despite the suffering and manifest injustice experienced by human beings, creation was not random, was not a meaningless chaos, as the rock on which was based the confidence of those 'natural philosophers' who set out to understand the natural world – metaphysicians from whom the physicists would ultimately derive. The reality of a transcendental as well as a material world remained very much alive in the minds of the sixth-century mathematicians and astronomers. Pythagoras, a resident of Ionia, was a mystic as well as a mathematician, a believer in immortality and the transmigration of souls, insisting that in numbers lies the key to the universe. His near contemporary in the latter half of the sixth century, Xenophanes, challenged the traditional polytheism, holding that men had envisioned god in their own image. He substituted a vision of a single, unstirring deity, swaying the universe through the power of thought.[*]

Cerebration, a priori reasoning rather than practical experimentation, the world of ideas rather than of matter, distinguished the early Greek scientific speculation. It was not wholly devoid either of empirical research or of practical application. Thales (a little before Thespis began the transformation of worship into drama), who probably learnt his geometry from Egypt, used it in conjunction with astronomy to assess heights from the length of shadows thrown at particular hours.[44] He turned his studies of astronomy and geometry to navigational use, both coastal and astral. The astronomer Anaximander at the same period is credited with inventing the sundial, and of fashioning a crude map of the world. Glaukos of Chios meanwhile was experimenting with welding techniques. These practical men living in Ionia, the small Greek states and islands of Asia Minor, were followed over the next century and a half by technicians who improved – or imported from Egypt improvements

---

[*] It was Xenophanes who, moving from the Ionian shores of Asia Minor to Syracuse in Sicily, was intrigued to find fossil imprints of seaweed and fishes in the stone quarries, and sea shells on the mountaintops. He realized, as Charles Darwin was to do more than two millennia later when confronted with similar phenomena on the high hills of Chile, that it was necessary to postulate a theory of geological change (Kitto (1957), p.179).

to – anchors (by adding flukes), bellows and potters' wheels, among them being Theodorus, a mathematician and reputed teacher of Plato.[45]

In the first half of the fifth century the Sicilian Empedocles gave practical demonstrations to illustrate his theories. With the help of a wineskin he proved that air is a material substance, and he demonstrated atmospheric pressure using a clepsydra,* a gadget with holes in the bottom in which liquid could be retained provided the aperture at the top was firmly closed.[46] He also toyed with a rudimentary atomic theory which was elaborated later in the same century by Democritus, a metaphysician who developed the theory that the universe was the result of an undesigned combination of atoms falling in space.[47] In the absence of the sort of sophisticated laboratory instruments that had yet to be invented, this remained an untested mental construct rather than an aspect of quantum physics. Nevertheless, Democritus set high store by specific, rational *observation*, and this was too materialist for Plato, for whom ultimate reality resided in the world of ideas, not of matter.

He ridiculed Democritus and his notions in *Timaeus*.

> What is that which is Existent always and has no Becoming? And what is that which is Becoming always and never is Existent? Now the one of these is apprehensible by thought with the aid of reasoning, since it is ever uniformly existent; whereas the other is an object of opinion with the aid of unreasoning sensation, since it becomes and perishes and is never really existent . . . as Being is to Becoming, so is Truth to Belief.[48]

For Plato, worse was to follow. Mathematicians who specialized in problems of geometry were coming perilously close to engineering. Archytas invented a form of screw, earning Plato's contempt for the cast of mind which sought to solve geometrical problems by the use of mechanical implements rather than pure cogitation.[49] As the Greek biographer Plutarch, writing in the first century AD, explained:

> The art of mechanics, now so celebrated and admired, was first originated by Eudoxus and Archytas, who embellished geometry with its subtleties, and gave to problems incapable of proof by word and diagram, a support derived from mechanical illustrations that were patent to the *senses* [italics added]. For instance, in solving the

---

* The name clepsydra was also applied to the later water-clocks, the early models of which also had holes at the bottom to let the water flow out. Empedocles's 'water-clock' was not a form of timekeeper. See Cohen and Drabkin (eds.), p.245, note 3.

problem of finding two mean proportional lines, a necessary requisite for many geometrical figures, both mathematicians had recourse to mechanical arrangements, adapting to their purposes certain intermediate portions of curved lines and sections. But Plato was incensed at this, and inveighed against them as corrupters and destroyers of the pure excellence of geometry, which thus turned her back upon the incorporeal things of abstract thought, and descended to the things of sense, making use, moreover, of objects which required much mean and manual labour. For this reason mechanics was made entirely distinct from geometry, and being for a long time ignored by philosophers, came to be regarded as one of the military arts.[50]

Plato's contemporary, the Ionian Isokrates, who opened a school of oratory in Athens in 392 BC, describes the young men of the early fourth century as delighting in astronomy and geometry,[51] and Plato's Academy maintained an emphasis on pure mathematics, but as the century wore on, Greek ingenuity became more and more interested in technology, applying mathematical analyses to five simple machines – lever, wheel, pulley, wedge and screw.[52] By the latter half of the century philosophic deliberations were firmly grounded in the natural world, with Aristotle's speculations pre-eminent. Between 335 and 330 BC he compiled (in addition to works on politics, ethics and aesthetics) his *Physics* and his *History of Animals*.

With innovation and creativity now increasingly centred on manipulation of the natural world, construction began of the magnificent stone theatres whose abundant remains litter the areas of the Mediterranean which once were Greek. None of the great playwrights of Greece's golden age, neither Aeschylus nor Sophocles, Euripides nor Aristophanes, ever saw their plays performed in these theatres, of which more than sixty-five have now been excavated.[53] None dates from earlier than the latter half of the fourth century BC.

Most scholars assume that the circular Greek theatre owed its origin to religious celebrations of the harvest home. To this day in Mediterranean islands may be seen the circular threshing floors of beaten earth, where mules or oxen (tethered to a patient woman standing in the centre while her men sleep in the shade) endlessly circle the strewn sheaves of grain. Certainly the Greek theatre developed round a central O, in which was placed a stone altar. The altar was not treated with exaggerated respect; it served as a 'prop', a throne perhaps, or the rock to which Prometheus was chained. In this circle (the 'orchestra' or 'dancing place') the chorus performed. Behind was a platform on which the principals acted, and beyond that some sort of wagon or hut serving as dressing room, though there may in some places have been a shrine or temple that formed a backdrop (and temporary dressing room). The audience surrounded the rest of the circle, initially on the grassy banks to which the orchestra was strategically adjacent, later on wooden benches. The only constructional stone in use was for retaining walls to terrace the slopes.[54] This was the rudimentary theatre that witnessed the first performances of Aeschylus's plays. It was none too safe. There are accounts of a nasty collapse of the scaffolding supporting the benches about 500 BC, and there is also the suggestion that a further collapse during a performance of *Agamemnon* in 458 BC, when Aeschylus was manager, led to the poet being exiled to Sicily, where he died two years later.[55]

About 450 BC a permanent wooden building (a *skene*) was erected behind the platform at Athens (which later acquired a decorated façade that could be changed, thus introducing *scenery*). The building was two storeys high, the façade half that height.[56] In 415 BC a similar structure was put up at Corinth.[57] The flying machine used for the *deus ex machina*, itself a product of advances in wheel and pulley technology, probably conveyed actors to and from the roof of this building.

In the 330s the Athenian Theatre of Dionysus was rebuilt in stone, and Epidaurus and Delphi date from the same period. About 274 BC Delos was reconstructed in stone, some twenty years after it had begun painting the panels of the façade, thus, according to some authorities, being the inaugurator of scenery,[58] though the evidence cited below from Athens suggests that scenery had long been employed. The theatre at Ephesus is of about the same date as Delos.[59]

The scientific cast of mind was now being brought to bear on technical aspects of staging plays. Aeschylus's stage director wrote a commentary which was taken up by the philosophers Democritus (of atomic theory) and Anaxagoras, who explored a theory of optics that tackled the problems of perspective in scenery.[*] Their objective was to show

> how, if a fixed centre is taken for the outward glance of the eyes, and the projection of the radii, we must follow these lines in accordance with a natural law, such that from an uncertain object, uncertain images may give the appearance of buildings on the scenery of the stage, and how what is figured upon vertical and

---

[*] The stage director, Agatharcus, was working on the presentation of the *Oresteia* trilogy (see Vitruvius, VII, Preface, 11 note), so this was presumably the occasion of the unfortunate collapse of the wooden benches.

plane surfaces can seem to recede in one part and project in another.[60]

At some uncertain date revolving prisms were introduced, called in Greek *periaktoi* (revolving wings). These were three-sided, painted with different scenes which could be displayed as need arose. They corresponded to the three dramatic *genres*, tragedy, comedy and satyric. 'There are three styles of scenery,' says Vitruvius, the first-century BC Roman civil engineer whose treatise on architecture covered Greek as well as Roman theatre.

> The tragic are designed with columns, pediments and statues and other royal surroundings; the comic have the appearance of private buildings and balconies and projections with windows made to imitate reality, after the fashion of ordinary buildings; the satyric settings are painted with trees, caves, mountains and other country features, designed to imitate landscape.[61]

Like the landscapes creeping into the background of fifteenth-century religious art, the natural world is claiming a place in religious celebration.

Applied science was brought to bear on acoustics as well as optics. Echo chambers or 'sounding vases' were installed. 'Bronze vases are to be made in mathematical ratios corresponding with the size of the theatre,' says Vitruvius. He gives lengthy instructions on how to determine their size, construction and siting, including a diagram based on a theory of harmonics elaborated late in the fourth century by the Greek musician Aristoxenus. The Greeks, he says, placed copper vases under the rows of seats in accordance with mathematical reckoning.

> The Greeks call them *'echeia'*. The differences of the sounds which arise are combined into musical symphonies or concords, the circle of seats being divided into fourths and fifths of an octave. Hence, if the delivery of the actor from the stage is adapted to these contrivances, when it reaches them, it becomes fuller, and reaches the audience with a richer and sweeter note.

For the sake of cheapness, many of the Roman theatres contemporary with Vitruvius substituted earthenware for bronze, producing, says Vitruvius, 'very useful effects'. Earthenware are the only remnants found by today's archaeologists, but bronze had certainly been used in

Greece. Vitruvius comments that the Roman general Lucius Mummius, who destroyed the theatre in Corinth in 146 BC, 'transported these bronze vessels to Rome, and dedicated them, from the spoils, at the temple of Luna'.[62]

Playwrights whose words this sophisticated technology amplified include no tragedians whose work posterity has thought worth saving. Revivals of the classics (the practice of reviving earlier successes appears to have begun in Athens about 387 BC)[63] enhanced the spectacular aspects of productions, and the use of stage effects such as the crane-and-pulley machine. The tragedies of the fourth and later centuries leaned heavily on the more superficial aspects of Euripidean technique: violence, showmanship, a love of spectacle for its own sake. Even more significant is the introduction of on-stage violence. In the original production of Sophocles's *Ajax*, the suicide takes place off-stage. By the late fourth century a telescoping sword has been invented for a sensational on-stage *coup de théâtre*.[*64]

While serious-minded people concentrated on philosophy and science, dramatists, abandoning theology and its accompanying deities and heroes, turned to comedy; and to comedy's dramatis personae: ordinary people.

---

[*] An example of the fourth century's increasing preoccupation with authenticity in the presentation of violence is the painter Parrhasius's conduct in buying an elderly war captive from Philip of Macedon, and subjecting this artist's impotent model to tortures (from which he died) in order the better to illustrate his painting of Prometheus having his liver destroyed by vultures. Lively debate ensued as to the ethics of this artistry, and of the possible corruption inherent both in the action and in its depiction (*The Times*, 12 April 1993).

Chapter 3

Hellenistic Pleasure and Prosperity: the Fourth to Second Centuries

Day-long performances of tragic drama had always included some light relief, some bawdy buffoonery originating with the phallic songs and ceremonies of the peregrinating revellers whose obscenities in perform-ance of the *kordax*[*] had been considered so shocking that it was impossible to take part except masked. The 'satyr' interludes of classical times, akin perhaps to (though much more raunchy than) the knock-about harlequinades traditional as end-pieces in English theatre as late as the 1930s, may seem a strange embellishment to what was essentially a religious occasion, but a striking parallel emerges in the account of another deeply religious society experienced by Heinrich Harrer during his years in Tibet in the 1940s.

> Every year dramatic performances are given on a great stone stage outside the inner garden. Vast throngs of people come to see the plays, which go on for seven days from sunrise to sundown. They are performed by groups of male actors and are almost entirely of a religious character. The actors are not professionals. They come from the people and belong to all sorts of professions. When the drama week is over they go back into private life. The same plays are performed year after year. The words are sung in a kind of recitative, and an orchestra of drums and flutes sets the rhythm for the dances. Only comic parts have spoken lines. The beautiful and valuable costumes belong to the Government and are kept in the Summer Palace.
>
> One of the seven groups of actors, the Gyumalungma, is famous for its parodies ... One could not but be astonished at their frankness. It is a proof of the good humour and sanity of the people that they can make fun of their own weaknesses and even of their

[*] The Peloponnesian 'single' dance of comedy.

religious institutions. They go so far as to give a performance of the Oracle, with dance and trance and all, which brings down the house. Men appear dressed as nuns and imitate in the drollest fashion the fervour of women begging for alms. When monks and nuns begin to flirt together on the stage, no-one can stop laughing and tears roll down the cheeks of the sternest abbots in the audience.[1]

Comedies, as distinct from the parodic satyr pieces, were staged not at the Dionysiac festival in March/April but at the earlier January/February festival known as Lenaea. However ribald their content and presentation, they competed for prizes with all the status and respectability of tragedies, and winners are recorded from 486 BC, though according to Aristotle they had to rely on unpaid amateur choruses much longer than did the tragedies.[*2] Only fragments from the comic playwrights survive prior to the middle of the fifth century BC, but in about 450 was born the outstanding writer of Athenian comedy – Aristophanes. Euripides had already enjoyed half a decade of activity, and was to win his first prize in 441. The earliest Aristophanes play was produced in 427, the earliest still extant (*Acharnians*) in 425, and the last in 388.[3]

In a spirit of robust indecency, Aristophanes satirized and parodied his respected contemporaries, including Euripides and Socrates (who, it is reported, took the ribbing in *The Clouds* in good part).[4] His topics were local and scurrilous, as in revue; the manner of presentation preserving 'as a trace of its phallic origin, an unbridled obscenity in its dances, songs and dialogue'.[5] Yet 'underlying his farce and vulgarity were a depth of thought and a seriousness of purpose for which we look in vain in later comedy,' says George E. Duckworth,[6] and the existence of a firm moral framework in the society which enjoyed the plays is implied in Kenneth Dover's comment that 'the comic characters of Aristophanes . . . give us vicarious satisfaction by breaking moral and social rules as we too would like to break them if only we dared'.[7]

With the defeat of Athens in 404 BC and the ending of the Peloponnesian War, political satire ceased – indeed, at about this time it was expressly forbidden with the introduction of political censorship. According to tradition, Greece produced 252 authors of comic plays, but with the exception of Aristophanes little but fragments survived until, in 1905, parchments were discovered in Egypt which proved to be copies of

---

[*] Probably until about 465 BC (Aristotle, *Poetics*, V.3 note).

the work of the late-fourth-century playwright Menander. Our knowledge of Greek comedy is heavily dependent on later translations made by Roman writers, twenty-six of whose translations are still extant.[8] It is evident that social relationships became the dominant theme, playwrights busying themselves with the activities of a cast of characters as stylized as any modern pantomime, though instead of principal boy and girl, dame, etc., the list included doddering old fathers, irresponsible sons, cunning servants, greedy hangers-on, swaggering soldiers, impudent prostitutes, all in their stereotype masks. To quote H.D.F. Kitto:

> Old Comedy had been political through and through, it was the life of the *polis* [city-state] that was criticized and burlesqued on the stage. Now it finds its material in private and domestic life, and makes jokes about cooks and the price of fish, shrewish wives and incompetent doctors.[9]

The chorus disappeared from comedy, though not from tragedy, after a period during which it had provided musical interludes, usually stock lyrics rather than new compositions related to the action. The extravagant costumes with their huge externally attached phalluses were phased out. The Athenian theatre, particularly after the conquest of the city by Alexander the Great in 336 BC, narrowed down to domestic comedy, plus revivals of the old classic tragedies (but not the old comedies, which were too politically dated).

A respectable if shallow moral rectitude pervades the New Comedy. Lovers do not appear unchaperoned on stage, a third person is always present.[10] The plot ensures that people get their come-uppance. But the theatre is no longer attempting to deal with the great issues of meaning and purpose in human life, and indeed the connection of the drama with its roots in sacred rite has become very tenuous. Performance is no longer limited to the great religious festivals, theatre has become entertainment rather than an aspect of religious observance. Actors have, by the fourth century, become fully fledged professionals; the stars are commanding high salaries, and touring companies are playing full time in one or other of the cities of Greece, Macedon and the Greek diaspora in Asia Minor, Sicily and southern Italy.[11]

There is an increasing emphasis on naturalism, on accurate representation of the material world. This led to a strange episode at Tralles, inland from Ephesus in modern Turkey, where there was a tiny theatre known as the Small Assembly (the name, incidentally, a reminder that in the Greek world the theatre building was also used as a political forum).

The stage director had gone over the top in ebullience, providing 'columns, statues or centaurs supporting the architraves, the orbed roofs of domes, the projecting angles of pediments, cornices having lions' heads which provided outlets for the rain from the roofs'. Moreover, 'the storey above the scenery had domes, porticoes, half pediments and every kind of roof, with varied pictorial ornament'. The audience were about to burst into applause when they were silenced by a certain Licymnius, who pointed out that the whole thing was a travesty.

> Who of you can have, above your roof-tiles, buildings with columns and elaborate gables? For the latter stand upon floors, not above the roof tiles. If therefore we approve in pictures what cannot justify itself in reality, we are added to those cities which because of such faults are esteemed slow-witted. [*12]

The abashed stage director removed the offending scenery, 'and when this was altered to resemble reality, he obtained sanction for his correction'.

Meanwhile a different theatrical art form, the mime, was making headway and was to become of paramount importance for both Greek and Roman culture, taking drama further from any concern with otherworldliness and anchoring it securely to the tastes and interests of *l'homme moyen sensuel*. We use 'mime' to designate mute performances, but the original Greek word *mimos* indicated rather a copy or imitation, the word having a faintly pejorative implication, as with the verb 'to ape'. Mime was intended to be a realistic but not respectful representation of scenes from everyday life. There was no chorus, the players were not masked, and they included actresses, contrary to the practice in the more formal theatre – indeed some authorities deem this the main factor distinguishing mime from other forms of comedy. The dramatis personae tended to be from low in the social scale – kings and heroes are not included. Performance of mime seems to have consisted of a series of amusing and, above all, indecent vignettes, sometimes sung, sometimes spoken, interspersed with acrobatics, puppetry or juggling – an entertainment akin to vaudeville or music hall. [13]

Mime originated not in Athens but in Sicily, among the Spartan emigrant colonists of Syracuse. Initially there were probably no scripts, the players improvising and ad libbing their way along, but Aristotle

---

[*] The date of this episode is problematic. Vitruvius calls Licymnius a mathematician. If he is identical with Licymnius the poet and professor of oratory, it can be dated to the late fifth century BC.

names a 'poet' called Epicharmus as the originator, in Sicily, of written comedies, though it is Aristotle's translator who identifies this work with the mime genre.[14] Epicharmus was writing early in the fifth century, and at that time, according to Bieber, the themes mirrored the old Doric (Spartan) comedy of the sixth century BC, travesties of mythology or daily life. At this stage it is not the myths themselves that are being burlesqued so much as the heavy handling of them in the tragedies.[15] By the second half of the century a playwright named Sophron was established churning out entertaining sketches on everyday life (of which some 170 fragments are extant), some focused on men, some on women, and known by categories which may be roughly translated as *The Masculinities* and *The Femininities*.

Not until the fourth century did the genre reach Athens. Plato had gone to Syracuse by invitation in 388 BC to advise on a new constitution, but was shortly deported, having 'exercized the right of free speech too freely'.[16] He greatly admired Sophron, and it is he who is credited with introducing the mime to his fellow Athenians on his return.[17] It became the rage, too, at the Macedonian court (Macedon and Syracuse were both allies of Carthage at the time), and Demosthenes was highly critical of Philip of Macedon for the amount of time he wasted on slapstick comedies.[18] The slapstick coarsened into a relish for simulated cruelty. When the Roman playwright Terence came to translate Menander's comedy *Perinthia*, about a century and a half later, he omitted a scene of slave torture which apparently went further than Roman taste at that time was prepared to accept.[19]

Philip was succeeded by his son Alexander the Great in 336 BC. Most of the Greek mainland, including Athens, had fallen to Philip's armies in 338. Alexander added the old Greek settlements of Asia Minor to his empire, and by his conquests in Syria, Mesopotamia and Egypt provided new outlets for Greek colonization and influence – the touring theatrical companies were now travelling as far afield as Persia.[20] When, after his early death in 323 BC, his Greek generals divided his empire among themselves, it was his new foundation of Alexandria, in the Nile delta, that was to play the principal role in carrying the torch of Greek civilization. Hundreds of Greeks of all classes migrated to the city, whose aristocracy and ruling house, the Ptolemies, were entirely Greek, by descent and by culture.

The Ptolemies certainly welcomed and encouraged Dionysiac 'artistes': the players were respected and were freed, along with Greek educational and cultural professions, from salt-tax. By now players were beginning to organize their own craft guilds. Artists, stage managers, actors, musicians, dancers and other professionals were eligible for membership. The first Dionysiac *technitai* appears to have been formed in Athens early in the third century; Egypt soon followed. In mainland Greece these guilds were self-governing corporations, possibly with some vestigial cult adherence to Dionysus, but in Alexander's successor states abroad there is evidence that they received subventions from the Hellenistic rulers and were court players, whose function was to entertain rather than to fulfil any religious role.[21]

Evidence of dramatic presentations in the next two centuries is scanty. The troupes repeated old classics, plus the work of a group of tragedians known as the Pleiad, four of whom worked in Alexandria, repeating such traditional themes as Heracles, Andromeda and Hyppolytos. But the treatment is comic parody and burlesque. Early in the third century, Theocritus, a Syracusan who had moved to Alexandria, wrote a poem describing a religious pageant manifesting the death and resurrection of Adonis (a god of Middle Eastern origin who, like Dionysus, symbolized vegetation and fertility), a pageant celebrated in the palace but open to the general public with a world-famous opera star in the lead.[22] Euripides's later plays had marked the start of the disintegration of myth and religion. After Alexander's time, says Kitto, the myths became

> a form of literary and artistic rabies, when pretty or scandalous stories of divine amours and surprising metamorphoses were told in elegant verse by poets who, poor men, found neither the inspiration nor the audience for anything more important . . . The mythologizing of these poets is at first charming, but it soon becomes an intolerable bore. It is dead . . .[23]

Instead Theocritus in Alexandria writes about private and domestic life;[24] the themes and motivations are the entirely personal ones of love, jealousy, avarice and the like.[25]

There is little evidence of original comedies. One scholar suggests that comedy needs 'a community of feeling . . . intimacy of contact and homogeneity of experience which were lacking in Alexandria' because of its New Town status, populated by streams of immigrants without common roots.[26] One writer who achieved a reputation as a comic dramatist in the late third century was Machon, whose work appears to have consisted chiefly of a series of *bons mots* uttered by notable prostitutes in the course of their professional encounters with distinguished figures. Repartee centred on the sexual meaning of words, and there was much emphasis on unusual sexual postures.[27] 'What a squalid party!' was the verdict passed by Queen Arsinoe III on the Dionysiac festival in Alexandria at the close of the third century.[28]

Undoubtedly the artistes continued to be familiar with the traditional tragic arias, as was rather gruesomely evidenced in 53 BC when a troupe of Greek actors were playing at the court of the King of Parthia. The Parthian cavalry had just defeated the Roman general Crassus at the battle of Carrhae, and during the performance the victors arrived at court carrying Crassus's head, which one of the actors immediately placed on a spear, bursting into Euripides's aria from *Bacchae*, beginning:

> From the mountains we bring it,
> The spoil of our hunting—[29]

But the classics were no longer performed as explorations of a theme. Impatience, the tendency to be readily bored which Sorokin identifies with the sensate phase of a culture, meant that dramatic entertainment now consisted of the less intellectually demanding 'An evening with . . .' type of theatre, in which a performer offered a series of solo monologues and arias.[30]

There is, too, the first hint of a development which is to reach its apogee in the Roman theatre. A poem at the end of the third century describes how a performer of traditional epic (*The Sons of Temenos*) is sent packing by an audience wielding rattles, while great applause is accorded to Aristagorus who 'danced the *Gallus*'[31] (the Galli were priests of the cult of Cybele, whose main claim on public interest was their ritual self-castration in frenzied ceremonies). The pantomime (meaning, from the Greek *panton mimos*, a performance in which a single player performs *all* the different parts, or *representations*) unfolded the drama wordlessly with dance and gesture. It was to become the vehicle for some of the most famous artistes of the ancient world. But the story of its flowering lies not in the increasingly bedraggled remnants of the old Greek world, but in the courts of Imperial Rome, when Cleopatra, last of the Ptolemies, lay dead, and Octavian, her conqueror, had inaugurated the Augustan Age.

Hellenism, then, made little contribution to the world's dramatic heritage. Contemporary literature, in Michael Grant's words, 'appealed less to the high matters of principle that had been contemplated by the tragic dramatists of the past than to the reality of [Hellenistic man's] own domestic and day-to-day interests'.[32] The educated people of the later Greek world continued to read and quote the playwrights of the Golden Age, but the well of inspiration from which they had drawn was dry. The

genius of Hellenism lay elsewhere, and is encapsulated in the foundation, by Ptolemy Soter, the general who took control of Egypt on
Alexander's death, of the Mouseion.

The inspiration for the Mouseion, the most important academic
institution of the Hellenic world, came from mainland Greece, from
Plato's Academy and Aristotle's Lyceum. The name 'Mouseion'
acknowledges a religious inspiration, an attribution to the Muses, the
goddesses of the arts. But the institution's emphasis was always literary
rather than worshipful, and though it retained a vestigial religious
connection, it was primarily a great teaching and research university,
borrowing from the Athenian academies the concept of an almost
collegiate common life,[33] its library a Mecca for scholars from all over
the Greek world.

The university developed into an institution with some 14,000
students, a Royal Academy of Science and Letters housed within the
royal domains. It included lecture halls, gardens for botanists, menag-
eries for zoologists, observatories for astronomers, and laboratories for
chemists and physicists.[34] Euclid, whose city of origin is unknown, was
already at work there by 320 BC,[35] but it is the next century that sees the
fullest flowering of the Hellenistic scientific genius. Rostovtzeff says of
the Greek ruling class in Egypt:

> their mentality was not exactly the same as that of their fellow-
> Greeks in continental Greece, on the islands, and in Asia Minor.
> The *homo politicus,* still alive in Greece, yielded place to the *homo
> oeconomicus* and to the *homo technicus* in Egypt.[36]

Alexandria was developing into a magnificent city, with its parks, walks,
theatres, temples, gymnasia, and racecourse, its colonnaded streets and
sidewalk arcades.[37] It was probably in Alexandria that, early in the third
century, the astronomer Aristarchus worked out his hypothesis that the
earth revolves about the sun, not vice versa, a theory which did not win
general acceptance.[38] Eratosthenes of Cyrene (to whom Queen Arsinoe
III made her comment about the squalor of the entertainment at the
Dionysiac festival) became librarian at the Mouseion in 245 BC,[39] having
been appointed from Athens, where he was currently working. He
produced *On the Measurement of the Earth*, abandoning the attempt to
measure the circumference of the planet on the basis of the supposed
distance of the constellations from two separate points on earth, and
substituting a method based on the length of the shadow cast by a

perpendicular of measured height compared with a similar perpendicular at the same time a measured distance away on the same meridian, at an hour when at the summer solstice no shadow was cast. His conclusion was that the circumference of the earth is 24,662 miles, its diameter 7,850 miles. Modern measurements are 24,862 and 7,900.[*] [40]

Archimedes visited Alexandria from his native Syracuse, and is thought to have there learnt of (not invented) the type of screw which came later to bear his name, and which was in use in Egypt for raising water. He maintained a serious correspondence with Alexandrian mathematicians after his return home. 'His extraordinarily accurate approximation to the value of *pi* in his work on the measurement of the circle is particularly striking',[41] and it was he who made the celebrated analysis of the lever: 'Give me whereon to stand and I will move the world.'[42] He shared the Platonic contempt for mechanics as compared with pure mathematics, but that did not prevent him, in 230 BC, from constructing for the ruler of Syracuse 'an enormous pleasure-boat, with sports-deck, garden deck and a marble swimming bath. It is said to have been a stadium (407 feet) in length and to have weighed 1000 tons.' It proved too expensive to run.[43] He willingly lent his skills to the development of military technology as Syracuse fought to stem the Roman tide rolling over Sicily, a tide in which Archimedes himself was ultimately to perish. He would not, however, demean himself by writing any practical treatise, 'regarding the work of an engineer and every art that ministers to the needs of life as ignoble and vulgar', but we know from other sources that his theoretical studies enabled him to make such practical calculations as the number of pulleys needed to lift a given weight with a given force,[44] and Plutarch records that he prepared 'offensive and defensive engines to be used in every kind of siege warfare'.[45] Third-century Alexandria was a noted centre for military technology. As a contemporary commentator remarked: 'the existence, for the first time, of abundant funds provided by an ambitious king, liberal to the sciences' enabled the technicians of Alexandria to concentrate on problems of calibration. Alexandria became a leading centre for ballistics research.[46]

Another third-century inventor, Ctesibius, the son of a barber, worked on applied pneumatics, and developed a catapult working on compressed air. A report, of which the Arabic translation still survives, describes some sixty-five machines using pneumatic or hydraulic

---

[*] There is difficulty in translating the Greek *stade* into miles, and thus a margin of error may enter into these comparisons. The problem is discussed in detail in Fraser, P.M., Vol II p.599, note 312.

principles.[47] Many of these tended to be toys or gimmicks – Vitruvius credits Ctesibius with devising toy singing blackbirds. But a highly useful gadget was the water-clock, on which Ctesibius is known to have worked, though the first description of it occurs in a document attributed to Archimedes.[48] These were sometimes embellished with rotating discs with holes responding to floats in which, at given intervals, the holes coincided to release balls which were discharged through the beak of a bird on to a cymbal, thus sounding the passing of the hours. Other decorations included flute players who, with the aid of an air-vessel, could be made to whistle and 'play'.[49] Water-clocks were of course a great advance on sundials, because they operated in bad weather as well as good. The anatomist Herophilus devised a portable version, which he used for measuring pulse rates in medicine.[50]

The most notable scientific advances achieved at the Mouseion were in the field of medicine. Traditional medicine had looked to Asclepius, god of healing, whose sacred snakes are the symbol of the medical profession to this day. Cures depended on miracle. In the mid-fifth century, in the island of Cos, Hippocrates initiated a revolutionary new approach. 'What is important is that the Hippocratic attitude toward medicine threw off the religious aspect of suffering and made a beginning toward the scientific study of disease. Clinical medicine had its inception . . .'[51] In his work *The Sacred Disease*, a study of epilepsy, Hippocrates says, 'It is not, in my opinion, any more divine or more sacred than other diseases, but has a natural cause, and its supposed divine origin is due to men's inexperience, and their wonder at its peculiar character.' 'With these words,' says V. Robinson, Professor of the History of Medicine at Temple University, Philadelphia, 'Hippocrates expels the gods from medicine . . . [This] marks the greatest revolution in the history of medicine. It enthroned the doctrine of the uniformity of nature, and Greek medicine became a science.' It was, however, a science that still recognized moral absolutes. The Hippocratic oath forbade the abetting of suicide or abortion.[52]

The essential point about Hippocratic medicine is stressed in an essay attributed to Hippocrates, *On Ancient Medicine*. In this he protests at the use of an a priori approach in any matter for which observation is a possibility, such as medicine. 'Conclusions drawn by the unaided reason can hardly be serviceable; only those drawn from observed fact.'[53] The observation of symptoms, diagnosis and prognosis had to be supplemented by an overall knowledge of anatomy and physiology.

The medical school which grew up round Hippocrates on the island of Cos encouraged dieting, baths and gymnastic exercise, and Hippocrates himself proved a good advertisement for his theories, dying about 357 BC at the age of 104. Forty or fifty years after his death, following the foundation of the Mouseion, there was established in Alexandria, probably by students from Cos, a medical school at which during the next century medicine reached levels which 'were not surpassed till the 17th century AD'.[54] More than six centuries later the Roman historian Ammianus Marcellinus, who died in 391 AD, was to write, 'it is sufficient as a recommendation for any medical man to be able to say that he was educated at Alexandria'.[55]

Basic to these advances was the institution of a crucial novelty – the dissection of human corpses. The School of Anatomy at the Mouseion was equipped with dissecting rooms, under the leadership of two Asian Greeks, Erasistratus the physician and Herophilus the anatomist.

In the days of Sophocles, desecration of a human corpse was an abomination. The prospect of such a fate befalling her brother is the crux of Antigone's defiance of Creon, the source of her insistence, in Sophocles's *Antigone*, on the right to give him decent burial. This, insists Kitto in *Form and Meaning in Drama*, is not for any ritual reason, such as the ordinances of the gods, or the restlessness of an unquiet soul inadequately laid to rest, but simply because human decency requires the protection of the corpse, and when the people of Thebes are portrayed praising Antigone for her stubbornness, they are lauding her simple desire to ensure that his body does not become a prey to animals.

> The religious and the human or instinctive motives are not sharply distinguished by Sophocles; indeed, they are fused – and for a very good reason: he saw no distinction between them; the fundamental laws of humanity and the *Dike* [Justice] of the gods are the same thing.[56]

During the century after Sophocles, dissection of animals had been practised, but Aristotle remarked that the internal organs of man are not known. Hippocrates and those who came after him in the medical school of Cos had not challenged the prejudice against human dissection.[57] By the third century, however, taboos were dissolving. Rumour had it that in Alexandria vivisection, as well as dissection, of human beings was practised. Celsus, a Roman encyclopaedist of the first century AD, wrote of the two researchers that 'they procured criminals out of prison by royal permission, and, dissecting them alive, contemplated, while they were yet breathing, the parts which nature had before concealed'. P.M.

Fraser endeavours to vindicate Herophilus with the somewhat ambiguous assurance that 'certainly Herophilus would not have permitted suffering in excess of scientific requirements'.[58] Huge strides were made, particularly on the brain, and on the distinction between motor and sensory nerves. Twentieth-century values wholly applaud the achievement. 'Any Faculty is fortunate to count a Herophilus on its staff,' comments Professor Robinson of Philadelphia, writing in 1931,[59] and Fraser sums up: 'In medicine, as in other branches of science, the Alexandrian emphasis on two distinct factors, the human and the rational, created in the third century a scientific humanism of the highest order.'[60]

In fields other than medicine, too, the speculations of the scientists were being put to good use. From the fifth to the second centuries, productivity rose. In the fifth century agriculture, industry, foreign and interstate trade flourished as never before. There was disruption and famine during the Peloponnesian War and the disorder of the fourth century. But the damage caused by the wars to mainland Greece was quickly repaired. The cultivated areas did not diminish, the soil was not exhausted, and though poor it was well farmed and productive, with surpluses for sale. Agricultural science was taken seriously, and treatises published. Crop rotation was introduced, implements improved, irrigation extended. Pergamum in Asia Minor became famous for advances in stock breeding. Textbooks were studied, the second-century ruler of Pergamum, who devoted his old age to horticultural experiments, being among the authors. In Egypt the Ptolemies introduced the substitution of iron for wooden implements, a move which Rostovtzeff deems 'tantamount to a revolution'. They were supervising research into wheat varieties, and importing improved seed corn; they extended the areas under cultivation, applying the Archimedes screw and other innovative techniques to irrigation. The screw was adapted for use too in wine, oil and cloth presses.[61]

International trade extended with the increasing knowledge of geography. Guides to routes and harbours were available to merchants and seamen of the fourth century BC, and with Alexander's conquests maps were extended to cover new areas, using Persian and Hellenistic military road records, and the work of mathematical geographers like Eratosthenes in Alexandria in the late third century. Towards the middle of the second century, Hipparchus applied the 360 degrees of the circle to the circumference of the earth, as a basis for cartography.[62] Late in the same century the discovery of the pattern of the monsoon winds gave a huge boost to trade between Egypt and India.[63] The vast extension of the

Greek world consequent on Alexander's conquests expanded the areas of trade in Greek goods, though not without temporary friction which harmed the mainland, as overseas settlements began to produce their own wine, oil, pottery, clothes, jewellery, woodwork and linen. Nevertheless, by the late fourth century Menander's plays are presenting a picture of prosperous middle-class families, comfortably housed and served by one or two slaves.[64]

Homo oeconomicus, Rostovtzeff remarks, is taking his place alongside *homo technicus*. An unknown author of the late fourth or early third century, probably a Greek Syrian, published a treatise on economic theory which Rostovtzeff calls 'the first attempt at a theory of Finance'. It covered public and private economic management, distinguishing between central and local government responsibilities. It dealt with monetary policy; commercial policy, including imports and exports; budgetary policy and taxation, including sources of revenue and types of tax, covering such options as excise duties, tolls, land tax, licensing and stamp duties.[65]

Discussing the mentality of the Hellenes, the Greek diaspora from Babylon to Alexandria, as the third century gave way to the second, Rostovtzeff sums them up as 'mainly concerned to secure for themselves and their families a life of material prosperity and if possible social prominence . . .'[66] Sorokin's sensate society is in full bloom. The material world is the repository of truth, whose tenets are unveiled by scientists applying reason to the observations of the senses; and the material world is the source for the fulfilment of human life, defined in terms of the enjoyment of consumption.

In the century that followed, fragment after fragment of the Greek world fell to Roman pressure. The educated Romans of the second and first centuries BC respected and studied the Greeks of an earlier epoch, but for their own contemporaries they had nothing but contempt. Something had gone wrong.

Chapter 4*

The Greek World Disintegrates: the Second and First Centuries

'The control of man by himself . . .' says Sorokin 'is impossible without a system of absolute values.'[1]

Belief in, and service to, the traditional deities of the Greeks was primarily a source of social cohesion rather than of personal ethics. Into one pantheon were welded the ancient life-giving powers, usually female, immanent in mountains and streams, and the guardians, usually male, of tribes and cities. There resulted a tangled tale of heavenly liaisons, as tribes coalesced and conquered peoples were absorbed, together with their gods.[2] Shared rites and festivals provided a basis for a communal identity.

In the great issues of life, human beings – and indeed the gods themselves – were governed by the ultimate imperatives of Fate, Justice and Necessity, forces which came in time to be identified with Zeus. To please the gods, and thus obtain their active benevolence, strict ceremonial purity had to be observed rather than any particular code of conduct. The gods required good treatment of heralds, guests, suppliants and the dead – they governed relationships between communities rather than between individuals.[3]

Personal conduct was governed by a traditional morality based on the four cardinal virtues of Justice, Courage, Self-Restraint and Wisdom.[4] Dover stresses the extent to which freedom (quite literally, for conquest meant enslavement) depended on the exercise of soldierly qualities. Self-discipline was of the highest importance, and wealth was suspect for the very reason that the softness engendered by luxury undermined the capacity for endurance on campaign and promoted cowardice; Aristophanes in *The Clouds* represents even the use of hot water for washing as morally decadent.[5] In Kitto's view the same restraint, exercised in frugal standards of living, accounts for the leisure which enabled the Athenians to participate so fully in civic responsibilities.[6]

Respect for self-control in the citizen soldier extended also to sexual

50

behaviour. Notwithstanding sexually explicit vase paintings, the Greeks were averse to public demonstrations of sexuality, and were disgusted when confronted by such exhibitions by barbarian peoples. In certain religious contexts, chastity was required, and intercourse in temples or sanctuaries was invariably forbidden. A male involved in adultery or seduction of an unmarried woman (other than a slave or a foreigner) could be imprisoned or even put to death.[7] Society was regarded as an aggregate not of individuals, but of families, each with its responsible head[*] – a concept, says Kitto, common not only to the Greeks, but also to the Roman, Indian, Chinese and Teutonic traditions.[8]

Personal morality was brought within the purview of religion by the swearing of oaths in the name of the gods, who were held to execrate perjury. At the age of eighteen an Athenian citizen swore on oath, 'I will not hand on my fatherland diminished, but larger and better.' Any failure in citizenship was a failure in religious as well as secular terms; increasingly, the life lived in accordance with civic virtues came to be equated with conduct approved by the gods.[9] Thus the loss of faith evident among the more thoughtful Greeks of the fifth and later centuries dissolved not only important aspects of shared identity, but also the taboos by which the community's conduct was regulated.[†]

It was done from the highest possible motives – the search for the good and the true. But there was, for many of the seekers, a crucial qualification: good meant good *for man*. 'Man is the measure of all things,' said Protagoras, the fifth-century Sophist. He himself is reputed to have accepted conventional moral teaching, but his aphorism, understood in antiquity to imply that no proposition, moral or scientific, could claim universal validity, opened the floodgates to relativism.

Protagoras began his career as a teacher of rhetoric in Athens in 450 BC. If truth was no longer a matter of revelation, persuasion was the instrument for a civilized new dispensation, and rhetoric was the art of persuasion, the art on which depended the success of the philosopher, the advocate and the democratic politician. The Schools of Rhetoric flourished (and continued to do so throughout the whole period of classical antiquity). Scepticism was fortified as it came to be recognized that the strength of a proposition lay more in the skill with which it was argued than in any absolute validity. By the end of the fifth century the Sophist Thrasymachus was throwing all moral restraint to the winds, and

---

[*] A detailed and persuasive account of the origin and ramifications of this social pattern is explored by Fustel de Coulanges in *The Ancient City* (1864) translated by Willard Small (1873).
[†] Aristophanes in *The Clouds* shows a character who has lost his faith quite willing to lie on oath, though he later repents of his conduct. See Dover (1974), pp.249, 261.

propounding a doctrine that amounted to little more than naked personal ambition.

Socrates, as presented to us by Plato, sought to find an unassailable logical foundation for virtue, 'to make it not a matter of traditional unexamined opinion, but of exact knowledge which could be mastered and taught'.[10] In the course of this attempt, he demonstrated that traditional morality had no foundation in logic – and 'the effect on some of the young men was disastrous; their belief in the tradition was destroyed, and they put nothing in its place. Faith in the *polis* too was shaken, for how could the *polis* train its citizens in virtue, seeing that nobody knew what it was?'[11] The city's old guard were correct when they recognized in Socrates a force subversive of traditional mores. In 399 BC they condemned him to death for irreligion and the corruption of youth.

About a decade later, Plato in *The Republic* shows the utmost contempt for the myths about the gods and their scurrilous behaviour, and would, in his ideal state, have them banned, together with oracles, signs and supposed apparitions.[12] In their place he substitutes a lofty vision of the divine nature, a perfection of goodness and truthfulness. But it is not his views that capture the imagination of his contemporaries. The virtue-through-knowledge that he extols assumes a context of citizenship, of civic duty. Among his contemporaries, however, the tide is setting firmly in the direction of personal happiness as the goal of human existence.

Kitto has drawn attention to the tragic decline of the Athenian spirit following the appalling twenty-seven years of the Peloponnesian War which ended in 404 BC. Early in the fourth century Diogenes, holding that the world of immediate physical experience is alone of any significance, developed a popular theory that happiness lies in satisfying only one's natural needs, and satisfying them, moreover, in the cheapest and easiest way. Elements of 1960s self-sufficiency entered into this philosophy. Another element was that 'what is natural cannot be dishonourable or indecent and therefore can and should be done in public'.[13] This earned the followers of Diogenes the nickname of Cynics, from the Greek word for a dog, *kuwv*, whose public behaviour was quite devoid of shame.

Significant of the changing evaluation of the gods was the introduction, in the late fourth century, of portraits of Greek monarchs on the coinage, replacing such symbols as the Athenian portrait of Athena and her owl, or Poseidon on the coins of Poseidonia, the city of which he was patron.[14] At the close of the fourth – or early in the third – century a

Sicilian historian, Euhemerus, resident in Alexandria, published *Sacred History*, in which he claimed that all myths had a historical basis, and the so-called gods were in fact long-dead heroes – men, in short. This had long been accepted with regard to certain special individuals, such as Asclepius, the god of healing, but Euhemerus challenged the whole concept of the pantheon of deities. In the course of the next century, demythologizing of the Olympian gods became commonplace among writers. The rulers seized upon the other side of the coin, and demanded to be accorded the status of gods, not merely in the next world, but already in this. Since the pharaohs of pre-Greek Egypt had already enjoyed the status of gods, it was a short step to according the same dignity to the Ptolemies. They were in any case claiming descent from Dionysus, whose drunken celebrations were 'a permanent feature of Ptolemaic devotions' in Egypt. Soon most of the recorded festivals were dynastic rather than Olympian, and 'the dynastic cult had very little religious significance at all'.[15]

A symptom of the disintegration of a Greek culture based on a shared inheritance was the increasing prevalence of attacks on temples. From time immemorial, the temples of the gods had been inviolate to pillage. As Heracles says in Sophocles's *Philoctetes*, 'When you capture Troy, respect the shrines of the gods. Reverence is what the gods prize above everything.'[16] Late in the fourth century, the King of Macedon was tempted to plunder Ephesus, but forbore, fearing his soldiers would refuse to obey his orders. In the third century, in spite of repeated appeals from temple guardians and the organizers of festivals requesting that the sanctity of sacred sites be respected, there were sackings by Gauls and Scythians, from whom, perhaps, no better could be expected. Sacrilegious sackings multiplied, and by the second century Greeks themselves were joining in.[17]

While the intellectuals of the fourth century debated, those of simple faith continued to believe in the old deities, to seek the guidance of oracles and to believe that the gods walked among them. A subtle change was occurring, however. Dover comments on the increasing interest in magic in the Hellenistic period (the third and later centuries).[18] The calling-up of occult forces to influence the physical world certainly manifests a belief in the Unseen Powers, but it also illustrates a profound change in the relationship between this and the 'other' world. No longer does the creature seek to do the will of its creator, but on the contrary the Unseen Powers are enlisted to manipulate the natural world, usually to the immediate physical advantage of the manipulators or their clients.

Paradoxically, the sphere in which religion was making its greatest impact was also to be the source of the transition from religion to philosophy. The terrible enigma of unwarranted suffering found a solution in the developing acceptance of universal immortality and personal accountability. Belief in some sort of shadowy afterlife (except for heroes, who shine in Elysium) had been evident in Homer's eighth-century *Odyssey*, and Homer envisaged punishment of perjurors beyond the grave. There are suggestions from the sixth century that initiation in the Eleusinian Mysteries[*] offered some sort of preferential treatment in the next world. Aeschylus, in *The Suppliants*, early in the fifth century mentions the prospect of a general judgement after death. During the fourth century BC the prospect of every soul surviving death, being individually judged, and punished or rewarded in the hereafter made an increasing impact.[19] The orator Demosthenes (in the prosecution of Timokrates) implies that the pious are separated from the impious in the underworld; and epitaphs from this same century suggest belief in a heaven (in the sky) and a hell (beneath the ground), replacing earlier suppositions consisting of Elysium for heroes, Hades for the very wicked, and the Shades for everyone else.[20]

By the end of the fourth century, however, terror at the prospect of the merited sufferings in the next world was replacing horror at the unmerited sufferings in this. In about 307 BC the philosopher Epicurus established himself in Athens. Though his name is now associated with the philosophy of 'eat, drink and be merry for tomorrow we die', he was far from being a hedonist. He lived at a time of catastrophe for mainland Greece, as first Philip of Macedon and then his son Alexander subjugated city after city. Political liberty and a life of civic duty and responsibility no longer seemed a worthwhile option. Epicurus aimed to help people as individuals to attain tranquillity of mind by liberation from fear and mental disturbance, especially from fear of the gods and of death. Scientific enquiry he regarded not as an end in itself, but as a means to that philosophic end. His system of thought was composed of three strands – a theory of knowledge; physics; and ethics. It remained a potent influence for some seven centuries.

Epicurus did not deny the existence of the gods, nor dispute the

---

[*] Eleusis was a town in Attica. From very ancient times, ceremonies associated with the earth's fertility had been carried out there. Sometime before 600 BC Athens took over responsibility for the Mysteries, which were by now connected with Demeter, the corn goddess, and Dionysus, the god of wine. The content of the Mysteries and associated rites is unknown, but they remained deeply venerated until the end of paganism. 'Moral notions came to be associated with the mysteries, and righteousness and gentleness were added to ritual purity' (*Oxford Classical Dictionary*, 'Mysteries').

possibility that intimations of their attributes might be vouchsafed in dreams. He maintained, however, that they had no relevance to human lives, it was pointless to try to propitiate or cajole them, and for all practical purposes they could be ignored. His philosophy is profoundly materialist. Sense-perception is the one and only basis of knowledge. Repeated sensation provides the foundation for generalization. Our senses are assailed by a stream of atomic particles given off by objects. 'Everything is due to the atoms and their movement: this perishable world as well as the infinite number of other worlds, including men and gods. At death the atoms of the soul are dispersed and sensation ceases immediately.' In life there are two basic feelings, pleasure and pain. Seeking the one and avoiding the other constitutes the basis of ethics.[21]

This was, however, no debauchees' charter. Pleasure resulted from imperturbability, not desire. Epicurus recommended a life of great simplicity which eschewed the pursuit of wealth, power or honour. He opposed involvement in public life, and thought it preferable that his followers should not marry or have children. Those in whom the flesh was too weak for this prescript to be followed were enjoined to remember that it was a mistake to pursue short-term pleasure at the cost of long-term pain, and that there could never be merit in the pursuit of insatiable desire.[22] Of course his philosophy was easily perverted. The message that went home in many cases was that pleasing oneself was the goal of life, and should be pursued without let or hindrance, as we would only pass this way once, and were not answerable, now or ever, to anyone but ourselves.

A few years after Epicurus began his mission (and he did see it as a mission – to reduce human suffering), the philosopher Zeno attracted students to his meditations beneath the *stoa* or portico in the marketplace in Athens, students who were to become known as Stoics. The philosophy of the Stoics laid stress on the underlying unity and rationality of a supra-sensible universe, beyond the reach of human manipulation, but supplying all creation with a spark of divinity which could guide the individual to right thought and action. The Stoic must learn through self-discipline to ride with destiny, responsibly and unselfishly, seeking within himself for the necessary reserves of courage. Stoicism approved of practical involvement in public affairs, but cautioned against emotional involvement, whether in public or private life. A detached independence of spirit was the Stoic ideal, where liberty of the mind could bestow dignity however catastrophic external circumstances might be. If life's circumstances became intolerable, then Stoicism had no objection to suicide as a rational and proper alternative.

This philosophy was to have immense influence on many outstanding figures of the classical world, but it was a sombre creed without mass appeal, nor did it lend itself to the sort of cheerful perversion to which Epicurus's ideas were prone. It is significant of its time of origin, however, for it was essentially a profoundly private, individualistic faith, symptomatic of the fragmentation of community that assailed the whole body politic in mainland Greece.

The third-century Athens which is depicted by the contemporary Roman playwright Plautus is one in which

> clever young men had penetrated beyond Epicurus's ethical sophistry to the logical naturalism of his premises; they had even waved aside the forced idealistic definition of 'nature' which Zeno was teaching them to follow and had learned to give allegiance to a simpler nature more responsive to immediate wishes . . . Young men saw no valid objection to doing as they liked . . . The *jeunesse dorée* of Athens, pleasure loving, undisciplined . . . not yet brutal-ized . . . usually had a gentlemanly code of a kind, and they were often generously devoted humans. But they had no anchorage in principles.[23]

An example of changing mores is to be found in the recorded attitudes to homosexuality – always a litmus paper in testing a society's response to the claims of personal fulfilment. The relationships between males portrayed in Homer's epics, usually ascribed to the eighth century BC, do not go beyond warm friendship. Even Zeus's abduction of Ganymede, which by the sixth century is being regaled as a tale of homosexual attraction, is in Homer inspired by a non-erotic response to absolute beauty. (In classical Greek, the very word *eros* was used, not necessarily in a sexual context, to mean 'passionate joy in', and was not synonymous with physical desire.)[24] Ibykos, a Sicilian lyric poet of the sixth century, introduced a sexual element into the Ganymede story, and also coupled two lesser-known heroes of mythology, Rhadamanthys and Talos. Not until Aeschylus, in the fifth century, are there references to an erotic element, absent from Homer, in the friendship of Achilles and Patroclos. The same century saw the introduction, by Pindar, of an overtly homosexual element into his story of the abduction of Pelops by Poseidon. Dover has described how the vase paintings of the sixth and early fifth centuries are frank in their depiction of homosexual as well as heterosexual relationships.[25]

Though Sappho in the island of Lesbos had been writing love poems to members of her own sex early in the sixth century, no one appears to have noticed the fact. At least six comedies entitled *Sappho* were produced in classical Greece, but her lovers are all depicted as male.[26] One can only assume that, whatever the case for males, female homosexuality was not an accepted concept. An analogous response is evident in the England of the early twentieth century, when homosexuality was not only illegal but unacceptable to most public opinion. Kegan Paul published, for a mass market, a series of highly successful volumes of verses by a Church of England vicar, the Reverend Edwin Bradford; verses which, to a more aware climate of opinion, are patently homosexual.[*] These were 'widely and favourably reviewed by the whole spectrum of the British press', the sexual orientation apparently passing quite unnoticed.[27]

Judging by the vases, and by the literature of the fifth and fourth centuries, moral attitudes to male homosexuality were by no means wholly permissive. There was a recognized framework of what was, and what was not, appropriate conduct. Beardless boys could be the beloved of adult males, but it was not proper for the relationship to continue once the beloved became an adult himself. A homosexual liaison could thus not aspire to permanency, and it was assumed that the role of beloved would be shed as adolescence progressed, to be replaced by the adoption of the role of would-be lover towards some younger beloved. The Greeks had separate words for the lover and the male beloved, words which cannot be exactly equated with active and passive sexual roles, since that would be to assume genital practices which in theory, at least, were not approved – even the vases, though totally uninhibited in their depiction of heterosexual intercourse, stop short of depicting penetration of males by males. 'Their pursuit of the subject to the stage of erection, let alone penetration, is very rare, whereas heterosexual intercourse in a variety of positions is commonplace.'[28]

The moral problem for Greek males was that it was utterly humiliating to be penetrated, shameful and unnatural to wish to be, but there was nothing unnatural about desiring to play the active role; indeed it squared with a 'macho' image of randy masculinity. This left the way open for any sort of conduct with slaves and foreigners, whose moral status and

---

[*] For instance, 'The Kiss':

> He never had done it to Geoff, or to Guy,
> Nor to Arthur – not one of the three;
>   And I thought that he never would, he was so shy!
>   But he did it – he did it to me!

standards were of no consequence, but it complicated matters among equal citizens. One way out of the impasse was the ethos, presented to us in Plato's work, of an adoring but protective sponsorship on the part of the older partner; a grateful, admiring acceptance of adoration on the part of the younger. The adoration is presented as a tribute to beauty – beauty in a particular individual as a symbol of physical beauty in general, ending in contemplation of beauty as an ultimate metaphysical good.

Plato, in both *The Republic* and *Euthydemos*, and Xenophon in *Memorabilia* represent Socrates as condemning homosexual copulation – as distinct from love as a metaphysical concept. There is a parallel in subsequent centuries – the romantic, idealistic, medieval idyll of courtly love, for ever beyond any prospect of consummation. If, for the Greeks, it was boys, not women, who filled the role of the adored, that may be partly because women were so protected as to be inaccessible (except when they were slaves or prostitutes, and thus not appropriate recipients of adoration). Of course the great majority of the men would settle down with wives, but the women's essential function was to be inseminated and provide the next generation – a rather coarse and unspiritual business, entered into with due regard to considerations of family and property, not under the enslaving influence of romantic passion.[29]

Later in the century Aristotle was to lend the weight of his authority to the view that women are spiritually inferior, their proper function being simply to serve humanity by bearing and rearing children. Reason, he held, is to be identified with the male, emotion with the female. Emotion is inferior to reason, and the male must therefore dominate the female. Such attitudes did not accord women the sort of attributes that could elevate them to soul-mate status. Dover believes that another factor was the ever-present threat of war and subjugation, making the hardy athleticism of the good soldier an essential ingredient of comradely love (Socrates served his time in the army, like Aeschylus and Sophocles before him).[30]

How far the concept of 'Platonic' love corresponded to any reality is a matter of conjecture. Writing not of Athens but of Sparta, Dover dates to 378 BC the formation at Thebes of the 'sacred band' of warriors, composed entirely of homosexual lovers. But 'If Spartans of the 4th century BC,' he comments, 'unanimously and firmly denied that their [lovers] ever had any bodily contact beyond a clasping of right hands, it was not easy for an outsider, even at the time, to produce evidence to the contrary . . .' and he adds drily, 'We are naturally tempted to believe that a society such as Sparta, capable of great cruelty and treachery, was guilty also of hypocrisy.'[31]

Certainly homosexual relationships in Athens were not without hazard. Presents and patronage could be accepted by the beloved, but anything smacking of payment risked the accusation of prostitution, which was not illegal (provided the appropriate taxes were paid) but did entail the loss of citizenship and all political rights. The original date of this provision is not known. It was certainly in force prior to 424 BC, when Aristophanes made reference to it,[32] it was an issue in the trial of Timarkhos, accused in 346 BC of homosexual prostitution,[33] and its existence in classical Athens was common knowledge a thousand years later, when the Palestinian schoolteacher Chorikios referred to it during his oration in defence of theatrical mimes.[34] Furthermore, it was permissible for wives to bring a 'suit for ill-usage' against their husbands for 'associating with boys and young men', and there is a record from the late fourth century of a wife seeking such redress.[35] At the end of his life, Plato in the *Laws* enjoined the forbidding of both homosexuality and relationships outside marriage. He held out little hope of the achievement of such continence, however, without the backing of an extreme sanction – the fear of God.[36]

There is a shift during the fourth century towards an admiration for feminine, rather than athletically masculine, characteristics in the beloved youth.[37] If there is anything in the theory that admiration for qualities appropriate in the soldier may have played a part in defining the characteristics of the beloved, then it is of interest to note that the change to a more effeminate definition coincided with the period when Athens began increasingly to rely on mercenaries, on paid troops rather than citizens, to fight her battles for her.[38]

The comic poets in the century and a half from Aristophanes to Menander (who died in 291 BC), writing not for the rarified atmosphere of the Academy but for the audience of 'bums on seats', robustly ridicule effeminacy. 'The reader who turns from Plato to comedy is struck not only by the consistent comic reduction of homosexual *eros* to the coarsest physical terms, but also by its displacement from the centre to the periphery of Athenian sexual life.' So says Dover of fourth-century Athens.[39] The fact that lower-class women were probably less segregated and therefore more available as recipients of affection may be relevant.[40] Among the by now routine comic burlesques of the gods are one or two comedies clearly concerned with homosexual *affaires*, but by Menander's time heroes fall in love only with women, though explicit references to homosexual prostitution occur.[41] The Greek first-century AD biographer Plutarch was among those commenting on the absence of homosexual relationships from the later comedies.[42]

In Alexandria, however, to which the cutting edge of Greek culture was by the third century BC being transferred, Asclepiades writes erotic epigrams to women and boys indiscriminately. His successor Dioscorides shows a preponderance of interest in boys, and in mid-century Callimachus, who became librarian of the Mouseion in 260 BC, is overtly exclusively homosexual, a new trait when compared with the bisexuality of the Athenian model. The most striking development, however, is the emotional quality of the relationships portrayed, from which all trace of Platonic idealism has vanished. Sexuality, not love, is the focus of interest, and Dover speaks of poetry preoccupied with 'sensual gusto'.[43] 'Some of the Hellenistic poems are more blatantly physiological than anything which preceded them,' says Dover.[44] Fraser says of Asclepiades and Callimachus that, though their themes were frequently obscene, they were not crude or obscene in expression, but Dioscorides was explicit in his descriptions of sexual intercourse, a matter on which Athenian poets of earlier generations had exercised restraint.[45] In the ripe senate society, sensation is not to be trammelled by the dictates of good taste.

'We notice at once the absence of deep emotion.' Asclepiades is, for the most part, 'concerned with the demi-monde, in particular with *hetaerae*, whose ways and whose power over men and over himself he illuminates brilliantly' . . . 'a world of venal love in which the young of both sexes refuse and grant their favours with equanimity and impartiality, on a cash basis'.[46] Callimachus, by his own admission a victim of 'the disease of loving boys', was unable to escape the enslavement of being in thrall to a succession of promiscuous and predatory rent-boys, selling to the highest bidder.[47]

Cash, comfort, consumption – these are the goals that are creeping to the forefront of Greek values during the fourth and third centuries. Demosthenes in mid-fourth-century Athens noted the splendid houses built by his wealthy contemporaries, comparing them unfavourably with the simple homes of the previous century. He

> struggled hard to persuade the people to devote to national defence revenues which they had been regularly placing to the 'theatre fund' – not a fund for producing plays, but one for enabling the citizens, free of charge, to attend the theatre and other festivals.[48]

To the Athens of the previous century, the age of Pericles, the idea of raising revenues to employ paid troops would have been extraordinary. In those days the rich served, with their own horses, in the cavalry, the middle class in the infantry, each providing their own armour, while the poorer citizens (not slaves) manned the oars of the fleet or served as army auxiliaries.[49]

But there had been 'a permanent change in the temper of the people: it is the emergence of a different attitude to life. In the fourth century there is more individualism.'[50] Rostovtzeff, an acknowledged authority on the ancient world, and sometime Professor of Ancient History at Yale, puts it more harshly when he says that there developed 'a growing individualism and selfishness, a strong tendency to concentrate effort on securing the largest possible amount of prosperity for oneself and one's limited family'. Of the Greek in the Egypt of the next century he says, 'material interests are uppermost in his mind, and his feverish activity is devoted mainly to enrichment, regardless of ways and means . . .'[51]

Athens may indeed have been a slave-owning democracy, but, Ellen Meiksins Wood argues in *Peasant-Citizen and Slave*,[52] agricultural and industrial production was the work of free citizens. Very few slaves were engaged in agriculture. They were domestics and miners rather than farm labourers. In craftwork, the disdain of technical capability manifested in ancient writings was a peculiarity of the literary class, and was not a widespread attitude.* Legislative texts show a high regard for skill and dexterity.[53] Basic production, in short, was achieved by free, self-governing citizens. As the war-torn fourth century gives place to the third, however, Rostovtzeff sees the mass of the population lapsing into proletarianism and unemployment. 'I use the term "prosperity",' he says, 'to describe the general conditions of a certain period: progress in production, brisk trade, accumulation of capital. General prosperity did not necessarily mean that the working classes enjoyed tolerably satisfactory conditions.' Wealth is becoming concentrated, large land-owners are increasing their estates at smallholders' expense. The second century sees conditions throughout mainland Greece deteriorating still further. There is progressive impoverishment.[54]

Sorokin envisages the collapse of sensate societies as stemming ultimately from their failure, notwithstanding their technological successes, to attain their most coveted objective – rising standards of living; and this failure he attributes to the anarchy and criminality which result from unbridled greed unfettered by moral constraints. He pays

---

* Kitto (1957, p.240) suggests that the contempt shown by Socrates and his circle for the artisan may well have owed less to snobbery about manual labour than to the fact that indoor, sedentary occupations, unlike the physically taxing outdoor life of the yeoman farmer, did not become the fighting man.

little heed to the possible impact of resource depletion on earlier civilizations.* Rostovtzeff, however, reports that the late Hellenistic period saw increasing deforestation, soil depletion and erosion, and the exhaustion of minerals in mainland Greece. He follows the fifth-century BC historian Thucydides in saying that the soil of Greece had always been poor, hence emigration and the development of commerce and industry with which to pay for food imports, a contingency which left the mainland impoverished only after the overseas settlements developed indigenous industries.[55] Vernon Gill Carter and Tom Dale, in *Topsoil and Civilization*,[56] present a different picture. 'The soils of Attica,' they say (remarking that the rest of Greece 'had land conditions similar to those of Attica'), 'were not always poor . . . The soil became poor only after the civilized Greeks started misusing it.' They provide a catalogue of deforested slopes, soil erosion and silting, with lowland marshes being created faster than they could be drained. 'Eventually the topsoil eroded from the slopes until the underlying limestone was practically on the surface of the ground, which is the way most of these hills are today, and which is the way many of them have been since the time of Thucydides.' Where once there had been excellent yields of barley, wheat and other crops, thinning soils had already, by the sixth century, led to the substitution of grapes and olives, crops that furnished wine and oil for export, but left the basic feeding of the homeland on imported grain vulnerable to the vagaries of overseas trade.

They quote Plato's verdict, as recorded in *Critias*:

what now remains of the once rich land is like the skeleton of a sick man, all the fat and soft earth having wasted away, only the bare framework is left. Formerly, many of the present mountains were arable hills, the present marshes were plains full of rich soil; hills were once covered with forests, and produced boundless pasturage that now produce only food for bees. Moreover, the land was enriched by yearly rains, which were not lost, as now, by flowing from the bare land into the sea; the soil was deep, it received the water, storing it up on the retentive loamy soil; the water that soaked into the hills provided abundant springs and flowing streams in all districts. Some of the now abandoned shrines, at spots where former fountains existed, testify that our description of the land is true.[57]

---

* Nor does he foresee the ecological anxieties that were to burgeon from the 1960s on.

The inability of the environment to sustain the pressure of rising material expectations intensified the social conflicts which Sorokin sees as the main agent of disintegration in a sensate society. Competition, unrestrained by the moral imperatives of a shared religious outlook, became ferocious, with increasing anarchy instituting a vicious cycle of worsening impoverishment. Fustel de Coulanges, in his magisterial survey of the evolution of religious influences on classical civilization, remarks of the Greek city-state: 'From the day when it was mastered by material interests, it was changed and corrupted', and writes of the nonstop civil wars that plagued Greece until suppressed by the Roman conquest.[58] Athens's attempts to maintain a semblance of social cohesion included periods of debt remission, and recourse to special levies ('liturgies') on the well-to-do to pay for food, for the obtaining and distribution of which citizens were conscripted into unpaid service as public officials.[59]

Revolutions alternated with mob rule, while according to Rostovtzeff, 'a dissipated club life flourished and produced a general lowering of moral tone'.[60] In an attempt to maintain living standards, Greek families began, according to Polybius, a Greek historian living in the second century BC, to limit their children, by abortion and the exposure of infants, to not more than two. Infanticide had been presented by Menander in the fourth century as a desperate resort of the poor, but Polybius upbraids his contemporaries for practising family limitation simply in order to raise their surviving children in luxury. The resulting depopulation he attributes to a greed for ostentation and an easy life.[61]

Rostovtzeff, however, reads into the declining population figures a psychological despair, prompted by the increasing uncertainty of life. For law and order was in the process of complete breakdown.[62] In addition to class war, the pirates whose pillage had been endemic in these waters now clustered round the coasts like aphids on a diseased leaf. Sporadic raids had led in the fourth century to the construction of defensive watch-towers, an activity which was intensified in the third century. Human beings, either for sale or ransom, became the preferred form of booty, and purchasing their freedom a favourite object of charity. By the late second century the pirates, operating from secure lairs in Cilicia and Crete, were in undisputed control of the eastern Mediterranean, and their depredations, even as far afield as the west coast of Italy, were to turn on them the full might of Rome, with results that were to clear the area of pirate ships and settlements for several hundred years.[63]

Egypt remained potentially rich, yet here too lawlessness was initiating the same vicious cycle of deterioration. Initially, after Alexander's conquests, the ruler, the ruling and middle classes, and the bulk of the urban population of Alexandria were Greeks, native Egyptians forming the rural masses. For the first hundred and fifty years of Greek settlement, both the ruling class and the Alexandrian middle class remained Greek, descended from the original settlers and amplified by recruitment from educated lower-class Greeks.

The Ptolemies had on their hands the problem of a large indigenous Egyptian population growing increasingly resentful of foreign domination. In 276 BC the ruler Philadelphus took a leaf out of the pharaohs' book and married his sister, which scandalized his Greek subjects but may have endeared him to the Egyptians. A Greek poet who protested was arrested and later executed. Whether for this reason, or because moral standards are very accommodating if not grounded in religious taboo, there appear to have been no protests when, two generations later, the ruler Philopater followed the same course and married *his* sister.[64]

Towards the end of the third century Egyptians were allowed to enrol in the army. This coincided with – and provided arms and training for – a strong growth of Egyptian nationalism. The first half of the second century witnessed increasing insecurity and mob rioting. The royal house began to play off the Greeks and Egyptians in support of its own dynastic quarrels, and the triumph of the Egyptian-supported faction led to a diminution of Greek influence.[65]

The first Ptolemy instituted, in close connection with the royal house, the worship of Serapis as patron deity for the Greeks of Alexandria, hoping thereby to weld them into a corporate unity notwithstanding their very diverse origins. The cult appears to have inspired little in the way of literature, and to have languished, particularly as native Egyptians infiltrated the Greek-Egyptian world.[*] In the third century the oath of the city was sworn in the names of the gods of central Greece, but as on the mainland the speculations of the philosophers took their toll. According to Fraser, by the first century BC,

> We are probably justified in assuming that by this time the spontaneous private worship of the Olympians had considerably declined . . . the over-all impression is that in most directions the religious life of the capital was much reduced in the last two generations of Ptolemaic rule . . . this decline in religious activity is

---

[*] The Egyptians identified Serapis with their own Osiris, and henceforward he became the spouse of their own Isis.

attested by Strabo, when he says that the old shrines of the city were largely neglected in the first days of Roman rule.

This reflects, says Fraser, both the increase in rationalism and also the uncertain religious loyalties of a racially mixed population. There was no common focus of religious emotion.[66]

As in the Greek homeland, civil disorder created conditions in which trade and even agriculture languished. Robbery was widespread and the police were losing the battle with criminals. The river police were unable to guarantee safety for river transport, soldiers were stationed on board the shipping, and by the second century units of the royal Egyptian navy were patrolling the Nile. In the countryside, alive with fugitives from justice living by pillage, villages were being abandoned, dikes and canals were unmaintained, irrigation was neglected. Famines occurred. In the cities, inflation was rampant. The Rosetta Stone, dating from 196 BC, betrays a nation, says Rostovtzeff, in which there was 'pressure of taxes, rapid accumulation of arrears and the concomitant confiscations, prisons full of criminals and public and private debtors . . .'[67]

By now, in Rostovtzeff's view, the strife in Egypt was due to class rather than nationalist rivalries, the Greek and Egyptian poor having assimilated to form one underclass. They were, during the second and first centuries, effectively governed not by the king and his ministers, but 'by a clique of selfish, greedy and lawless officials'.[68] Fraser is equally harsh about the mob.

> The tale of disturbance and racial and political intolerance which marks the history of later Ptolemaic and of Roman Alexandria, both under the Principate and much later, may be assigned to a single fundamental cause: the excitable and savage temper of the Egyptian and mixed Greco-Egyptian population which predominated in the city from the 2nd century BC onward.[69]

By the start of the second century Rome had had enough of international lawlessness. Already, with a view to stamping out piracy in the Adriatic, Rome had established a protectorate over the Dalmatian coast, thereby arousing such apprehension in Macedonia that an alliance was formed with Rome's bitter enemy Carthage, whose colonies in Sicily were under attack from Rome during the Punic wars of the third and second centuries. In the course of the second century Rome conquered Macedonia, absorbed mainland Greece (which became an appendix to the Roman province of Macedonia) and received Pergamum, the most

Hellenized part of Asia Minor, by bequest. Other small kingdoms of Asia Minor followed. Only Alexander's great successor states of Egypt and Syria remained independent, and by the middle of the first century BC they too were Roman provinces.

The Greek hegemony in the eastern Mediterranean was at an end. The Greeks, no longer citizens but subjects of a foreign power, were helpless as Greece was mulct of such wealth as remained in pursuit of interests other than their own. If enslaved, they had to watch their families sundered, their wives and children sold. They themselves, though the educated among them might become tutors or stewards in their masters' households, lost control of their destiny, even to the point that, if attractive, they could be castrated and kept as sexual toys for the remainder of their days. They were, in Roman eyes, an effete and effeminate people who deserved nothing better.

Chapter 5

Sententious to Saucy: the Roman World, Third Century BC to First AD

The Rome that absorbed the anarchic Greek world of the second century BC was peopled by hardy, frugal, rather stern people. Polybius, the contemporary Greek historian, considered them very admirable compared to his compatriots, and he had no doubt what made them superior.

> The quality in which the Roman commonwealth is most distinctly superior is in my opinion the nature of their religious convictions. I believe that it is the very thing which among other peoples is an object of reproach, I mean superstition, which maintains the cohesion of the Roman State. These matters are clothed in such pomp and introduced to such an extent into their public and private life that nothing could exceed it, a fact which will surprise many.[1]

The origins of Roman religion lay in the nature worship of their distant ancestors, long before the Latin tribe founded Rome in, as they were to claim, a date corresponding to 753 BC. 'Generations passed,' says J. Wight Duff, 'during which the Latin gods had no image and no temples. The worshipper sometimes knew no more than that he addressed a spirit of power, a *numen*, of whose very name and sex he might be ignorant.'[2] Once the Latins came into close contact with the Etruscans they absorbed Etruria's 'olympiad crew' so swiftly that, according to Tenney Frank, they 'stepped almost from primitive animism to sophistication'.[3] Their festivals had, according to their own beliefs, originated in the religious calendar drawn up by Numa, who became king in 715 BC, and the observances were concerned with the vicissitudes of the country-man's life, placating benign and averting malignant influences on the crops.[4] A programme of temple building began, including the dedication, in 509 BC, shortly before the final expulsion of the Etruscan kings, of the temple to Jupiter, Juno and Minerva on the Capitol. An elaborate ceremonial of sacrifices and rituals sought to divine the will of the gods, and enlist their support. Already by the time of King Numa, thirty-seven festivals were supposedly in being.[5]

These festivals were originally devoted to athletics and horse-racing, but they went on to incorporate music and dancing, then dramatic interludes, hunting episodes, exhibitions of exotic animals and, much later, gladiatorial shows and public executions. What began as solemn ceremony on a Roman holy day evolved over time, as in the Hellenic world, into obstreperous entertainment. The Roman passion for chariot-racing is symbolic. It began as a religious rite. Every year in mid-October, when the war horses had returned from summer campaigns to spend the winter at home, the harvests of grain and grape gathered in, a chariot race was held at the great race-track, the Circus Maximus, first constructed by about 600 BC. The right-hand horse of the winning team was ceremonially slaughtered, and various rituals were performed connected with its head and blood. The blood was preserved until the following April, when it was used in ceremonies intended to promote crop protection and fertility.[6] By the early days of the Empire, some half-millennium later, chariot-racing was a spectator sport to which the populace was passionately addicted, adoration attaching more ostentatiously to the charioteers than to the gods, while the level of gambling greatly distressed the early Christian divines. The fanaticism of the fans of different teams caused endless street violence, culminating in the horrific six days of rioting when the Green and Blue factions clashed in Constantinople in AD 532, which ended with thousands being crushed to death in the hippodrome.[7]

The inclusion of dramatic displays at the festivals had its origin in the need to placate the Unseen Powers. The Roman historian Livy, writing in the first century BC, tells how, in 364 BC, the Romans sent to Etruria for a troupe of dancers and musicians to perform for the delectation of the gods, in the hope of so propitiating them that they would remove from Rome the curse of a devastating plague. The performance was entirely rhythmic, devoid of song, speech or plot; nevertheless it was the first time that a religious festival had included a 'spectacle', a novelty, says Livy, for a warrior nation that had hitherto known on its festival days only the 'contests of the Circus'. The performers brought with them into the Latin language their Tuscan name of 'histriones'; and thus were the histrionic arts formally inaugurated at Rome.[8]

Livy, who was no friend of the theatre of his own day (some three and a half centuries later), commented that this innovation, though intended as a means of religious expiation, entirely failed to relieve either the mind from religious terrors or the body from the inroads of disease.

However, as in Greece two centuries earlier, dramatic performances became of increasing significance to the festivals. According to Livy, songs in the form of disciplined chants were added to the dances. Sketches were presented (there was no overall plot), but we have no clue as to the content of these *saturae* – or 'medleys'.

The third century BC brought the Romans into close touch with their Greek neighbours to the south. For the twenty-three years of the First Punic War, from 264 to 241 BC, the legions were campaigning in Sicily and south Italy against the Carthaginians and their Greek allies. On their return to Rome there was instituted, at the victory celebrations included in the Roman Festival of September 240 BC, the first presentations of comedy and tragedy in the Greek mode, with scripts and a developed plot. Perhaps it was an acquaintance with Greek drama formed during the campaign that encouraged the change. Certainly the playwright and actor-manager responsible for the new departure came from Greek Tarentum, on the instep of Italy, and was presumably himself a Greek. He had been captured and enslaved during an earlier campaign in 272 BC, and though sometimes referred to as a prisoner of war, was only twelve at that time, so was more probably a child slave. He took his master's family name, and is known to subsequent generations as Livius Andronicus. He offered translations into Latin of existing Greek plays.[9]

In the second half of the third century the Romans were to have a further opportunity of gaining first-hand acquaintance with Greek drama, as renewed hostilities with the Carthaginians took them back to Sicily in the Second Punic War, which continued from 219 to 201 BC, and ended with a further defeat for Carthage. Syracuse fell to the Romans in 212, notwithstanding the superior military technology devised for the defenders by Archimedes, who was killed in the siege.[*]

The fashion for adding theatrical performances to the customary festival horse-racing and athletic contests gradually spread. In addition to the September Roman Festival, of great antiquity and dedicated to the worship of Jupiter, there were introduced during the latter half of the third century the Festival of the Goddess Flora, dating from 238 BC; the Festival of the Plebs (also dedicated to Jupiter) in 230; that of Apollo, first celebrated in Rome in 212 BC but of much earlier date elsewhere in Italy; of Ceres, not proven before 202 BC but again almost certainly of much earlier origin; and finally, in 204, the Festival of Cybele, the Great

---

[*] Livy and the Greek historian Polybius tell similar stories of how the old man was discovered working out mathematical calculations in the dust, and killed by a Roman soldier, much to the distress of the Roman commander, Marcellus, who had been intent on making the acquaintance of the famous mathematician and engineer.

Mother, brought from Greek Asia Minor and known by the Greek name of Megalesia. Following its presentation at the Roman Festival of 240, drama was introduced at most of these festivals within the next few decades – to the Festival of the Plebs in 200 BC, the Great Mother in 194 and the Apollo in 169. In 160 BC came the first recorded private use of actors, again in a religious context, when a dramatic performance was included at the funeral ceremonies of a certain Paullus.[10]

Tenney Frank suggests that already by 240 BC the Roman Festival was a matter more of entertainment than of worship, not even the races having any sacred associations.[11] It seems evident, however, that there was at least a superstitious formalism, for where there were flaws in the ritual, or unfavourable omens, there might have to be complete or partial repetition of some elements. Livy records that at the Roman Festival in 201 BC, two whole days of performance had to be repeated.[12] The festival performances remained part of a religious ceremony, with free admission, the costs being defrayed by the state and by contributions from those with political ambitions.

The hundred years from 240 to 140 BC were the zenith for the creativity of Roman playwrights. Works by the two principal comic writers have come down to us. Twenty of the plays written between 204 and 184 BC by the Umbrian poet Plautus have survived, all based on Greek originals which are now lost. Six works by the Carthaginian freed slave Terence, produced between 166 and 159 and also all based on Greek originals, are still extant.[13]

Of the work of the tragedians, only fragments have survived, and our knowledge depends largely on what later Latin authors had to say about them.[14] It seems obvious, however, that their inspiration derives from the more humanistic Euripidean tradition rather than that of the theologically austere Sophocles and Aeschylus. Most of the known translations and adaptations are based on Euripides rather than on his forerunners. Dill comments that 'a writer like Euripides, who had a great popularity, must have influenced many by the audacious skill with which he lowered the dignity and dimmed the radiance of the great figures of Greek legend'.[15]

The Romans' staunch religious observance, on which Polybius comments with such approbation, was under challenge even as he wrote, for educated Romans were already becoming familiar with the translation into Latin, made earlier in the century by the playwright Ennius, of Euhemerus's *Sacred History*, with its claim that the gods were only men, heroes of an earlier epoch. 'As a channel for the questionings of Euripides and the rationalism of Euhemerus, [Ennius] distilled into the *zeitgeist* the sweet poison of doubt', as one scholar puts it.[16] Ennius showed no awe of the Olympian gods. In his play *Telamo* his protagonist is represented speaking of the gods' indifference to human affairs.

Right conduct was determined not so much by direct religious injunction (as in the Judaeo-Christian Ten Commandments, for instance) as by tradition, 'the done thing', a consensus on which the upper classes were expected to set a good example. The standard for thought and action was based on ancestral conduct.[17] But it was religion that provided the ultimate sanction. Polybius observed Roman society in the first half of the second century BC from the standpoint of a Greek Stoic, and the Stoics, though believing in divine providence, rejected the crude old pantheon. However, they recognized a social value in the traditional creeds. Commenting on the universality of Roman religious practices, Polybius says:

> My own opinion at least is that [the Romans] have adopted this course for the sake of the common people. It is a course which perhaps would not have been necessary had it been possible to form a state composed of wise men, but as every multitude is fickle, full of lawless desires, unreasoned passion, and violent anger, the multitude must be held in by invisible terrors and suchlike pageantry. For this reason I think, not that the ancients acted rashly and at haphazard in introducing among the people notions concerning the gods and beliefs in the terrors of hell, but that the moderns are most rash and foolish in banishing such beliefs. The consequence is that among the Greeks, apart from other things, members of the government, if they are entrusted with no more than a talent, though they have ten copyists and as many seals and twice as many witnesses, cannot keep their faith; whereas among the Romans those who as magistrates and legates are dealing with large sums of money maintain correct conduct just because they have pledged their faith by oath. Whereas elsewhere it is a rare thing to find a man who keeps his hands off public money, and whose record is clean in this respect, among the Romans one rarely comes across a man who has been detected in such conduct . . . [18]

The reference to correct conduct being the product of an oath is a reminder that here, as in the Greece of an earlier epoch, though it is the state which defines what constitutes moral conduct, it is the gods who provide the sanction when the citizen pledges his oath. Cato the Elder, a contemporary of Polybius, recognized the danger to Roman standards inherent in Greek free-thinking. He despised Socrates as 'a babbler and a man of violence who attempted in whatever way he could to tyrannize over his country by destroying its customs, and enticing and diverting the citizens into opinions which conflicted with the laws'.[19]

While religion concerned itself with propitiation and divination, it was the playwrights of Rome who for many generations filled the role if not of preacher, at least of articulator of contemporary morality, encapsulating through their delineation of character and their trenchant maxims the approved philosophy of life.[20]

The old legends of Greece, Troy and the Olympian deities, and the Greek plays that celebrated them, continued to be quarried for Latin language drama, but in addition Roman playwrights turned to the epic tales of Rome's own heroes. The first to do so was Naevius, a poet who had seen service in the First Punic War, and who wrote on the obvious subject – Romulus – but also on the Roman campaign in Cisalpine Gaul in 222 BC.[21] Ennius, born in 239 BC, a former centurion and one of the foremost Latin language dramatists, much respected among later writers for the wisdom of his philosophic poems,[22] wrote plays about the Rape of the Sabine Women, and about the campaign, in which he himself took part, fought in Greece in 189 BC under the command of Marcus Fulvius Nobilior.[23] Ennius's nephew Pacuvius is known to have written one Roman historical drama among a selection of other tragedies based on Greek originals; and Accius, who died in 85 BC, wrote, in addition to a large number of plays based on Greek themes and originals, two Roman dramas, one of which, *Brutus*, about the expulsion of Tarquin from Rome in the sixth century BC, remained a firm favourite (at least with Brutus's distant descendants, one of whom tried unsuccesfully to stage it as a piece of political propaganda during the confused political situation following the assassination of Julius Caesar in 44 BC).[24] These historical plays take a high moral tone, extolling such civic qualities as honour, courage, loyalty and patriotism.

With the comedies, Roman drama moves from heroics to human relationships. Comedy, too, developed in an atmosphere of cautious moral rectitude, and even scurrilous characters are made the mouthpiece for moralizing maxims. Dialogue readily proffers improving exhortations, such as 'A stout heart in misfortune is half the battle'; or 'Moderation is the most valuable rule in life'.[25] None of the works of Caecilius, who died in 168 BC, are now known, but he was said by the poet and critic Horace to be distinguished by moral earnestness.[26] Familiar Terence tags – such as 'fortune favours the brave'; 'other times, other manners'; 'I am a man, nothing human is alien to me'; 'a word to the wise is sufficient' – have a flavour about them of Victorian confidence and optimism. The comic dramatists have stood the test of time; tags from Terence have, until the recent demise of a classical education, been almost as familiar as some of Shakespeare's, while twentieth-century revivals of Plautus (*A Funny Thing Happened on the Way to the Forum*) cap a long history of similar 'rediscoveries', in addition to such borrowings as the many reworkings of *Amphitryon*, or Shakespeare's *Comedy of Errors*, based on Plautus's *Menaechmi*.

The Roman society for which these authors wrote was, in the late third and early second centuries BC, if not prim, at least proper. As in the Greek New Comedy on which so much Roman comedy was based, bad conduct gets its comeuppance. The outcome of setting to partners is marriage, and, in marked contrast to later centuries, adulterous wives are not a topic of humour and ribaldry. As Duff points out:

> Despite the plots, there is a feeling for the value of morality . . . The Plautine theatre is no carnival of unredeemed profligacy. The worst vices are made repulsive. The morality of Plautus is undeniably better than that of Congreve and Wycherley. Depravity in the aged is derided, and the sanctities of family life are respected . . . It is not unintentional that he puts in the mouth of his most maidenly character the thought that a single wall will serve a city, if it is free of the Ten Deadly Sins, which she enumerates. This is 'the righteousness which exalteth a nation'.*[27]

In the treatment of their themes, Plautus and Terence were circumscribed by convention. The love interest is an important element, but neither in Greece nor in Rome would a young woman of marriageable age be free to meet a young man unchaperoned, least of all out of doors and in the street, which the stage represented.† As a result, 'there are few ardent love scenes in Terence's comedies since his heroines so often do not appear on the stage'.[28] Respectable wives and older women could be portrayed on stage, but if the girls (actually, of course, male actors) were to appear in speaking parts, they had to be represented as either slaves or courtesans. This made them unsuitable marriage partners, and the plot frequently turns on the revelation that the girl is really of good

---

* The reference is to *Persa*, 554ff. The sins are enumerated by Duckworth (p.301) as 'treachery, graft, greed, envy, political corruption, gossip, perjury, laziness, fraud, wickedness'.

† The convention that required the length of the stage to represent a street led to some plot contortion, and far-fetched episodes, such as a harlot bringing her make-up table out into the street (Arnott, p.108).

family after all, having been lost or abandoned in childhood, or enslaved through no fault of her own. Thus the path of true love finally runs smooth, with marriage its proper outcome.[29]

Loyalty and fidelity triumph. A true love who is so irredeemably compromised that marriage is impossible nevertheless remains the faithful mistress of her lover, but 'whenever marriage is possible, the youth in almost every instance marries the girl of his choice'.[30] In a number of plays, a respectable girl is violated before the start of the drama, but she ends up married to her violator, the overimpulsive hero.* [31]

By retaining the Greek settings, Plautus could get away with a bawdiness which Romans would not have accepted as applicable to their own society, presenting an essentially frivolous world which Frank describes as utterly different from Rome's universal military service and 'the harsh frugality of the Punic Wars', though he adds that 'the time was to come, and sooner than could have been expected, when the characters of these plays were to take on a semblance of realism even at Rome'. Duff remarks that so long as faults and foibles, knavery and intrigue were staged as Greek and not Roman, they could be held to amuse rather than shock.[32] Frank makes the further point that it would have been an insult to Roman womanhood to ascribe virtuous qualities to a Roman courtesan; even in a Greek setting Plautus's *hetaerae* have a limited appeal. But the times they were a-changing, and Terence, twenty years after Plautus's death, though still restricting himself to wholly Greek settings, could risk portraying Bacchis, the courtesan in *Hecyra*, as a noble and generous character.[33]

Terence's contemporaries, meanwhile, were developing an indigenous Roman comedy which, venturing into the provinces and rural areas in search of lower-class settings, freed the boy-meets-girl theme from the restrictions of urban middle-class respectability.[34] In short, a touch of the 'kitchen sink' was apparently introduced, though since only fragments of this genre survive, it is not possible to be confident. It is evident, however, from subsequent references, that there was an exploration of more daring themes. There are references to such erstwhile shocking notions as adultery on the part of Roman wives.[35]

But the most concerted attack on traditional morality in the early second century came not from literary free-thinkers exploring Greek

---

* Illicit couplings in Roman literature usually involve rape rather than seduction. Relationships in Ovid's *Metamorphoses* seem to consist of little else. This is not to be construed as macho aggression, however, but rather as a tribute to feminine virtue, which the Romans liked to regard as incorruptible.

examples, but from a non-traditional form of religion. In 186 BC it was discovered that there was a widespread cult of secret orgies. Livy described them as Bacchic, but some scholars suspect a connection with the importation in 204 BC of the cult of the Phrygian Great Mother, which as practised in Asia included orgiastic rites.[36] Whatever the deity being worshipped, those involved in the scandal of 186 BC were accused of crimes ranging from fraud and forgery to sexual depravity and ritual murder. In the orgies 'there were more lustful practices among men with one another than among women'. Practitioners in the cult were executed; those who had 'been initiated but not practised any form of corruption' were imprisoned. Livy's summary was that the seriousness lay not so much in practitioners rendering themselves effeminate by their wrong-doing – that was their personal dishonour, though it unfitted them for military service. The main danger lay in the overthrow of the state by conspiracy.[37]

Unlike Greece, Rome did not pass through a stage of idealizing or romanticizing homosexual love. Early reactions were wholly disapproving. According to Livy, Romans of the fourth century BC thought homosexual copulation an outrage on nature, and for citizens it was punishable by imprisonment. Though there were degrees of depravity, varying from the minor misdemeanour of making use of a boy slave to the major disgrace of being the recipient of the attentions of an adult social inferior, all participation was regarded as shameful. References to so-called 'Greek love' are couched in pejorative terms, and accusations of homosexuality provide a weapon for character assassination.[38]

The Bacchic orgies, though punished at the time, heralded a new era. In Polybius's view, Greek moral 'laxity' spread to the youth of Rome as a result of contact with Greeks during the Macedonian campaign, brought to a successful conclusion in 168 BC. Young men were abandoning themselves to 'the society of courtesans' and 'amours with boys', paying up to a talent for a male favourite. The indignant Cato commented that the Republic was surely deteriorating when 'pretty boys fetch more than fields, and jars of caviar more than ploughmen'.[39]

The new permissiveness was soon made explicit in the theatre. A playwright called Afranius, who flourished in the mid-second century, introduced what Quintilian (writing two centuries later, when some of Afranius's forty plays were still being revived) referred to as 'indecent paederastic intrigues'. Homosexuality had been mentioned on stage before, but usually in a context of vulgar abuse. Now it became a theme. What was more, Afranius abandoned the Greek settings with which

Plautus and Terence had camouflaged their bawdiness, and gave his plays Italian backgrounds.[40]

It was at about this time that the question arose of establishing a permanent playhouse in Rome. By 169 BC all the major Roman festivals were incorporating drama, the last to be mentioned being the Festival of Apollo in that year. Livy remarks that ten years earlier, in 179 BC, the Pontifex Maximus commissioned the building of a *theatrum* and proscenium buildings at the Temple of Apollo, and if this was done, it was the earliest permanent theatre in Rome. There is no further reference to it, and possibly it was used solely for cult purposes, since *theatrum* may, in this context, mean no more than 'auditorium'.[41]

Both Virgil and Ovid envisaged their supposed ancestors in primitive theatres – Aeneas in a wooded valley forming a natural theatre, Romulus and his people sitting on steps made of turf, 'chance leaves covering their unkempt hair'.[42] Once spectacle was added to athletics at the festivals, temporary *ad hoc* stages were erected, probably, at least in the early days, using some part of the temple façade as a backdrop.[43]

Greek-settled areas of Italy which were later conquered by Rome had, of course, their stone theatres; Pompeii's, one of the nearest, being in use before 200 BC.[44] But among the Romans there was a powerful prejudice against the building of any permanent playhouse. In part this was because of the uncomfortable possibility that the populace might start trying to use the opportunity of mass assembly for political purposes, as indeed they ultimately did. In any case, dramatic performances were initially presented on only a very few festival days, and, as Tacitus explains:

> the games had usually been exhibited with the help of improvised tiers of benches and a stage thrown up for the occasion; or, to go further into the past, the people stood to watch: seats in the theatre, it was feared, might tempt them to pass whole days in indolence.[45]

A permanent theatre seemed all too likely to encourage an unseemly waste of time. Above all, for serious-minded Romans, drama was too closely identified with Greek decadence. When in 151 BC work started, by order of the authorities, on a new permanent theatre for Rome, there was an outcry from the old guard, and the Senate ordered the building demolished as injurious to the public character.[46] Later generations were to record Scipio Nasica's plea to the Senate that 'they should not allow the luxury of the Greeks to overrun the manly practices of the fatherland', nor 'by favouring foreign frivolity to allow Roman manhood to be undermined and sapped'.[47]

The perceived threat to Roman manhood came in large part from the fact that the performers, professional dancers, were regarded as fops and nancy-boys. Roman theatre had never been the vehicle for worshipful (male) community participation as in the early Greek theatre. On the contrary, as Livy was later to point out, there was from the start an unbridgeable gulf between the professional performers and the amateurs, who steered clear of dancing, concentrating on bucolic buffoonery known as Atellane farces, 'a species of comedy,' says Livy, which 'the young men kept . . . for themselves, and would not allow it to be polluted by the professional actors'. As a result, the amateurs suffered from no social stigma, and, unlike the professionals, were not disenfranchised and could serve in the army.[48]

Not only was there to be no permanent building, the opposition also obtained a commitment to the exclusion of seating and the provision of standing room only in the temporary structures, a restriction which cannot have applied in Plautus's time, for the Prologue to one of his plays includes the injunction: 'Slaves! Don't sit down but leave the seats for free men.'[49] A wooden structure with tiers but no provision for seating was put up in 145 BC, but was demolished after use.[50] The building is credited to Mummius, who was celebrating his victories of the previous year in Greece, during which he had looted from the theatre in Corinth the acoustic bronzes developed in the Greek theatre to intensify sound. There being obviously no permanent place for them in his temporary wooden playhouse, they were deposited as trophies of war in the Temple of Luna.[51]

But the tide of Greek influence could not be stemmed. A generation after Scipio Nasica's successful stand against the construction of a permanent theatre, his distant adopted cousin Scipio Africanus Aemilianus, the destroyer of Carthage, though he had far more respect for Greek culture than had Nasica, was shocked to discover, in 129 BC, that respectable Roman families were allowing their children to go to dancing classes.

> In the company of effeminate fellows, and carrying zither and lute, they go to a school for actors . . . When someone told me this I could not bring myself to believe that men of noble birth taught their children such lessons. But when I was taken to the dancing school, I saw, upon my word, more than fifty boys and girls in that school and among them . . . a boy still wearing the amulet of a

freeborn child, the son of a candidate for public office, a boy less than twelve years old, dancing with castanets a dance which it would have been improper for a shameless little slave to dance.[52]

The reputation of these 'effeminate fellows' may be gauged from Scipio's account, a few years earlier, of a perfumed contemporary with plucked beard and eyebrows reclining on a couch at banquets with a lover, indubitably 'doing what ballet-boys commonly do'.[53] In 102 BC Marius punished, in some cases with death, troops under his command found guilty of homosexuality, but this may have been in the special context of military service.[54] Attitudes at the top of society were undergoing further relaxation, and by the start of the first century BC the dictator Sulla was prepared to challenge public opinion by openly associating with actors, and flaunting his affection for one female impersonator in particular.[55]

The show-business coterie with which Sulla surrounded himself included mime actresses. Mime must have been among the entertainments to which the legions were introduced during the Punic wars, but however acceptable to the contemporary Hellenic world (in Syria in 168 BC the king himself was a performer),[56] mimes were in the Roman world considered disreputable, with their female performers, their absence of masks, and their willingness to wander irreverently and salaciously over any subject, sacred or profane. They were not included in the festival dramas of the third and second centuries, with the exception of the Floralia in late April/early May, with which no serious drama seems ever to have been associated.[57] The Floralia developed as a licentious celebration of nature, fertility and sex, especially the latter, the goddess Flora being established as the patroness of prostitutes, from whom mime actresses were not very clearly distinguished.

At the Floralia there was much stripping on the part of the mime actresses, but as late as the middle of the first century BC there was a general sentiment that this, though not inappropriate to the occasion, was rather naughty. It is recorded that in 55 BC, Cato, a magistrate known to be of strict moral standards, was applauded at the Floralia when he ostentatiously left the theatre, thus freeing the audience from the sense of embarrassment under which it laboured in the presence of a citizen of such moral authority.* [58]

---

* Shortly after this episode, Cato found himself organizing dramatic festivals when he deputized for a friend who was supposed to be in charge. Plutarch (*Cato*, 46) records that when he came to distribute the prizes, he 'gave to the actors crowns not of gold, but of wild olive, as was done at Olympia, and inexpensive gifts – to the Greeks, beets, lettuce, radishes and pears; to the Romans,

By the end of the first century BC mimes had become the preferred dramatic entertainment. Their infiltration was gradual. Bieber says that mimes had become the most important part of the Floralia by 173 BC. The acceptance of mime as fare for festivals other than the Floralia is placed by Grysar towards the end of that century, when he believes mimes were used as after-pieces, being performed not on the main stage but in the orchestra (dancing) area in front of the stage. He believes they were raised to stage status around the start of the first century, but even so did not make use of the traditional stage buildings, being performed in front of a special curtain which was draped at the back of the stage after the main drama was over.[59] Certainly by this period mimes were being performed at private functions.[60]

Traditionally, it had been the Atellane farces that supplied the after-piece, the slot filled in the Greek theatre by the satyr plays. These rumbustious romps, also called Oscan farces, are associated with the Oscan town of Atella, where they may have derived from the burlesque mimes of Greek southern Italy. But north of Rome, Etruria also had its tradition of improvised bawdy banter, the so-called 'Fescennine verses', which had been performed since time immemorial at wedding and harvest celebrations. Livy says that after the Etrurian dancers had come to Rome with their propitiatory performances, young Roman citizens 'imitated the dancers, adding burlesque words and actions', which sounds like some less-than-adulatory mimicry, and it was in these amateur effusions that he saw the genesis of the later Atellane farce.[61] Initially, the distinguishing features appear to have been improvisation and amateurism, but improvisation gave place to written scripts towards the end of the second century BC.* Scholars dispute whether the

jars of wine, pork, figs, melons and faggots of wood'. This was done 'to show that in sport one must adopt a sportive manner and conduct matters with unostentatious gladness rather than with elaborate and costly preparations, where one bestows upon trifling things great care and effort'.
* The improvisation was to return. The Atellane farces are widely (though not universally) regarded as one of the principal well-springs of the *commedia dell'arte*, Renaissance theatricals of Italian origin which, like the farces, recycled a small cast of about four masked stock characters including, as did the Roman versions, a hunchback who has come down to us, via his later Italian name of Pulcinello, as Mr Punch. Another stock character, the servant Harlequin, may have had a more sinister origin. *Encyclopaedia Britannica* ('*Commedia dell'Arte*') traces him from a devil featuring in legends in France in the Middle Ages, but he, too, may have stemmed from antiquity. In the amphitheatre a clowning attendant known as Charon (boatman to the underworld) was responsible for removing the corpses. Tertullian (*Apologeticus*, XV.5) calls him 'Jove's brother', i.e. the ruler of the underworld. He in turn stemmed from an Etruscan official who had responsibility for the man/beast fights – a figure shown in Etruscan art wearing the tatterdemalion clothing of the Harlequin, which developed into the neat diamond patchwork of the later Harlequin. The Etruscan is known as Phersu, the 'persona' or masked one, which Heurgon (p.213) identifies with the mask of the demon who reigns over the Etruscan hell.

performers continued to be amateurs. Mime artistes apart, the old contempt for the theatrical profession was fading, and tragedians and comedians were becoming wealthy and respected members of society. Aesopus the tragedian left a fortune when he died equivalent to fifty times the property qualification for knighthood; and Roscius the comedian not only became a rich man, he was actually knighted by Sulla.[62] Both were friends of Cicero and frequently mentioned with admiration by other writers. It is quite possible that professional comedians were by now no longer denied participation in the farces.

Competition from the mime companies did not extinguish the farces, which, with their sharp political innuendoes, continued to irk authority and delight audiences for many generations, though some scholars maintain they never again achieved the eminence they enjoyed in the mid-first century BC.[63] It was the traditional comedies that lost ground to the mimes, as the latter won acceptance not just as after-pieces, but as the principal entertainment of the festival. In the earlier part of the last century BC traditional comedies were still being performed; Roscius, much praised for the beauty of his voice, established a considerable reputation in revivals of Plautus's work. But the contemporary authors whose names have come down to us are writing mimes, the distinguishing features being of course the inclusion of actresses, the absence of masks, and a cheerfully irreverent approach. Plays on a great variety of subjects came to be described as mimes. *Laureolus* concerned the exploits of a highwayman; Quintilian describes a play involving the testing of a poison on a dog, who was trained to feign giddiness and death, recovering to great applause at the end of the action.

The mimes replaced the comedies as repositories of the jingles of improving or sagacious intent, comparable to the verses that used to find their way into British children's autograph books.[*] The mimes burgeoned with saws and adages which were remembered across not merely generations, but centuries. Seneca considered the maxims of one mime author, Publilius,[†] sufficiently profound to warrant declamation by 'the buskin-clad actors, as well as by wearers of the slipper', in other

---

[*] For example:

> *Never let your chances*
> *Like sunbeams pass you by*
> *For you'll never miss the water*
> *Till the well runs dry.*

[†] Publilius came from (Greek) Syria, which according to Grysar remained a cradle of good mime and mime artistes right up to the fourth century AD.

words by tragedians as well as comedians. He particularly admired the wisdom encapsulated by 'the gifts of chance are not to be regarded as part of our possessions'. Other tags he recorded appreciatively include 'Whatever can one man befall, Can happen just as well to all'; and 'The poor lack much; the greedy man lacks all' – a salient comment, incidentally, for a sensate society. His father, also a great admirer of Publilius, quoted variants on the same theme: 'The greedy lack what they have as much as what they do not have'; and 'Luxury lacks much, avarice everything'.[64] Macrobius, whose date is uncertain, but probably some four centuries later, is still quoting tags supposedly from Publilius, such as 'On a journey the merry talk of a companion is as good as a lift', but there is a sharp if not cynical twist to many of them. 'The tears of an heir are a mask to hide a grin'; 'Patience too often abused turns to anger'; 'To put up with an old wrong may be to invite a new one'.[65]

Respect for script-writers did not extend to the players in the mime companies, who, notwithstanding the patronage of Roman grandees such as Sulla, were regarded as tarts and rogues and thoroughly disreputable. Several classical authors recount the story of the mime-writer Laberius, a knight compelled by Julius Caesar to appear on stage in one of his own mimes, who lamented in the prologue 'For twice thirty years I have lived without reproach, and left my household gods today a Roman knight; I shall return home – a mime. In very truth, today I have lived a day too long.' He got his own back on Caesar, inserting into his play the line 'Many he needs must fear whom many fear', and had the satisfaction of seeing the audience turn as one man and look at Caesar, 'Thus indicating that this scathing gibe was an attack on his despotism.'[66] It was a brave action, but he got away with it, and later had restored to him the knighthood which his public appearance as a mime had forfeited.

Topical political references and sketches, along the lines of *That Was The Week That Was*, were integral elements in an evening of mime – but caution was necessary. There had been political censorship of what was said on stage for the last two hundred years of the Republic, in other words almost from the start of scripted drama. Naevius, third-century writer of epics, had gone to prison for his attacks on Roman statesmen, and had died in exile. The lampooning indulged in by the burlesque farces had been even more harshly threatened – according to Cicero, traditional Roman law had provided for the death penalty for singing or composing slanderous or insulting material.[67] Horace says that the Fescennine verses, which had started 'innocent', became so wounding that 'at last a law was carried with a penalty, forbidding the portrayal of any in abusive strain', and Tacitus remarks that 'the old Oscan farce [came] to such a pitch of indecency and power that it needed the authority of the senate to check it'.[68] Neither makes clear the date to which he is referring. In 115 BC the *ars ludicra* were banished from Rome, and though this phrase later came to apply to all dramatic entertainment, Frank suggests that at this period it refers only to 'coarse or obscene' performances, not to serious drama, which evidently continued in Rome.[69] The implication of the comments by classical writers is that the offence lay in the attacks on prominent individuals rather than in the obscenity itself – in short, the censorship was basically on political not moral grounds.

It is evident that the farces and the mimes, with their tradition of improvisation, continued to poke fun at the Republic's authorities. Under the Empire the capricious response of individual emperors made political barbs risky. Some accepted taunts and innuendo, some did not. A writer denounced for scurrilities against Tiberius committed suicide, together with his wife. Caligula had the author of an Atellane farce containing an ambiguous line burnt to death in the arena; Nero was less stern and preferred, when offended, to impose exile rather than execution. Domitian executed the author of a farce which he thought covertly criticised his divorce.

Writers sought protective colouring by camouflaging contemporary politics in distant settings, just as, in Nazi-occupied France, Anouilh's *Antigone* could represent the struggle of the French resistance movement. But it did not always work. The author of a play which had been read to, and approved by, Augustus himself was put to death by Tiberius, and his work destroyed, for supposedly slandering Agamemnon in a tragedy – obviously some pointed contemporary reference was detected.[70] It was safer to stick to the old authors – under the emperors a revival of Euripides could make a contemporary political point, for example staging Jocasta's exchange with her son: 'What is worst in exile?' 'Not to enjoy free speech.' 'This is slavery, not to say what you think.'[71] Philo in the first century AD tells of an audience cheering boisterously at a line in a Greek play referring to 'freedom'.[*][72]

Imperial sensitivities were understandable, for after the suppression of the democratic institutions of the Republic, the theatre came to offer a splendid opportunity for demonstrations of public sentiment. There were

---

[*] There is a contemporary echo. The German writer Bernt Engelman tells of an occasion at which he was present in Nazi Germany when 'a performance of Schiller's *Don Carlos* was halted by thunderous applause at the line "Sire, grant us freedom of thought"' (*The Independent*, 16 January 1988).

many examples of disorders fomented by remarks from the stage, and claques were organized among the audience.* This is the context in which, in AD 17, the Senate forbade senators from entering the house of a *pantomimus*, and barred knights from associating with them in public.[73] From time to time emperors banned public theatre and expelled the actors from Rome, even from Italy, though these banishments always proved temporary. Even when public performances were banned, performances in private houses might be permitted, as they were by Domitian, for instance; again suggesting that it was public disorder that was the problem, not public morality.[74]

It was safer to stick to the topic of sex, for which the climate of opinion was increasingly tolerant. Any excuse for a parade of female flesh was welcome, and nothing served this purpose better than the old myth of Paris selecting the most beautiful from among three rival goddesses. Apuleius, albeit in a work of fiction, gives what reads like an eye-witness account from the second century AD of the entry of Mercury, Juno, Minerva and the delectable Venus:

> to show her perfect figure to fullest advantage she wore nothing at
> all except a thin gauze apron which inquisitive little winds kept
> blowing aside for an amorous peep at her downy young thighs, or
> pressing tight against them so as to reveal their voluptuous
> contours . . .[75]

The old coyness about love scenes on stage had long since gone. Once public opinion had accepted such scenes, producers and performers moved on to on-stage simulations of sexual intercourse. Marseilles, which Tacitus late in the first century AD described as a place where 'Greek refinement and provincial puritanism meet in a happy blend', had in the early part of that century banned mimes whose plots included love scenes, 'lest the habit of watching such things should assume the freedom of imitating them as well', an argument which the bishops of the as yet embryonic Christian Church were also to employ.† [76] But Marseilles seems to have been exceptional. The favourite theme of the

---

* Suetonius (*Nero*, 20) describes how Nero, as an aspiring performer, organized his own admiring claque from a group of visiting Alexandrines whose leaders he paid. They had a special technique of rhythmic applause. Today's football crowds are practising an ancient art. Other writers (see Tacitus, *Annals*, XIV.15, and Dio Cassius LXI.20) describe his claque as Roman, numbering thousands, and sporting a special appearance, with pomaded hair and left hands devoid of rings.
† It has been suggested that the ban was invoked because of the practice of actual, as distinct from simulated, intercourse. The Latin is ambiguous, as indeed is the English word 'performance'. For reasons discussed later, I doubt the suggestion.

mime was adultery, as in the great hit of the second century AD, *The Cuckold.*[77]

Playwrights, however, are of decreasing significance in imperial Rome. There are revivals of old material, but little mention of new plays. The emphasis switches from the realm of ideas to the realm of personal magnetism; from the author to the performer, who increasingly enjoys star status. Already in the last days of the Republic in the middle of the first century BC the mime actresses were achieving profitable liaisons. Horace was shocked when a certain Marsaeus 'gave his paternal home and farm to an actress'.[78] Mark Antony made no secret of his attachment to Cytheris, mime actress and former mistress of several other prominent citizens, who used to accompany him on his official travels.[79]

During the first century AD, adulation for the stars of the stage spread, at least among the more sophisticated, to a new type of performer, one who dispensed with words and relied entirely on gesture and movement to project meaning and emotion – the *pantomimus*.

The Roman enthusiasm for 'pantomime' began when the dancers Pylades and Bathyllus arrived in Rome from the Greek east in the last decades BC, Pylades supposedly giving the first performance in 22 BC.[80] Pantomime was *par excellence* a form of dance, and has therefore sometimes been equated with ballet, albeit a ballet consisting of one principal and no *corps de ballet*. As late as the eighteenth century, when pantomime had long signified not a one-man performance but a stylized format with many players, dancing remained of the essence, and the set pieces were indeed arranged by a *maître de ballet*;[*] but this evolution probably conceals more than it reveals of the classical pantomimists. We can only guess, but for dexterity of movement and gesture, for emotional pathos and the ability to communicate without words, perhaps Charlie Chaplin of the silent films is the closest we can come to appreciating something of the appeal of the classical pantomime.

Normally there was musical accompaniment, from flutes to full orchestra and from solitary vocalist to full choir, recounting the tale being unfolded. But this was not essential, and the greatest pantomime artistes took pride in proving that they could communicate without any assistance from either words or music. Two examples of this, both dated to Nero's reign, are cited by Lucian, a staunch second-century defender

---

[*] A memoir of the great Italian pantomime clown Joe Grimaldi, first published in 1838, describes both his grandfather Joseph and his father Giuseppe as eminent dancers. 'The father of our Joe was originally a pantomime actor at the fairs in Italy and France, at the time these fairs supplied the French Theatre with some of the finest dancers that have conferred distinction on that stage.' Giuseppe became *maître de ballet* at Drury Lane in 1758 (Grimaldi, pp.2–3).

of pantomime. A member of a foreign royal house, accompanying Nero to see a pantomime but unable to understand the singing, was so amazed at the clarity of meaning expressed by gestures that he asked for the pantomime to be given to him, to act as interpreter in his dealings with neighbouring foreign countries. The other incident was even more telling. The Cynic Demetrius derided the pretensions of the pantomimes, saying that the impact lay in the music, not the dancing, whereupon the leading pantomime of the day put on a performance in which 'time-beaters, flutes and even chorus were ordered to preserve a strict silence' while a complicated story was enacted. Demetrius was entranced, saying ' 'tis as if your hands were tongues'.[81]

The pantomimes danced masked, varying masks being one of the props used to differentiate the many roles enacted in each performance, so movements of the head, body and hands had to replace facial expressions in conveying meaning. There must have been a huge vocabulary of gestures, something which modern Italians can relish more easily than Britons, whose range scarcely extends beyond the V-sign and its obverse, the childhood obscene 'long nose', the referee's wagging finger, a recently introduced habit of drawing quotation marks in the air to indicate detachment from the statement being made, and a general agitation of the hands which conveys little other than that the speaker is animated.[*]

The themes portrayed by the pantomimes were drawn chiefly from Greek mythology. Competent pantomimes were expected, according to Lucian, to have an enormous repertoire, memorizing the most minute details of ancient mythology – 'the history of the world from Chaos to Cleopatra' – and it is part of Lucian's defence to maintain that confronted with humanity in all its breadth and depth, the spectator could not help but come away with his self-knowledge profoundly enriched.[82] As with the mimes, however, attention soon focused on tales with erotic potential. Venus and Mars, Leda and the swan, Pasiphae and the bull, Danae and the shower of gold, Cinyras and Myrrha – adultery, rape and incest became the favoured topics, with stage performances of increasingly explicit salacity.

Clearly the pantomimes (male so far as public performances were concerned, though women were performing at private parties) were stars of great personal magnetism. Sex appeal was the strongest weapon in their armoury. They attracted the adoration of fans of both sexes,

---

[*] C.J. Grysar, in 'Über die Pantomimen der Römer' (*Rheinisches Museum für Philologie*, 1834), p.42, comments that the existence in old languages of special verbs to express gestures by eye, nose, lips, fingers or other limbs shows how frequently they were used.

including emperors and their spouses, with resulting jealousies that led to the murder of at least three famous performers: Mnester, whom Caligula kissed in public, came to grief in the next reign when Claudius discovered he was the lover of his wife Messalina; Paris, murdered on Nero's instructions; and another Paris, murdered by Domitian on discovering his empress was in love with him.[83]

Because the early pantomimes covered the same topics as the old tragedies (and may well have had the same traditional stage sets),[84] they have been regarded as in direct descent from classical tragedy. It is true that dramas of profound horror were reinterpreted by the pantomimes, including *Agamemnon*, *Thyestes* and *Procne and Tereus*, the last offering scope for rape, mutilation *and* cannibalism.[85] But there is evidence that for some audiences at least there was a hilarity of response incompatible with a truly tragic performance. Among other examples, Lucian describes heckling from the sophisticated audience in Antioch with such shouts as 'Step over! You don't need a ladder!' when an exceptionally tall player was supposedly scaling the walls of Thebes.[86]

Tragedy, with all its pity and its fear, had taken a different route. The theatre of the first and succeeding centuries AD concentrated on the celebration of concupiscence.

Chapter 6

Pity and Fear? Or Brutalization?
The Rise and Rise of the Amphitheatre

It is apparent that as late as the middle of the first century BC there was a widespread familiarity, at least in Rome, with classical tragic drama. There are copious references in the works of the great advocate and orator, Cicero. He was familiar with the playwrights of classical Greece, probably from reading them in the original, and although, of the subsequent Latin versions, it is not always clear whether the plays to which he refers are still in the repertoire of the first century BC, or whether he knows them only from reading the texts, in many instances he clearly assumes that the juries who are the frequent recipients of his comments are familiar with them.[1]

But Roman audiences were becoming as bored by traditional tragedy as by traditional comedy. Already in 167 BC during festivities (for which a huge stage had been constructed at the racecourse) to celebrate victories in the Dalmatian campaign, an imported troupe of distinguished Greek tragedians and musicians had been subjected to the indignity of having, by public request, to call off their performance and substitute a mock fight. At one point,

> when one of the dancers girt up his robes on the spur of the moment, and turning round lifted up his hands in boxing attitude against the flute-player who was advancing towards him, there was tremendous applause and cheering on the part of the spectators. And while they were thus engaged in a pitched battle, two dancers with musicians were introduced into the orchestra and four prize-fighters mounted the stage accompanied by buglers and clarion-players, and with all these men struggling together the scene was indescribable.[2]

Terence himself, whose plays were produced during the following six or seven years, had to contend with audiences who made plain their preference for boxing matches, and this must have become a traditional way of signifying boredom, for Horace a century and a half later reports dramas interrupted by shouts of, 'We want bears', 'We want boxers'.[3]

Producers in the mid-first century BC tried to engage public interest and fight off the challenge of the mime by changing both the format and the staging of tragedy. The chorus (which had disappeared from comedy) was brought from the orchestra area on to the stage, texts were cut, singing extended.[4] This resulted in a change of design in Roman as compared with Greek theatres. Lacking the need for a large 'dancing' area in front of the stage, the stage was allowed to encroach much further upon the orchestra area, cutting it to a semicircle and resulting, of course, in a longer stage in proportion to the auditorium. The remaining orchestra area was filled with seats, and it was in order to ensure that those seated in them should still have a good view that Vitruvius specified the stage should not exceed five feet in height.[5]

As in the Greek tragic theatre, the type of music used in Roman drama developed over time a more emotional, less austere timbre. Cicero comments in particular on the moving aria in which, in the *Iliona* of Pacuvius, a drowned youth returns to beseech his mother for burial – pouring out 'splendid, subdued and mournful strains' to the music of the flute. On the whole, though, Cicero was not a great admirer of the music of his time compared with the more severe style of the period of Andronicus and Naevius, even suggesting that some of the audience would have welcomed a return to the simpler music of the past in preference to the florid effusions of the contemporary theatre, with their surfeit of sensuousness and the actor-dancer's exaggerated responses.[6] (The music of the comedies he considered trivial, notwithstanding his great admiration for Roscius, who sang to it.)[7] Sorokin says that the impact of Hellenistic culture on Rome propelled Roman music (and the other arts, too) from ideational to sensate virtually without benefit of an intermediate, idealistic phase. 'It skipped this greatest stage and from the predominance of the primitive Ideational jumped directly to the superannuated and overripe Sensate music which was imported from Greece.'[8]

It had been the custom in the early Greek theatre for the singer to accompany himself on the lyre. Later the lyre had frequently been replaced by a flute, which of course necessitated an accompanist, since the principal could not both sing the lyrics and blow on the flute. Flutes were the customary instruments in the Roman theatre,[9] but here, too, there was a change towards a stronger impact, towards the more –

literally – brassy. Horace records how the simple flute was replaced by brass flutes to rival trumpets.[10]

Music was taken extremely seriously in classical culture. It was regarded as having a moral dimension. A play by Pacuvius, *Antiopa*, dating from the second century BC but still very popular when Cicero was a young man, included a celebrated discussion on the respective merits of music and philosophy. The proper aim of both was to promote 'virtue'. Two commentators born during the first century AD lament the increasing stridency and sensuality of contemporary music. Quintilian, the Roman lawyer, recommending musical training as part of the accomplishment of the well-educated man, remarks that it should not be 'our modern music, which has been emasculated by the lascivious melodies of our effeminate stage, and has to no small extent destroyed such manly vigour as we still possess'.[11] The Greek philosopher Dio Chrysostom comments that only the 'strong parts' of tragedy remain, 'I mean the iambics, and portions of these they still give in our theatres, but the more delicate parts have fallen away, that is the lyric parts.'[12]

In Alexandria it was apparently impossible to put on serious drama at all. 'Into your theatre there enters nothing beautiful or honourable, or very rarely; but it is always full of the strumming of the lyre, and of uproar, buffoonery and scurrility . . .' Dio is particularly scathing of the music. '[T]hese performers . . . are unmusical offspring of Disharmony herself, having perverted and shattered the majesty of song and in every way outraged the grand old art of the Muses'. With their 'effeminate ditties', 'music-hall strummings of the lyre' and 'the drunken excesses of monsters', they 'have turned you human beings into savages and made you insensible to culture'.[13]

In addition to changes in the type of music performed, audiences were wooed with increasingly spectacular productions, catering for that 'love of spectacle for its own sake' which Arnott describes as 'the hallmark of Hellenistic tragedy'.[14] At Pompey's games in 55 BC a historical play (not now identifiable) included a pitched battle with infantry and cavalry. A performance of Accius's *Clytemnestra* built up the scene of Agamemnon's return from Troy by including a huge parade of six hundred mules laden with booty – Cicero found it most distasteful.[15] Horace later in the same century complains of performances during which, for four hours,

troops of horse and files of foot sweep by: anon are dragged in kings, once fortune's favourites, their hands bound behind them: with hurry and scurry come chariots, carriages, wains and ships; and borne in triumph are spoils of ivory, spoils of Corinthian bronze. Were Democritus still on earth he would laugh, whether it were some hybrid monster – a panther crossed with a camel – or a white elephant that drew the eyes of the crowd – he would gaze more intently on the people than on the play itself, as giving him more by far worth looking at.

Obviously there was little prospect of sustained dialogue.

... for the authors, he would suppose that they were telling their tale to a deaf ass. For what voices have ever prevailed to drown the din with which our theatres resound? One might think it was the roaring of the Garganian forest or of the Tuscan Sea. Amid such clamour is the entertainment viewed, the works of art, and the foreign finery, and when overlaid with this, the actor steps upon the stage, the right hand clashes with the left. 'Has he yet said anything?' Not a word. 'Then what takes them so?' 'Tis the woollen robe that vies with the violet in its Tarentine dye ...

A sight for sore eyes, no doubt, but by now neither arias nor dialogue are of any importance.[16]

Throughout this progression from poetry to spectacle, the topics of tragic drama continued to be horrific. Subjects found particularly attractive included the story of how Tereus raped Philomela and then cut her tongue out to prevent her reporting what had happened, and the ever-green account of the House of Atreus, with Atreus serving to Thyestes a meal made from the flesh of his own sons. What is significant, from the viewpoint of the changing values of society, is the way these themes are handled.

What evidence there is from the early Roman theatre suggests that there was little on-stage violence. A rape occurs during the course of Terence's *The Eunuch*, but it is off-stage, and the audience learns of it by report. Slaves who refer to whips, chains and crucifixions are seldom depicted actually undergoing chastisement.[17] In the theatre of classical Greece, violence almost always occurs off-stage and is reported, the on-stage staking of Prometheus to a rock in Aeschylus's eponymous play being the exception rather than the rule. Death occurs behind the scenes, and the inert corpse is then frequently brought on to the stage on the wheeled pallet which was one of the earliest pieces of stage equipment. However sensational Euripides may have been compared with his predecessors, he did not depart from tradition in this respect. Throughout such plays as the *Oresteia* of Aeschylus, the *Ajax*, *Elektra* and *Antigone* of Sophocles, or Euripides's *Madness of Hercules* and *Hyppolytus*, victims of violence are wheeled on to the stage only after their deaths have been encompassed.[18] Medea murders her children behind closed doors on which the chorus beat in desperation.

Commentators have sought to explain this by reminding us of the size of Greek theatres, in which, thanks to their superb acoustics, it was easier to follow the action with the ears than with the eyes, hence the preference for reported action; or alternatively that reported horrors worked more powerfully on the imagination, not being limited by what was feasible on-stage.[*] [19] Others have suggested that if the corpse was played by an extra, allowing the deceased principal to reappear (masked, of course) in another leading role instead of having to lie dead on stage, more characters could be introduced with the few players available, so the off-stage deaths were an economy measure. But non-violent deaths do occur on-stage – as in Euripides's *Alcestis*.[20]

So the question arises whether the avoidance of on-stage violence was a matter of pragmatism or of taste. Commentators favouring the latter view draw attention to an account by Plutarch, the first-century AD historian and biographer, of how an audience leaps to its feet in dismay at a scene in which a mother is about to kill, in ignorance, her own son,[†] [21] an action which they interpret as stemming from shocked abhorrence at the proposed on-stage slaughter. The context in which Plutarch introduces the anecdote, however, is a disquisition on the merits of vegetarianism, his point being that we should err on the side of caution before killing for food, since there may be truth in the theory of the transmigration of souls, the moral of his story being that we may in ignorance kill what is precious to us. His story illustrates not general horror at on-stage violence, but at the particular victim involved; and the scholars who prefer to attribute the audience reaction to Greek emotionalism rather than to any form of protest are probably right.[22]

That there was a critical prejudice against on-stage violence is evident. Aristotle, in *Poetics*, makes clear that he thinks it crass.

The plot should be so constructed that even without seeing the play, any hearing of the incidents happening thrills with pity and fear as a

---

[*] There is merit in this argument. When Christ is nailed to the cross in full view of the audience in the Oberammergau passion play, the effect is far less moving than if hammer blows were audible from off-stage, for inevitably the audience, knowing that the actor is not actually being nailed to the cross, begins to wonder how the effect is produced.

[†] The play was *Chresphontes*, by Euripides, of which the text is now lost. It is referred to in Aristotle's *Poetics*.

result of what occurs. So would anyone feel who heard the story of Oedipus. To produce this effect by means of an appeal to the eye is inartistic and needs adventitious aid, while those who by such means produce an effect which is not fearful but merely monstrous have nothing in common with tragedy.[23]

In the first century BC the Roman poet Horace, in his *The Art of Poetry*, was maintaining a similar point of view. The eyes, he admitted, respond more vividly than do the ears, but even so 'you will not portray on stage what should be performed behind the scenes. Medea is not to butcher her children on stage, nor Atreus cook human flesh . . . Whatever you thus show me, I discredit and abhor.'[24]

Horace spoke for the last generation that would defend such a proposition. Seneca, born in 3 BC, was to pack his tragedies with sensational horrors paraded in full view of the audience – if, indeed, there was an audience, a point which is much disputed, many scholars holding that Seneca was read, not performed. A comparison of his plays with those on the same subjects by the Greek dramatists illustrates how much more sensational the approach has become. In Sophocles's *Oedipus*, a messenger tells that Jocasta, the queen, has killed herself, and in some eight lines he describes how Oedipus clutches the brooches from the dead queen's robes and uses them to blind himself. In Seneca's version Jocasta commits a form of hara-kiri on stage, crying, 'Strike here, my hand, strike at this teeming womb which gave me sons and husband!' Oedipus has already blinded himself off-stage, but the messenger expands for some eighteen lines on the gory details. In *The Madness of Hercules*, Euripides's version has the children murdered off-stage, to the accompaniment of cries and sounds of battering, followed by graphic description by a messenger including a poignant account of their mother's attempt to save them. Seneca has Hercules put an arrow through one child on-stage, then take another off-stage and kill him by whirling him round and bashing him with a stone, all to the accompaniment of an on-stage running commentary, not a retrospective account by a messenger. The commentary continues as the mad Hercules seizes his wife, kills the baby she is sheltering, clubs her to death and bashes her head off. Euripides's Medea murders her children off-stage, they are heard crying, then in the succeeding silence blood oozes from beneath the closed door. In Seneca Medea kills one child on-stage, leads the second to the roof where she kills him, then throws the corpse to her husband on the stage below before departing in a flying machine.

Aeschylus's *Agamemnon* includes a description of how Agamemnon's forebear Atreus killed the sons of Thyestes and served them as a meal to their father. Seneca, in *Thyestes*, uses a messenger to describe, in revolting detail, the slaughter and cooking of the children, in which 'the liver sputters on the spits', and then proceeds to show, on stage, the father enjoying, in all ignorance, his gruesome banquet. 'He belches with content', and, half-drunk on a potion of wine to which his sons' blood has been added, he tries to sing and make merry, but is burdened by a terrible premonition of evil. This is followed by the arrival of Atreus bearing a covered platter which he opens to reveal the children's severed heads. The text then works through Thyestes's agonised questioning of whether their bodies lie exposed to the wild beasts, to the horrifying realization that he has himself eaten them.

The contrast between Euripides's *Hyppolytus* and Seneca's *Phaedra* underlines the doubts about whether Seneca could have been staged. In Euripides's version, Phaedra's off-stage death is reported by the chorus, and a messenger comes to report the terrible injuries suffered by Hyppolytus in the chariot accident. He is carried on and sustains several pages of dialogue with his father before expiring. In Seneca, Hyppolytus is killed in the accident of which a messenger gives a detailed and gory description, including battering by rocks and mutilation by trees and brambles as the maddened horses career about with their driver entangled in the reins – a sight which contemporaries no doubt hoped to enjoy in actuality when they went to the races. The several battered remnants are then brought on-stage, and the father instructs himself to 'take in your arms these relics – all you have that was your son', which leaves one wondering whether, if it ever was staged, joints of pork were by this time scattered about the stage. At this juncture, Phaedra kills herself on-stage.

Whether any of this was publicly performed is doubtful. Ronald Vince claims that the last recorded *performance* of a new Roman drama (as distinct from mimes and farces) was in 31 BC, though Quintilian praises a version of *Thyestes* performed at the games in 29 BC to celebrate Octavian's victory at the battle of Actium, for which the author, L. Varius Rufus, was paid a million sesterces.[25] Tacitus refers obliquely to a playwright who is known to have written a Roman historical drama some seventy or eighty years later, during the reign of Claudius, and Carcopino accepts this author, Pomponius, as the last known serious writer to have his work performed on the Roman stage. Quintilian considered him the best of the writers of tragedy he had himself seen, polished and eminent in learning, though 'his older critics thought him insufficiently tragic'.[26] From the time of Nero, there is no proof of the performance, as distinct from private readings, of plays by serious contemporary dramatists such as Seneca. Tacitus's friend, the stage-struck advocate Maternus, though he neglected his legal work in order to compose Greek tragedies, dreamt only of performing dramatic readings – as indeed he did, courting the displeasure of the Emperor with an undiplomatically heartfelt rendering of Cato's opposition to Caesar.[27]

Indubitably public recitals of favourite tragic arias continued to be given, not least by the Emperor Nero, who was of course an inveterate performer, the undisputed victor in every contest for which he entered. But professional performances seem to have become increasingly melodramatic, earning respect for neither the player nor the play. Seneca himself points the contrast between the lofty declamations of the tragedians and their pathetic existence off-stage, living on a daily pittance and sleeping on a pile of rags – a far cry from such wealthy stars as the tragedian Aesopius, friend of Cicero in the closing years of the Republic.[28] In the next century Lucian dismisses tragedy as ridiculous – it has clearly become a parody of itself. He castigates

> the hideous, appalling spectacle that the actor presents. His high boots raise him up out of all proportion; his huge mouth gapes upon the audience as if he would swallow them;* to say nothing of the chestpads and stomach pads with which he contrives to give himself an artificial corpulence, lest his deficiency in this respect should emphasize his disproportionate height. And in the middle of it all is the actor, shouting away, now high now low – chanting his iambics as often as not; could anything be more revolting than this sing-song recitation of tragic woes?[29]

The tragedians did not entirely disappear; Suetonius records that Vespasian (AD 69–79) rewarded a tragedian called Apelles with 400,000 sesterces – the level of wealth necessary to qualify for knightly status – but this may well have been for private performances at the palace; Hadrian early in the next century is recorded as presenting plays of all

---

* Mary Renault, in *Mask of Apollo* (p.375), points out that 'the grimacing, flat-faced masks of Tragedy and Comedy which are a cliché of today's commercial art bear no relation to anything worn on the Greek stage. Masks covered the whole head and included a wig mounted upon cloth, the front only being rigid material . . . [I]n the 5th and 4th century, masks followed the trend of sculpture, idealizing or enhancing nature; from the few representations that survive, they seem to have had great subtlety, variety and often beauty. The mouths were not, as with late examples, opened in a vast dolorous gape, but parted as if in natural speech.'

kinds 'in the ancient manner' in the public theatre, permitting his court players to appear in them; and certainly he included readings from tragedies at his banquets.[30] But tragedy no longer had much popular appeal. Violence was now relished for its own sake. The potential audience had moved even further along the road to authenticity and was in the amphitheatre; watching real blood flow.

The gladiators, too, began as a solemn religious rite. Yet again, according to a writer in imperial times, the inspiration came from the Etruscans, whose early custom of sacrificing prisoners to the shades of dead warriors had long been commuted into permitting them to fight one another, with the victors allowed to live.[31] Livy gives the first recorded Roman incidence as dating from 264 BC, when a modest three pairs of gladiators fought at the obsequies performed by Decimus Junius Brutus in honour of his dead father. The fights were not 'games', but bore the special title of *munera*, oblations to the gods. Livy records two similar funeral celebrations in the next half-century – one in 216 BC when 22 pairs fought, and one in 206 BC, offered by Scipio in Spain on behalf of his father and uncle. We may infer, however, that there were other occasions, for Livy comments that the combatants on the latter occasion were not the usual class of slaves and impecunious freedmen, but were all unpaid volunteers, either settling legal disputes (a form of trial by combat?) or demonstrating courage on behalf of their tribe.[32] The numbers involved were not large. As the second century progresses, Livy notes funerals engaging 25 pairs (200 BC), 60 pairs (183 BC), and a modest 37 pairs in 174 BC, a year in which Livy comments that several small exhibitions of gladiators were given.

King Antiochus of Syria, who had been a hostage in Rome, returned home in 175 BC and introduced gladiatorial combat to his subjects. They were appalled. The king managed, however, to acclimatize his population to what was obviously, by now, entertainment rather than oblation. At first the fights were stopped at the wounding stage. By frequent repetition and the continuation of some bouts until death supervened,

> he rendered such kind of shows not only familiar to people's eyes but even agreeable, and kindled in most of the young men a passion for arms; so much so that although at the beginning he was obliged to entice gladiators from Rome by high rewards, he soon found a sufficient number in his own dominions willing to perform for a moderate hire.[33]

In Rome the *munera* proved so successful that in 105 BC they were instituted as a state enterprise.[34] The authorities welcomed an activity that promoted martial arts and qualities, in preference to the effete gymnastics of the Greeks.[35] During the first century BC candidates for office sought to curry favour with the voters by sponsoring fights, with the result that in 63 BC the Senate disqualified from the elections any magistrate who had financed shows in the previous two years. After the demise of the Republic, the Emperor Augustus required the magistrates to give two *munera* annually of not more than 120 gladiators, thus leaving it to the emperor to bestow on the public much larger and more splendid shows of his own.[36]

The introduction of exotic animals was at first solely for purposes of exhibition. In 289 BC the Romans campaigning in Sicily and south Italy had had their first experience of being confronted by elephants,[37] and they lost little time in acquiring these fascinating beasts for exhibition back home, four in 275 BC, well over 100 by 250.[38] A spectacle in 186 BC, staged by Marcus Fulvius Nobilior (hero of Ennius's play *Ambracia*), included, according to different authorities, lions, panthers, leopards and ostriches. Two decades later, some 40 bears were on display, together with 63 panthers and leopards and several elephants. For over a century these animals of African origin were the only ones to be exhibited alongside the indigenous European stags, boars and bears. Ambitious politicians demonstrated their largesse by searching for fresh novelties, as in 58 BC, when a temporary reservoir was built to accommodate a hippopotamus and five crocodiles, followed three years later by the first arrival of a rhinoceros (the single-horned Indian variety), an anthropoid ape and a Gallic lynx. In 46 BC the first giraffe was on display. In 11 BC came another non-African beast, a tiger, exhibited in a cage. Nero, in the first century AD, is credited with obtaining polar bears and displaying them chasing seals. Some of these animals were not to be seen again in Europe until the nineteenth century, others only as rare and costly gifts to medieval princes.[39]

It is not clear when the foreign beasts first became the victims of staged hunts – they were, after all, difficult and expensive to collect, and only a wealthy society could afford to slaughter them. Hare-coursing and the hunting of indigenous animals such as deer became customary at the Festival of Flora, who, though an old Italian deity, is not listed in the festival records prior to April of 238 BC. Friedländer gives 186 BC as the date at which staged hunts – *venationes* – began.[40] Ferocity builds up in the last century BC. Pliny says that the Senate had passed a law against the importation of African elephants, but that this was rescinded in 114 BC. Elephant fights were staged in 99 BC; and in 79 BC the elephants were pitted against bulls.[41] Early in the same century the dictator Lucius Sulla exhibited lions, and Seneca makes the point that this was the first time lions were turned loose, rather than being in chains as at previous exhibitions.[*] He further explains that they were dispatched by javelin-throwers supplied by King Bocchus (of Mauretania), which suggests that this was an innovation and Rome had no home-grown supply of lion-slaughterers.[42] But the crowd was not yet quite comfortable with indiscriminate animal slaughter. Cicero was present at Pompey's games in 55 BC when elephants were pitted against javelin-throwers. 'The last day,' he remarks in a letter to a friend, 'was that of the elephants, and on that day the mob and crowd were greatly impressed, but manifested no pleasure. Indeed, the result was a certain compassion and a kind of feeling that the huge beast has a fellowship with the human race.'[43]

The occasion was obviously not readily forgotten. The elder Pliny and the younger Seneca, neither of whom had even been born at the time, give accounts of it (and so, some two and a half centuries after the event, does the historian Dio Cassius, but by then an accretion of myths is clinging to the tale). According to Pliny:

> twenty, or as some record, seventeen, fought in the Circus, their opponents being Gaetulians armed with javelins, one of the animals putting up a marvellous fight – its feet being disabled by wounds, it crawled against the hordes of the enemy on its knees, snatching their shields from them and throwing them into the air, and these as they fell delighted the spectators by the curves they described, as if they were being thrown by a skilled juggler and not by an infuriated wild animal ... [T]he whole band attempted to burst through the iron palisading by which they were enclosed and caused considerable trouble among the public ... Pompey's elephants, when they had lost all hope of escape, tried to gain the compassion of the crowd by indescribable gestures of entreaty, deploring their fate with a sort of wailing, so much to the distress of the public that they forgot the General and his munificence, carefully devised for their honour, and bursting into tears rose in a body and invoked curses on the head of Pompey, for which he soon afterwards paid the penalty.[44]

Seneca's version is interestingly different.

---

[*] Pliny the Elder (VIII.53) agrees that Sulla was the first to exhibit 'a combat of 100 maned lions' (in 93 BC) but maintains that two years earlier Quintus Scaevola had organized 'a fight with several lions at once'.

Pompey was the first to exhibit the slaughter of 18 elephants in the Circus, pitting criminals against them in a mimic battle. He, a leader of the State, and one who, according to a report, was conspicuous among the leaders of old for the kindness of his heart, thought it a notable kind of spectacle to kill human beings after a new fashion. Do they fight to the death? That is not enough! Are they torn to pieces? That is not enough! Let them be crushed by animals of monstrous bulk![45]

Seneca assumes the men involved are criminals (*noxii*). But the huntsmen, the *venatores*, who had performed at the early festivals, were skilled operators, akin to matadors.* At some stage there were added the *bestiarii*, who, like the gladiators, were a mixed bag of condemned criminals, slaves and prisoners of war, plus a few ne'er-do-wells willing to hire themselves out, and even a few volunteers intent on death or glory. They trained at professional schools and enjoyed the same dubious glamour as the gladiators. But there was also a category of criminal deemed unsuitable or too venal for such leniency (a category which was to include many Christian martyrs), who were sent into the arena unarmed or inadequately armed, or with their hands bound, or tied to a stake, to suffer capital punishment by being torn to pieces by the wild beasts.[46]

Most societies have considered public executions a salutary exercise in social control; public hangings were not abolished in Britain until 1868, though the hiring of seats and vending of sweetmeats suggests that on the whole the populace set out to enjoy the experience.† At what period the celebratory entertainments at Roman festivals came to include execution by being savaged by wild beasts is not clear. The earliest documented use of the term *bestiarii* occurs in Cicero, in the first century BC, and Dio Cassius (writing more than two centuries after the event) says that men condemned to death as well as prisoners of war took part in all the contests staged at Julius Caesar's games in 46 BC.[47] Incidents are recorded from a century earlier of military commanders in the context of campaign discipline having (non-citizen) deserters thrown

---

* Bull-fights were in fact introduced at Caesar's games in 46 BC: Balsdon (1969), p.307.
† Friedländer (Vol.II, pp.76ff.) recalls the fashionable ladies calling for sherbets and ices to be served at a witch-burning in 1787. It would not be long before *tricoteuses* were watching the heads of fashionable ladies roll from the guillotine. The execution of Frederick and Maria Manning on the roof of Horsemonger-lane Prison in 1849 attracted, according to *The Times* of 13 November, over 10,000 spectators, some of whom had waited all night, and for whose comfort and convenience local householders sold ladders and rooftop seats. 'I felt as if I were living in a city of devils', wrote Charles Dickens.

to the beasts or even crushed by elephants, and Friedländer comments that the use of wild beasts to execute criminals was a form of punishment then already in use.[48] Carcopino suggests that inclusion of such executions in the festival entertainments may have begun in Augustus's reign, at the start of the Empire, but we have an earlier eye-witness account of one such execution during a gladiatorial show in the late Republic, in 35 BC.[49] They were certainly common in the first century AD, forming the usual opening sequence of the day's entertainment (and attracting the avid dawn presence of the Emperor Claudius, so sanitized in Robert Graves's fictionalized autobiography).[50] One thing was obvious – the fact that uncaged, unchained, dangerous animals were now roaming free necessitated another innovation: the construction of special buildings.

The earliest gladiatorial funeral fights, back in the third century BC, had been staged in the Forum. When they were incorporated in the public festivals they were held at one of the race-tracks, of which the Circus Maximus was the oldest, tradition claiming that it had been laid out in the reign of the elder Tarquin about 600 BC.[51] Scaffolding was erected at festivals to provide seating for many thousands of people – Julius Caesar in 56 BC supposedly arranged for 150,000 to be seated, but later enlargements took the figures much higher. Including standing room, a figure of 385,000 was being claimed by the fourth century AD.[52] The animals were penned in enclosures, hence Pliny's reference to the desperate attempts of the elephants to charge the palisades, as a result of which Caesar later had a moat constructed to improve security. In 46 BC Caesar constructed a special wooden hunting theatre which had seats all round and no stage – hence its name, first documented about a generation later: the 'double theatre', or *amphitheatre*.[53]

The town of Pompeii had constructed a permanent stone amphitheatre early in the century, but probably for gladiators, not animal-baiting, as there were no underground passages or storage cages.[54] Rome's first purpose-built stone amphitheatre dates from 29 BC, and it served till its destruction in the great fire of AD 64, after which the notorious Colosseum was constructed. The stage was set for that orgy of blood-letting, human and animal, with which the Roman Empire is indissolubly linked.

The scale is hard to visualize. It was the Emperor Augustus's proud boast, in the testament he left to his presumably grateful people, that in the course of eight spectacles he had given in Rome, 10,000 men had fought and 3,500 animals been slain.[55] At the dedication of the Colosseum later in the first century AD, 5,000 animals were killed on the first day alone, 9,000 by the end of the celebrations.[56] The Emperor Trajan was responsible for the slaughter of 11,000 animals at a spectacle lasting 123 days in AD 107, and between AD 106 and 114 some 23,000 men fought to the death.[57] Some of the bouts involved skill, but the lunch-hour intermission was devoted to simple killing, when those of the condemned who had not been fed to the animals at dawn were brought on, one with a weapon, the other defenceless, the victor entering the next bout unarmed in his turn until all malefactors had been disposed of for the day. The emperor Claudius was particularly fond of these lunch-hour sessions.[58] The same timetable was certainly in use at the end of the following century, when the Christian apologist Tertullian remarked how his fellow-citizens enjoyed laughing at 'the noon's blend of cruelty and absurdity'.[59]

Enthusiasm spread in non-Roman lands, just as it had in Antiochus's Syria. Greeks were as receptive as Romans, mainland Greece and western Asia Minor even more enthusiastic than the less Hellenized areas inland, to judge by remaining inscriptions and epitaphs; though this may merely have reflected a link between gladiatorial shows and urbanization, since paucity of evidence tends to be linked with the more rural areas. Evidence of the direction in which taste had moved comes from Sparta; as Martin Nilsson explains:

> Spartan lads had to prove their fortitude by being scourged at the altar of Artemis Orthia. But it is significant of the age, that what previously was a part, if a barbaric part, of religion and training, was now a sensational spectacle not far above the level of a common combat of gladiators. Around the altar was erected a theatre, so that a better view could be obtained of the scourgings, the endurance of the lads, the sanguinary scenes.[60]

Louis Robert, in *Les Gladiateurs dans L'Orient Grec*, lists the Greek towns where the purpose-built amphitheatres went up, among them Antioch, Beirut and Alexandria; he cites eighteen where existing theatres were adapted, including Ephesus (converted about AD 140) and Pergamum. Athens was converted sometime between AD 55 and 62, by the insertion of a marble parapet in front of the lowest circle of seats, enabling the orchestra area to be used for animals and gladiators.[61]

The Greek philosopher Dio Chrysostom watched with disgust as the people of Athens in the first century AD converted their ancient Theatre of Dionysus to the new form of entertainment.

Whereas the Corinthians watch these combats outside the city in a glen, a place that is able to hold a crowd but otherwise is dirty and such that no-one would even bury there any freeborn citizen, the Athenians look on at this fine spectacle in their theatre under the very walls of the Acropolis in the place where they bring their Dionysus* into the orchestra, and stand him up so that often a fighter is slaughtered among the very seats in which the Hierophant and the other priests must sit.[62]

It was not long before Corinth, by now a Roman colony, had constructed a purpose-built amphitheatre, greatly admired into the fourth century.

City by city and town by town the Empire's centres of population began either to build amphitheatres or to insert high barriers in front of the lowest tier of seats in their existing theatres so that they could introduce animals. Some were on the scale of modern football stadia. The Colosseum itself held at least 45,000. In Pompeii 20,000 spectators could be accommodated, in Verona 22,000, or according to some estimates, 30,000. Arles, in Gaul, went up to 25,000; Nîmes to 24,000, and in Aquitaine Poitiers held 40,000 seated, 12,000 standing. On the outskirts of the Empire, in Britain, Germany, Switzerland, Hungary, Transylvania and Spain, stone ruins are less common, but documents attest the existence of wooden structures.[†] Friedländer gives the dimensions of 71 stone ruins.[63]

The appetite grew by what it fed on. The subterranean vaults beneath the amphitheatre at Capua had room for some 1,000 people in addition to the beast cages and the mechanisms for lifting the animals.[64] It was difficult to keep up the supply of gladiators. For prisoners of war the arena provided an alternative to being directly put to death as a sacrificial offering – a practice indulged in as late as the victory celebrations of Julius Caesar.[65] Claudius lost no time after his successful conquest of Britain, and had British captives into the arena by AD 47.[66] There were cases of prisoners committing suicide rather than going out to kill or die with the roar of the crowd in their ears: Seneca (commenting that 'the foulest death is preferable to slavery') reports the case of a German

---

* A statue formally escorted into the orchestra.

† Foundations of a Roman amphitheatre were discovered beside London's Guildhall in February 1988, oval in shape, some 100 yards long, and probably built between AD 70 and 140. It brought to twelve the number of known amphitheatres in Britain, including those at Chester, Cirencester, Chichester, Dorchester and Silchester. Archaeologists expressed the view that there were undoubtedly at least ten more, in such towns as York, Winchester, Colchester, Exeter and Lincoln (*The Independent*, 29 February 1988).

prisoner-gladiator who slipped away from his guard on the pretext of going to 'relieve himself', and then choked himself to death by thrusting down his windpipe the sponge-tipped stick normally 'devoted to the vilest uses'; and in the late fourth century a group of Saxon prisoners strangled one another rather than enter the arena.[67] However, as is evident from Livy's comments about the earliest contests in the third century BC, gladiators had initially been drawn from slaves and impoverished freemen. At some stage, obviously, malefactors were included, those condemned to death providing the quarry for the beasts and the material for the lunchtime bouts, while those guilty of less serious crimes who were sentenced to proper training either as gladiators or as *bestiarii* might, if they were lucky enough to survive for three years, be discharged and ultimately regain complete liberty.[68] Under the more bloodthirsty emperors it was always possible, if there was a serious shortage of fighters, to lower the degree of criminality warranting sentence to the arena – in one huge naval battle (staged on a lake) Claudius used 19,000 condemned men on each side. He sent men to face the beasts even for incompetence at work. His predecessor Caligula, 'when short of criminals for the wild beasts ... had some of the spectators thrown in, after cutting out tongues to prevent protest'.[69]

Roman citizens were not at first liable to punishment in the arena, and though this was later rescinded, knights (*equites*) and senators remained exempt.[70] There was nothing to stop a Roman citizen from volunteering, however, and Caligula knew how to obtain 'volunteers'. In AD 38 he forced some of the knights to enter the ring as gladiators. Twenty-six of them were killed, people being less shocked by their demise than by Caligula's 'excessive delight in their death and his insatiable desire for the sight of blood'.[71] The knights were back in the arena in AD 55, in Nero's reign, and by AD 63 senators, too, were fighting, to Tacitus's great disgust.[72]

But appetites became jaded. The search was on for something spicier. One idea was to send women into the ring. During the Republic a rich man had purchased some women slaves for the express purpose of having them fight at his funeral games, but public opinion had required the annulment of the relevant clause in his will.[73] Times changed. Tacitus records the presence in AD 63 of 'women of rank'.[74] They were used as animal-dispatchers at the ceremonies accompanying the dedication of the Colosseum in AD 80, though the reporter remarks that on this occasion they were not women of prominence.[75] At the Saturnalia festivities in December AD 88 the Emperor Domitian had women and dwarves as gladiators, though one reporter thought little of them, writing to a friend, 'women untrained to the sword take their stand daring – how recklessly! – men's battles'.[76] A relief from Halicarnassus shows two women ('The Amazon' versus 'Achillia') fighting without the helmet customary to their type of armament, no doubt to emphasize their sex.[77] Women fought on throughout the second century, but the use of female fighters was forbidden in AD 200.[*][78]

At some time during the first century AD a brilliant new idea occurred for intensifying the emotions experienced at these extended exhibitions of public execution. The innovation wedded the amphitheatre to the theatre.

Dramatic embellishment of straightforward execution by wild beasts had already been staged in 35 BC, before the first purpose-built amphitheatre had even been constructed. Strabo the Geographer, as a young man of about twenty-eight, had been visiting Rome and had witnessed, during a gladiatorial show, the execution of a Sicilian bandit who styled himself 'Son of Etna'. In the Forum a mock Mount Etna was constructed of scaffolding, on which the miscreant was placed, with cages of wild beasts situated beneath it. The scaffolding was made to collapse and precipitate the robber to his doom among the animals below him.[79]

Now a more sophisticated approach was introduced. The evidence for this next phase comes from the poet Martial, who arrived in Rome from his native Spain in about AD 63; and from the Christian apologist Tertullian, born about a century later into a Carthage which was by that time largely peopled by Italian immigrant stock. The inspiration may well have arisen in Nero's reign (AD 54–68), when a nasty accident occurred during a performance in the arena by 'Pyrrhic dancers'. These song-and-dance interludes, akin perhaps to the band concerts during the interval at a football match, included performances of episodes from mythology, which on this particular occasion featured the story of Pasiphae (who was raped by a bull; in this performance a bull supposedly mounted a wooden heifer in which Pasiphae was concealed, or 'at least many spectators thought so'). There followed the story of Icarus, doomed when the wax in his wings melted because he flew too close to the sun, presumably a tightrope display, but Icarus fell near Nero and 'bespattered the emperor with his blood'.[80]

The next step was to put on dramas involving death or mutilation, but

---

[*] The reason is somewhat obscure. Dio Cassius (LXXVI.16) says of a certain contest in AD 200 that 'women took part, vying with one another most fiercely, with the result that jokes were made about other very distinguished women as well. Therefore it was henceforth forbidden for any woman, no matter what her origin, to fight in single combat.'

to use condemned criminals in the victim roles, and instead of simulating death and disaster, putting it into actual effect. There was, for example, the epic tale of one of Rome's early heroes, Mucius, who in 508 BC muffed his mission to kill the Etruscan king Lars Porsena, and, in a scene reminiscent of Archbishop Cranmer, deliberately thrust his offending right hand into the fire – thus, incidentally, earning such respect from Porsena that he was freed, his family bearing thereafter the proud title of Scaevola, left-handed. Martial describes how this story was re-enacted in the Colosseum, and applauds the panache of the criminal playing Mucius, but adds that perhaps it took less courage than the alternative – to go to his execution in the *tunica molesta*, a garment smeared with pitch in which criminals were sometimes burnt as Nero did the Christians.* [81]

A favourite drama was *Laureolus*. The original Laureolus was no hero, but a runaway slave, who became leader of a gang of highway robbers, and was captured and executed by being crucified and attacked by wild animals. The play about him was written either by Lentulus, an actor who certainly starred in the title role, or by Catullus (generally assumed by scholars to be a first-century mime-writer, but Wiseman makes out a strong case for the claims of the late-Republican poet to be the author concerned).[82] It was a great favourite, remained in the repertoire for decades, and was still being read as late as the fourth century.[83] It was performed in Caligula's presence on the day before his assassination, together with *Cinyras*, a tale of incest from Greek mythology, probably a pantomime since it was performed by Caligula's favourite, Mnester, the renowned pantomime dancer. The evening provided the occasion for copious effusions of the Roman equivalent of tomato ketchup, since Laureolus not only dies messily but vomits blood when endeavouring to make his escape.† 'Several understudies so vied with one another in giving evidence of their proficiency that the stage swam in blood',‡ and this, coupled with the fact that a version of *Cinyras* had also been performed during a festival at which Philip of Macedon had been assassinated (in 336 BC), was with hindsight held to have been, for Caligula, an ominous concatenation of circumstances.[84]

Clearly the whole thing was a simulation. But within a few decades

---

* A modern parallel is the 'necklacing' of political opponents in South Africa.

† Josephus in *Jewish Antiquities* (XIX.94, 95) says that the quantities of mock blood were amplified by the fact that Cinyras and his daughter Myrrha are killed, but if so this is a departure from the legend, in which Myrrha is turned into a tree.

‡ It was the custom for the actors 'secundarum partium' to entertain spectators at the conclusion of a play by imitating the performance of the stars. See footnote to Suetonius, *Caligula*, 57.

the Emperor Domitian had the idea of staging the play in the amphitheatre with a condemned criminal in the role of Laureolus. Martial records his crucifixion and how he 'gave up his vitals defenceless to a Caledonian bear'. Another scene portrayed Orpheus, surrounded by a scenic spectacular of woods and cliffs, a 'grove of the Hesperides'. Wild animals are loosed on to the scene, and Orpheus too is mangled by a bear – a departure from historical accuracy, comments Martial, presumably because in legend he is torn apart not by animals but by Thracian women.[85] A hundred years later the same picture of theatrically staged death and mutilation is recorded with detestation by Tertullian. 'We have seen at one time or other Atys, that god from Pessinus, being castrated; and a man who was being burned alive had been rigged out as Hercules.'[86]

Naturalism could go no further.

Chapter 7

The Ascendancy of the Senses: the Late Republic and Early Empire

Though public entertainment in imperial Rome was to have little to offer but orgies of sex and violence, the closing years of the Republic did witness the construction, at last, of Rome's first permanent theatre. In 55 BC Pompey organized, on the Field of Mars, the building of a huge theatre, in the upper circle of which he craftily incorporated a Temple of Venus, thus averting the threat of demolition, which would have involved the sacrilege of temple destruction. The theatre stayed. Whatever arguments the old guard may still have wished to deploy, drama – or anyway, theatricals – was immensely popular, and even the old guard had to admit that building and demolishing temporary theatres every year was very extravagant.[1]

So, a century after the death of Terence, Rome at last acquired its first permanent theatre. But for the Romans, as for the Greeks, the great age of dramatic creativity was finished before work even began on the construction of any of the Roman stone theatres whose ruins we can trace today. As Duckworth points out, engineering and architectural skills made possible the construction of spacious theatres and ornately decorated stage buildings at a time when the most creative phase in drama was long over. In the imperial theatres, greater splendour of staging was accompanied by increasing triviality of content.[2]

The festivals at which the theatres and amphitheatres were open for business were still nominally holy days, the ceremonies beginning with parades of images of Rome's deities. Augustus mentions in his testament that his Theatre of Marcellus, opened in 11 BC, was built 'near the Temple of Apollo'.[3] There were, as Harold Baldry has pointed out, no special seats reserved for the priests, as there were in the Greek theatre,[4] but the Roman priests were secular, holding other offices of state, and they had reserved seats in their capacity as knights or senators.[*] The

---

[*] Special seating arrangements were a matter of social, not sacerdotal, eminence. In 194 BC seats

religieuses of Rome were the Vestal Virgins, and it is inconceivable that they did not have special places allocated to them, for otherwise they would have been stuck at the back, to which, in a firmly segregated auditorium, the women were relegated.* Certainly when Augustus extended segregation to the amphitheatre, where it had not been enforced prior to his reign, he made provision for the Vestals to have special seats at the front, 'opposite the praetor's tribunal'.[5]

An altar figured somewhere among the stage properties. When Caligula was assassinated during a festival in late January of AD 41, soldiers wreaked immediate vengeance on the conspirators, and burst into the theatre (where the audience, who had heard of the murder, still

for senators were reserved at the games, and later, when theatres were built, these were located in the orchestra area. In 67 BC the People's Tribune, Lucius Roscius, obtained a law (*Lex Roscia*) setting aside for the knights the first fourteen rows behind the senators (Livy, XXXIV.44; XCIX). Both Cicero and the historian Velleius Paterculus refer to this as a restoration, not an innovation, but if so the date of its original institution is not known (Velleius Paterculus III.xxxii.3 and note). The law was extremely unpopular with the ordinary people, and there are reports of street riots against it four years later, but it was not revoked, though not always stringently enforced (Pliny the Elder, VII.117 note). Part of Laberius's disgrace, when Caesar made him appear on stage in a mime, was that by losing his status as a knight, he lost the right to sit in the 'fourteen rows'. On having his status restored, he went to take his accustomed place, but the knights, uncertain perhaps of Caesar's temper, failed to move up to make room for him (Seneca the Elder, VII.3). Distinguished foreign visitors were also permitted in the privileged area. Tacitus tells the story of two Frisians sightseeing in a Roman theatre in AD 58 where 'to kill time (they had not sufficient knowledge to be amused by the play) they were putting questions as to the crowd seated in the auditorium – the distinctions between the orders – which were the knights? – where was the Senate? – when they noticed a few men in foreign dress on the senatorial seats. They enquired who they were, and on hearing that this was a compliment paid to the envoys of nations distinguished for their courage and for friendship to Rome, exclaimed that no people in the world ranked before Germans in arms or loyalty, went down, and took their seats among the Fathers. The action was taken in good part by the onlookers, as a trait of primitive impetuosity and generous rivalry. Nero presented both with the Roman citizenship, (Tacitus, *Annals*, XIII.54) Seneca comments on his right to a seat among the knights, 'not to sell, not to let, not to dwell in, but to use only for the purpose of viewing the spectacle' (Seneca, *Moral Essays*, 'De Beneficiis', VII.12.4). Provision was not always made for segregation by rank. In the temporary theatre which Caligula erected annually in front of his palace, 'no seats had been set apart either for the Senate or for the *equites*, so that the seating was a jumble, women mixed with men and freemen with slaves' (Josephus, XIX.85). By Domitian's time imposters were always trying to sneak into the fourteen rows, and the Emperor took steps to reinforce the law. One man who usually wore green switched to red or purple in an attempt to be mistaken for a knight, but the usher was not deceived. Others, after being removed, loitered about in the adjacent gangway pretending that they were just standing (Martial, *Epigrams*, V.8, 14, 23). The wearing of green, incidentally, did not persist. Originally, audiences were required to wear white. This provision had been rescinded, but Domitian revoked the permission for people to dress in a choice of colour, and enforced the wearing of white, scarlet or purple (Friedländer, Vol.II, p.8).

* If, as seems probable, the Vestals sat in the orchestra area like the senators, this is an example of their status as 'honorary' males, discussed by Mary Beard in 'The Sexual Status of Vestal Virgins', *Journal of Roman Studies*, 1980, pp.12ff.

sat petrified in their seats) and placed the heads of their victims on the altar.[6] But it sounds, from Quintilian's advice to any advocate proposing the erection of a theatre, as if the religious function had become a bit of an afterthought:

> the orator will consider the advantages to be derived from relaxation from toil, and the unbecoming and undesirable struggle for places which will arise if there is no proper accommodation; religion too has its place in the discussion, for we shall describe the theatre as a kind of temple for the solemnization of a sacred feast.[7]

There was nothing very solemn or sacred about the bedlam and bawdiness with which the theatres in fact resounded.

The first century BC had seen traditional religion at a very low ebb. From the end of the third century BC to the middle of the first is, in W. Warde Fowler's opinion, the period of decay and downfall of the old Roman religion.[8] The educated minority had ceased to believe in the gods. The lack of faith extended well beyond a small élite, encompassing at least that section of the population prepared to attend revivals of classic dramatists. When a revival was staged in the first century BC of Ennius's play *Telamo*, in which the protagonist is represented speaking of the gods' indifference to human affairs, the sentiment was greeted, according to Cicero, with applause from a sympathetic audience. He elaborates on the theme with the reflection that if the gods did care, the righteous would prosper and the wicked would not, which is clearly not the case.

The distinction between mankind and the Unseen Powers was becoming blurred, as heads of state began to award themselves attributes hitherto reserved for the gods. As early as 196 BC, some century and a half after the Greeks had set the example, a portrait of a prominent citizen had replaced a deity on the coins of Rome,[9] precursor of that penny which, some two hundred years later, was to be rendered to the Caesar whose likeness appeared on it. The festival instituted in 81 BC in perpetual honour of Sulla's victory was dedicated not to a god, but to Sulla. When a further festival was instituted in 46 BC in similar commemoration of Julius Caesar's prowess, the dedication was to Caesar.[10] Caesar, though keen to establish divine honours for himself, was not overawed in relation to existing gods. When, two years later, he started work on his never-completed theatre, there were complaints that he cleared the site of numerous dwellings and temples, 'burning the wooden statues and appropriating the hoards of money';[11] Augustus himself, when, as Octavian, he had erected in Greece a monument commemorating his great victory over Antony and Cleopatra at the battle of Actium, commissioned an inscription which gave his own name, as victor, pride of place over Mars and Neptune to whom the site was nominally consecrated.[12]

The poet Propertius, who died just before Augustus came to power, had spoken of neglected shrines and deserted groves, piety vanquished and all men worshipping gold. 'Gold has banished faith, gold has made judgement to be bought and sold, gold rules the law, and once law has been undermined, chastity as well.'[13] His near-contemporary Sallust, in Alföldy's words, 'traced the whole crisis of the Roman Republic back to these moral weaknesses', seeing in the love of money and of power 'the root of all evil. Greed undermined loyalty, honesty and the other virtues. In their place it taught arrogance, cruelty, disregard for the gods and the view that everything was for sale.'[14] It was a repetition of Polybius's Greece, where, as he had pointed out, 'bribery, and the notion that no one should do anything *gratis*, were very prevalent . . . they were ignorant of the Roman principles and practice in this matter . . .' Writing in the early second century BC, Polybius had feared, as he ruefully contrasted Roman standards of integrity and incorruptibility with those of his venal fellow countrymen, that Rome might go the same way. 'If I were dealing with earlier times,' he wrote:

> I would confidently have asserted about all the Romans in general that no one of them would do such a thing [peculate public funds]. I speak of the years before they undertook wars across the sea, and during which they preserved their own principles and practices. At the present time, however, I would not venture to assert this of all, but I would with perfect confidence say of many particular men in Rome that in this matter they can retain their faith.[15]

In the course of the second century BC the rampant materialism of the Greeks engulfed Rome. Greed and opulence became socially acceptable. Livy, writing a century and a half after Polybius, was to date the change from the booty brought home from the campaign of 189 BC in Asia Minor. The victory parade included, besides marble and bronze statues, 18,000 lb. of silver and 3,714 lb. of gold.[16] Pliny, too, blamed 'the conquest of Asia' for the introduction of 'luxury'.[17] In the austere old world of the early third century BC, even Roman generals had been forbidden to own more silver than a dish and a saltcellar,[18] and later in the third century, during the punishing years of the first and second Punic wars, severe measures limiting consumption had been introduced, including, in 215 BC, the *Lex Oppia* with its provision that no woman, whatever her social status, should own more than half an ounce of gold, or wear multicoloured garments.[*] The law was still in force in the 150s BC, when the Senate was besieged by women successfully demanding its repeal.[19]

From then on, conspicuous consumption gained in public esteem. Seneca's laments about the ostentatiousness of his contemporaries' villas compared with those of their forebears parallel those of Demosthenes in the Athens of the fourth century BC.[20] Old-fashioned puritans like the elder Pliny were also distressed by the vulgarity (as he saw it) of contemporary opulence. He noted that the ceiling in the Capitol building was gilded with gold leaf in 146 BC, though the extension of the gold leaf to the bronzed tilings some seventy years later did not win universal approval. However, the fashion soon spread even to private houses, with walls and vaults as well as ceilings being gilded.[21] This progression was just what Pliny feared. He distrusted the argument that public affluence was morally acceptable – in his opinion, it inevitably led to ostentation on the part of private citizens, too. He drew his argument mainly from the enormous extension in the use of marble (instead of simple brick), but there were other examples. 'What route is more commonly taken by vices in their surreptitious approach than the official one? How else have ivory, gold and precious stones come to be used in private life? Or what have we left entirely to the gods?' But he recognized that there was nothing the law could do about it. 'When it was seen that there was no effective way of banning what had been expressly forbidden, it seemed preferable to have no laws at all rather than laws that were of no avail.'[22]

This was also the conclusion reached by Tiberius when, in AD 22, the magistrates requested new laws on gluttony. Sporadic sumptuary laws (including one believed to date from 169 BC forbidding the serving of dormice at dinner) had found their way on to the statute book from the second century on, endeavouring, in an attempt to cut down on gourmandising, to limit how much could be spent on what items.[†][23] The Emperor Claudius's potions of dissolved pearls[‡] or Vitellius's

---

[*] Austerity regulations in Britain in World War II included similar provisions with regard to women's fashions – e.g., limiting the number of pleats a skirt could contain.

[†] Dormice are a particularly expensive delicacy, as they are nervous breeders and hard to raise in captivity. They cost £84 per edible pair in England in December 1989 (BBC Radio 4, *Farming Today*, 13 December 1989).

[‡] Both Pliny and Horace refer to this extravagance. An acid strong enough to dissolve pearls would be undrinkable, but could be diluted to potable quality. See Beckmann, Vol.1, p.259.

flamingo tongues and peacock brains were excesses quite untypical even of the rich Romans,[24] but indulgence in food, virtually to the brink of bankruptcy, was condemned only by the old-fashioned, among whom may be numbered such ascetics as Varro and Pliny the Elder, and moralists such as Seneca and Juvenal – the latter three all Stoics, and Varro, though somewhat eclectic in his philosophy, more often than not a supporter of Stoicism. In the first century AD, overindulgence in alcohol was resulting in drunkenness becoming a familiar public nuisance – with increasing numbers of people turning up drunk at the baths, for instance.[25]

Conspicuous consumption, then, was beyond the reach of the law. Bribery and corruption were another matter. In 59 BC Julius Caesar introduced laws aimed at controlling the growing perversion of standards of public conduct, laws which by 46 BC were beginning to bite. In the following year he initiated action in another field of morality, executing his favourite freedman for adultery.[26]

Early Roman society had viewed marriage very strictly. According to subsequent belief, the first Roman divorce occurred in 235 BC,[27] but marriage remained a very solemn and permanent undertaking – not even failure to provide children being regarded as adequate reason to terminate it. A husband could kill his wife if she committed adultery. By the first century BC divorce was commonplace among the aristocracy on the initiative of either spouse, and was being frankly pursued as a means of fortune-hunting, with prominent citizens getting married and divorced up to four or five times. As divorce got easier, adultery ceased to be taken very seriously.[28] Catullus, in his dalliance with Lesbia (his love poems to her were published in mid-century), is typical of his period in expressing no qualms about seeking to seduce her during her husband's absence.

When Augustus achieved sole power in 27 BC, in a country devastated by two generations of civil war, he set about the reconstruction of the nation's morals. He introduced new controls on consumption. He decreed heavy fines on both parties where adultery was proved – replacing the old, and presumably no longer exercised, freedom for husbands to put guilty wives to death.[29]

Alarmed at the evident propensity of the well-to-do to remain childless, something which Polybius had remarked on among the Greeks of two centuries earlier, Augustus in 18 BC introduced penalties for celibacy (*Lex Julia*), and when they proved ineffective, 'sharpened the penalties of celibacy', as Tacitus put it, with the *Lex Papia Poppaea* of AD 9. (It was all to no avail. 'Childlessness remained the vogue.')[30]

Homosexuality remained a criminal offence under the *Lex Scantinia*, whose date of origin is unknown. It was being applied in 50 BC, when Cicero's friend Caelius wrote to tell him of charges and countercharges being brought at Rome by rival political aspirants, but the personal reputation of the president of the court seems to have opened the proceedings to ridicule.[31] Cicero, sharing the Stoic commendation of sexual restraint, considered homosexual passion an 'unseemly emotion', and could not believe his ears when he was openly propositioned on a visit to Laodicea in Greek Asia Minor.[32] But the beau monde of Rome was rapidly abandoning the old moral standards. To enact the passive role was still considered degrading, but there was nothing immoral or unmanly about being a raunchy stud. There are increasingly explicit references in the work of the poets to homosexual *amours* and practices. Catullus, in mid-century, consciously takes Callimachus of Alexandria as his model and scatters among his more sensuous poems episodes involving studiedly obscene images and the coarsest possible language. 'Only thus,' says Wiseman, 'could Catullus get his message through to sensibilities so much cruder than his own.'[33]

It is in the late first century BC, too, that literary references first occur, in the works of Horace and of Ovid, to Sappho's homosexuality. 'No-one,' says Dover, 'who speaks of Sappho's eros for her own sex can be dated with complete certainty before the Augustan period.'[34] Hitherto, the name of the island that was her home, Lesbos, famed for the beauty of its women, had carried nuances of coquetry and dalliance, but not of homosexuality; nor does any such suggestion attach to the pseudonym, Lesbia, for whom the poet Catullus, a generation earlier, pours out his insatiable desire.

In this climate of sexual permissiveness, the old reservations about show-biz dancers, who even in mid-century were ranked by Cicero among the lowest in social status,[35] evaporated. Augustus's moral legislation sought to reassert their inferior status – it included the provision that 'men and women who had senatorial blood even three generations back were forbidden to marry actors or the children of actors'. But Roman aristocrats, women as well as men, were even appearing on stage themselves. Augustus tried to put a stop to it – in 16 BC senators, knights and members of their families were prohibited from appearing on stage or in the arena, but the regulations were constantly flouted, even in the presence of Augustus himself.[36] Dio Cassius recounts how the famous pantomime Pylades paid for a festival in 2 BC in which he did not himself perform, being by then a very old man, but 'it was on this occasion that knights and women of distinction were brought upon the stage'.[37] The nominal ban appears to have continued in effect, however, for Suetonius reports that in the next reign, under Tiberius, 'the most profligate young men of both orders voluntarily incurred degradation from their rank, so as not to be prevented by the decree of the Senate from appearing on the stage and in the arena',[38] and Quintilian bases a legal disquisition on the tricky question of whether a person who has merely performed in a praetor's private garden has or has not 'exercised the profession of an actor', and has or has not thereby forfeited knightly status.[39]

Contemporaries maintained that being part of the audience was just as liberating (or corrupting – depending on one's point of view) as being on the stage itself. Men and women had always had segregated seats at the theatre (Augustus extended the practice to the amphitheatre),[40] but that did not prevent the theatre being a happy hunting ground for forming liaisons – 'to chastity that place is fatal', as Ovid encouragingly urged in *The Art of Love*. He even maintained that it was an ancient tradition, starting with the Rape of the Sabine Women, which had been planned to take place at a festival celebration; and he reminded the ardent that with so many theatres in the city, it was not difficult to outwit the chaperons.[41]

Like Catullus before him, the young Ovid was an Epicurean of the sensual, hedonistic variety. He took abundant delight in dalliance; his *The Art of Love* was a manual less of sexuality than of seduction and permissive morality – and as such, was considered to be pernicious in its influence.[42] The atmosphere, says Duff, 'is that of a reckless pursuit of the voluptuous in a society amid which the demi-monde reached a pitch of polished luxury unsurpassed in history', and where the author is undisturbed by qualms of conscience, patriotism or religion.[43] The antidote, *Remedies for Love*, deals with human sexuality with an unabashed (and unromantic) frankness that some have called obscene – but this, too, was in keeping with a relentlessly materialist philosophy. Shortly after Catullus published his love poetry, the less lyrical, if more profound, Epicurean poet and philosopher Lucretius had firmly constricted passion to physicality, devoting a chapter of his *On the Nature of Things* to demolishing the ruinous and extravagant pretensions of what was only a physiological process.[44]

A decade after the publication of *The Art of Love*, Ovid was exiled by Augustus, partly for a scandal never fully explained, but possibly involving the Emperor's granddaughter; and partly for the immorality of his poetry.[45] Ovid tried to justify himself by saying that the women for whom his work was intended were courtesans. From exile he addressed heartfelt supplications to Rome, pointing out (in *Tristia*) that nothing in his poetry could compare in depravity with the 'foul-jesting mimes' devoted to 'forbidden love' viewed in the theatres by 'the marriageable maiden, the wife, the husband, and the child. Even the Senate in large part is present.' Striking even closer to home, Ovid apostrophized the Emperor himself:

> Run over the expenses of thine own games, Augustus, and thou wilt read of many things of this sort that cost thee dear. These thou hast thyself viewed and oft presented to the view of others . .·. thou hast gazed undisturbed at these adulteries of the stage.[*] If 'tis right to compose mimes that copy vice, to my themes a smaller penalty is due.[46]

It was to no avail. Ovid was never pardoned. He died on the coast of the Black Sea, pathetically in his old age helping to man the walls of his primitive town of exile against the assaults of savage Goths.

In addition to his attempts to legislate improvements to Roman morals, Augustus sought to fortify and restore respect for the traditional religion of Rome, and in 12 BC had himself appointed Pontifex Maximus, head of the state religion, a post which subsequent emperors held until it was specifically repudiated by the Christian Gratian in AD 375.[47] He rebuilt eighty-two temples, and restored old rites and ceremonies which had fallen into disuse.[48]

Given the tenuous connection between the religious beliefs of the Romans and their ethical standards, the link between Augustus's two-pronged approach to Roman conduct has been questioned. J.H.W.G. Liebeschuetz, in *Continuity and Change in Roman Religion*, strongly maintains that 'it was felt that the gods could not be piously asked to maintain the State, while the Romans were behaving in a manner that must undermine it'. The disasters of the civil wars were presumed to be due to the loss of the gods' favour; Augustus saw the moral reforms as an integral part of restoring a right relationship with the gods. Horace, a little earlier in the century, had attributed Italy's wretchedness both to neglect of the gods and to immorality, particularly that of the women, who had failed in their duty of bringing up responsible citizens.[49] The institution of the Vestal Virgins, guardians of the sacred flame, and the

---

[*] Tacitus (*Annals*, I.54) remarks that Augustus's acquiescence in 'theatrical exhibitions' was in deference to the aristocratic Maecenas, patron of the arts, who was violently in love with Bathyllus, one of the earliest pantomime artistes. Tacitus's comment may refer not so much to Augustus's moral campaign as to toleration of the disturbances to public order associated with the theatre, which led to the intermittent banishment of actors.

severity of the punishment to which they were subjected if they forsook their vows of chastity, is evidence enough of the Roman conviction that there was a connection between sexual purity and religious duty.

Augustus's attempt to restore traditional observances had to contend with the burgeoning cults brought in initially by the slaves and foreign settlers. The poet Propertius wrote of the long-gone time when 'no man sought to bring in strange gods, when the folk trembled in suspense before the ritual of their sires',[50] but the sires of the Roman population of the late Republic and early Empire were in large part of alien descent, slaves, settlers and their children, loyal to the devotions of *their* forefathers. As Scipio remarked of the crowd he faced in the Forum in the second century BC, most had come to Rome as slaves.[51]

Greek settlement in southern Italy meant, of course, that the Romans had long been familiar with the gods of Greek Olympus, with whom indeed they identified their own deities; and the newer cult of the Greek Aesculapius had been established on an island in the Tiber by 293 BC. Although the Bacchanalia had been proscribed in 186 BC, restrained homage to Bacchus, as the Romans called Dionysus, had been exempted from the proscription provided not more than five worshippers were present.[52] The innumerable local gods of the Syrians, whose presence as slaves, soldiers and merchants was ubiquitous throughout the Empire, were easily accommodated as assorted manifestations of Jupiter.

In the exigencies of the Punic War, Rome had in 204 BC imported from Greek Asia Minor and solemnly erected a sacred stone, representative of Cybele of the Phrygians, an action which, as W. Warde Fowler puts it, 'illustrates the far-reaching policy of the Senate in enlisting Eastern kings, religions and oracles in the service of the State at a critical time', and, he adds, 'also the curious readiness of the Roman people to believe in the efficacy of cults utterly foreign to their own religious practices'.[53] Whatever belief the Romans may have had in the goddess's efficacy, the Senate firmly restrained the fashion in which she was worshipped at Rome. 'By a law and decree of the Senate, no native Roman walks in procession through the city' at her festivals 'or worships the goddess with the Phrygian ceremonies', says the historian Dionysius of Halicarnassus, and though Roman officials performed the proper sacrifices at her festival, the Megalesia, no Roman was permitted to join Cybele's priesthood, whose members, the Galli, castrated themselves in frenzied ceremonies.* 'So cautious are they,' continues Dionysius,

---

* Using for the purpose, according to Pliny the Elder (XXXV.165), a piece of the superior and highly prized Samian pottery.

'about admitting any foreign religious customs and so great is their aversion to all pompous display that is wanting in decorum.'[54]

Other exotic cults were no more readily assimilated. Isis, the Egyptian goddess, was being worshipped in Greece by the fourth century BC (by which time Macedonian Greeks had conquered, and were emigrating to, Egypt); a Pompeii temple to Isis was in existence by about 105 BC. But when altars to her were erected in Rome, they were, by order of the Senate, destroyed on five occasions between 59 and 48 BC, the 'devotees of this Egyptian cult' being 'repeatedly suppressed by the Roman Senate because of their political activities'. A surprising proposal in 43 BC to allow her a temple was apparently not put into effect; possibly because of a change in the convoluted relationship between the government and Cleopatra.[55] Further restrictions were put in the way of this cult in 28 and 21 BC.[56]

In seeking to generate a renewed sense of patriotism and of social cohesion, Augustus made the person of the emperor the focal point of loyalty. Augustus's adoptive father, Julius Caesar, attracted by the example of the Hellenistic world, not least as experienced in Egypt during his affair with Cleopatra, had initiated moves to have himself recognized not merely as a monarch, but as a divine monarch. Given the indifference of the educated to the traditional gods, the divine element was of little consequence – it was the monarchic principle that stuck in their gullets, and led ultimately to Caesar's assassination.

The Senate which accorded Caesar the dignity he sought was, according to Lily Ross Taylor, packed by Caesar with men of freedmen stock, not deeply imbued with respect for Roman traditions.[*] Insofar as they were of oriental descent and culture, god-kings were not unfamiliar concepts to them. Augustus did not discourage, but he carefully avoided acceding to, such claims on his own behalf, being anxious to preserve the trappings of the Republic – an empty shell given that the militia of earlier times was now replaced with a standing army pledging allegiance to the person of the emperor.[57] Nevertheless, under Augustus state worship subtly changed. In addition to the vows made every 1 January for the preservation of the Republic, vows were instituted, on 3 January, for the gods' protection to be vouchsafed to the emperor. The Senate decreed that honours be paid to the emperor's *genius*, a combination of his guardian angel and the life force within him, and the distinction between worship of, and worship on behalf of, the emperor became increasingly

---

[*] Lily Ross Taylor, in *The Divinity of the Roman Emperor*, gives a fascinating picture of the incremental steps by which Julius Caesar achieved his objective.

blurred. Emperors were pronounced gods only after their demise, but they began to enjoy in life the trappings of godhead.

> The loyalty of the inhabitants of the Roman Empire was re-created by the ceremonies taken from religion: festivals, processions, temples, statues, altars, sacrifices, even very occasionally mysteries, focussed men's attention on their remote sovereign as in their original context they had focussed it on remote gods.[58]

The threat from alien cults was averted – at least for the time being. There were the traditional philosophies to contend with. Neither the Stoics nor the Epicureans set any store by the Olympic gods, though the Stoics retained a respect for a principle of transcendent divinity. Cicero had found frequent occasion to comment on the significance, from the Stoic point of view, of various elements in the classic dramas he witnessed. A passage in Ennius's *Eumenides* describing the abundance of the varied life on earth illustrates, for Cicero, the diversity of the divine mind. He quotes a fragment from Pacuvius's *Chryses*, 'the physical philosopher condemns the auspices and the haruspices [soothsayers], and yet in clear words sets forth the unity of the world', the implication being that if everything in creation is a manifestation of the same underlying reality, it is illogical to deny the possible validity of omens and auguries. What is objectionable is for prophecy to be based not on rational forecasting but on some sort of second sight. He distrusts the implications of Ennius's *Alexander*, in which Cassandra is portrayed raving about the future fate of Troy, fearing that delight in the attraction of the music and dancing may charm audiences into accepting the play's dubious implications of divine revelation.[59] A critic of the Epicurean belief in the pursuit of pleasure, Cicero finds opportunities in the tragedies he attends to ridicule the adequacy of Epicureanism as a philosophy of life, and to validate the Stoic ideal of transcending suffering by self-discipline. He prefers the approach of Roman writers such as Ennius, Pacuvius and Accius, all of whom portray heroes who endure pain with dignity, to the wailing of such Greek heroes as Sophocles's Odysseus.[60]

From the Stoics, with their ethic of public service, Augustus's reassertion of tradition had little to fear. Regarding religious rituals as socially wholesome, the Stoics did not set out to destroy respect for the state religion. But Rome's traditional gods were nevertheless being irreparably undermined. In the last decade BC, Dionysius of Halicarnassus had remarked on the good sense with which traditional Roman religion (he ascribed the impulse to Romulus in the earliest times) had eschewed

> all the traditional myths concerning the gods that contain blasphe-
> mies or calumnies against them, looking upon these as wicked,
> useless and indecent, and unworthy, not only of the gods, but even
> of good men; and he accustomed people both to think and to speak
> the best of the gods and to attribute to them no conduct unworthy of
> their blessed nature.[61]

Less than two decades later, just before his banishment, Ovid completed for publication his great collection of poems, *Metamorphoses*. It exemplifies the flippancy with which the educated classes viewed the old religious myths. *Metamorphoses* is 'full of gods, empty of reverence'.[62] The traditional gods are presented as trivial and capricious, and it is probably to Ovid's essentially frivolous portrayal that subsequent generations owe their disrespectful picture of the Olympian deities, for the work achieved lasting popularity. Whether it was so popular with Augustus is a matter of doubt. The treatment of its author contrasts markedly with that of the pious Virgil, who was profoundly respected under Augustus's dispensation, and who supposedly left instructions to his executors to burn the *Aeneid*, for fear of being condemned on moral grounds for representing Venus begging from her lawful husband a gift of armour for her illegitimate son.[63]

Metamorphoses explores the implications of the Epicurean belief in a universe constantly changing, constantly in flux. Ovid departed from orthodox Epicureanism in that he clung to the belief that beneath the manifestations of change an essential identity persisted. In a section on the doctrines of Pythagoras, he explains:

> Nothing retains its form; new shapes from old
> Nature, the great inventor, ceaselessly
> Contrives. In all creation, be assured,
> There is no death – no death, but only change
> And innovation; what we men call birth
> Is but a different new beginning; death
> Is but to cease to be the same.[64]

This emphasis on continuity, however, does not depart from the essential Epicurean tenet, that the ultimate manifestation of reality is of this world, is material. Lucretius had published *On the Nature of Things*, his magnificent poetic exegesis in defence of Epicureanism, in 58 BC. Here, in terms that could appeal to the finest contemporary intellects, was restated the whole Epicurean philosophy, the creation of the world through the chance agglomeration of atoms, the dissolution of the individual at death (with no fear of survival into any kind of hell or judgement), the ultimate indestructibility of matter, the conservation of energy, and the prospects for evolutionary improvement through change, for (to borrow Sorokin's paraphrase) 'all things are in incessant flux. Only Becoming is real. Unchangeable Being is an illusion.'[65] Serenity is the primary goal of philosophy, and to its achievement gods, demons and all other supernatural powers are an irrelevance.

Unlike his mentor Epicurus, who, living at a very disturbed time in Greek history, had advised a policy of withdrawal from worldly concerns, Lucretius preached an essentially optimistic doctrine of progress. In addition to his missionary zeal to free suffering humanity from the miseries of superstition in this world (such as Agamemnon's appalling sacrifice of his daughter Iphigenia at the supposed behest of the gods) and the terrors of judgement in a life to come, Lucretius was prepared to contemplate the possibility of a golden age not in the past, but in the future (albeit only temporary of course, destined in its turn to perish), when survival of the fittest would ensure improvement in every aspect of life, artistic as well as technological. He traced the gradual evolution of our world from chaos, the establishment of first the vegetable, then the animal kingdoms, and the development of the human species from the hunter-gatherer phase ('Early man did not till the soil – they wandered, eating berries. They did not know how to make fire or use animal skins for clothing . . . They hunted animals with stone and clubs') through the development of language, the discovery of metal-working, first in bronze, then in iron, to the sophistication of societies with settled agriculture, horticulture, law, and arts such as music and dancing.[66] Admittedly there are ambiguities in his text: at one stage he writes that our world is in an advanced stage of its inevitable decay, but later he commits himself to the belief that 'the world is young and new, and it is not long since its beginning. Therefore even now some arts are being perfected, some also are in growth; today many improvements have been made in ships, yesterday musicians invented their musical tunes . . .' What he bitterly doubts is his contemporaries' moral qualities, fearing that 'mankind labours always in vain and to no purpose, consuming its days in empty cares, plainly because it does not know the limit of possession', and he discerns in man's restless pursuit of novelty and wealth a cupidity that can only lead to war.[67]

119

The achievement of further evolutionary progress required a cast of mind that looked outward not inward, that proceeded by induction from observable data, 'a cosmology', in Tenney Frank's words, 'that substituted sense perception for vague mystery'.[68] Reasoning cannot supersede sense perception, for it proceeds from it. 'It is from the senses,' says Lucretius, '. . . that the concept of truth has come.'[69]

'The periods when the Ideational culture begins to decline and the Sensate to rise are marked by the beginning of the improvement of the economic situation of the social system as a whole (though not necessarily of all its parts),' says Sorokin. 'The highest levels are attained, however, at the time of the fullest development of the sensate culture, just before its subsequent decline.'[70] It is no coincidence that the centuries during which Lucretius's Epicureanism was a dominant influence on Roman thought encompassed the most materially prosperous years of the whole Roman epoch.

Chapter 8

The Fruits of Materialism: the Late Republic and the Early Empire

In part, as contemporary writers were not slow to point out, the rising affluence of the last century BC and the first two centuries AD was thanks to the loot of successful wars, but these successes in themselves owed something to applied technology. The main impetus for the tremendous achievements of the highway engineers, for instance, was the need for efficient movement of troops.

The first of the great Roman highways, the 162 miles of the Appian Way, with its gravelled surface and its sixteen-mile embankment across the Pontine Marshes, was built in 312 BC primarily to connect Rome with the military base north of Naples at Capua; later it was extended to Brindisi.[1]

In 295 BC the Appian Way was paved with polygonal basalt blocks, and these were afterwards used for all roads leading out of Rome. The paving was 'two wagons wide, and filled without mortar'. A writer in the sixth century AD, that is, almost a millennium later, was to remark that 'after sustaining so much traffic' there was no separation at the joints, nor was the surface worn down.[2] Towards the end of the century, in 220 BC, the Flaminian Way was constructed, linking Rome with the Po Valley.* The second century BC saw roads pushing out into Dalmatia (145 BC), into Asia Minor (130 BC), and by the 120s into southern Gaul. Trajan linked Syria to the Red Sea. By the second century AD a huge network stretched from Morocco to the Euphrates, from Scotland to the Sahara[†] – extending in all to some 186,000 miles.

---

* Three hundred years later it was to be the location for a monument to Paris, the adored pantomime put to death by the jealous Domitian. 'The delight of the city and the wit of Nile, incarnate art and grace, frolic and joy, the fame and affliction of Rome's theatre, and all the Venuses and Cupids are buried in this tomb', said Martial (*Epigrams*, XI.13).
† After the French conquest of north Africa in the nineteenth century, General St Arnaud endeavoured in 1850 to drive a road through the very difficult terrain of the Kanga Pass in the Atlas Mountains. He was not the first. On the rock face was an inscription by the Roman Third Legion, whose road had passed that way in AD 145. (Nilsson, p.219).

Roads in and near cities in the European provinces were paved. References to paved streets in the older Italian cities go back to 400 BC, and by 300 BC the Romans had learnt the use of lime mortar from the Greek cities of southern Italy.³ Rome itself had been paved by 174 BC. In the open countryside roads were gravelled, with cambered surfaces and rainwater ditches at the side. Major roads were six metres wide, minor roads three.* There were milestones every 1,000 paces (equating with 1,620 yards, and thus rather shorter than an English mile). The miles were measured out through a geared series of revolving drums attached to a carriage, in which a stone was released into a bucket at the end of each mile, a system first described by Vitruvius in about 20 BC.† ⁴

Military imperatives impelled improved sea communications, too. In pursuit of the German campaigns, the Romans in the late first century BC constructed a canal through the Zuider Zee to the North Sea. A hundred years later reconstruction was effected of the old Persian-built Suez Canal between the Nile and the Bitter Lakes, thereby creating a waterway from the Mediterranean to the Red Sea.‡ ⁵

Rome's civil engineers produced, in addition to the road network, an incomparable infrastructure of sewers and piped water. The beginnings were modest. In 312 BC came the first simple aqueduct into Rome, the Aqua Appia, built by Appius Claudius Caecus (also responsible for the earliest highway, started in the same year) for Rome's most populous quarter.§ It was fed by springs east of Rome. Most of its ten miles ran underground in cut stone, but the water emerged into a channel raised on arches as it entered Rome.⁶ The secret of the arch and the vault was learnt from the Etruscans; it was a technique unknown to the Greeks, and it was to liberate the Roman genius for civil engineering.**

* The minimum width stipulated for an English highway was eight feet until 1773.
† The Emperor Pertinax, who reigned briefly in AD 192–3, sold off the goods of his predecessor Commodus, which supposedly included carriages that not only measured the distance travelled, but also 'told the time' (*Lives of the Later Caesars*, p.185).
‡ According to Herodotus, Greek historian of the fourth century BC, the Pharaoh of Egypt had started the canal in the late seventh century BC, but had desisted on receiving cautionary prophetic utterances – though not before 120,000 Egyptians had perished in the attempt. Darius the Persian completed the work a century later, in 515 BC, digging it wide enough for two triremes to row abreast, and of a length which took four days to traverse (Herodotus, II.158).
§ The Romans did not invent aqueducts. The Assyrians were using them as early as the eighth century BC (Singer, C., et al. (eds.), Vol.I, p.469).
** 'The arch and the vault were constantly used in Tuscany and enabled local architects to attempt constructions of a magnitude which the linear construction of the Greeks would not have permitted. At a very early period Rome inherited the essentials of Etruscan technical knowledge, and therein lies the origin and explanation of the monumental character of Roman architecture' (Bloch, pp.164–5).

122

In 272 BC a second aqueduct, the Anio, brought water from the River Anio (the modern Aniene) to Rome via a forty-mile-long underground stone channel. By the middle of this century wealthy Romans were beginning to install private bathing halls in their homes.[7] It was over a century before a third aqueduct was constructed, but in 144 – 40 BC, the Marcia was built to bring water from a group of springs over 56 miles distant. The last six miles of this aqueduct were carried on arches above ground. Fifteen years later the fourth aqueduct into Rome joined the Marcia, using the same arches but running in a separate channel. By now there was enough water to permit the construction of public bath-houses, which were instituted during the second century BC. A census in 33 BC revealed 170 such public amenities.[8]

Three more aqueducts, lined with durable hydraulic cement, were constructed in the last third of the first century BC. By this time there were some 700 reservoirs serving Rome, plus 500 fountains and 130 distribution tanks, many of them ornately decorated with statuary. Four more aqueducts had been added by AD 226, and these were, by the start of the fifth century, feeding 1,212 fountains, eleven huge *thermae* (leisure centres including pools, restaurants and other facilities), and 926 bath-houses. Similar provision was being made elsewhere. Constantinople had nine leisure centres and 153 bath-houses.[9]

Pliny, writing when nine of the eleven Roman aqueducts were in operation, could not contain his satisfaction.

> If we take into careful consideration the abundant supplies of water in public buildings, baths, pools, open channels, private houses, gardens and country estates near the city; if we consider the distances traversed by the water before it arrives, the raising of arches, the tunnelling of mountains and the building of level routes across deep valleys, we shall readily admit that there has never been anything more remarkable in the whole world.[10]

All over the Empire, in Spain and France, in north Africa and the Near East, dales and valleys were being straddled as the civil engineers strove to bring water by gentle gradients from distant mountains. Their surveying instruments permitted assessment of the gradient to an accuracy of 1:2,000, and they maintained watercourses, including those tunnelled through hills, at gradients of between 1:200 and 1:1,000. They knew of (though they did not invent) techniques for inverse siphoning to take water down one side of a valley and up the other, and where any bridge would have had to be more than 200 feet high, they used

123

siphoning instead (nine siphons supplied Roman Lyons). Siphoning was very expensive, however, because of the huge quantities of lead (up to 2,000 tons of metal for one siphon) required for the pipes to withstand the pressures involved, and they preferred to build bridges.

Arched masonry bridges were first constructed in 145 BC when the simple wooden road bridge across the Tiber at Rome was replaced by a stone structure. In the following year the Marcia aqueduct included a bridge. Aqueducts crossing valleys could need great heights. The Pont du Guard in Provence, taking water to Nîmes and built about 20 BC, achieved its 160 feet by stacking three rows of brick arches one above the other. With the development of concrete, stacking ceased to be necessary. Soaring structures were erected during the first century AD, including bridges at Tarragona and Merida in Spain, the latter in conjunction with dams which are still in use; an arch in upper Mesopotamia in AD 70 with a single span of 112 feet; and Trajan's six-arch bridge over the Tagus, the two central arches of which have spans of 87 feet.[11]

As a result of all this activity, ample supplies of water were available to the Empire's citizens. At the end of the aqueducts were cisterns or distribution tanks from which pipes discharged to three sub-cisterns, serving (a) the baths; (b) the public cisterns and fountains, public buildings and army barracks; and (c) private customers, domestic and industrial. Records compiled in about AD 97 by Frontinus, the highly competent ex-Governor of Britain who was in that year appointed Commissioner for Water, show that in Rome at that time the baths absorbed some 17 per cent of the water, private customers some 39 per cent, and general public uses the remaining 44 per cent, including 13 per cent for the public cisterns and fountains. Calculations of the amount of water flowing into Rome suggest that in 50 BC there was a per capita consumption of some 198 gallons per day, rising by AD 100 to 300 gallons. This may be compared with London's 1936 consumption of 35.5 gallons per head per day. Galen, the second-century doctor, recorded that a daily bath was common practice, even for country people.[12]

Access to the water in the public fountains and cisterns was free, and this was the source from which the poor would have been supplied. For piped water there was a charge, on a scale determined by the capacity of nozzle fitted, for which there were fifteen standard choices. All but the smallest homes in Pompeii had water laid on. In some of the private houses there were more than thirty taps. Apartment houses contained secondary storage reservoirs into which water was pumped. In Britain, the Silchester supply arrived below ground level and was raised by pumps; in Worcester, private houses were supplied by separate sluices for each house. In Antioch in the fifth century Libanius remarked that 'our public fountains are mere ornaments, as everyone has his own water supply at home'. In some cases hot-water boilers were installed. In Hadrian's reign hot water was provided for miners' baths.[13]

By the first century AD there was water available in quantities which permitted the flooding of the amphitheatres, providing whole new ranges of entertainment. At the opening of Balbus's theatre in 13 BC the nearby Tiber had flooded, with the result that it was impossible to get into the theatre except by boat.[14] Perhaps this introduced the idea of staging in the amphitheatres the *naumachiae*, the naval battles (with real casualties) such as Claudius had staged on a lake. Claudius's successor, Nero, built a wooden amphitheatre in AD 57 for which his engineers devised plumbing that permitted the arena to be flooded for naval battles, then drained for the reappearance of gladiators, and these performances could be repeated several times in the course of one series of spectacles. This amphitheatre was burned down in the great fire of AD 64, but the ideas were incorporated when the Colosseum was built in the 70s, the basement originally containing a complex of water-filled cisterns and pipes to permit the flooding and draining of the arena. At the inauguration in AD 80, Nero's programme was repeated. Later, purpose-built amphitheatres were constructed for water entertainments; Domitian, for instance, who gave a number of naval shows at the Colosseum, also had a special pool surrounded with seats dug near the Tiber, for 'sea fights of regular fleets'. Ramps, hoists and cages replaced the plumbing in the basement of the Colosseum.[15]

The *thermae* were a central aspect of Roman social life all over the Empire. In 13 BC (in the same year that Balbus provided his theatre) Augustus's wealthy friend Agrippa had opened, at his own expense and without any entry charge to the public, the first of the grand bath-houses with extra facilities (including library, restaurant, surrounding park) which were to turn them into leisure centres rather than hygienic resources. The public baths provided by Maecenas at this time included a heated swimming pool. The leisure centres, variously including shops, restaurants, gymnasia and exercise rooms for athletics, lecture rooms and libraries, in addition to the cold pool, hot pool, sauna and massage room, were among the most magnificent buildings of the Roman Empire. They were lavish in their use of marble and mosaic, with decorative sculptures and colonnaded walks set in parkland. Caracalla, in the early third century, covered 27 acres with his leisure complex, which included a cross-vaulted hall measuring 185 feet by 79 feet and containing a pool. The vaulting, supported by iron girders, was regarded as 'inimitable' by contemporaries. It became the prototype of the vaulted naves of medieval cathedrals. Part of the beautiful complex erected at the end of the century by Diocletian on a 32-acre site in Rome was to become, long afterwards, the Church of Santa Maria degli Angeli. The leisure centre built at much the same time in Trier, with its three arched apses and recessed window frames, shows clearly the influence of these buildings on later ecclesiastical design. Even the curved mosaics of Byzantine church ceilings have their experimental forerunners in the tile decorations of some of the 'baths'.[16]

In the last century BC, in a Rome immensely enriched by conquests in Greece and Asia Minor, theatre-building at last came into its own. Extravagant decoration in silver, gold and ivory was lavished on the temporary theatre built by Claudius Pulcher in 99 BC. For a festival in 63 BC, a whole theatre was roofed.[17] The building put up in 58 BC by Sulla's stepson, Marcus Aemilius Scaurus, almost beggared description. Pliny says that the backdrop to the stage consisted of three storeys comprising 360 columns, the lowest level of marble, the middle one of glass and the top of gilded planks – and all this for 'an improvised theatre that was intended to be used barely for a month'. Pliny presumes the columns are solid marble, since he has heard of no other evidence of the use of marble veneer at as early a date as this. The marble columns of the lowest storey were 38 feet high, and dotted among the columns were 3,000 bronze statues. There was costly painted scenery, and dresses of cloth of gold. The scale of the enterprise is indicated by the fact that Scaurus suffered huge losses when discontented servants burned down his house, to which he had removed from the theatre such 'surplus knick-knacks' as 'could be put to ordinary use'.[18]

This theatre, like its predecessors, was pulled down, and Pliny, who was shocked by vulgar ostentation, recorded with distaste that Scaurus carted off the marble pillars to embellish his own house, an undertaking that alarmed the local sewerage contractor, who demanded to be indemnified by Scaurus against any possible damage to the drains when the columns were being hauled about.[19]

Three years later, in 55 BC, Pompey built on the Field of Mars what was to be Rome's first permanent stone theatre. Vitruvius devotes several chapters to the siting and construction of theatres. He comments that 'if the theatre is on a hillside, the construction of the foundations will be easier',[20] but, in notable contrast to the Greek theatre, this was no longer essential for the production of a raked auditorium. The Romans did use hillsides when occasion offered, but most of their theatres were built on level ground – thanks to their mastery of the vault and the arch. Using these to produce rising banks of seats, Vitruvius was free to devote pages to discussing such matters as salubrious siting (avoiding southerly aspects, for instance, that would permit excessive sunshine and resulting heat prostration) or the best design of gangways for safe crowd entrance and exit (no small consideration when audiences could number, as they did in Pompey's theatre, as many as 40,000);[*] and to give detailed attention to construction in relation to acoustics.[21]

Julius Caesar planned a huge stone theatre, and in 44 BC actually laid the foundations, but by the time of his assassination he had completed only the wooden amphitheatre for gladiatorial fights. That temporary wooden theatres had become commonplace is evident from comments made by Vitruvius, who, writing in the reign of Augustus, remarks on the useful resonance not only of the wooden scenery, but also of the theatres' 'several wooden floors'.[22] Rickety temporary scaffolding could collapse just as it had done in the early Greek theatres. Suetonius recounts how Augustus calmed an incipient panic at the theatre by leaving his place and taking his seat in the area deemed most unsafe. Suetonius says this was during games put on by Augustus in the name of his grandsons.[23] These occurred in 28, 16 and 12 BC. Dio Cassius says that in 28 BC Augustus had had a temporary wooden structure erected on the Campius Martius, and this may well have been the scene of the near panic.[24]

Before the century was out, two more permanent stone theatres had been built in Rome. Augustus named his building, completed in 11 BC on Julius Caesar's old foundations, after his much-loved nephew and son-in-law Marcellus, who died young; the other was built by Cornelius Balbus, following Augustus's plea to rich Romans to 'embellish their city'.[25] They probably had wooden stages, as there are many subsequent references to their destruction in fires, and to the uncertain largesse of various emperors in rebuilding and re-equipping them.[26] Given the dates at which they were constructed, it is unlikely they witnessed productions other than mime, pantomime, farce and perhaps revivals. They were the forerunners of hundreds of beautiful theatres built across the Empire, often by private benefactors. By the second century they were being roofed. Herodes Atticus, tutor to the Emperor Marcus Aurelius, roofed the theatre he built at Corinth, and used cedar wood for his intimate 6,000-seat theatre beneath the Acropolis at Athens.[27]

---

[*] This is Pliny the Elder's figure, given in *Natural History*, XXXVI.115. Estimates of capacity varied. Carcopino (p.243) quotes the following figures: Pompey:27,000; Marcellus:14,000; Balbus:7,700.

Backstage, the theatres became more elaborate (there were fourteen rooms at the theatre of Minturnae, south of Rome), and the façades of the buildings more ornate, richly decorated with niches and statues, which were continued even on the façade of the stage itself down to ground level in the floor of the orchestra. The figure of the Emperor Augustus was frequently included, as may be seen to this day on the façade at Orange. Tiberius added a statue of Augustus over the 'royal' (central) door in the façade of Rome's Theatre of Marcellus. These statues were frequently gilded, and Nero, when entertaining the King of Armenia, went further. 'Not merely the stage but the whole interior of the theatre round about had been gilded, and all the properties that were brought in had been adorned with gold, so that people gave the day itself the epithet ''golden''.' Ovid thought the gilding in Augustus's own time meretricious – 'Look closely,' he said, 'at the images that shine all golden in the decorated theatre, and you will think them worthless; foil covers up wood; but neither may the people come nigh them, till complete'; in other words, you will not be given a chance to realize that they are a con.[*][28] The Roman craftsmen were superbly skilful, and made gold leaf to a thinness of 0.0002 mm, an achievement which was not surpassed until the eighteenth century.[29]

The period from the mid-second to the mid-fourth centuries is adjudged the climax of Roman architecture. There was, says Robin Lane Fox of the opening phase, 'a splendid baroque vitality' which made the upper classes of this period 'the modern sightseers' best friend'.[30] By the late third century, says Vogt:

> Roman architecture now reached its zenith . . . this generation of Roman architects achieved full mastery over the technical and constructional problems presented by their art, and by their barrel and cross-vaulting lifted to impressive heights the great halls the emperors commissioned them to build.[31]

Housing, too, was becoming more comfortable as well as more opulent. Augustus was to say that he inherited a city of brick, and left it of marble, and certainly in his time marble, which had not been used in Rome prior to 92 BC, poured in from the quarries of Greece and Asia Minor as well as from those of Italy itself, special sand for its cutting being fetched, according to Pliny, from as far away as Ethiopia and India.[32] Tibullus,

---

[*] The context of Ovid's remarks is his advice to women that in applying their make-up they should do it privately, out of sight of the men they are seeking to impress.

who died in 18 BC, noted that the streets of Rome were crowded with wagons loaded with marble.[33] But the real revolution, second only to the Etruscan arch and vault in significance, was the development of concrete. The Romans discovered that the volcanic earth known as pozzolana occurring in a thick strata on the Alban Hills near Naples, if mixed with lime, water and with broken stones as an aggregate, set into an exceptionally tough and durable concrete, capable of hardening even under water.[*][34]

Until Augustus's time the normal building material was brick, at first sun-dried, later kiln-dried. Before the importation of marble, the brick was usually faced with plaster. From the first century BC on, however, concrete became the preferred material for mass construction. Vitruvius, writing in 20 BC, shows detailed knowledge of mortars and concretes. By Caligula's reign (AD 37–41) there is evidence of pre-cast concrete being used in the construction of a harbour mole, and this was soon extended to the pre-casting of walls between timber shuttering. Concrete was extensively used for cores which were faced with brick or marble veneer – Nero's Golden House was of brick-faced concrete, as was the Pantheon, built between AD 120 and 124 and still standing today with its 142-foot dome intact.[35]

For Rome's middle class, houses were simple, built round a courtyard. Land was expensive, and for the less well off blocks of flats, three to five storeys in height, were favoured, each flat having a separate staircase. Augustus limited the height of tenements for the poor to seventy feet, Trajan reduced the limit to sixty.[36]

Cavity walls to exclude damp had been recommended by Vitruvius, but he did not have the opportunity to discuss an important innovation introduced just after he wrote – the installation of glazed windows. Before the use of glass, window spaces had been protected with shutters, gratings, slabs of crystalline gypsum, mica or specially prepared parchment, methods to which post-Roman Europe was to return for the next millennium.[37] Seneca, in the first century AD, refers to the use of 'glass windows which let in the full brilliance of day through a transparent pane' as something which had 'appeared only within our own memory'.[38]

Some of the windows were small rounds of blown glass of the type with which we are familiar from medieval leaded windows, but there

---

[*] Pozzolana is also credited with giving Stradivarius violins their exquisite tone and exceptional longevity. In 1988 Cambridge scientists discovered that the violins are painted under the varnish with a layer of pozzolana, probably made into a paste with water and egg white (*Nature*, 24 March 1988, p.313).

were also panes of cast glass. Pompeii has yielded evidence of panes 21 by 28 inches in size, though rather smaller ones, 12 inches by 24, seem to have been more usual, the bronze metal window frames anticipating, by almost two millennia, today's replacement window salesmen. At Pompeii's central baths (where, incidentally, the doors were hung on inclined doorposts, so that they closed automatically to exclude draughts and retain warm air) the windowpanes measured 40 inches by 28, were half an inch thick, and were frosted on one side. Equally large windows have been found in the villas of the rich. Carcopino, in his *Daily Life in Ancient Rome*, suspects that glass windows were a rarity, and that the apartment blocks were dark. Among the well-off, however, the amenity was not limited to the heartland of the Empire; Romano-British homes had glazed windows.* Nor was the use of glass confined to windows. The elder Pliny seems to envisage glass roofs when he says that 'Agrippa, in the baths he built at Rome . . . would certainly have built vaults of glass if such a device had already been invented.' Martial, in AD 93, refers to glass conservatories ('your vineyard blooms shut in transparent glass, and the fortunate grape is roofed and yet unhid'); and Pliny the Younger describes the sun-parlour at his house near Ostia, with adjacent alcove equipped with folding glass doors.[39]

Seneca brackets with glazed windows, as things which have 'appeared only within our own memory', 'the pipes let into [the] walls to distribute heat and preserve an equal warmth above and below'.[40] The hypocaust, the system for circulating hot air through pipes, had been invented in the first century BC by Sergius Orata, an oyster farmer, who installed heated oyster-beds for his commercial production. Seneca is referring only to bathroom heating, to which the idea soon spread, but by the end of the first century AD the hypocaust system was being widely used as a form of general heating in public buildings and in the homes of the well-to-do; Pliny the Younger describes the 'floating floor over a stove which runs underneath, and pipes in the walls' at his newly constructed villa. Initially there was a risk from poisonous fumes, but by AD 70–80 chimneys were being built against an *inner* wall, thus conserving heat before discharging the fumes at roof level. The hypocaust was, naturally enough, gratefully installed across northern Europe, in Gaul, in Germany and in Britain, but there is no evidence of such central heating in the multiple-occupancy blocks of the Roman

---

* Fragments may be seen at Brading Roman villa on the Isle of Wight. Clearly glass windows were a novelty to the locals; the Welsh, i.e. Romano-British, word for a window is *ffenestr*, of obvious origin.

poor, where the ground-floor or basement heat chamber would have been quite inadequate to heat six or seven storeys.[41]

Arrangements to collect and dispose of sewage dated from long before the aqueducts. The original great sewer had been started, according to Pliny, when the Etruscan king Tarquin ruled Rome in the early sixth century BC, and thus he claimed it was already nearly 700 years old in his own time. The Roman sewer was in use right up to the late nineteenth century (when a more modern system was substituted), but so far as structures apparent today are concerned, none pre-date the third century BC, so clearly there had been extensive rebuilding. Today's evidence shows the huge scale of the main sewer, which was 10 feet 6 inches wide, and 14 feet high to the crown of the vault. Baths, washbasins and latrines on the ground floors of buildings, and, in Pompeii, Herculaneum and Ostia, on some upper floors also, were connected to the sewers, which were flushed with water from the aqueducts. The multi-occupancy blocks were not connected, and occupants had to rely on the large public latrines.

Latrines for public use are mentioned in Rome as early as 161 BC. The contractors who ran them sold off the contents for manure, and were being taxed for the privilege by Vespasian in the first century AD. As water became more abundant, arrangements were made for public toilets to drain into the sewers. Though offering no privacy, they could be fairly grand, with attractive decorations and rows of marble seats positioned over a channel of running water; and some were on a generous scale – the Puteoli public toilet, for instance, accommodated 45 people; in Timgad, in north Africa, 28 seats were provided. In some cases, they were heated. By AD 315 there were 144 water-flushed public toilets in Rome. A small charge was payable for their use, relegating the very poor to cesspits and dunghills.[42]

All cities worthy of the name had a drainage system and a public water supply.[43] Rome's streets were regularly cleaned with water, and the dropping of litter was forbidden. Wheeled traffic was permitted only at night. References to lighting in Rome suggest that the streets were not lit at night, though specific events or festivals had been lit since at least 17 BC, including Nero's ghastly use of Christians as human torches.[44] At the Floralia in AD 31 5,000 torch-bearers were present to guide people home after dark.[45] Caligula 'exhibited stage plays continually . . . sometimes even by night, lighting up the whole city'.[46] The Emperor Severus Alexander, in the third century AD, donated oil for the lighting of baths, which previously 'were not open before dawn and were closed before sunset'.[47] The cities of the old Greek world, however, notably Alexandria, had been lit at night, and in the Roman Empire it is again the old Greek cities of which mention is made in connection with streetlights. In one Pompeii street there were lamps, either on shop counters or over doors, at intervals of less than six feet (285 in a 500-metre stretch of road); in the next street there were 396 lamps over a stretch of 576 metres. On Pompeii's Stabiae Road there were lamps every four to five feet – 500 lamps in a 700-metre stretch. In Antioch there are accounts, from both early and late in the fourth century, of street-lighting by means of lamps suspended from ropes, and the same system was in use in other towns of Asia Minor, such as Caesarea and Edessa, in the fourth and fifth centuries. By the fifth century, Antioch was using tarred torches.[48]

In short, to quote Rostovtzeff, writing in 1926, 'As regards comfort, beauty and hygiene, the cities of the Roman Empire, worthy successors of their Hellenistic parents, were not inferior to many a modern European and American town.'[49]

Levels of consumption were also rising. Trade burgeoned, not only because of the excellent road network, but also because the imposition of Roman order on a widening area of the Mediterranean brought a decline in brigandage and piracy such that, as Balsdon points out, for the first two centuries of the Roman Empire conditions for travel were better over a wider area than they were to be again until nineteenth-century Europe, with inns and restaurants to ease the journey.[50] As Italian demand for goods increased while that from the conquered and impoverished Greek world diminished, the trade routes began to realign from the Anatolian to the Phoenician ports of Asia Minor.[51] Roman Italy began to benefit from the ingenuity and innovation that had characterized the Greek world of the third century BC. The water-clocks, for instance, that had been invented in 245 BC, had found their way to Rome by 159 BC and were displayed in public buildings at public expense. At some stage they were installed in the law courts (where, incidentally, by the middle of the first century BC the court reporters were using shorthand)[*] and advocates were required to limit their pleas to prescribed time limits.[52]

Greek glassware captivated the Roman world. Glassmaking was a very ancient skill,[†] and glassware had long been known to the Greeks. Bowls of glass are mentioned by Aristophanes in 425 BC. Cast glass was produced in the Persian Empire before the time of Alexander the Great.

---

[*] Devised, in Seneca's opinion, by 'the lowest grades of slaves' (*Epistles*, XC.26).

[†] 'By about 2500 BC, craftsmen in Mesopotamia had begun to manufacture the first real glass objects, crudely fashioned beads' (Marcus Chown, 'Glass in Antiquity', *New Scientist*, 18 February 1988).

Beautiful vases cut from solid glass have been found dating from about 200 BC, and probably originating in Alexandria. Sometimes the glass was embellished with gold ornament and inset with precious stones.[53] By the time the Roman legions were marching into Asia Minor and Egypt, moulded glass was being widely made.

Late in the first century BC came the discovery, probably in Syria or Phoenicia, of techniques for blowing glass. The resulting explosion in the manufacture and use of glass extended throughout the Empire, and by AD 50 blown glass was in use all over the Roman world. Entrepreneurs, often immigrant Syrians or Jews, settled in Rome, and a huge trade in manufactured glass developed. Manufacturing sites proliferated, and the recycling of broken glass was organized, the trade being in the hands of itinerant collectors who offered households sulphured fire-sticks in exchange.[54] Blown glass from southern Italy surpassed in beauty, according to Rostovtzeff, that from Syria or Alexandria.[55] By the second century AD there were production units in Cologne and Trier, and in Britain at Colchester, Warrington and Caistor-by-Norwich. Gaul was producing a particularly fine transparent variety. Egypt was sending quantities of glass to Rome (as well as paper, linen and hemp) as a form of revenue-in-kind. Already in the first century AD Pliny remarks that 'for making drinking vessels, the use of glass has indeed ousted metals such as gold and silver', but he cautions that 'it cannot bear heat unless cold fluid is first poured into it'.[56] Soon glassware spread throughout the social scale. So universal was it on Roman tables that in the third century the Emperor Gallienus refused to use it. 'He always drank out of golden cups, for he scorned glass, declaring that there was nothing more common.'[57]

Apart from the application of mass production methods, no advance in glass technique comparable to the introduction of blown glass occurred until 1959, when Pilkington developed float glass.[*] So far as blown glass is concerned, the techniques have never been bettered. Roman glass contained fewer bubbles than most other glass made prior to the nineteenth century, indicating the achievement of very high firing temperatures, and the artistry and elaboration rivalled Renaissance Venice. In the 1870s it took a Victorian craftsman, John Northwood,

---

[*] Pliny the Elder (XXXVI.195) recounts the story that in the reign of Tiberius a method of glassmaking was invented which rendered it flexible and thus unshatterable. 'The artist's workshop was completely destroyed for fear that the value of metals such as copper, silver and gold would otherwise be lowered. Such,' adds Pliny, 'is the story, which, however, has for a long period been current through frequent repetition rather than authentic.' In Petronius's version, in *Satyricon* 51, the inventor is beheaded. Dio Cassius (LVII.57) tells the same tale.

three years of full-time work to produce a copy of the Portland Vase, the original of which was made about 30 BC; and in the 1960s a German craftsman, using a modern diamond drill, worked for eighteen months in his spare time to reproduce a single example of Roman cage glass, in which an apparent cage encloses an inner glass vessel, both layers being cut from the same blank.[58]

Clothing was improving too. Cotton and muslin had been coming from India since early in the second century BC, with textile dyeing benefiting, according to Rostovtzeff, from the contemporary advances being made at that time in chemistry in the Greek world, to add to the traditional dyes of vegetable, insect and mollusc origin.[*] Large-scale production of cotton goods was developed in Malta, but Indian cotton was preferred. Flax, initially imported from Egypt, was later cultivated in north Italy. Weaving was disappearing from individual households by late republican times, ample supplies of woven cloth being available in the market, which was the usual source of clothes for the huge numbers of slaves.

The linen into which the flax was made provided not only tunics for the populace, but also huge awnings to give shade. Awnings had first been used, according to Pliny, when Quintus Catulus dedicated the Capitol rebuilt after the destruction of the civil wars – a ceremony that occurred in 69 BC. Their use spread rapidly to the theatre, the first installation coming only six years later.[†] Julius Caesar stretched awnings 'over the whole of the Roman Forum, as well as the Sacred Way from his mansion and the slope right up to the Capitol, a display recorded to have been thought more wonderful even than the show of gladiators which he gave'; in 23 BC 'curtains' were stretched over the Forum for the whole summer.

In the theatre the awnings were strung from the backstage buildings, and supported round the auditorium by masts whose sockets can still be seen – a classical big top. This may have encouraged the huge increase in the height of the backstage buildings, to which Scaurus's theatre bore witness, and which is evident today in such well-preserved ruins as those at Orange in Provence, or Aspendos in modern Turkey, a 25,000-

---

[*] Rostovtzeff (1941, p.564) cites the large-scale mining which began at this time of the red rubrica sinopensis and the orange-red sandarake. Rubrica sinopensis was a form of red ochre, the best mine being, according to Pliny, in Cappadocia. Sandarake, now called realgar, is a natural orange-red sulphide of arsenic. Again, the best mine was in Asia Minor, but the wretched slaves who mined it died off rapidly from the fumes (Forbes, Vol.III, pp.205ff.). These are pigments rather than dyes, and there is some doubt whether they would have been applied to textiles.

[†] According to Pliny, their first theatrical use was at the Games of Apollo.

capacity theatre where the top of the stage buildings equates with the top of the colonnaded walk above the highest circle of seats. Sailors and marines did the job; for the immensely complicated task of roofing over the Colosseum with awnings, a detachment from the fleet at Misenum was permanently stationed in adjacent barracks; some one hundred were on maintenance work, but it is calculated that a further thousand were needed to raise and lower the huge 'velarium' of the Colosseum.[59]

Pliny records that when people began to use awnings for the courtyards of their homes, to protect the moss from the heat of the sun, red was the favoured colour, otherwise awnings were usually white; but Lucretius, writing in 58 BC and therefore referring, presumably, to the wooden theatres, provides evidence that quite early on there were multicoloured awnings. He writes of 'yellow and red and dark purple awnings'.

> [W]hen outspread in the public view over a great theatre upon posts and beams, they tremble and flutter; for then they dye, and force to flutter in their own colour, the assembly in the great hollow below, and all the display of the stage, and the glorious throng of the Fathers;[*] and the more the walls of the theatre are enclosed all round, the more all within laughs in the flood of beauty when the light of day is thus confined.

He writes, too, of how the awning which 'cracks flapping between poles and beams, sometimes tears and flies wild under the boisterous winds'.[60] 'Rippling', 'waving' awnings feature in the poetry of the Augustan Age Propertius. A century after Lucretius the problem of the wind had not been solved. The alternative of wearing a hat for protection against the sun was not permitted until Caligula relaxed the law in AD 37 and allowed senators to use Thracian 'parasol' hats.[61] Martial writes of the need to take a broad-brimmed hat to Pompey's theatre (he mentions a special high-crowned, wide-brimmed Macedonian fashion, worn by fishermen and sailors, presumably the same Thracian style) 'for blasts of wind are apt to deny the people an awning'.[62] By Martial's time the awnings had become more resplendent. Nero's amphitheatre boasted sky-blue spangled with stars. In the theatre itself, for the state visit of the King of Armenia, 'the curtains stretched overhead to keep off the sun were of purple, and in the centre of them was an embroidered figure of Nero driving a chariot, with golden stars gleaming all about him.'[63]

[*] The senators seated in the orchestra.

Also during the first century BC arrangements were made for a curtain between the stage and the seats. It was hung from the high buildings whose façade formed the backdrop to the stage, which were now extended across each extremity of the stage to form wings with entrances in them. When not in use the curtain was rolled into a trench in front of the stage, and thus was lowered at the start by being wound down, and raised (by pulleys) at the end of the performance. Ovid gives a graphic description of the curtain rising at the end of a play:

> So when on festal days the curtain in the theatre is raised, figures of men rise up, showing first their faces, then little by little all the rest, until at last, drawn up with steady motion, the entire forms stand revealed, and plant their feet upon the curtain's edge.

He compares the experience to Cadmus's sowing the dragon's teeth so that there 'spring up from the furrows the points of spears, then helmets with coloured plumes waving; next shoulders of men and beasts and arms laden with weapons come up, and the crop grows with the shields of warriors'. It is tempting to believe that Virgil was describing the same scene when he remarked on the purple curtain with its 'inwoven Britons', in which case it was probably Pompey's theatre, for Virgil was dead before those of Marcellus and Balbus were built.[64]

A particularly gauzy, transparent material known as 'Coan silk' was made up in the island of Cos, and was worn by fast women; Horace commented in the late first century BC that they looked naked, and Seneca, a couple of generations later, congratulated his mother on *not* wearing it.[65] By the first century AD silk was coming from China, much favoured by the women, though men who wore it were considered effeminate. At first, of course, only the rich could afford silk, but by the third century it was being worn in all classes. Wool production benefited from a significant Roman innovation, the harvesting of wool by shearing instead of plucking, for which purpose the two-bladed shear with a U-shaped spring, as used today, was invented.[66]

For inspecting their appearance, the citizens of the Empire had metal mirrors, including full-length, often a base metal coated with silver, but solid silver mirrors were common and were owned even by slaves. Pliny refers to the development at the Sidon glassworks of glass mirrors, but whether they were the modern metal-backed variety is not clear. The first certain description of a genuine glass mirror backed with tin does not come until AD 220, but Pliny was certainly familiar with the idea of backing glass with a layer of gold for a 'more reliable reflection'.[67]

Silver was becoming common in the last century BC. Pliny remarks that Caesar was the first person to use nothing but silver for the appointments of the arena: 'criminals made to fight with wild animals had all their equipment made of silver, a practice nowadays rivalled even in our municipal towns'. He goes on to describe the soldiers' accoutrements of his own time, in the first century AD, with sword hilts of chased silver, 'even ivory not being thought good enough', scabbards jingling with silver chains, belts with silver tabs. As for the women, they were insisting on silver for their washbasins as well as for their tableware. By the late first century only the poorest Romans were eating from ordinary earthenware, though luxury decorated pottery continued to command high prices and confer a reputation for artistry on towns specializing in its production.[68]

Food and drink became more varied. Viticulture was an ancient skill, but by the end of the second century BC it was becoming sophisticated, with date and place of origin marked on the amphorae containing the wine, and recognition among connoisseurs of exceptional vineyards and vintages. Julius Caesar, in 46 BC, was reputedly the first host to offer four different wines on one occasion. Wines were shipped over considerable distances, the amphorae protected by plaited straw such as persists on today's Chianti bottles. By imperial times, snow and ice cellars were in use for chilling wine in summer.[69]

According to Livy, it was in the second century BC that interest in food developed to the point where cooking became an art instead of a chore, and by the reign of Tiberius the notable chef Apicius was compiling and publishing his recipes.[70] During the first century BC cherries,[*] apricots and peaches were introduced to Roman orchards from the Orient, supplementing the indigenous crops of apples, plums, figs and pomegranates, and by the first century AD they were being harvested in Italy along with melons and pistachio nuts. The olive, imported from Greece, had long been naturalized, and by the reign of Augustus, oil as well as wine was being produced on a mass-production scale by the large farms attached to the country villas, many of them second homes, of his prosperous subjects.[71] Refined white flour was being used for breadmaking, though the effect on their bowels worried the whole-food fanatics.[†]

---

[*] They were brought to Britain in AD 47.

[†] In the first century AD Petronius, in *Satyricon* (66), depicts a guest who, when offered white bread, remarks that he prefers wholemeal, which 'puts strength into you, and when I do my business, I don't grumble'. Some 600 years earlier, Hippocrates ('On Ancient Medicine', 14) had taken the question of refined flour very seriously: 'And this I know, moreover, that to the human body it makes a great difference whether the bread be fine or coarse; of wheat with or without the

Baking, like weaving, had become a marketable trade. Professional bakers had been in operation since about 170 BC, though whether they did their own milling, or merely baked loaves for which the flour was prepared within private households, is not clear. By the first century AD convict labour was grinding the grain into flour.[72] Professional millers do not figure in the records until later, when watermills had been harnessed to the milling process.[73]

All over Italy at the start of the first century AD small market towns were changing their character and becoming industrialized, with shops and workshops springing up. It was a time of mass production and mass consumption, with centres specializing in pottery, metal goods, silver plate and ready-made clothing. Capua was pouring out a stream of lanterns, lit by oil or candles and fitted with horn or mica plates; for the huge candelabra (those in public buildings could have as many as 350 wicks) there was specialization of labour, the sockets being made in Aegina, the stems in Taranto. Those who could not adorn themselves with real jewels had ample supplies of costume jewellery to choose from, counterfeit beryls, opals, emeralds, garnets and turquoise initially imported from India. Pliny was particularly impressed by the mock opals, so skilfully crafted in glass that the only way to tell the difference was to hold them up to the sun, whereupon in the false opal 'one colour predominates steadily, unlike the genuine article, in which the radiance of the colours changes'. The other gemstones were so realistic that the only test was 'to knock off a piece of the stone so that it can be baked on an iron plate, but dealers in precious stones not unnaturally object to this, and likewise to testing with a file'. By the second century AD, to quote Rostovtzeff's summary:

> . . . better brands of coloured woollen and linen stuffs and of leatherware, more or less artistic furniture, fine silver plate, perfumes and paints, artistic toilet articles, spices and the like . . . became more and more necessities of life for the city population throughout the Empire . . .[74]

Slaves shared in the rising material standards. As in Greece, the bulk of the productive work in agriculture was done by freeborn tenants, but slaves were extensively employed as artisans, in domestic work, in state enterprises such as mining and public works and, at a later stage, in the

hull . . . Whoever pays no attention to these things, or, paying attention, does not comprehend them, how can he understand the diseases which befall a man?'

138

chain of publicly owned bakeries (of which, by the mid-fourth century, there were 274 in Rome to supply the state distribution of free bread). For the last two hundred years of the Republic and the first century of the Empire there was extensive manumission of skilled slaves, many of whom achieved positions of considerable wealth and influence, taking over the houses of the old aristocracy and redecorating them with *nouveau riche* abandon. By the second century AD the material standard of living of those still enslaved matched that of the freeborn, and slaves were indistinguishable in dress from their masters. In the households of the well-to-do, in particular, they were living well, enjoying wine and wheaten bread.[75] For the freeborn, climbing the social scale was by no means impossibly difficult; a centurion's pay was sufficient to accumulate the capital necessary to qualify for the rank of a knight.[76]

There were other avenues to riches. During the festivals, lotteries were conducted in theatres and amphitheatres, carrying prizes some of which were equivalent to a big win on the football pools. Nero had tokens thrown among the audience which could be redeemed for horses, pack animals, slaves, gold, silver, clothes, furniture, jewellery, pearls, pictures, paintings ... even ships, lodging houses and country estates. Titus followed a similar policy. Under Domitian 'it rained figs, dates, nuts, plums, cakes, cheese and pastry' in the morning, pheasants and partridges at night. At the dedication of the Colosseum, Diocletian had tokens thrown to the people, and an extra fifty thrown to each of the areas where the senators and the knights were sitting, to ensure they also benefited. Spectators died in the scramble, and some deliberately left before the distribution rather than be caught up in it.[77]

The huge strides in material standards, made in particular in the period 100 BC to 200 AD, resulted from the ingenious application of existing scientific theories. There was little in the way of fresh speculation, and most contemporary scientific literature – such as Pliny's *Natural History*, compiled, he claimed, from some one hundred authorities – consisted of encyclopaedic summaries of existing knowledge rather than pioneering work. But experimental application continued. While the Roman architects and civil engineers were transforming living conditions, the Hellenistic Greeks were pursuing their laboratory researches into the uses of cogwheels, gears and crankshafts.* In Alexandria, in the

---

* One result was an instrument of extraordinary complexity, made at Rhodes during the first century BC and salvaged from a sunken vessel in 1900. The Antikythera calculator, an astronomical instrument for indicating the position of the planets and the phases of the moon, comprised an intricate system of differential gearing.

first century AD,[*] Hero picked up where the practical-minded Ctesibius left off in the third century BC. His contribution included, but was not limited to, devising improved water organs and a series of gimmicks to amaze the credulous, such as hot-air pneumatic doors which opened automatically. The *Oxford Classical Dictionary*, which credits him with solving weight-lifting problems and with the invention of sighting instruments, says of him: 'While classical "Euclidean" mathematics aimed at constructing theorems, "Heronic" mathematics was directed at solving practical problems.' According to Bertrand Gille:

> Modern machine-practice may be regarded as taking its rise at Alexandria, for the school there represents the transition from very simple mechanisms, involving hardly more than primary combinations of levers, to the far more complex devices which later ages understood by the word 'machines'.[78]

Adapting such inventions,[†] the Romans developed powerful treadmills, operated by animals, convicts and slaves. Instead of hand-grinding the grain, large millstones, employing rotary motion, were introduced during the first century BC, and were soon extended to grape and olive crushing. Concentrations of mills began to appear; in several areas of north Africa olive oil was processed on a mass industrial scale. Combined with the Archimedean screw, the treadmills were developed into highly effective machines for draining water from the mines, and raising it from wells for extensive irrigation works: 'it was in pumping devices that Roman mining showed the greatest advance on Greece', says C.N. Bromehead in *A History of Technology*, and Derry comments that 'in Spain mines were dug deeper and more ingenious in their construction than any known in post-Roman Europe for the next 1000 years'. With men and animals treading inside them, cranes increased enormously in power, and were put to use in the construction industry and at the docks.[79]

Pliny tells an extraordinary story, which some scholars entirely

---

[*] His date is disputed. Mellersh (p.197) places him in the middle of the third century BC, but Vitruvius does not mention him, though he includes Ctesibius in his comprehensive survey of earlier scientists and engineers, which suggests that Hero postdates Vitruvius. Most authorities assign a date in the first century AD.

[†] Experiments which failed included a reaping machine, of which an illustration has been found in Belgium and which is described by Pliny in the first century AD, involving a sharp steel comb harvesting the heads of grain into a wagon pushed by oxen; and an attempt, in the fourth century, to power a boat by using oxen to turn a capstan attached to a paddle-wheel. (R.J.Forbes, 'Power', in Singer, C., et al. (eds.), Vol.II, p.607; Hodges, p.199).

discount,* of the construction in 52 BC (seventy-five years before Pliny's own birth, so he was not an eye-witness) of two adjacent wooden theatres 'poised and balanced on a revolving pivot', which could be swung round to face one another, thus forming one amphitheatre. He states specifically that

> during the forenoon, a performance of a play was given in both of them, and they faced in opposite directions so that the two casts should not drown each other's words. Then all of a sudden the theatres revolved (and it is agreed that after the first few days they did so with some of the spectators actually remaining in their seats) . . . and thus Curio provided an amphitheatre in which he produced fights between gladiators . . . When the pivots of the theatres were worn and displaced he altered this ostentatious display of his. He kept to the shape of the amphitheatre, and on the final day gave athletic displays on the two stages as they stood back to back across the middle of the arena. Then suddenly the platforms were swept away on either side, and during the same day he brought on those of his gladiators who had won their earlier contests . . .

Pliny was appalled at the folly of the spectators who continued to sit in their places while this exercise was going on.

> Here we have the nation that has conquered the earth, that has subdued the whole world, that distributes tribes and kingdoms, that dispatches its dictates to foreign peoples, that is heaven's representative, so to speak, among mankind, swaying on a contraption and applauding its own danger! What a contempt for life this showed! . . . What a disaster it could have been! . . .[80]

Whether this really happened or not, it is not the only claimed example of revolving structures. When Nero built his huge palace, the Golden House, he installed a circular main dining room, which according to Suetonius revolved 'day and night like the heavens', though Rolfe, his translator, presumes that it was only the spherical ceiling which revolved.[†81]

---

* Ludwig Friedländer (Vol.IV, p.512) is not among the sceptics. Among other authorities he quotes Professor Rudolf Bergau as saying, 'The construction and technical execution of Roman buildings compel us to presuppose a very high degree of elaboration in the machinery, the manual work and the technique generally.'

† There is another possibility. Seneca (*Epistles*, XC.15) writes (disparagingly) of the man who 'so

Feats of engineering were certainly put at the disposal of the production staff in the theatres. Seneca in AD 65 speaks of stage mechanics 'who invent automatically rising platforms, stages that noiselessly sprout upwards storey upon storey and various other surprises – solid floors that yawn, great chasms mysteriously closing, tall structures slowly telescoped'.[82] Martial, a decade or two later, describing the pageant in the amphitheatre in which Orpheus was torn to pieces, gives a picture of the mechanisms in action: 'Cliffs crept, and a marvellous wood sped swiftly on.' Some of this ingenuity went into such projects as sophisticated devices for hoisting animals from their underground cages to spew them directly into the arena: 'the earth yawned suddenly,' says Martial, 'and sent forth a she-bear to attack Orpheus'.[83] From the next century Apuleius gives us a picture of a major production supposedly (his *The Golden Ass* is fiction, but with resonances of personal experience) in the amphitheatre at Corinth, with a reconstruction of Mount Ida, 'an imposing piece of stage architecture, quite high, turfed all over and planted with scores of trees. The designer had contrived that a stream should break out at the top of the mountain and tumble down the side. A herd of she-goats were cropping the grass . . .' At the end,

> a fountain of wine mixed with saffron* broke out from a concealed pipe at the mountain top, and its many jets sprinkled the pasturing goats with a scented shower, so that their white hair was stained the rich yellow traditionally associated with the flocks that feed on Mount Ida. The scent filled the whole amphitheatre; and then the stage machinery was set in motion, the earth seemed to gape and the mountain disappeared from view.[84]

Exercises in technological wizardry continued for several centuries – there is an account from late in the third century of an accident when the mechanized scaffold caught fire and demolished the stage.[85]

An advance instituted in the first century BC was the use of water as a

---

cleverly constructs a dining-room with a ceiling of movable panels that it presents one pattern after another, the roof changing as often as the courses', a remark which some commentators suspect may have been prompted by the Golden House.

* The use of saffron and balsam, as sprays or washes, to sweeten the theatres persisted across centuries. Propertius ([I], IV) in the first century BC writes of Aeneas's time when 'no rippling awnings hung o'er the hollow theatre, nor reeked the stage with saffron, as 'tis wont today'. Suetonius (*Nero*, 31) recounts that Nero installed plumbing in the ivory ceilings of his Golden House to sprinkle guests with 'flowers and perfume'. For Hadrian's reign, AD 117–38, see *Lives of the Later Caesars*, p.78.

source of power, an innovation which led the Augustan Age poet Antipater of Thessalonica to declare in 30 BC, 'Cease from grinding, ye women who toil at the mill; sleep late even if the crowing cocks announce the dawn', for the water nymphs are henceforth to grind the corn.[86] The earliest wheels were floated horizontally in the stream. By the late first century BC Vitruvius was describing geared vertical water wheels, giving five revolutions of the millstone for one of the wheel. They were undershot by the water; not till the third century is there evidence, in a mural, of the much more efficient overshot wheel. After this date there appears to have been a rather more rapid spread of water wheels, particularly in north Europe where the rivers were more reliable than those of the Mediterranean, but Donald Hill believes they were probably mostly of the undershot variety, which was much simpler to install.[87]

One result of the use of water power was the concentration of processing plants. Near Arles on the Rhône there was installed during the fourth century a major complex of 18 sets of grindstones activated by 14 water wheels drawing on the stream at seven successive levels. The whole mill was capable of producing 28 tons of flour per ten-hour day, which was so in excess of local requirements that it is presumed to have been the basis of a considerable export trade. A similar installation in Burgundy supplied the army in north Gaul. Equally, however, the new technology enabled a number of private entrepreneurs to set up as millers with their own small mills, and milling joined baking as a specialized trade. Where there were streams, millponds began to be constructed. More and more millers began to take water from the aqueducts, and the law, which first concerned itself with watermills in AD 398, increasingly during the following century and a half sought to control this illicit diversion of water.[88]

There was now an established source of power other than human and animal muscle. Roman technology stopped short of harnessing it to hammers or bellows, but its use went further than simply grinding corn.* By the fourth century watermills to cut marble were in operation near Trier.[89]

There the great technological achievement of the classical world,

---

* R.J. Forbes (Vol.II p.104) speculates on, but dismisses, the suggestion that water power could have been the agency for turning Nero's revolving banqueting hall. Nero was certainly interested in vast water engineering projects. For his villa on the River Aniene near modern Subiaco, about fifty miles east of Rome, he had huge masonry dams constructed to create artificial lakes. The largest soared to at least 130 feet, the highest dam built up to that date anywhere in the world; and not to be rivalled for another 1,500 years (Hill, p.53).

Roman practice grounded in Greek theory, ossified. Wind power was not harnessed to the mills, as water had been. In Alexandria, Hero had invented a small steam turbine, but it was never developed beyond curiosity status. Its industrial exploitation would, of course, have required a source of fuel, such as the industrial revolution of the eighteenth century found in coal. The Romans in Britain knew of, and used, coal; it was not mined, but in Somerset surface coal was burnt, even by the poor, and in the north the military forts on the Scottish border used coal from Cumberland, Scotland and the Tyne valley. The coal remained in Britain, the steam turbine in Egypt.[90] 'Long before Rome fell,' as Hodges puts it in *Technology in the Ancient World*, 'all technological innovation had ceased.'[91]

The classical world's failure to proceed to a fully mechanized industrial society is often seen as the result of deliberate choice rather than of factors outside their control. The isolated story is quoted of Vespasian's refusal of an engineer's offer to install a water hoist for transporting some heavy columns, on the grounds that it would deprive the poor of work.[92] F.W. Walbank is one of many economic historians who found the explanation in the institution of slavery, which both removed any incentive to lighten labour through technological inventiveness, and, at the same time, by preventing technological advance, prolonged its own indispensability. Seneca, speaking with personal experience of a slave-owning society, did not share the dismissive assumptions of later historians about slave passivity; his theory was that ingenuity was the fruit of engagement in practical tasks.[*] Hammer and tongs were both invented by 'some man whose mind was nimble and keen, but not great or exalted, and the same holds true of any other discovery which can only be made by means of a bent body and of a mind whose gaze is upon the ground'. Little though he respected such preoccupations, it was precisely the slaves whom he was prepared to credit with innovation. After a catalogue of ancient examples, he cites current inventions like windows, central heating and shorthand, all, in his opinion, devised by slaves. R.J. Forbes comes to the categoric conclusion that 'there is no basis for the sweeping assertion that [slavery] impeded the use and evolution of machinery and engineering', and A.H.M. Jones agrees, citing the manpower shortage that assailed the

---

[*] Fanny Trollope (p.157), visiting America in the early nineteenth century, comments on the Washington patent office. 'This patent office contains models of all the mechanical inventions that have been produced in the Union, and the number is enormous . . . They chiefly proceeded from mechanics and agriculturalists.'

later Empire. Rostovtzeff, too, dismisses the slavery argument, maintaining that Hellenistic industry was at its most vibrant at a time when it was entirely based on slavery; he seeks the explanation in a decline in purchasing power which made investment in higher productivity unattractive.[93]

There is another potent disincentive to investment of any kind: lack of confidence in the future. There is no point in sowing if there is no hope of reaping. Kenneth Clark, identifying the destroyers of civilization, gives pride of place to fear – 'fear of war, fear of invasion, fear of plague and famine, that make it simply not worthwhile constructing things, or planting trees or even planning next year's crops'.[94]

Rostovtzeff had postulated just such a collapse of morale among the Greeks of the second century BC, prompted by increasing insecurity. By the start of the third century AD the warning signs were evident in the lands under Roman jurisdiction. Law and order were breaking down, and confidence in the future was evaporating. The sensate society's suicidal tendencies were everywhere manifesting themselves.

Chapter 9

Paying the Price: the Second and Third Centuries

The later centuries of the Empire witnessed such a plethora of internal weaknesses that scholars are more surprised by the capacity of the Western Empire to survive in the face of external attack for as long as it did than by its final defeat and subjugation. A falling birth rate did not preclude excessive demands on a deteriorating environment from an ever-expanding migrant populace in Rome; but hampered rural recruitment to an army made the more necessary by increasing reliance on the produce of overseas possessions. Social cohesion vanished. The multiplicity of subject peoples which expansion had incorporated into the Roman state, and in particular into the Roman army, increasingly demanded recognition for their indigenous cults, while the secularized Roman intelligentsia had little loyalty to their own traditional religion. Above all, prosperity succumbed to social tensions generated by the greed, rapacity and selfishness which are the natural and logical outcome of untramelled sensate goals and values.

Since the fifth century BC the authorities of Rome had sought tranquillity on the home front by striving to ensure that there was an adequate supply of corn for sale at an acceptable price, though state action was only initiated when bad harvests threatened scarcity and profiteering.

At first it was not a form of welfare, but a right of citizenship. In 123 BC the *Lex Sempronia* enacted that all Roman citizens be entitled to corn (later, and possibly from the start, up to a total of five bushels per month) at a fixed price. It was not a heavily subsidised price, but treasury intervention prevented speculation. There were, of course, political repercussions, with jockeying between those who sought to reduce the price, and those anxious to hold costs.[1]

Corn politics intensified during the civil wars that ended the Republic. In 58 BC a free distribution was introduced for citizens resident in Rome (Cyprus was summarily annexed to pay for it). Place of domicile was an important qualifying factor. There were some unforeseen results. Impecunious smallholders began to move in from the country, and masters freed their slaves to enable them to qualify, both developments resulting in an increasing pool of urban unemployed. Pompey, in 57 BC, obtained enough grain to feed 486,000 people, and in 56 BC tried unsuccessfully to establish a register and definite tally of those entitled, hoping at least to control the enthusiasm for freeing slaves.[2] Caesar, in 46 BC, found 320,000 people on the list, which had swollen 'not by lawful methods but in such ways as are common in times of strife', and Dio Cassius says he struck out half the names.[3] He managed to reduce numbers to 150,000, partly by dispatching some 80,000 Roman citizens to form colonies elsewhere, partly by closing the list and entering new names only on the death of an existing beneficiary, with the result that two classes of citizens came into existence, those with an entitlement to corn dole, and those without. Veyne remarks that if a good many of the displaced 170,000 died of hunger, it would not have bothered Caesar.[4] In a bid for popularity, he also made a cash distribution to those on his corn list, gave them more than the usual amount of corn, and added oil to the free distribution. Augustus abandoned the attempt to limit numbers, and found himself with 250,000 beneficiaries. Numbers crept up, and by 5 BC were again back to the 320,000 figure.

With the failure of the attempt to limit recipients to a definite number, the alternative was tried of defining entitlement more closely. At some stage senators and knights ceased to be eligible, but other evidence of means-testing is lacking. Augustus limited the emancipation of slaves to a set proportion of the total number of slaves, and separated the emancipated into two classes, those with, and those without, right of corn benefit. According to Van Berchem, he redefined 'domicile' to mean domicile at time of birth, thus debarring all immigrant citizens from qualifying, but Rickman is dubious whether the available evidence justifies this conclusion. Both accept that there was, by the latter part of Augustus's reign, a limit not exceeding 200,000 to the number of recipients. They were issued with vouchers which by the middle of the first century AD were stating the day of the month on which they could collect their entitlement, and the number of the arcade at the distribution portico to which they should report.[5]

As Rome became more wealthy, huge disparities in living standards manifested themselves. The emperors set out to buy the loyalty of the urban underlings. Nero abolished the free issue, but flooded the market with cheap grain, thus winning the gratitude of the non-citizens. Subsequent emperors restored the citizens' privileged position, though there were continuing efforts to control costs by limiting access to citizenship. Soldiers from the provinces, for instance, were entitled to citizenship on completion of their period of service, but since their wives also qualified automatically, the privilege to apply was limited to only one wife, thus obviating the temptation to enrol extra settlers in the privileged category through a series of divorces and marriages of convenience.[6]

The old nominal responsibility of the Senate for the corn distribution evaporated as the emperors took over control, and as a result there occurred a change in the recipients' status – no longer was access to corn a basic privilege of a free citizen, it was one aspect of imperial largesse, for which the appropriate response was gratitude to the emperor in person. After a while the largesse came to be taken for granted and resented when it seemed stingy, so the emperors became the prisoners of their own policy. In the reign of the Emperor Septimus Severus (193–211) olive oil brought from Tripolitania was dispensed ('a free and lavish daily supply', according to *Lives of the Later Caesars*) in addition to the free corn. Occasional presents of oil and wine had from time immemorial been distributed at special celebrations, but the new distribution was a permanent feature. Severus had accumulated such vast stocks of both grain and oil that on his death he left the equivalent of seven years' tribute of grain, and oil in quantities sufficient to meet the needs of the whole of Italy for the next five years.[7] From this period all references to domicile disappear; the criterion is poverty; the distributions are a form of social security for the urban proletariat in a disintegrating economy. During the late third century a daily ration of bread replaced the monthly grain issue, and pork was added to the free rations. The Emperor (Aurelian) wanted to include free wine, his plan being to buy uncultivated land in Etruria and settle it with prisoners of war and their families, producing wine at cost for free issue to the Roman population. His Prefect of the Guard opposed the idea, enquiring what was to be next on the list? Free chicken? Free goose? Some wine was produced, but Aurelian had been murdered by then, and the wine was sold, albeit cheaply, not given free.[8]

In addition to the urban food programmes, intermittent distributions of cash were made. This began with an exercise of unmitigated demagoguery on the part of Julius Caesar, who promised the people money in 49 BC; and in 46 BC, instead of consigning the booty from his victories to the treasury, as was customary, made a direct distribution to the people, comprising grain (ten bushels), oil and a sum in cash equivalent to four months' pay for a legionary. In his will he left a further cash bounty of the same size. This example was followed by subsequent emperors, who used distributions on birthdays or other family occasions to reinforce loyalty to the imperial line. The sums involved were huge. Domitian on three occasions handed out sums three times as much per capita as Caesar's bequest had been. Trajan paid out nearly nine times as much per capita. The recipients were the same as those entitled to grain, except that senators and knights were not excluded from the cash largesse, and children were sometimes included, though they did not qualify directly for corn.[*9]

The proletariat of Rome were not the only beneficiaries of this policy. In AD 134 Hadrian instituted a state dole in Athens.[10] Marcus Aurelius supplied grain from the city of Rome to communities across Italy when there was a famine.[11] At least three of Egypt's cities enjoyed a corn dole.[12] By the fourth century free food provided by the state was being distributed to the urban poor of Alexandria, probably Antioch and, after AD 332, in newly renamed Constantinople, where there were 80,000 recipients.[13] In areas without a free issue, local officials all over the Empire were responsible for ensuring the availability, at accessible prices, of wheat and oil.[14]

Virtually all the grain required for Rome had to come from outside Italy. By the end of the third century BC, the mainland was failing to produce adequate supplies. Though the north of Italy and the Po valley remained highly productive, the soils of central and south Italy were degrading by the second century BC, and, as in Greece at an earlier date, grape and olive production began to replace the more demanding grain crop.[15] Deforestation of the Apennines, particularly to build ships for the wars against Carthage and the Illyrian pirates, precipitated, though not on a wide scale, the familiar saga of soil erosion, silt-filled rivers and the creation of coastal marshlands – this is the period when the bulk of the malaria-ridden Pontine marshes were created. South of present-day Salerno, the harbour of the splendid Greek-founded commercial centre which the Romans had renamed Paestum became clogged with silt, malaria-infested marshlands spread, and by the end of the Empire Paestum was no more than a village with some impressive Greek ruins.[16] Lucretius, in *On the Nature of Things*, comments on eroding soils, and the need for farmers to work harder to achieve the same result. Livy

---

[*] The age at which people qualified for the corn dole depended on the age of majority, hence citizenhood, which varied in the different tribes from twelve to nineteen. Augustus set ten as the qualifying age, but later emperors lowered the age limit (Van Berchem, p.33). Trajan went to some pains to have 5,000 extra children enrolled on the tribal lists (Pliny the Younger, *Panegyricus*, 25)

remarks on the depopulation of once rich soils, and Domitian, in an effort to halt depopulation, tried to forbid the switch to vineyards.[17]

Deforestation, and the consequent soil erosion, accelerated as demand grew for fuel for the hypocausts and the baths, and although damage did not become catastrophic until long after the Roman period, the production of corn became increasingly inadequate. Victory in the second Punic War had given Rome access to tribute from the erstwhile Carthaginian corn lands of Sicily, Sardinia and eastern Spain. By the middle of the second century BC, the great wheatlands of Carthaginian north Africa were also Rome's to command. Supplies from the valley of the Nile were obtainable by trade until, with Egypt's absorption by Rome in the first century BC, its abundance became available to the emperors, who retained Egypt as their personal fiefdom. Ships carrying well over 1,000 tons of grain plied between Egypt and Rome, cargo vessels that might also be carrying up to 600 passengers.[18] In Augustus's time, a third of the corn was coming from Egypt, a third from north Africa and the rest from Spain, Gaul and Sicily,[19] but Africa was of ever-increasing importance, and by Nero's time was said by a contemporary to be feeding Rome for two-thirds of the year.[20] (The port of Ostia could not handle the necessary tonnage. Claudius started work on a new port, to be connected by canal with the Tiber. Nero finished it, but it silted up, and Trajan had to construct another.[21] Among Rome's rural population there lingered from an earlier piety pockets of superstitious dread about interfering with watercourses – a flood prevention scheme in the Apennines some fifty miles north-east of Rome had to be cancelled when the locals, during Tiberius's reign, demanded that consideration be accorded to 'the altars of their country streams'.[22] Down on the coast no such considerations intervened.)

Much of this imported corn was revenue in kind from subjugated territories, rather than the more costly product of international trade. Access to it depended on continued control by the Roman authorities – in short, on a strong and loyal army.

Army officers were drawn from the senatorial and knightly classes. The legions and the NCOs of auxiliary regiments were recruited from among the citizens, the rank-and-file auxiliaries from freeborn subjects who lacked citizen status, though they were expected to understand Latin, and they were awarded citizenship at the end of their period of service.[23] Slaves, whose loyalty presumably could not be assured, were not enrolled in the early Roman armies (though they must have been ubiquitous as camp followers; all NCOs had personal slaves, as, in the Guards, did even private soldiers).[24] As early as the second century BC it was observed, with disquiet, that the native population of Italy was diminishing relative to the slaves, partly at least because slaves stayed at home and begat offspring while the wretched citizens and freeborn were off campaigning and getting killed.[25]

In the ensuing century extensive manumission of slaves enhanced the pool of potential recruits, and there was also a constant broadening of the categories recognized as citizens. By Caesar's time, the whole of Italy had been enfranchised, though in practice few could journey to Rome to exercise the vote to which, under the Republic, they were entitled.[26] But prosperous though the early centuries of the Empire were, the citizens of Italy, particularly the classes from which the officers were drawn, manifested an inability, or unwillingness, to bear and raise children.

Augustus had assumed unwillingness, and had legislated against single blessedness. It was ineffective. Of 45 patrician families restored by Julius Caesar, only one remained after 165 years.[27] Abortion was widespread – Seneca especially praised his mother for her unusual conduct in never having 'crushed the hope of children that were being nurtured in your body';[28] not until the end of the second century, however, did the law forbid the practice.[29] Scholars disagree as to how far contraception was known and practised, the difficulty being that it is not clear whether references in contemporary texts are to contraceptive, as distinct from abortional, practices. However, Professor John Riddle, a medical historian at North Carolina State University, in his *Contraception and Abortion from the Ancient World to the Renaissance*, recounts modern researchers' rediscovery of the effectiveness of many of the ancient herbal impediments to conception.

Polybius had lamented the depopulation of his country, complaining that his contemporaries in Greece at the beginning of the second century BC had refused to raise more than one or two children 'so as to leave these in affluence'.[30] In the first century AD the Stoic philosopher Musonius Rufus was to level exactly the same charge at the Romans: 'they impiously contrive the prosperity of their children by the murder of their siblings; that is, they destroy their brothers and sisters, so that the earlier children may have a greater share of the inheritance'.[31]

At the end of the first century AD Nerva and Trajan initiated programmes, further developed under their successors, of child benefit in cash for the freeborn children (girls as well as boys) of Italian parents. In further efforts to boost the Italian population, Nerva bought land for distribution to the poor. Trajan forbade emigration from Italy, and forced senators to own land in the mother country, for which purpose he made cheap loans available to landowners. It was the interest on these loans, for which the land constituted the security, that financed the child benefits, a system of which Rostovtzeff says, 'the financial operations of this department might be compared *mutatis mutandis* with those of modern state-banks which lend on landed security'.[32]

Whatever incentive this may have provided to those able to have children, ample evidence of regret over barrenness raises the question of involuntary sterility. Among the emperors themselves, sons were a rarity. Trajan, Hadrian, Antoninus Pius, Lucius Verus and Marcus Aurelius – all were 'adopted' sons of their predecessors.[33] There was grief, too, for numerous children dying young, even in prosperous households. Fronto, in the second century AD, lost five young children. Balsdon discusses the possible impact of lead poisoning, which reputedly conduces to miscarriage in females and to sterility in males. The pewter used by the Romans for household goods was a lead/tin alloy containing one part of lead to 2.5 parts of tin.[*34] Some Romans were wary of lead. Warnings about lead pollution dated back at least to Hippocrates in the fifth century BC. Pliny alluded to the dangers, and Vitruvius urged the use of earthenware wherever possible for water pipes and storage, but much of the distribution system, including the cisterns, were of lead.[35] Bones of Romans of the classical period have been found to contain lead. Balsdon, however, questions whether this is a likely explanation of failing fecundity, in view of the great disparities between different families, all presumably at equivalent risk.[36]

Venereal infections are frequently a source of sterility. The *British Medical Journal* of 10 November 1990 reported that among women suffering ectopic pregnancies, 76 to 78 per cent showed antibodies to chlamydia trachomatis, and in a controlled study 32 per cent showed the presence of gonococcus, compared with only 4 per cent of the control group.[37] We know that sterility in women can be one of the consequences of gonorrhea, but we do not know whether gonorrhea was particularly prevalent at this period. The Greek physician Galen (another of those who warned about the danger of lead poisoning), who practised in Rome in the second century AD, has traditionally been credited with the first use of the term 'gonorrhea',[38] but a recent analysis of the diseases of the classical world disputes the assumption that the word meant then what it means today.[39] We do know, however, that sexually transmitted disease became a matter of concern to the Romans during the first century AD.

---

* As may be seen in the Museum of Roman Civilisation in Rome, Roman household goods such as four-egg poachers, wine filters and cheese graters would not look out of place in a modern kitchen. The decorative placing of the holes in Roman colanders made them things of beauty as well as utility.

Plutarch had described Sulla as suffering from a revolting disease of the bowels, resulting from his sexual proclivities, but there is no suggestion that at that time (the early first century BC) it was at all widespread.[40] By the reign of Tiberius an edict had been passed forbidding kissing, in the hope of combating the spread of skin disease.[41] It cannot have been very effective. In the same century Pliny was describing skin infections, passed on, he says, by kissing, in which a scaly eruption covered face, neck and chest.[42] Martial remarked that people would keep on kissing, undeterred by skin infections.[43]

Nicolo Leoniceno, describing in 1497 the syphilis pandemic which was then sweeping Europe and which has since been widely attributed to infection brought back from the Americas by Columbus's crews, identified the symptoms with the skin infections described by Pliny in the first century AD. Was Roman Italy also suffering from syphilis, and could this account for the sickness and death of children in prosperous homes? Pliny himself thought the disease he described was new to Italy, having been brought from Asia Minor, but Leoniceno equates it with a disease known to Hippocrates, and suggests that it was the medical skill to diagnose it that was new to Pliny's Rome, not the disease itself.[44]

The description in Hippocrates is vague, amounting to no more than the suggestion of ulcerated genitals.[45] A first-century AD Roman physician, Scribonius Largus, also refers to ulcerated genitals, and so does Galen in the second century. But these may not have been syphilitic lesions, involving the whole system as syphilis does. There is, however, independent evidence that, whatever may have been the case in antiquity, syphilis existed in the Empire by the fourth century AD. The court physician to the Emperor Theodosius gives an account of a sickness stemming from 'venereal poison' which is a classic description of tabes syphilis, including the late-stage paralysis. Subsequent centuries include various references to venereal infections which contemporaries call 'leprosy', but the symptoms described accord more closely with syphilis than with what is today called leprosy.[46] One school of thought maintains firmly that skeletons from classical times betray late syphilitic lesions, but those upholding the Columban theory dispute the diagnosis, holding that the lesions are due to leprosy.[47] Excavations of burials of Greek colonists in southern Italy, published in 1992, show clear evidence of conditions for which the medical researchers consider 'syphilitic-like infections' the likeliest explanation, a clear repudiation of the Columban theory. The burials date from about 580 to 250 BC, but there is no indication whether the syphilitic traces cluster in any particular period.[48]

153

The case remains unproven, as does the possibility that a disease comparable to AIDS was, by the late fourth century, ravaging Rome.[*] The historian Ammianus Marcellinus remarked on an incurable condition from which childless and unmarried men suffered.

> Since among them, as is natural in the capital of the world, cruel disorders gain such heights that all the healing art is powerless even to mitigate them, it has been provided, as a means of safety, that no-one shall visit a friend suffering from such a disease, and by a few who are more cautious another sufficiently effective remedy has been added, namely that servants sent to inquire after the conditions of a man's acquaintances who have been attacked by that disorder should not be re-admitted to their master's house until they have purified their persons by a bath. So fearful are they of a contagion seen only by the eyes of others.[49]

Modern experience, informed by statistics for sexually transmitted diseases based on the fact that notification of their incidence is compulsory, confirms what common sense would suggest – that they are (at least in the absence of adequate prophylaxis) more prevalent when morality is permissive. Chlamydial urethritis in males and chlamydial cervicitis in females (both of which can result in sterility) are very prevalent among promiscuous people.[50] The morality of the early Empire had been not a whit chastened by Augustus's 'back to basics' crusade. His successors on the imperial throne, Tiberius and Caligula, soon acquired reputations for debauchery of various kinds. Caligula's successor Claudius (in an echo of the Greek Ptolemies' adoption, in the early third century BC, of Egyptian brother-sister marriages) determined to marry his niece – a union which previous practice had classed as incestuous. Tacitus reports that Claudius hesitated for some time, fearing public disaster might result, but a crony, claiming that although uncle-niece marriage was a novel idea for Rome, it was quite customary among other nations, prevailed on the Senate to call for the union as politically judicious, whereupon Claudius had no difficulty obtaining the necessary change in the law.[51] Public opinion was not won over. Suetonius remarks that in fact only two other men were known to have availed themselves of the liberty thus afforded them.[52] In other respects,

---

[*] Scientists at Amsterdam University have for some years been investigating DNA from ancient Egyptian mummified baboons to establish whether they were then harbouring viruses of the type implicated in the development of AIDS (*The Times*, 12 July 1990, an article which also asserts that syphilis was 'rampant' in ancient Egypt; *Egyptian Archaeology*, 3, 1993, pp.31–3).

however, permissiveness became increasingly the order of the day. Seneca a few years later spoke of 'unchastity, the greatest evil of our time', and remarked that chastity had become 'simply a proof of ugliness'. There were women, he said, who reckoned their years not by the number of consuls, but by the number of their husbands.[53] The poets Martial and Juvenal, one with relish, the other with disgust, were to catalogue the sexual restlessness, opportunism and experimentation of their time.

At the turn of the first century, Tacitus was to castigate his own society by pointing the contrast with the Germans, among whom:

> The marriage tie is strict. One wife apiece. The bond between them is in their eyes a 'mysterious sacrament' hedged in divinity. Their life is one of fenced-in chastity . . . adulteries are very few for the number of the people . . . no-one laughs at vice there; no-one calls seduction, suffered or wrought, the spirit of the age . . . To limit the number of their children, to make away with any of the later children, is held abominable . . .[54]

Whether the lack of recruits from mainland Italy stemmed from a failure to raise children, or whether, as other analysts suggest, the population decline was due to plague or to emigration to more fertile soils abroad, the result for the army was an increasing proportion of troops drawn from provincial sources.[55] Already by the start of the second century AD the legions were recruiting not in Italy but at their frontier headquarters, a third to a half the recruits being the children of the legionaries.[56] Early in the next century, in 212, the Emperor Caracella extended citizenship to almost everyone in the Empire;[57] the distinction between the legions and the auxiliaries disappeared.[58]

There were cultural adjustments to be made. The antagonism to foreign deities was abandoned. Tiberius had continued to persecute the followers of Isis, who had a reputation for immorality, but Caligula gave state sanction to the cult when he erected a temple to the goddess in about AD 38. It remained a substantially immigrant, or immigrant-descended, cult. Analysis of inscriptions associated with Isis reveal that in the Roman port of Ostia 85 per cent of the names are of non-Italic origin, in Campania some 43 per cent, and this excludes non-Italian women married to Italian men.[59] Claudius approved an enhanced standing for Cybele, permitting Romans to join her self-mutilating priesthood, and allowing the festivals of deities associated with the cult to be celebrated, a move which may have been made to reduce the relative privileges accorded to Isis in the previous reign. In the second century an important concession was made to the legions, probably by Commodus (180–92) when the provincial armies, by now consisting almost entirely of men raised in the locality, were allowed to promote the cults of their local native gods.[60]

The oriental cults were polytheistic and not exclusive or jealous, so their incorporation into the Roman religious calendar did not pose insuperable problems. The monotheistic Jews could not be similarly assimilated, but after the suppression of their national revolt and the destruction of Jerusalem in AD 70,* followed by the dispersal of the Jews from their Palestinian homeland, they do not seem to have been regarded as a serious threat, perhaps because they did not proselytize. There remained the challenge of the breakaway Jewish sect known as the Christians. Tertullian, a century and a half after the supposed event, claims that Tiberius, on receipt of news from Pilate (himself now a 'Christian in his secret heart') in Palestine, enrolled Christ in the pantheon, but the Senate refused to ratify the endorsement, out of pique at not being consulted in advance; a story not widely believed after the classical period.[61] Instead, the Christians, with their refusal to sacrifice to the *genius* of the head of state, and their propensity to proselytize whenever circumstances allowed, came to be regarded with the same suspicions of subversion and conspiracy as had attached to the Dionysian orgies of the early second century BC – and to be accused of some of the same crimes. Intermittent persecution was the consequence. Tertullian complained bitterly at the lack of toleration extended to Christians, when the cults of other non-Roman deities were allowed to flourish, even when they were not practised in Rome itself.[62] But the trouble with the Christians was that the emperors doubted their political reliability. When Pliny the Younger was Governer of Bithynia he wrote to Trajan saying that except for the problem of the Christians refusing to sacrifice to the Emperor, they seemed a pretty harmless bunch, swearing oaths to abstain from theft, robbery and adultery, and meeting to eat quite harmless food. Trajan replied sternly that any such assemblies would soon turn into a political club, and must be forbidden.[63]

The attachment of the provincials to their native deities was not matched among the sophisticated Romans and Greeks. The *mouseia*, the institutes of learning based on the Alexandrine model that had sprung up in many Greek cities, were strictly secular foundations.[64] Augustus's

---

* The resulting supply of prisoners provided both the labour force for the building of the Colosseum, and a source of victims for the festivities surrounding its dedication.

efforts to restore traditional Roman piety had had no more success than his parallel attempts to restore traditional standards of conduct. (Sorokin calls the Augustan Age 'pseudo-ideational'.) Literate circles after Ovid's time showed little interest in the native gods of Roman mythology,[65] nor was there respect for their supposed protection. Lucan's epic of the first century AD on Julius Caesar and the civil war departed from previous convention by entirely omitting the gods from the action. Indeed, he voiced the opinion that 'There are no gods: to say Jove reigns is wrong. 'Tis a blind Chance that moves the years along.'[66] Nero saw to it that when the sacred theatre dedicated to Dionysus at Athens was remodelled, his own name was added as an additional dedicatee – though he drew the line at having a temple erected to himself during his own lifetime.[67] The younger Pliny, writing from Greek Asia Minor, reported that the temples were falling into disuse.[68] There are accounts of roofs fallen in, idols missing, the whole sanctuary in a tumbledown condition. Even the shrine of the ineffable Diana at Ephesus is reported neglected in both the first and second centuries AD.[69] 'The altars of Zeus are as cold as Chrysippus', wrote Lucian in the second century. 'Religion is absurd . . .'[70] Dozens of blasphemous graffiti preserved for our inspection at Pompeii include insults to Venus (the patron deity of the town) as well as to Isis.[71] Drawings of a crucified donkey are identified by some scholars as lampoons on the Christians.[*] The sardonic Juvenal at the start of the second century remarked that anyone displaying faith in temple or altar was a target of derision.[72] 'Wealth,' as he tartly put it, 'is our divinity.'[73]

In the early Empire prosperity, and pride in a shared secular citizenship, more than compensated for the absence of any cohesive religious allegiance. Assimilation to Roman culture and customs was expected of the educated classes. When Sertorius, the Roman general, campaigned in Spain in the early first century BC, he encouraged Spanish officials to wear the toga, and started a school to teach the Latin and Greek languages,[74] a process that led to grants of citizenship to individual Spaniards. Increasingly, provincials gained access to the Senate. Senators were originally all from the Italian mainland (though many were of foreign origin; Caesar had packed the Senate with eastern

---

[*] According to Tacitus (*Histories*, V.4) there was a belief among the Romans that the Jews had consecrated the 'likeness of an ass', out of gratitude to wild asses which had guided them to water when they were dying of thirst during their wanderings in the desert. He maintains that when Pompey conquered Jerusalem, he had sought for such an image in the Temple. The ass symbol was associated with the Christians simply because they were originally regarded as a Jewish sect. See Tertullian, *Apologeticus*, XVI.

ex-slave stock sympathetic to his oriental-style personal ambitions).[75] By the late first century AD 80 per cent were still Italian, but Trajan, himself a Spaniard, readily admitted provincials from Spain and Gaul. By the end of the second century AD less than half the Senate were Italians, the majority hailing from the provinces, including north Africa and Asia Minor. Nor were they an impermeable class of hereditary grandees. Knights, army NCOs, even former private soldiers were being created senators, and the distinction between knights and senators disappeared. Macrinus, the emperor who assumed office in 217, was not himself of senatorial rank.[76]

Pride in shared Roman citizenship produced a high level of patriotism and civic generosity. Wealth was increasing throughout the first and the first half of the second centuries, much of it flowing into new hands, and the *nouveaux riches* were as assiduous as the diminishing numbers of the old aristocracy in seeking public honour by disbursements in the public interest.[77] The rich citizens of the Empire joined with the emperors in an Empire-wide programme of civic liberality, including the purchase of food for distribution in their local municipalities beyond the metropolises served by the State; hospitality at public banquets; the endowment of professorial chairs and institutions for the education of the poor; and the provision of public buildings such as libraries,* theatres and, above all, 'baths', from wash-houses to leisure centres.[78]

Rivalling the baths as an object of munificence was the financing of entertainment, racing, athletics, gladiatorial shows or theatricals, celebrating the traditional festivals and national commemorations. When not financed by the emperor, these were the responsibility of the civic dignitaries, whose period in office required them to dig deep into their own pockets. Widely distributed plaques commemorating benefactions testify to the fact that they were proud to do so. All over the Empire, in provincial towns and cities, benefactors provided wild beast and gladiatorial shows, and footed the bill to buy in criminals for the arena. Largesse to the stadium and the theatre was the principal route to immediate popular acclaim,[79] and, as an instrument of social control, even more important, according to one contemporary, than welfare provision. As Fronto said, early in the second century:

the Roman people are held fast by two things above all, the corn-

---

* By the fourth century Rome had twenty-nine lending libraries, and there was library provision in at least seven other Italian country towns. Six Greek cities boasted libraries, as did five in Asia Minor; Pergamum, Cyprus, Carthage and Timgad (in north Africa) had libraries, and there were several in Alexandria (Balsdon (1969), p.148).

dole and the shows ... food-largesse is a weaker incentive than shows; by largesses of food, only the proletariat on the corn register are conciliated, singly and individually, whereas by the shows the whole population is kept in good humour.[80]

They served the purpose of 'obliterating, at least for a short space, class distinctions based on property', to quote Joseph Vogt in *The Decline of Rome*.[81]

The two hundred years starting in the late second century have, in their profusion of grand ruins, left a splendid testimony to the ambitions of contemporary taste; in this, 'the climax of the Empire', huge halls and domes, apses and vaults rose in response to the maturing skills of architects and engineers.[82] But behind the architectural triumphalism, social cohesion was evaporating. Government edicts are concerning themselves with outbreaks of lawlessness – as yet only localized – from the 130s AD.[83]

Manpower shortages had much to do with it. Already in Hadrian's time (117–38) the policy began, though much deplored by the Emperor himself, of preventing tenants from leaving their agricultural tenancies, the start of what, in the fullness of time, was to develop into medieval feudalism.[84] Devastating plagues in mid-century are presumed to have further depleted the numbers available to work the land. Severus, who became emperor in 193, barred Italians from joining the army.

Elsewhere, however, he made military service compulsory.[85] The resulting regiments of provincial conscripts were to prove a source of disaffection. From the end of the second century there are increasing reports of brigandage, much of it the work of conscript soldiers who, stationed in their own locality, deserted the army, found shelter among the local peasantry and embarked on a life of pillage and rapine. Robbers were rampant on land and sea, says Rostovtzeff, travel ceased to be safe and piracy made commerce practically impossible.[86]

Severus unashamedly used his army command as his power base, ignoring the Senate's nominal role in the appointment of emperors. Others were to follow his example, with the result that the third century witnessed a chaotic succession of claimants and counterclaimants to the imperial throne, each supported by some element of the provincial armies. In the 73 years from the death of Severus to the accession of Diocletian, there were 24 more or less legitimate emperors, and many more usurpers. In the face of these challenges, emperors had to keep elements of the provincial militia in Italy to protect their backs from challengers, thus depleting the forces desperately needed on the frontiers.[87] Barbarian invaders intent on loot, sometimes enthusiastically abetted by local soldiers and peasantry, sacked peripheral towns and even penetrated to Rome itself, where defensive walls had to be built.[88] Cities emerged into the fourth century, remarks Robin Lane Fox, behind their distinctive late-antique emblems: solid towered walls. And the funds to supply these walls diminished what was available for games and entertainments.[89]

In the East, a reinvigorated Persia renewed an old threat. To the north, the multiplicity of Germanic tribes were federating into agglomerations – the Franks and the Alemanni – increasingly conscious of their common Germanic identity. 'It became much harder for Roman diplomacy to contrive divisions among men who now had much in common', says Edward Luttwak, in *The Grand Strategy of the Roman Empire*.[90] The cultural identity of the citizens of the Empire, on the other hand, was fragmenting, and by the end of the third century the acquisition of citizenship was without cultural implications. 'The cities', as Rostov-tzeff puts it, were no longer able to 'hellenize or romanize the masses'.[91] The throne, which Augustus had sought to establish as a focal point of loyalty, now commanded fear but not respect, and in these circumstances the great system of voluntary service and benevolence in the public interest broke down. The inscriptions, laudatory or self-congratulatory, commemorating acts of beneficence disappear.[92] There is speculation that perhaps a cultural change, such as a decline in the intercity rivalries prompting the vaunting of local achievements, may have been responsi-ble;[93] but there are other indications that the propertied classes (other than the Senate, which exempted itself) were overwhelmed by the huge taxes being exacted to pay for defence expenditure.

By now, in addition to their traditional obligations to fund expensive entertainments, civic dignitaries are being made responsible not merely for the collection of taxes, but for making good any tax deficit out of their own pockets.[94] The council minutes of the late third century are exclusively preoccupied, says Rostovtzeff, with the problem of civic responsibilities which are tantamount to ruin. The well-to-do flee the municipalities rather than be eligible for duty. Anyone with a country estate retires to it, fortifying it against the depredations not only of bandits, but of imperial tax demands. The tenantry are more closely tied to the land than ever, both by their need to be protected by powerful landlords, and by the landlords' tax obligations, which are based on labour as well as land. Their prospects in the unprovisioned cities are even worse. When Aurelian, behind the huge newly erected walls of

Rome,[*] increased the dole to its citizens, it was not to dispense affluence but to avert starvation.[95] Rich and poor alike abandoned the towns. When the walls of towns razed by insurrection and insurgency were rebuilt, they enclosed urban areas shrunk to one third or even one quarter of their former size. In Gaul, Autun, a town formerly covering some 500 acres, was reduced to a settlement no more than 25 acres in extent.[96]

Whereas in the second century the state had paid for the levies of goods, the food, fodder, clothing and arms requisitioned as an emergency measure for the troops, there now began a policy tantamount to confiscation.[97] This was the more onerous because, in the disruption of the times, productivity was falling. The exactions became so ruinous that land was abandoned, it was uneconomic to continue to retain it in use.[98] In an attempt to keep the army and the civil service supplied, the emperors set up state factories, using slave, convict and directed labour, which was paid in kind.[99] The craft guilds, which had started life as voluntary burial societies, were now suborned by the State as instruments for the direction of labour, neither the members of crafts designated essential nor their children being permitted to change their occupation. Over the course of the next century these reserved occupations came to include armourers, weavers and dyers, miners and agricultural workers, merchant seamen, shippers, bakers, butchers, purveyors of wine and oil, entertainers, and stokers for the fires at the baths. Wives had to be chosen from families within the same guild. Husbands from outside the designated crafts had to join the guild of their wife's family.[100]

Private enterprise virtually ceased. In the absence of business activity, interest rates fell. Commerce was disrupted not only by the lawlessness of the trade routes and the decay of the ill-maintained highways, but also by instability in the financial markets. From time to time the managers of the banks of exchange stopped dealing.[101] Inflation began to menace the whole economy. So stable had prices been in the early Empire that in over two hundred years, from Augustus to Septimus Severus, the army had only had one increase in pay.[102] But from the start of the third century the currency began to suffer rapid debasement. Old money of higher intrinsic value was hoarded, and fresh supplies of silver were impeded by the difficulty in obtaining miners, compounded towards the end of the century by the loss of the Dacian silver mines, when the legions had to evacuate Transylvania in the face of Gothic invasion. Worthless token

---

[*] Beyond which the city was not to grow for the next sixteen centuries (Sumption, p.217).

money was issued, which was widely distrusted, and there was a run on goods. By the end of the century inflation was out of control.[103]

In AD 301 Diocletian promulgated a prices and incomes policy. The preamble to the edict blamed the economic troubles on speculators, and threatened with capital punishment anyone withholding goods or exceeding the maximum stipulated price. It proved impossible to implement.[104]

Twenty-six years before the edict, in 275, there had gone out into the Egyptian desert a solitary Christian named Antony, the first of the anchorites. Twenty-four years after the edict, in 325, Pachomius, concerned that solitude might be a form of selfishness, founded an abbey at Tabenne in Egypt, and gathered the desert hermits into a community of monks. The complexities of the Empire and its assailants held no interest for them. They were seeking for a kingdom that was not of this world. It was their ideals that were to shape the next millennium in Europe.[105] A new ideational culture was about to be born.

Chapter 10

The Shattering of the Mirror: the Fourth to Sixth Centuries

Lucretius's vision of progress, of a golden age lying not in the past but in the future, had by the end of the second century AD lost its power to attract and inspire. Epitaphs, says Sorokin, indicate a widespread debased Epicureanism of despair. 'Baths, wine, and love impair our bodies, but baths, wine, and love make life'; 'what I have eaten and what I have drunk; that is all that belongs to me'; 'I was; I am not; I do not care'. Lucian, who had dismissed religion as absurd, found philosophy vacuous and concluded, 'therefore let us enjoy the moment, eschewing enthusiasms'.[1]

By the third century, the disintegration of society as law and order collapsed was to make a mockery of hedonism. This, says Franz Cumont, an authority on Roman religious belief, is a period of such suffering, anguish and violence, of so much unnecessary ruin and so many unpunished crimes, that the Roman world took refuge in the expectation of a better existence in the hereafter.[2] The seeds of this religious revival, however, pre-date the social collapse. Robin Lane Fox sees the resurrection of interest beginning in the second century with, as he puts it, 'flamboyant building for the gods'.[3] Though there is, in the third century, a marked diminution in the building of temples and the carving of inscriptions, this appears to be a reflection of the poverty and insecurity of the times rather than any failure of devotion. 'It is not the priest who is stilled but the stonecutter', says Ramsey Macmullen in his *Paganism in the Roman Empire*.[4]

Scholars are agreed that the new spiritual fervour differed in quality from the old state pieties. It was the mystery religions of the East that could assuage 'the growing spiritual anxiety which the orthodox religion of Rome neither recognized nor catered for'.[5] They offered worshippers a more personal relationship with the object of their devotion, and reassurance not only for this world, but for the next. In this climate, even the stern resolution of the Stoics, with their commitment to a belief in a rational, if not particularly cosy or accessible, Providence, began to fail. Faith in the cool ratiocination of the philosophers is replaced by an acceptance of revelation. In AD 176 the Stoic Emperor Marcus Aurelius was initiated in Greece into the Eleusinian Mysteries,* 'that he might prove himself to be free of guilt', says the *Augustan History*,[6] and though perhaps the motive is anachronistically interpreted by the fourth-century author, it is clear that a widespread feature of the Eastern religions is the inclusion of elaborate rituals, such as baptism and ceremonies of purification, whose purpose is not the temporal prosperity of the city or the State, but the eternal salvation of the worshipper. Apuleius, a contemporary of Marcus Aurelius, in his novel *The Golden Ass*, left an almost certainly autobiographical account of his initiation into the cult of Isis 'of the Myriad Names, Lady of All, Queen of the Inhabited World, Star of the Sea', as M.I. Finley describes her.[7] A ritual bath and sprinkling with holy water is followed by ten days of frugal meals from which meat and wine are excluded, after which come ceremonies in the inner recesses of the sanctuary too holy to be revealed, the whole period accompanied by a series of visions of the goddess.[8]

Others were seeking transcendent experiences in the wisdom of the Orient. Already in the first century Apollonius of Tyana was pursuing an interest in Indian mysticism, though his concerns were not much emulated in his own time. By the third century, however, his ideas had become fashionable. Philostratus, who stressed self-discipline and purity rather than ritual sacrifices as the proper route to salvation, wrote a *Life of Apollonius* in 214. Thirty years later Plotinus of Alexandria was in Rome, having returned from a visit to the East in pursuit of contact with Hindu philosophy. His message preached a continuum from divine mind to material body, spiritual advance was to be achieved by rapturous contemplation, by turning the attention from 'the things without to look within', to seek contact with the inner being, and, reabsorbed into the One, partake of a reality immune to material suffering.[9]

This neo-Platonist idealism, says Macmullen, went beyond philosophy. What was being offered was salvation. Philosophy no longer implies calm deliberation; instead it is the path to ecstatic absorption into the ultimate. The seat of power is the soul, not the mind, which from the second century on 'comes under increasingly open, angry and exasperated attack'.[10] To quote E. Kornemann, contrasting the third century BC, 'then the high point of exact science', with the third century AD: 'In half a millennium, antiquity had transformed itself from a world of knowledge

* See p.54.

164

into a world of belief; from philosophy it had gone over . . . to theology, from astronomy to astrology; it was now ripe for a purely hieratic [priestly] culture.'[11]

Devotees of mystical practices were an élite, distinguished by their long hair and their commitment to vegetarianism – indeed, a near contemporary of Plotinus was at pains to explain that 'a vegetarian diet helped Plotinus four times to attain nirvana'. Levitation was among the marvels with which some practitioners were credited.[12] The uninitiated may not have aspired to such esoteric behaviour. But the fact that it had become respectable to believe in the palpable reality of a spiritual dimension to life unleashed upon society at large a flood of occult practices that a few generations previously educated people would have dismissed as peasant superstition. Necromancy flourished, resort to magicians, oracles and astrologers became commonplace, and there was universal belief in, and fear of, witches and demons.[13] The long-established practice of divination had sought the intentions or advice of the Unseen Powers; neo-Platonism was easily degraded into an occultism in which reverent obedience played no part, but which sought rather, through spells and rituals, to manipulate spiritual forces and bind them in the secular interests of the petitioners.[14]

This fevered commerce with the Unseen Powers was highly individu-alistic. State religion underwent a different metamorphosis. Early in the troubled third century Heliogabalus, emperor for four adolescent years prior to his murder at the age of eighteen, imported to Rome from Syria the religion of his Syrian mother, which included the worship of the Invincible Sun. By the third quarter of the century, the Emperor Aurelian had proclaimed this deity supreme, so superior to other challengers for the title that *Sol Invictus* becomes the precursor of monotheism. Sunday is pronounced his sacred day, 25 December his birthday. Aurelian's establishment of pontiffs of *Sol Invictus* senior in the hierarchy to all other high priests marks the formal end of the old Roman religion.[15]

By the end of the century the Invincible Sun had merged with another oriental deity – the austere figure of Mithra. Mithra absorbed into himself all the old pagan deities except those of the Isis cult.[16]

It is possible that Mithra, a god of Persian origin, had obtained a temple in Rome as early as 67 BC, serving a small foreign settlement,[17] but he made slow progress. As Macmullen points out, Mithra had no 'home base' within the Empire, was patron of no area, tribe or ancestry within its borders.[18] The cult was not open to women, wives and daughters of Mithraists being received into Cybele's mysteries.[19] It was soldiers, presumably initially those whose service had taken them to the eastern front, who encouraged interest in the cult of Mithra. It remained a particular favourite among the military, the legions spreading the faith 'from the mouth of the Danube to the Solway'.[20] The Emperor Commodus received initiation late in the second century.[21] State endorsement came in 307, when Diocletian, who had retired as Emperor of the Eastern Empire,* together with his successor Galerius and an emperor-in-waiting Licinius, dedicated a sanctuary at the Danube town of Carnuntum to Mithra, according him the status of 'protector of their Empire'.[22]

According to Franz Cumont, Mithra, or Mithras, introduced to the spiritual life of the Empire the ancient Persian Mazdean concept of a duality of good and evil, of righteousness and wickedness.† There were powers of light, and there were others, demons, who were powers of darkness. For a human being to be among the righteous required watchfulness and self-discipline. 'Mithra is chaste, Mithra is holy, and for the worship of fecundity he substitutes a new reverence for continence', says Cumont. 'This perfect purity distinguishes the mysteries of Mithra from those of all other oriental gods.' Eternal salvation was the reward for those who fought the good fight.

> [B]y divesting themselves of all sensuality and lust in passing through the planetary sphere . . . they become pure as the gods whose company they enter . . . After time had run its course, Mithra would raise all men from the dead, pouring out a marvellous beverage of immortality for the good, but all evil doers would be annihilated by fire . . .[23]

Four years after participating in the dedication of the sanctuary to Mithra, Galerius in 311 issued an edict of toleration with regard to the one sect which had had to struggle against continuing, if intermittent, bouts of hostility from the Roman state: the Christians. The following year, in 312, Constantine, Emperor of the West, believing that he had been instructed in a vision to fight under the banner of Christ, ordered his troops to emblazon on their shields the Greek initials for Christ's name, Chi Rho; and above them Christ's emblem, the cross. The ensuing battle

---

* For administrative convenience, Diocletian had in AD 286 divided the Empire into an eastern and a western sector, each under a different emperor, with a 'caesar' as his deputy.

† Cumont's long-accepted identification of the Roman Mithras with the Persian Mithra has been challenged in recent years. See, for instance, David Ulansey's *The Origins of the Mithraic Mysteries*, which offers an analysis linking Mithras to Perseus and to Greek perceptions of the significance of the precession of the equinoxes, rather than to Persian Mazdean antecedents.

of the Milvian Bridge at Rome, at which Constantine triumphed over his enemies, was to be celebrated in Christian art – in the Eastern Church at least – down the centuries. It marked the moment at which Christianity began its by no means unchallenged alliance with the secular power – the tentative origins of Christendom.

The third century had been a harsh trial of faith for the Christians. As anarchy and wretchedness spread, the authorities had turned in increasing desperation to supplications to the gods of the various localities. Local magistrates were not concerned with what Christians chose to believe, but it was vital that everyone should conform to the proper formulae of propitiation, and accede to the necessary sacrificial animal slaughter. In December 249 Decius, having in that year seized the throne from the reputedly Christian Philip (killed on the battlefield), gave the order for a nationwide ceremony of sacrifice – a national day of prayer, as it were. The Christians refused to join in, an omission to which the pagans attributed the continuing misfortunes of the Empire. The Decian persecution ensued. A brief interlude of toleration in the 260s was followed by renewed persecution, culminating in the Empire-wide Diocletian persecution of the first decade of the fourth century, during which Christians were purged from the army and excluded from courts of law; and scriptures and churches were destroyed.[*24] Constantine's victory did not put an end to Christian martyrdoms, but future executions were the result of heresy-hunts by fellow Christians, not the proscription of Christianity as a whole.

The Empire did not become Christian overnight. Constantine's triumph did not constitute a revolution. Probably no more than 4 or 5 per cent of the population were Christian at the start of the fourth century, even less in Constantine's army and among the ruling class.[25] The institutions of the state were, and for some time remained, pagan; and though the head of the Western Empire was now a Christian, and had embarked on an ambitious programme of basilica-building for the Church, he and his successor emperors, most of whom were Christians, continued until 375 (when Gratian refused the office)[26] to fulfil the functions of Pontifex Maximus, titular head of the pagan state religion.[†] The Church reached an accommodation with unregenerate state institutions by allowing prominent citizens among its members to fulfil their civic duties, often involving formal acquiescence in pagan cults, such as the provision of festival entertainments. The Council of Eliberis

---

[*] This was the persecution in which, in Britain, Alban lost his life.
[†] Augustus had inaugurated this practice as part of his religious reforms. See p.114.

in Spain in 305 had stipulated life-long penance and excommunication until 'the hour of death' for Christians performing such functions,[27] but a compromise was now worked out, requiring the magistrates concerned merely to absent themselves from the Church community during their year of office.[28] Constantine exempted Christian clergy of the magisterial class from such civic obligations, but had to rescind the exemption, as it resulted in an unmanageable exodus into the priesthood from the highly expensive responsibilities of rank.[29]

Until the last quarter of the century, paganism continued not merely to be tolerated, but to receive state support. But in 382 Gratian, who died in 383, withdrew the estates and endowments from the pagan sacred colleges. State payments for the upkeep of the old priesthood were terminated; the Vestal Virgins lost their privileges.[30] In 384 the statue and altar of Victory were removed from the Senate House in Rome. A resolution for their restoration from the predominantly pagan Senate did not receive the Emperor's assent.[*31]

Theodosius, a Spaniard who became Emperor of the East in 379, and was briefly, in 394–5, Emperor of the West as well, set about the imposition on all imperial subjects not merely of Christianity, but of its Catholic variant. The Bishop of Rome was given jurisdiction over the whole Empire. In 391 came the first of a series of edicts that were to ban pagan sacrifices, close the temples, and forbid, even in the privacy of people's homes, the lighting of votary lamps, the burning of incense or the hanging of garlands in honour of the old gods; though the frequency with which the laws were later re-enacted suggests that paganism still enjoyed considerable vitality, even into the period of Islamic conquest – not least, perhaps, because animal slaughter followed by a good ritual meal of roast meat was an attractive social occasion for an impoverished underclass.[32] Heresy and paganism alike became treasonable, and paganism was banished, if not universally, at least from public life. Theodosius's reasons were akin to those which had led to the earlier persecution of the Christians – appalling political and military disasters from which only stringent pursuit of divine favour could rescue the State.[33] A contemporary pagan historian, Zosimus, reached precisely the opposite conclusion, seeing in the Emperor's neglect of the old gods explanation enough for the continuing ruin of the Empire.[34]

---

[*] Symmachus, respected leader of the pagan senators, argued for religious toleration. Among those most anxious to see pagan rites, particularly the murderous gladiatorial games, banned by law was the Spanish lawyer and poet Prudentius (see his *Contra Orationem Symmachi* I.385ff.; II.1114ff.) whose 'Of the Father's love begotten' and 'Earth has many a noble city' are still to be found in *Hymns Ancient and Modern*.

Long before the law supervened, however, the bishops were striving to inculcate among the growing community of Christians standards of conduct that set them apart from the majority of their fellow citizens. Though Christianity was to tolerate the imposition of hideous suffering on those judged guilty of crimes, a strong body of Christian opinion had from the start been appalled by the pursuit of violence as an entertainment. They were not entirely alone; there were Stoics who were repelled by blood-lust – the Emperor Marcus Aurelius had 'limited gladiatorial shows in every way' and had preferred contests in which the men duelled with foils that did not injure one another. He had also insisted on the provision of nets and mattresses beneath the tightrope walkers.[35] But it was the Christians from whom came the most sustained and vociferous opposition to what they did not hesitate to categorize as murder. Tatian, writing around the middle of the second century, had condemned those who sold themselves as murderers, but even more he condemned the rich men who bought in the gladiators for the purpose of perpetrating murder, and Tertullian declared that there could be no place in the Church for those who trained them to fight.[36] 'A man who is a gladiator or a trainer of gladiators, or a huntsman [in the arena] or one concerned with wild beast shows or a public official who is concerned with gladiatorial shows, either let him desist or let him be rejected [from baptism]', warned Hippolytus in his treatise summarizing the Church's administrative practices.[37]

As for the spectators, Christian polemicists from the late second century on were warning of the moral pollution inherent in deriving enjoyment from watching others suffer. 'There is little difference between seeing such murders and committing them', wrote Athenagoras in AD 177; his contemporary Tertullian took much the same view, saying, 'If we can plead that cruelty is allowed us, if impiety, if brute savagery, by all means let us go to the amphitheatre.'[38] 'Murderers with their eyes', Cyprian, Bishop of Carthage in the mid-third century, calls the spectators.[39] The harm lay in the very act of enjoying the show, quite apart from what influence the watching of such scenes might have on the character of the viewer – though that aspect was also the subject of comment, when at the end of the fourth century Chrysostom, Archbishop of Constantinople, deplored the opportunity which the arena provided for inculcating in the populace 'a merciless and savage and inhuman kind of temper'.[40]

Lactantius, a friend of Constantine, who entrusted his son's education to this teacher of rhetoric, considered all forms of killing to be un-Christian, whether in war (he was a pacifist); as capital punishment, whatever the method; or through the exposure of infants. 'He who reckons it a pleasure that a man, though justly condemned, should be slain in his sight, pollutes his conscience', he wrote.[41] Perhaps it was under his influence that Constantine moved, in 325, to ban gladiatorial contests, condemning criminals to the mines instead of to the arena.[42] But the ban could not be made effective. Throughout the fourth century the contests continued, and so did the Christian campaign against them. The *Constitutiones Apostolicae*, a compilation of ecclesiastical law dating from the latter half of the century, includes gladiators among those debarred from baptism,[43] but the allure of the shows, even to those who disapproved of them, is illustrated by Augustine. Describing his friend Alypius's visit to Rome, he recounts how he is propelled by friends to the amphitheatre, protesting that he will not watch. But inadvertently he opens his eyes when attracted by the 'mighty cry of the people', who are 'hot with hideous gloating'. In no time, he, too, is 'drunk . . . with that bloodthirsty joy', and becomes an habitué.[44]

Ultimately the opposition was to prevail. In the East, where Christianity permeated society more widely than in the West, there are no records of gladiatorial games after 400. At Rome there are indications, from medallions featuring gladiators, of sporadic contests as late as 434–5. How far their demise was due to Christian influences, how far to barbarian invasions, including the sack of Rome itself in 410, and the increasing impoverishment of the West, is open to question. In the turbulent conditions of the fourth century, Christian dignitaries were discovering that gladiators had their uses, and both Pope Damasus in the West and Bishop Marcel in the East employed troops of gladiators as fighting men.[45] What is indisputable is that gladiatorial games did come to an end; and that for their last three hundred years they had been the target of sustained attack from Christian polemicists.* Wild beast shows lasted longer. In the East, Anastasius forbade the contests of men against beasts in 498, though the pitting of beasts against other beasts continued. No examples of fights against animals are recorded in the West after 532.[46] Instead, malefactors faced execution by a method that was to have a protracted future: burning at the stake.

---

* The traditional belief that the imperial gladiatorial schools were closed in 399, and the games themselves terminated in 404, is disputed by G.Ville in 'Les Jeux de Gladiateurs dans l'Empire Chrétien' (*Mélanges d'Archéologie et d'Histoire de l'École Française de Rome* 1960, pp.322–5, 331). He makes out a strong case for his contention that the closure applied only to private establishments, which were threatening the security of the State by furnishing trained troops of personal retainers to senators. As when similar action was taken against private gladiatorial schools in the early days of the Empire, the motives for the closures were political rather than moral.

The renewal of religious belief among both Christians and non-Christians greatly strengthened the passions evoked by the festivals. The Christians did not dismiss the various deities in whose names the celebrations took place as figments of the imagination; on the contrary they accepted them as powerful occult forces – but forces of evil, demonic presences. The Church debarred from baptism those who had truck with them – magicians, enchanters, astrologers, diviners, magical charmers, makers of amulets and phylacteries, fortune-tellers, observers of the motion of birds or weasels, and a number of other categories of 'curious arts'. Amulets, ribands with texts or spells inscribed on them, hung round the neck to cure disease or protect from danger, were particularly popular, even the clergy conniving in their production, a practice for which the Council of Laodicea in 361 ordered them to be 'cast out of the Church'. Three centuries later, councils were still debating the matter, and in 692 a penalty of six years' penance was prescribed.[47]

With the increasing political ascendancy of the Church as the fourth century progressed, these prohibitions passed into law. Constantius II, Valentinian and Valens all legislated against divination, astrology and magic, Constantius enacting the death penalty for the wearing of amulets.[48] But the practice of magic continued. Augustine tells how in his unregenerate youth in north Africa, a magician approached him when he was competing for a prize in the theatre, offering by animal sacrifices to enlist demons to ensure his success.[49] The contemporary historian Ammianus Marcellinus has left a graphic description of the witch-hunting of those suspected of dabbling in magic. Torture and execution, even for trivial gestures, were not uncommon.[50]

Increasingly it was the world of the spirit that seemed real and permanent, the material world a snare and a delusion.* Among the Gnostics[†] were many who regarded the whole material creation as irredeemably fallen, destined for destruction; for some, the material world was actually a terrible travesty of the 'real' world, and owed its

---

* Many centuries later, at the beginning of the twelfth century, St Anselm was to maintain that 'things were harmful in proportion to the number of senses which they delighted, and therefore rated it dangerous to sit in a garden where there are roses to satisfy the senses of sight and smell, and songs and stories to please the ears' (Kenneth Clark, *Landscape into Art*, John Murray, London, 1949, p.2).

† The Gnostics held that salvation is achieved through knowledge, through enlightenment. Gnostic sects claiming to be Christian were regarded by second- and third-century patristic writers as heretics. By the eighteenth and nineteenth centuries, Roman Catholic theologians were regarding Gnosticism not as heresy but as a form of paganism, and noting its links with Buddhist and Hindu doctrines (*The New Catholic Encyclopedia*, McGraw-Hill, New York, 1967).

171

creation not to God but to the demons of whose hovering presence the age was so acutely aware. Mani, an immensely influential Persian mystic of the third century, inherited the Gnostic tradition, and preached a doctrine of rival realms of darkness and of light, equal in creative power. Pursuit of the realm of light required a rigorous asceticism. Augustine was for fifteen years a Manichean, and just before his conversion to Christianity in 385 a Spanish bishop, Priscillian, the first Christian to be executed for heresy, was burnt at the stake for preaching Manichaeism, though Ambrose, Bishop of Milan, who was so soon to receive Augustine into the Church, disapproved of the execution.[51] The influence of Mani was to echo down the centuries, reappearing among the Cathars and Albigensians of medieval France, who in their turn were to suffer martyrdom.

At its most extreme, revulsion at the material world led to a cult of celibacy on the grounds that to beget children was to collude in prolonging the sufferings of a corrupted creation. But most Christian asceticism had a positive rather than a negative motive – to purify the soul and fit it for heaven, perhaps even for the anticipatory experience of eternal bliss within the confines of this temporal life. Material self-indulgence, gluttony as much as concupiscence, would forfeit that hope. Throughout the fourth century the interest in and attraction of monasticism grew, for both women and men. Among them was Jerome, who in 386 settled in Bethlehem, where, among many other scholarly tasks, he pursued the huge undertaking, already embarked upon during his sojourn in Rome as secretary to the Pope, of translating the scriptures into Latin, the version known as the Vulgate. Communities of intellectual men and women gathered round him, and pilgrims from all over the Roman world visited him for advice. A hundred years later, in Umbria, was born a boy whose later years of schooling in Rome left him with such a revulsion against the lasciviousness of Roman society that he withdrew to the mountaintop of Monte Cassino; there Benedict, drawing heavily on the advice and example of the desert fathers, fashioned his Rule, and founded the order of monks that were to be the guiding influence of Western European monasticism.

Contemporary texts advising and exhorting on the overcoming of temptation catalogue the intensity of the personal sacrifices involved in the practice of chastity, poverty and obedience. Stemming largely from the Coptic communities of Egypt, these practical guides were to remain, in Aline Rousselle's opinion, the inspiration of monasticism in the East and in the West. 'One might even regard them,' she says, 'as one of the chief sources of inspiration, perhaps in a less conscious fashion, of

European civilization since the 4th century.'[52] So alien are the values to twentieth-century ideas that modern scholars find it hard to account for what was going on. Robin Lane Fox suggests that those who departed into the Egyptian desert in the early fourth century may have been perfectionists unable to tolerate the compromises indulged in by Christian communities during the Diocletian persecution.[53] Rousselle, trying to account for the Greek and Roman emulation of the Egyptian example, suspects a revulsion from sexual intercourse on the part of Roman mothers, forced to marry in their teens and willing to inculcate in their sons and daughters an aspiration to celibacy; coupled with a long-standing antipathy to matrimony on the part of Greek males,[54] an analysis which perhaps says more about twentieth-century attitudes than about those of the early Christians.

Whatever truth there may be in these explanations, there was also abroad a widespread disgust at the greed and debauchery of contemporary society, a disgust not unique to Christians but shared by such groups as Stoics, Manicheans and Mithraists. The pagan Ammianus Marcellinus commented late in the fourth century that from the praetorian prefects downward, all 'were inflamed with a boundless eagerness for riches, without consideration for justice or right', and Augustine spoke for thousands when he inveighed against a society which thought 'human affairs are prosperous when men are concerned about magnificent mansions and indifferent to the ruin of souls'.[55]

Those who sincerely believed that the spiritual world was more real and permanent than the material looked to revelation, not human experience, least of all human preference, to determine standards of conduct. The spirit, not the flesh, was the final arbiter of morality. Human bodies belonged not to the personalities manifested in them, but to God who created them.* 'The temple of the Holy Spirit', Paul had called the body.[56] He, like all but the most extreme of the early celibate sects, recognized that the majority of Christian people would marry and have families. But the sexual impulse was deeply distrusted by the Christian divines, for nowhere did human wilfulness, that fatal flaw separating man from a right relationship with God, manifest itself more powerfully than in sexual behaviour; hence the preoccupation of the Church leaders with trying to frame the rules of right sexual conduct.†

From the time of Constantine, the Church endeavoured to back its

---

* The Stoic philosopher Epictetus had made a similar point: 'What says Zeus? . . . this body is not thine own, but is only clay, cunningly compounded' (Brown, Peter, p.26).
† Brown, in *The Body and Society: Men, Women and Sexual Renunciation in Early Christianity*, provides a compelling account of the exploration of this theme.

173

moral standards with the force of law. In keeping with the new respect for celibacy as the highest spiritual calling, Constantine abolished the long-standing penalties on childlessness. He forbade the keeping of concubines by married men.[57] In 331 he penalized bastardy and tightened the law on divorce. Later emperors were more liberal, ultimately permitting divorce by consent,[58] but where adultery was concerned punishments remained harsh. Constantine instituted the death penalty for adultery, and there is a reference in the late fourth century to the beheading of a senator for this reason,[59] and in the sixth century, in the Eastern Empire, to the execution of adulterous women – who, in the early days of the Empire, had to face nothing more drastic than divorce plus the loss of their dowry.[60] In the fifth century prostitution was forbidden (the ban proved unenforceable), the tax normally levied on it, as on all other trades, being abolished.[61]

Under Constantine, homosexuality became a capital crime, punishable by the sword.[62] Several emperors had during the preceding centuries banned one adjunct to homosexuality, the castration of slaves. Pretty boy-slaves were sold ready-castrated by the slave dealer.[63] Seneca had commented on slaves 'kept to satisfy the master's lust', required to dress as women, their beards plucked at the root. He found the practice offensive. 'I do not wish to discuss the treatment of slaves, towards whom we Romans are excessively haughty, cruel and insulting.' 'Treat your inferiors as you would be treated by your betters', was his prescription for good conduct.[64] The fact that Domitian's ban in AD 83 was re-enacted by Nerva a few years later, with Hadrian increasing the penalties* in the next century, suggests that the ban was more honoured in the breach than the observance.[65]

The demand for eunuchs was not solely for homosexual purposes, and even when, under Christian rulers, the ban was more strictly enforced, it was always possible to evade its consequences by importing ready-castrated slaves from Persia and Armenia.[66] Handsome boys in the area east of the Black Sea were kidnapped by tribes who sold them to dealers, frequently killing their parents in order to avoid vengeance; but their final price was very high, because of the large proportion who died before sale as a result of the surgery they underwent at the hands of the dealers (Domitian, when he forbade castration of slaves, had at the same time limited the price that could be paid for eunuchs as yet unsold). In the

---

* Under Domitian, infringement of the ban was punishable by confiscation of half the transgressor's property. Hadrian doubled the penalty.

174

sixth century Justinian suppressed this trade, but illicit castrations continued within the Empire.[67]

Few emperors, however, instituted proceedings against homosexuality *per se*, and though the *Lex Scantinia*, the old law against homosexual practices (*De nefanda venere*), was not repealed, the penalties for infringement were not severe – a fine of 10,000 sesterces sufficing for sexually assaulting a freeborn boy, even in the hypothetical case, postulated by Quintilian, in which as a result of the assault the boy hanged himself. Quintilian discusses this in the interesting context of cases where 'there is no question of guilt, but only of law'.[68] The last vestiges of restraint on the subject of homosexuality vanished in the literature of the early Empire. The novel *Satyricon*, from the first century AD, includes lengthy scenes of students on the prowl looking for rent-boys, and in the ensuing horseplay buttocks are 'almost dislocated with poking'. (When a married man joins in, however, his wife makes her disapproval very clear.)

Domitian undertook a brief moral crusade. In 83 AD he condemned several men, some senators, some knights, for offences under the *Lex Scantinia*.[69] But his successors resumed their permissive attitudes. Many emperors were themselves reputedly homosexual, at least two, Nero and Heliogabalus, contracting homosexual marriages.* Homosexual orgies in the imperial palace are reported of a number of emperors. However, classical biographers (not only the authors of the *Augustan History*, written when the Empire was Christian, but also Suetonius writing during the second century, and Dio Cassius in the third) tend to be censorious; they refer to homosexual proclivities, certainly where the paramour is an adult, in pejorative terms such as 'unnatural desire' or 'immoral relations', and think worthy of special comment any predilection for anal or oral sex.[70] Just before the start of the third century, the emperor Clodius had persecuted those accused of 'unnatural' sex practices, and during the third century Severus Alexander

> had in mind to prohibit catamites altogether – which was afterwards done by Philip – but he feared that such a prohibition would merely convert an evil recognized by the state into a vice practised in private – for men when driven on by passion are more apt to demand a vice which is prohibited.

* According to Dio Cassius (LXXX.16), who moved in contemporary court circles, the tormented adolescent Heliogabalus even tried to bribe his court physicians into performing a sex-change operation on him, including construction of a vagina.

About two decades later, Philip the Arab, reputedly a Christian, did attempt to ban homosexuality, but his reign was brief.[71]

Constantine's edict, reflecting the implacably hostile attitude of the Church to homosexuality, was followed by harsher punishments. Towards the end of the fourth century, Theodosius substituted burning at the stake for beheading.[72] 'For the first time in history, in 390, the Roman people witnessed the public burning of male prostitutes, dragged from the homosexual brothels of Rome.'[73] In sixth-century Byzantium offenders were paraded through the streets – minus their 'privates'.[74]

The close connection between the theatre and homosexuality was a factor in the intense opposition of the Church to the former. The female roles in pantomime and farce were played by men, and both the transvestite dancer and the buffoon 'dame' were offensive to Christian standards – Deuteronomy 22:5 clearly condemned cross-dressing.[*] Christian protagonists from the second century on deplore the lascivious cavortings of eunuchs and ballet boys, 'gesticulating and writhing in an unnatural way', as Tatian put it. The supreme charm of the theatre, said Tertullian, is above all contrived by its filth – 'filth in the gestures of the actor of the farce – filth acted by the buffoon playing the woman, banishing all sense of sex and shame ... filth that the pantomime undergoes in his own person from boyhood to make him an artist'.[75] 'A human being broken down in every limb, a man melted to something beneath the effeminacy of a woman', said a treatise from the middle of the third century, attributed, probably wrongly, to Cyprian, Bishop of Carthage.[76]

Celebrations of eroticism, plots apparently devoted exclusively to seduction, incest and adultery: these had been the staple theatrical diet since the late Republic. By Christian moral standards the theatre was a sink of unrelieved iniquity. There was only one topic – lust, whether dressed in the magnificent robes of the pantomime or the flimsy chiffons of the mime. Not only were the mime actresses prostitutes, their price, address and record were publicly announced from the stage.[77] It was a theatre completely unacceptable to the leaders of the Church. How could good Christian people hope to be modest or chaste if they spent their leisure hours feasting their eyes on obscenities?[78] If only the faithful would gaze instead at the wonders of nature – the sun and moon and stars, the mountains, the flowing rivers, the pure air, the birds and fishes –

---

[*] 'The woman shall not wear that which appertaineth to a man, neither shall a man put on a woman's garment: for all that do so are abomination to the Lord thy God.'

'What theatre built by human hands could ever be compared to such works as these?'[79]

Furthermore, the spectacles were organized in honour of pagan gods, and those gods were demons, fallen angels, out to encompass the eternal ruin of God's people. To attend such festivals was idolatry, quite apart from the obvious incitement to lewd conduct which the performances could not help but arouse. The baptismal vow of the Christian initiate included the words 'I renounce Satan and his works and his pomps [*spectaculis et operibus eius*] . . .', and those who could not promise to stay away from pomps and shows were not eligible for baptism. Those who lapsed after baptism were excommunicated.* [80]

By the start of the third century a treatise summarizing what was already traditional Church practice on baptism stipulates that 'If a man be an actor, or one who makes shows in the theatre, either let him desist, or let him be rejected.'[81] In the middle of the century it was made clear that those who tried to reconcile the ban with continued employment by retiring from the stage and becoming teachers of dramatic arts must equally be debarred from Church membership. Those who renounced the stage for baptism, but subsequently returned to it, were excommunicated. These provisions were re-emphasized at councils held in Spain in 305 and in Carthage in 397.[82] Once entertainers had been included in the hereditary professions, however (as they had been by the beginning of the fourth century),[83] their options were closed. During the fourth century the Christian bishops petitioned the Emperor to release actresses who converted to Christianity, and in AD 380 permission was given, with the proviso that if the actress lapsed 'into vice', she would have to return to her hereditary calling. Legislation in 428 permitted prostitutes (from whom actresses were not distinguished) to leave their hereditary calling.[84]

The Christian repugnance at theatrical morals mirrored that of the early Roman Republic. A strand of disapproval had persisted into the early Empire. Caligula, who 'wished to dance and act a tragedy and for this purpose announced three more days of the entertainment' (though he was assassinated before his ambitions could be fulfilled), shocked

---

* Some of the faithful protested, and demanded scriptural chapter and verse for these prohibitions. Tertullian admitted that there was no actual commandment 'Thou shalt not go to the theatre, thou shalt not look on at contest or spectacle.' But he suggested that Psalm I:1, 'Happy is the man who has not gone to the gathering of the impious', met the case. He took his objections to the theatre to very literal lengths. By placing the actor on the high-heeled buskin of tragedy, he said, the devil endeavoured to make a liar of Christ, who had said that nobody could add a cubit to his stature. Also, every word uttered and gesture made on stage was false, every portrayal a counterfeit, all of which offended against the 'author of truth' *(De Spectaculis*, III, XXIII).

respectable opinion when he gave free rein to aristocrats who wished to appear in public performances, but they were punished by the next emperor, Claudius, who

> forced to appear on the stage any knights and others, together with women of similar rank, who had been accustomed to do so in the reign of Gaius [Caligula], but he did this not because he took any pleasure in their performance, but to expose and reprove their conduct in the past; certain it is at least that none of them appeared again on the stage during the reign of Claudius.[85]

The stage-struck Nero sought to silence opponents by making them accessories.

> The noblest families were forced to disport themselves on stage – Aelia Catella, an octogenarian, danced in a panto. The sick and old had to be in the chorus . . . Out of shame, some put on masks, but Nero forced them to take them off. Thus the magistrates were exhibited to the rabble.

On another occasion he presented a huge festival covering five or six theatres, in which knights and senators appeared in both the race-track and the arena, acted in tragedies and comedies, played the flute and sang to the lyre; some against their will, but others, the historian Dio Cassius tells us, willingly.[86] Tacitus 'as a debt due to their ancestors' refrained from recording the names of the 'scions of great houses' involved, 'whom poverty had rendered venal'.[87] Juvenal in the second century was appalled at the enthusiasm to tread the boards by then being shown by men of noble family, even though 'no Nero compels them',[88] but the tide of popular opinion was against him. His younger contemporary Lucian, from Greek Syria, which was the main recruiting ground for professional pantomimes, put up a spirited defence of pantomime as an art form, defending the playing of women's parts by men ('equally applicable to tragedy and comedy'), the breadth of knowledge of classical mythology required of the dancer, and the generally beneficial effects on the temper of the spectator. He included the classic dilemma of those who venture to disapprove:

> Have you seen these performances yourself, that you are so hard on them? Or do you decide that they are 'foul mire' without personal experience? If you have seen them, you are just as bad as I am, and

if not, are you justified in censuring them? Does it not savour of over-confidence, to condemn what you know nothing about?[89]

Throughout the second and third centuries there is little evidence of contempt for entertainers. They formed part of the households of emperors and aristocrats, and were lavishly rewarded, not only by their employers but also by adoring fans, whose liberality was chastised by the censorious fourth-century authors of the *Augustan History*.[90] Pliny the Younger thought very highly of his freedman, Zosimus, 'an honest fellow, obliging and educated', who entertained the household with readings of history and poetry, recitals on the lyre, and 'his talent for comedy, where he has great success'. His health was frail, and Pliny went to considerable trouble and expense sending him on holiday, first to Egypt, and then, when there was a recurrence of what sounds like TB, arranging for him to go and stay with friends of his, the family of the Roman procurator in Provence, where 'the air is healthy . . . and the milk excellent for treating this kind of case'.[91]

By the fourth century, however, opinion among pagans as well as among Christians was hardening against the moral turpitude of the entertainment world. The pagan professor Libanius, who supervised his students in Antioch outside as well as inside the lecture room, endeavoured to steer them away from the dissipations of the big city, including the theatre. He was one of the circle advising the Emperor Julian (361–3). Julian abandoned Christianity and returned to the worship of *Sol Invictus*, whose priests were, like the Christians, now forbidden to frequent the stage or the arena.[92] At the turn of the century, Macrobius, a senior official but not, apparently, a Christian, remarks with seeming surprise that 'we have the evidence of Cicero to show that [actors] were not looked upon as being among the disreputable classes of society, since it is common knowledge that he was on such friendly terms with actors Roscius and Aesopus', the inference being that they certainly were regarded as disreputable in his own time.[93]

In 389 Theodosius abolished all pagan festivals. Certain Christian festivals were introduced (25 December was reassigned from *Sol Invictus* to Christ), and Sunday was designated the Lord's Day (though pagan loyalties lingered on; there is evidence from Spain as late as 575 of the celebration of Thursday as Zeus's day).[94] A hint of what might lie ahead for the traditional institutions of Rome had been given earlier in the century when Constantine in 321 forbade the holding of legal proceedings on a Sunday, the tentative start of the observance of Sunday as a day of holy rest; an observance which, when the urban masses came to benefit from it, was not enjoined on the toiling rural peasantry.[95] Furthermore, he had failed, on coming to power, to convene the Centennial Games,* an omission which committed pagans regarded as a disturbing portent for the future well-being of the realm.[96] But the normal pagan holidays had continued. The total number of days of public holidays had increased gradually over time, especially when the emperors began to add family anniversaries to the list. Scholars are not in complete agreement about the calendar, but from Rome's earliest days to near the end of the Republic, public holidays had totalled about 58 days a year, Augustus inherited about 66, after which there was a steady inflation, plus bursts of non-recurring festivities such as the 100 days with which Titus celebrated the opening of the Colosseum, or the 123 days of Trajan's victory celebrations after the Dacian campaign. Marcus Aurelius in the mid-second century limited public holidays to 135, but two centuries later the number of days had reached 200, so in Rome more than half the year consisted of non-working days.

Not all of the days of festival qualified for free entertainment. Friedländer assesses the 66-day calendar at the start of the Empire as 14 of races, two of horse trials, two of sacrifices and 48 of theatricals (with no gladiatorial contests, which were not yet part of public entertainment, but only of private funeral ceremonies). Of the 200 days in the fourth century, about 175 were entertainment days, with theatricals on 101 days, and gladiatorial shows on ten.[97]

It was politically impossible to deprive the people of the Empire of this source of relaxation and enjoyment. In Carthage, where paganism was strong, the attempt to suppress pagan festivals led to serious rioting, houses being set on fire and some of the Christian clergy killed. Pagan celebrations continued, Christians being compelled to join in, which led, in 401, to supplications to the Emperor Honorius from the Church leadership to enforce the law more strongly. Some among the laity, who greatly enjoyed drinking and dancing at the festivals, gave, to Augustine's profound grief, covert support to the pagans, and as late as 692 the Council of Trullanum specified excommunication for those celebrating pagan festivals such as the winter solstice or 1 May.[98]

The festival entertainments continued, the only change being that the junketing was no longer even nominally in honour of pagan deities. Augustine laments that some Christians were substituting the names of

---

* These games were supposed to be held every *saeculum*. The *saeculum* represented the longest human life-span, which the Romans reckoned at about 110 years (see Zosimus, II.i.1). In fact the intervals, though long, were erratic. They had lapsed entirely under the Republic; Augustus had revived them as part of his campaign of religious renewal.

Christian martyrs for those of the pagan deities, and 'acting all the impurity of the heathen festivals under the name of Christian'. But 'their multitudes in Afric were so great, that though their crimes deserved the severity of excommunication, yet St Austin in such circumstances could not think that the proper remedy', and instead counsels education.[99]

It could no longer be argued that attendance at the shows constituted idolatry and devil worship, and by the fifth century it appears that attendance no longer incurred excommunication.[100] Spirited diatribes against the moral pollution of the theatre continue, however preachers like Augustine, Bishop of Hippo (reformed from a youthful passion for the stage),[101] and John Chrysostom, Bishop of Antioch and later Archbishop of Constantinople, opening the fifth-century attack, while in mid-century Salvianus, Presbyter of Marseilles, sustained the town's puritanical reputation with a condemnation of the theatre which was to be translated and circulated in sixteenth-century England by a forerunner of the Puritan opposition.[102] All watched in sorrow as their congregations sped from the pew to the playhouse. 'You will notice also,' wrote Augustine, 'that the very crowds fill the churches on the festival days of the Christians which fill the theatres also on the solemn days of the pagans.'[103] People said they were too busy to read the scriptures or attend church, but they had time for 'loitering in the theatres, and the parties they make to see horse-races'.[104] For Salvianus,

> Whenever it happens, as it does only too often, that on the same day we are celebrating a feast of the church and the public games, I ask it of everyone's conscience, which is it that collects greater crowds of Christians, the rows of seats at the public games or the court of God? ... For on every day when the fatal games are given, whatever festival of the church it may be, not only do men who claim to be Christians fail to come to the services, but any who do happen to have come unwittingly, if they chance to hear, while in the church, that games are being given, leave the building at once. The temple of God is scorned for a rush to the theatre; the church is emptied, and the circus filled.[105]

'Lo each day I rend myself with crying out ''Depart from the theatres'' ...', lamented Chrysostom, 'numberless are our exhortations and there is none to hear us'.[106] The one discipline which the Church did try to impose was the prohibition of attendance at public games and stage plays during Lent.[107]

Much of the entertainment could be castigated for no stronger reason than that it was a waste of time, or of money which would have been better spent on the poor.[108] In the absence of sustained plots, shows consisted (as had the early Greek mimes) of a series of turns, in which spicy sketches (Jove's various seductions were still a staple diet),[109] jugglers, acrobats, tightrope walkers and performing animals offered the minimum challenge to sustained concentration. Augustine refers to people who (presumably in the context of entertainment, though he does not actually say so) 'can swallow an astonishing number of different objects and then, with a very slight contraction of their diaphragm, bring forth, as though from a bag, whatever item they please in good condition'; and to others who 'produce at will without any stench such rhythmical sounds from their fundament that they appear to be making music even from that quarter'.[110] A popular genre was the so-called 'noise' plays, in which the plot revolved round some sort of dispute, resulting in energetic kicking and pummelling, and the dialogue consisted largely of swear words. One mime actor of the early fifth century achieved great fame because of the extraordinary toughness of his head, which could withstand kicks, punches, boiling pitch and even assault by a battering ram. The public adored him.[111]

The lascivious performances from which decent people were abjured to absent themselves are frequently assumed to have been live sex shows in the sense that sexual intercourse actually took place in front of an audience. The report of the exceptionally debauched Heliogabalus, that 'when adultery was represented on the stage, he would order what was usually done in pretence to be carried out in fact',[112] suggests that such was not the usual practice. The Christian divines who thunder through the centuries deploring stage obscenity primarily attack the moral depravity of the *themes* presented – adultery and incest. In attacking the *presentation* for provoking sexual arousal, and thus conducing to unchastity, they almost always refer to 'representation' (i.e. mimicry), or 'feigned actions'. 'Why should I speak of the actors of mimes, who hold forth instruction in corrupting influences, who teach adulteries while they feign them, and by pretended actions train to those which are true?' said Lactantius.[113] About a century later, Augustine, writing *City of God* in north Africa where pagan rites clearly still flourished, makes several references to obscenities performed in actuality in the temples and counterfeited in the theatres, and refers to those who love 'in plays to see vices counterfeited'.[114]

The clearest evidence comes in a long dissertation made in defence of the mime by Chorikios, an orator in the Eastern Empire, probably early in the sixth century, when the legal survival of the mime was in doubt.

Discussing the accusation that actors do what is not fit to look at, and say what it is not honourable to listen to, he says:

> if they were seriously doing these actions and making these remarks, I would certainly be ashamed to undertake their defence, indeed not to be indicating my disapproval; but as their practice is mere playacting ... what can you see in them that calls for blame?[115]

Similarly, the assumption that there were public exhibitions of bestiality seems to be unfounded. Copulation between human beings and gods in animal form, such as Jupiter's bull-guise wooing of Europa, was of course a staple of classical mythology – and Jupiter's swan-guise seduction of Leda was a favourite pantomime theme for centuries. Had animals really been involved in the stage presentations, however, it seems inconceivable that the Christian polemicists would have omitted to mention them – bestiality was a sin for which the Council of Ancyra stipulated harsh appropriate penance.[116] Bestiality features in Daniel Mannix's imaginative reconstruction of the arena, *Those About to Die*, but the only source references given are to twentieth-century porno-graphic films made in Mexico, and to Apuleius's novel *The Golden Ass*, which does indeed include a scene involving intended copulation between an ass and a female criminal sent to the arena on a capital charge; but as the ass is a man temporarily transmogrified, like Bottom in *A Midsummer Night's Dream* (who escapes before the proposed show has been enacted), this does not justify the conclusion that public displays of bestiality formed part of Roman entertainment.[117] Apuleius modelled his tale very closely on an earlier story, 'Lucius or the Ass', which includes the same scene in the amphitheatre, but again there is no bestiality, as the ass is magically transformed back into a man and the whole episode terminated.[118]

However, that a great deal of explicit posturing went on, with simulations which included on-stage masturbation,[119] is indubitable. Precise descriptions are rare, but the sixth-century Byzantine historian Procopius of Caesarea wrote a fairly explicit account of the performance of his contemporary, the famed theatrical prostitute Theodora, who was 'neither a flute-player nor a harpist nor a dancer' but just paraded her beautiful body. Her performance consisted of lying down near-naked (G-strings were required by law) with grains of barley scattered on her genitals, which geese would then peck up. Among her other turns was to simulate sexual intercourse, including oral sex, with actors on stage.[120]

During the fourth century a new entertainment of even more debauched potential began to attract attention – the *maiuma*, or water-show. This seems to have begun at Gerasa in Syria, again under the umbrella of some sort of religious rite. Women were required to go to a sacred pool in the suburbs, and there bathe naked under the gaze of the townsfolk.[121] The idea was taken up in other areas, where the small theatres and concert halls, the *odeon*, were adapted to provide flooded orchestra areas in which the nymphs could disport themselves. They went too far in lasciviousness even for emperors anxious to find a compromise between (in some cases) their own Christian conscience, pressure from the divines, and the need to avoid provoking public unrest. *Maiuma* were alternately banned and licensed ('on condition decency is preserved and modesty maintained with chaste morals') by eight changes in the law during the fourth century, and were finally abolished by Arcadius (395–408).[122]

Censorship on moral grounds had not previously been exercised. When the mimes and pantomimes had been banned from Rome, as from time to time they were, even under their devotee Nero, it was more for political than for moral reasons: for provoking civic disturbances such as rioting by fans or, in the case of individual performers, for seditious comments or ribaldry that brought ridicule on prominent citizens, rather than for obscenity in itself.* Arcadius's predecessor Theodosius, who was himself inordinately fond of pantomime, had a court official, a guardian of public morals, but there is no evidence of stage censorship.[123] A disputed section of the *Codex Theodosianus*, the codification of Roman state law published in 438 in Byzantium, may imply that all staging of plays and other entertainments was forbidden during Lent,[124] and a number of edicts between AD 392 and 469 testify to the emperors' various but apparently not very successful attempts to stop Sunday performances.[125] Otherwise the State does not appear to have tried to incorporate Church standards with regard to the shows into state legislation.

Early in the sixth century, Anastasius, Emperor in the East, banned mimes, possibly less on moral grounds than because of the general disorder and rioting associated with the factions championing the stars.[126] Clearly the ban could not be made effective, but that the performances were felt to be under threat is obvious from the impassioned dissertation made in their defence by Chorikios, one-time fan of the theatre, but now debarred from attending by a by-law of his

* See p.83.

local city, Gaza, in Palestine, which forbade schoolmasters from attending theatres, horse-racing and various other pastimes.[127]

Chorikios dealt with every one of the arguments deployed by those who disparaged the theatre. Yes, there are disorderly actors – but the same goes for every profession. Most actors are good family men, only pretending to be rent-boys, which makes their performances much funnier;* and if they really are rent-boys, well what harm does watching them do? People can in real life meet rent-boys with ruined bodies, but they catch no harm thereby themselves.[†] They are not going to be corrupted by displays of what is against nature. True, the plays are always about adultery, but punishment usually threatens, and it's all good for a laugh, which we need in this anxious world. The classical myths – and the tragic actors – deal with much worse themes. Mimes must ape what is bad in life as well as what is good, but no one is going to be influenced by the theatre into behaving in a way contrary to his or her nature. We do not copy the theatre. Maidens are not going to be seduced by listening to suggestive ditties! And if some people are aroused, it's because they were that way inclined anyway. As for the argument that the mimes encourage idleness, the reverse is the case – people are working at night so as to be free to attend the shows. Everyone is the better for a good laugh, including those whose spirits the doctors have failed to lift. Chorikios even dealt with the sensitive souls who were upset by the episodes of bald-pate bashing, saying that logically they should be opposing boxing as well.[128]

It was to no avail. In 526 the Emperor Justinian closed the theatres of Byzantium. Four years earlier he had persuaded the then emperor, his uncle, to abrogate the ancient law forbidding senators to marry actresses, and in 523 he had married the notorious Theodora.[129] He had himself staged a show in the theatre which was called *The Tarts*.[130] But after his marriage he and his wife became fanatical Christians. In 529 he ordered all pagans, on pain of exile and confiscation of property, to come to church and be baptised, and there were a number of executions of prominent pagans during his reign.[131]

Whether it was his faith that impelled him to close the theatres is, however, disputed. Procopius accuses him of a miserly neglect which led the theatre to die of attrition. There is no known regulation in which Justinian expressly bans the mimes, but there are regulations restricting the interests and honours of actors.[132] Something survived, for the

---

* Cf. the boys from the rugger club dancing *Swan Lake*?
† Does this relate to the condition described by Ammianus Marcellinus – see p.154? If so, realization had obviously dawned that it was less contagious than had earlier been supposed.

Church's Council of Trullanum, meeting in Constantinople in 692, included a canon forbidding all public performances in perpetuity.[133]

In the West, the tide of barbarian invasion eroded the urbanity which underpinned the theatre. During the fifth century Salvianus of Marseilles, arch-enemy of the theatre, saw it die, but derived no satisfaction from a demise due not to a change of heart, but to conquest and impoverishment. As the alien tide swept over the old towns of Gaul and Spain, theatre after theatre fell not merely into disuse but into dereliction, followed by demolition. In Italy, where the playhouses still stood, only Rome and Ravenna could boast an active theatre, which in the case of Rome even survived the sack by Vandals and Berbers from north Africa in 455.[134] Elsewhere, 'the collapse of the imperial fiscus and the beggary of the Roman treasury do not permit money to be lavished on trifling matters that make no return'.[135] By the start of the seventh century the theatre was only a memory throughout the Western Empire.[136]

A millennium of classical theatre that began with Thespis ended with Theodora. The dancers and singers, the jugglers and tightrope walkers, the buffoons, animal trainers and gymnasts joined forces with the displaced horse-acrobats of the race-track, that Circus where in Rome the last recorded chariot race was run in 549, with Totila the Goth giving the starting signal from the imperial seat of honour.[137] Loading their gear and their finery on to carts, they set out to wander the crumbling roads of the old Empire. As vagabonds the remnants of an erstwhile proud and wealthy profession plod towards the Middle Ages.[138]

Chapter 11

Through a Glass Darkly: the Sixth to Tenth Centuries

Those who lived during some part of the Roman Empire's prolonged – and, in the case of the Western Empire, unsuccessful – struggle for survival include several whose writings closely link the theatre with the disasters that were befalling their times. For some, it was simply that attachment to the theatre was equated with the sort of soft, self-indulgent living that made for poor soldiering. Zosimus blamed the failure of the campaigns against the Goths marauding into Greece at the end of the fourth century on the fondness of the Roman general Stilicho and his troops for 'mimes, buffoons and shameless women',[1] an association of ideas that had been made before – the first-century poet Silius Italicus, for instance, had considered Hannibal and his army much debilitated by the stage plays and enfeebling music with which his allies the people of Capua had regaled him and his troops during his unsuccessful attempt to conquer Italy.[*2]

Christian writers went beyond the cause and effect of effete character on military prowess; they saw also the corrective hand of God at work. Orosius was a Christian priest in Portugal, born towards the end of the fourth century. It was the Eastern rather than the Western Empire that was under pressure during his early childhood, but Visigoths, Ostrogoths, Vandals, Franks and Huns were all turning their attention towards the riches of western Europe. In 401 the Gothic commander Alaric marched on Milan which had, since Diocletian's division of the Empire, replaced Rome as the administrative capital of the West. Stilicho defeated Alaric, but nevertheless the Emperor Honorius shortly thereafter withdrew the capital to Ravenna, which was considered impregnable, thus leaving open the route to Rome. On 24 August 410 (Stilicho had by then been assassinated) Alaric took Rome, aided by a traitor who

---

[*] At the start of World War II the governors of the BBC had considered dispensing with the services of Vera Lynn, fearing that her sentimental melodies might sap the martial ardour of the British Expeditionary Force. (*The South Bank Show*, 'Dame Britain', ITV, 9 November 1991).

opened the gates from within.* The Palace of the Caesars had been deserted for the best part of a hundred years,[3] but the city still symbolized the Empire, and its fall spread fear and despair from Hadrian's Wall to Palestine, whence Jerome wrote to friends that he was 'so confounded by the havoc wrought in the West, and above all by the sack of Rome, that, as the common saying has it, I forgot even my own name. Long did I remain silent, knowing that it was time to weep.'[4] Already the hard-pressed legions had been withdrawn from Britain, and in 411 Honorius informed the British that henceforward they must defend themselves. The Roman army would not return. Up on the northern frontiers, on 31 December 406, some three and a half years before Rome fell, a hard winter and a frozen river Rhine had smoothed the path for Vandals and other Germanic tribes to cross into Gaul. By 409 they were pouring into the Iberian peninsula, looting the rich cities of Roman Spain.

Orosius fled his Portuguese home in about AD 414 and set sail for north Africa, to visit Augustine in Hippo. Both were wrestling with the problem of why such disasters should overwhelm the Empire at a time when it had become officially Christian, and persecutions (which might have been expected to kindle the wrath of God) had ceased. Augustine began work on his *City of God*, anxious to counter the pagan contention that it was the abandonment of the old gods that was the source of Rome's troubles. Orosius travelled on for a sojourn in Jerusalem with Jerome, and on his return to Hippo was encouraged by Augustine, who felt he had not done full justice to his theme, to embark, by way of a supplement to his own Book III, on an exploration of the fate of all the four empires then recognized, those of Babylon, Macedon, Carthage and Rome, in order to demonstrate that disasters were even more prevalent in pre-Christian times. From these researches came Orosius's *Seven Books of History Against the Pagans*.

In an appalling catalogue of disasters, Orosius chronicled the miseries of previous civilizations, laying considerable stress on the wretchedness of the conquered whose life of toil and slavery sustained the great empires.[5] He drew particular attention to the moderation of conduct shown by the Christianized (albeit heretical Arian) Gothic conquerors of Rome,† who had remained but briefly, had done far less physical

---

* According to Balsdon (1969, p.26) Alaric had the bad manners to attack, contrary to accepted convention, during the 12 noon to 1.15 p.m. siesta period universally observed during the hot Roman summer.
† 'If anyone asserts that the Romans . . . were much more tolerable enemies to our forefathers than the Goths are now to us, his knowledge and understanding of conditions are quite at variance with the facts' (Orosius, V.1).

damage than had Nero's fire, had respected church treasure and left unmolested those who had sought sanctuary. 'The Roman people, indeed,' he remarks, some eight years after the city's capture, 'have unmistakably borne witness that the disturbance which for a short time interrupted their customary pleasures was of but slight importance for they freely cried out "If we are given our circus back again, we have suffered nothing." ' It is part of Orosius's thesis that the people *deserved* chastisement for their frivolity and for their addiction to the theatre with all its lewdness and blasphemy ('they should blame the theatres and not the times'), and he goes so far as to say that the Goths were meting out punishment with, if anything, too light a touch, so that it became necessary for God to intervene and strike the Forum with lightning.[6]

Orosius was optimistic that the influx of barbarians would be assimilated and Christianized, and that a new and noble future lay in store for the Empire. Augustine was less sanguine, and in his *City of God* sought consolation for the loss of earthly security in the reflection that Rome could not be the Eternal City; for the Christian had here no abiding home. He watched with incredulity as refugees from Rome streamed into north Africa still preoccupied with shows and theatres. 'This will quite possibly be incredible to our descendants', he wrote:

> when the City of Rome was sacked, those who were so possessed by this disease [a frenzy for stage plays] and were able to reach Carthage, after fleeing thence, were daily in the theatres, indulging the craze of partisan support for favourite actors . . . What insanity was this, when, as we have heard, the nations of the East and the largest states in the uttermost parts of the earth were bewailing your destruction with public lamentation and mourning, it was theatres that you sought, entered, packed, and far outdid your previous lunatic behaviour.[7]

The Roman refugees had fled the Goths only to encounter the Vandals. In 429 the Vandals crossed from Iberia to north Africa, and by 430 had invested and conquered Augustine's Hippo. The Bishop himself, now well into his seventies, died during the siege. A decade later Carthage suffered the same fate. In the twenty years since the refugees from Rome had so shocked Augustine with their nonchalant disregard for the tragedy engulfing their city, their predilection for stage shows clearly had not changed – it was reported of both Cirta and Carthage that the populace were at the circus and the theatre even as the Vandals were besieging the walls.[8] If they hoped for the sort of relatively mild treatment Rome had experienced at the hands of the hymn-singing Goths, they were mistaken. Not only did the Vandals subject Carthage to an orgy of pillage, murder and massacre, but, unlike the Goths in Rome, they had come to stay. With puritanical fervour, they rooted out the pimps and prostitutes of the city's easy-going way of life, firmly forbidding not only prostitution and the effeminacy for which Carthage was especially notorious, but even fornication and adultery.[9] Twenty-five years later, with north Africa as their base, they raided Rome, and looted it of all movable valuables (including the treasure from Solomon's temple in Jerusalem which Titus had brought back from his Jewish wars), returning to Carthage with the Empress and her two daughters among their captives. (The imperial family had abandoned Ravenna and returned to Rome as a result of attacks by the Huns in northern Italy.)[10]

Salvianus, the Presbyter of Marseilles, writing a decade after Orosius, could no longer sustain his predecessor's optimism that the Empire would be reborn under the impact of Christianity. Christianity had, in his view, entirely failed to regenerate the vice-ridden Roman world, of which the theatre was a prime example. True, poverty and disruption had largely put an end to the shows, but in so far as plays were in abeyance, it was because the towns were either conquered or too impoverished to fund them, while the former wickedness had grieved God to the point where (as Jeremiah had put it) ' "for the abominations which you have committed" ... the greater part of the Roman world is become "a desolation and an astonishment and a curse" '.[11] Echoing Tacitus some three hundred years earlier, Salvianus contrasted Roman depravity with Germanic piety and purity, their respect for marriage and the family, their sense of justice and their comradely concern for one another. Not for Germans the naked greed of the Empire's rich, their ceaseless oppression of the poor, forced into slavery or the near-slavery of tied tenantry on the big estates. Salvianus, like Augustine when he witnessed the arrival of the refugees in north Africa, found the studied flippancy of the Romans in the face of calamity particularly depressing. Rome, he said, was laughing as it died – but there is a note of horror behind the remark, for he links it to 'Sardonic herbs', poisons which had the property of constricting a victim's jaws into a simulacrum of laughter as they killed.[12] The future, Salvianus accepted, lay with the barbarians. 'They increase daily while we diminish; they gain in power while we are humbled; they flourish and we wither away.'[13]

A similar tribute to barbarian piety and moderation emerges in the writings of a contemporary of Salvianus, Sidonius, a third-generation

Christian born in Lyons about 430, and later to be Bishop of Clermont (though for a while expelled from his see by invaders). He was well connected: his wife was the daughter of one of the swiftly changing and rapidly assassinated emperors of the period. To his brother-in-law, the Emperor's son, he sent a description of a visit he made to the court of one of the Gothic chiefs, Theodoric II, who from 453 to 466 ruled a kingdom carved out of part of Gaul.

Theodoric, he reports, attends a religious service daily before dawn (though Sidonius suspects that this is more out of custom than conviction). Dinner, except on festival days, is 'just like that of a private household', food is good but neither ostentatious nor costly, and the goblets are refilled so infrequently that thirst is more of a hazard than the temptation to tipsiness. Very occasionally comedians are permitted to perform at the evening meal, but 'are not allowed to assail any guest with the gall of biting tongue'. Languorous music and female performers are alike excluded, but the King does enjoy 'string music which comforts the soul with virtue just as much as it soothes the ear with melody'.[14]

There were Romans, eminent and cultivated men according to Salvianus, who preferred life among these Germans, in spite of the stench of their clothes and bodies, to the unremitting greed and avarice that characterized the civilization of Rome.[15] Salvianus did not actually claim that hot baths and the use of body lotion contributed to Rome's downfall, but it may be mentioned in passing that in the Greece of the fifth century BC, when living standards began to permit hot baths, Aristophanes in *The Clouds* had presented such self-indulgence as morally decadent;[16] and when Rome reached a similar level of affluence, moralists held that daily baths represented Hellenic contamination.[17] Seneca, paying a reverential visit to the humble home of Scipio Africanus, a hero dead some two and a half centuries previously, had commented on the small and simple bath, remarking that the Romans of those days washed only their arms and legs daily, and bathed all over just once a week. And if it was held that they must have been smelly, his retort was that they smelled of the camp, of the farm – and of heroism.[18] There was a significance to be read into the pervasiveness of barbarian body odour!

Certainly the physical discomfort and hardship of a soldier's life had long ceased to attract recruits to the Roman army. Vegetius, a military strategist whose writing is dated to the crucial years of the late fourth century or the first half of the fifth, says that the Roman infantry would no longer wear helmets or breastplates, because they were too heavy. He explains that when, because of negligence and laziness, parade ground drills were abandoned, the customary armour began to seem heavy, since the soldiers rarely ever wore it. Therefore they first asked the Emperor to set aside the breastplates and mail, and then the helmets. So our soldiers fought the Goths without any protection for chest and head, and were often beaten by archers. Although there were many disasters, which led to the loss of great cities, no-one tried to restore breastplates and helmets to the infantry. Thus it happens that troops in battle, exposed to wounds because they have no armour, think about running and not about fighting.[19]

Arthur Ferrill, in *The Fall of the Roman Empire: The Military Explanation*, comments of this work that 'more than anything else . . . Vegetius emphasized drill, drill and more drill – in every weapon including sword, javelin, sling and bow, and in every militarily useful activity such as digging, marching with heavy pack, swimming and precision parade ground exercises'.[20] But nothing was done, and to this lack of discipline and application Ferrill in large part attributes the elimination of the Roman army as a fighting force. As late as the mid-fourth century the close-order tactics of the Roman infantry had enabled a Roman force of only 13,000 to defeat an army of Alemanni numbering 35,000, but the tactics were inoperable without the necessary discipline, when, as Ferrill remarks, close order was worse than no order at all. 'Romans,' he says, 'could be expected to huddle behind their screen of shields; Visigoths and Alans would do the fighting.' This army was last seen in action at Chalons in 451, attempting to stem the advance of Attila and his Huns. Attila told his troops to ignore them, and concentrate on the danger facing them from the associated Visigoth and Alan troops.[21]

The truth was that Roman fighting prowess was now, and had for some time been, dependent on foreign mercenaries. The difficulty of raising Roman troops had long been acute, in spite of vigorous annual conscriptions, and a reduction, in the late fourth century, of the minimum height for recruits from five foot ten inches to five foot seven.[22] An anonymous author of the period produced a work, *De Rebus Bellicis*, advocating assorted new inventions in warfare to save on manpower.[23] The unreliability of the peasant militias had resulted, by the late third century, in an increasing reliance on professional foreign mercenaries, mostly Germans, attracted by levels of pay unmatched at home.[24] As time passed, much of the urban population came in any case to be in reserved occupations debarred from military service, and the civil population came increasingly to assume that a professional army would look after them.[25] Germans or other barbarians came to hold the top military offices – Stilicho himself was a Vandal. They were, as Nilsson puts it, masters of the Empire long before it fell.[26]

To the unreflecting, this was a source of pride. The Christian Sidonius, addressing a paean of praise to Majorian, emperor 457–61, catalogues the different groups: 'Bastarnian, Suebian, Pannonian, Neuran, Hun, Getan, Dacian, Alan, Bellonotan, Rugian, Burgundian, Visigoth, Alites, Bisalta, Ostrogoth, Procrustian, Sarmatian, Moschan have ranged themselves behind thine eagles.'[27] It is reminiscent of those hour-long radio link-ups of the British Empire that used to precede the royal broadcast on Christmas Day – 'Come in, St Kitts and Nevis!'

It is a roll call such as might have delighted Orosius, whose vision of the Empire's future of Christianized, assimilated barbarians embraced

> the width of the East, the vastness of the North, the great stretches of the South and the largest and most secure settlements on great islands, all have the same law and nationality as I, since I come there as a Roman and Christian to Christians and Romans . . . One God, who established the unity of this realm in the days when He willed Himself to become known, is loved and feared by all. The same laws, which are subject to this one God, hold sway everywhere. Wheresoever I go, stranger though I be, I need harbour no fear of sudden assault as would a man without protection. Among Romans, as I have said, I am a Roman; among Christians, a Christian; among men, a man. The State comes to my aid through its laws, religion through its appeal to the conscience, and nature through its claims of universality.[28]

Ever since Augustus and the early Empire, there had been Germans serving with the imperial armies, and indeed when, in 312, Constantine had dissolved the Praetorian Guard, the 'Household Brigade', and replaced it with a personal imperial bodyguard of Germans, few if any Italians were in fact still serving with the Guard.[29] What shattered Orosius's vision of harmony was an influx of Gothic and other Germanic peoples into the Empire on a scale that completely overwhelmed Roman law and custom.

So long as the response to external Gothic pressure was to cede territory, withdraw the legions and redraw the frontiers, as was done, for instance, when Dacia (in modern Romania) was abandoned to the Goths in AD 271 (the name Dacia being transferred to territories south of the Danube), Roman law remained paramount within the Empire. Late in the fourth century, however, pressure from the Huns on the Ostrogoths to the north and east of the Black Sea led to their flight west, disrupting the Visigoths of Dacia. These incursions brought to the borders of the Eastern Empire unprecedented numbers of Gothic refugees fleeing war and poverty. Dill numbers them at a million, Ferrill at more like a quarter of that figure, but still in the hundreds of thousands.[30] They pleaded for, and were granted, asylum in Thrace.

The historian Ammianus Marcellinus was a soldier in the Eastern Empire and a contemporary witness of these events. In AD 376 the refugees poured across the Danube in boats, on rafts, in hollowed-out tree trunks, some attempting to swim and drowning in the process. Their leaders had promised the Emperor that they would serve as auxiliaries in the Roman army, but other motives facilitated their passage – a much smaller influx who had attempted unsuccessfully to settle some twenty years earlier had been found to be carrying quantities of gold, which they were willing to part with in return for *not* serving in the army, and venal Roman officials (Polybius's incorruptible Roman civil servants were long since gone) hoped to make a similar swift fortune from the new tide of displaced persons. Ammianus is sardonic in the extreme. 'Diligent care was taken that no future destroyer of the Roman state should be left behind, even if he were smitten with a fatal disease', he comments. 'With such stormy eagerness on the part of insistent men was the ruin of the Roman world brought in.'[31]

The refugees were mercilessly exploited by the local Roman officials, their women assaulted, food made available only in return for children sold into slavery. In despair they went on the rampage, pillaging the country estates in the vicinity, aided by the fact that although it had normally been a condition of entry that immigrants should lay down their arms, these had not done so.[32] The forces of law and order were marshalled against them, and succeeded in chastising but not subduing them. Two years later, abetted by fresh waves of immigrants entering without permission, they killed the Eastern Emperor himself in battle.[33] When, in 382, a peace treaty was concluded, granting them permanent settlement rights not only in Thrace but also in Macedonia, they were permitted to retain their political and military cohesion, instead of, as in the case of earlier immigrants, serving under officers of the Roman army or working on Roman estates.[34]

Scholars down the ages have questioned the wisdom of allowing this massive settlement, and Ammianus Marcellinus was not the only contemporary to be alarmed – the pagan Zosimus regarded the evolution of the Roman Empire into a 'home of every barbarous tribe' as punishment by the gods for their abandonment by the Christian emperors. But the truth was, there was no option. The newcomers were too numerous to be either expelled or destroyed.[35] As the fifth century dawned, with bands of marauding Goths cruising, sometimes in search of settlement, sometimes merely as raiding parties, through the Balkans into Greece, through Gaul and Spain and into Italy itself, other groups began to carve out settlement areas for themselves.

Assimilation as Roman citizens was impossible. Instead, the government sought to contain the newcomers within Roman structures by giving the barbarian armed forces the status of federates, allied troops with access to Roman supplies and armouries.[36] The old mercenary units had been constituent elements of the Roman army. The federates served under their own officers and followed their own strategic and disciplinary techniques.[37]

Ferrill speaks of the federates as 'a cancer'.[38] By 418, by which time Rome's Gallic administrative headquarters had, as a result of depredations in the north, been withdrawn from Trier to Arles, the Goths of south-east Gaul had negotiated a treaty with Rome granting them local autonomy, and thereafter the system spread to other petty kingdoms.[*] Nominally they accepted, at least at first, Roman sovereignty. Their home-minted coinage, for instance, continued to show the image of the head of the Roman state. But they were never satisfied with the rewards paid to them, and what began as subventions by Rome escalated into something indistinguishable from tribute.[†] By 435 even the Vandals in north Africa had been accepted as federates, which did not prevent them going on to attack Carthage and sack Rome, as well as gathering into their fold Corsica, Sardinia, Sicily and the Balearic Islands. By 474 they had obtained recognition as an independent state.[39] This was the background to the assorted warring armies of the fifth century, culminating, so far as the West was concerned, in the deposition and exile, in 476, of the last of the Roman emperors (the Senate managed to dispatch the imperial regalia east to Constantinople).[40] Henceforth,

---

[*] Vortigern, Celtic King in forsaken Britain, tried a similar policy. He allowed the Anglo-Saxons settlement rights in Kent, in return for promises of help against the Picts and other enemies of the State – hence the retention of the old Roman name for the county (Cantium), unlike the surrounding counties which succumbed to direct Saxon conquest and took the names of the East, West, South and Middle Saxons (Essex, Wessex, Sussex and Middlesex). Saklatvala (pp.74–6) refers to the settlers as 'treaty troops'.

[†] The dissatisfaction of the newcomers to Britain with the rewards accorded to them is recorded by Bede (1968, p.56–7). They 'threatened that unless larger supplies were forthcoming, they would terminate their treaty and ravage the whole island', a threat which they rapidly put into effect, destroying with 'fire and sword'.

overtly as well as covertly, a succession of Germanic warlords were masters of the West.

The cost of supplying the federates and buying off their discontent was prodigious. Jerome in Bethlehem had seen what was at stake, and in 409 spoke of Rome 'fighting within her own boundaries not for fame but for existence, nay, not even fighting but buying her life with money and goods'.[41] Taxes had doubled during the fourth century, largely to meet the defence budget,[42] and Jones reckons that by Justinian's time, in the sixth century, the peasants were paying a third of the gross product in taxes.[43] The senatorial landlords (by the fifth century, 'senator' was a social grade rather than a political responsibility)[44] evaded paying their share, either by passing the costs on to their tenants or by corrupting the local justice system,[45] but for the middle classes there was no escape. All small proprietors came into the category of municipal* magistrates (*curiales*), charged not only personally with such civic duties as public entertainment, but also with the collection of taxes, making good from their own pockets any shortfall. Promotion to senatorial rank provided no escape, for the children born before the promotion then became responsible for discharging the debt. Nor did death offer any relief – the heirs inherited the liabilities to the State. If a *curial* died childless, three-quarters of his estates were forfeit to the treasury. They escaped into the army, the civil service, the trade guilds – they even went as serfs on the big estates. The State responded, early in the fifth century, by ordering all those of *curial* descent back to their municipalities. They were forbidden to travel or to live in the country.[46]

Not surprisingly, faced with such rapacity, many erstwhile Roman citizens preferred a barbarian overlord.[47] Salvianus commented that 'all the Romans in [the Gothic country] have but one desire, that they may never have to return to the Roman jurisdiction', and there is a record of a fugitive Greek who even preferred life under the Huns to the ruthless taxation and unprincipled conduct of his superiors within the Empire.[48]

Men of property paid a heavy price. By 418 the Goths who had settled in the Bordeaux and Toulouse areas of Gaul were benefiting not only from the rules under which Roman soldiers were billeted – that is, one third of the 'host's' house – but from an amendment extending to them one third of all the householder's immovable property – a proportion which appears to have grown to two-thirds over the course of the next half-century.[49]

After the deposition of the last Roman emperor of the West, in 476,

---

* The municipality included its agricultural hinterland.

Italian householders in the vicinity of Gothic garrisons (mostly in northern Italy) suffered the same fate, having to give up one third of their estates to the federate invaders; and although the Emperor in the East sent another Gothic federate army to dispossess the first, this second army, under the Goth Theodoric the Great,[*] succeeded on similar terms – the troops being entitled to one third of the houses and estates, including the workforce, of their 'hosts'.[50] Theodoric accepted the continuation of Roman law for Roman citizens, but his Goths lived under Gothic law, and intermarriage between the two groups was forbidden.[51] In the north Gallic territories of modern Belgium, by now occupied by Frankish settlers, and in the area of the west Rhine and the Rhône, where Burgundians had established themselves, the invaders' legal system was established alongside the Roman (though the Franks were not averse to intermarriage), penalties differing for the same crime; Roman law was, for instance, far more severe on rape, for which the penalty could be death, whereas Burgundian law specified only a fine; and in view of the repeated references to the much higher moral standards of the barbarians, it is arguable that this reflects the greater prevalence of – and therefore concern about – the offence among Romans compared with the more relaxed punishment specified by the barbarians.[52] Orosius's hopes of an Empire dominated from end to end by the rule of law, one law, the Roman law, were not to be fulfilled.

It was in everyone's interest that law, some sort of law, should prevail. The century preceding the establishment of the federate states had seen little improvement over the chaotic conditions of the third century. In East and West alike brigandage had continued rife, trade and travel unsafe. At Rome the devout pagan senator Symmachus[†] no longer felt safe in the enjoyment of his country seat, and people were very hesitant about endeavouring to traverse the roads to the imperial court at Milan. The highways were in any case falling into disrepair, the organization of the relays of post-horses neglected; sometimes the horses in the public stables were not even fed.[53] Thrace and parts of north Italy had become no-go areas,[54] which may have some bearing on the probability that the Goths who were given settlement rights there in 376 were allowed to retain their weapons. Fifteen years later, in 391, the general prohibition against civilians carrying arms was rescinded to enable citizens to look to their own defence against robbery with violence,[55] and in the course of the next decades vigilante groups were being constituted; the Christian

---

[*] An Ostrogoth, not the Visigothic Theodoric whom Sidonius had visited earlier in the century.
[†] Who had so stoutly objected to the removal of the Winged Victory from the Senate House – see p.168, above.

Bishop of Ptolemais in Egypt was one of the organizers.[56] In the countryside the bailiffs were conniving with the rustlers in removing sheep,[57] while in the cities drunk and disorderly conduct had become a public menace, exacerbated, so far as Rome was concerned, by the removal to Milan of the emperor's bodyguard, who had previously been able to exercise some sort of discipline in the streets. Towards the end of the century the urban prefects intervened, for the first time in about three centuries, in the wineshop trade, limiting opening hours and delineating what could be sold.[58]

Inevitably in these conditions the public welfare system suffered. In the late fourth century Symmachus was responsible for the distribution of the corn dole, an increasingly difficult task, for the ships were not arriving as expected from north Africa. He had to obtain supplies from the East, recording his great relief when the corn fleet arrived from Macedonia.[59] The Egyptian harvest was by now earmarked for the cities of the Eastern Empire, north Africa being the normal supplier for the West, but with the Vandal conquest of the African grainlands, tribute from that area, with the possible exception of Mauretania, ceased to be obtainable.[60] Supplies depended on the much more expensive option of trade; and even trade became increasingly difficult as Vandals operating from what was later to become the notorious Barbary Coast turned pirate, and virtually terminated sea-going commerce in the western Mediterranean.[61]

The population of Rome had been diminishing for a long period. Estimates of Rome at its imperial peak in the first and second centuries are in the range of a million to a million and a half, but by the start of the fourth century the numbers are put at not more than three-quarters of a million, and by the time of the Vandal sack in the mid-fifth century, at perhaps a third of a million.[62] Jones estimates that by then there were only about 120,000 recipients of food dole in Rome, which had long ceased to be the capital city, though still a centre for games and circuses, served by a floating population of charioteers, grooms and popular entertainers.[63]

Nevertheless, huge efforts were made to keep up supplies, with continuing hereditary direction of labour for all the trades associated with the distribution, including the shippers, merchant seamen, bakers, butchers and purveyors of wine and oil. The young Sidonius, before he turned to the Church and became a bishop, was Prefect of the city of Rome about a decade after the Vandal sack, having the Prefect of the Food Supply as one of his subordinates. He wrote a graphic description to a friend of how he sent this officer post-haste to the harbour on hearing that five ships laden with wheat and honey were approaching the Tiber from Brindisi (a port of departure that again suggests an Eastern origin for the supplies), with orders to unload and distribute the cargoes with all possible dispatch, 'for I am afraid that the uproar of the theatre benches may sound the cry of ''starvation in Rome'' and that the general famine may be put down to my luckless management'.[64]

At the end of the fifth century, when Goths had succeeded the Roman emperors, Theodoric the Great strove to continue the largesse to the city. His near-contemporary biographer, writing in the mid-sixth century, says that Theodoric, visiting Rome in some state from his capital at Ravenna, gave 'a hundred and twenty thousand measures of grain' annually to 'the Roman people and to the poor of the city'. He also financed the rebuilding of the city walls, restored the old disused palace, repaired Trajan's aqueduct at his home base of Ravenna and that of Verona, both of which had been out of commission for some considerable time, and embarked on other initiatives such as a new palace, amphitheatre and baths at Pavia; and at Rome he had Pompey's ancient theatre restored.[65]

Men hoped for a *Pax Gothica*. A chronicler recounts that Theodoric forbade Romans to carry any weapon larger than a small knife, but whether this was because self-protection was no longer necessary, or whether it was to disadvantage Roman citizens in comparison with Goths is not clear.[66] In any case, the lull proved temporary. Orosius's dream of an Empire united by Roman law and the Christian religion went unfulfilled in the religious as in the legal domain. The barbarians were indeed progressively Christianized, but into different Christian factions. Most of the Goths either were, or became, Arians, heretics in the eyes of the traditionalists of both East and West.[*] On the whole the Gothic Arians were fairly tolerant of the Roman Catholics (by the late fifth century the epithet 'Romanus' was coming to imply 'Catholic' as much as 'citizen of the old Empire'),[67] but the Vandals of north Africa, recent converts, were fanatic in their Arianism, and the Catholics of Carthage had to suffer the loss of all their churches and the destruction or confiscation of their books and liturgical vessels following the Vandal conquest. For much of the next hundred years the practice of any religious allegiance other than Arianism was forbidden in Vandal north Africa.[68]

---

[*] Arius was a Libyan theologian who, in 321, anxious to avoid a seeming departure from monotheism, propounded the doctrine that Christ was not 'consubstantial' with God the Father. Catholicism proved more attractive in the long run, the conversion of the by then militarily dominant Franks from paganism to Catholicism in 498 setting a trend to which the Burgundians responded in 516, the Goths in the latter part of the same century (Vogt, pp.237, 266).

In the sixth century, Justinian, Emperor in the East, failing to reciprocate the Arian Goths' tolerance, set out to reconquer the Arian lands for Christian orthodoxy. Once more Italy was devastated by war, from which yet another Gothic warlord, Totila, he who presided at the last recorded races at the old Roman race track, the Circus Maximus, emerged briefly victorious. His ultimate defeat, and the expulsion of the Goths from Italy, came at the hands of a new group of mercenaries in Justinian's service – the Lombards. In less than twenty years the Lombards were back as conquerors, seizing the agriculturally rich northern plains and thus depriving urban Rome of what little fertile corn-growing land was left within Italy.

By the end of the Gothic wars, Italy was pauperized. Once more the aqueducts fall into disrepair, and the baths cease to function. There is no further mention of the appointment of consuls in the West, no further convening of games, no further record of state largesse to the poor. By mid-century Rome's population has sunk to about 40,000, and the Senate vanishes from the records.[69] The Church had for many decades been deeply involved in helping the destitute through purchasing the tokens or vouchers entitling the holder to free grain, and distributing the proceeds. Henceforth religious charity replaced the welfare state, with about a quarter of church revenues going to provide such 'good works' as almshouses and orphanages.[70]

Lecky, in his magisterial *History of European Morals From Augustus to Charlemagne*, sees in 'this vast and unostentatious movement' of Christian charity almost the sole redeeming feature of post-imperial Europe. Little though he respected the monkish asceticism which in his eyes went to lunatic extremes, he paid tribute to the devotion which

> inspired many thousands of men and women, at the sacrifice of all worldly interests, and often under circumstances of extreme discomfort or danger, to devote their entire lives to the single object of assuaging the sufferings of humanity . . . the poor protected, the sick tended, travellers sheltered, prisoners ransomed, the remotest spheres of suffering explored

even down to 'the solitary hermit . . . with his little boat by a bridgeless stream' for whom 'the charity of his life was to ferry over the traveller'.[71]

The context in which this charity operated was one of deepening anarchy. 'The mind is fatigued,' says Lecky, 'by the monotonous account of acts of violence and of fraud', the perpetrators of which tended to be praised or reviled by the worthies of the Church not for the intrinsic moral quality of their actions, but according to whether their professed allegiance was to orthodox or heretical doctrines.[72]

Anarchy and insecurity were certainly playing their part in destroying the prosperity for which, it must be assumed, both the new arrivals and the established populations longed. But there was a more profound influence at work, one which was to determine the shape of things to come. Arian and traditional Christians alike had in common what Vogt refers to as 'the alteration in men's spiritual outlook ... we have seen how overwhelming was the surrender to new divine powers which bound men inwardly, and how crucial, even for leading spirits, was the revelation of a suprahuman and supraterrestrial reality'.[73] The thinkers of the period were not much interested in unravelling the secrets of the physical world, nor in feats of environmental manipulation. To quote Vogt again: 'The supreme task of Christian scholarship was to apprehend and deepen the truths of revelation.'[74] Augustine's *City of God* is grounded in the conviction that God's purpose is to bring man to eternal salvation, an end to which worldly benefits are irrelevant.

Some commentators see in the advent of Christianity a liberation from the taboos which ancient animism interposed between humanity and the exploitation of the natural world.[75] Robin Lane Fox remarks, *apropos* the felling of the sacred groves, 'the triumph of Christianity was accompanied by the sound of the axe on age-old arboreta'.[76] But paganism imposed few inhibitions either on the intellectuals or on the engineers of Rome's economic zenith, whereas the early Christians actively rejected scientific speculation. The scientific study of the heavens could be neglected, said Ambrose, Bishop of Milan at the time when it was the Western Empire's capital, 'for wherein does it assist our salvation?'[77] The Romans had been comfortable with the idea, already explored by the Greeks, that the earth must be a planet, and in his *Natural History* Pliny had noted contemporary learned opinion 'that human beings are distributed all round the earth, and stand with their feet pointing towards each other, and that the top of the sky is alike for them all and the earth trodden underfoot at the centre in the same way from any direction', though he admitted that 'ordinary people enquire why the persons on the opposite side don't fall off – just as if it were not reasonable that the people on the other side wonder that we do not fall off'.[78] Some three hundred years later, Lactantius directly challenged this belief:

How is it with those who imagine that there are antipodes opposite to our footsteps ... Is there anyone so senseless as to believe that there are men whose footsteps are higher than their heads? ... that the crops and trees grow downwards? That the rains, and snow, and hail fall upwards to the earth?[79]

Lactantius's view became the accepted doctrine. Four centuries later, in 748, a Christian priest named Vergilius was convicted of heresy for his persistence in believing in the existence of the Antipodes.[80]

Experimental science was seen not simply as superfluous, but as dangerous, having truck with demonic forces. Books were a source of deep suspicion. Not only might they be erroneous, they might record such commerce with the occult. Ammianus Marcellinus, chronicling the fourth-century persecution by the Eastern Emperor Valens of those suspected of superstitious practices, says that 'as a result, throughout the Oriental provinces owners of books, through fear of a like fate, burned their entire libraries; so great was the terror that had seized upon all'. 'In this way,' comments his editor, 'Valens greatly diminished our knowledge of the ancient writers, in particular of the philosophers.'[81]

Already by the middle of the fourth century, says Canfora, historian of the ancient library in Alexandria, Rome was virtually devoid of books. The famous lending libraries had been closed.[82] In Alexandria the Christian archbishop in 391 destroyed the great library of the Temple of Serapis, second only to the ancient Mouseion in size and prestige. 'The burning of books was part of the advent and imposition of Christianity.'*[83] Hypatia, pagan daughter of one of the mathematicians associated with the Mouseion, herself an eminent philosopher and mathematician, and lecturer at the university, was in 415 lynched in the street by a mob of Christian fanatics, egged on by Cyril, their bishop, who was later to be canonized.

For the moment the Mouseion survived. In his book *The Vanished Library* Canfora argues persuasively that the writers of antiquity who credited Caesar with its original destruction during his Egyptian campaign against Pompey were mistaken, since the great conflagration in which it was supposedly destroyed was confined to the docks, and the loss was probably that of a warehouse of scrolls awaiting export. Similarly, he believes that Ammianus Marcellinus's account of the destruction of the Serapeum Library misled Gibbon into thinking it was the Mouseion that then suffered. But there is evidence that the district in which the Mouseion stood was very badly damaged during disturbances

---

* And was to continue down the centuries. The first Spanish Archbishop of Mexico burnt all Aztec manuscripts that could be found, thus substantially destroying all evidence of Aztec learning and literature. On the capture of Granada from the Moors, Arabic manuscripts suffered the same fate (see Prescott, Vol.I, pp.84–5).

in the late third century, and Canfora suspects that most of its later contents postdated these events, and were not of much value. It had become a repository of largely Christian sacred texts, ill-copied parchments 'crawling with errors, for Greek was increasingly a foreign language'.[84] But it, too, was doomed, for now a new religious fanaticism threatened the Eastern Empire.

No traitor opened the gates of Constantinople to invaders, and the city and its government survived for a millennium after the sack of Rome. But much of the territorities ruled from the Eastern capital had passed into alien occupation within two centuries of Rome's fall. Goths and Huns had been successfully deflected West, but Bulgars and Turkish Avars were seizing and settling in Constantinople's agricultural Balkan hinterland from the late sixth century on. In Arabia an even more implacable enemy was on the move – the newly begotten whirlwind of militant Islam.

The Saracens invaded Palestine in 635, and took Jerusalem three years later. Within another hundred years they had taken Persia, Syria, Egypt and the whole of north Africa (where Salvianus's estimable Vandals had soon lapsed into degeneracy and had in the mid-sixth century suffered defeat at the hands of Justinian), had crossed into Spain and then on over the Pyrenees into Languedoc and Provence. They were stopped at Tours, and by 759 had been forced back over the mountains into Spain, where they were to remain for the next seven centuries. By 680 the Eastern Church had no choice but to accept that the patriarchates of Jerusalem, Antioch and Alexandria no longer formed part of the imperial Christian world. In 699 Arabic replaced Greek as the language of administration in Damascus.

Amrou Ibn el-Ass conquered Alexandria just before Christmas in 640. It was still a flourishing city, with some 400 theatres and 4,000 public baths. At the Mouseion the chief librarian pleaded with the city's conqueror to spare the books in the library, and he in turn passed the request on to the Caliph. 'If their content is in accordance with the book of Allah,' replied the Caliph, 'we may do without them, for in that case the book of Allah more than suffices. If, on the other hand, they contain matter not in accordance with the book of Allah, there can be no need to preserve them. Proceed, then, and destroy them.'[*85]

The books were distributed round the public baths as fuel for the

---

[*] Gibbon, in his *Decline and Fall of the Roman Empire* (Chapter 51) recounts this story but registers his doubts as to its authenticity. However, he added a footnote citing further research, which convinced him the account was true.

stoves. So huge was the quantity that for six months the bathwater of Alexandria was heated by the burning scrolls.

One author's books were not burnt. The omission was to prove of profound significance.

The works of Aristotle escaped the flames.

Chapter 12

Scholars and Scientists: the Tenth and Twelfth Centuries

The successor states established in Europe in the corpse of the old Empire witnessed what Sorokin calls the 'destruction of economic values', with de-urbanization, de-industrialization and de-commercialization.[1] Religion inspired a proliferation of beautiful artistic achievements, Anglo-Saxon England, for instance, developing a magnificent culture of illuminated manuscripts, carved ivories, exquisitely worked reliquaries, embroideries and metalwork, almost all, even when destined for secular use, embodying religious symbols, first pagan, then Christian. Meanwhile the technological expertise of Roman Europe not merely stagnated. It went into reverse.

After the fourth-century spread of watermills, six hundred years were to pass before there was any marked increase in their use. From AD 450 to 1000, no substantial secular buildings were erected in western Europe, and only two or three significant churches. By then even Europe's richer inhabitants had reverted to wattle-and-daub homes, the poorest to rough stone bothies sunk in the ground. No bricks were being made or used, apart from those pillaged from old Roman sites. The technique of stone-cutting fell into decay in Britain on the departure of the Romans; defensive structures regressed from the magnificent stonework of Hadrian's Wall and its fortresses to earthworks. Travellers waded through fords or crossed rivers on timber planks – for six hundred years after the deposition of the last Roman emperor there was no major bridge construction within Europe.[2]

A few fortunate settlements retained their Roman water and sewage systems; in Nîmes, for instance, the aqueduct across the Pont du Gard did not silt up terminally until the ninth century; Segovia was obtaining water from its Roman aqueduct as late as 1804, Naples until 1885;[3] in Rome the main sewer functioned until supplemented by a new system late in the nineteenth century, Pavia's was still operational in the 1980s.[4] In most settlements, however, the population reverted to cesspits, and to fetching its water from rivers and wells, the latter all too often polluted from the cesspits.

A knowledge of glass-making survived in Gaul, whence in 675 glaziers, 'who were at this time unknown in Britain', were summoned to show the Anglo-Saxons of Monkwearmouth how to glaze windows for their church; but window glass in private houses was unknown, and remained a rarity even in churches. The glaziers of Monkwearmouth evidently did not re-establish their craft in Britain, for some hundred years later the Abbot of Jarrow was sending to the Rhineland for glaziers for his church.[5] The whole technology of central heating, too, disappeared, warmth being supplied by open fires in braziers or on the floor, and chimneys were abandoned, replaced by a simple hole in the roof to let the smoke out.[6]

In craft after craft, expertise was lost and skills deteriorated. In the north-west of the old Empire, including Britain, the large-scale production of good pottery made on a potter's wheel ceased, though Roman methods lingered in the Rhineland and parts of Gaul and Italy, whence they were reintroduced to Britain in the ninth century.[7] Italian carpenters retained skills in woodwork, though the plane, well known in antiquity, seems to have disappeared from their tool-kit.[8] Outside Italy, no one seems to have attempted so complex a task as the construction of wooden drawers, though they were almost certainly an item of Roman furniture.[9]

Walbank has commented that the Middle Ages were to benefit from 'a whole series of innovations which they owed, not to the classical world, but to the northerners', and he cites the heavy plough, stirrup, horseshoe, soap and butter, cloisonné jewellery, the making of tubs and barrels, felt-making, skis and the cultivation of rye, oats, spelt and hops.[10] Virtually all these contributions had been made, however, in imperial times or even earlier; though the rigid metal stirrup only came, via the steppes, in the sixth century, whereupon it was immediately adopted by the Byzantine cavalry.[11] In the eighth century the padded horse-collar resting on the animal's shoulder bones was introduced, replacing the inefficient old collar which half-strangled the horse and therefore severely limited its use as a draught animal. This important advance reached Europe via Siberia, probably from China, where it had been devised in the mid-seventh century, but for several further centuries*

---

* The eleventh-century Bayeux Tapestry is the earliest known depiction of horses working in the fields (Gimpel (1988), p.33).

there was little use of the horse in agriculture, oxen being much cheaper.[12]

The half-millennium following the institution of Christendom is almost barren of technological innovation. The sixth and seventh centuries are cited as the economic nadir of post-Augustan Europe.[13] Sorokin hesitated to make too simple a connection between economic prosperity and the dominant culture. Too many other variables enter into the calculation, such as wars, plagues or vagaries of climate erupting into flood or famine.[14] All these factors, however, are transitory, waves within the tides of history. In the longer run, cultural values assert themselves. Hill, in *A History of Engineering in Classical and Medieval Times*, notes the marked decline in intellectual activity and the falling off of standards in sanitation, water supply, communications and domestic comfort that occurred from the fifth to the eighth centuries, and he quotes Professor Price of Yale University who, in discussing Greek engineering, had remarked that a 'mechanistic philosophy led to mechanism' rather than vice versa.[15]

Tentatively, Greek mechanistic philosophy was stealing back into Europe. It came, paradoxically, through Christian influences, but they were highly circuitous. During the fifth century two groups of eastern Christians, the Nestorians and the Monophysites, had been excommunicated as heretics. The essence of their quarrel, with the Church and with one another, lay in their differing interpretations of the relationship between spirit and matter, as actualized in the person of Christ. The Nestorians held that the baby born to the Virgin Mary was a human child, who only later became imbued with divinity; and hence they denied to Mary the title of 'Mother of God'.[*] The Monophysites believed that Christ's humanity and divinity were inseparable, and the more extreme among them took this to the ultimate conclusion that His human nature was so far subsumed into His divine nature that He must have been immune to earthly pain and suffering.

The Orthodox Church reached a compromise position to which neither contestant would submit, and both groups withdrew from the Byzantine Empire into Persia and Mesopotamia, there to pursue their loyalties without persecution and harassment (except intermittently from one another). The Nestorians – and perhaps it is not fanciful to see in this a reflection of their belief in the reality of Christ's physical humanity – became renowned for the practice and teaching of medicine,

---

[*] 'I will not,' said Nestorius, 'call him God when He was two or three months old' (O'Leary, p.183, note 3).

retaining in their academies the whole corpus of Greek knowledge as taught at the medical school at Alexandria, whose reputation they were to eclipse.[16] The Monophysites, as perhaps befitted their attachment to the superior reality of transcendence, founded monasteries, rather than academies. This may have made their scholarship less readily accessible to their non-Christian neighbours, but both they and the Nestorians embarked on a diligent programme of translating their legacy of Greek scholarship into the Syriac language of their new abodes.[17]

An essential feature of these heretical scholars was their refusal to rest content with revelation. They sought to engage reason in the defence of the faith. Aristotle's work on logic was a treasured possession, for it provided the intellectual framework within which doctrinal debates were pursued, tools for the rational defence, not demolition, of the faith. The cerebral sciences of astronomy and mathematics were studied, aspects of natural science which, as O'Leary points out in *How Greek Science Passed to the Arabs*, philosophy would weld into a unified whole, through the medium of a logic applicable to all.[18] Of profound significance for the future was their preservation of Aristotle's *Physics* and *Metaphysics*, with his theories on the ultimate identity of all matter, and explanation of the influences through which matter takes on the different forms apparent to our senses.

When the Arabs in the seventh century conquered Persia, Syria and Mesopotamia, they found these nests of scholarship well ensconced. Initially their reaction was suspicious. 'The continued and undiminished hostility of official orthodoxy against the ancient sciences remained as characteristic of Islam as it was of Christianity until deep into the Middle Ages,' comments Martin Plessner. 'Knowledge not founded on revelation and tradition was deemed not only to be irrelevant but to be the first step on the path to heresy.' The attractions of the excellent Nestorian medicine were obvious, but 'there were doubts about its practice in religious circles: it was regarded as an interference with God's counsels'.[19] However, a tradition held that the Prophet himself had referred the sick to a doctor trained by the Nestorians at their principal medical school at Jundi-Shapur in Mesopotamia. When in 762 the Caliph moved the Arab capital from Syria to the newly founded city of Baghdad, close to Jundi-Shapur, Nestorian doctors were in high demand, not only as court physicians but to provide general medical services, including regular medical rounds in the prisons.[20] Wealthy Arabs began to endow hospitals throughout the Arab domains (Cairo's main hospital in 1284 held some 8,000 patients, separated into wards according to sex and type of illness),[21] and Arab medical standards were to confound the

Europeans when they encountered the Saracen armies during the Crusades.

During the late eighth century, under the caliphate of Harun ar-Rashid, a systemic programme of translating the Greek works into Arabic began at Baghdad, where a special institution, under Nestorian supervision, was set up for the purpose, moving on to original Greek texts when the supply of Syriac versions was exhausted. Mathematical and astronomic treatises and works on logic and medicine were followed, somewhat later, by translations of the Greek philosophers, providing an opportunity for the Monophysites to make a particular contribution from the mystical literature dear to their traditions. Greek philosophy was a problem. It was found to be incompatible with the Koran, and Arab philosophers who developed Aristotle's theories were regarded as heretics. A solution was found by treating the Koran as having two levels – a face value appropriate for the untutored masses; and a hidden, symbolic significance reconcilable with rational philosophy.[22]

This opened the way for further study of Aristotle's explanation of the nature of matter. If all matter was ultimately identical, it ought theoretically to be possible to break it down into its basic constituents and reconstitute it in a new – and more precious – form. The search was on for the ingredient that inspired the particular form in which the matter manifested itself. It was envisaged as a sort of breath or spirit, the creative essence of being, but a spirit which could be condensed (our dual meaning of the word 'spirit' is indicative) into something tangible for practical application – the philosopher's 'stone'. The task of *alkimia*, as the Arabs called the pursuit of this knowledge, was to deconstruct matter by the application of heat and solvents, preparatory to reconstituting it in a finer form.[23]

Tradition believed that alchemy was an ancient wisdom which had been lost. The more recent forerunners of the Arab alchemists were experimenters known to have been working in Alexandria since about 200 BC, their texts having been included in the learning preserved by the heretical Christian sects. Set in a context which envisaged all matter as unified and permeated by the creative spirit, alchemy not only had obvious strong links with medical theory, it was also a highly spiritual undertaking, tightly connected to astrology (and therefore mathematics) through the belief that man is the microcosm of a macrocosm that embraces the very heavens. The attempt to transmute base metal into gold was only one aspect of alchemy. The perfection of human beings was as much part of the task as the improvement of grosser material, and much alchemical literature is written in such an allegorical form that modern investigators often do not know whether they are dealing with accounts of laboratory experiments or of mystical experiences.[24]

Alchemy was to provide the bridge to modern experimental science. In the late ninth century the Persian alchemist Razi

> brought about a revolution in alchemy by reversing the relative importance of experiment and speculation; whereas earlier adepts had swamped practice in floods of unsupported hypothesis, Razi felt that if success were to be obtained, it would be from work in the laboratory and not from lucubrations in the study.[25]

This pre-eminence accorded to observation reflects a growing respect for the material world as the repository of 'reality'.

Europe was not entirely ignorant of scientific and philosophic developments within the Arab world. Though Barcelona had been recaptured from the Moors as early as 801, before Islamic thought had benefited much from its cross-fertilization with Greek scholarship, the monasteries of Catalonia apparently kept in touch with developments in Moorish Spain to their south, and are known to have obtained Latin translations of Arab scientific works.[26] The real impetus came, however, with the Christian capture of Toledo in 1085, followed by the Norman conquest of Moslem Sicily in 1091, exposing libraries of Arab literature to Christian inspection.

Within a few decades twelfth-century Toledo had become a centre of intellectual ferment such as Baghdad had been in the ninth century. Just as in Baghdad a 'House of Wisdom' had been founded to produce translations from Syriac into Arabic, so now Archbishop Raymond of Toledo established his College of Translators,[27] where the work of rendering Arabic texts into Latin proceeded without remission. The Italian scholar Gerard of Cremona, who died in 1187, spent most of his working life in Toledo, where he translated some seventy-one books, including medical texts and works on philosophy, astronomy, geometry and alchemy.[28] Toledo became a Mecca for Christian scholars, who arrived from all over Europe, among them the Englishmen Adelard of Bath and Robert of Chester. So great did the respect for, and sense of dependence on, Arab civilization become, that by the thirteenth and fourteenth centuries professorships in Arabic were being provided for in universities at Salamanca, Bologna, Oxford, Paris and Rome.[29]

The theologians, particularly at the new University of Paris, where Peter Abelard was a leading exponent of Greek philosophy, now set about reconciling Aristotle's rationalism with a faith based on revelation. The task proved difficult; indeed, so far as those of a mystical tradition were concerned, it was shocking. 'He deems himself able by human reason to comprehend God altogether,' declared Bernard of Clairvaux of Abelard.[30] Three major tenets of Aristotelianism proved particularly indigestible: that the world has always existed, which denies the Creation: that the soul does not survive the body; and that miracles are impossible. The ecclesiastical authorities took fright, and in 1210 the teaching of Aristotle was forbidden in Paris. By 1245 a similar ban was in force in Toulouse. Meanwhile, in 1233, the Inquisition for the rooting out of heresy had been established at Rome, though not till 1255 was it authorized to use physical torture in pursuit of its enquiries. Averroes, the twelfth-century Spanish Arab who was the acknowledged authority on Aristotelian studies in the Islamic world, followed his master's teaching in largely accepting that man is essentially an intellectually superior animal, an approach which was contested in the next century by Thomas Aquinas.[31] In 1270 Averroes's ideas were formally condemned by the Church, and were among the 219 'execrable errors' being studied in the arts faculty of Paris University which in 1277 were condemned by the Bishop of Paris.[32]

But the genie of scientific method was out of its bottle. Adelard of Bath, who had been among the first to visit Toledo, 'favoured scientific investigation and set reason above authority'.[33] He proved to be 'one of the most influential pioneers of the scientific spirit'.[34] His English contemporary, Robert of Chester, who had become Archdeacon of Pamplona, had in 1144 translated the first alchemical work. A hundred years later Robert Grosseteste, Bishop of Lincoln and sometime Chancellor of Oxford University, was another who emphasized the importance of observation and experiment.[35] His protégé and fellow Franciscan, Roger Bacon of Ilchester, took his stand on the contention that 'there are two modes of acquiring knowledge – namely by reasoning and experimentation'.[36] In addition to his respect for the experiential wisdom amassed by generations of craftsmen, he was convinced that alchemy would ultimately prove successful in its search to unlock the secret of the universe, and once that had been done Bacon foresaw a time of plenty and prosperity, in which men would produce, among other wonders, ships without rowers, cars 'made so that without animals they will move with unbelievable rapidity . . . flying machines . . . bridges across rivers without piers or other supports . . .'[37] A year after the condemnation of the 219 errors, Bacon too suffered condemnation by the Church authorities, though the reason is not known.[38]

The challenge of the material, physical world was once again attracting the attention of able people. Augustine, enjoying Rome's twilight days, had given glory to God for endowing human minds with the ingenuity to produce 'such progress in agriculture and in navigation', such a multiplicity of clothing, buildings and goods of various kinds, drugs and remedies, seasonings and appetizers, skill in measuring and reckoning, and a host of other achievements, including sophisticated entertainment and complex engines of war. But he dismisses much of this as 'superfluous, nay more . . . dangerous and suicidal'.[39] Lynn White, in an article 'Cultural Climates and Technological Advance in the Middle Ages',[40] charts the changing attitudes of Christian thinkers in the Western, though not the Eastern, Church to the gospel story of Martha and Mary, unquestioning acceptance of Mary's role as symbolizing the superiority of a life anchored in contemplation giving place to an appreciation (rather in the face of Christ's reported teaching) of the rightness, for this world, of a life of practical activity. He quotes a monk who died in 875 as exceptional in his contempt for the mechanical arts, but perhaps he was not untypical of his time, for White also points out that about the year 1000 a significant change came over the portrayal of God the creator. Iconography which had hitherto displayed God as passive majesty, activating the cosmos by the power of thought, is replaced by God the master craftsman, shown with the tools of the civil engineer's trade, actively designing the material world. He cites too the changing emphasis in pictures illustrating the seasons of the year, where the practice of portraying the months as 'static personifications holding symbolic attributes' gives place to active scenes of 'plowing, haying, the harvesting of grain, wood chopping, men knocking acorns from oaks so that pigs can eat them, pig slaughtering' – illustrations that 'breathe a coerciveness towards nature . . . Technological aggression, rather than reverent co-existence, is now man's posture towards nature.'

Whatever the precise interaction between science and technology, the generations that thirsted so avidly to share the heritage of Arab scientific scholarship were also the generations that turned their minds to the condition of their material existence, and strove to improve it. The long technological stagnation was coming to an end. Some expansion in the application of water mills had begun already in the ninth century, when their use was extended from grain-milling to making mash for beer. In the next century cams (known to, but not exploited by, the Romans) were applied to tilt-hammers and used in leather tanning and for fulling cloth. By the twelfth century a huge expansion was taking place both in the number of mills and in the uses to which they were put, including the metal trades, in which, though not for another two centuries, water-powered bellows raised furnace temperatures to levels which could liquify iron ore.[41] The Cistercian order recognized the labour-saving potential of water power, and encouraged the siting of monasteries near to rivers, in order that the monks might be freed for longer periods of prayer and meditation. A monastery could be organized like a craft workshop, in which the same water ground corn, made beer, operated fulling and tanning machines and finally swilled away the waste.[42]

Late in the twelfth century come records of the construction of dams to control water-flow, and almost simultaneously, first in Normandy and Yorkshire, and shortly thereafter in the Low Countries, windmills are mentioned – possibly an importation from Persia or Afghanistan where they had been known for several centuries, but since they make their first appearance so far from the Mediterranean and are rather different in design, some scholars consider it more likely that in this instance they are a north European innovation.[43]

To the enhanced power of wind and water was soon added coal, fuelling what R.J. Forbes does not hesitate to call 'the medieval industrial revolution'.[44] There are references to the use of coal in eleventh-century France, and over the next two centuries English coalfields in Newcastle-upon-Tyne, Derbyshire, Nottinghamshire, Shropshire and the Midlands, as well as those in Wales and Scotland, were being mined. From the thirteenth century on, industry was converting to coal, and recent archaeological research in Leicestershire shows that by the mid-fifteenth century coal was being deep-mined with sophisticated galleries and pit-props.[45]

The result of all this increased industrial activity was, of course, pollution. Paris began to pipe in clean water, in lead pipes, towards the end of the twelfth century, an example which other towns set out to emulate; for the rivers were running foul with industrial as well as domestic waste.[46] Coal effluent was a more intractable problem. In 1257 Queen Eleanor of England had to vacate Nottingham Castle, so pervasive were the fumes rising from the industrial city below her. Fifty years later, the inhabitants of Southwark, Wapping and East Smithfield were forbidden to burn sea-coals in their kilns, so much distress and injury was it causing to fellow-citizens.[47]

The reverse side of the coin of pollution was that throughout the twelfth, thirteenth and early fourteenth centuries, material living standards were rising. The use of brick for building revived in southern France in the eleventh century,[48] reaching England in the late thirteenth, when bricks were brought from Flanders for building within the Tower of London – the first use of new (as distinct from purloined old) bricks in England since Roman times, when the 20th Legion had operated tile-kilns in Denbighshire, stamping their production with the legion stamp.[49] By 1335 bricks were once more being manufactured in England.[50] Workers from Normandy reintroduced a glass industry to Surrey and Sussex in the thirteenth century, producing both windows and domestic glassware, though the latter remained a rarity.[*] Even in churches window glass had not been the rule, and the oldest surviving stained glass in England dates only from the latter part of the twelfth century; but in the course of the next three centuries, glass was installed in most church windows and in the grander residences.[†] However, as late as the fourteenth, fifteenth and early sixteenth centuries most European houses were still relying on shutters, gratings or specially treated parchment, recipes for the preparation of which continued as late as the eighteenth century.[51]

Chimneys were reinvented. The first known in England dates from 1130, when a rudimentary flue discharging sideways just above the fire was constructed. Fireplaces and hearths soon followed, but, as with glass windows, it was not until the sixteenth century that their installation spread much beyond the homes of the most wealthy.[52]

Other thirteenth-century innovations include the spinning wheel and spectacles. Contact with Arabs during the Crusades, which lasted for approximately two centuries, from the first capture of Jerusalem in 1099 to its final reconquest by the Muslims in 1291, resulted in the introduction to Europe of previously unimagined accoutrements to gracious living, such as scents and silks, jewels and ivories; the acquisition by European armies of such superior Arab equipment as chain mail and the crossbow; and gunpowder, knowledge of which had passed to the Arabs from China. Two other Chinese inventions reaching Europe by the same route were wheelbarrows and the art of paper-making, which had been known in China since the second century AD. The Arabs had begun to use paper instead of papyrus during the eighth or ninth centuries; the first known paper mill in Europe outside Moorish Spain is first recorded in France in 1157, whence the art spread to Italy in the thirteenth century, Germany in the fourteenth and England in the fifteenth, with water mills operating rag-pulping hammers. Whether the

---

[*] Sussex continued to specialize in glassware. The sixteenth-century alchemist Thomas Charnock had to travel from his Somerset home to a glassmaker in Chiddingfold, Sussex, in order to obtain appropriate equipment for his chemistry laboratory (Taylor, F. Sherwood, pp.133–7).

[†] Countess Isabella de Fortibus, who became chatelaine of Carisbrooke Castle in the Isle of Wight in 1263, was one of the first people in England to use glass for windows.

compass, first referred to in European sources in the late twelfth century, was a Chinese, Arab or European invention is a subject of scholarly dispute, but it was certainly in widespread use by the late thirteenth century.[53]

One other Arab achievement, familiar to Europeans both from the work of the translators and from European experience of the Crusades, met with a more mixed reception. Medicine raised difficult issues of the relationship between body and soul which the importation or imitation of technological novelty had been able entirely to ignore.

The tone of the traditional Christian attitude to medicine had been set by Tatian in the second century, when he expressed his conviction that though pharmacy might have some capacity to heal, trust in God would be even more efficacious.[54] Such a view was entirely at odds with the prevailing attitudes in contemporary society which, highly distrustful when the first Greek doctor set up practice in Rome in 219 BC, had by Tatian's time come to accord great respect to medical practitioners – who were by then undergoing very rigorous training.[*55] By the fourth century health services were in operation not only in Rome but in other major cities, with, while the Empire lasted, state-salaried doctors providing a free service to the poor.[56] The developing Christian doctrine, however, was that sickness was a symptom of the malfunction of the whole personality, stemming ultimately from sin, a condition which applied to all humanity as a result of the Fall and Satan's ensuing power over the created world. 'There is no doubt,' John Chrysostom had said in the fifth century, 'that sin is the first cause of bodily disease.'[57]

Sickness was seen as the positive infliction, by some spiritual agency, of punishment for wrongdoing. A simple equation of sin with suffering was unsatisfactory – it was too evident that some sufferers were relatively innocent; and at the extreme of spirituality, suffering afflicting the saintly was viewed as a privilege, a sacred opportunity to share in Christ's redemption of the world by paying the price of sin. Most people did not aspire to be saints; for them the antidote to pain and sickness was repentance, and the invocation of help from saints and martyrs. Reports of their intervention, and the resulting miraculous cures, were frequent. Gregory, Bishop of Tours in the late sixth century, wrote extensively on the miracles wrought at the tombs of the saints and martyrs, particularly that of his fourth-century predecessor at Tours, Martin, at whose tomb he

---

[*] An encyclopaedia published by Celsus in the first century AD revealed extensive medical and surgical knowledge. Galen, physician to Marcus Aurelius in the second century AD, studied for eleven years before starting to practise (Balsdon (1969), p.132; Fraser, P.M., p.350).

had himself been miraculously healed. He made no secret of his preference for religion over medicine.[58]

In the monasteries there were monks who, notwithstanding official discouragement, studied the old texts of Hippocrates and Galen.[59] A medical school of obscure origin, but probably active by the eleventh century, developed at Salerno, where Arab medical literature was translated.[60] In the twelfth century a Latin version of the *Canon of Medicine* of the great Persian doctor Avicenna,* who died about 1037, was published, and became the dominant influence in the teaching of medicine until at least the end of the sixteenth century. Henceforth, most authorities cited in subsequent texts are Arab rather than Greek.[61]

But all this was peripheral. Doctors, with their blood-letting and butchery were heartily distrusted in practice, while healing solely through the manipulation of material substances was regarded by the Church as in principle perverse. Jonathan Sumption, in his *Pilgrimage: An Image of Mediaeval Religion*, quotes Jacques de Vitry who in the thirteenth century pointed out to his congregations that

> their only hope of good health was to look to the salvation of their souls, to which the instructions of doctors were positively deleterious. 'God says to keep vigils; the doctors say go to sleep. God says fast; the doctors say eat. God says mortify your flesh; the doctors say be comfortable.'[62]

In 1215 the Lateran Council forbade doctors to pay return visits to patients unless they had been seen by the priest first, for it was a spiritual not a physical physician of which patients were held to stand in need. Similar injunctions were repeated by synods over the next two centuries.[63]

Like a compulsive gambler constantly giving Lady Luck one more opportunity to show she is on his side, medieval people longed to be the beneficiary of a miracle, and interpreted every chance turn of events as due to miraculous interventions.† They were not, after all, so very unlikely. Augustine had accepted that Nature itself is full of occurrences beyond our understanding, and God, who far transcends mere matter, is the final cause of everything, the ultimate law of Nature. 'The final

---

* Avicenna's studies led him to conclude that the alchemical transmutation of elements was not possible. Majority opinion was against him (Holmyard, pp.95–6).
† Perhaps it is not overfanciful to see the medieval reliance on trial by ordeal in the pursuit of justice as owing something to the belief that God could be counted on to intervene on behalf of the truth.

reason for believing in miracles,' he says, 'is the omnipotence of God . . . God is the author of all natural substances . . . He is assuredly called almighty for no other reason except that he can do whatever he wishes.'[64]

Particularly potent for purposes of intercession were the sites associated with the life, and even more the death, of saints and martyrs, and any relics associated with them. Early Christian authorities had, like their pagan Roman contemporaries, regarded the bodies of the dead as inviolate, and continued to do so – for instance, where medical dissection was concerned. But mass enthusiasm for relics overcame this delicacy. As early as the fourth century the Eastern Empire was awash with relics, many entirely bogus, and by the seventh century opposition collapsed in the West as well. At the start of the ninth century, mysterious lights shining in a field in north-west Spain (claimed to be the origin of the name that was soon to resound through Christendom: Compostela – *campus stellae* or Field of the Star) led to the discovery of a Roman sarcophagus, declared to be that of the apostle James.* Great wealth and prestige accrued thereafter to Santiago de Compostela, but there were many aspiring competitors. Local and national pride was at stake as relics were traded and looted, the Crusader sack of Constantinople in 1204 providing a positive cascade of relics westward-bound. So ubiquitous were relics that some favourite saints could have been reconstituted more than once.[65]

The dissemination across Europe of the tombs and relics of saints provided magnets to which the faithful in distress were drawn for comfort and in the hope of cure. Pilgrimage was an enterprise of ancient lineage, indulged in as much by pagans of the classical world as by medieval Christians. It reached a climax of intensity at the start of the second Christian millennium. Throughout Europe the highways and byways were crowded with pilgrims seeking out shrines and reliquaries, while the most dedicated embarked on perilous journeys even to the Holy Land itself. The Camino de Santiago of the early twelfth century is described as 'the busiest trunk road in Christendom'.[66] Half a million pilgrims a year trudged over the Pyrenees and through the Galician mud to reach it, numbers that could swell to two million in jubilee years.

This was the spiritual context in which were constructed the great medieval cathedrals, the supreme architectural achievement of Christendom.

In England the stone-cutter's art virtually disappeared after the

---

* James 'the Greater', the son of Zebedee, as distinct from James 'the Lesser', the kinsman of Christ.

Romans left, but it did not vanish from the European mainland, and masons were among the craftsmen summoned to Monkwearmouth from France in the seventh century.[67] But even on the Continent skills were rudimentary, and though there is some documentary reference to the use of stone in bridge-building in the mid-eleventh century,[68] not until the twelfth is there work comparable with that of the Romans. The celebrated Pont d'Avignon, its 22 arches spanning 3,000 feet of river and marsh, was built in 1177. The 926 feet of Old London Bridge were in place by 1209 – the construction supervised by a French architect summoned by King John, who had been much affected by the beauty of the bridges he had seen in France.[69]

The construction of major stone churches and cathedrals began early in the eleventh century, when two Romanesque abbeys were built in Normandy, whence the conquering Normans brought the style to England, restoring to their province a use of masonry which had been in little evidence in Saxon times.[70] Romanesque, as its name implies, owed its aesthetic inspiration to Roman sources. The medieval civil engineers adopted the forms not of Rome's temples but of their secular buildings, the columned nave and aisles of the baths and basilicas. To guide them, they had not only the crumbling remnants of Rome's grandeur, they also had copies of Vitruvius. Gimpel notes that there are fifty-five Vitruvius manuscripts extant dating from the tenth to the fifteenth centuries, and Frank Granger, translator of the Loeb edition of Vitruvius, remarks that a manuscript had been taken from Italy to Jarrow as early as the sixth century, whence knowledge of its contents was spread by English Benedictine missionaries to the Frankish kingdom, there to influence the development of Gothic architecture.[71] What the Europeans lacked was a capacity to understand and solve the geometric problems involved in large-scale construction, but with the availability, after the mid-twelfth century, of translations from Arabic of the work of the Greek mathematicians (Adelard of Bath translated the complete works of Euclid), plus the Arabs' 'magnificent synthesis of the knowledge of classical antiquity and of India', where modern numerals had been pioneered, the way was clear.[72]

For the next three centuries the great cathedrals rose over Europe, higher and higher as one technical problem after another was overcome. Strasburg's spire soared to 466 feet – the height of a 44-storey skyscraper – unchallenged in Europe until the introduction of iron and steel into stone construction enabled the Eiffel Tower, late in the nineteenth century, to surpass medieval ambitions.[73]

As the buildings grew more magnificent, another though less

immediately obvious change was taking place. At the heart of the faith there is, as Jonathan Sumption puts it, a 'growing emphasis on the humanity of Christ in the spiritual literature of the 11th and 12th centuries', resulting in new devotions to Christ's nativity and childhood as much as to his death and resurrection. 'The formal, stylized, infinitely distant God of the Mosaic tympanum gave way to the human God of Chartres cathedral, and thus to the suffering God of Cimabue and Giotto . . .'[74]

Not only the material world, but the human beings within it were being accorded increased significance. By the thirteenth century the great cathedrals, albeit to the glory of God, did not scruple to include magnificent tombs and inscriptions in honour of the masons, architects and civil engineers who had fashioned them.[*] Man, himself, was moving towards centre stage.

Quite literally, in fact. In about 1262 there was written in Arras the first secular play of which western Europe has record since the closure of the Roman theatres. It was the work of Adam de la Halle, and he called it simply *Adam's Play*.[75]

---

[*] On the basis of known examples, Gimpel questions the accepted belief in the anonymity of medieval craftsmen. None of the instances he cites, however, pre-date the thirteenth century (Gimpel (1983), pp.41, 72; (1988), pp.116–17).

Chapter 13

From the Mass to Melodrama: the Twelfth to Fifteenth Centuries

No doubt the jugglers and songbirds, dancers and swashbucklers who rolled up their bundles and departed from the empty theatres of the dying Empire had tumbled and strutted their way through the Dark Ages, but they left little trace of their passing, and no dramatic literature. We catch glimpses of them in references, invariably disapproving, in ecclesiastical documents; in 791 'disturbing the mind of the people', according to Alcuin, the Yorkshire scholar who became adviser to Charlemagne. 'Low and obscene' performances were reported to the council at Châlon-sur-Saône in 813; three years later priests were forbidden to attend them. The Archbishop of Lyons in 836 found fault with his King for neglecting the needs of the poor while wining and dining the 'vainest and most turpitudinous' of the show-biz set.[1] The diligent Puritan William Prynne, who in the seventeenth century compiled a voluminous catalogue of Church references to players through the ages, cites numerous prohibitions and castigations by councils and synods from the earliest times to the ninth century, which suggests that there was at least a presence for them to rail against.[2] There is then a lacuna until the thirteenth century. That hopeful entertainers were still endeavouring to ply their trade is evident from the fact that an itinerant troupe turned up at the wedding in Germany of the Emperor Henry III to Agnes of Poitou in 1043 but were sent packing, and in the following century Philip August II of France banished the strolling players not only from his court but from the whole of France.[3] Henry piously enjoined that the money which might otherwise have been spent on maintaining, rewarding and adorning the players should be distributed among the poor.[4]

We think of these troupes of entertainers as wanderers; and travellers they probably were. But the implication of rootless, aimless, vagabondage is, as John Southworth points out in his *The English Medieval Minstrel*, probably largely false. Fairs and festivals had set dates, and it is reasonable to envisage the entertainers following a regular annual circuit, like later fairground barkers. There is little evidence of the content of their performances. Southworth sees them as in direct line of descent, even to the costumes favoured, from the Roman *mimae*, with rope-walkers, puppeteers and performing animals among the jugglers, conjurers and striptease artistes.[5] Many of the players would have been musicians, singing and playing instruments before and after, as well as during, the set-piece performances. Any sketches performed were probably, as with the actors of early Rome, impromptu, the dialogue improvised, a tradition that was to surface in Italy in the *commedia dell'arte,*[*] though Southworth points out that improvisation does not preclude a good deal of rehearsal, and even memorizing of lines.[6] There is almost no surviving evidence of scripts, which may reflect a society where literacy was the prerogative of a disapproving Church, but possibly the type of entertainment provided did not call for them. Grysar suspects that the acting consisted chiefly of vulgar and scurrilous comedy, in which dubious gestures played a large part, and he says that these gestures had their own term – *mimaritiae*.[7]

A literate drama was about to develop, but not out of the old theatre. Just as it was innovations in worship that led to the evolution of Greek drama, so now, in the ninth century, changes occurred in the celebration of the Mass which were to have equally dramatic consequences. The sung antiphonies of the liturgy began to be elaborated with interpolations in the form of dialogue from the Scriptures.[8]

The great drama of Christ's death and resurrection, implicit in every offering of the Mass, was played out before the people on one special day of the year – at Matins on Easter Sunday. The text, in Latin, was taken straight from the words of the New Testament, where the exchange of dialogue between the angel and the women at the empty tomb, beginning 'Quem queritis?', provided a holy script. The earliest extant text dates from 950, and comes from St Gall in Switzerland. Lengthy stage directions in the form of rubrics are incorporated in the 970 version supervised by the Bishop of Winchester, which required a cast of four to play the three women and the angel. The players were all monks – neither lay people nor of course women were included.[9] There was no suggestion of naturalistic representation. The dialogue was intoned in

---

[*] The first descriptions of these improvised Italian comedies date from 1568, at the wedding of Duke William of Bavaria. Their connection with Roman antecedents (see p.79) is tenuous, as there is no certainty that any such drama persisted alongside the liturgical drama of the Middle Ages. However, there are many close parallels, including the identity of the stereotyped protagonists, and the use of masks and improvisation (see, for instance, K.M. Lea, *Italian Popular Comedy*, Clarendon Press, Oxford, 1934).

plainsong, the participants wore ecclesiastical vestments. The three 'Marys' carried not the scriptural spices, but thuribles filled with incense. 'The whole manner of the performance,' says Richard Axton in his *European Drama of the Early Middle Ages*, 'seems distinguished as little as possible from the "office" in which it takes place.'[10]

By the next century, mirroring the increasing devotion to Christ not only as Saviour but also as Mary's son, comes the first evidence of a nativity play, introduced, like the Easter material, as an interlude in the Mass, the dialogue still in Latin, and still derived from scripture. No human actor was so blasphemous as to attempt to portray the Madonna, who for another two centuries was represented by an image, usually depicted holding a child.[11]

Between the eleventh and twelfth centuries this liturgical drama evolved towards increasing naturalism. Additional characters were introduced – at first from scripture, such as Herod and the Magi; then as ancillary to the story, such as the apothecary selling the spices for the anointing of Christ's body, though these non-scriptural parts had no lines to speak. The priests and monks who composed the cast began to project an image of daily life: cooking pots were stirred, fires tended. Realistic props appeared – such as a genuine spade for Christ when he is mistaken for the gardener.[12]

With the twelfth century come the first of the Mystery plays – though this description, a corruption from the Latin *ministerium sacrum*, 'holy action', or 'drama', was not applied for another three centuries. These were not simply liturgical re-enactments of Christ's nativity and passion, they began to explore the Old and New Testaments, debating man's redemption. The oldest known, *The Representation of Adam*, deals with the sin of Adam and Eve and the murder of Abel by Cain, concluding with a procession of prophets foretelling the coming of Christ. It cut new ground in another way, too; the dialogue was in Norman-French,* though the choral chants and the stage directions continued to be given in Latin. Furthermore, it was performed outside, at the doors of the cathedral.[13] The church building, however, remained central to the action of the 'Adam' plays, with God emerging from its portals to deliver his lines, and the choral music sung within.[14]

This was no longer liturgical worship, it was instructional entertainment, albeit solemn in tone, and the Church recognized the distinction. Previously *ordo* or *officium* had been used in describing the priestly

---

* According to Axton, experts dispute whether the play's language is Continental or insular, the possibility remaining open that it originated in Norman England rather than in France (Axton, p.113).

enactments, but by the twelfth century the word *representatio* is creeping in, and for the 'representations' of biblical narrative the Church soon accepted *ludus*, which had centuries previously shed any religious connotation.[15] In Spain in the thirteenth century King Alphonse X forbade the clergy to stage 'scenic representations' in church. Only the enactments of the Nativity and the Passion were permitted.[16]

Meanwhile, a parallel development was introducing drama from another source. There had always been, in the noble houses of Celts and Saxons as of many other peoples, bards who, to the accompaniment of the harp, had sung the genealogies of their tribal masters and borne witness to the great deeds of their ancestors. Their relationship with their employers is signified by the name, first recorded in the twelfth century: 'menestrel', or minstrel, derived from the Latin *ministrellus*, a minor court servant.[17] Often the household minstrels had other tasks, such as doing the baking or supervising the hounds; they acted as heralds and messengers, a task which, among the senior and literate minstrels, could shade off into diplomatic missions.

These the Church did not despise. Indeed, a penitentiary of the early thirteenth century, written for the guidance of confessors, clearly distinguishes between these minstrels and other categories of entertainers. Three grades of entertainer are delineated. Those who are to be damned unless they abandon their calling include those who 'transform and transfigure their own bodies by base contortions and base gestures, or by basely denuding themselves, or by wearing horrible masks';* buffoons who hang about the courts of great men, 'backbiting the absent opprobriously and ignominiously in order to please others'; and musicians who 'haunt public drinkings and wanton assemblies, where they sing divers songs to move men to wantonness'.

However, there is a subsection of the musician category 'called *jongleurs* who sing the deeds of princes and the lives of saints and solace men in their sickness or in their anguish, and do not those innumerable base deeds which are done by dancing-men and dancing-women ...'[18] These latter escape Church condemnation; indeed they were often recruited from among boy choristers. Five of the choirboys serving Edward, Prince of Wales, later Edward II, went on to become minstrels.[19] John Rutherford, in *The Troubadours*, maintains that 'it is certain that the ranks of the troubadours were largely recruited from the cloisters', aspirants to the religious life who changed their minds about their

---

* The horror of masks, with their liberating anonymity, has found a late-twentieth-century echo in the English law courts hearing allegations of ritual sexual abuse of children.

vocation.[20] Many returned to the cloth when their professional lives were over.[21]

The term *jongleur*, though often used interchangeably with 'minstrel' or 'troubadour', tended to signify the less reputable balladmonger, and in France the troubadours jealously guarded their superior reputation. A late-thirteenth-century troubadour petitioned the King of Spain to protect the status of his calling by giving a clear ruling on the nomenclature to be used.[22] An ex-soldier, aspiring to be a troubadour, was admonished, 'bethink you, for instance, how terribly you swear when you happen to lose your last coin at the gaming table; that, my friend, is a trick that society will not tolerate in a troubadour'. Only if the ex-serviceman can give up this 'and other uncleanly habits of the camp' can he hope to be accepted as a troubadour.[23]

The troubadours wrote in the Langue d'Oc and were thus at home in the whole swathe of territory that stretched from Catalonia, up into Aquitaine, and through Provence into northern Italy. Through Henry II's marriage to Eleanor of Aquitaine, individual troubadours in her service are known to have visited England, too.[24] Like the minstrels, they had antecedents in the household poets who wrote metrical histories of families, lauding the beauty of the ladies and the heroism of the men, lamenting deaths and celebrating weddings and births. The epithet 'troubadour' (or, in its northern variant, *trouvère*), however, describes not the relationship of the musician with his employer, but with his material – he was an innovator, a discoverer, a composer as much as a performer. The description was not limited to professional musicians; noblemen (and women) could – and did – qualify as troubadours.

The troubadours surface in the twelfth century and are at the peak of their influence in the thirteenth. At the period when men of a scientific cast of mind were laying the intellectual foundations for the medieval industrial revolution, the troubadours were leading those of an artistic and emotional temperament to a similar preoccupation with this, rather than some other, world.* It is Bernard of Clairvaux, using the psychology of love to clarify what he is trying to say of the mystical ascent of the soul to God, who, says Jack Lindsay, comes nearest to

---

* In Umbria, Francis of Assisi, the son of a Provençal mother, aspired to be a troubadour. Seared by an incandescent experience of God, he became instead a *jongleur de Dieu*, dedicated to the Lady Poverty. Yet in him, too, can be traced the troubadours' celebration of the physical world, though for the Franciscans it was a manifestation of, not a substitute for, spiritual realities. To quote the *New Catholic Encyclopaedia* (Catholic University of America, New York, McGraw Hill, 1967, on 'Franciscans'), a characteristic of Franciscan spirituality is 'incarnationalism'. 'Because God has become man, natural creation has value already in time . . . nature is in its very creation orientated to the supernatural order.'

explaining the courtly love that was the troubadours' main theme. As Lindsay (himself a materialist of Marxist persuasion) sees it, the troubadours

> translated the mystical experience of the soul alone with God into the ecstatic experience of lover alone with lover. But by substituting for a cosmic and social abstraction a real[*] person, they had taken the decisive step of breaking from metaphysics and making the life-process itself the source of all knowledge and self-realisation. They drew back into life the energies that had alienated into God.[25]

Courtly love was a distillation of single-hearted devotion to a loved one who is the epitome of beauty and nobility of character – and of distance; a grail ever pursued and ever eluding capture. The idea of the quest, of the gap between what is longed for and what is, makes it impossible for troubadour poetry to handle the theme to which the longing is addressed – copulation. The passion, the jealousy, the joy of unfulfilled desire make courtly love incompatible with marriage.[26] The object of adoration was usually a married woman, and if the romance showed signs of real-life consummation, particularly where the participants were unequal in rank, rapid steps were likely to be taken by the woman's husband or kinsfolk to terminate matters mercilessly.[27]

Late in the twelfth century a chaplain named Andreas wrote, at the behest of Marie of Champagne, a treatise on love, *De Amore*. Ovid's work of that title had been a guide to flirtation and seduction based on the premise that promiscuity is the natural inclination of the human race. Andreas too took nature as the determinant of right conduct, but rejected promiscuity as an impulse of animal, not human, nature. In Lindsay's paraphrase of Andreas: 'Human nature is thus what separates man from animal nature and enables him to see that love is not just a random response or impulse, but the greatest and only steadfast good.' Furthermore, Andreas accepted that such love should reach its proper fulfilment.[28]

Could such a position be reconciled with the Church's teaching that love of God, of transcendent reality, was the sole source of goodness and virtue? Andreas seems to have abandoned the attempt. The third volume of his treatise relegated courtly love to a wholly inferior status. This did not save his work from condemnation. In 1277 it was included with those

[*] I.e. physical, material.

other 'manifest and execrable errors' in which Averroes and his mentor Aristotle had sought to elevate the primacy of the natural world as the source of truth.[29] By then the Provençal troubadour tradition was already nearing its end. The first half of the thirteenth century had seen the crusade against the Cathar heretics of Provence, backed by the Inquisition now in possession of full powers to use physical torture to extract confessions, bring devastation to the once smiling lands of the Midi. Troubadour heresy had nothing in common with the Manichean beliefs of the Cathars, but the sledgehammer of orthodoxy frightened them as thoroughly as it disposed of the Cathars. The Provençal troubadours of the thirteenth century retreat from courtly love into a safe adoration of that even more distant paragon of beauty and virtue, the Virgin Mary.[30]

In the north, however, the condemnations of 1277 were as ineffectual in the emotional as they were to prove in the intellectual sphere. Romance had become respectable, and it is the subject chosen for the second play by the northern troubadour, the *trouvère* Adam de la Halle, who in the thirteenth century provides the first evidence of sustained secular drama.* His works are described as 'delicious operettas' by Gustave Cohen in his *Histoire de la Mise en Scène dans le Théatre Religieux Français du Moyen Age.*[31] That the title of his first known work, *Adam's Play*[†], so closely mirrors a religious drama is perhaps fortuitous, for it derived its name from its author, whose life it depicted in a series of autobiographical vignettes, satirizing the way of the world in his home town of Arras and introducing complications in the form of diverse interventions by the denizens of Fairyland. His next known production, *Robin and Marion*, written some time before 1288, was a musical romance of which Mantzius says (in 1903) that 'the old music in its triple time, as also the text, are still enjoyable to modern ears on account of the peculiar grace which distinguishes this pastoral play'. 'Robin' and 'Marion' became, to generations who had yet to hear of Romeo and Juliet, the stock names for tender lovers.[32]

These are no more than harbingers of frivolities to come. As Sorokin points out, referring to the non-theatrical literature of this epoch, the secular and the religious remain deeply entwined. The heroes are human

---

* There is an earlier reference – a Provençal troubadour who served Richard Coeur de Lion in the twelfth century was apparently composing 'tragedies and comedies', organizing a company of actors, selling scripts to other troubadours and taking money from an audience, but the scholarly consensus seems to be that at so startlingly early a date these must have been 'farcical sketches having neither head nor tail'. (Rutherford, pp.228–30).
† It was also known as *Le Jeu de la Feuillée*.

beings – as in the Arthurian romances, or Dante's *Divine Comedy* – but human beings dominated by moral and religious values.[33] Most drama was still wholly religious in subject and tone, but it was changing, emancipating itself from close reliance on scripture. Non-biblical walk-on parts like the apothecary are being given a few dignified lines to speak, the text still in Latin. The central figure of Christ is, for the first time, a speaking part, instead of being treated purely symbolically. New scenes are introduced: Doubting Thomas, the Road to Emmaus; and inventive drama develops with the incorporation of scenes implicit but not explicit in scripture, such as Pilate admonishing the watch. The whole physical space of the church is engulfed by a series of playlets making up the totality of the play.[34]

The Church is, however, beginning to lose control of the drama. The custom developed of mounting the various playlets on wagons and presenting them one after another at different sites around the town. About the middle of the thirteenth century four-wheeled wagons began to replace the two-wheeled cart of the Dark Ages, permitting, over the course of time, the development of pageant wagons, miniature travelling theatres of two storeys, with the actors' curtained dressing room below and a hard roof over it on which to stage the show.[35] In 1311 the observance of the Feast of Corpus Christi (instituted in 1264 but never elaborated, because of the death of the Pope responsible for the innovation) was enjoined on the faithful.[36] The processions associated with this summer festival lent themselves well to street theatre. Corpus Christi processions in England were including pageant wagons by about 1318. Teachers and scholars as well as clerics joined in the writing and production, there is increasing use of the vernacular, prominent lay people began to defray the expenses, and in England the various guilds undertook special responsibilities according to their craft: the shipwrights, for instance, building Noah's Ark.[37] Special fraternities were founded to perform the plays, though 'the most sublime parts, such as God, Jesus and the Virgin Mary' tended to be monopolized by the clergy, sometimes to the detriment of their ecclesiastical duties.[38]

As the fourteenth century progresses, the event

is no longer a ritual, but a play; the setting is no longer in the church, but in the town; it is no longer organised and performed by members of the clergy, but by men who are, for the most part, members of the urban community. Finally the audience is composed not of the faithful attending a religious service, but of the general public.[39]

The part of Herod had been permitted a certain burlesque quality even in stricter days. Now other parts were written up to give comic relief. The apothecary acquired a wife and assistants, and developed – though not without some ecclesiastical disapproval – into the stereotype of a wily merchant, the dignity with which he formerly reflected the solemnity of his place in the Easter rituals having been displaced by a more lively characterization.[40] Opportunities for gratifying secular tastes included portraying Mary Magdalene (played, of course, by a youth, not a woman) as a courtesan and allowing 'her' to sing a profane song.[41]

In the changes that these developments introduced, Axton sees evidence of the absorption into mainstream drama of a little-noticed tributary – folk festivals long pre-dating Christianity. Rituals of death and renewal, of fertility, of seed-time and harvest had been enacted by the people in due season, and though the Church tried to sanctify and Christianize these rites, it had frequent occasion to lambast them – as, for instance, in 1244 when Bishop Grosseteste banished from his Lincoln diocese plays 'bringing in May or Autumn'.[42] No extant text of any folk play pre-dates the eighteenth-century versions of a mummers' play, but Axton suspects that, for instance, the mummers' quack doctor who restores a seeming corpse to life dates from the earliest dramas of death and renewal, and that this character transferred readily into the spice-merchant-cum-quack-doctor who sells life-restoring ointments to the Marys of the Corpus Christi cycles. In scene after scene of the evolving 'cycles', in the buffoonery, in the doctrinally unnecessary elaboration of the role of the shepherds, in the 'plough-drama' vestiges in the treatment of Cain and Abel, Axton detects the possible influence of the old rural folk celebrations.[43]

There is a marked change of tone in the drama of the later Middle Ages. Without appreciating the danger, suggests Cohen, the Church allowed religion to be portrayed increasingly materially. Heaven and Hell both take on wholly material illustration – Hell is not alienation from God, but burning vats in which Satan requires people to be cooked.[44] Contemporary drama seeks not to transcend but to mirror the material world. 'The medieval dramatic author,' says Mantzius, 'aims directly at everyday life, picks up and takes note of every detail, and retails it in the most ordinary language of real life.'[45] Turds drop from the rear of the hobby-donkey bearing Christ into Jerusalem, to the great delight of the audience.[46]

The distinction between the type of drama purveyed by the amateurs and by the professionals was closing. Charles Mills Gayley, in his *Plays of our Forefathers*, made a careful analysis of the manifold 'playlets' making up the York, Chester and Wakefield (Towneley) cycles of mystery plays in order to assess their evolution over time. His conclusions are an interesting corroboration of Sorokin. In the 'transmutation of the spectacle from liturgy to popular drama' he traces a progression from 'the humour of the incidental, then of the essential or real, and gradually of the satirical; afterwards the accession of the romantic, pathetic and sublime; the wonderful, the allegorical, and the mock-ideal; and finally of the scenic and sensational'.[47] As in the tragedies of late republican Rome, scenic spectacle became of prime importance. The later mystery plays included huge numbers of 'extras' swelling the trains of grand personages, and by the sixteenth century the cast were bedecked with a stunning wealth of furs, silk and jewels.[48]

The status of the performers – amateur craftsmen and clergy, salaried minstrels and self-employed strolling entertainers – remained distinct, but the edges were blurring. The mime who used Salome to provide a biblical framework for the old striptease was a girl, whereas almost without exception the female parts in the 'religious' dramas were still played by men, though by the late fifteenth century even that was changing. An estimable character such as a female saint could be played by an actress, though old and comic female roles were still monopolized by men.[49] In the royal and noble households the minstrels, whose ballad recitations had grown less acceptable in a time of spreading literacy,[*] were replacing their musical interludes with dramatic performances. There is fragmentary evidence of such a sketch late in the thirteenth century; certainly by the fourteenth *miracula* were being performed at court to divert Edward I's young second wife.[50]

Minstrels began to specialize, some as players of musical instruments, some as players of dramatic interludes – though for at least the next two centuries, performers were expected to show great versatility, acting, dancing, juggling, vaulting and tumbling as occasion demanded.[51] By the early fifteenth century companies of full-time player-minstrels emerge, performing *miracula* which Southworth categorizes as only ostensibly religious. 'They were the popular entertainments of their day, generally disapproved of by the Church.' Some of these were in royal service; Henry VII had a small company of players, his son a group of chamber minstrels, but the execution of a number of them for supposed adultery with Anne Boleyn symbolized the end of the medieval-style minstrel.[52] Noblemen followed the monarch's example – by the late

---

[*] 'People prefer chatterers,' lamented Chandos Herald in the late fourteenth century, 'false liars, jongleurs or jesters who will pull faces and imitate a monkey to make them laugh, to someone who can tell true stories' (Southworth, p.98).

fifteenth century the records show more than fifty lords owning troupes of players.[53] Others belonged to specific towns and cities, having developed out of the old companies of town waits who had combined the duties of watchmen and civic musicians. The companies were permitted to tour when not required at their home base by their patron.[*54]

The minstrel companies kept a jealous eye on the activities of the non-salaried troupes, demanding (in effect) a 'closed shop'. Their main complaint seems to have been against part-timers, who made a killing at fairs and festivals, but depended on some other trade for their main living.[55] Official prejudice against the old-style pros was waning. By the fourteenth century there is ample evidence that they had become prized adjuncts to royal celebrations, especially weddings. Grysar quotes a series of entries in Continental chronicles cataloguing the generous gifts lavished on comedy actors, including in one instance no fewer than 7,000 valuable dresses to mime actresses. There were 1,500 performers present at the festivities put on by the Duke of Malatesta in 1324.[56] Although the pious Henry VI objected, in his youth, to topless female French dancers, sexy striptease was becoming acceptable entertainment in the best circles. In 1461 Louis XI was welcomed to Paris with poems from beautiful naked girls, and in 1468 the city of Lille put on that hoary old favourite *The Judgement of Paris*, with three naked goddesses, for the entertainment of Charles the Bold.[57]

The integration of the professional players into the main dramatic stream was helped by the fifteenth-century development of secular plays. Their subject matter leaned heavily on the eternal pabulum of light comedy – unfaithful wives and cuckolded husbands – and to this typical late Roman amalgam the Middle Ages added hypocritical priests, avaricious tradesmen, cunning lawyers and a gallery of other characters.[58] They were played as farces, but Mantzius insists that the characters portrayed were not stock stereotypes, as in the Greek and Roman comedies. On the contrary, 'the ruling principle is to copy the characters of real life' and to allow the actor 'to make use of his observations of everyday-life, of gestures and accents which strikingly reminded the spectator of the class to which the character belonged; in short, variegated superficial pictures of real life'.[59] The farces also managed to work in some veiled political and social comment, for which

---

[*] It was on or after one such out-of-London tour to Stratford-on-Avon a century later, that Lord Leicester's Men took on as call-boy a stage-struck young man called Will Shakespeare *Dictionary of National Biography* (Vol.XVII p.1292). It is a reminder of the versatility expected of them that when, in 1586, the company visited Denmark, they were described as singers and dancers (Bradbrook, p.97).

purpose the character of the Fool, complete with jester's cap and bells, was invaluable. The main aim, however, was simply entertainment, and this was pursued by scraping the bottom of the barrel of lavatorial humour and sexual crudity. Some of the French plays, like the 'noise' plays of late classical times, were virtually plotless, simply providing opportunities for an assemblage of coarse allusions.[60]

These farces shared the stage with, and were played before or after, the Mystery play. The acting fraternities had included citizens of some standing in the community as well as artisans and churchmen. Neither the content nor the presentation of this developing secular theatre was appropriate to the dignity of the former or the vocation of the latter. Particularly in France, performance of the farces came to be the prerogative of 'fool companies'. The origins of these companies are obscure and may have been very ancient, but only in the late Middle Ages did the fool companies establish themselves as dramatic societies. The actors were still amateurs, and, unlike the strolling players, they had permanent urban bases where their main employment was situated; but unlike the old devotional drama in which *naïveté* was acceptable provided it was sincere, the farces demanded sophisticated professional performance. It was a further impetus towards the blurring of the once prized distinction between the professionals and the amateurs.[61]

To Sorokin, the very development of a secular theatre is symptomatic of a sensate culture, corresponding in its frank acceptance of illusion to that satisfaction with sense perceptions, with appearances, which he regards as the essence of the sensate society's understanding of reality.[62] Religion, however, still bulked large in the lives of men and women, but increasingly it was being reinterpreted to serve, rather than to command, human convenience. Though the fourteenth-century development of 'miracle' plays still had a religious context, the central figure is not biblical, but a secular hero, drawn perhaps from legend or from near-contemporary courtly romance. The dramatic tension arises from the conflict between self-expression and divine law, from which trap the hero is conveniently sprung by the miraculous intervention of the Virgin Mary.[63] Her timely appearance achieves the rescue of all who call on her, no matter how heinous their conduct.[64]

Alongside this taste for miracles benignly bestowed rather than manfully merited came, as in the world of late antiquity, a great increase in that bane of debased supernatural belief, occultism; the determination to manipulate unseen powers in the interests of the manipulator. The once noble profession of alchemy became infected. Sorcery and demonology were everywhere rife – or thought to be. Since early in the fourteenth century 'the Papacy had been taking an increasingly punitive view of recourse to the supernatural', but not until the latter half of the century were campaigns against witches and sorcerers vigorously pursued. Towards the end of the century the theology faculty of Paris University issued a statement of twenty-eight articles warning of the increasing threat to society from the black arts. Sorcery was aligned with heresy as liable to the most severe punishments the Church could inflict; and the way was open for the next century's destruction of such 'witches' as Joan of Arc and the production of the notorious *Malleus Maleficarum*, the handbook for their recognition.[65] Testimony abounded (most of it extracted under torture) of sexual debauchery, of satanic rites, of the ritual killing and sexual exploitation of young children – a crime for which Joan of Arc's companion Gilles de Rais was executed in 1440.[66]

The fourteenth century is seen, says Sumption, as a time of appalling spiritual decay. The pilgrimages have become roistering package holidays, as much an occasion for acquiring tourist souvenirs as holy relics. Travel guides are being published, the well-to-do, far from journeying in penitential penury, travel in pomp, accompanied by comfortable retinues.[67] Sunday is losing its significance as a holy day. In 1311 the Bishop of Angers in France fulminated against such recent innovations as the holding of fairs, trials and assizes on Sundays, complaining that 'the churches remain empty while law courts, taverns and workshops echo with quarrels, noise and blasphemy . . .'[68] In England, where during the thirteenth century there had been at least fifteen statutes and canons on the suppression of Sunday markets, the Archbishop of Canterbury was by 1362 complaining that the reverence of earlier centuries was 'now turned into blasphemy, seeing that assemblages, trading and other unlawful pursuits are specially followed upon those days'.[69] The Rector of Paris University complained that the churches were empty and Mass meagrely attended. 'People kept vigils in church not with prayer but with lascivious songs and dances, while the priests shot dice as they watched.' Another observer denounced the hawking of lewd pictures in church, to the detriment of the young.[70] An English monk 'reported that certain barons of England believe "that there is no God, and deny the sacrament of the altar and resurrection after death, and consider that as is the death of a beast of burden, so is the end of man himself" '.[71] William Langland,[*] in *Piers Plowman*, remarks

[*] Information about Langland is scanty. He is thought to have been born in the Malvern area about 1332.

that in the halls of the nobility, scoffing at the mysteries of religion was acceptable table-talk in the intervals of waiting for the minstrels to strike up again.[72] Gimpel notes that in 1306 a radical sculptor made for a London church a statue of Christ so untraditional that the bishop refused to install or pay for it. 'This independence of the sculptor from tradition was unthinkable a century earlier,' he comments, 'and coincided with the waning of religious faith.'[73]

'The contrast between the 13th and 14th centuries,' remarks Boccaccio's biographer Thomas Bergin,

> may be illustrated by the works of the great doctors of the respective ages: the serenity – one might fairly say the optimism – of the great *Summa* of St Thomas Aquinas was challenged by the scrutiny of Duns Scotus and William of Ockham, whose perceptions, however admirable in showing the way to a new world of intellectual emancipation, were *au fond* corrosive of traditional values.[74]

Gimpel develops a theory that one particular technological triumph was instrumental above all others in secularizing society – the achievement, after long years of endeavour, of the mechanical clock. Astronomic research rather than the demands of routine timekeeping had fuelled the search, which probably obtained success during the closing decades of the thirteenth century, with mechanical clocks becoming widespread during the fourteenth. The chimed[*] definition of equal hours was, he claims, of far-reaching intellectual, commercial and industrial consequence. Hitherto, through all the ancient civilizations of Egypt, Greece, Rome, Byzantium and Islam, water clocks had been designed to indicate hours of differing lengths at different times of the year, so that there were always twelve hours of daylight and twelve between sunset and sunrise, a system that led to much larger variations in northern latitudes than in the Mediterranean basin. 'Time' was not a man-made discipline, it was a flexible response to the natural world, 'real time' was the eternity of God.[75] In Lewis Mumford's words:

> The clouds that could paralyze the sundial, the freezing that could stop the water clock on a winter night, were no longer obstacles to time-keeping: summer or winter, day or night, one was aware of the measured clank of the clock . . . The bells of the clock tower almost

---

[*] The first record of the striking of equal hours was at the Church of St Gothard in Milan in 1335.

defined urban existence. Time-keeping passed into time-serving and time-accounting and time-rationing. As this took place, Eternity ceased gradually to serve as the measure and focus of human actions.

'The clock,' adds Mumford, 'not the steam-engine, is the key-machine of the modern industrial age.'[76]

In the east of Europe the Orthodox Church stood its ground against this assault on eternity. For them it would have been blasphemy, 'would have contaminated eternity with time', in Lynn White's phrase. The western Church detected no threat and gladly installed clocks on towers and steeples,* thus in Gimpel's view subordinating its own liturgical practices to the increasingly materialist outlook of a society for whom 'time is money'.[77]

In other respects, too, the western Church was succumbing to the sensuous delights that previous ages would have thought too worldly. The early Church fathers of both east and west had deeply distrusted the intrusion of instrumental music into church services, and had sought to limit worship to the purity of the human voice alone. After Louis the Pious obtained an organ for his own personal use in 826 their application to church services spread rapidly in the west, and in the following century the Benedictines installed a huge organ of 40 pipes in Winchester Cathedral, requiring 70 men to pump its 26 bellows.[78] By the fourteenth century (by which time secular music was using as many as 36 different instruments)[79] a variety of string, wind and percussion instruments was being permitted in church, though the singing was still limited to plainsong.[80] In the fifteenth century trumpets were allowed to announce the elevation of the Host.[81] A compilation of liturgical music believed to date from the reign of Henry V in the early fifteenth century strongly suggests that by then lay ministrels were at work composing music for use in church.[82]

The increasing challenge to traditional pieties was reflected in the intellectual content of a new dramatic genre which developed late in the fourteenth century, the 'moral interlude', or, as it came much later to be called, the morality play, which reached its zenith in the fifteenth century.[83] Abstractions – Gluttony, Lust, Justice, the Church, Peace – were personified in earnest allegories. Many of the plays involved

---

* Though the belief that there was something blasphemous about imposing an artificial grid on time lingered on, to surface again when the development of the railways led to 'God's time' being replaced with a nationwide synchronization of clocks on noon as registered at Greenwich, instead of 'noon' following the sun west across the country.

disputations and trial scenes, and they provided a vehicle for points of view not hitherto advertised, attitudes that challenged the whole basis of the Age of Faith. 'Throughout the continent of Europe, the morality plays were increasingly invaded by scepticism: truth is rejected everywhere in the world, faith is sought but never found . . .' as Margot Berthold puts it.[84]

In this atmosphere, a significant change came over the presentation of the erstwhile 'religious' drama. Whether in pursuit of enhanced 'realism' or to gratify some other requirement, stage nudity became acceptable during the fourteenth century. In the early Adam plays, Adam and Eve had appeared modestly draped even before the Fall. By the fifteenth century they are appearing nude, as is Christ at His Crucifixion, and indeed scenes of His being stripped are played out with, says Mantzius, 'the intention of producing a half comic, half brutal effect'.[85]

Biblical re-enactments had inevitably dealt with violence, and had presented it, not off-stage as in the early Greek theatre, but in full view of the assembled faithful. Cain had killed Abel on stage in the twelfth-century Norman-French drama, but the stage directions had required Abel to wear a saucepan under his garment to ensure he was not hurt in the fray.[86] By the fourteenth century stage violence in the religious dramas was taking on a ghoulish and even sadistic quality. An enactment of the destruction of Jerusalem managed to work in the cooking and eating of a baby, and Nero ripping open his mother's womb to see where he came from, 'gory entrails, supplied by the local pork butcher, spilling from the victim', to quote Tuchmann.[87]

Discussing the English Towneley cycle of plays, Mantzius remarks:

> on the whole, the chief attraction of these plays . . . consisted of scenes of torture . . . the medieval mystery represented the horrors before the eyes of the audience, who did not wish to be spared a single detail . . . Not even a situation of the sublimest nature, such as the crucifixion of our Lord, escapes the general desire for vulgar realism. The act of nailing our Saviour to the Cross is spun out with long dialogues between the executioners, who pull his limbs with all their might to make them reach the place where the nails are to enter, and the hard work is accompanied by merry jokes.[88]

Cohen speaks of anguish being dragged out in the mystery plays almost beyond its real-life equivalent.[89] On the whole, clever substitution of dummies and copious supplies of ox-blood protected the actors from injury, but there was always the hope that someone would suffer real harm in the course of these simulations. 'All the tortured saints had constantly to be prepared for some serious physical injury', notes Mantzius. Priests playing the part of Christ were at maximum risk, and there are reports from the fifteenth century of performers losing consciousness, and even of mishaps that could come near to costing the life of a Judas or a Jesus.[90]

Sex accompanied violence. 'Sex and sadism were relished in the rape of Dinah, in the exposure of Noah naked and drunk, the sins of the Sodomites, the peeping of the Elders at Susanna', says Tuchmann,[91] and for Cohen, 'simulations of rape are taken to their limits with a shameless absence of all delicacy and reserve, a reversion to primitive pack instincts'.[92]

Sexuality – not the chaste, romantic yearning of the troubadours, but a more rumbustious approach to the delights of the flesh – had begun to surface in literature by the mid-thirteenth century, when, shortly before the first secular drama, there had appeared that celebration of wine and women, the *Carmina Burana*, 'one of the best known testimonies to unadulterated medieval sensual pleasure', as Berthold summarizes it.[93] By the mid-fourteenth century, Boccaccio, an avowed atheist (though late in life he was converted), wrote the *Decameron*, a bawdy romp whose contrast with the *Divine Comedy* of a generation earlier is highlighted by Thomas G. Bergin's comment that 'motivation is strictly worldly and pragmatic; the roll call of protagonists includes no saintly figure whose thoughts are on eternal things . . .'[94] Literature has begun its sensate progression from Platonic romanticism to crude physiology.

The uninhibited conduct of Boccaccio's characters mirrors a change in accepted moral standards which appears to have developed over the course of the late thirteenth century – in the public bath-houses, for instance,* behaviour became so promiscuous that the very word for bath-house, 'stew', came to mean brothel. Legislation, believed to date from the fourteenth century, sought to control the situation by insisting that the sexes be segregated, and that proprietors run their establishments for one sex or the other, but not both.[95] Homosexuality was, in the thirteenth century, far from tolerated (the body of the murdered Edward II was refused burial by 'most of the abbeys of the West [of England]' before being accepted by Gloucester at the behest of Edward's former friend, Abbot Thokey),[96] but the belief that it was becoming more generally practised was widespread, and was one of the many

---

* Rather rudimentary compared with their Roman predecessors. Baths were taken in wooden tubs with cloths along the bottom to protect from splinters (Gimpel, (1988), p.91).

accusations of sexual scurrility on which was based the suppression, early in the fourteenth century, of the Order of Knights Templar.[97] Roger Bacon, who died late in the thirteenth century, had attributed to 'unnatural debauchery', allegedly very prevalent at the time, the aetiology of a disease which B.L. Gordon, author of *Medieval and Renaissance Medicine*, equates with syphilis.[98]

As in imperial Rome, descriptions of, and anxiety about, venereal diseases begin to be voiced. Because there is no consistent medical terminology, it is impossible to be sure what malady or maladies are being discussed. The word 'syphilis', for instance, was not used before 1546, when it appeared in a poem as the name of a shepherd suffering from a disease to which his own name was subsequently transferred. Medieval writers refer to 'leprosy' and a 'burning disease' variously called by such names as 'Persian Fire' or 'St Anthony's Fire', a condition for which, in the twelfth century, brothel-keepers were required to dismiss any prostitute so affected.[99] Tuchmann writes of the fourteenth-century 'St Anthony's Fire' as a 'terrible rash . . . which by constriction of the blood vessels . . . could consume a limb as by some hidden fire and sever it from the body'. She says, however, that modern diagnosis tends to assume it was either erysipelas or ergot poisoning.[100] Fourteenth-century descriptions of so-called 'leprosy' frequently refer (in contradistinction to the disease called leprosy today) to genital ulcers and to the sexual transmission of the disease, and the medieval abhorrence of leprosy has in it a sexual element akin to today's horror of AIDS. Descriptions of 'Persian Fire' also appear to be describing syphilis, and it is these hints that lead some commentators to believe that syphilis was endemic in Europe prior to Columbus's return from the Americas, though his sailors may well have brought back the virulent strain which was to wreak havoc from end to end of Europe at the close of the fifteenth century.[101] People had feared the Black Death as the wrath of God, and there had been mass outbreaks of penitential hysteria. Now the same message was preached. Ulrich von Hutten, a young man who was himself to die of syphilis at the age of thirty-five, wrote resentfully of the divines who

imputed this disease to the wrath of God sent from heaven as a scourge for our wickedness, and took upon them thus to preach openly, as they had been admitted of council with God, and came to understand thereby, that men never lived worse, or so bad, as we.[102]

It may well be that as the great syphilis pandemic of the late fifteenth and early sixteenth centuries took its toll across Europe, such sentiments played their part in promoting the Puritan strand in the Reformation. Meanwhile another aspect of personal self-indulgence was becoming manifest – the increasing employment of contemporary craftsmen by the rich for purposes of personal gratification rather than to embellish churches and religious foundations. As Gimpel puts it, the 'rich and powerful . . . began to use their money to improve their personal comfort and satisfy their appetite for pleasure . . .'; and he confirms Sorokin's thesis when he adds:

> It was the kind of thing that must have happened in Athens in the fifth and fourth centuries BC . . . Throughout the fifth century sculptors had worked on buildings like the Parthenon; then, in the fourth century, Athens was ruined and rich individuals attracted sculptors like Praxiteles to pander to their egotistical tastes.[103]

Paraphrasing a contemporary writer, Barbara Tuchmann in *A Distant Mirror* reports that the new generation of knights 'sleep late between white sheets, call for wine on waking, eat partridges and fat capons, comb their hair to perfection, know nothing about the management of estates, and care for nothing but making money. They are arrogant, irreligious, weakened by gluttony and debauchery . . .' She produces ample evidence of the spectacular extravagance of the nobility of western Europe in the fourteenth century. Sumptuous banquets and ostentatious displays of clothing and jewels accompanied every ceremonial occasion. A description of one banquet is reminiscent of Nero's Golden House:

> The ceiling painted like a sky opened to allow the dinner to descend on machines resembling clouds, which raised the dishes again when they had been emptied. An artificial storm lasting half an hour accompanied dessert, dropping a rain of scented water and a hail of sweetmeats.

Contemporary recipes were offering forty kinds of fish and thirty different roasts. By the second half of the fourteenth century 'conspicuous consumption became a frenzied excess'[104] and spread to other classes than the aristocracy. 'In Germany and England . . . city life came to be distinguished by a boastful and competitive materialism.'[105]

Yet, as in the later Roman Empire, this opulence coincided with the cessation of the growth in general prosperity which had been evident over the preceding three centuries. Gimpel ascribes to a worsening climate and disastrous harvests the economic depression which was to last to the Renaissance.[106] Bad harvests and malnutrition may have lowered resistance to the devastating assaults of bubonic plague that intermittently swept across fourteenth-century Europe, though some scholars consider the Black Death may at least have improved the economic condition of the peasantry by enhancing their value as scarce labour. But there was another factor pauperizing and demoralizing the populace, and it, too, is an echo of late Rome – anarchy and brigandage.[107]

In England a statute of 1285 had required landowners to clear scrub and fill in ditches for a distance of 200 feet each side of the highway in order to deprive lurking robbers of cover. Some thirty years later, Oxford students, normally forbidden to carry weapons, were permitted to go armed when travelling.[108] Across Europe, brigand companies composed of outlaws, exiles and bankrupt adventurers had been on the increase throughout the thirteenth century, hiring themselves out to kings and courts, their commanders oscillating from odium to respectability as current employment prospects dictated. The knights, comfortable between their white sheets, had gone soft, the warriors were no longer willing to endure discomfort, they were 'unfit for the profession of arms'.[109] The solution was that adopted by both Greece and Rome in their period of decline: mercenaries. The wars of the fourteenth century, especially the Hundred Years War between England and France with its intermittent truces and demobilization of fighting men, greatly swelled the marauding bands of pillaging, deracinated ruffians.

In Italy these *condottieri*, or contract men, were to become a permanent feature of the social landscape. Tuchmann quotes from the letters of Francesco Datini, a merchant of Prato, who lived 'in daily dread of war, famine, pestilence and insurrection, believing neither in the stability of governments nor in the honesty of colleagues. ''The earth and the sea are full of robbers, and the great part of mankind is evilly disposed.'' '[110] Boccaccio's biographer speaks of the fourteenth century as a time of 'endemic crime on a continental scale'.[111] In England the House of Commons strove to mitigate the evil, petitioning the King that

whereas it is notoriously known throughout all the shires of England that robbers, thieves and other malefactors on foot and on horseback, go and ride on the highway through all the land in divers places, committing larcenies and robberies; may it please our Lord the King to charge the nobility of the land that none such be maintained by them, privately nor openly; but that they help to arrest and take such bad fellows.[112]

But 'robberies remain unpunished ... the land is inundated by homicides', declared the Bishop of Rochester.[113]

In France they

imposed ransoms on prosperous villages and burned the poor ones, robbed abbeys and monasteries of their stores and valuables, pillaged peasants' barns, killed and tortured those who hid their goods or resisted ransom, not sparing the clergy or the aged, violated virgins, nuns and mothers, abducted women as enforced camp-followers and men as servants. As the addiction took hold, they wantonly burned harvests and farm equipment and cut down trees and vines, destroying what they lived by, in actions which seem inexplicable except as a fever of the time or an exaggeration of the chroniclers.

Plague and brigandage had between them reduced the population of Europe by 50 per cent by the end of the century.[114]

'In the distracted 14th century ... the need for communion with God was never greater, nor less satisfied by His appointed agents', writes Tuchmann.[115] The Church had lost all claim to moral authority. Not only did rival popes contend for supremacy from their respective bastions in Rome and Avignon (where the walls of the papal study featured hunting and nude bathing in preference to devotional art), the Church itself was engulfed from top to bottom in 'worldliness'. Nor did the next century presage improvement. Holy poverty and clerical celibacy alike were jokes. Even the supposedly mendicant friars were living like lords. Every office was up for sale. Traffic in bogus relics reached unprecedented levels, the wonders of technology were prostituted, as in late pagan times, to deceiving the credulous with phoney miracles. At Boxley there was 'a lifesize figure of Christ which rolled its eyes, shed tears, and foamed at the mouth.' In Kent a similar device* 'nodded its head, winked its eyes, and bowed at the waist to receive the prayers of pilgrims'.[116]

The travail of pilgrimage that earned an indulgence for the penitent sinner had been commuted into a cash payment. Indulgences were bought and sold, and men paid others to complete the pilgrimage on their

---

* Possibly the same one. The source reference is ambiguous.

behalf. Pardoners criss-crossed the land, peddling salvation at a price. For an appropriate payment, release of the dead from purgatory could be arranged.[117]

Wave after wave of reformers had sought to purify the Church. The orders of both Carthusians and Cistercians dated back to the late eleventh century, and the Cistercians in particular, under the inspired leadership of Bernard of Clairvaux, and with renewed dedication to the Rule of St Benedict, founded numerous monastic communities throughout the twelfth century. Early in the thirteenth came the Franciscans, and shortly thereafter the Dominicans, another mendicant order, soon to earn a terrible reputation as zealous inquisitors. For now the Church was facing not just movements of renewal from within, but total rejection by disillusioned puritans who saw no hope of redemption for an institution so saturated by worldly greed and lust.

The Cathar heresy of southern France, suppressed by the Dominicans with the utmost ruthlessness during the course of the thirteenth century, was rooted in that disgust for the material world that had inspired the Manicheans of late imperial times, and had for a while seduced Augustine of Hippo. Their destruction failed to ensure the security of the Church. It was not just that the corruption and manifest abuses of a degenerate hierarchy were too notorious to be overlooked. In the midst of the rampant secularism of the fourteenth century, individual seekers after spiritual fulfilment turned increasingly to mysticism, to the deliberate attempt to transcend the material world in the pursuit of direct union with the unseen, a pursuit to which the priesthood was seen as irrelevant. The threat to the authority of the Church was obvious. But in spite of papal condemnations, devotional works streamed from the pens of such fourteenth-century mystics as the German Dominican Meister Eckhart who died in 1327, the English Richard Rolle (d.1349) and his contemporary, the author of *The Cloud of Unknowing*. In Thomas à Kempis may be found, in Tuchmann's words, 'a prolonged rhapsody on the theme that the world is delusion and the Kingdom of God is within . . . the life of the senses is without value . . . the world is an exile, home is with God'.[118]

'Mysticism,' says Frederick Artz, 'is . . . the tap-root of the Protestant Reformation.'[119] In England John Wycliffe, himself ordained, explicitly condemned the intervention of the priest between the soul and God, and set about translating the Bible into English to provide every soul with its direct guide to right living. Rejection of the priesthood led on, by logical steps, to the rejection of such sacraments as transubstantiation and confession, and ultimately of the Pope himself, or rather of the two popes, for this was the Avignon period. Wycliffe came to the conclusion that both were antichrists.[120] He escaped a martyr's death in 1384 only because a stroke cheated the executioners, but thirty years after his death his bones were ceremonially disinterred and burnt, and a year later the Czech Jan Hus, who had adopted many of Wycliffe's tenets, was burnt at the stake.

Sumption detects some attempt by the Church of the fifteenth century to assert unworldly values. There was in Rome, in 1424, a 'great bonfire of playing-cards, lottery tickets, musical instruments, wigs, and "such like effeminate vanities" '.[121] But the real scandals continued. Within a century of the death of their founder, Franciscan friars were being linked with the priests as venal, lecherous, grasping, frivolous and disrespectful of God.[122] Throughout the fifteenth century ecclesiastical acquisitiveness flourished unabated, the sale of indulgences and bogus relics ever-burgeoning.

On 31 October 1517 an Austin (Augustinian) friar named Martin Luther nailed to the door of the church in the university town of Wittenberg a paper listing 95 theses attacking current Church practices, largely in connection with the grant of indulgences. Christendom, at least as Europe had known it since the demise of Rome, was at an end.

Chapter 14

Post-Reformation Ambiguities: the Sixteenth to mid-Seventeenth Centuries

The Reformation convulsed Europe, as state by state the authorities took their stand for or against the papacy. Religion was the ostensible catalyst of the explosion, but Sorokin, far from regarding Protestantism as the start of a fresh otherworldly ('ideational') phase in the cultural cycle, saw in it rather a further development towards the sensate society whose sphere of influence had been gradually increasing since the twelfth century.[1] It is a view not shared by some of those who otherwise accept much of his thesis. Talcott Parsons, for instance, Sorokin's successor as chairman of the Harvard Department of Social Relations, challenged Sorokin's view that the Reformation in itself represents a turning to more secular values, holding that, on the contrary, the Reformation constituted an attempt to bring the secular world more fully into harmony with the religious.[2] Of far greater significance in the move towards more sensate values was Renaissance humanism, which affected all aspects of the religious divide.

The 'humanism' of the Renaissance carries no necessary connotation of human values or human welfare. It is false to see Renaissance humanism through the distorting glass of modern usage of the word, which was not applied to Renaissance developments until early in the nineteenth century, and was made more ambiguous by its later implication of atheism, of an ethical system derived solely from human norms.[3] The humanism of the fourteenth to seventeenth centuries remained fundamentally Christian, at least nominally.[4] The word 'humanista' came into use in the late fifteenth century by analogy with such designations as 'legista' or 'jurista', to indicate a professional teacher of a specific branch of learning; in this case, one concerned with *studia humanitatis*, an expression from classical Rome, where it signified the literary education worthy of a gentleman. It was an educational programme, not a philosophic attitude.[5]

The discipline developed within well-established systems of vocational training for government service and diplomacy, in particular the
ars dictaminis, which included the study of prose and poetry to foster
spoken and written articulacy and style, the composition of formal
documents, and the preparation of speeches and orations (ghost-writers
were as necessary to the medieval as to the modern statesman and
politician). There were links with the study of law, history and moral
philosophy.[6] The vocational strand was cross-fertilized in France by a
developing interest in classical Latin poetry, and in Italy by increasing
links with Greek-speaking Byzantium. Greek scholarship had begun to
make an impact even before the Turkish conquest of Byzantium in 1453
precipitated the westward flight of refugees – some of the Byzantine
scholars attending the Council of Florence in 1440, for instance, had
chosen to remain in the West.[7]

What distinguished the humanists from their professorial predecessors was their insistence on a return both to the language and to the
literature of classical Greece and Rome. The material available for study
rapidly expanded, as searches were instituted in monastic and royal
libraries, and a wealth of texts unearthed, including Lucretius, Tacitus
and hitherto unknown works by Cicero.[8] Scholars began to study Greek,
and to render Greek texts into a purified Latin, the language of western
scholarship.[9]

Many students of the Renaissance find puzzling this insistence of the
humanists on a return to the pure sources of classical Latin. Their verdict
tends to be that it was some sort of 'mysterious urge' or 'spontaneous and
natural development'. George Makdisi, in *The Rise of Humanism in
Classical Islam and the Christian West*, accuses them of 'Eurocentrici-
ty', and sees in humanism a late reflection of a development that had
taken place in Islam some centuries earlier, where the same insistence on
the purity of classical texts had been introduced in order to maintain the
pre-eminence of the Koran in uncorrupted form, and where a similar
curriculum had formed the basis of the education of the cultivated
Moslem and the government official. The high standards and evident
usefulness of Arab culture, well known and highly esteemed among the
Spaniards under Moorish rule, and easily accessible to Europeans at the
Spanish and Italian frontiers of contact with the Arabs,[*] induced among
Europeans a spirit of emulation that led them to seek a corresponding
well of excellence in their own past.[10]

---

[*] In Sicily, the conquering Normans modelled their state administration on their predecessors'
Islamic example.

Paul Oskar Kristeller, a leading authority on the subject, resists the suggestion that Renaissance humanism constituted a new philosophical insight; indeed, he remarks that humanist scholarship is not usually concerned with philosophical subjects, and when it is, it tends to be shallow.[11] But he does say that the humanists' respect for the culture of antiquity altered their viewpoint.

> When the Renaissance humanists called their studies the 'humani-
> ties', or *studia humanitatis*, they expressed the claim that these
> studies contribute to the education of a desirable human being, and
> hence are of vital concern for man as man.* They indicated a basic
> concern for man and his dignity, and the aspiration became quite
> explicit in many of their writings.[12]

'The assimilation of the moral and political theories of the Greek philosophers, and of the social and ethical assumptions implicit, for example, in the speeches and writings of Cicero, led inevitably to a conception of man as a rational and socially conscious being in his own right', says Antonia McLean in her *Humanism and the Rise of Science in Tudor England*.[13] A Florentine humanist of the mid-fifteenth century, Giannozzo Manetti, made extensive use of quotations from Cicero and Lactantius in his treatise on the dignity and excellence of man; and this became a favourite topic. Platonists and Aristotelians shared with humanists an increasing absorption in, and respect for, mankind. 'The three major intellectual currents of the early Renaissance were all concerned with the purpose of human life and with the place of man in the universe . . .'[14]

Whatever the connection between the return to classical roots and the scholarly exaltation of man, or between Arab and European scholarship, for Sorokin the pre-eminence in the scheme of things accorded by humanism to human beings is a further development of the progressive humanization of religion, a natural evolution in a species capable of self-consciousness and self-concern.†

---

* The humanist faith that man could be improved by education encouraged a mass demand for schooling. There was widespread lay generosity in the endowment of new schools and colleges. However, these institutions now came under lay, i.e. secular, rather than ecclesiastical supervision. Tawney makes the damning comment that 'King Edward VI's Grammar Schools are the schools which King Edward VI did not destroy' (Tawney, p.148) but McLean presents a rather different picture, saying that the old chantry schools whose assets passed to the Crown at the Dissolution were part of a system in decline, and where the schools really were in existence, they were largely restored and refounded as secular institutions (McLean, pp.75–83).
† This is a superficial summary. Sorokin's 'principle of immanent change' is complex, and is part

That there was a meeting of minds between the Arab and European humanists is evident from the opening words of the oration on the dignity of man delivered by the eminent fifteenth-century humanist scholar Giovanni Pico della Mirandola, which began by citing a Moslem intellectual, Abdala the Saracen, who, 'when asked what he regarded as most to be wondered at on the world's stage', answered that 'there was nothing to be seen more wonderful than man'.[15] This is the intellectual climate in which Shakespeare's Hamlet was to exclaim, 'What a piece of work is man! How noble in reason! how infinite in faculties! in form and moving, how express and admirable! in action, how like an angel! in apprehension, how like a god! the beauty of the world! the paragon of animals!'[16]

Indubitably, humanism exalted the individual human being. It was a characteristic tendency of the age, says Kristeller, 'to express and to consider worth expressing, the concrete uniqueness of one's feelings, opinions, experience, and surroundings', and with this tendency he equates the novel contemporaneous enthusiasm for portrait-painting.[17] But Renaissance humanism was not a simple endorsement of egotism. In spite of Sorokin's tart remark that humanist thinkers, particularly in France and Italy, were 'notoriously sensual in their ethical systems as well as in their conduct';[18] in spite of the unattractive picture painted by Artz of the vanity, arrogance and malevolence of some of the Italian humanists, 'who exhausted the resources of the Latin language to befoul each other's characters and explored the lowest depths of human nature to find fresh accusations', a pursuit of 'literary dunghills' which, says Artz, 'became for centuries a tradition of humanist scholarship';[19] there was a serious concern to appraise, in universal terms, the moral implications of man's privileged position in the universe. Ficino, a late-fifteenth-century philosopher-priest, had recognized the man-centred-ness with which 'man worships the eternal God for the sake of the future life', but his salvation was to be worked out by proving himself a worthy member of the human race, by loving other men as his equal, by being humane.[20] For Erasmus, the great but ultimately defeated humanist champion of toleration, freedom of conscience was the essential condition in which the exercise of a mature morality of personal responsibility could be enacted.[21]

Protestantism strongly endorsed humanism's stress on individual

of the validation of his theories which, as mentioned in the Preface, this book is not attempting to elucidate. The theory is dealt with in detail in Volume IV of his *Social and Cultural Dynamics*.

responsibility, but rejected its sunny exaltation of humankind. Theologians had returned with as much enthusiasm as educationalists to the study of the classical authorities – in their case, the patristic Fathers, including those who wrote in Greek, some of whose work now became available to the West for the first time.[22] The Protestant renewal of emphasis on the Fall, on the intrinsically depraved nature of man and his helplessness in the face of the omnipotent but inscrutable purposes of God, gave to the reformed religion that total submission to supernatural authority which Sorokin saw as constituting the essence of an ideational society.[23]

There was, however, a unique component in the Protestant re-emphasis on the reality and pre-eminence of godliness, and it goes far to explain Sorokin's conviction that the Reformation, despite its emphasis on spiritual regeneration, enhanced rather than hindered the rise of sensate values. This was the conviction that man's salvation is to be worked out not by withdrawal from the world but by the deepest possible engagement with it. Luther's 'conception of the calling', as Max Weber describes it in *The Protestant Ethic and the Spirit of Capitalism*, is, he says, unprecedented among ancient or medieval people. Catholicism had offered an honours degree in salvation, to be sought through pursuing a religious vocation, but for most of the rest of humanity there was only the pass degree of secular activity redeemed by a striving to minimize sinfulness. For Luther, 'the fulfilment of duty in worldly affairs [was] the highest form which the moral activity of the individual could assume . . . every legitimate calling has exactly the same worth in the sight of God'.[24]

A second revolutionary influence, explored in depth both by Weber and by R.H. Tawney in *Religion and the Rise of Capitalism*, stemmed from Calvin and the Puritan tradition, and it concerned the lending of money in return for interest; usury, in the language of the time. Diligent, sober, honest hard work was the hallmark of the elect of God, idleness almost as heinous a sin as drunkenness, lechery or theft, for at the day of reckoning all would be called to account for how they spent every second of their time on earth. It was right and proper that such labour should reap rewards in this world as well as in the next, and no blame attached to the enjoyment of a modest sufficiency. Monks and nuns who idled their time away in contemplation, and then expected the community to support them when they went round with the begging bowl, were among the most contemptible in this version of citizenship, and poverty a badge not of holiness but of failure, disgrace – even of classification as one of the horde of God's rejects: a goat, not a sheep. It was not a compassionate attitude, but mercy was not a dominant characteristic of the God of the Puritans – or of any other deity in the early ideational phase of a culture.

That is not to say that the elect were to luxuriate in the fleshpots of this world. The temptations to sin, not least the sin of idleness, proffered by possession of the wealth which diligence and temperance were likely to generate, were not underestimated. The obvious conclusion was that riches were not to be used for luxurious personal consumption, still less for ostentation or display. Simplicity and frugality were to be the watchwords of the Puritan. So what was to be done with the savings that inevitably accrued?

In some cultural settings, there would have been intermarriage with impoverished elements of the nobility, and the money would have found its way into land. The Puritan ethos sought to keep it productively employed.[25] To argue that the long-standing prohibition against usury, against lending money at interest, deserved to be interpreted with considerable liberality was not a Protestant innovation. The Roman Catholic Church had for long been struggling with the minutiae of what did, and what did not, constitute usury. Councils pronounced their verdicts, and Church courts, even as late as the sixteenth century, struggled to discipline the usurers, but it was, after all, in Catholic Italy that the great banks of the Lombards had developed, and for Luther, who maintained a total opposition to usury, the Church had already compromised too far.[*][26] Calvin's treatment of capital was, says Tawney, a watershed. It was no longer 'a matter to be decided by an appeal to a special body of doctrine on the subject of usury', but 'a normal and inevitable incident in the life of society', and Calvin dismissed biblical precepts to the contrary as being peculiar to their own time and place.[27] The Calvinists, who were on the whole townspeople engaged in manufacturing and commerce rather than the agricultural activities of the countryside, 'started,' says Tawney, 'with a frank recognition of the necessity of capital, credit and banking, large-scale commerce and finance, and the other practical facts of business life'.[28]

Sorokin, who was familiar with the work of Weber and Tawney, remained unconvinced by their claim that it was the theology of Protestantism that uniquely gave birth to capitalism. On the contrary, the acquisitiveness of capitalism and the emphasis on the concerns of this world as the arena of principal interest he sees as among the multiplicity of developments signifying the evolution towards an ever-more sensate

---

[*] The debate continues. Under the headline 'Call for laws to curb loan sharks' *The Times* of 25 September 1991 summarized the report *Unjust Credit Transactions* issued by the Office of Fair Trading.

society which was already manifest well before the Reformation.[29] His view is corroborated by the onward march of science, in the teeth of objections from all sides of the religious divide.

The humanist rediscovery of antiquity seized upon just those aspects of classical culture that Sorokin categorized as sensate. A. Wolf, in *A History of Science, Technology and Philosophy in the 16th and 17th Centuries* says that

> Modernism was essentially a revival of antiquity, brought about with the help of the literature of antiquity. And modern science, in its early stages, was helped more specifically by the astronomical, mathematical and biological treatises transmitted from ancient times, and most of all perhaps by the mechanical treatises of Archimedes and the technological works of Hero of Alexandria and Vitruvius ... modern science was a return to the implicit reliance on natural knowledge that was felt by the ancients. And the attention which the stubborn facts of Nature received at the beginning of the modern era, the stress laid on experience and more particularly on experiment were largely prompted by the spirit of naturalism exemplified and encouraged by the recovered literature of pagan antiquity ...[30]

'The rise of mathematical and astronomical studies in the West is linked also with the translations of Greek and Arabic scientific writings made during the 12th and 13th centuries ... Yet it appears certain that some of the most advanced Greek treatises on mathematics were translated only in the 16th century', says Kristeller.[31]

Parallel with the renewed enthusiasm for the naturalism of Greek science came a resumption of the late Hellenistic desire to short-cut the whole process of understanding, and thus mastering, the natural world: by recourse to the occult, to magic. In 1471 there had been published a Latin translation of the *Corpus Hermeticum*, the supposed writings of 'Hermes Trismegisthus', a guide to astrology and magic, utilizing the supposed properties of colours, minerals, etc. This hotch-potch of Greek, Jewish, Persian and Egyptian ideas enjoyed enormous prestige in the mistaken belief that it was of great antiquity, though by the early seventeenth century it had become clear that the compilation was not earlier than about the second to fourth centuries AD.[32]

Hermetic philosophy expounded the alchemical belief in a direct causal link between God and matter, exercised through the medium of the *pneuma*, the vital spirit, evolving from the most subtle manifestations of the celestial sphere to the gross manifestations of the material plane. In some developments of the theory, Christ himself came to symbolize the *pneuma*, the Philosophers' Stone, the symbol and instrument of perfection.[33] In sympathetic magic these Renaissance alchemists sought not to deny natural laws, but by the acquisition of arcane knowledge to understand the hidden relationships governing natural phenomena. Paracelsus, the influential Swiss physician, developed in the early sixteenth century a theory of medicine which, abandoning Galen (whose works he publicly burnt), saw man as a microcosm embodying all the influences of the macrocosm, sickness being the result of chemical imbalances.[34] He saw the fundamental elements not in the fourfold classic definition of fire, air, earth and water but in the trinity of sulphur, mercury and salt.[35]

Hermetic science attracted many Renaissance scientists who felt uneasy with descriptions of the natural world which excluded God. The sixteenth-century scholar-scientists were unwilling to accept a total split between scientific truth, proved by empirical observation and mathematical calculation; and moral or aesthetic truth subject to no such validation. They sought to bridge the gap by according a mystical significance to numbers, a sort of code communicated directly by God. The *Corpus Hermeticum* laid great stress on cabbalistic magic, on the power of numbers and the numerical significance of the letters in the Hebrew alphabet. 'Cabbala was in itself a sterile type of intellectual gymnastics [but] the belief in the importance of number as the basis of scientific knowledge was correct', says McLean, quoting Frances Yates's statement that ' "the subsequent history of man's achievements in applied science has shown that number is indeed a master-key, or one of the master-keys, to operations by which the forces of the cosmos are made to work in man's service" '. [*][36]

Numbers, liberated by the increasing use of Arabic/Indian numerals in place of the cumbersome Roman symbols, were the building blocks of Renaissance science. Medieval thinkers had sought, with Plato, to elucidate purposes, ends which things were designed to serve (the teleological approach). The Renaissance looked, with Democritus and the other classical atomists, for causes. They followed Pythagoras in preferring quantitative measurement to the Aristotelian exploration of qualities, a preference which, says Wolf, harmonized well with their rejection of analysis in terms of purpose, for 'mathematics was the one

---

[*] A fascinating account of the intellectual networks whereby cabbalistic enthusiasms came to percolate into scientific investigations is contained in Frances A. Yates's *The Art of Memory* (Routledge and Kegan Paul, London, 1966).

department of knowledge in which teleology had obviously no place'.[37] The question to be asked was not 'Why?' but 'How?', a tenet that has remained characteristic of science to our own day.

Mathematics were of immediate relevance to the development of navigation and astronomy. Technological improvements in sea-going vessels progressed during the fifteenth century from single-mast ships to three-masters in the course of fifty years.[38] The Greek geographers Ptolemy and Strabo were translated for the first time during the same century, and inspired a frenzy of exploration.[39] John Cabot visited Newfoundland in 1496, Vasco da Gama pioneered the sea route to India in 1497–9, Columbus explored across the Atlantic to America in the years 1492 to 1506, Amerigo Vespucci in 1499 and 1501 pushed south along the seaboard of the Americas, and in 1519–22 Magellan's ships completed the circumnavigation of the globe. The world was definitely round. There was a desperate need for new maps. Mathematicians, not least those of Tudor England, had an immense influence in furthering navigation and exploration, as they strove to incorporate new knowledge and to solve the problem of projecting a round world on a flat surface, a task whose solution by the sixteenth-century Fleming, Gérard de Mercator, had been generally adopted by the middle of the next century, though the problem of how to assess longitude when at sea without an accurate timekeeping device remained unsolved.[* 40]

Reliable astronomical tables were vital for navigation. The idea that the sun, not the earth, was the centre of our solar system had already been postulated about 250 BC by Aristarchus of Samos. Now Copernicus, a canon of the Church in Poland, pursued the notion, elaborating the hypothesis with 'a coherent planetary theory capable of furnishing tables of an accuracy not before obtained'. He realized the threat posed to religious orthodoxy, and only on his deathbed, in 1543, was his work published, attracting immediate condemnation from reformers and traditionalists alike. The noted Italian scholar and Dominican friar Giordano Bruno was convinced by Copernicus's arguments; and in 1600 was burnt at the stake in Rome for his heresy. When Galileo, in 1613, published articles betraying a sympathy with the Copernican viewpoint,

---

[*] The first necessity was to know, wherever the ship was, what o'clock it was by Greenwich Mean Time. The motion of the sea made pendulum clocks unreliable, and, with Britain's extensive maritime investment suffering a serious haemorrhage by shipwreck, Parliament in 1714 established a prize of £20,000, with a 'Board of Longitude' to supervise it, to be awarded for the solution of the problem of timekeeping at sea. It was won by John Harrison, who by 1773 had perfected a chronometer that not only solved the problem for seafarers, but was also the progenitor of generations of wristwatches.

he was warned by the Pope not to 'hold, teach or defend' the Copernican theory. In 1632 Galileo published a dialogue (a frequent method of airing, while distancing the author from, controversial views) 'concerning the two chief systems of the world, the Ptolemaic and the Copernican'. Initially this work received the Church's 'imprimatur', but when it was realized that one of the protagonists lampooned the Pope, Galileo was summoned to Rome, threatened with torture, forced to recant, and imprisoned.[41]

The invention of printing made it doubly difficult to control the spread of ideas. The art of papermaking was well established in Europe; the constriction on book production posed by the use of expensive animalskin in the form of parchment or vellum had long since gone. But throughout the medieval period, book production continued to be the work of the scribes. Knowledge of the early use of printing in China did not accompany the manufacture of paper west to Europe, probably because Islam insisted that handwriting was alone appropriate to reproductions of the Koran, and thus Islam posed a barrier to the onward transmission of the art of printing. European direct contact with Genghis Khan in the thirteenth century introduced knowledge of the carved wooden block, long used for printing textiles. The earliest book printed by carved block dates from 1423. Then came the great technological breakthrough, the European invention of movable metal type,[*] a consummation sought all over Europe, and first successfully achieved by a goldsmith of Gutenberg. Ancillary difficulties over inks and suitable paper surfaces were similarly overcome, and by 1500 there were some 1,700 printing presses operating in 300 towns, including Caxton's press set up in London in 1476.[42]

There were hundreds of print types and founts – Gothic, Italic, Roman, Greek, Hebrew. The market was predominantly secular. The reading public increased, and with it the demand for books in vernacular languages, ultimately fracturing the old international fraternity of Latin-educated scholars. This explosion of printed material, with its obvious potential for propaganda and subversion, frightened the authorities. Initially, the attempt to license publication rested with the Church. In 1529 Henry VIII issued a list of books prohibited for reasons of heresy, and in 1538 tried to extend the power to cover secular topics. The result was a mushrooming of illegal printworks. In England in 1550 an Act against Superstitious Books led to a holocaust of libraries comparable to that which Ammianius Marcellinus had reported in the fourth century

---

[*] The Chinese had invented a movable ceramic type by the mid-eleventh century.

AD. 'Every book with a cross was condemned for Popish; with circles: for conjuring.'[43] On the Continent, the Council of Trent, the Council of the Roman Church charged with the duty of countering Protestantism, instituted the Index of Prohibited Books in 1555. Copernicus's *De Revolutionibus* was immediately listed; Galileo's dialogue was to remain on the Index until 1822.[44]

The initial beneficiaries of the new spirit of enquiry were trade and commerce. The new wealth and rising inflation of the sixteenth century owed more to exploration and conquest than to technological innovation in industry or manufacturing, where change was modest. Knitting became popular in the fifteenth century – its anonymous inventor is not recorded, but during the 1590s William Lee[*] invented a mechanical knitter, a 'stocking frame', which was soon in general use and 'was the basis of all subsequent inventions in the field of knitting and lace-making machinery'; but the necessary improvements in its design did not occur until the eighteenth century.[45] Other improvements were being made in the textile industry, such as a foot-operated spindle leaving both hands free to manipulate thread, and there were various advances in the design of looms. Glassmakers of the sixteenth and seventeenth centuries rediscovered some of the lost arts of making coloured glass and imitation gems, coloured right through and not just on the surface, as was the case with much medieval stained glass.[46] But the real triumph of applied science lay in the future. Of this period Wolf concludes, and the editor of *A History of Technology* concurs, that 'though scientific progress has sometimes promoted practical applications, yet more often pre-existing technical methods have supplied the data for scientific discoveries; and perhaps most frequently technical inventions and improvements were made without any help from pure science', a judgement which he considers holds good until the late eighteenth century.[47]

It was the theatre that made the most flamboyant use of new technology. At Milan in 1490 Leonardo da Vinci had impressed his contemporaries with revolving scenery – perhaps a rediscovery of the Greek tri-sided revolving flats, though the description by his collaborator, Bellincioni, of a 'paradise with all the seven planets, and it turned in a circle' has led some to suppose that it was a form of revolving stage.[†] New editions of Vitruvius, replete with illustrations, were published in

---

[*] Widely but incorrectly reputed to be a clergyman. See the Rt. Revd Richard Rutt, 'The Genius of William Lee and the Knitting Industry Worldwide', *Knitting International*, Vol.96, No.1145 (May 1989), pp.90–2.

[†] The modern view is that a genuine revolving stage was not invented until 1896, when Max Reinhardt used it in Munich with electrically operated machinery (Berthold, p.607).

1521 and 1556, intended not for scholars but for general appreciation, and his descriptions of the traditional stage sets became familiar: palatial columns and statues for tragedy, urban street scenes for comedy, trees and mountains for *pastorales*.[48] Italian architects constructed stage sets based on his advice, and in 1565 Palladio went further, and at Vicenza built the magnificent Olympian theatre in imitation of the Roman theatre at its grandest, a stage backed by three great arches through which can be seen a perspective of streets, not painted on a flat but built in relief and in perspective, the furthest houses only two feet high. The problems of optical illusion that had taxed Democritus and Anaxagoras in the Greek theatre were back on the agenda. Palladio's theatre was unique, but the impact of the use of perspective was highly influential.[49] The dramatic packaging seems, however, to have been at the expense of the content. 'The more magnificent the stage became,' comments Berthold of this period of Italian theatre, 'and the more attention was claimed by its visual aspects, the more worthless became the literary content.'[50]

The spectacular scenery employed in the Italian theatre did not reach England until well into the seventeenth century – Shakespeare's theatre was still largely dependent on draped curtains – but England shared in the Continental enthusiasm for gimmickry and wizardry. Mystery plays specialized in technological feats in which, balanced by counterweights, people and scenes flew up and down, and platforms floated surrounded by clouds.[51] John Dee, alchemist and fellow of Trinity College, Cambridge, produced Aristophanes's *Peace* in 1546 and in one scene transported a man to heaven on the back of a bee to such good effect that it was reputedly done by magic.[52] In Germany a mid-sixteenth-century performance included the arrival and departure of a ship.[53] Minor miracles were achieved in which people suddenly appeared and disappeared, a fig tree withered and grew dry when cursed, two loaves and five fishes multiplied, and water turned to wine before people's very eyes. Continental producers scoured the land for engineers and 'fakers', and paid highly to engage them.[54] A passion play performed in Vienna in 1510 utilized the services of no fewer than eight 'masters of machinery'.[55]

In the end, says Cohen, the ingenuity defeated its own purpose so far as the mystery plays were concerned. The infinite grandeur, goodness and power of God had somehow become encapsulated in a man entangled in flying machines and trap doors.[56] For Mantzius, 'now the machinery took up a principal share of the general interest and degenerated into mere conjuror's tricks, which were enjoyed as such by the wondering public'.[57] A familiar criticism surfaces yet again: 'It is particularly the . . . 16th century, which presents at the same time the decline of the [ecclesiastical] drama and the highest perfection in the domain of scenery.'[58]

The days of the traditional religious plays were in any case numbered. One reason was the escalating costs of the spectacular productions now in demand. Gratuities – gifts rather than fees – to minstrels helping with the productions are recorded from the early fourteenth century, and token payments had been made to other participants, presumably to compensate for lost wages. At York by 1561 the Minstrels' Guild was itself responsible for one of the plays, a Herod play which formed an introduction to *The Three Kings*, and the assumption is that they contributed as paid professionals. From the early fifteenth century, however, other production costs took on increasing prominence, with the guilds protesting that they could not afford the levies being raised on them. By the sixteenth century, both the Church and the civic authorities were desperately seeking benefactors to pay off the creditors. Their fragile success could not survive the doctrinal dissensions of the Reformation.[59]

Corpus Christi day and its associated festivities had been instituted in veneration of the doctrine of transubstantiation. Since this doctrine was denied by the reformers, its celebration was inadmissible. The feast of Corpus Christi was abolished in England in 1548, and although briefly revived under Queen Mary in 1553, it was finally suppressed under Elizabeth in 1558. The play cycles maintained some vestiges of life, records in York persisting until 1579, Kendal recording a performance as late as 1612 – but Chester was prohibited from continuing in 1594. Much of the subject matter was becoming unacceptable, replete in the eyes of the reformers with superstition and idolatry. Plays celebrating the miraculous achievements of various dubious saints were equally suspect, and vanished within about a decade of the abolition, in 1537, of all feast days other than Christmas, Easter, St John (midsummer) and St Michael; a move inspired by Puritan horror of the red-letter days' tendency to promote the dreaded 'idleness'.[60]

Nor was it only in Protestant England that medieval religious drama came to an end. Counter-Reformation Catholicism was equally appalled by the depths to which the plays had sunk. By the fifteenth century one council of the Church was enacting that, while not prohibiting honest and devout representations, severe fines were to be imposed on clergy who permitted filthy verses, scoffing speeches and other such tumults as had come to disturb worship in church at the season of the Nativity.[61] By the mid-sixteenth century active attempts to suppress the performances were widespread. In Paris in 1542 the Procurator-General attacked the principal performing guild, the Confrères de la Passion, as ignorant and incompetent artisans, whose play, 'instead of elevating the minds of the people, becomes a scandal and a mockery'. Within a few years they had been deprived of any licence to perform sacred drama – though, significantly, they were specifically not prevented from putting on secular plays, at which they did not prove particularly successful, for by that time competent professional companies were at work in the secular theatre. 'The mysteries now definitely expired, not only in France, but everywhere', says Mantzius.[62]

The secular theatre, too, had its critics, but for the moment they were without decisive influence. On the contrary, for the first time since the demise of imperial Rome, purpose-built public permanent theatres were constructed, the earliest being the Hôtel de Bourgoyne in France, opened about 1550.[63] The first in England, the Theatre, opened in 1576, followed soon after by the Curtain. The Rose opened some eleven years later, and by 1600 there were five London theatres, plus some with names like the Red Bull which may have been inn yards.[*] [64] They were a development of the amphitheatrical bear-pit, and usually served the dual purpose of housing both theatrical performances and animal-baitings; indeed, the contract for the building of the Swan Theatre in 1595 and of the Hope about 1613 stipulated that the construction must provide for bull- and bear-baiting as well as for the performance of plays – the Hope was in fact a rebuilding of a pre-existing structure called the Bear-Garden.[†] [65] Actor-managers such as Philip Henslowe and Edward Alleyn owned lucrative bear-gardens, and Alleyn, who held the appointment of 'Master of the Royal Games of Bears, Bulls and Dogs', died a wealthy landowner, able to found and endow Dulwich College.[66]

In the early part of the sixteenth century, morality plays like *Everyman* provided a bridge between ecclesiastical and secular drama – many even calling for the same settings with Heaven and Hell hovering just off-stage. Having no particular anchor in the Church calendar, they were attractive to professional actors, who could perform them at any place and time. Their allegorical personifications allowed for humanist exploration of individuality, and although they risked a unidimensional

---

[*] Red Bull Yard, between St John's Street and Clerkenwell Green, was the site of a ruined priory. The monastic ruins may well have been used for a theatre, as was the case with the Blackfriars site near St Paul's, put to the same use by the company which included Shakespeare (Dryden, 1903, p.150, note 28).
[†] The Swan, the Globe, the Rose and the Hope were all clustered on Bankside, the Shaftesbury Avenue of Shakespeare's day.

characterisation that paved the way for such dramatis personae as Sheridan's Sneerwell and Backbite, Mantzius credits them with being 'the first to catch hold of the prominent features of the human character and expose each of them to contemplation, thus laying the foundation of future great pictures of character'.[67] The seeds of that exploration of character which was to come to such glorious fruition in the plays of Shakespeare were thus being sown.

The morality plays were essentially didactic – they were intended to be edifying and instructive. With the Reformation they became highly polemical, arguing the religious controversies of the day, and some began to substitute the desirability of learning for the previous pursuit of virtue as the theme. In the late sixteenth century, for instance, *The Marriage of Witte and Science* dealt with the mishaps of Wit in his endeavour to win the hand of his lady Science, the daughter of Reason and Experience.[68] A certain dreariness was infecting the genre, and as the century came to a close 'the drift of the drama was setting steadily away from the useful and toward the pleasant'.[69]

The increasing interest in human, rather than divine, concerns witnessed the transition from a drama featuring man struggling with the transcendental forces of good and evil to the hero contesting with the elements of history – the period, in terms of the evolution of Roman drama, of the lost plays of Naevius, Ennius, Pacuvius and Accius. These 'chronicle' plays date, in England, from about 1538, hymning the sources of national pride, and featuring such legendary heroes as King Arthur as well as the more recent monarchs who are the protagonists of so many of Shakespeare's historical plays.[70]

The comedies of Terence and Plautus had been approximately contemporaneous with Rome's chronicle plays. The synchronicity was to be repeated. Terence had been known, if not well known, in the early Middle Ages; indeed, the tenth-century German nun Roswitha had written some plays in imitation of him.[71] Now the humanists discovered Plautus. Some comedies based on his work were written in Italy during the fifteenth century, but the first evidence of actual performance comes in 1484 with the staging of a Plautus play on the Quirinal.[72] By 1520 both Terence and Plautus were being studied in English schools (in Latin), while in Italy endless modernized adaptations of Plautus were being staged.[73]

'Italian comedy . . . came into existence at the beginning of the 16th century under the direct stimulus of the two Roman playwrights', says Duckworth.[74] The same was not quite true of England, where John A Wodde, court singer and player of virginals to Henry VIII, more familiar under the name John Heywood, was writing farces credited with marking the transition from medieval interlude to such Elizabethan comedies as *Gamma Gurton's Needle*.[75] However, the 1552 success, *Ralph Roister Doister*, derived from Plautus's *Miles Gloriosus*; and Shakespeare took the plot of *A Comedy of Errors* from the Latin *Menaechmi*.[76]

The comic playwrights were not the only legacy Rome bequeathed to the dramatists of the Renaissance. 'In the course of one century,' remarks Berthold, 'the Renaissance theatre went through a quick-motion repetition of the development of the Roman theatre.'[77] Interest moved forward two or three Roman centuries, and fastened on Seneca, whose influence becomes detectable by the fourteenth century – the library of Charles the Wise of France was among those to include Seneca's works.[78] As early as 1314 there is evidence from Italy of a play called *Ecerinis*, written in Latin and based on Seneca.[79] The first stage performance of Seneca is dated to 1486 in Rome.[80]

The attraction of Seneca is another indication of the extent to which the Renaissance was permeated by the sensate values of imperial Rome. As J. Wight Duff points out in his *Literary History of Rome in the Silver Age*: 'As a force at the birth of modern drama [Seneca] completely eclipsed the other dramatists of antiquity: Sophocles counted for very little, Aeschylus for less, and Euripides mainly for as much of his spirit as operated through Seneca', whom contemporary taste rated well above Euripides.[81] Duckworth remarks that

> It seems rather ironical that the doubtless superior tragedies of Ennius, Pacuvius and Accius were lost and that the Italian, French and English dramatists of the Renaissance and after found in Seneca the very qualities they desired and could use to create a drama greater than their model. It is very possible that Seneca's plays appealed far more to the Renaissance playwrights than the less sensational and less rhetorical tragedy of the early republic would have done, had it survived to modern times.[82]

Gareth Lloyd Evans, in his essay 'Shakespeare, Seneca and the Kingdom of Violence', after cataloguing the many respects in which the Elizabethan playwrights echoed Seneca in both the content and the structure of their plays, adds that Seneca's most compelling appeal for them lay in his exploitation of the themes and usages of blood, revenge and cruelty. He postulates 'the possible existence in humanity of a primordial streak of cruelty', but does not explore why different epochs should vary in the extent to which they regard indulgence of the streak as acceptable.[83]

The flood-tide of Senecan blood that surges through the drama of the sixteenth century was fed by streams that had been gathering force for several generations. The introduction of Hell into the mystery plays had already opened up an appropriate setting for the exploration of violence and horror. In the new century the plays became more horrific than ever – reports of a performance in France in 1547 speak of the bodies of the Holy Innocents made to spurt blood, saints having their eyes gouged out, and when a victim is 'burnt alive', the artificial body was filled with real bones and bowels to produce the correct smell.[84] Cohen even holds the mystery plays in part responsible for the relish with which the torturers and executioners of the Reformation and Counter-Reformation went about their business of discouraging heresy.[*]

Elizabethan audiences loved brutality with a relish reminiscent of the Roman amphitheatre. They delighted in the sight of dogs mauled by lions, a bear set on by huge bulldogs, a terrified monkey tied to the back of a pony as it kicked out at attacking dogs, a blind bear whipped by seven or eight men.[85] Fearing that the attraction of the theatre might pose some threat to animal-baiting as a recreation, the Privy Council in 1591 forbade theatrical performances on Thursdays, the usual bear-baiting day, but the threat cannot have been very serious. When in 1613 the Bear-Garden was rebuilt as the Hope Theatre, Tuesdays and Thursdays were reserved for animal-baiting, but these occasions became so popular that the name Bear-Garden was reinstituted.[86] Advertisements wooed audiences by emphasizing the goriness of the plays, playbills for *Henry IV* mentioning inclusion of 'the battell at Shrewsburie'; *The Merchant of Venice* sought playgoers with promise of 'the extreme cruelty of Shylocke the Jew towards the said Merchant, in cutting a just pound of his flesh'.[87]

Gorboduc, the first recorded full-length tragedy in English, was produced in 1560, just before English translations of Seneca began to appear.[88] It tells the story of a king's son who kills his elder brother, whereupon the mother kills the murderous son, the people rise in revolt

---

[*] Since the tortures portrayed in the mystery plays were based on the accounts of the sufferings of the martyrs of the Roman Empire, Lecky's comment is apposite. 'There was a time when it was the just boast of the Romans that no refinements of cruelty, no prolongations of torture, were admitted in their stern but simple penal code. But all this was changed. Those hateful games, which made the spectacle of human suffering and death the delight of all classes, had spread their brutalizing influence wherever the Roman name was known, had rendered millions absolutely indifferent to the sight of human suffering, had produced in many, in the very centre of an advanced civilization, an exultation in watching the spasms of extreme agony' (Lecky, Vol.1, p.467).

and kill both the queen and the king, the nobles annihilate the rebels, then quarrel over the crown and kill one another. All these deaths, in the tradition of Greek tragedy, take place off-stage and are reported by messengers.[89]

A generation later, when Thomas Kyd, in *The Spanish Tragedy*, set out to elaborate a similar tale of revenge, he ensured that the mayhem occurs in full view of the audience. Characters are hanged and stabbed, commit suicide, and one bites out his tongue in order to be incapable of responding to torture. Kyd's debt to Seneca is undisguised, and he quotes him directly, using Senecan tags in translation. The date at which this play was written is uncertain, possibly in the late 1580s. It enjoyed enormous success in the period 1592–7,[90] during which, on 23 January 1595, Shakespeare's *Titus Andronicus* was staged. Here is murder and rape, the hands and tongue cut from the rape victim, the hand cut from Titus in return for the promise that his sons will be ransomed, but they are murdered, so is their nurse, as is the messenger, and the sons of a villainess who is also murdered but not before she has been served (*à la* House of Atreus) with a pie containing her murdered sons; various murders follow, including that of the rape victim by her father. 'The piece,' says the theatre critic J.C. Trewin, 'a shocker to outmatch *The Spanish Tragedy*, triumphed in its own period. Its violence, 13 deaths of one kind and another, and more to come, transcended Kyd's: Hieronimo biting out his own tongue was no real competitor to the involuntary cannibalism of Tamora, the final Thyestean feast.'[91] The corpses piling up in the last scene of *Hamlet*, the atrocious on-stage blinding of Gloucester in *Lear*, repeat the theme, and Webster's *Duchess of Malfi* and *The White Devil* enjoy similar wallows. The Elizabethans, says Trewin:

> wanted a few direct hours of murder and rapine: it was nothing odd to them to watch a bear-baiting while lute music drifted across the river; and they saw nothing strange when Marcus Andronicus, instead of bringing a surgeon to his niece, the ravished and lopped Lavinia, addressed her in a stream of classical conceits.[92]

There was even the excitement of the on-stage violence spilling over into the audience; in November 1587, when a scene in *Tamburlaine* required the Governor, hanging in chains from his own walls, to be shot, the actor missed his (presumably suitably padded) target, killing a child and a pregnant woman, and hurting another man in the head 'very sore'.[93]

Dramatic critics have argued ever since as to whether the 'revenge' tragedies were grounded in any coherent view of life, or whether they were simply playing to the gallery of essentially ghoulish contemporary taste. Glynne Wickham, writing of the secular drama of the late fifteenth and early sixteenth centuries, considers the ethic of plot and moral conclusion to be Christian,[94] but this is far from evident in post-Reformation English drama. The frame of reference of *The Spanish Tragedy*, for instance, though the setting is vaguely contemporary, is entirely pagan; all the deities referred to by name are pagan (Flora, Cupid, Venus, Mars, et al.); and the only overtly Christian reference occurs when a character is offered a sword-hilt and invited to 'swear on this cross'.[95] Isabella, wife of the Marshal of Spain, mentions cherubins (*sic*) and voices comfortable sentiments:

> The Heavens are just; murder cannot be hid;
> Time is the author both of truth and right,
> And time will bring this treachery to light.[96]

But time does no such thing, the Heavens do not prove just, and Isabella goes mad and kills herself. Moelwyn Merchant, in *Creed and Drama*, detects in the 'revenge' dramas a 'morbidity of tone' combined with the ostensible moral purpose, and in the case of one dramatist in particular, Cyril Tourneur, who wrote *The Revenger's Tragedy*, 'a constant shifting of tone between moral judgement and depravity'. 'The mind of the dramatist moves along the traditional way of penitential purgation, but his senses are committed to the rank decadence.'[97]

Kyd himself was arrested, and probably tortured, on suspicion of atheism and blasphemy in 1593 – a date subsequent to the production of this play, so the experience does not account for his preoccupation with violence. He maintained that the incriminating papers found in his room were not his, but Marlowe's, and he was released.[98] Marlowe flaunted himself as an atheist and a blasphemer; he was arrested shortly after Kyd, and though released, was stabbed to death in a tavern brawl a few days later, in May 1593. Flamboyant in his homosexual refusal to be constrained by Christian morality, he campaigned actively against Moses and Jesus as frauds, and dismissed religion as appropriate only for primitive peoples.[99]

Yet his best-known work, *Dr Faustus*,[*] is riddled with spiritual

---

[*] The first recorded performance dates from 1594, after Marlowe's death, but this may have been a revival. It is uncertain when it was written, but probably in 1592 (Marlowe, pp.6–8). It may be mere coincidence, but one of Faustus's feats is to free from papal confinement a character called 'Saxon Bruno', who is spirited over the Alps to Germany. It was in 1592 that Giordano Bruno (see

ambiguity. The protagonist, symbolic of Renaissance man's proud aspirations, seeks through knowledge to obtain power over the whole created world. A hundred years later such an ambition would be universally esteemed, but for Marlowe its satisfaction involves conspiring with the Devil; 'a lurking sense of damnation *precedes* the invocation to Mephastophilis . . . The free-thinking Renaissance humanist only hides a traditionalism which is basically mediaeval,' says Steane in *Marlowe: A Critical Study*.[100] Throughout the play Faustus argues with himself as to whether he should or should not repent of what he is doing, pitting his refusal to believe in an afterlife that can condemn him to Hell ('No, these are trifles and old wives' tales')[101] against an inner conviction that wrings from him the chilling cry, 'See, see where Christ's blood streams in the firmament!'[102] 'Faustus,' sums up Steane, 'is about evil living and consequently desperate dying.'[103] The play's power to project an atmosphere of transcendent evil was attested in its own time by a performance in Exeter during which the actors sensed the presence on stage of an extra character, and, believing they had in truth raised the Devil, aborted the performance, everyone, actors and audience, fleeing for the door. The players, 'contrary to their custom, spending the night in reading and in prayer, got them out of the town the next morning'.[104] Prynne, writing in the next century, has heard a similar story, 'the truth of which I have heard from many now alive, who well remember it', concerning the 'visible apparition of the Devil on the stage at the Belsavage Playhouse in Queen Elizabeth's days (to the great amazement both of the actors and spectators) while they were there profanely playing the *History of Faustus* . . .'[105] A generation later, when Ben Jonson wrote *The Alchemist*, the whole topic of acquiring magical powers by dabbling in the occult was to be treated as a romp, the cozening of gullible dreamers by charlatans.

For George Steiner, writing in *The Death of Tragedy*, Shakespearian tragedy, like that of the Greeks, inhabits a world where 'mortal actions are encompassed by forces which transcend man'. Men still hold to such concepts as the presence of the supernatural in human affairs, to belief in grace and divine retribution, to the notion that the structure of society is a microcosm of the cosmic design, and that history conforms to patterns of justice and chastisement as if it were a morality play set in motion by the gods for our instruction. Not until Racine, in Steiner's opinion, is the watershed reached after which the triumph of rationalism and secular metaphysics marks a point of no return; in England he considers Milton

p.251, above) was betrayed to the Inquisition while on a visit to Venice.

the last major poet to assume the total relevance of classic and Christian mythology.[106]

There is little that is overtly religious in Shakespeare, a lacuna which has left his admirers free to claim his allegiance to all denominations and none. In his *Landmarks of Contemporary Drama*, Chiari, discussing twentieth-century gratuitous dramatic violence, contrasts it with sixteenth-century usage, acknowledging that though the religious substrata had disintegrated at the Renaissance and was never explicitly stated in Shakespeare, nevertheless the violence is not meaningless. The violence of Othello, he says, is intent on destruction in order to purify; Lear's world is the violence of chaos let loose – archetypal, a mirror of man *sub specie aeternitatis*; Gloucester's blinding is symbolic – of the loss of truth in the world of Lear.

> The violence of tragedy is a violence which is neither social nor gratuitous or sadistic, but part of the means to restore the temporarily disrupted poetic justice of a timeless world. This violence has been given a style which excludes any possible naturalistic interpretation . . .[107]

Kitto, while recognizing that such naturalistic touches as the true-to-life juxtaposition of tragic and comic scenes and the introduction of character vignettes in Shakespeare's tragedies mark a departure from the canons of the Greeks, nevertheless sees *Hamlet* as concerned fundamentally with the problem of evil, and therefore a profoundly religious play in the Greek mould. 'The conception which unites these eight persons [who die] in one coherent catastrophe may be said to be this: evil, once started on its course, will so work as to attack and overthrow impartially the good and the bad.' To reduce the play to a character study of a man with a fatal flaw, to whit procrastination, is, in his view, to secularize and romanticize it.[108] For Lloyd Evans, on the other hand, while a play such as *Richard III* indeed expresses a 'significant truth about the relation of mankind to the forces of evil in the world', it is Shakespeare's 'concern to put man in the foreground of his plays, and to explore the often agonizing irony of potential wrecked by weakness' that justifies the evocation of evil and violence.

> [N]ot only is the relationship of a man to something outside himself being explored, but . . . the man himself is being explored . . . In the final analysis, it is simply the word 'humanity' which distinguishes

Shakespeare's work from that of Seneca and Seneca's Elizabethan followers.[109]

Bernard Crick believed that Shakespeare deliberately excluded all references to Christianity, and even Christian suppositions, from his *Lear* in order to free the play from any specific historical dimension. *Lear*, says Crick, remains an exposition of 'the doom of tragedy and grief ... of man's mortal and perhaps salvationless lot'.[110] It was this very aspect of Shakespeare that Dostoevsky, writing from the bosom of Holy Mother Russia, found intolerable. 'The ancient tragedy was a form of worship, but Shakespeare was despair ...'[111] George Bernard Shaw, too, considered that Shakespeare incorporated no philosophy other than despair at the human condition. 'He would really not be great at all,' he wrote in the preface to *Back to Methuselah*, 'if it were not that he had religion enough to be aware that his religionless condition was one of despair.'[112] 'As flies to wanton boys are we to the gods', he had written in *King Lear*. 'They kill us for their sport.' Life, says Macbeth, 'is a tale told by an idiot, full of sound and fury, signifying nothing'.[113]

If we can endure so bleak a message, it may be because the sublimity of Shakespeare's poetry acts to console us, as Nietzsche saw the music reconciling the Greek soul to the plays of Aeschylus and Sophocles. As Shaw put it, Shakespeare's word-music is irresistible to the English.[114] Tolstoy was deaf to Shakespeare's poetry.

> No living men could or can say, as Lear says ... that the heavens would crack with shouting, or that the winds would burst, or that the wind wishes to blow the land into the sea, or that the curled waters wish to flood the shore ...[115]

For fifty years, he says, he has read Shakespeare, seeking in English, and in Russian and German translations, to understand the veneration in which Shakespeare is held. Unentranced, he finds fault with Shakespeare for plagiarizing his plots; for manipulating into ludicrous and impossible situations a cast of characters all of whom speak 'Shakespearian', a language limited to a small range of interchangeable stereotypes; and for the dreary mirthlessness of his comedy. Then he comes to the real burden of his song: Shakespeare exemplifies the view

> that no definite religious view of life was necessary for works of art in general, and especially for the drama; that for the purpose of the drama the representation of human passions and characters was

264

quite sufficient; that not only was an internal religious illumination of what was represented unnecessary, but art should be objective, i.e. should represent events quite independently of any judgement of good and evil.

And he concludes, 'The fundamental inner cause of Shakespeare's fame was and is . . . that his dramas . . . corresponded to the irreligious and immoral frame of mind of the upper classes of his time.'[116]

For Tolstoy, drama should serve the development of religious consciousness, a task for which it had failed to find a form in post-Reformation Christianity.[*] 'The drama which has no religious element at its foundation is not only not an important and good thing . . . but the most trivial and despicable of things.'[117]

Sixteenth- and seventeenth-century Puritans entirely agreed.

Disquiet about the degeneracy of secular entertainment resurfaces in the decrees of councils and synods of the pre-Reformation Church during the thirteenth-century, including the provision that clergy indulging in scurrilous rhymes as jesters and stage-players should have their heads shaved, thus losing their clerical tonsures.[118] Warnings about the use of churchyards and other church property for unseemly cavortings, and exhortations to clergy to mend their ways on pain of assorted forfeitures of stipend were issued at intervals during the fourteenth, fifteenth and sixteenth centuries.[119] The Bishop of Exeter in 1352 prohibited 'lewd' plays in his diocese.[120] Usually it was only the clergy who were abjured to abstain from theatricals, others being put under similar injunctions only on Sundays and holy days, but in 1571 a Protestant council at La Rochelle had taken the further step of pronouncing it unlawful for a lay Christian, too, 'to act, or to be present at any comedies, tragedies, plays, interludes, or any other such sports, either in public or in private chambers'.[121]

Control of dramatic performances by the civic authorities, as distinct from ecclesiastical exhortation and discipline, was provoked in Tudor England, as in ancient Rome, by political rather than moral considerations. Public order was at stake, for in addition to the usual disturbances such as pickpocketing associated with large assemblies of people, the stage polemics of the morality plays after the Reformation provoked responses of glee or indignation among spectators that soon led to fisticuffs, and rumpus in the streets.[122] In 1533 'interludes' on controversial matters were forbidden.[123]

[*] For a full development of his theme, see his *What is Art?*.

Three different authorities appear to have been involved in permitting or forbidding performances: the Master of Revels, a court official appointed to the Lord Chamberlain's office by Henry VIII in 1544 with the task of promoting mirth while preserving good order; the Privy Council, issuing instructions whose enforcement was the task of the local magistrates; and the local civic dignitaries. Licences to perform were introduced in the City of London in 1527. In 1547 the Privy Council prohibited all performances for two months on the grounds that they were seditious. Evidence that there was active enforcement of censorship comes in 1552, when a poet was 'thrown into the Tower for the offence of "making playes" '.[124]

Censorship continued under Mary and Elizabeth, and in 1559 it was enacted that no play be performed unless it had been approved by the mayor, two justices of the peace and the Lord Lieutenant, general oversight of whom was later accorded to the Master of Revels. A royal licence issued to five of Lord Leicester's servants in 1574 permitting them to perform all kinds of stage plays, provided they had first been submitted to and approved by the Master of Revels, makes it clear that his authority was by then extending beyond the court, and in 1581 he was formally empowered to vet all stage plays, and could remove oaths, profaneness and obscenities, personal attacks and political indiscretions. In addition, the Commissioners for Religion had responsibility for licensing the publication of scripts.[125]

For the Puritans, these powers were inadequate to control what they saw as a socially and spiritually pernicious institution. The arrival in northern Europe during the sixteenth century of touring companies from the Italian *Commedia dell'Arte* had introduced a new licentiousness. Essentially, the performances were based on improvisation, not scripts, which carried the danger that 'the more artless improvisation becomes, the more trite the jokes and the more obscene the subjects, the closer is the danger of decadence, of debasement into mere vulgarity', to use Berthold's words.[126] Moreover, they employed actresses, and every excuse was sought – such as scenes of madness, shipwreck or rescue from fire – to present them denuded of their clothes. It is probable that the actresses were seen at Queen Elizabeth's court, but there is no contemporary record of public performances.[127] In Paris the *Confrères de la Passion*, the actors who had been barred from further performance of mystery plays, were working cheek by jowl with these touring companies. A petition to the King of France stated that

there is also another evil committed and tolerated chiefly in your city of Paris on Sundays and holidays . . . viz, the public plays and performances which are exhibited on the said Sundays and holidays by foreign Italians as well as by Frenchmen, and, above all, those which are represented in a cesspool and house of Satan, named the Hôtel de Bourgogne, acted by those who unjustly call themselves Passion Brothers of Jesus Christ. In this place thousands of scandalous meetings are held, to the prejudice of respectability and female chastity, and to the ruin of poor artisans' families, of which the low hall is quite full, and who more than two hours before the play commences pass their time in indecent talk, with card and dice, in revelry and drinking . . . out of which arise many quarrels and fights.[128]

The Privy Council had, in 1572, introduced an Act for Restraining Vagrants. 'All bearwards, common players of Enterludes, counterfeit Egyptians etc.' were to be 'adjudged and deem'd rogues, vagabonds and sturdy beggars', and were to be branded 'R' (for 'rogue') on the left shoulder, though liveried troupes attached to the household of a baron or above were exempted from this provision.[129] In the same year, and again in 1574–5, plague gave the magistrates in the predominantly Puritan city of London an excuse to ban all theatrical performances. In 1575 actors were expelled from the city. It may well have been this denial of access to the inn-yards which had hitherto provided their stage that prompted Richard Burbage, of Lord Leicester's Men, to set about the construction, in 1576 on Finsbury Fields outside the Lord Mayor's jurisdiction, of England's first permanent playhouse, the Theatre (where the company were still playing when Shakespeare joined them some years later).[130]

In the following year came the first tract in what was to become a sustained attack on the whole secular theatre. John Northbrooke, a Devonian and a clergyman of Puritan persuasion working in Gloucester-shire, was more moderate than some of his successors, for while he thoroughly disapproves the popish institution of 'idle holidays', he does not share the view of some of his Puritan contemporaries that *all* games and pastimes are forbidden the true Christian. 'I will not be so straight or scrupulous, for I say with St Augustine that it is the part of a wise man sometimes to recreate himself and rejoice the mind, that he may . . . more cheerfully return to his ordinary labour and vocation.'[131] However, he considers it would be all to the good if 'dicers, mummers, idlers, drunkards, swearers, rogues and dancers, and such as have spent and made away their living in belly cheer and unthriftiness were straightly

punished',[132] along with blasphemers, tosspots, whoremasters, 'enter-
lude players' and considerable further categories of undesirables.[133] The
theatre he regards as a wholly sinful waste of time. There

> you will learn how to be false, and deceive your husbands, or
> husbands their wives, how to play the harlots, to obtain one's love,
> how to ravish, how to beguile, how to betray, to flatter, lie, swear,
> forswear, how to allure to whoredom, how to murther, how to
> poison, how to disobey and rebel against princes, to consume
> treasures prodigally, to move to lusts, to ransack and spoil cities
> and towns, to be idle, to blaspheme, to sing filthy songs of love, to
> speak filthily, to be proud, how to mock, scoff and deride any nation
> . . . shall you not learn then at such enterludes how to practise
> them?[134]

He backs his opinions with copious references to the authority of the
Primitive Church.

The recently built Theatre and its younger sister the Curtain
Northbrooke equates with brothels and stews. Far better do as Scipio
Nasica had done, and have these dens of iniquity destroyed.[135] The next
pamphleteer, Stephen Gosson, himself a repentant actor and playwright
who was later ordained, was more concerned about this aspect of the
contemporary theatre than about the content of the plays, some of which
he thought perfectly harmless in themselves, if read rather than put into
production. Nor was he against the indulgence in music and clothes
which accompanied performance – it was the opportunity afforded by
live theatre for disorderly conduct on the part of the audience that led him
to call for restrictions. Ovid's account of Roman theatre was paralleled
in the theatre of his own time, Gosson averred, with prostitutes searching
out customers among the audience even if there was not, as at Rome,
'any filthiness in deed . . . committed within the compass' of the theatre.
Taverns in the vicinity were renting out every spare room, not to mention
private houses pretending to be giving music lessons should the frequent
comings and goings of clients attract the attention of the authorities.[136]

Next to enter the lists, in 1580, was an anonymous author generally
believed to have been Anthony Munday, like Gosson a reformed
playwright. Unlike Gosson, who defended many of his fellow players as
decent, modest and of good reputation,[137] Munday castigated every
aspect of the theatre, including the actors, whose private lives mirrored
their stage roles as roisterers, brawlers, ill-dealers, boasters, lovers,
loiterers and ruffians. He too is disgusted by the behaviour of the

audience, contradicting Gosson and maintaining that the harlots press to the forefront and, without respect of the place and company which behold them, 'commit that filthiness openly which is horrible to be done in secret . . .' Worst of all were the plays supposedly portraying Biblical stories, wherein 'these blasphemous players are so corrupted with their gestures of scurrility and so interlaced with unclean and whorish speeches that it is not possible to draw any profit out of the doctrine of their spiritual moralities'. He translated and published Salvianus's diatribe against the late Roman theatre, and much of his own *Blast* repeats the accusations of blasphemy, lechery and general debauchery advanced by the fifth-century Marseilles presbyter.[138]

Munday's recourse to Salvianus illustrates that the tract-writers, like the scientists and the theologians, were finding in the return to the literature of antiquity ample ammunition for their cause. Phillip Stubbes, although not himself in Holy Orders, was a devout Calvinist, and in the ten (out of 200) pages of his 1583 publication *The Anatomy of the Abuses in England* devoted to ills for which the theatre could be held accountable, he quotes from the writings of Tertullian, Augustine, Chrysostom and Lactantius, as well as showing familiarity with the judgements of the early Church councils. His descriptions of performance are vivid: 'such wanton gestures, such bawdy speeches, such laughing and fleering, such kissing and bussing, such clipping and culling, such winking and glancing of wanton eyes and the like . . . as is wonderful to behold'. All this enacted, of course, by boys. Small wonder that after the show 'they play the Sodomites'.[*][139]

Munday concludes with a reminder of the 20,000 killed when God in his wrath permitted the collapse of the Roman amphitheatre at Tidena.[†] An earthquake on a Sunday in 1580 caused a panic in English theatres, leading to casualties and some heightened guilty consciences. The English theatres were wooden structures, suffering the structural instability that had undermined confidence in the older type of Roman theatre. When, on a Sunday in 1583, the upper gallery of the Paris (Bear) Garden collapsed with loss of life and numerous injuries, many believed it a direct punishment for profaning the Sabbath. The incident figured widely in the growing pressure, as much from traditionalists as from Puritans in the Church, to keep holy the Lord's Day, a pressure which

---

[*] Ben Jonson, in *The Devil is an Ass* (Act II, Scene viii), includes a dialogue describing the off-stage behaviour of a youth playing female roles, who continues to wear female clothing and 'talk bawdy' at an off-stage party (Mantzius, Vol.III, p.233).

[†] During the reign of Tiberius.

ecclesiastical discipline was incapable of enforcing, and Parliament was prevented, by royal veto, from endorsing.[140]

Throughout Elizabeth's reign, the attempts by Sabbatarians to enforce Sunday observance had been largely thwarted. Neither local parish officials nor potential witnesses were avid in ensuring that ecclesiastical discipline was observed, and although there were a number of initiatives in Parliament aimed at preventing Sunday trading and entertainment, these failed when opposed by the Sovereign, whose opposition was probably grounded in an anxiety to prevent Parliament involving itself in the highly contentious subject of religious jurisdiction. During the last two decades of the reign, however, opinion at parish level was hardening noticeably, a general concern for moral purity replacing the previous somewhat academic disputes on the implication of Sabbath-keeping. Charges in the ecclesiastical courts against people accused of trading, dancing, piping and otherwise desecrating the Sabbath became more frequent.[141]

The court made some attempt to respond to Puritan sentiment; indeed, in 1600 it was decreed by the Privy Council that in view of the theatre's propensity to encourage idle, riotous and dissolute living, only two theatres should be licensed, the Fortune north of the Thames, and the Globe to the south, a theatre to which Burbage's company had repaired in 1598 when the lease on the old Finsbury Fields Theatre ran out. Nothing was done to put the decree into effect, and a year later the players at the Curtain were being disciplined for libellous plays. The Privy Council, in receipt of petitions from the City's Lord Mayor to do something about theatrical disorders, reissued the command to the magistrates to imprison those responsible for performances outside the two designated theatres, but again nothing was done, an indication, says Mantzius, of the powerful behind-the-scenes influence of magnates at court, where the Queen herself was a known devotee of the theatre – an example, perhaps, of the upper-class tastes that so dismayed Tolstoy.[142] James I, having been petitioned by 1,000 ministers of religion, in 1603 ordered 'that no bearbaiting, bullbaiting, enterludes, common plays or other like disorders or unlawful exercises or pastimes be frequented, kept or used at any time hereafter upon the Sabbath day', but an unsuccessful attempt three years later, in 1606, to put teeth into the Act suggests it was being flouted.[143] There was, however, in that year, an Act to Restrain the Abuses of Players, providing for a fine of £10 for jestingly or profanely referring on stage to God, Jesus or the Holy Ghost.[144]

The 1606 Bill was revived in 1614 and again failed to pass into law as a result of the dissolution of Parliament. With amended punishments, it passed both houses in 1621, only to be vetoed by James I, who approved a certain amount of Sunday recreation and considered the Bill too severe, a stance which he repeated in 1624, saying that he did not intend (though in 1603 he had done so) to suppress the recreation for 'poor men that labour hard all the week long'. Charles I, however, in search, presumably, of some sort of accommodation with Parliament, rapidly approved bills restricting Sunday activities, a succession of increasing severity being enacted in 1625, 1626 and 1627.[145]

Stubbes's summary had been that plays, sacred or profane, are 'sucked out of the Devil's teats to nourish us in idolatry, heathenry and sin'. This vocabulary, inspired by his reading of early Christian writers battling in pagan antiquity, figured largely in the work of the most influential of the pamphleteers, the barrister William Prynne, whose *Histriomastix, or The Scourge of Players* appeared in 1633. Prynne says he went to the theatre in his impressionable youth, but now deeply regrets it. In over 1,100 pages there is none of Stubbes's vivid description; the whole work smacks rather of midnight oil, as he ploughs his way through Scripture, 55 synods and councils, 71 Fathers of the Church prior to 1200 and over 150 since, both Protestant and Popish; and 40 heathen philosophers, plus an assortment of historians and 'poets', preachers and magistrates, both of England and elsewhere, from whom he culls authority to disapprove of everything, including women who cut their hair and men who do not, with a scrupulousness that even Tertullian's objection to the high heel of classical tragedy could hardly match. To have accomplished this, working by candlelight with quill pen over the years 1624 to 1630 'as well', he writes, 'as my poor ability and other interloping employments would permit', must indeed have been a mammoth task, accomplished in the sincere belief that he laboured in the Lord's vineyard.

The court was no more appreciative of the Puritans than Elizabeth's had been. Prynne knew he wrote at his peril; he had faced the dilemma 'whether to sit mute and silent still, and mourn in secret for these overspreading abominations . . . or whether I should lift up my voice like a trumpet and cry against them?' But he had decided 'to endure the cross and despise the hate and shame which the publishing of this *Histriomastix* might procure me'. His forebodings were well founded. He was tried for sedition, spent a year in prison, was fined the huge sum for those days of £5,000, had his upper ears cropped, was expelled from Lincoln's Inn and deprived of his degree in the University of Oxford.[146] His intemperate attacks on the magistrates (among whom he included monarchs) for failing to suppress the various abuses and illegalities perpetrated by the players and their sponsors were taken as an attack on Charles himself. Worse, Prynne was held to have attacked the person of Her Majesty the Queen.

Something new had come into the English theatre just as Prynne was nearing the end of his task. At Michaelmas 1629 at the Blackfriars Theatre some French *women* appeared and 'attempted', according to Prynne, to act a French play. Mantzius says they were pelted with rotten eggs and apples. Prynne discusses which is worse, the 'mannish impudency' of the 'woman actors', or the 'inducements to sodomy' of continuing with boys in women's roles, and concludes that there is no virtue in identifying which is the lesser evil. Evil is simply not tolerable.[147] Unfortunately, by 1607–8, 'the new and splendid form of the Jacobean Masque' as Bradbrook puts it, 'had evolved at court',[148] a genre associated with private parties which had found its way from Italy, where it had been growing in popularity for over a century.[149] Women freely took part in masques, and Charles's Queen, Henrietta Maria, was in the middle of rehearsals as Prynne finalized his book for publication. She took exception to his remarks about women actors, and was not mollified by his plea that, his book having been written in advance of her first appearance, he could not have been referring to her.[150]

When, after an eleven-year obligatory recess, Parliament reconvened in November 1640, Prynne's sentences were declared illegal, his degree and his membership of Lincoln's Inn were restored, and 'pecuniary reparation' was awarded to him though long delay ensued in actually paying it. Puritan sentiments were in the ascendant. Much controversy had surrounded the question of whether certain activities could be pursued after the evening service had been held on a Sunday, but in September 1641 that question was settled in the strictest possible manner. In that year the Commons resolved that 'The Lord's Day should be duly observed and sanctified; that all dancing or other sports, either before or after divine service be forborne and restrained . . .'[151]

Tensions between Court and Calvinists soon reached breaking point. The outbreak of the Civil War in August 1642 was followed within less than a fortnight by the Puritan Parliament's edict closing the theatres. This time the law was strictly enforced, and successive orders permitted actors to be flogged and spectators fined. Ostensibly, the closure was in virtue of the 'distressed Estate of Ireland . . . steeped in her own Blood, and the distracted Estate of England . . .' The wording does not imply that the closure was necessarily intended to be permanent, but magistrates were authorized to demolish buildings. Shakespeare's old Globe Theatre had already gone, burnt down in 1613 when the firing of a ceremonial cannon during a performance of *Henry VIII* went wrong and set the roof-thatch on fire. It was rebuilt (with a tile roof) and stood until 1644. In that year the Puritans pulled it down.[152]

Chapter 15

Rights Supplant Rites: the mid-Seventeenth to Late Eighteenth Centuries

There had not been much capering in the Puritan Commonwealth. Diligent perusal of the Patristic Fathers and the councils of the early Church had revealed that in the fight against the Devil, masquerading in various pagan disguises, such heathenish practices as New Year gifts, decking houses with laurel and green boughs, lighting fires for the New Moon and jumping over them, and celebrating the first of March must all be suppressed.[1] Worst of all was 'Maying'. Bishop Grosseteste of Lincoln had banished ceremonies 'bringing in May or Autumn' from his diocese in 1244, and in the next century the chapter of Wells Cathedral were trying to expel Maygames from their precincts.[2] But some sort of accommodation between folk practices and the Church was obviously reached, for expenditure on Maygames not infrequently appears in churchwardens' accounts.[3] However, they must have grown ever more bawdy for late in the sixteenth century a preacher in England complained of Lords of Misrule, Morris dancers, Maygames, who were not ashamed 'in the time of divine service, to come and dance about the Church', some of them stark naked – 'most filthy: for the heathen that never had further knowledge, than the light of nature, have counted it shameful for a player to come on the stage without a flop'.[4] Stubbes has a vivid description of the nocturnal departure of lads and lasses for the woods, ostensibly to gather greenery but (he sadly comments) 'scarcely the third part of them returned home again undefiled'. In the morning all trooped back with a maypole decked with ribbons and pulled by oxen with sweet nosegays of flowers on their horns, round which the villagers danced as 'heathen people did at the dedication of the Idols'. Once the Puritans were in power, they put a stop to such blasphemous revelry.[5]

Even before the Restoration, however, Puritan discipline was weakening. There is a suggestion that surreptitious theatrical performances, though of a poor standard, had been staged at the Red Bull during the Commonwealth.[6] In addition a Royalist officer, Sir William d'Avenant, whose father was innkeeper at an Oxford hostelry where Shakespeare had often stayed (leaving it open to d'Avenant carefully not to contradict rumours that he was Shakespeare's bastard), was not only pardoned by the Puritans for his Royalist sympathies, he managed to get permission to stage patriotic 'entertainments', which Hazlitt later described as 'dramatic in everything but the names and form; and some of them were called operas'.* Richard Cromwell in 1658 (it was the year in which the Puritans abolished Christmas) demanded an explanation from Drury Lane as to what was going on.[7]

With the Restoration known to be imminent, the Red Bull and the Salisbury Court began openly to stage plays, and early in 1660 a licence was obtained by John Rhodes for the reopening of the Cockpit, Drury Lane – but he was to have a very short run for his money.[8] On his return from France in May 1660 Charles II licensed only two London impresarios, William d'Avenant, who opened the Duke's Theatre (patron: the Duke of York) in a former tennis court in Lincoln's Inn Fields; and Tom Killigrew, who, after a short tenure of the Bull and then of another former tennis court in Vere Street, built the King's Theatre, Drury Lane, ten of whose players, known as 'the Gentlemen of the Great Chamber', or 'the King's Servants', wore the scarlet and gold uniform of the royal household – a last echo of the old royal minstrelsy, made more poignant, perhaps, by the fact that the company was led by a former Royalist officer, Charles Hart, who was Shakespeare's great-nephew, a grandchild of Shakespeare's sister.[†][9]

The post-Restoration theatres were constructed on the Italian model, no longer dual-purpose amphitheatrical bear-pits, but roofed halls with semicircular seating, a proscenium arch, painted wings and back curtain, stages that protruded much less deeply (and by early in the eighteenth century, not at all) into the auditorium, and front curtains that closed from each wing. The architect and designer Inigo Jones replaced these with a drop curtain, at first modelled on the Roman style which dropped

* The first woman known by name to have acted professionally on the English stage was a Mrs Coleman, who in 1656 played Ianthe in d'Avenant's so-called first English 'opera', *The Siege of Rhodes* (Mantzius, Vol.II, p.280; see also Dryden, [1903] p.171 note 88.4).

† By royal warrant, Charles Hart and thirteen other actors were in July 1661 issued with 'four yards of Bastard Scarlett for a Cloake' and 'a quarter of a yard of Crimson Velvett for the cape of itt, being the usuall Allowance of every second yeare to commence at October last past'. In June 1666 the same provision was made for ten actresses. An order of March 1672 required the Master of 'His Majesty's Comedians' to issue Charles Hart and two others with 'two perruques to begin with for the first yeare; one perruque yearely afterwards, to begin a yeare hence; two Cravatts yearely; one Lace or point Band in two yeares, the first band to be now provided; three paire of Silk Stockins yearely; four paire of shooes yearely; three Hatts yearely; two plumes of feathers yearely; three Shirts with Cuffs to them yearely' (Nicoll, Vol.I, pp.363, 365).

into a trench or slot, but this was later replaced by overhead pulleys.[10] From Italy, too, came such innovations as flat sliding wings, introduced in 1618 in their country of origin and spreading across western Europe by mid-century, together with lights that could be dimmed for special effects.[*][11] Ever more ingenuity was poured into technological feats – in France an unused opera house acquired (after his death) by Molière's troupe in Paris was richly equipped with machinery, enabling the staging, in 1675, of an elaborate, highly expensive, but immensely successful production of Corneille's *Circe* as a super-spectacle.[12]

The elaborate Italian machinery and scenic effects were costly. In Spain the playwright Lope de Vega voiced a familiar comment, recording his sadness that the technical ingenuity of the purpose-built theatres, and the rich décor and costumes, attracted far more audience attention than did his words. Spanish dramatists like de Vega and Calderon were still held within the medieval framework of Christian belief, and Calderon, in particular, cared far more about the 80 sacred works in which he explored the relationship between God and man than about his 120 comedies.[13]

In England, as in France, taste was demanding that drama should as closely as possible represent the world of every day. John Dryden, playwright and poet, in 1668 published *An Essay of Dramatic Poesy*, a serious critique in dialogue form of the methods and purposes of dramatic art.[†] Much of this is taken up with technical discussion of the supposed classical unities of time, place and action. Considerable further attention, however, is given to the topic of whether the use of 'poesy', either in rhyming form or in blank verse, is compatible with naturalism, 'the lively imitation of nature being in the definition of a play', as the *Essay* puts it. Actors were exercised over the other side of the same coin – how to declaim poetry. Already in Shakespeare's time criticism of bombastic delivery had been voiced – most explicitly by Hamlet in his complaint that 'it offends me to the soul to hear a robustious periwig-pated fellow tear a passion to tatters'; he 'would have a fellow whipped for o'erdoing Termagent; it out-Herods Herod' – a dig here at the overacting of the latter-day passion plays.[‡] In France Molière's protegé

---

[*] Lighting at this time was from chandeliers. Footlights had not been introduced (Mantzius, Vol.V, p.341).

[†] It is an interesting comment on contemporary assessments of the Elizabethan dramatists that Dryden puts forward his personal preference for Shakespeare over Ben Jonson almost diffidently. Jonson, he allows, is 'the most learned and judicious writer which any theatre ever had . . . I admire him, but I love Shakespeare'. He remarks, however, that there are twice as many current revivals of Beaumont and Fletcher as there are of either Jonson or Shakespeare (Dryden (1903), pp.67–71).

[‡] Mantzius suggests that Alleyn was the butt of this sally. Termagent and Herod were in his

Baron was to champion Molière's contention that natural delivery was right even in tragedy, in place of chanted declamation ('he speaks, he does not declaim', said a contemporary), but this school of acting was criticized by the Italian Elena Riccoboni for adopting the tone of the most commonplace talk.[14] Dryden permitted himself the conclusion that although verse was unsuitable for comedy, it was allowable for 'nature wrought up to an higher pitch' in tragedy.[15]

The play as the 'just and lively image of human nature, representing its passions and humours, and the changes of fortune to which it is subject'[16] had been the practice but not the avowed objective of the later medieval scriptwriters, and Dryden's definition echoes the 'representation' that gave birth – and name – to the mime in the century following the great Greek tragedians. As with the classical mimes, this approach signalled the arrival of the professional actress. Charles II returned from France with a well-developed taste for theatricals, and an appreciation of 'women actors'. He promptly bestowed on Sir William d'Avenant a licence permitting women to replace boys in female roles; and among the beneficiaries of the new policy was a pretty young actress named Nell Gwynn, who first appeared at Drury Lane in 1666.[17]

In his essay, Dryden remarked of drama that it was 'for the delight and instruction of mankind'.[18] Instruction had, of course, been a prime objective of the morality plays that succeeded liturgical drama, and even as late as the early seventeenth century an English strolling player, seeking leave to play in Frankfurt, had stressed his intention of giving spectators 'cause and occasion to pursue propriety and virtue'.[19] This was also the message of a defence of theatricals published in 1662. Its author, Sir Richard Baker, had written it as a riposte to Prynne's *Histriomastix*, but he had died in 1645 leaving the work unpublished, presumably neither he nor anyone else daring to publish it during the years of Puritan supremacy. In brief, he dismisses Prynne's work as having relevance only to the idolatrous pagan communities in the midst of which most of his witnesses, such as Tertullian, were writing, and he takes Prynne's lavish citing of canonical prohibitions against performances in churches or on Sundays as evidence of their acceptability at other times and in other places – or, if the councils really meant to ban them altogether, then no more worthy of obedience than the equally disregarded prohibitions on New Year gifts or on decking the house with greenery. Even more strongly than Lucian, defending pantomimes from accusations of obscenity in the second century, Baker contends that

repertoire (Mantzius, Vol.III, pp.190ff.).

'obscene sights' are troubling only to 'obscene hearts'. 'It is not so much the player that makes the obscenity as the spectator himself . . . it is the spectator's fault and not the player's, if any evil or corruption be contracted by them.'[20] In the last resort, he defends plays as morally uplifting. 'The very scope of plays in Christian times has ever been addressed to the magnifying of virtue; or to make notorious the foulness and deformity of vice . . . plays do not only show us the right, but lead us in it.'[21]

A more honest apologia was about to emerge. In a defence of his *Essay*, published later in 1668 in response to criticisms of the original, Dryden declares:

> [D]elight is the chief, if not the only, end of poesie: instruction can be admitted but in the second place; for poesie only instructs as it delights . . . I confess my chief endeavours are to delight the age in which I live. If the humour of this be for low comedy, small accidents, and raillery, I will force my genius to obey it . . . To please the people ought to be the poet's aim, because plays are made for their delight.[22]

The people – initially in the person of the King – soon made their tastes apparent. Charles had restored to his office as Master of Revels Sir Henry Herbert, who had diligently and for a hefty fee excised oaths and blasphemies in Charles I's time; but he was deprived of his powers of censorship. These were transferred by royal warrant to, of all people, the impresarios Sir William d'Avenant and Tom Killigrew (who after Sir Henry's death became Master of Revels in name as well as in function).[23] The author of *The Stage Censor* comments:

> The man whose conscience on the matter of oaths was so nice that it moved him to enter a personal protest against the retention by Charles I of the 'asseverations' of *faith* and *slight* in a play-book, was little likely to be in accord with Charles II, in the matter of licensing Restoration comedies. That merry monarch ordained d'Avenant and Tom Killigrew, for the masters of his 'revels'; and the period of their dual authority is still notorious as that in which the English stage touched its lowest depth.[24]

'The drama of the Restoration', comments Mantzius,

> when it made its entry on the stage, had picked up from the French

their keen wit and bright conversation, though not their gift of handling gallant and amorous subjects with the polished and imperturbable grace which prevents them from giving offence. English people are by nature chaste in their speech;[*] if they throw off their natural bashfulness and give way to frivolity, they are apt to become coarse. This was what happened with the drama of that time; its authors, in the attempt to copy the shuttlecock playing of the frivolous French writers, tossed out atrocious indecencies among the public, who after the long Puritan abstinence, greedily caught at this coarse amusement.[25]

Post-Restoration drama delighted in one theme – seduction; and the treatment was in no whit inhibited by the fact that Killigrew and d'Avenant had authority to prevent the production of any play or opera containing profane, scurrilous or obscene material. Any hint of political criticism was another matter, and the King himself intervened in 1667 to ensure that a play, *The Change of Crowns*, about corruption in high places did not enjoy a second performance.[26] As in ancient Rome, such influence only served to enhance the preoccupation of dramatists with the politically safer subject of sex. Witty women writers of *demi-monde* reputation who joined in the fun included Aphra Behn (who made 'extraordinary efforts ... to write as uncleanly as any of her male rivals'), Mrs Manley (whose taste for slander and intrigue led to her arrest in 1709), and Susannah Centlivre, an actress credited with the authorship of 'ingenious and sprightly' comedies.[27]

The theatre-going public was not numerous, Puritan sentiment was widespread and managers were hard put to it to fill their houses. Patrons, on the prowl for sexual partners, were violent and quarrelsome, murders in the auditorium not unknown. Nicoll remarks that:

> Hardly any of them had a faith beyond vague attachment to royalty; every one of them was eager for the day's pleasure, eager for love and cynical laughter and the enjoyment of the senses ... [T]he love of pleasure which had come as a reaction to the restrictions of the Puritan régime led towards a recrudescence of brutality. No one in that age could possibly conceive of such a thing as innocence ... Sexual disease ... was treated half as a joke, half as a glory ... Incest and similar relationships are referred to again and again ... Occasionally, even, the spectators were content, perhaps eager, to

[*] Mantzius was writing in the early years of the twentieth century.

see more than mere themes of incest. Unnatural sex relationships
... too were reflected in the dramas.* [28]

Not only the theatre but public morality as a whole had now reached a
pitch of indecency that was outraging a considerable section of the
population, and among Christians a campaign of evangelization was
embarked upon, with the foundation in 1698 of the Society for
Promoting Christian Knowledge, followed three years later by its
missionary sister, the Society for the Propagation of the Gospel. In 1692
there was founded a Society for Reformation of Manners (i.e. of moral
conduct, not of social etiquette), and the movement spread across the
country – the Wendover Society, for instance, met to hear their first
sermon in 1701, and by the time of the 39th Account of the Progress of
the London and Westminster Society in 1733 it was reported with
pleasure that 'Thanks be to God, many such combinations and public
confederacies are now in being.'[29]

The purpose of these societies was 'furthering the execution of the
laws against prophaneness and immorality'. The movement was not, this
time, Puritan in origin.† The societies were of Anglican inspiration, and
bishops frequently accepted the invitation to give the annual January
sermon at St Mary-le-Bow in London. Their objective was pursued in
some cases by one of the societies itself taking legal action against
offenders, but they preferred amendment to be sought through drawing
the attention of the authorities to breaches of the law (enduring with
fortitude the 'odious associations of the word Informer stemming from
its use in political tyrannies')[30] and endeavouring to stiffen the resolve of
the magistrates who, in the societies' opinion, were often excessively
lax. In their first forty years the London and Westminster Society were
responsible for prosecuting nearly 100,000 people for offences including exercising their trades or ordinary callings on the Lord's Day,
drunkenness, profane swearing and cursing, keeping bawdy, sodomiti-
cal and disorderly houses, keeping common gaming houses, and plying
their trade of prostitute or sodomite on the streets.[31] An account of the

---

* Both in drama and in real life (Sharpe (1983), p.69), much of seventeenth-century incest
reflected laws which, until well into the twentieth century, included in the prohibited degree of
relationship step and in-law connections which would not now be regarded as incestuous. Their
inclusion in Elizabethan and Jacobean drama, however, was intended not to suggest changes in the
law, but to provoke the horror and tension that so thrilled what Nicoll does not scruple to call 'the
depraved tastes' of Elizabethan and Jacobean audiences.
† In the confusion of sixteenth-century ecclesiastical affairs, Calvinists/Presbyterians had formed
part of the post-Reformation Church in England. The seventeenth century saw their withdrawal
and reconstitution as Dissenters.

activities of the societies published in 1698 attributes to the playhouses much of the blame for the current debauchery, for in them 'Virtue and Vice had . . . changed their Names; it was reckoned Breeding to Swear, Gallantry to be Lewd, good Humour to be Drunk, and Wit to despise Sacred things . . .'[32]

In France somewhat similar developments were occurring, with a 'Society of the Holy Sacrament' endeavouring to raise moral standards, and in the process acquiring a reputation for spying and general nosy-parkering. Not all its members were of spotless reputation themselves, and it was the hypocrisy of this wing of the Church that Molière set out to lampoon in *Tartuffe*. The play was taken, however, as an attack on the Church in general; Louis XIV enjoyed it in private but forbade public performance, and the Church reacted with the utmost severity. In February 1673, as Molière lay dying, his parish priest refused to visit him, thus denying him the opportunity (which admittedly he might not have taken, though it was a common and accepted practice among theatre people) to abjure his theatrical career, a calling which at that time in France, as in the Primitive Church, barred practitioners from the sacraments. Dying thus outside the bosom of the Church, his body was denied Christian burial by the Archbishop of Paris, who was, however, overruled by Louis, who managed to obtain a surreptitious night burial, though without a church service.[33]

In 1694 an Italian-born priest in the French Catholic Church, Father Francisco Caffaro, ventured to publish a defence of stage-plays, claiming, as had Sir Richard Baker's paper in England some thirty years previously, that patristic polemics to the contrary were based on the excesses of the *pagan* theatre, not the theatre *per se*. He found theological precedents in Augustine and Thomas Aquinas for approving entertainment that refreshed the mind, provided the actors 'neither speak nor act anything which is unlawful; mix nothing that is sacred with profane, and never act in a prohibited time'. This provoked a swift and powerful riposte from J.B. Bossuet, Bishop of Meaux, defending the traditional stance of the early Church.[*] [34] No doubt the controversy was followed in England by Jeremy Collier, who in 1699 introduced Bossuet's work to an English readership, and was probably himself responsible for its translation.[35]

Collier had, in the previous year, 1698, published a polemic of his own – *A Short View of the Immorality and Profaneness of the English Stage*.

---

[*] The following year, 1695, the Bishop of Arras, the diocese where secular European drama had had its origin, forbade all performances in his diocese in Advent, Lent, or at any time of public calamity, and reiterated the excommunication of all players, male and female (Collier, pp.247–9).

Collier had been an Anglican priest of the High Church faction, until, together with the other Nonjurors who had adhered to their oath of allegiance to James II and therefore had refused to swear a fresh oath to William of Orange, he lost his living.* Like his predecessors, he made copious reference to the opinions of the Patristic Fathers and the councils of the early Church.[36] His diatribe covered complaints familiar from Puritan times – a theatre distinguished by 'smuttiness of expression, swearing, profaneness and lewd application of scripture . . . abuse of the clergy . . . making their top characters libertines and giving them success in their debauchery . . .', and he contrasted these abuses not only with the moral decency of the Greek tragedians, but also with the comic writers Plautus and Terence, who limited their obscenities to the mouths of slaves and prostitutes (even Terence's strumpets were better behaved than contemporary portraits of women of quality), and who showed no debauching of married women, no contempt for priests and no unpunished disrespect for the gods.[37]

Collier went much further than his predecessors in detailing the plays and the characterizations that were the butt of his objections. William Congreve's *Love for Love*, *The Old Bachelor* and *The Mourning Bride*, John Vanbrugh's *The Relapse* and *The Provok'd Wife*, William Wycherley's *The Country Wife* and Dryden's *Amphytrion* are among plays accused, *inter alia*, of extinguishing shame and making lewdness a diversion – 'The modern poets seem to use smut as the old ones did machines† to relieve a fainting invention.'[38] Dryden, whose plays had been staged since 1663, was his *bête noir*. He picked up Dryden's claim that delight was the chief aim of comedy, saying, 'he should have said debauchery, that's the English word'; and he noted in particular Dryden's remark that 'our minds are perpetually wrought on by the temperament of our bodies, which makes me suspect they are nearer allied than either our philosophers or School Divines will allow them to be'.[39] 'The meaning is,' says Collier, 'he suspects our souls are nothing but organized Matter. Or, in plain English, our souls are nothing but our bodies . . . [so] the prospect of the other world [is] almost shut up'.[40]

A Short View enjoyed enormous support. 'It made a mighty noise with us in Staffordshire,' wrote one less than enthusiastic reader, 'his arguments were cried up as invincible, and all the precise old folks here (who perhaps had never seen a play in their lives) joined in a loud outcry against the wicked stage.'[41] Congreve attempted a defence, including a

---

* The group included an archbishop, eight bishops, some 400 clergy and substantial numbers of their parishioners. The schism lasted for over a century.
† I.e., the *deus ex machina*.

feeble attack on Collier for misusing the verb 'to learn' when he meant 'to teach'; and another witness for the defence averred that Collier's attack had simply resulted in *The Mourning Bride* enjoying 'the greatest audience they have this winter had'. But enough of the public were on Collier's side for a jury at Middlesex Quarter Sessions to indict Congreve, his printer and the playhouse concerned for *The Double Dealer*; and in 1701 the players from the Lincoln's Inn Playhouse were indicted for the language used in *Love for Love* and in Vanbrugh's *The Provok'd Wife*, the jury finding them guilty without even retiring to consider their verdict. As a result, players took evasive action, changing 'God' as an oath to 'Gad!', 'God's wounds' became 'Zounds!', 'God's body' 'Ods Bodikins!', and so on.[42]

The pamphlet war, much of it conducted anonymously, raged on over the following years, with the defence reiterating that it was merely reflecting society, and if what society delights in is immorality, then it is the clergy who have failed; while the prosecution maintained, as the Bishop of Winchester did, that 'most considering people have the fairness to own, that the Stage has gone furthest in running us down to this low and almost brutal condition . . .'[43] Vanbrugh, Congreve and D'Urfey stoutly defended themselves, though Dryden, to the puzzlement of contemporaries, did not.[44] The dispute was not above descent into personal abuse – such as the accusation that Collier's 'dwelling so long on the subject of debauchery argues something of delight and pleasure in the case', or the claim that the seeds of the mischief were sown under those very Stuarts to whom Collier, as a Nonjuror, remained loyal.[45] On the other side, revoltingly explicit charges of bodies rotting with venereal disease were thrown at the players.[46]

To the dismay of the reformers, Vanbrugh was in 1702 made manager of the new Haymarket Theatre. Several appalled members of the Society for Reformation of Manners petitioned the Archbishop of Canterbury on the unsuitability of this appointment, unmindful, perhaps, of the fact that he had been the preacher at Nell Gwynn's funeral.[47] In spite of these protests, it was Vanbrugh and Congreve who, in December 1705, were appointed, by letters patent, to oversee plays, and 'take care nothing should be acted to the prejudice of religion and good manners'.[48]

In November 1703 a great storm of unprecedented severity struck southern England, a phenomenon not rivalled again until the hurricane of October 1987. The Eddystone Lighthouse was swept away, together with its designer Henry Winstanley, 700 vessels on the Thames were driven into one confused tangle of spars and sheets, and salt spray was blown so far inland that sheep were near to starving on the inedible grass of the Sussex Downs. More than 8,000 people are thought to have died. It was looked upon as a chastisement from God, and a day of public fasting and humiliation was decreed, which the clergy used for a spate of sermons against the stage, though one playwright pointed out that it was rather hard that such storm-battered cities as Cologne, Hamburg and Danzig should also have had to suffer for the iniquities of the English theatre.[49]

However, in the teeth of opposition from at least some sections of the population, plans were announced to build playhouses in both Bristol and Bath. A touring company arrived in Bristol and, having assured the citizens of their intention to stage nothing but the most inoffensive of plays, proceeded in July 1705 to put on *Love for Love* followed in August by *The Provok'd Wife*, the very plays which the London jury had condemned. As a result, professional theatre came to a premature, if temporary, end in Bristol,[50] and a local vicar, Arthur Bedford, was moved to join the ranks of pamphleteers. In sermons preached to the Society for Reformation of Manners and in a number of publications, he showed a diligence to rival Prynne's as he proceeded, in the course of a general discourse on blasphemy, lewdness and scriptural standards of morality, to cite no fewer than 1,400 instances of swearing, cursing and blasphemy in plays printed in 1704 and the first ten weeks of 1705, a total that had mounted to 7,000 by the time of his 1719 publication, *A Serious Remonstrance in behalf of the Christian Religion . . . against . . . English Playhouses*.[51] Translations of French and Italian plays were being spiced with extra swearing and profanity for an English audience, said Bedford, and revivals of such sixteenth-century favourites as Beaumont and Fletcher concentrated on plays distinguished from their contemporaries by the amount of swearing, cursing, profanity, smut and assaults on authority that they contained.[52] Bedford takes serious stock of an argument that had not had much previous currency – freedom of expression. The 1689 Act of Toleration had freed Dissenters from the obligation to attend Anglican services, and had permitted them to hold their own assemblies. Liberty of conscience, said Bedford, was being distorted into liberty to act without any conscience at all.[53]

Public opinion continued to side with the reformers. John Dennis, whose comedy *Gibraltar* came in for particularly harsh criticism at Bedford's hands, said that managers had treated him so badly since he sprang to the defence of the theatre that he had no choice but 'to take leave of the playhouse for ever'. Vanbrugh's work, much of it translations and adaptations of French originals, was being published and staged anonymously.[54] Scholars seem agreed that a marked

difference came over the theatre following the Collier – and subsequent
– attacks. 'The language of comedy was drastically revised and
emended', claims Anthony.[55] And some at least of the participants
expressed sincere contrition. Among them was John Dryden. Collier
may have thought he had no time for the soul – but in 1686 John Evelyn
reported that Dryden, five years after writing a scathing attack on priestly
licentiousness in *The Spanish Friar*, had been seen attending a Roman
Catholic Mass. He had indeed become a convert, together with his sons,
one of whom was to become a Dominican. A year after Collier's great
denunciation, Dryden wrote, in the preface to *The Fables*:

> I have pleaded guilty to all thoughts and expressions of mine, which
> can be truly argued of obscenity, profaneness or immorality, and
> retract them. If [Collier] be my enemy, let him triumph; if he be my
> friend, as I have given him no personal occasion to be otherwise, he
> will be glad of my repentance.[56]

In the last three weeks of his life he was to write, in an epilogue he
composed for a revival of Fletcher's *The Pilgrim*, a wry defence of
playwrights for treating of the human condition in all its fallen
propensity; but still he expressed no rancour against Collier, and indeed
pleaded guilty, on behalf of his fellow poets, to seeking to profit from the
debauched example of the court.* [57]

Socially and culturally a battle – or perhaps, in the overall scheme of
things, only a skirmish – had been won by the proponents of
otherworldly priorities. But in the intellectual sphere, the war was in the
process of being lost. The pre-eminence of that 'organized matter',
belief in which could, in Collier's words, shut up the prospect of the
other world, had received a significant boost from the foundation, in

---

* Perhaps the Parson stretch'd a point too far,
  When with our Theatres he wag'd a War.
  He tells you, That this very Moral Age
  Receiv'd the first Infection from the Stage.
  But sure, a banisht Court, with Lewdness fraught,
  The Seeds of open Vice returning brought.
  Thus Lodg'd, (as Vice by great Example thrives)
  It first debauch'd the Daughters and the Wives.
  London, a fruitful Soil, yet never bore
  So plentiful a Crop of Horns before.
  The Poets, who must live by Courts or starve,
  Were proud, so good a Government to serve;
  And mixing with Buffoons and Pimps profain,
  Tainted the Stage, for some small Snip of Gain.

1660, of the Royal Society, incorporated by charter from Charles II in 1662.

The Society had a precursor in Gresham College, founded in the City of London through a bequest from Sir Thomas Gresham, a financier to Tudor royalty. The college had a strongly scientific bent, and served as a meeting place for men of science; and it was radical for its time in providing for lectures in English as well as in Latin. There were chairs in rhetoric, civil law and divinity as well as in medicine[*] and mathematics.[58] However, the charter of the Royal Society, in its amended 1663 form, though it announced that its activities were 'to the glory of God the creator, and the advantage of the human race', and its officers were required to take their oath of appointment 'upon the holy Gospels of God', stipulated that the topics with which the Society was to concern itself were exclusively 'the sciences of natural things'. Its purpose, as expressed in a document drawn up in 1663, was

> to improve the knowledge of all natural things, and all useful arts, manufactures, mechanic practices, engines and inventions by experiments – (not meddling with divinity, metaphysics, morals, politics, grammar, rhetoric or logic) ... this Society will ... question and canvass all opinions, adopting nor adhering to none, till by mature debate and clear arguments chiefly such as are deduced from legitimate experiments, the truth of such experiments be demonstrated invincibly.[59]

Though he was, by then, dead, the founding genius of the Royal Society was Sir Francis Bacon, who had hoped to see established a 'House of Solomon' or, as he put it in *New Atlantis*, a College of the Six Days' Works, 'for the finding out of the true nature of all things (whereby God might have the more glory in the workmanship of them, and men the more fruit in the use of them)', as the 1629 posthumous translation from the original Latin put it; in short, where the proper end of knowledge should be to provide 'a rich storehouse for the glory of the Creator and the relief of Man's estate'.[60] Absorbed in the Renaissance confidence in 'man's universal skill in the arts and sciences', Bacon exemplified a sanguine assurance at the prospect of the reign of man over Nature, 'the ideology,' to quote Kristeller 'that still underlies the technological aspect of modern natural science'.[61] He it was who, desiring 'to extend

---

[*] The Royal College of Physicians, the oldest medical institution in England, had been granted its royal charter by Henry VIII in 1518.

more widely the limits of the power and the greatness of man', had laid down that in order 'to look into and dissect the nature of this real world', the natural philosopher must 'consult only things themselves'. The method to be followed must be inductive reasoning based on trained observation and verification by experiment.[62]

Sorokin has tabulated the exponential increase in scientific and technological discoveries and inventions which followed the adoption of this approach to knowledge.[63] It was religious attitudes of mind that paid the price. In his passionate advocacy of systematic observation and experiment, Bacon insisted on a self-disciplined attempt to eliminate from the mind the distortions which traditional pre-judgements inevitably inspire, such as teleological assumptions about there being a purpose which phenomena are designed to serve; or habits of thought derived from outmoded authorities. 'He rendered valuable help towards the secularization of natural knowledge', remarks Wolf.[64]

This secularization was not, at the time, aggressively anti-religious. A judgement applied by Kocher to Elizabethan science and scientists continued to hold good:

> It was not irreligious but non-religious. They merely took religion for granted. But this point itself was ominous of a future divorce between religion and science, once so closely wedded. The quiet indifference of the scientists was to work worse mischief to religion in the long run than the conjuring of a John Dee or the blaspheming of a Christopher Marlowe.[65]

When the Royal Society was founded, a contemporary reported a scattering of 'over-zealous Divines' who 'do reprobate Natural Philosophy as a carnal knowledge, and a too much minding worldly things', but early supporters and members untroubled by such reflections included bishops among their number.[*] Because of the need to raise as much money as possible, a high proportion of the early membership of the Society was drawn from people prominent for their interest and wealth rather than their scientific achievements. Dissenters tended to be more friendly to science than the established Church (Gresham College, too, had had the reputation of appealing particularly to Puritans) and by the next century many of the increasing proportion of scientific fellows

---

[*] The Accademia del Cimento, founded in Florence in 1657, was less fortunate. It was disbanded in 1667, by which time one of its researchers had committed suicide, on being apprehended by the Inquisition (Wolf (1950), p.55).

came to be drawn from the Presbyterian and Puritan wings of Christianity, or were Quakers.[66]

Prominent among the founders of the Society was Robert Boyle, the distinguished chemist, who endowed an annual lecture in defence of Christianity which is still given by a lecturer appointed by the Bishop of London.[67] Yet paradoxically Boyle was himself responsible, by destroying the claims of alchemy, for severing the essential link which had sustained earlier generations of scientists in their belief that the spiritual and the material were inextricably entwined through the mysterious agency of the *pneuma*. In 1661 Boyle published *The Sceptical Chymist*, in which he denied Aristotle's theory of the four elements. The number of elements, he said, is unknown, but each is homogeneous and irreducible into other substances. Metals cannot be converted into one another.[68]

Boyle's thesis was found incontrovertible, and belief in alchemy began to dissipate, though pockets of alchemical belief lingered for another century.* Hermetic philosophy, belief in the unity of all material things within a single scheme the author of which is God, with whom the seeker after knowledge is in partnership in pursuit of perfection, has never ceased to have its adherents, though not, on the whole, among scientists. The nineteenth-century Theosophists took their inspiration from Paracelsus's sixteenth-century followers.

The legacy of the alchemists to science was the laboratory techniques they had evolved; indeed, prior to the late sixteenth century there were virtually no laboratory workers other than the alchemists. This was rapidly to change. Scientific chemistry inherited the mantle of the alchemists. Though Paracelsus's hermetic mysticism was dropped, his insistence on the chemical composition of living matter was retained, and interest in the efficacy of pharmacy developed.[69]

The most significant change in the approach to laboratory work was, however, in biological science, especially anatomy. Dissection became commonplace.

The Romans had initially clung to the taboo against the dissection of human corpses. Celsus, the first-century medical encyclopaedist, strongly supported the case for human dissection, but it is not clear that it was practised. He also explored the case for vivisection (on condemned criminals) but rejected it on grounds of cruelty, holding that adequate

---

* James Price, who was elected a fellow of the Royal Society in 1781, claimed to be able to produce silver and gold by transmutation. He committed suicide when unable to verify the claim at the behest of the Society. Since the investigation into his claims, 'no learned scientific body has been willing officially to notice alchemical claims' (Holmyard, pp.267–8, 273).

knowledge could be gained by surgeons in the course of treating victims of violence.[70] The medical school in Roman Alexandria, Herophilus's old stamping ground and one of the teaching institutions attended by Galen, the renowned second-century physician,[71] included anatomy in the curriculum, but even there it is not clear whether dissection was practised, or merely the use of skeletons. Galen himself lectured on anatomy in Rome in the late second century, and there are several hints in his practical handbook on dissection, *On Anatomical Procedures*, that he dissected human corpses as well as lecturing on skeletons and dissecting animals. He disassociated himself from Celsus's view that adequate information was available through the treatment of wounds, and though he specifically stated that of two corpses to which he had access, one had been cleaned of flesh by its long immersion in a river, the other by the attention of scavenging birds, there are other references which suggest flesh was available for his inspection.[72]

Christians had from the first rejected human dissection. Tertullian referred to Herophilus of Alexandria, dissection's pioneer, as 'that butcher who cut up innumerable human beings so that he could study nature'.[73] In his *City of God* Augustine remarks that

some doctors called anatomists with a cruel zeal for science have dissected bodies of dead men, and even of men who have died while the doctor was cutting and examining them. Thus they have not humanely, but in human flesh, explored every secret place in order to gain new information about such parts and the kind of treatment to employ and in what spot.[74]

Only gradually had the revulsion against the use of human corpses been overcome. Perhaps as a result of observing Arab treatment of wounds during the Crusades, interest in surgery developed. As late as 1163 ecclesiastical decree had forbidden the teaching of surgery, but in 1252 a book on the subject was published, and notwithstanding Church opposition, students at Salerno medical school studied anatomy on the bodies of executed prisoners,[75] permission for one dissection every five years having been granted by the thirteenth-century ruler, the Emperor Frederick II.[76]

Autopsies to discover the cause of inexplicable deaths were carried out in the thirteenth century, and in the fourteenth the Avignon Pope Clement authorized dissection of the dead as a desperate measure to discover the origins of the Black Death.[77] Contemporaneously, the direct study of human anatomy for research and teaching purposes spread,

Montpellier medical school receiving permission for biennial anatomical dissection in 1340.[78] Such studies 'became more or less habitual in various medical schools in Italy',[79] where the University of Bologna was probably the first, using for the purpose the bodies of executed non-Bolognese criminals. Venice followed in 1368, Florence in 1388, Siena in 1427, Perugia in 1457, Genoa in 1482 and Pisa in 1501.[80] Leonardo da Vinci in the fifteenth century made some 750 anatomical sketches, but they were not published.[*][81]

In 1531 there was published a Latin translation of Galen's *On Anatomical Procedures*, which was largely based on the dissection of animals, especially monkeys, and projecting the results on to human beings.[82] This work directly inspired the Belgian anatomist Andreas Vesalius, teaching at Padua,[†] who in 1543 published a revolutionary treatise, *On the Structure of the Human Body*, which replaced the authority of Galen and the philosophic analogies of hermetic medicine with his own clear account of human anatomy as revealed directly by the scalpel. 'It was Vesalius who revived the direct study of anatomy, initiated the revolt against mere authority in the realm of biological science, and introduced new methods and instruments for the effective pursuit of anatomical and physiological studies.'[83]

Vesalius's work aroused strong opposition, not least because of his challenge to Galen, and he judged it prudent to leave Padua. But his proved to be the voice of the future. Rembrandt's powerful painting *The Anatomy Lesson of Dr Deyman*, dating from 1656, was commissioned by the Surgeons' Guild, and though much damaged in a fire in 1723, the remaining fragment, including the pale, half-dissected corpse of a young Flemish thief, is eloquent testimony to the interest the subject aroused.

---

[*] Da Vinci declared himself to be 'a disciple of experience', insisting that visual scrutiny of nature – as recorded in direct representations – comprised the only certain route to true knowledge of the world (Martin Kemp, 'Leonardo Da Vinci', *National Art Collection Fund Review,* 1992, p.19). 'Those sciences are vain and full of error,' declared Da Vinci, '. . . that have neither at their beginning, middle nor end passed through any of the five senses', a sentiment which, together with 'other rigorous assertions of the primacy of experience and the necessity of sensory knowledge align Leonardo's thought', Martin Kemp points out, 'with prominent aspects of the Aristotelian tradition in Mediaeval science' (Kemp, 'Disciple of Experience', in *Leonardo Da Vinci*, catalogue to the South Bank Exhibition, 1989).

[†] Where the statutes required the rector and councillors to procure one male and if possible one female cadaver of a legally executed non-Paduan and non-Venetian criminal. If no suitable executed criminal was locally available, one was to be sought in an outlying area. Vesalius, habituated perhaps to the gallows by the fact that his childhood home in Brussels was hard by the execution hill, obtained specimens as a student by risking nights locked outside the walls of Louvain while he stole bones from the gibbets. Once established in his profession, he petitioned judges to delay executions to times suitable for dissections (O'Malley, pp.27, 78, 222).

The members of the Royal Society were fascinated by dissection. 'One of the privileges of the Society was the right to claim the bodies of executed persons for dissection, and in 1664 a committee was formed to undertake dissections upon every execution-day.'[84]

Dissection soon failed to slake the thirst for knowledge. Wolf remarks laconically of Vesalius's work: 'Perhaps the most original part of the book is the last chapter, in which he describes his method of vivisection', presumably on animals, though Wolf does not make this clear.[85] The first edition of Vesalius's book had injudiciously mentioned the still-pulsating heart of one of the human subjects of his investigations, and he hastened to clear up any ambiguity on this topic in the second edition, explaining that one subject had died in an accident, the other by execution. He had no inhibitions about practising vivisection on animals, however, exploring, for instance, the results of severing the optic nerves of live dogs and other large animals.[86] The Royal Society avidly followed his example. Robert Hooke demonstrated that the heart of a dissected dog could be kept beating for over an hour by injecting air from bellows into its lungs through an opening in the windpipe.[87] Richard Lower, elected a fellow in 1667, transferred blood from one animal into another, and went on to elucidate the problem of why arterial blood differs in colour from that in the veins.[88] Inspired by this example, other members of the Society experimented with 'transfusions of blood between similar or dissimilar animals, including dogs, sheep, foxes, and pigeons'. They injected liquids such as mercury and tobacco-oil into the veins of animals, removed organs and severed nerves.[89]

Vivisection on animals had formed a substantial proportion of Galen's work, and he had indeed published a text, *De vivorum dissectione*, which has not survived;[90] the Rome of his time, saturated in the culture of the amphitheatre, was hardly likely to concern itself over cruelty to animals. But the Judaeo-Christian tradition introduced what C.W. Hume, in *The Status of Animals in the Christian Religion*, calls a 'neighbourly' attitude towards the animal kingdom. He cites Biblical injunctions on animal welfare in both Old and New Testaments, the whole symbolism of the Good Shepherd, the place of animals in the story of the Nativity, and numerous Lives of the Saints, of which the life of Francis of Assisi was perhaps the culmination, to illustrate his point.

Elizabethan Puritans had expressed concern at cruelty to animals. So far as hunting was concerned, Church canons had long forbidden the sport to priests, but this was more to preserve the soul of the priest from the frivolity of the chase than out of concern for the quarry. Similarly, much of the Puritan criticism of cock-fighting and bull- and bear-baiting hinged on the fact that it frequently occurred on the Sabbath. But Stubbes, in his *The Anatomy of the Abuses in England*, went much further. Of the killing of beasts by hunting, he said:

> If necessity, or want of other meats, inforceth us to seek after their lives, it is lawful to use them, in the fear of God, with thanks to his name; but for our pastimes and vain pleasures' sake, we are not in any wise to spoil or hurt them. Is he a Christian man, or rather a pseudo-Christian, that delighteth in blood?[91]

As for tormenting animals as entertainment, he was even more severe:

> For is not the baiting of a bear, besides that it is a filthy, stinking and loathsome game, a dangerous and perilous exercise? ... What Christian heart can take pleasure to see one poor beast to rent, tear, and kill another, and all for his foolish pleasure? And although they be bloody beasts to mankind, and seek his destruction, yet we are not to abuse them, for his sake who made them, and whose creatures they are. For notwithstanding that they be evil to us, and thirst after our blood, yet are they good creatures in their own nature and kind, and made to set forth the glory and magnificence of the great God, and for our use; and therefore for his sake not to be abused. It is a common saying amongst all men ... love me, love my dog: so, love God, love his creatures.[92]

Stubbes does not discuss the use of animals in science, but it is highly doubtful whether vivisection was occurring in England at the time; or if it was, it was behind closed doors. Bacon, in *The Advancement of Learning*, published in 1605, some twenty years after Stubbes's polemic, recommends animal vivisection in terms which imply that such was not the practice in his time.[93] In 1636, however, came the publication of a book which was to liberate consciences from any qualms about the infliction of suffering on animals. René Descartes, in *Discours de la méthode*, proved, to the satisfaction of a sufficiency of his contemporaries, that animals were automata, animal-machines, incapable of feeling pain.[94]

The cogitations that led Descartes to this conclusion arose out of the dissatisfaction many thinkers were experiencing at the wholesale confidence in observation and experiment which was one of the fruits of the Renaissance. 'I call that knowledge which we receive when the senses are properly brought to observe things', Juan Luis Vives, the

Spanish educationalist who taught at Oxford and served in the household of Catherine of Aragon, had written in the early sixteenth century, prompting the judgement that 'Vives points the way to the empirical materialist philosophy of the 17th century'.[95] What worried Descartes was the evident fact that observation can mislead – the senses are unreliable. 'I had always,' wrote Descartes, 'an extreme longing to learn how to distinguish the true from the false.'[96] When he had stripped away every proposition that could possibly be considered doubtful, he was left with the awareness of a doubting consciousness and nothing else; I think, therefore I am. Twentieth-century philosophers were to complain that even this pared-down statement made unwarranted assumptions – that there was an 'I' with a continuing identity through time, for instance; but Descartes was satisfied that he had arrived at the ultimate bedrock of certainty. The problem was how to link his basic proposition to any sort of scientific certainties about the material world, including even his own physical being.

This is not the place to pursue a full account of the steps whereby Descartes bridged the gap which resulted from his strict separation of mind from body, but a brief resumé includes the following tenets: the mind is not only self-conscious, it is capable of an intuitive grasp of the primary axioms of mathematics and physics, and of their logical application, resulting in the delineation of certain mechanical laws of matter and motion. Certainty requires that both the intuitions and the observations supplying the raw material of scientific enquiry (the intimations of material reality impinging on the mind through the questionable agency of the senses) are trustworthy. Descartes had to postulate the existence of God, the fount of truth, as the guarantor who could be trusted not to be deceiving his creation, provided the human beings involved exercised proper care and discipline in their use of observation. Much of his philosophy consists of the necessary proofs for the existence of such a deity.

The self-consciousness which is the first principle of Cartesian philosophy is supplied by the soul, in communication with God. 'Feeling' is a condition only possible where there is self-consciousness, and self-consciousness is only possible where there is a soul. Since animals do not have souls, they cannot feel, and the physical signs which suggest that they do are merely mechanical reflexes.[97]

Their consciences clear, scientists embarked on the path which, in the sacred pursuit of knowledge, was to sacrifice millions more animals than the altars of ancient piety had ever required. 'The theory of the animal-machine is a grim foretaste of a mechanically minded age,' says Boyce

Gibson, in *The Philosophy of Descartes*, 'and it brutally violates the old kindly fellowship of living things.'[98] A long step had been taken along the road to the assumption that human beings are entitled, either in their own interest or in the interest of knowledge in the abstract, to exploit to the limit the resources of the natural world around them. It only remained to deny the existence of the soul, and the way was open for human beings, too, to be classed as animal-machines, as was to happen a century later in theory,* and three centuries later in hideous practice.

In spite of the central role played by God in his philosophy, Descartes contributed to the growing autonomy of the individual which Sorokin sees as a concomitant of a developing sensate society, an individualism which, as Bertrand Russell points out, distinguished the Cynic and Stoic philosophy of antiquity, as well as the seventeenth to nineteenth centuries of the modern era.[99] 'No amount of criticism on points of logic and detail,' says Boyce Gibson, 'should blind us to the revolutionary importance of Descartes' approach to philosophy. For the first time in the history of thought, personality (not experience as a content but the personality which asserts it) is taken as the primary philosophical concept.'[100] The Reformation had asserted the right of the individual to direct access to God. Now a whole theory of knowledge was being based on the primacy of the concept of individual self-consciousness.

It was to this same 'self' that the philosophers now turned for guidance in constructing a system of ethics derived not from authority, but from reason. Descartes's near contemporary, Thomas Hobbes, was a thoroughgoing materialist, for whom matter and motion were the only ultimate realities, the basis of everything including feeling and thought. The primary problem of existence has become, not to fathom man's place in the universe, but to elucidate how we can be sure of anything. 'There is no conception in a man's mind which hath not at first, totally or by parts, been begotten upon the organs of sense', concluded Hobbes in *Leviathan*.[101] Rookmaaker, in *Modern Art and the Death of a Culture*, points to a developing change of emphasis, wherein *reason* is being supplanted by *rationality*, in other words, the exclusion, or rejection, of all that is not rationally verifiable. 'Rationalism . . . means that there is nothing more in the world but what the senses can perceive and reason apprehend.'[102]

Man is wholly the measure. Given this premise, Hobbes concludes

---

* La Mettrie, *L'homme machine*, first published 1748 (Gibson, p.207). An English version, *Man a Machine* and *Man a Plant*, translated by R.A. Watson and M. Rybalka, was published in 1994 by Hackett, Cambridge and Indianapolis.

that 'good' and 'bad' signify no more than the distinction between sensations we experience as pleasurable, and those which are painful.

> Whatsoever is the object of any man's Appetite or Desire; that is it, which he for his part calleth *Good*: And the object of his Hate, and Aversion, *Evill*; And of his Contempt, *Vile and Inconsiderable*. For these words of Good, Evill, and Contemptible, are ever used with relation to the person that useth them: There being nothing simply and absolutely so; nor any common Rule of Good and Evill, to be taken from the nature of the objects themselves.[103]

Ethically, this leaves human beings in a permanent state of conflict with one another, with no overarching moral imperatives restraining their conduct; and it was from this condition that Hobbes derived his political conception of the necessity, if peace and security were to prevail, of an absolute and all-powerful ruler. God is introduced at this point in the argument as the ultimate omnipotent ruler, author of the command to obey the earthly powers-that-be, but this in no way undermined the principle that morality is based on self-interest, since eternal life or eternal damnation depended on compliance with the final omnipotent power.[104]

John Locke, towards the end of the seventeenth century, spent the best part of twenty years struggling with the question of the reliability of sense perception, cogitations which finally appeared under the title *An Essay on Human Understanding*. He concluded that ethical and mathematical propositions, being based on the relationship of ideas and thus fully subject to rational scrutiny, could claim a validity to which propositions about external reality could not aspire.[105]

Locke based his ethical theory on the premise that happiness is the principal goal of conduct, and in his *Second Treatise of Civil Government* explored the implications of this conclusion for the relations between government and governed. Locke himself, like Descartes, accepted, indeed required, the existence of God, as author of the natural law, evident to all through the exercise of reason, which asserts that 'being all equal and independent, no one ought to harm another in his life, health, liberty, or possessions'.[106] It is historically evident, however, that powerful individuals will do exactly that, and Locke sees the institution of civil government as stemming from the need to defend natural rights against the assaults of tyrants and oppressors. His political theories explore how best to construct the necessary instruments of government.

The mankind eulogized by Renaissance humanism had in reality been not humanity in general, but an idealized image; scholarly, virtuous, healthy and noble. Locke envisaged 'all being equal and independent' (though it is only males with property to safeguard who are specifically mentioned as qualifying to give or withhold consent to government. If in the context of his treatises 'men' and the masculine pronouns are to be taken as 'embracing women', he does not say so, nor is there any reason to suppose that he intended they should). His ideas were immensely influential among the colonists of the thirteen American states; indeed, it was Locke, then serving as secretary to the Council of Trade and Plantations, who in 1673 drafted the *Fundamental Constitutions for the Government of Carolina*.[107] Though he was not directly involved in the preparation of the English Bill of Rights of 1689 (he was abroad at the time), it had much in common with his thinking. A century later, early in 1776, Tom Paine, in *Common Sense*, launched into a diatribe against the tyranny and oppression rife in Europe, lambasted monarchy and the hereditary principle, and called upon the American people to make themselves independent of England and establish republicanism with representative government, objectives of which he regarded the independence issue as secondary, but necessary in view of the prevailing political circumstances.[108]

The process was in train which was to lead, in July 1776, to the promulgation of one of the most influential documents in human history – the American Declaration of Independence.

We hold these truths to be self-evident, that all men are created equal, that they are endowed by their Creator with certain inalienable Rights; that among these are Life, Liberty and the pursuit of Happiness;[*] that to secure these rights Governments are instituted among Men deriving their just powers from the consent of the governed; that whenever any Form of Government becomes destructive of these ends, it is the Right of the People to alter or to abolish it, and to institute new Government, laying its foundation

---

[*] Earlier drafts of the declaration, and the declarations of rights being drawn up in individual colonial states, followed Locke even more closely, specifying the right to 'life, liberty and property', the version that Jefferson preferred, though Franklin persuaded him to change it. This reading was retained in the constitutions of several states – not least because property was seen as the sheet anchor guaranteeing life and liberty (Commager, pp.83, 103, 107; Becker, pp.121, 240). After the collapse of Communism in eastern Europe, the Polish prime minister placed huge significance on the right to the ownership of property as a bulwark of liberty.

on such principles and organizing its powers in such form, as to them shall seem most likely to effect their Safety and Happiness.[109]

It is true that 'the Creator' gets a mention, both here and in the preceding paragraph, which refers to the assumption by the colonists of 'the separate and equal station to which the Laws of Nature, and of Nature's God, entitle them'. God, however, is there to justify rights rather than to enjoin duties.* There has been a complete reversal of the order of priorities in which the basic documents of the previous Post-Reformation centuries had dealt.

After the cataclysms of the Reformation, old and new religious institutions had felt the need to clarify where they stood in relation to their rivals, and catechisms proliferated. When the Calvinist Geneva catechism asked, 'What is the chief end of human life?' the reply was not 'To seek happiness', but 'To know God, by whom we have been made human beings.' The Westminster Confession, the result of deliberations by English Puritan commissioners to the Assembly of Divines at Westminster in 1647,† asked, 'What is the Chief End of Man?' and provided the answer, 'Man's chief end is to glorify God and to enjoy him for ever.' When the Church of England incorporated in the 1549 Book of Common Prayer a catechism expanding on the duty of the Christian to God and to his neighbour, it made no mention of rights, but instructed that:

My duty towards my Neighbour is to love him as myself, and to do to all men as I would they should do unto me: To love, honour, and succour my father and mother: To honour and obey the King, and all that are put in authority under him: To submit myself to all my governors, teachers, spiritual pastors and masters: To order myself lowly and reverently to all my betters: To hurt nobody by word nor deed: To be true and just in all my dealing: To bear no malice nor hatred in my heart: To keep my hands from picking and stealing, and my tongue from evil-speaking, lying and slandering: To keep

---

* When Fanny Trollope was travelling in America early in the next century, she heard discussions as to whether George Washington was or was not a Christian. His farewell address on declining re-election to the presidency settled the issue, in her eyes, in the affirmative. 'Of all the dispositions and habits which lead to political prosperity, religion and morality are indispensable supports . . . And let us with caution indulge the supposition that morality can be maintained without religion, reason and experience both forbid us to expect that national morality can prevail in exclusion of religious principle' (Trollope, pp.192–3). This reads very like Polybius's defence of Roman religion – not that it is true in itself, but that it is a necessary adjunct to civil society.

† Later adopted by the Scottish Presbyterians.

my body in temperance, soberness, and chastity: Not to covet nor desire other men's goods; but to learn and labour truly to get mine own living, and to do my duty in that state of life, unto which it shall please God to call me.

The casting of the final phrase in the future tense saves this confession of faith from the charge of advocating total submission to the status quo, since (and here is an echo of the Protestant innovation of the secular calling) there is no knowing to what destiny the call may summon. Nevertheless, it is obvious that, whatever its merits in seeking to promote honesty and decency, the whole tenor of this catechism is to safeguard the existing order of society, with all its entrenched privileges. The American Revolution had already challenged this complacency. Now France was to deal it a terminal blow.

Jean Jacques Rousseau had published *The Social Contract* in 1762. His basic tenet is that all men are born equal and have an equal right to liberty from oppression and exploitation. 'Man is born free; and everywhere he is in chains' are the words with which the first chapter resoundingly opens. The political philosophy Rousseau erected on this foundation, with its distrust of private property, its appeal to a somewhat mysterious 'general will' (not necessarily identical to majority opinion) and its confidence in emotion as a satisfactory guide to right conduct, was to pave the way for a totalitarianism that expunged all prospect of individual liberty, but such unforeseen consequences were for the future to unfold. For his immediate contemporaries, the clarion call was to establish liberty and equality.

French troops had served with the American revolutionary armies, and in the 1770s had witnessed both the triumph of the rebellion and the political steps involved in its prosecution. Tom Paine, whose writings had made so significant an impact in the American colonies, now turned his attention to the needs of France, where shifting coalitions of interests were bringing pressure to bear on the King to abandon absolutist royal rule. By August 1789 a National Constituent Assembly had adopted a 'Declaration of the Rights of Man and the Citizen'. The American Declaration had addressed itself to a specific and localized problem – the relationship between the colonies and the King of England. The French sought a declaration of universal significance. As Jacques Godechot puts it in *France and the Atlantic Revolution*:

The French deputies . . . desired to prepare, in Mirabeau's words, 'a declaration applicable to all ages, all peoples, all moral and

298

geographical latitudes'. In it are to be found neither the name of a nation nor the description of a system of government; it is as valid for a monarchy as for a republic. It is truly universal.[110]

The Declaration of the Rights of Man and the Citizen promulgated seventeen '*sacred* rights', of which the most basic stated: 'The end of all political associations is the preservation of the natural and imprescriptible rights of man; and these rights are Liberty, Property, Security and Resistance of Oppression.' The remaining rights elaborated the various ways in which this basic principle was to be implemented (such as freedom from arbitrary arrest, freedom of religion and of expression, limitation of the law to such restrictions as are necessary to guarantee free exercise of the rights of others, the right to concur, either personally or by representation, in formation of the law),[*] ending with a resounding insistence that 'the right to property being inviolable and sacred, no one ought to be deprived of it, except in cases of evident public necessity, legally ascertained, and on condition of a previous just indemnity'.[111]

At this stage the French revolution was anti-Roman Catholic, but not anti-religious. The enormous wealth and economic privileges of the established Roman Catholic Church resulted in deliberate legislative curbs on the Church as an institution. The abolition of tithes and the nationalization of Church property were accompanied by assurances of state support, the price of which was an oath of loyalty to the State and severance from obedience to Rome – a price which virtually all the bishops and about half the clergy refused to pay, leading, after a brief period during which there were two functioning churches, to unbridled persecution of nonjurors, their massacre or flight into exile. As for the religious orders, they were viewed as largely parasitical, and anyway the ethos of self-sacrifice was totally contrary to ideals of liberty and the pursuit of happiness. All future taking of religious vows was forbidden, and recognition of existing religious vows was withdrawn from all but educational and charitable orders; though by 1792 all teaching by monks and nuns was forbidden. Erstwhile monks found that their only hope of survival was to take the oath of allegiance and vie for a living vacated by an ejected nonjuror.[112]

---

[*] The deputies to the Constituent Assembly soon hedged this last right. Women, black slaves and Jews were excluded, and a minimum level of tax paid, as well as conditions as to age and length of domicile, was soon incorporated in the qualifications for franchise (Schama, pp.497–8). The universal direct suffrage incorporated in the constitution of 1793 (not implemented because of war) did not include women (Godechot, pp.165–6).

Influential elements in French society were intent on a campaign of de-Christianization, in which civic celebrations and commemorative holidays like Bastille Day replaced religious festivals. Marriage was declared a civil contract (a development precipitated by a church refusal to perform the marriage ceremony for an actor), divorce was legalized, and when the remains of Voltaire were disinterred from the abbey where he had been buried (the site being up for sale), no clergy were invited to participate in the obsequies of his reburial in the Pantheon.

But the need for some sort of transcendental authority figured in the calculations of even the most radical political philosophers. Tom Paine's philosophy needed God (though not, as was soon to become apparent, the Christian God):

> . . . man came from the hand of his Maker . . . we are now got at the origin of man, and at the origin of his rights . . . men are all of one degree, and consequently . . . all men are born equal . . . His natural rights are the foundation of all his civil rights

he wrote in *The Rights of Man*.[113] 'Even to Rousseau . . . a state religion was a necessity; he saw the *religion civile* as the heart of the moral machinery by which the inherent vices of civilization could be eradicated',[114] and 'for all his personal deism, Voltaire had always thought religion, stripped of its legally coercive power, indispensable for public morality . . . they envisaged a church dissolved into the general purposes of the public realm: a useful, rather than an ineffable institution'.[115] The Declaration itself, like its American counterpart, nodded in the direction of religious sanction, with the inclusion of a phrase to the effect that the National Assembly laboured 'in the presence of the Supreme Being, and with the hope of his blessing and favour'.

It was, however, a theology that indubitably gave priority to what human beings wanted. To Rousseau, man was naturally good, it was corrupt institutions that led him astray. 'The essential, unifying conviction of the Enlightenment . . .' writes John McManners in *The French Revolution and the Church*, 'was the rejection of the idea of original sin . . . Everyone agreed that man had an inalienable right to pursue happiness here on earth . . . Enlightened self-interest was the well-spring of moral conduct.'[116]

God was still there, but Christ and his redemptive mission had become redundant. The God of the Enlightenment was to be divined in nature, and in natural law. In the second part of *The Rights of Man*, published in 1792, Paine is crediting Nature with purposes and intentions, and personifying her as female.* In August 1793 a colossal statue of the Goddess of Nature was unveiled, with invocations, and in October the Christian calendar was superseded by a new system based on Nature, evoking cycles of the weather and the seasons, introducing a ten-day week which obliterated Sunday, and dating the years from the birth not of Jesus Christ, but of the French Republic.[117]

Even the state Church now ceased to have a role. The Paris Commune had tried to ban the celebration of Midnight Mass at Christmas 1792. By late 1793 priests were being forced to abjure their vocation and churches were being destroyed. Though hundreds of the nonjuring clergy had been rounded up and imprisoned in mass arrests in September 1792, large numbers had had time to emigrate. Now the 'constitutional' priests were trapped, and thousands were executed or imprisoned.[118]

On 10 November 1793 Notre Dame was the scene of a great festival, during which the cathedral was rededicated as the Temple of Reason. The Christian God was officially dethroned and in his place was installed the principle of Reason, to whom the Goddess of Liberty, played by an actress from the Opéra, made obeisance before seating herself upon a bank of flowers and plants. In Lyons an antihymn celebrating 'Reason as the Supreme Being' was sung.[119] At ceremonies all over France vestments and confessionals were burnt, while effigies of the Goddesses of Reason, Liberty and Nature were carried aloft.[120]

The supreme being who hovered behind these metaphorical personifications was a vague and shadowy concept, and Tom Paine was becoming alarmed at the speed with which all transcendental authority was being jettisoned. In November and December of 1793, in Paris, Paine completed for publication the first part of his *The Age of Reason*,† laying down his pen only hours before, as by then he fully expected, he was himself arrested. 'In the general wreck of superstition, of false systems of government and false theology,' he wrote, 'we lose sight of morality, of humanity and of the theology that is true.' His attack on Christianity was unconstrained, but he affirmed his faith in 'the only idea man can affix to the name of God . . . that of a *first cause*, the cause of all things'.[121] The true word of God, the true revelation, is the Creation we

---

* 'As nature created [man] for social life, she fitted him for the station she intended . . . She has gone further. She has not only forced man into society by a diversity of wants . . . she has implanted in him a system of social affections, which . . . are essential to his happiness . . .' (Paine (1915), pp.157–8).

† Internal evidence, including his failure to include Uranus, discovered in 1781, among his list of planets, leads to some supposition that the bulk of this part was written much earlier (Paine (1910), p.3).

behold. 'Search not the book called scripture, which any human hand might make, but the scripture called Creation.'[122] True theology lies in the study of the eternal and immutable mathematical principles underlying Creation – science should replace Latin and Greek in the schools. The moral message from the Almighty is 'Learn from my munificence to be kind to each other';[123] moral duty consists of imitating the goodness and beneficence of God manifested in the Creation towards all his creatures.[124] 'Nature red in tooth and claw' was a manifestation of creativity in action which Paine, like his contemporaries the Romantic poets, preferred to ignore.

Paine was not alone in his alarm at the complete social breakdown accompanying rampant atheism. Assumptions of basic human virtue and evolutionary perfection were fading as the excesses of revolution and civil war took their toll.* Intellectuals were coming to the reluctant conclusion that 'only the educated man could practise social virtues by rational choice', a conclusion much like that which had assailed Polybius two millennia earlier. For the people as a whole, belief in God and in life after death were necessary to social control – without it, men would be 'ravening wolves'.[125] Various useful cults and rituals were proposed, the most influential of which, 'Théophilanthropie', explicitly denied any doctrine of original sin, but proffered a cult of the supreme being and an assurance of immortality.

The cults generated little in the way of loyalty or enthusiasm, and with civil unrest continuing while only a desultory bureaucracy celebrated such rites of passage as marriage and death, First Consul Napoleon accepted that a reconciliation with the Pope was the most sensible course to follow. By 1800 nursing nuns were being urgently sought for the depleted hospitals. The 'constitutional' Church held its last council in 1801, a concordat with the Vatican was negotiated, and on Easter Sunday, 1802, a solemn Te Deum was sung in Notre Dame in celebration of the return of France to her Roman Catholic roots.[126]

---

* *The Times* of 12 September 1792, for instance, printed the following, claimed as an eye-witness account: 'At the Place Dauphin, the mob had made a fire, and before it, several men, women and children were roasted alive. The Countess Perignan with her two daughters, the daughters first, and the mother after, were stripped of their cloaths, washed with oil and roasted alive, while the mob were singing and dancing round the fire, and amusing themselves with their cries and sufferings. After the repeated prayers of the eldest girl, not more than 15 years old, that some one would with a sword or a pistol put an end to her horrid existence, a young man shot her through the heart, which so irritated the mob, that they immediately threw him into the fire, saying, he should suffer in her place. When the mother was roasted, the mob brought six priests to the same fire, and then cutting some flesh from the body, ordered the Priests to eat it . . .'

The exaltation of deism had miscarried, the triumph of atheism had been aborted. But it had been a prophetic pregnancy.

Chapter 16

Technology Triumphant: the Eighteenth Century

The theatre of the Age of Enlightenment was unashamedly sensate; it was there to entertain. The last thing the devotees of the Goddess of Reason wished to do was to involve – even if they accepted the existence of – their souls. 'It was a facile, elegant world,' writes Mantzius of the later eighteenth-century drama,

> with good manners and good clothes, sharp-tongued and witty and not without sentimental leanings; eminently fitted for the brilliant presentation of lightly-touched, elegant comedy, but containing absolutely no-one, whether man or woman, capable of going below the surface in search of the deeper things of the soul, the very existence of which seemed for the time to have been forgotten.[1]

So the eighteenth century witnessed a prolonged diet of farces, burlesques, parodies (the theatre companies preyed incestuously on one another) and superficial social comedies. Dr Faustus, for instance, had metamorphosed into a farce by the late seventeenth century, and *The Tempest* had been reworked with the characters recast as degraded Londoners, Prospero himself appearing as 'Duke of my Lord's Dog Kennel'.[2]

'Nature' as the ultimate repository of truth dominated dramatic criticism. Shakespeare was constantly praised for what was seen as his 'naturalism'; Dryden (who had, incidentally, been one of the first members of the Royal Society)* had in his *An Essay of Dramatic Poesy* stressed Shakespeare's truth to nature ('he needed not the spectacles of books to read nature'), and Samuel Johnson, almost exactly a century later, harped on the same theme in his *On Shakespeare*. 'It is the great

* He was elected on 26 November 1662 (*Dictionary of National Biography* Vol.VI, p.65).

excellence of Shakespeare that he drew his scenes from nature and from life . . . Shakespeare is above all writers . . . the poet that holds up to his readers a faithful mirror of manners and of life'.[3] The actor Thomas Dogget won particular renown for seeking to 'characterize each of his figures with naturalistic precision in dress and speech. Above all, he was successful in reproducing the ways and manners of the lower classes.'[4] Equally popular was the upper-class comedy of manners. Dogget's colleague Colley Cibber excelled early in the eighteenth century as the quintessential Lord Foppington; later the actor James Dodd became the

> acknowledged darling of the public as the impersonator of the more or less idiotic coxcombs, the brainless idlers, lineal descendants of Lord Foppington without one of whom no comedy was complete. In the art of wearing an ultra-fashionable costume, poising a cane, offering his porcelain snuff-box and helping himself to a pinch, he stood unrivalled.[5]

The excessive profanity and obscenity of the late seventeenth century had been curbed, but the 'reformation of manners' was, according to Allardyce Nicoll, entirely superficial.

> A new viciousness was arising . . . The men and the women of 1685–1700 who professed to abhor the immoralities of Charles's court appeared to love hearing the enunciation by lisping infants of sexual ideas not usually referred to even by adults in polite society . . . Children . . . made up for the comparative innocence of the body of the play by uttering the most filthy obscenities in the licence of the epilogue.

He cites examples as recited by six- and eight-year-old girls.[6] The eighteenth century continued these episodes. 'Cynicism, callousness, external veneer of morality and inner viciousness' is Nicoll's summary of contemporary comedy.[7]

Sensate predilection for sauciness and spice led to some rewriting of Shakespeare. John Dennis in 1702 had added some titillating material to *The Merry Wives of Windsor*, and Dryden had rewritten *The Tempest* to provide, among other new characters, 'a sexy twin sister named Dorinda' for the innocent Miranda, adding 'scenes in which Prospero warns them both against men'.[8] This version was highly successful, dominated eighteenth-century productions of the play, and was still being performed well into the nineteenth century, until Macready in 1838 finally laid Dorinda's ghost to rest.[9]

On the whole, Shakespeare's comedies were not nearly as popular as those of the Restoration (superficially verbally expurgated), and most were seldom performed prior to the 1720s and 1730s.[10] To make them more palatable, they were presented as musicals. Song and dance invaded production after production – the popular *A Midsummer Night's Dream* did not receive a 'straight' performance from 1642 until 1840.[11] In an assessment reminiscent (as is much else in this period of the English theatre) of the Roman theatre in the first century BC, when Cicero questioned the artistic influence of sweet airs on the profundity of the drama, Dane Farnsworth Smith writes that

> a superfluity of music ... in focussing the attention upon the emotions interferes with thinking and tends to injure the intellectual life of the nation. Certainly when music has the seductive quality which it evinced during the first appearance of *The Beggar's Opera** it does not prepare the public for the reception of great drama.[12]

Two other innovations – both, again, characteristic of the Roman theatre towards the end of the last century BC and the start of the first AD – now conspired to dominate eighteenth-century productions. Prodigious investments of talent and treasure were devoted to spectacular stage effects and settings; and pantomime was reintroduced.

The seventeenth century had already witnessed lavish productions stemming from the court masques, for which Inigo Jones had introduced fabulous scenic effects, with clouds and flying chariots.[13] A magnificent theatre in Dorset Gardens, designed by Wren and decorated by Grinling Gibbons, had been opened by d'Avenant's old company from Lincoln's Inn Fields in 1671 (d'Avenant himself was by then dead), fully equipped with all the latest technology. This grand and much-praised edifice, initially inheriting the Lincoln's Inn Fields name of the Duke's Theatre but renamed the Queen's Theatre after the Duke of York became James II, had later to be abandoned, being too close to the river, and in 1709 it was demolished.[14] During its brief supremacy, however, Dorset Gardens popularized Shakespeare with highly operatic productions that had Macbeth's witches singing, dancing and flying; a version of *The Tempest* engulfed in thunder and lightning during which the ship is wrecked in

---

* John Gay's 'ballad opera' was first staged early in 1728 (by the new calendar; 1727 by the old).

tempestuous seas ('in perpetual Agitation') while 'several Spirits in horrid shapes' hover over the sailors, later reappearing in more friendly guise attending upon Ariel who is also hovering in the air; and a version of *A Midsummer Night's Dream* (under the title *The Fairy Queen*), the description of one scene of which, as quoted by Odell in his *Shakespeare from Betterton to Irving*, could almost be interchanged with Apuleius's account from the first century AD:

> A Sonata plays while the Sun rises, it appears red through the mist, as it ascends it dissipates the Vapours, and is seen in its full lustre: then the Scene is perfectly discovered, the Fountains enrich'd with gilding, and adorn'd with Statues: The View is terminated by a Walk of Cypress Trees which lead to a delightful Bower. Before the Trees stand rows of Marble Columns, which support many Walks which rise by stairs to the Top of the House; the Stairs are adorn'd with Figures on Pedestals, and Rails and Balasters on each side of 'em. Near the top, vast Quantities of Water break out of the Hills, and fall in mighty Cascades to the bottom of Scene, to feed the Fountains, which are on each side. In the middle of the Stage is a very large Fountain, where the Water rises about twelve Foot . . . a Machine appears, the Clouds break from before it, and Phoebus appears in a Chariot drawn by four Horses.[15]

Odell's source concludes: 'The Court and Town were wonderfully satisfy'd with it; but the Expences in setting it out being so great, the Company got very little by it.'

Fortunately another, but somewhat less financially daunting, opportunity to amaze and dazzle audiences made its appearance. Allardyce Nicoll sees modern pantomime as owing its genesis in England to a series of performances of 'Harlequin and Scaramouche, after the Italian manner' which were advertised from August to September of 1702.[16] These characters stem from the *commedia dell'arte*, and if they have a Roman origin, it lies in Atellane farce, not in pantomime in its Roman sense.* But the performances had in common with classical pantomime a predominance of music and dancing, and a story initially in dumb show. The impresario John Rich, 'the perfecter, if not the inventor of English pantomime', was particularly noted for 'his mimetic skill as Harlequin', his pantomimes being performed initially at Lincoln's Inn

---

* See p.79.

Fields,* but later moving to Covent Garden, a theatre built by Rich in
1731. One of his most successful performances consisted in being
'hatched by the rays of the sun from a large egg on the stage. His
pantomime, after leaving the shell, was wonderful.'[17] Conjuring,
acrobatic tricks and other musical-hall type diversions were soon added
to the pantomime repertoire.[18] Dr Faustus now emerged in a new guise –
Harlequin Dr Faustus, using his magic skills to run the gamut of the stage
technicians' ingenuity. At Lincoln's Inn Fields in 1723 Rich had a
dragon belching flames which descended towards the stage, dropping
demons from its claws, and finally swallowing Faustus. This was such a
success that Drury Lane, the rival house, also put on a Harlequin Dr
Faustus, in an attempt to win back trade.[19]

Interludes of dancing and singing were interspersed in the intervals of
serious drama. Odell finds rather shocking an advertisement dating from
1704 which promised the audience that during the presentation of 'a Play
called *Macbeth*' there would be 'several Sonatas on the Violin by
Signior Gasperini. Also several Entertainments of Dancing by the
Famous Monsieur Du Ruel.'[20] The Harlequinades, however, were played
as after-pieces (a tradition that continued in the West End theatres as late
as the 1930s). Financially, they proved essential. It was they, rather than
the main drama, that brought in the paying public.

Actors found this an embarrassment. The public, explained a
travelling player in *The Vicar of Wakefield*, only go to the theatre 'to be
amused, and find themselves happy when they can enjoy a pantomime
under the sanction of Jonson's or Shakespeare's name'.[21] According to
the biographer of Barton Booth, Shakespearian actor with the Drury
Lane company, Booth had confessed that

> there were many more spectators than men of taste or judgement;
> and if, by the artifice of a pantomime, they could entice a greater
> number to partake of the *utile dulci* of a good play . . . he could not

* The original Duke's Theatre, Lincoln's Inn Fields, from which d'Avenant's company had
moved to Dorset Gardens, was used by the King's Men for a time in 1672 while their own Theatre
Royal, Drury Lane, was being rebuilt after a fire. It was refurbished and reopened in 1695 by a
group of actors who were quarrelling with the Drury Lane management, and who succeeded in
obtaining from the Lord Chamberlain a licence to set up a separate company. In 1705 this company
moved, initially to Vanbrugh's new theatre in the Haymarket, and later back to rejoin the Drury
Lane company. John Rich took over the Lincoln's Inn site and rebuilt it, opening his new Lincoln's
Inn Theatre in 1714 on the strength of d'Avenant's old patent from Charles II, which had come into
his father's possession and passed to him by inheritance. Later he bought Killigrew's patent, and
used it to develop Covent Garden (Nicoll, Vol.I, pp.322, 335–6; Vol.II, pp.271–2; Liesenfeld,
pp.171, 197, 197, note 12; Smith, D.F., pp.59–64).

see any great harm in it; that as they were performed after the play, they were no interruption to it, and gave the people of fashion a better opportunity (if they left the house before the farce began) of getting to their coaches with more ease than if the whole audience poured out together. For his part, he confessed he considered profit as well as fame; and as to their plays – even they reaped some advantage from the pantomimes, by adding to the accounts, which enabled the managers to be more expensive in habits, and other decorating of the theatre in general, and to give better encouragement to their performers.[22]

The century that witnessed the formal recognition of the pursuit of happiness as a primary goal of human existence was uncomfortable with tragedy. Already in the late seventeenth century *Romeo and Juliet* had been rewritten to provide a happy ending, and although this version did not last, a *King Lear* as rewritten by Nahum Tate in 1681, in which Lear is restored to his kingdom, the part of the Fool excised, and Cordelia, far from perishing, has a love affair with Edgar and lives happy ever after, entirely superseded Shakespeare's original for the whole of the eighteenth century.[23] An attempt was made at Covent Garden in 1768 to stage a pre-Tate version, possibly even including the original ending, but it was a failure. As one contemporary critic said:

> We think his having restored the original distressed catastrophe, is a circumstance not greatly in favour of humanity, or delicacy of feeling, since it is now rather too shocking to be borne; and the rejecting of the episode of the loves of Edgar and Cordelia, so happily conceived by Tate, has, beyond all doubt, greatly weakened the piece . . .[24]

As late as 1820 the producer of a *Lear* starring Edmund Kean explained that 'the public taste long ago decided against the sublime, but terrible catastrophe of the original . . .'; not until 1845 was the tragedy again staged as Shakespeare wrote it.[25]

Dr Johnson was among those who considered Shakespeare's *Lear* intolerable. He found Cordelia's death so affecting that 'I know not whether I ever endured to read again the last scenes of the play till I undertook to revise them as an editor.' Shakespeare, he says, allows the virtuous Cordelia to perish 'contrary to the natural ideas of justice'; and 'since all reasonable beings naturally love justice, I cannot easily be persuaded that . . . the audience will not always rise better pleased from the final triumph of persecuted virtue'.[26]

There are echoes here of Plato and Aristotle, who in a period which similarly sought to domesticate Providence in accordance with human-centred ideals of natural justice, rejected as infamous the unmerited, arbitrary suffering in the tragedies of Aeschylus and Sophocles, demanding that any character meeting with disaster should, through some personal flaw or inadequacy (as in the dramas of Euripides), deserve it. Kitto sees similar cultural forces at work at their period of antiquity, and in the seventeenth and eighteenth centuries.

> In each case the human mind seems to have achieved its new clarity
> by contracting its field of vision; in each case, a classical tragedy,
> poetry at its most comprehensive, almost disappeared over the
> horizon . . . leaving as its successors Heroic or a rhetorical tragedy,
> and either witty or sentimental comedy.[27]

Attempts to popularize Shakespearian tragedy took a form for which, again, there is a precedent to be found in Rome in the first century BC, when, to the disgust of Cicero and Horace, a lavish cast of extras was introduced into classical Greek tragedy, dazzling the senses with opulent processions.* Funerals and coronations provided excellent opportunities. 'Though not absolutely essential,' wrote a contemporary of Juliet's funeral in a 1770 production of *Romeo and Juliet*, 'nothing could be better devised than a funeral procession, to render this play thoroughly popular.'[28] Contemporary Ciceros and Horaces were not lacking to object to 'all this pomp, shew, and farce', but public taste prevailed. 'The very idea of a triumphal procession at Covent-Garden struck terror to the whole host of Drury', wrote a critic of the 1745–55 period,[29] and the two theatres spent the century out-processioning one another, the processions on offer forming an important element of the advertising playbills.[30]

A *Coriolanus* of 1755 included 'in the military Procession alone, independent of the Civil', 108 persons, including lictors and incense-bearers, captive generals in chains, gold and silver 'spoil', and assorted standard-bearers. Priests, flamens, choristers, senators, tribunes and 'matrons' figured in the civil procession.[31] The real-life coronation of George III in 1761 inspired coronation processions at both playhouses in 1762, Drury Lane performing *Henry VIII* with a coronation for Anne

---

* See above, p.89.

Boleyn that involved at least 136 attendants, from choristers, musicians and 'the Queen's herb-woman strewing flowers' to representatives of every aspect of the judiciary, military, aristocracy and church.* It was not a success – the public thought the clothes tawdry, but were delighted by the 'fine cloaths, of velvet, silk, sattin, lace, feathers, jewels, pearls, etc.' paraded by Rich at the rival Covent Garden coronation scene.[32]

A feast of another kind was sought in a thoroughgoing emotional wallow. A 'weepy' was much enjoyed: 'the ladies delighted in tears and pathetic situations', writes Nicoll.[33] This did not include any agonizing over the injustice of fate, reflections that perhaps lie 'too deep for tears'. Chance was all – as an anonymous tragedy of 1704, *The Rival Brothers*, explained:

> Our Life is all a Journey in the dark
> Where every step we take is on the Brink
> Of some most horrid dreadful Precipice.
> And now we Pass on safe, and now we fall,
> We know not how, All Chance, at least in us.[34]

Shakespeare's tragedies and historical dramas were milked and when necessary rewritten to feed the appetite for tears. Thomas Otway, late in the seventeenth century, wrote a new scene for *Romeo and Juliet* in which Juliet awoke in the tomb before Romeo died, thus permitting a heart-rending farewell. This formed part of a completely revamped version of the tragedy which was grafted on to a tale of the Roman civil wars of Marius and Sulla, Romeo being translated into young Marius. In spite of the change of period and name, the play was basically Shakespeare's, and, under the title *Caius Marius*, ousted the original until Theophilus Cibber's hybrid revival of 1744. Otway's new and affecting scene was retained and continued to be played until well into the nineteenth century, and when David Garrick, four years after the Cibber production, returned substantially to Shakespeare's play, he too retained the idea of the deathbed reunion (which he rewrote), a scene of which a contemporary declared, 'Romeo's distraction, and her tenderness, are so excellently wrought up, that we cannot suppose any heart so obdurate as not to be penetrated.'[35]

Tate rewrote the end of *Coriolanus* to provide a scene of 'affected pathos' in which Coriolanus's little son, unable to understand that his

---

* Some half-century later, Covent Garden virtually paralleled this procession, attaching it this time to the christening of Princess Elizabeth (Odell, Vol.I, p.425).

mother is dead (Tate had introduced the novelty of her suicide), fears that some misdemeanour of his own has inclined her not to speak to him.[36] This enthusiasm for tear-jerking was still evident in 1814, when Edmund Kean produced a version of *Richard II* using Lear's lament over Cordelia (redundant in the revised original) to provide a new scene in which the Queen grieved over the slain Richard.[37]

While pathos sentimentalized the tragic austerity of Aristotelian catharsis-through-pity-and-fear, melodrama coarsened violence into ghoulishness. The French theatre had stuck to classical precedents, but English audiences continued into the eighteenth century their long-standing relish for on-stage violence.[38] Nicoll comments on stage directions of the late seventeenth century that 'equal in bloody suggestion even some of the passages in *Titus Andronicus*', citing scenes of execution and mutilation, of torture and impaling.[39] Even the original version of *Titus Andronicus* was found insufficiently bloodthirsty, and in the late seventeenth century it was reworked, providing a version that 'transposes scenes, changes motives, piles on extra horrors'.[40] The sensitive Dr Johnson declared that 'the barbarity of the spectacles, and the general massacre which are here exhibited, can scarcely be conceived tolerable to any audience . . . that Shakespeare wrote any part . . . I see no reason for believing'.[41] In the nineteenth century the play was to disappear from the repertoire of the English stage, but it enjoyed a certain vogue in the early eighteenth century, becoming increasingly rare after about 1725.[42] *Coriolanus* was subjected to similar treatment by Tate, who introduced the threatened rape and suicide of Coriolanus's wife, the collapse into madness of Coriolanus's indomitable mother Volumnia, and her gratuitous braining of a further member of the cast. Throughout the eighteenth century most productions replace Shakespeare's dignified Volumnia with a figure waving a dagger and threatening to kill herself in order to put pressure on her son not to harm Rome – 'a sickening cheapening of the character', says Odell; but it enabled actresses to strike pleasing tragic attitudes.[43]

In *An Essay of Dramatic Poesy* Dryden had defended the tradition of off-stage deaths, pointing out, with examples drawn from classical and Elizabethan authors, that 'death is far more affecting if narrated'; indeed, except where the deaths are real, as in the gladiatorial shows, they may tend to cause hilarity when merely simulated in public view. To his regret, 'whether custom has so insinuated itself into our countrymen, or nature has so formed them to fierceness, I know not; but they will scarcely suffer combats and other objects of horror to be taken from them'.[44]

This zest on the part of Dryden's contemporaries for gratuitous violence was not confined to the theatre and was to persist throughout most of the next century. Cock-fighting, bear-baiting and goose-throwing were as popular as ever.[45] By the end of the seventeenth century the upper-class young blades who formed a substantial section of London audiences were notorious for street rowdiness.[46] These 'mohocks', as by the early eighteenth century they were called,[*] showed mercy to neither age nor sex. Thoroughly drunk, they

> employed their ample leisure in forcing prostitutes and old women to stand on their heads in tar barrels so that they could prick their legs with their swords; or in making them jump up and down to avoid the swinging blades; in disfiguring their victims by boring out their eyes or flattening their noses; in waylaying servants and . . . beating them and slashing their faces.[47]

Violence was constantly erupting among members of theatre audiences. There were localized, personal quarrels, sometimes resulting in people being killed or seriously injured. Occasionally something more like a general riot occurred.[48] After a disturbance at Lincoln's Inn Fields in 1721, grenadiers, paid for by the management, were habitually stationed at the side of the stage in London's theatres, a practice that continued for about fifty years.[†49] It did not prevent further outbreaks of rioting. In the spring of 1737 riots at Covent Garden were followed by disturbances at Drury Lane during which twenty-five members of the audience were injured, culminating in the reading of the Riot Act, and the subsequent augmentation to fifty of the number of grenadiers on theatre duty.[50]

The Riot Act had been passed in 1715, re-enacting provisions which had existed in earlier reigns, and although later used to deal with disturbances in general, its primary purpose in 1715 had been to counter the threat to the state from Jacobite supporters of the exiled Stuarts. The Act required assemblies of twelve or more persons to disperse within an hour of the reading of the Act, and empowered magistrates to call in the military if the crowd failed to obey.[51]

Fear of subversion dominated relations between the authorities and the theatre in the period between the Jacobite rebellions of 1715 and 1745. Though subject, like all printed material, to the libel laws, the *written* script of a play was free of censorship after 1694, when the

---

[*] John Gay's play *Mohocks* dates from 1712 (Smith, D.F., p.90).

[†] There is a reference to soldiers on duty in the theatre as early as 1715, but the practice does not appear to have become universal until later.

Printing Acts lapsed.* However, control of *performed* material by the Lord Chamberlain's office still nominally applied, and was intermittently enforced, sometimes for political reasons, occasionally at the behest of an influential aggrieved individual.[52] The Lord Chamberlain had in 1704 reminded managements of their duty to submit material for advance approval, and although the response seems to have been patchy, managers specifically ordered to submit a play normally did so. However, when Richard Steele, in 1715, refused, the Master of the Revels apparently did not insist. Since profanity remained a criminal offence, and indictments included the players, managers with qualms about their material tended to protect their actors by obtaining prior approval, but prosecutions for profanity ceased to be pursued after 1725, with a consequent diminution of that particular spur to the submission of scripts.[53]

The principal control over the stage was exercised, now as previously, through the issue of patents. The original Killigrew and d'Avenant patents, both of which specifically required the exclusion from dramatic performances of any profane, obscene or scurrilous material, were both in the ownership of John Rich, at Covent Garden. A third royal patent had been issued to a group of prominent actors who in 1695 had seceded from a company run by John Rich's father, and who by 1710, after some peregrinations and changes in the licence holders, were established at Drury Lane. These constituted the only legitimate London theatres.† Vanbrugh's Haymarket, originally built to house the dissident actors, had since their departure to Drury Lane become an opera house.[54]

In the 1720s additional theatres began to open without benefit of patent or licence. Goodman's Fields Theatre, which opened in Whitechapel in 1729, was ordered to close, but did not do so.[55] In 1720 a second Haymarket theatre, the Little Theatre, had opened opposite the opera house, initially catering mainly for visiting companies from abroad.[56] However, by the end of the decade the Little Theatre, swiftly emulated by Lincoln's Inn Fields, had embarked on a studied programme of subversive drama, the Government's riposte to which was ultimately to trammel the theatre for over two centuries.

---

* In 1728 John Rich, then running the Lincoln's Inn Fields theatre, submitted John Gay's *Polly*, only to have it banned, but Gay still made money out of the printed version (Liesenfeld, p.12).
† The legality of Lincoln's Inn Fields theatre at this time is not clear. Liesenfeld states (p.197) that it was operating under one of Rich's patents until 1741, but it was not under his management after his departure to Covent Garden in 1732. According to the *Oxford Companion to the Theatre* (p.579) Rich's departure signalled 'virtually the end of its career as a regular playhouse'. It was subsequently let for balls and concerts, later was used as a barracks, did a stint as an auction room, and was finally pulled down in 1848.

John Gay's *The Beggar's Opera* was staged at Lincoln's Inn Fields in 1728 (having been turned down by Drury Lane), and had a prodigious success, both immediately and in numerous revivals. Its message, spelt out in the last few minutes, that 'it is difficult to determine whether (in the fashionable vices) the fine gentlemen imitate the gentlemen of the road, or the gentlemen of the road the fine gentlemen',[57] did it no harm with the public, but the suggestion that the highwayman falls foul of the law while the peculator remains a respected member of society was not appreciated in the corridors of power, where corruption in high places had, particularly since the South Sea Bubble scandal of 1720, become a sensitive issue. Plays such as *The Fall of Mortimer* at the Little Theatre in 1731, a thinly disguised attack on Walpole, the Prime Minister, and Henry Fielding's *The Welsh Opera*, which ridiculed both the Prime Minister and the Hanoverian royal family, prompted a Government response. Action was taken against the players not under the libel laws, but under the old Vagrancy Acts, consolidated in 1714 in Queen Anne's reign, under which 'common players of interludes' continued to be categorized as rogues and vagabonds, subject to heavy penalties[*] if they took part in any production without a royal patent or a licence from the Lord Chamberlain. The actors managed to evade arrest, and there were no prosecutions, but the use of the Vagrancy Act attracted the attention of the theatre managers who held patents, and who wished jealously to guard their monopoly status. An action was started by a Drury Lane patentee against a principal player at the Little Theatre, who successfully defended himself on the grounds that he was no vagrant, but held settled property in Surrey and London. With the failure of this action, the attempt to use the Vagrancy Act to control unlicensed performances came to an end, together with any hope of controlling seditious plays or the burgeoning of new playhouses. 'The last legal obstacle to independent theatres had been removed.'[58]

A concatenation of interests now emerged in support of the status quo ante, and in search of means to reinstate it. In defence of the new liberties were ranged, of course, the managements and shareholders in the independent theatres; the actors, happy to escape from the servitude imposed by a very limited range of potential employers; and the political opposition, determined to defend its right to freedom of speech. Aligned against them were the existing patentees; a considerable body of sober-sided middle-class citizens anxious to preserve their neighbourhoods

---

[*] They could be whipped until bloody, or sent to hard labour, or ordered to undertake seven-year apprenticeships in Britain or overseas (Liesenfeld, p.163).

from contamination by the intrusion of playhouses, in whose wake, they averred (not without some justification, judging by reports of conditions in the vicinity of Covent Garden and Drury Lane), came pickpockets, pimps, prostitutes and the conversion of private houses to brothels at rents with which decent citizens could not compete; and the Government, convinced that Stuart subversion underlay the demands for the abolition of controls.[59]

A modest Bill to restrict the number of playhouses was introduced in Parliament in 1735, provoking numerous petitions, both pro and anti. It attracted considerable support in Parliament, until Walpole tried to tack on to the general prohibition of profane, obscene or scurrilous material tighter provisions as to passages offensive to piety and good manners, with fines for violations and a statutory reintroduction of the requirement for all plays to be submitted to the Lord Chamberlain prior to performance. A coalition of political opponents and those with an economic interest in the new theatres defeated the proposed Bill.[60]

The anti-Establishment faction took the defeat as a licence to throw all caution to the winds. Indifferent to traditional religious observance, the Little Theatre had in 1733 opened on Ash Wednesday (with a performance of *The Beggar's Opera*), a day on which, together with all other Wednesdays and Fridays in Lent, theatres were required to remain closed. Worse still, it played throughout Passion Week. By 1736 all the London theatres were opening on forbidden days. In 1737 the Lord Chamberlain successfully intervened to insist on the Lent closures, an order with which all the theatres, with and without patents, complied.[61]

Throughout 1736 and 1737, not just at the Little Theatre, but at Drury Lane and Lincoln's Inn Fields as well, production after production lampooned the administration and the royal family,* until the Government became convinced that 'enemies of the State, particularly Jacobites' were manipulating the London stage 'as part of their larger plan to create disaffection in Britain and overthrow the Government and ultimately the Crown itself'.[62] It was a time of widespread civic disturbance, with local riots in protest at the institution of toll gates and turnpikes on the highways, Shoreditch and Spitalfields convulsed with riots against the immigrant Irish, troops patrolling the streets of London and the Government suspecting the covert influence of the Jacobites fomenting trouble on every hand. The Hanoverian cause was hardly helped by the expensive and disreputable conduct of George II, who

---

* Obliquely, so that the playwright Henry Fielding was always able to claim that if scurrilous parallels were detected, they were in the minds of his critics; he himself had meant no such offence (Liesenfeld, p.119).

spent much of his time out of the country with his mistress; the notorious corruption of the administration; and the political machinations of the Prince of Wales, seeking to build his own basis of support among the politicians in opposition to his father.[63] It was in this atmosphere that the theatre riots at Covent Garden and Drury Lane occurred in the spring of 1737, the Prince and Princess of Wales being themselves present at the most serious.[64]

A dummy run for measures to control the London theatre now presented itself in the form of a dispute between Cambridge University and a local impresario who sought to establish a permanent booth where previously only temporary entertainments during the September Fair had challenged the university's disapproving jurisdiction. Parliament agreed to a 'Bill for the more effectual preventing the unlawful playing of interludes within the precincts of the University of Cambridge, and the places adjacent'. The Bill completed its third reading in May 1737. Instead of prohibiting the building of playhouses, the Universities' Theatre Act* plugged the loophole that had rendered Drury Lane's action against the Little Theatre ineffective – it reiterated the universities' power to arrest players and punish them[†] as rogues and vagabonds, regardless of their claims as to residence or settlement.[65]

Initially, plans to reassert control in London followed similar lines, the intention being to categorise as rogues and vagabonds, whether or not they possessed 'legal settlement', all those involved in theatrical productions, including management and backstage staff, unless they had letters patent from His Majesty or a licence from the Lord Chamberlain. As on the occasion of the abortive 1735 Bill to 'restrain the number of playhouses', Walpole then sought to add clauses imposing theatrical censorship. It was proposed that no new play or rewriting of an old play be performed unless a copy, signed by the manager, had been submitted to the Lord Chamberlain fourteen days in advance of the performance; and that the Lord Chamberlain should have authority to prohibit performances. Offenders were to be fined £50, and if they failed to pay, they, too, were to be subject to the harsh provisions of the 1714 Vagrancy Act.[66]

In support of his proposal, Walpole proceeded to read extracts from a play, *The Golden Rump*, which had supposedly been submitted by the manager of Goodman's Fields,[‡] with some suggestions that the

---

* Oxford University had by now been included, at its own request (Liesenfeld, p.111).
† With a month's hard labour in prison.
‡ Who was also, at the time, staging plays at Lincoln's Inn Fields, and was reputedly in dire financial straits as a result of trying to run two theatres (Liesenfeld, pp.117, 133).

management of the Little Theatre was also implicated – it being subsequently rumoured that money had changed hands in promoting the submission. The play was never published or performed, though it may possibly have gone into rehearsal. Its authorship is in doubt, and Walpole has been accused of *agent provocateur* tactics, but, whether it was ever seriously intended for production or not, there seems little doubt that it was a dramatized version of an allegory, 'The Vision of the Golden Rump', which was published in two parts at the end of March 1737 in a new weekly journal, *Common Sense*. This publication, whose editor was an Irish Roman Catholic, was reportedly founded by James III, the Old Pretender, to attack the Hanoverians by carrying 'to a larger audience than could be reached by a London play the social and political ridicule which has been so effective on the stage of the Little Theatre in the Haymarket'.[67]

'The Vision of the Golden Rump' portrayed the King, the Queen and the Prime Minister as, respectively, a pagan idol, a goddess and a magician. In the course of a general disparagement of the court and its adherents, a central theme was the volcanic eruptions from the idol's golden rump (the King was known to suffer seriously from haemorrhoids), requiring explicit ministrations from the goddess.[68]

The House that listened to Walpole's denunciations, shocked at such an amalgam of blasphemy, profanity, obscenity and sedition, offered little opposition to his Licensing Bill. Certainly anxiety was voiced that censorship of the theatre risked precipitating a general attack on freedom of speech, since banned plays could still be printed, and their 'refused' status might attract not only enhanced public interest and sales, but ultimately a concomitant extension of controls – and then 'we may bid adieu to the liberties of Great Britain'. But virtually no one regarded the contemporary theatre as defensible, and those who opposed the Bill, as Lord Chesterfield did in the House of Lords, did so on the grounds that there were already adequate safeguards, provided prosecutions were actively pursued under the existing libel laws.[*69] Even the players appreciated the change in public opinion. The Drury Lane and Covent Garden companies had campaigned actively against the 1735 Bill on the grounds that limitations on new playhouses left them vulnerable in the face of harsh management cartels, especially where they themselves had contracted (as had the Drury Lane company) to pay the rent of a theatre where the patentee might arbitrarily elect to move his patent elsewhere,

---

* Liesenfeld (pp.218–19) points out that 'The Vision of the Golden Rump' was clearly a seditious libel under eighteenth-century law, but there was no prosecution.

leaving the lessees with no means of meeting their financial obligations. In their 1737 petition, while reiterating the same anxieties, the players now declared themselves 'well persuaded a regulation of the stage . . . may be . . . of great advantage to the stage in general, by preventing the exhibiting any licentious or scandalous pieces', and they concluded with assurances that they themselves, 'as far as lay in their power, discountenanced anything that had the least tendency to vice, immorality or disaffection'.[70]

The Bill came into effect on 24 June 1737. Lincoln's Inn Fields took to staging musical entertainments; for some five years, until the management at Drury Lane managed to get it stopped, Goodman's carried on by selling tickets for concerts, during which an exceptionally long interval enabled a play to be performed, for which no charge was made.[*71] Fielding's company at the Little Theatre was disbanded, and the theatre remained shrouded in darkness until it reopened in the autumn of 1738 with a company specially imported from France at government behest. The London theatrical clientele, who were of course incensed at Government interference, vented their fury on the wretched foreigners who, notwithstanding the presence of two files of grenadiers with fixed bayonets, were prevented from performing by a thoroughly excitable audience, who burst into choruses of 'The Roast Beef of Old England' throughout the evening, and showered the stage with (presumably hard-dried) peas when the unhappy visitors attempted to dance.[72]

In the first five years after the passing of the Act, censorship was toughly exercised. There was a repeat of the device indulged in by the Roman theatre under similar constraints, with revivals of classic dramas in which audiences boisterously identified lines carrying contemporary relevance; and even some attempt to write new work on classical themes having covert contemporary significance.[73] In 1742 Walpole fell from power, the opposition were appeased, and for the following twenty years no play was suppressed for political reasons, there being no burning seditious attacks on the new administration.[74]

Many of those who supported the Act, however, detected in it a wider context than party politics. During its passage through Parliament, the *Daily Gazetteer* had doubted whether 'the present spirit of tumult, contempt of laws, sacred and civil, and that proneness to sensual pleasures which deform the manners of the present age, could ever have taken place but for the licentiousness of the stage for many years past'.[75]

---

* It was Goodman's which, in these circumstances, gave David Garrick his London start. On the closure of Goodman's in 1741, he moved to Drury Lane.

Others blamed the theatre for directly encouraging crime, *The Beggar's Opera*, with its promiscuous rogue of a highwayman presented as hero – and reprieved at the end, to boot – being considered particularly reprehensible.[76] John Gay's intended target, the iniquitous practice of informers inciting to crime and then claiming reward,[*] seems to have escaped critics and audiences alike.

Certainly London street crime escalated during the eighteenth century, and was to intensify in the twenty years after 1751, when Henry Fielding, then serving as a Bow Street magistrate, published his *Inquiry into the Causes of the Late Increase of Robbers*, complaining that innocent citizens were being beaten, threatened with pistols and hacked 'without any respect to Age or Dignity or Sex', laments that were still being voiced in 1775.[77] Footpads, sometimes operating in gangs, not only waylaid pedestrians but, lurking at locations such as bridges where coaches were forced to slow down, ensured that the privileged, too, knew no security. Highwaymen infested the approach roads to London, Hounslow Heath being especially notorious, but they were less feared than the footpads as they were not so prone to violence; indeed, the 'gentlemen of the road', though they included 'nasty thugs' like Dick Turpin, tended to cultivate a reputation for gallantry, a luxury in which the footpad, lacking a horse for speedy withdrawal from the scene of his crime, was perhaps less inclined to indulge.[78] Cheap gin and drunkenness added to the unpleasantness of London's streets, while the proliferation of public houses of dubious repute provided safe havens for, and strengthened the power and influence of, networks of gang bosses, fences and brothel-keepers – a professional criminal subclass already evident in Elizabethan and Jacobean London.[79]

In the countryside poaching was widespread among a peasantry which had never accepted the many centuries of post-Conquest limitations on the right to pursue game, and was resentful of more recent enclosures. In coastal regions, especially Sussex, smuggling was universally practised, excise taxes being regarded as a wholly unwarranted intrusion. Both these activities attracted the participation of professional gangs supplying the black market, and they were not averse to acting with considerable violence if interrupted.[80] Pickpockets, burglars, horse-thieves and sheep-stealers cluttered the assizes. Commentators seem agreed, however, that serious crime in the eighteenth century was overwhelmingly a London phenomenon.[81] Outside London, levels of

---

[*] An Act of 1692 provided for payment of £40 to any person who apprehended and prosecuted to conviction one or more highwaymen.

violence in pursuit of crime were low. J.A. Sharpe's examination of criminal records in seventeenth-century Essex concludes that 'the relative absence of violence (and in particular homicide) being used as a means to further another crime is striking, suggesting that even habitual criminals in this period were neither very brutal nor very violent', and in his extended general study of the period 1550 to 1750 he comes to a similar conclusion: 'Physical violence was rarely resorted to.' Even isolated areas were not unsafe, and 'it would seem more sensible to regard the criminal as an irritant to honest people rather than a menace'.[82] Frank McLynn, too, in *Crime and Punishment in Eighteenth Century England*, comments on the low level of serious violence, whether directly against the person or in association with thefts and burglaries, and says that foreign observers were unanimous in the judgement that, as compared with continental Europe, 'the homicide rate was remarkably low . . . even in the early years of the century'.[83]

Eighteenth-century crime was motivated largely by sheer, desperate, absolute poverty. There was no evidence of the sort of envious malice at relative affluence that leads the twentieth-century thief to urinate and defecate all over his victim's immovable property. Nor did women, apparently, feel insecure. A traveller in the latter part of the century noted that 'London crowds were in general very considerate towards women and children.' Roy Porter, in *Rape – An Historical and Cultural Enquiry*, remarks that research on pre-industrial England showed sexual assaults to be only a tiny proportion of those indicted for crimes. Assessments of the prevalence of rape in any society are inevitably bedevilled by the likelihood that most are not reported; and the fact that the penalty in the eighteenth century was death, and juries were all the less likely to convict, would not have encouraged the lodging of complaints. But there does not appear to have been any obsession with rape – reformers in the feminist cause do not mention it, nor do the polemics of contemporary moral crusaders include it. Journals and diaries of the period betray no preoccupation with rape. 'Heroines traversing country fields,' remarks McLynn, 'worry that their gowns will be dirtied, not that they will be raped', and he further comments that though highwaymen may have made travel insecure, their code of conduct excluded rape. Both Porter and Sharpe make the point that unmarried mothers seeking help for their bastards frequently complained of breach of promise of marriage, but not of rape.[84]

In tracing changes in the incidence of crime and violence, criminologists seek correlations with social and demographic conditions: with the ending of wars, for instance, demobilizing aggressive and possibly unemployed young males into the home country; with 'baby bulges' producing high proportions of adolescents, notoriously the least law-abiding age group; with population shifts, disorientating family relationships and overstraining housing provision; above all, perhaps, with patterns of punishment. In the period 1688 to 1815 one crime after another was made punishable by death. Not more than fifty crimes, including treason, murder, rape and arson, figured in the 1688 list; by 1765 there were 160, and during George II's reign almost two offences a year were added to the capital category, so that by the end of the Napoleonic Wars there were about 225 in all. The law was, furthermore, becoming increasingly severe. Grand larceny, which attracted the death penalty, was defined as theft to the value of more than twelve pence – a figure which had not been upgraded since Saxon times.[*85]

This extension in capital offences, mostly in defence of property, does not appear to have been the result of any precisely formulated policy, or any particular hysteria about crime. The 'Bloody Code' accrued piecemeal over the decades.[86] Its severity was mitigated by the fact that it was seldom invoked for crimes added to the list after 1688, though forgery and thefts accompanied by violence or intimidation were severely punished. It fell to juries to assess the worth of goods stolen, and they frequently pronounced values below the crucial figure: a sheep at ten pence, for instance, when it was really worth six shillings.[87] Horrendous though the execution figures sound to modern ears, they constituted only a fraction of those nominally eligible to be hanged. Sharpe estimates that despite the huge increase in capital statutes, the number of people executed for felony in the early eighteenth century may have been about a tenth of the figure a century earlier,[88] and McLynn, researching the statistics for London and Middlesex, found that hangings diminished from some 140 a year in 1600 to 20 in 1800. In the period 1700 to 1750, only about 10 per cent of those indicted in London were actually executed.[89]

Whatever the deterrent effect of the criminal code (and even if the likelihood of execution was statistically low, the alternatives offered by transportation or the prison hulks cannot have been very attractive),

---

[*] Our ancestors never experienced inflation on the scale Britain has suffered since World War II, but even so there had been depreciation of the currency, particularly in the late sixteenth century, and the twelve pence which represented wealth to a villein was by the eighteenth century the equivalent of only about a twentieth the weekly wage of a skilled man. When reform of the 'Bloody Code' at last began, early in the nineteenth century, one of the first Bills to be presented to Parliament remarked on the uncertainty of conviction, given the extreme severity of the law occasioned in part by 'the great diminution in the value of money' (Radzinovicz, Vol.1, pp.498–9).

Sharpe sees the fundamentally orderly quality of eighteenth-century life as stemming from a contemporary culture in which law and religion were closely entwined. 'Most contemporaries . . . would have had some difficulty in differentiating sin from crime.'[90] The essentially sensate dynamics of the world of fashion and of entertainment did not permeate the community as a whole.

In a society in which the vast majority of people were virtually without power or political influence, riot was not seen, by participants, as a sin. The century was punctuated by riots. Even in the heat of riot, however, restraint appears to have been exercised. In general, says Sharpe, and McLynn's survey confirms his conclusions, riots centred on specific grievances.

> Even when they were involved in tumult and disorder, it is evident that they were thinking men and women with the ability to formulate their grievances, to act in ways appropriate to gaining redress for them, and to combine together when so doing . . . Even when local authority is being defied, the mob rarely loses respect for all forms of hierarchy and order, for all forms of legality.[91]

There was considerable destruction of property; riots against enclosures destroyed fences, those against tolls and turnpikes destroyed gates and toll-houses, labour-saving machinery was wrecked – Arkwright's carding and spinning 'engines' were among those to suffer. The frequent riots about the price of food led to the destruction of mills, and to widespread looting of sacks of flour, flitches of bacon and other commodities. Even in these circumstances, however, the mob could display a sense of fair play. At Tetbury in 1766 the rioters looted bacon and cheese and sold it at reduced prices – but handed the takings over to the farmer from whom the produce had been stolen.[92]

Very seldom did the rioters kill anyone. In an analysis of the frequent riots in Colchester between 1550 and 1750, Sharpe says that 'despite manhandling and threats, there is no evidence that anyone was killed or seriously injured by the mob: the crowd appreciated the rules of the game'.[93] R.F. Wearmouth's analysis covering the country as a whole during the eighteenth century gives a not dissimilar picture – there was an occasional burning-in-effigy, but when casualties did occur it was the rioters themselves who suffered, when the military (there was as yet no police force) were called on to restore order. In the first half of the century, fatalities were rare. Disturbances in the later years of the century were both more frequent and more serious. A riot at Hexham in 1761 over the provisions of the Militia Act resulted in over 100 'killed or wounded'. In the Gordon Riots, which began as an anti-Roman Catholic protest following the Toleration Act of 1778 but which were taken over by troublemakers with more general grievances, over 200 rioters, most of them, according to McLynn, under twenty years old, were killed; a further 75 died later of their wounds.[94]

Even in that six-day general rampage, which escalated into the most serious civil disorder since Monmouth's Rebellion of 1685, the mob exercised discrimination, selecting the properties of wealthy Roman Catholics before broadening the assault to target symbols of authority, destroying the Lord Chancellor's house as well as four prisons (Newgate, Fleet, King's Bench and New Bridewell), and releasing the prisoners – some nine years before a French mob was to storm the Bastille.

It was, says McLynn, a 'revolution *manqué*'.[95] The absence in England of the revolutionary fervour that inspired France is widely[*] attributed by historians (with approval or dismay, according to their political predilections) to the advent, in the mid-eighteenth century, of a fresh wave of otherworldly enthusiasm and commitment; the movement that came to be known as Methodism.

John Wesley was an ordained priest of the Church of England, intellectually a convinced Christian with a record of missionary endeavour in America already to his credit when in 1738 he underwent the experience that launched him on his vocation as an evangelist. He became suffused with the joyful certainty that (contrary to the Calvinist doctrine of predestination) salvation through God's love was freely and readily available to all who by faith and amendment of life opened themselves to receive it. Into an Anglicanism half-paralysed by intellectual attempts to come to grips with the deism of the Enlightenment, by legislative restrictions on the development of new parishes to minister to the shifting population of the early industrial age, and by the idleness of a comfortable clerical hierarchy enjoying a plurality of livings, Wesley endeavoured to inject the enthusiasm of a vibrant, living faith in Jesus Christ, the very Saviour-from-sin whom deism found so superfluous.

The progression by which the Methodists and Anglicans became gradually estranged from one another, until formal separation proved inescapable, lies outside the scope of this work. Within both groups

---

[*] But not universally. E.F. Hobsbawm doubted if there were enough Methodists to achieve the necessary influence.

evangelical fervour fired the hearts and minds of men and women from top to bottom of society, the Anglicans, being socially more influential, tending to work for reform at a parliamentary level, the Methodists concentrating on works of personal philanthropy. Methodists visited the poor, the sick and the imprisoned, risking contagion in the fetid garrets and prison cells, courting opprobrium as they rode in the carts to Tyburn, befriending the condemned. They set up Stranger's Friend societies for the relief of poverty and distress among all, Protestant or Roman Catholic, foreigner or fellow-citizen. They were noted for their kindness towards animals, and the influence of John Wesley is credited with the closure, in 1756, of London's bear-gardens, as well as the suppression of prize-fighting. The later eighteenth century shows, says McLynn, an increasing 'tenderness in domestic relations, and less tolerance for the vicious beating of wives and children. There was also increasing distaste for slavery, blood sports and capital punishment, and gathering concern with prison reform', and he cites Methodism as one of the principal influences contributing to this change.[96] By 1790 the American Methodist Conference, inspired by John Wesley's *Thoughts upon Slavery*, had concluded that slavery was contrary to God's law, and almost the last action taken by Wesley himself before his death in 1791 was to write to William Wilberforce in support of his anti-slavery campaign.[97]

Enlightenment ideas, which rejected the concept of sin and ascribed to society the main responsibility for crime, no doubt played a major part in achieving the huge improvement in levels of crime and disorder evident by the end of the century. Improved law enforcement (the establishment, for instance, of the Bow Street Runners in 1749), better street lighting, improvements in drainage and sanitation, all contributed to the amelioration of conditions. But Methodism, too, induced a profound change in attitudes.[98] Smuggling, for instance, was in Wesley's eyes tantamount to picking pockets – the pockets of one's honest fellow-citizens who would have to make up, in their taxes, for lost revenue. Trafficking in 'uncustomed' goods was strictly forbidden to Method-ists.[99] 'Arguably,' says McLynn,

> it was Methodism that did most to break up the Cornish contraband gangs. After 1750 Wesley's preaching began to make a distinct impact on Cornwall, even though his moral prescriptions struck at the roots of the local economy by outlawing both smuggling and wrecking. Although smugglers began by stoning his meetings, they

soon had to acknowledge that the mass conversions to Methodism made their position precarious.[100]

Methodists were enjoined not to use tobacco or 'spirituous liquors' (except for medicinal purposes). State attempts in the period 1736 to 1743 to control drunkenness by manipulating the licensing laws had not proved successful, but fresh efforts embarked upon from 1751 on had the full weight of Methodist opinion behind them. Methodists were to avoid street brawling and fighting. Soberness of demeanour was to be matched by soberness of attire – no extravant clothing, no rings, earrings or necklaces, no curls and crimping. And no idle wasting of time reading plays and romances.[101]

Evangelicals, whether Methodist or Anglican, had a profound distrust of the theatre. Wilberforce, in his *A Practical View of . . . Christianity*, demanded, in terms which reveal how the whole theatrical milieu was still viewed, whether we should

> seek our pleasure in that place which the debauchee, inflamed with wine, or bent on the gratification of other licentious appetites, finds most congenial to his state and temper of mind? In that place, from the neighbourhood of which . . . decorum, and modesty, and regularity retire, while riot and lewdness are invited to the spot, and invariably select it for their chosen residence! where sentiments are often heard with delight, and motions and gestures often applauded, which would not be tolerated in private company, but which may far exceed the utmost licence allowed in the social circle, without at all transgressing the large bounds of theatrical decorum! where, when moral principles are inculcated, they are not such as a Christian ought to cherish in his bosom, but such as it must be his daily endeavour to extirpate . . .

and so on, ending with a condemnation of those willing to find their pleasure 'in spectacles maintained at the risk at least, if not the ruin, of the eternal happiness of those who perform in them!'* [102] In his youth

---

* Wilberforce cited the sorry example of Geneva, where theatre had recently been introduced 'to corrupt the simpler morality of purer times'. Geneva had been the focus of a furious mid-century dispute between Rousseau and Voltaire (hiding behind a 'front' composed of M. D'Alembert), Voltaire seeking to subvert the animosity of the local Genevois to the establishment of a theatre, Rousseau passionate in his – initially successful – opposition. In 1782 the city was forced to accept the establishment of a theatre as a result of the intervention of France and other *'puissances garantes'*, a previous attempt in the mid-sixties having failed when the wooden shack in which the company were performing burned down, as a result, it was suspected, of arson (Wilberforce,

Wesley, like Augustine, had been greatly attracted by the theatre, but he came to regard the English theatre as 'the sink of all profaneness and debauchery'.[103] Petitioning the Mayor and Corporation of Bristol, who were debating the request to build a theatre in their city, he warned against 'present stage entertainments' as (among other things) 'sapping the foundation of all religion . . . naturally tending to efface all traces of piety and seriousness out of the minds of men' and 'giving a wrong turn to youth especially, gay, trifling and directly opposite to the spirit of industry, and close application to business'.[104] Methodists and Quakers in Bristol who in 1764 opposed the projected construction of the Theatre Royal warned that it would 'diffuse an habit of idleness, indolence and debauchery throughout this once industrious city';[105] and in 1777 Birmingham refused a licence to a theatre on the grounds that it would be conducive to slothfulness and hence unfavourable to trade.[106]

Max Weber noted that the Methodist revival preceded the great economic expansion of the eighteenth century.[107] Tawney quotes authorities for the assertion that 'the most eminent ironmasters of the eighteenth century belonged as a rule to the Puritan connection', and that 'the leading Lancashire clothiers were often Nonconformists'.[108] Like the Puritans of the sixteenth and seventeenth centuries, evangelical otherworldliness was rooted in an ethical rejection of sensual self-indulgence, not in contempt for the material world as such. John Wesley himself was interested in experimental science, greatly admired Francis Bacon, and compiled a *Compendium of Natural Philosophy*, a work much of which was taken verbatim from the writings of John Ray, a seventeenth-century fellow of the Royal Society. In it Wesley expounded upon 'the wisdom of God in the Creation', ranging from 'the ant . . . a very beautiful creature' to descriptions of the eruptions of Etna and Vesuvius.[109] Higher education in the old universities was restricted to members of the established Church,* but non-denominational dissenting academies were springing up throughout the provinces, and Musson and Robinson, in *Science and Technology in the Industrial Revolution*, draw attention to the importance of these academies in preserving and disseminating the scientific information on which the Industrial Revolution was to draw.[110]

---

p.261; Rousseau, *passim*, especially pp.xxxix-xli).

* And restricted in subject matter to theology and *literae humaniores*, which combined classics, philosophy and ancient history. Mathematics was hived off into a faculty of its own only in 1807, the natural sciences not until the second half of the nineteenth century (*Oxford Today*, Vol.3, No.3, p.6). Cambridge established a Chair of Applied Mechanism and Applied Mechanics in 1875, but not until 1907 was there a Chair of Engineering at Oxford (Williams, T., p.3).

In the seventeenth century, the Royal Society had drawn together scientists of all kinds. In the eighteenth, according to Musson and Robinson, they were joined by industrialists, and there was constant interaction between the laboratory and the workshop; the 'knowledge of mathematics and natural philosophy ... was much more widespread among leading millwrights and engineers than has hitherto been appreciated'.[111] 'The pioneers of the new kind of worldly knowledge,' says Wolf, 'believed in the possibility of harnessing the forces of nature to the chariot of human progress by means of science and art. They valued knowing as an aid to doing, science as an aid to technics.'[112] Scientific clubs began to meet all over the country, listening to invited speakers and seeking the solution to practical problems. They flourished not only in such major cities as Manchester, Derby, Liverpool, Bristol and Leeds, but were to be found also in such relatively minor towns as Spalding and Maidstone. Birmingham's Lunar Society included Darwin's grandfather Erasmus among its members, along with Josiah Wedgwood and other manufacturers. Class distinctions were irrelevant – semi-literate craftsmen were to be found in coffee-house clubs 'discussing equations'. Millwrights with a background in carpentry and smithying proved themselves well versed in arithmetic, geometry and practical mechanics.[113]

Out of one of the London coffee-house clubs developed the Society for the Encouragement of Arts, Commerce and Manufactures, later abbreviated to the Society of Arts,[*] which was founded in 1754 entirely by private subscription to stimulate and reward innovation and invention. Among the skills it encouraged, for the sake of commercial usefulness, was drawing. The Royal Academy was set up under its auspices in 1768, but as a separate institution; it was the artisan, rather than the artist, who was the focus of the original society's interest.[114]

While the chemists were revolutionizing the bleaching and dyeing of cloth,[†] men with a background knowledge as clockmakers, carpenters and blacksmiths were devising 'engines' to lighten labour and increase productivity. Carding 'engines' were the first successful textile machine, in use from the 1750s. In 1758 came the first improvements to the knitting frame devised in 1589, in 1765 a spinning jenny enabling one operator to supervise not eight but eighty spindles; in 1771 Richard

---

[*] It did not receive the prefix 'Royal' until 1908.

[†] One of the innovations was a form of rubberized cotton, known, after the firm that produced it, as 'macintosh'. A rubber ball given to Macintosh's niece, and copied in her husband's factory in France, led ultimately to the development of the Michelin works (D.W.F. Hardie, 'The Macintoshes and the Origins of the Chemical Industry', in Musson (ed.), Chapter 7).

Arkwright's water-powered spinning machine, in 1796 the first power loom for weaving. In agriculture, in which the introduction of the four-course no-fallow rotation of clover, wheat, turnips and barley was expanding food production, ploughs were redesigned and, by 1788, a threshing machine was brought into operation.[115]

All these activities were about to be transformed by the successful harnessing of steam as a source of power. Treatises on the theoretical aspects of the use of steam had appeared as early as the sixteenth century, and in the seventeenth, in 1663, a device using steam had been erected at Vauxhall which raised water forty feet, but no one proceeded with the idea for another generation. Then, in 1699, a demonstration was given to the Royal Society of a steam engine for pumping out mines, and a patent obtained for its development. By 1712 a successful engine was on the market, but the danger of explosion in fact inhibited its use in the pits.[116] Improvements were achieved, and for the first three-quarters of the eighteenth century the steam engine drained mines and lifted water on to overshot water wheels, the water powering the machinery both for the multiplicity of uses – the milling, fulling, pulping, bellows-operating, hammering, rolling – traditional since the early Middle Ages; and for the machines being newly devised, especially in the textile industries. Between 1769 and 1776 James Watt perfected his improved engine, far more economical in its use of coal; and in the 1780s developed the rotative engine which made it possible to dispense with the water wheel and apply steam directly to the powering of machinery. 'They are now used in cotton mills and for every purpose of the water wheel, where a stream is not to be got', said a 1795 report.[117]

The additional power available made possible tasks for which the traditional machinery of wood and leather was inadequate. In Lancashire there developed, alongside the textile industry, an engineering industry, producing, among other things, cast-iron machinery – all hand-made, at this stage; not till the next century were the problems of precision engineering and the production of machine tools satisfactorily over-come. In 1772 the term 'engineer' began to appear in the press.[118]

British pre-eminence in the Industrial Revolution was not based on any monopoly of ingenuity. The excitement of discovery and the diffusion of technical information was occurring throughout north-west Europe, and British developments owed much to political refugees and immigrant entrepreneurs and inventors, attracted by economic and political liberty, and the protection of British patent laws. Observers in the early nineteenth century considered that the English genius lay more in the application of new ideas than in their invention. It was 'for diffusing the knowledge and facilitating the general introduction of useful mechanical inventions and improvements, and for teaching, by courses of philosophical* lectures and experiments, the application of science to the common purposes of life' that in 1799 the Royal Institution of Great Britain was established – not by government initiative but, like the Society of Arts, by subscriptions from the public. Lectures on technical and scientific subjects were given, working models displayed and intensive craft courses arranged.[119]

The triumph of the pursuit of scientific and technical knowledge was manifest. Yet there were still thinkers haunted by an atavistic unease at mankind's arrogance in seeking to probe the secrets of, and thus control, the created world. In Germany in 1759 the playwright Lessing, refusing to accept that (as the *Oxford Companion to the Theatre* puts it) 'man's noblest impulse could lead him to eternal pain', began work on a new version of Faust, and although he died leaving it incomplete, it is clear that he was not going to allow Faust to suffer eternal damnation. Some fifteen years later Goethe took up the same theme. For almost sixty years he worked on his version of the Faust legend. A performance of the final drama would last for twenty hours, and some scholars regard it as a purely literary work, but performances of Part I were given in Goethe's lifetime, though the author himself made drastic cuts for the theatre.[120] It was presented in London at the Coburg Theatre[+] in 1824, Drury Lane staged an adaptation in 1825, and there was a third production at Sadler's Wells in 1842.[121]

Although Part I was not finished until 1801, and Part II shortly before his death in 1832 (it was published posthumously), 'the whole plan of Faust was fairly complete in Goethe's conception long before the publication of Part One', says his translator, Philip Wayne.[122] This many-stranded, many-layered work has inspired numerous commentaries and interpretations, most of which are not relevant to the theme of this work: Faust's dissatisfaction with an academic approach to knowledge and his determination to run the whole gamut of experience, for instance; Goethe's exploration of the wedding of the values of Greek Hellenism, symbolized by Helen of Troy, with the Gothic spirit of north Europe, symbolized by Faust; the decision of the laboratory-created manikin Homunculus to eschew individuality and seek peace in absorption back into the infinite, as symbolized by the sea; the ultimate failure of the ideal of beauty in art, represented by Faust's and Helen's doomed son, to offer

---

* I.e., natural philosophy, or science.
+ The Coburg, later renamed the Royal Victoria Theatre, was built in Waterloo Road in 1816. It is now known as the Old Vic (Nicoll, Vol.IV, p.230).

satisfaction to the thirsting human spirit; even the strange flirtation with political power, with its prescient forecast of the inflation resulting from the uncontrolled issue of paper money. 'What gives coherence to the whole drama,' says Wayne, 'is the fate of Faust's immortal soul . . . the main coherence is seen in the fact that the much-erring Faust is saved.'[123]

In this version of his pact with the Devil, Faust defies Mephistopheles ever to provide him with satisfaction, with an end to yearning. Part I explores his seduction and abandonment of the simple-hearted Gretchen, and her subsequent execution for infanticide. At the end, voices are heard proclaiming that Gretchen is 'saved'; Faust proceeds to the symbolically more complex temptations of Part II. The challenge to his restless spirit upon which he finally determines is to master the sea, 'to bend Nature to the service of Man', as Bayard Taylor puts it in the introduction to his 1890 translation. Faust 'now determines to enter into conflict with a colossal natural force, and compel its submission to the imperial authority of the human mind'.[124] He will, by the construction of dykes, dams and drains, bar the sea from a sweep of low-lying territory, and create verdant land in its place.

At first his success is enjoyed entirely for his own sake. Just as in Part I he had not scrupled to destroy the simple Gretchen for his own convenience, so now he destroys the hard-working peasant family who have created a thriving smallholding on land which he particularly covets. But in his final speech, he extends his vision to include his fellow-men – 'I work that millions may possess this space'. His dying words are:

> Then to the moment could I say:
> Linger you now, you are so fair!
> Now records of my earthly day
> No flight of aeons can impair –
> Foreknowledge comes, and fills me with such bliss,
> I take my joy, my highest moments this.[*][125]

He rests content. It would appear that Mephistopheles has won the wager.

But Goethe had no intention of allowing Faust to be damned, and the final scene deals with the translation of 'the immortal part' of Faust to the

---

[*] These and subsequent lines are taken from Philip Wayne's translation of Goethe's *Faust* (see Bibliography) and are reproduced here by permission of Penguin Books Ltd.

threshold of heaven, where Gretchen is pleading his cause. In spite of the concluding lines of the play,[*]

> Here the ineffable
> Wins life through love;
> Eternal Womanhood
> Leads us above[126]

few commentators are content to reduce the complex strands of this play to a simple 'saved at the last by his true love'. As R.D. Miller points out, in *The Meaning of Goethe's Faust*, the quality of Gretchen's unselfish love has won her *own* redemption, it cannot avail for Faust. Nor is Miller satisfied with the suggestion that it is the recognition of the claims of his fellow human beings that redeems Faust. He has had noble impulses before, but they have never lasted long. The circumstances of Faust's death do not constitute a denouement.[127]

George Steiner, in *The Death of Tragedy*, contrasts Faust's redemption with the horrific perdition to which Marlowe's Dr Faustus is consigned, and sees in Goethe's version the Enlightenment's basically optimistic assumption that crime is essentially social in origin, and redemption follows upon better understanding.[128] But there is a more disturbing implication, one which moves Goethe's *Faust* in the direction of classic tragedy.

The angels who in the last scene convey Faust's soul are heard singing:

> For he whose strivings never cease
> Is ours for his redeeming.[129]

'Deep in Faust's nature, as in Goethe's,' says Wayne 'was a belief in the redeeming sanity of action; . . . "In the beginning was the Deed".'[130]

But the Lord of Heaven observes, in the Prologue, that

> man must strive, and striving he must err.[131]

In the prologue to the entire work, it is from the Lord in Heaven that Mephistopheles obtains permission to enter into his bargain with Faust. 'Man's efforts,' says the Lord, 'sink below his proper level.'

---

[*] Best known to modern audiences through Mahler's setting as the finale of his Symphony No.2, the Resurrection Symphony.

> And since he seeks for unconditioned ease,
> I send this fellow, who must goad and tease
> And toil to serve creation, though a devil.[132]

Good and evil are inextricably entwined. Mephistopheles, in promoting evil, cannot help promoting good at the same time. By inciting activity, he promotes, but is not the cause of, evil. 'The real bugbear is not Mephisto, but human nature and the nature of all forms of life; that is the only reason he is allowed a free run on earth', says Miller.[133]

It was a sombre message to offer to the nineteenth century, as it embarked on the great task of the conquest of Nature. For the next century and a half, few were to heed it.

Chapter 17

Propriety and Prosperity: the Nineteenth Century

A prominent feature of eighteenth-century theatre, and one which mirrored the later ages of the classical theatre, was the increasing idolization of individual performers and the focusing, both by dramatists and managements, on suitable 'vehicles' in which they could star. This primacy was, in Steiner's view, one reason for the declining quality of new dramatic literature.[1] Stars commanded far higher rewards than playwrights; the art of acting came to overshadow the art of the dramatist. The public, says Mantzius, would tolerate virtually any mutilation or distortion to the existing dramatic repertory, provided only that it was performed by 'accomplished actors'.[2]

Voluminous biographies and memoirs by and about actors and actresses found an increasing readership.[3] The profession was embarked on the long voyage to respectability. While the French Church still abominated players, and condemned the distinguished tragedienne Adrienne Lecouvreur to burial from a cart at night in an unrecorded grave, Anne Oldfield, who died some seven months later, in October 1730, was laid to rest in Westminster Abbey.[*4] By the end of the century stars such as David Garrick and Mrs Siddons were socially accepted in the most respectable circles.

The theatrical milieu, however, was changing compared with previous post-Reformation centuries. Earlier generations of the devout had refused to frequent the theatre at all alongside the pimps, prostitutes, raffish aristocrats and other ne'er-do-wells who were its supposed clientele. Many persisted in this attitude, but in the second half of the eighteenth century, managers had to cater for 'the increasing presence of a sober-minded (outwardly at least) respectable middle-class element in

---

* Jean Jacques Rousseau, who had the utmost contempt for the theatre, and wrote a protracted diatribe against it, assured his readers that Mrs Oldfield's august committal in no way detracted from an equally robust contempt for comedians among the Londoners, who were honouring her talents, not her calling (Rousseau, p.101).

the theatre audiences'.[5] It is arguable that it was the very operation of the censorship imposed by the 1737 Licensing Act that had emboldened them to come.

The primary purpose of the Act had been political, and performances of a number of plays had been prohibited on political grounds in the first five years of the Act's operation. But in the twenty years after the fall of Walpole's administration in 1742, no plays were suppressed for political reasons. Then, in 1763, a modern version of *Electra* was banned, Orestes being seen as a prototype Bonnie Prince Charlie come to wreak vengeance on the usurping Hanoverians. Throughout the 1770s there were further politically motivated interventions, and after 1789 the Lord Chamberlain showed some sensitivity about any discussion of affairs in France, a reflection of Foreign Office scruples about giving offence to foreign governments at a time when it was uncertain which of the factions in France would emerge triumphant. In Nicoll's view, such censorship as was effected was chiefly to protect individuals against satire rather than on general political grounds, and he concludes that the lack of active censorship between 1750 and 1800 is 'almost inexplicable'.[*6] One explanation may be that even if some individual playwrights felt aggrieved at interference with performances of their work (which in any case often served to improve sales of the unexpurgated texts), managements were doubtful of audience support for controversy. 'The theatre is no fit place for politics', said Sheridan.[7] So widespread, especially after news of atrocities began to spread, was the public abhorrence of revolutionary France that managers, without recourse to the examiners, rejected plays exuding the slightest whiff of egalitarianism or republicanism, though the censor did intervene occasionally (such as in 1795 when *The Whim* was offered dealing with a role-reversal Saturnalia) to ban works satirizing the aristocracy.[8]

As for moral and religious censorship, audiences were if anything more sensitive to offence than the authorities. A devout Methodist who held the office of Examiner of Plays from 1778 to 1824 cut a passage ridiculing Methodist lay preachers, averring that 'the Government did not wish the Methodists to be ridiculed', but this same examiner was reproached by audiences for excessive laxity in carrying out his duties.[9]

Methodism in mid-century, Anglican evangelicalism towards its end, were major influences in this change in public taste. As Ford Brown points out in *Fathers of the Victorians*:

---

* As a matter of good taste, performances of *King Lear* were banned when George III was suffering one of his recurrent bouts of madness.

As the moral campaign of Wilberforce and his associates had no illusions about obliterating wickedness, but had as a prime Evangelical purpose its removal from public view to avoid the further contagion of evil example, all conspicuous vice was peculiarly important. Hence an emphasis that at first seems exaggerated on the thoughtless or deliberately wicked vulgarity, 'freedom' or actual foulness of speech that was so much a matter of course in 'good society' at the beginning of this period that it was hardly noticed until the Evangelicals pointed it out . . . Only a few years later such language was barred in circles of any respectability.

Physiological and biological functions 'should never be mentioned', and scoffing at religion was a practice that by 1815 'would not be tolerated a moment in any company'. Brown quotes Walter Scott's story of his grandmother blushing as she sat in privacy reading an Aphra Behn novel that she remembered reading aloud in mixed company when she was a girl.[10]

The steadfast determination of the ticket-purchasing public to purify the drama, both in content and expression, was by now shared by many within the profession. Decency, decorum and delicacy were the watchwords, pushed to extremes that introduced Victorian levels of prudery many decades before Victoria herself ascended the throne.

Blasphemy and profanity had always shocked religious people. In the late eighteenth century Shakespeare came in for considerable criticism on this score, much of his profanity being conscientiously excised.[*] Dr Johnson, commenting on *The Merry Wives of Windsor*, considered that 'the great fault of this play is the frequency of expressions so profane, that no necessity of preserving character can justify them'. Worse still was Hamlet's speech concluding:

> That his soul may be as damn'd and black
> As hell, where to it goes.[11]

'This speech,' says Johnson, 'in which Hamlet, represented as a virtuous character, is not content with taking blood for blood, but contrives damnation for the man that he would punish, is too horrible to be read or to be uttered.'[12] By George IV's reign the censor (though having a

---

[*] Sir William d'Avenant had in Charles II's reign briefly pruned some of Shakespeare's profanities in a bid to appease Puritan tastes, but they proved irreconcilable, and Sir William's gesture lapsed (Perrin, p.88).

personal reputation for prolific recourse to bad language) would not allow the use on stage of 'damn' as a swear word; and he excised the word 'angel' from a love scene, maintaining that an angel was 'a character in Scripture, and not to be prophaned on the stage by being applied to a woman'.[13]

A similar sense of outrage about sexually explicit language had not, provided the context in which it was used was morally acceptable, been a hallmark of Christian piety. Medieval mystics adopted highly erotic language, and the early Church Fathers had not scrupled to discuss matters sexual with the utmost frankness.*

By the turn of the eighteenth century, anything having 'the least tendency to indelicacy and indecorum' came to be seen as unacceptable. Among the copious translations of the Fathers made during the nineteenth century, passages of dubious delicacy are left untranslated, decently cloaked in the original Latin.† As early as 1744 John Wesley had published an anthology of some 250 poems, of which about 100 had been pruned, together with editorial amendments in the interests of decency such as the substitution of 'children' for 'bastards'. Smollett's *Peregrine Pickle* of 1751 excited so much adverse criticism that he removed some 80 pages before printing a second edition in 1758. In 1795 the first expurgated Chaucer was published. Dr Bowdler's *Family Shakespeare*, covering 20 plays and expunging everything 'which may not with propriety be read aloud in a family', appeared in 1807,‡ coinciding with the publication of Charles Lamb's *Tales from Shakespeare*, intended for the innocent ears of children. Both these books were in fact the work of the ostensible authors' sisters, but Dr Bowdler brought out his own version in 1818, extending the total of plays from 20 to the full 36, and cutting even more drastically than his sister had done, since he had a more acute apprehension of what might be deemed suggestive. By 1850 seven different expurgated Shakespeares were in

---

* In advice on sexual conduct within marriage, for instance, as in Clement of Alexandria (late second century): '*Quaenam de procreatione liberorum tractanda sint.*' Clement actually wrote in Greek, but his mid-Victorian translator felt unable to offer an English translation, explaining that 'For obvious reasons, we have given the greater part of this chapter in the Latin version' (*The Writings of Clement of Alexandria*, tr. the Revd. William Wilson, T. & T. Clark, Edinburgh, 1867).
† A practice which persisted well into the twentieth century. At my school, passages such as Caesar's comment on the Britons having their wives in common were left untranslated in the classroom – leading, of course, to a scramble to the library for cribs as soon as the lesson was over. Delicacy required that a passage on 'smelly dogs' be translated as 'odiferous hounds'.
‡ The work illustrates changing ideas as to which oaths were most shocking. The government censor of 1611 had cut 'S'blood' and 'by the Mass' as offensive to Catholics, but Bowdler's nineteenth-century excisions did not include them; presumably they were too theologically remote to trouble Protestants (Perrin, p.74).

circulation; by 1900 there were nearly 50. Evangelicals were prominent among enthusiastic 'bowdlerisers', and the SPCK embarked on the retailing of secular texts to encourage sales of the results of their labours.[14]

In the theatre, the censor deleted suggestive, passionate, physiological or coarse references (the word 'bitch', for example), but he scarcely needed to play a major role, so fervent was public opinion in favour of purity. It was the avoidance of embarrassment rather than any fear of corruption that prompted employment of the blue pencil – or rather, the red ink. 'No *double entendre*, no smart innuendo admitted', declared a character in Sheridan's *The Critic*.[15] The established comedies of Vanbrugh, Wycherley and Congreve were 'not merely cut', they were 'entirely altered' and, in the words of one of Nicoll's sources, were 'acted almost without their dialogue' (perhaps it was hardly surprising that they 'seldom filled the house'). Mrs Siddons simply refused to speak an epilogue she considered indelicate, and in 1813 declined an invitation to play Cleopatra, saying she would hate herself if she played it 'as it ought to be played'.[16] So far did language depart from the robust vocabulary of the sixteenth century, Papist and Puritan alike, that by 1823 a critic was referring to an actor attired in 'a pair of *unmentionables* coming halfway down his legs'.[*17]

Eyes, as much as ears, were to be protected from shock. Ostensibly naked feet gave offence, even though in fact clad in flesh-coloured stockings. The author of a play in which an actor, kneeling in impersonation of a small woman, had to rise to his full height, thus revealing himself in too short a skirt, helpfully added a note to his text to explain that 'there is no indecency in this, as he has stockings etc. on underneath'.[18]

Themes were as closely scrutinized for moral rectitude as was the language in which they were couched.

> Licentious follies rarely intervene
> And truth and sense and honour claim the scene

---

[*] Sensitivities about underclothing were in for a long run. Perrin (p.220, note) reports that an audience 'broke up in disorder' at the first performance in 1907 of Synge's *Playboy of the Western World* on being confronted with the word 'shift' (Benedict Nightingale gives a full account of the incident in *The Times* of 29 December 1993). Variety artistes working for the BBC in World War II were not permitted to indulge in such vulgar *doubles entendres* as 'Winter draws on' (the relevant guidance booklet was not withdrawn until 1963; see Munro, pp.162–3), and even in the latter years of the twentieth century comics short of inspiration can usually count on an audience reaction to the word 'knickers'.

declared the prologue of a play produced in 1806.[19] *The Golden Pippin*, about the perennial favourite, the judgement of Paris, submitted to the examiner in 1772, only received a licence after extensive cuts of both dialogue and whole scenes, in order to eliminate an attempted seduction and promises from Venus of erotic delights to come.[20] In 1819 the manager of Covent Garden refused – to Shelley's surprise – even to submit his *The Cenci* for licence; a stark contrast to the Elizabethan and Jacobean Italianate revenge tragedies, in which incest was so prominent an ingredient.[21] An 1828 production dealing with the marriage of a couple on discovering that they were not, as they had previously thought, brother and sister, was condemned as 'one of the most immoral and dangerous dramas'.[22] The theatre was seen as the vehicle for direct exhortations to good conduct. *The Tragical History of George Barnwell*, a traditional ballad dating from at least the mid-seventeenth century, and probably much earlier, about an apprentice 'undone by a strumpet that caused him to rob his master and murder his uncle', was given dramatic form in the eighteenth century and staged to great enthusiasm on such holidays as Boxing Night and Easter with the purpose of edifying young apprentices. It was last performed in London in 1819, but had much longer currency in the provinces.[23]

Violence was sanitized. When Kemble in 1809 revived *King Lear* (in Tate's sentimentalized version) the blinding of Gloucester was kept off-stage.[24] The 1838 production cut the episode entirely.[25] *Titus Andronicus* no longer featured in the repertoire.[26] From the early 1840s, it is true, public taste felt able to bear, once more, the full weight of Shakespeare's tragedies, and one after another the original versions were restored.[27] Nineteenth-century poets, however, proved quite unable to provide a new tragic drama. Poets of the Romantic movement had felt moved, for the first time since Milton, to explore metaphysical themes, but their plays either failed in the theatre, or were 'literature', not seriously intended for performance. Wordsworth, Shelley, Keats and Coleridge all wrote uninfluential plays, Byron essayed a serious study of the implications of God's rejection of Cain's sacrifice, and later Browning and Tennyson both wrote worthy but unsuccessful dramas.[28] Nicoll is scathing of the imitative blank verse, the antiquarian subjects, the lack of dramatic talent. Even Byron, one of the few who at least seemed genuinely interested in the theatre and who served for a time on the board of directors of Drury Lane, is dismissed as backward-looking and manifesting 'absolutely nothing . . . of conscious endeavour on his part to devise something which will grip and interpret the temper of his time'.[29]

Nicoll blames the failure of the Romantic poets to write successfully for the theatre on Romanticism's excessive preoccupation with the individual self. George Steiner, too, in *The Death of Tragedy*, regards the Romantic vaunting of the ego as inimical to great drama, but he also takes a more profound, even metaphysical view. The Romantics, he says, desire

> to enjoy the privileges of grandeur and intense feeling associated with tragic drama without paying the full price. This price is the recognition of the fact that there are in the world mysteries of injustice, disasters in excess of guilt, and realities which do constant violence to our moral expectations.

In Romantic drama, remorse is sufficient to ensure a happy reconciliation of the issues; but remorse does not, in truth, wipe out the evil done. To Steiner, 'near tragedy is, in fact, another word for melodrama'.[30]

It was still the law that straight drama could be staged only by the 'patent' theatres: Covent Garden, Drury Lane and the former Little Theatre in the Haymarket, which, after its disastrous experience of uproar in 1738,* had been used as a dramatic school for some years, finally obtaining its own patent (for part-year performances) in 1766, and being rebuilt as the Theatre Royal.† [31] The unpatented theatres were always free to stage the ever-popular pantomime, and these provided a partial escape from what must, to some at least of the performers, have been a stiflingly decorous atmosphere. By Christmas 1830 every theatre, patented and unpatented alike, was putting on a seasonable pantomime. Though Harlequin continued to dominate the cast until the 1850s, increasingly characters from English history, nursery rhymes and folklore began to put in an appearance, as well as literary figures like Aladdin and Robinson Crusoe.[32] Spoken dialogue had to be submitted to the examiner, but there was a good deal of ad libbing and 'business' which contrived to make comments on such contemporary topics as Luddite riots, Catholic emancipation, the Poor Laws and the Corn Laws. (By the late nineteenth century the censor was attempting to have all stage 'business' written down and submitted for approval.)[33]

During the later eighteenth century, small unpatented theatres probed the law by staging 'burlettas', musical dramas, with sung dialogue, largely in rhymed couplets. There was no move to prevent this, so the

---

* See p.319.
† The current Theatre Royal, Haymarket, is a Nash rebuilding dating from 1821 (*The Times*, 16 April 1994).

managements began to take serious plays, transpose the dialogue into rhyme, and minimize the musical accompaniment – the orchestra was progressively diminished until sometimes only a piano remained, and even that might be reduced to sounding occasional dramatic chords. Then Covent Garden staged a spoken entertainment with a handful of songs, incautiously describing it as a 'burletta'. Immediately the non-patented theatres seized on the precedent to stage what were virtually straight plays, and provided they were embellished with a few songs, claiming they were merely producing 'burlettas'. The word 'melodrama', drama with songs, dates from 1809. In the end the Lord Chamberlain permitted a three-act piece (five acts remained within the purlieu of the patented theatres) to count as a burletta provided it included songs. Under this umbrella the minor theatres staged more or less anything they liked, including Shakespeare (under a variety of fancy titles) and other esteemed writers of the 'legitimate' theatre.[34]

Descriptions of the melodramas read rather like silent cinema: stereotyped characters very broadly portrayed, 'dark villainy and purest innocence', plenty of action, preferably including some explosions, mood heightened by orchestral (or, at a pinch, piano) accompaniment. Dialogue was an optional extra; incident was the central attraction, not subtle delineation of character.[35] The one essential was that virtue be exalted, wrongdoers abased, by the time the curtain came down.[36]

A happy outcome for a character who misbehaved was deplored, in melodrama as elsewhere. Nicoll quotes a review from the start of the century which complains that

the hero of this play is a man who first deserts his country and then seduces the object of his love; and the heroine is a woman who has not merely violated the purity of her sex, but has done it in defiance of a solemn vow. Yet, in contempt of every principle of morality these characters are made happy, and that without their having shown the most trifling marks of contrition.[37]

This play was a translation of a German original. Playwrights like Schiller were exploring daring domestic themes which the London theatre refused to countenance. 'The explanation of this neglect [of German authors],' says Nicoll, 'no doubt is to be traced in that moral mood which had greeted the earliest translations in the preceding age. During the first decades of the nineteenth century this moral mood was growing in intensity . . .'[38]

One disreputable old favourite proved impervious to reform. In 1773

Sir John Fielding, Westminster magistrate, had endeavoured to persuade Garrick not to perform *The Beggar's Opera*, and in 1776 a critic wrote: 'The public were little aware of the injury they were doing to society by giving countenance to an entertainment which has been productive of more mischief to this country than any would believe at the time.' In the following year an alternative version was staged (unsuccessfully), in which Macheath is sentenced to the prison hulks and his doxies resolve to lead virtuous lives. Dr Johnson, though not persuaded that any man 'was ever made a rogue by being present at its representation', nevertheless regretted the play's potential influence in 'making the character of a rogue familiar and in some degree pleasing'. A critic writing in 1835 remarked that 'its still continuing to be performed, in defiance of public decency, says little for the boasted improvement in the morality of the stage'.[39]

The huge size of the old patent theatres had predisposed them to large-scale musicals and spectaculars – Kemble had been known to lament the 'coarsening' of his art in which he had to indulge in order to be heard, and although he had done his best to draw audiences to *Julius Caesar*, theatre-goers preferred '*Timour the Tartar*, an "equestrian melodrama", or *The Cataract of the Ganges*, an extravaganza on which the manager of Drury Lane lavished £5000'.[40] Drury Lane had been rebuilt in 1794 on an even grander scale than before, and although this building burned down in 1809, the slightly smaller one reopened in 1812 was still a large playhouse. Edmund Kean, who joined Drury Lane in 1814, succeeded by pouring his immense vitality into Shakespearian roles of Protean dimensions, and wallowing in Renaissance villainy. Gothic romanticism, in 'horrific blood curdling castle romances', was considered his forte. But his soliloquies were not considered successful.[41] Covent Garden burned down in 1808, and again was rebuilt on a grand scale.[42] Both houses were in perpetual financial difficulty, both from the vast costs of the spectaculars, and from the inflated salaries demanded by the stars.[43] The new, expensively constructed Covent Garden introduced higher prices, which led to two months of mob riots until the management agreed to return to the old pricing structure;[44] Drury Lane, before its incineration, had been reduced to trying to fill seats with performing dog acts. Whitbread, of brewery fame, financed the 1812 rebuilding, but committed suicide in the financial débâcle that ensued.[45]

In 1843 the Licensing Act of 1737 was superseded by a Theatres Act. This Act ended the monopoly of the patent theatres – henceforth all theatres, whether in London or beyond, could receive a licence for performances from the Lord Chamberlain, provided the intended material was acceptable.[*] Texts had to be submitted not less than seven days in advance of production.

Full advantage of the new opportunities provided by the 1843 Act was not immediately taken. Sadler's Wells switched almost at once to 'legitimate' drama, the Princess's (in Oxford Street) followed in 1850. Then came the explosion. Whereas in 1851 there were only 22 theatres in London, of which two were opera houses and one confined to French drama, by the end of the century there were 61, of which 38 were in the West End, 23 in nearby suburbs, and 39 were music halls.[46]

The Act paved the way for new dramatic departures. The great playhouses struggled on, filling their pantomimes with elephants and clowns, their Shakespeare with stage wizardry, flying machines and pageantry. In 1847 Covent Garden dropped out of the competition, becoming an opera house.[†] Drury Lane, after importing a circus in 1848, tried staging Shakespeare again in 1850, but lost so much money that it reverted once more to the circus.[47] Interest was switching to the newer theatres, better suited to the sort of developments that had been taking place on the Continent and were now to proliferate in England – a theatre of intimate, domestic drama.[48]

The theatre of the last half of the nineteenth century embodied two traits which Sorokin identified as typical of a civilization in the ripening of its sensate phase: an absorbed, almost obsessive, attention to authenticity, to naturalism; coupled with an increasing focus on the concerns of ordinary human beings.

Both in historical and in contemporary drama, immense pains were taken to achieve accuracy. The habit of staging Shakespeare in whatever garments the players thought most becoming came almost to an end, though some of the actresses proved incorrigible. From early in the nineteenth century, says Nicoll, 'the movement towards the extreme of naturalism was constant', indeed 'this tendency . . . proved to be the most determined and the most persistent of its age . . .'[49] Some of the early productions were, perhaps, only approximate; Kemble's *Coriolanus* of 1811 displayed a marble Rome which was not to materialize until the time of the Emperor Augustus, but it made its point, as did an 1820 *Lear* rooted in 'an early Saxon period'.[50] There were anxious cogitations as to whether 'authenticity' really demanded the Elizabethan costume of Shakespeare's own time.[51] More recent events posed fewer problems –

---

[*] Supervision of other matters, such as the safety of the buildings, was the responsibility of local authorities. The Lord Chamberlain was the responsible officer only for theatres in London and Windsor, excluding Drury Lane and Covent Garden (*Oxford Companion to the Theatre*, p.194).
[†] The present house dates from 1856, when rebuilding followed yet another fire.

shipwrights from H.M. Dockyards were summoned to build and rig the stage ships for *The Siege of Gibraltar*.[52] In 1859 a renowned actor-manager was proud to boast that 'in no single instance have I ever permitted historical truth to be sacrificed to theatrical effect'; by the 1870s, for a production of *Rachel the Reaper*, live pigs, sheep, a goat and a dog were propelled on to the stage, imaginative construction on the part of the audience rendered virtually superfluous.[53] Larger potential audiences, the result of improved transport as well as the increasing popularity of the theatre, made long runs possible,* and encouraged managers to invest time and trouble in stage sets which would have been impracticable under the old repertory system.[54]

'Real life' issues drawn from daily experience began to compete with the ever-popular farces. The melodramas that delighted the working- and lower-middle-class patrons, especially in the fringe theatres developing towards the East End of London, featured the struggle against poverty, homelessness and crime; above all, horrific portrayals of the suffering caused by drink, a succession of plays on the subject of temperance flowing throughout the last three-quarters of the century. The patriotic and idealistic portrayal of England's soldiers, sailors, traders and country people (as distinct from aristocrats and townees) with which the century had opened was replaced, in Victorian times, with dramas of middle-class home life, in which women tempted to seek wider horizons than their own hearth were brought to see the error of their ways.[55] 'The theme of married boredom was one which attracted much attention during this time', says Nicoll; in *Broken Ties*, of 1872, for instance, a hero's happiness is almost wrecked by a wife intent on pursuing a career of her own. All is saved, however, when she sobbingly realizes that Home is what matters.[56]

The second half of the century, while less prissy than the first, remained attached to Christian moral standards. Where a play about the court of Charles II performed in about 1820 'endeavoured to demonstrate that affairs of the heart at Whitehall were of the purest and most honourable; a little flirtation perhaps, but positive evil, never', by 1845 *The King's Rival* admits that Charles has mistresses, and 'that there might be danger for a young girl in his court'.[57]

Censorship played a part in the prevailing standards – the *Dame aux*

---

* It was the end for the old stock companies, both in London and in the provinces, where, so far as the major theatres were concerned, the local company was replaced by companies on tour from London with the latest London success. The resulting loss of any training in versatility for young entrants to the profession was a powerful impetus towards the establishment of drama schools (Nicoll, Vol.V, pp.56ff.).

Camélias, for instance, was suppressed in 1853, and an attempt in 1886 to stage Shelley's *The Cenci* was vetoed.[58] The main obstacle, however, to playwrights seeking to explore daring domestic and sexual themes remained public opinion. An 1875 English version, *Love and Marriage*, of a French original dared not seek the sympathy and forgiveness of an English audience for an adulteress, and vitiated the weight of the original by making her the victim of a sham marriage.[59] Two years later a review regretted that the light-hearted treatment of conjugal infidelity in a contemporary play hindered proper respect for dramatic art.[60] In 1885 a Pinero version of a French original was criticized for permitting its married heroine to entertain the thought of straying from the path of strict virtue when she learns of her husband's infidelities.[61] English productions of Ibsen and Strindberg were poorly received; indeed, Ibsen, whose earliest success, *Pillars of Society*, dated from 1877, was hardly performed in London prior to the 1890s. Contemporary critics accused him of selecting his subjects 'from the most sordid, abject, even the most revolting corners of human life', of inhabiting a 'moral leper house', of being a 'provincial pornographer'; and he was exhorted to say something 'of the trials and struggles of the just, the sorely-tried, the tempted and the pure'.[62]

The very fact that performances eliciting such comments were being given is evidence that censorship was being exercised more liberally in regard at least to themes. Of 19,304 stage plays submitted for examination between 1852 and 1912, only 103 were refused a licence, though texts remained minutely scrutinized and oaths were excised – and of course it is impossible to assess to what extent playwrights censored their own work in the light of known policy in the Lord Chamberlain's office.[63] References to censorship for reasons of political ideology are sparse. An example early in the century was notorious – the refusal of a licence to *Alasco*, a historical tragedy about Poland which made what were held to be injudicious references to freedom and tolerance; and amendments were apparently required in a dramatic version of Disraeli's *Coningsby* in order to delete anything suggestive of class antagonisms.[64] However, plenty of melodramas voiced class conflict openly, whether, like *The Factory Lad* of 1832, they dealt with the Luddite smashing of new machinery, or, as in *The Workman's Foe*, with the depiction of the capitalist as selfish, vicious, arrogant and uncaring.[65] Wealth and poverty, capital and labour were commonplace themes on the West End stage by the 1890s.[66]

Public figures, especially the royal family, were firmly protected from lampooning (and of course could not be portrayed on stage), but W.S.

Gilbert, for instance, lost only one or two lines from an early libretto, most of his satire passing unscathed – perhaps, says Richard Findlater in *Banned*, because it was fundamentally good-humoured, 'it joked but never jeered'.[67] Complaints about the Lord Chamberlain's office centred on inconsistency and arbitrariness, the misapplication of the rules in particular cases, rather than on any objection to censorship in principle. In 1832 a select committee had listened to representations that censorship had become redundant, it being so unlikely 'in these enlightened times' that the public would tolerate anything offensive. Others suggested that the matter be left entirely to the good sense of the theatre managers. In the end majority opinion favoured 'an interposition well warranted by the interests of public morals and peace'. Among playwrights, support for censorship was more prevalent than was opposition, while many contemporaries considered the drama to be, if anything, inadequately controlled. Indeed, a select committee which looked into the question in 1892 expressed not only approval of the existing arrangements, but a preference for them to be extended to music halls and other places of public entertainment.[68] 'Public opinion and the press,' in the words of a later author quoted by Nicoll, 'were as fussily intolerant' as the fussiest reader of plays.[69]

In this moral climate, the formal heirs of the Reformation began a *rapprochement* with the theatre. Protestant religion never embraced drama as a form of worship as Catholicism had done (though only after a millennium of repudiation). But by the 1870s prominent churchmen were publicly giving their blessing to the secular stage. The Bishop of Manchester, in addresses to audiences both at Drury Lane and at the Prince's Theatre, assured his hearers that his intentions were not to abolish the theatre but to purify it. In the same year, a cleric referred to 'the desire to give the player the social status which his calling, if properly pursued, most justly demanded', and twenty years later that desire was fully consummated when in 1897 Henry Irving received a knighthood.[*][70] Queen Victoria, the paragon of rectitude, felt able without shame both to patronize the West End theatre and to invite London players to perform before her at Windsor.[71] Undeniably, a scintilla of moral unease lingered on,[†] but far from blanket condemna-

---

[*] By the late twentieth century, even long-retired minor Hollywood performers were being accorded several inches of obituary in *The Times*, a tribute either to the eminence to which the profession had by then ascended, or to the relative ease of amassing facts about the denizens of show-business.

[†] And was still doing so, in the mid-twentieth century, when players of Protestant backgrounds

tion, the Church now looked to the stage to measure up to the highest moral standards. 'The stage is a profession like other professions', wrote J.E.C. Welldon, Dean of Durham, in an appendix to his 1924 translation, for the SPCK, of Augustine's *City of God*.

> All that the State, or indeed, the Church can desire is that the theatre, which is not only an exponent but a creator of moral sentiment in the community, should, in the plays which are acted, in the manner of acting them, and in the personal lives of the artists who take part in them, maintain the highest possible level of moral dignity.[72]

However lofty the sentiments expressed from the stage, the area of London surrounding Covent Garden and Drury Lane continued to enjoy its sleazy eighteenth-century reputation as the domain of thieves and prostitutes.[73] In the teeming London slums there flourished a very different dramatic entertainment from that on offer in the fashionable theatres. Tales of notorious criminals 'formed the principal part of the repertoire of the low theatres and singing rooms in which boys and girls spent much of their time', notes J.J. Tobias in his *Crime and Industrial Society in the Nineteenth Century*. 'Such places do not seem to have blossomed in full vigour until the 1820s but thereafter they were much patronized. Boys and girls would make a visit to the theatre their first business on release from gaol.'[74]

In the burgeoning towns of the early nineteenth century, especially London, destitute orphans, deserted children and young runaways,[*] casualties of the shifting populations and disrupted societies of the Industrial Revolution, formed into gangs and were trained in crime by a new element on the social scene – professional thieves who had no other trade than crime, and no intention of acquiring one. A criminal subclass peculiar to the towns was emerging, distinct from the opportunistic thieves who tended to multiply or diminish in numbers in response to contemporary levels of employment.[75] Social cohesion, even among the poor, was disintegrating. The great characteristic of large towns, wrote an observer in 1837, is that the lower classes 'do not feel towards each other any of those kindly emotions which are so visible . . . in small towns'.[76]

Except in the period immediately after the Napoleonic Wars, few

were proportionately far less numerous than those from Roman Catholic homes.

[*] A survey of 600 juvenile delinquents found that over 40 per cent were fatherless (Tobias, p.191).

observers blamed crime on poverty, but rather on the demon drink, for whose consumption a certain minimum level of prosperity was required, except when the price of a drink was itself the motive for theft. Numerous migrants from country villages, most of them under twenty years old, deprived of the support of their old communities and dossing down in appalling living conditions, had every incentive to seek out the conviviality of the gin-shop. In some areas, a drinking-house lay behind every fifth or sixth door, with corrupt magistrates bribed to turn a blind eye, and sometimes owning the establishment themselves.[77]

A huge increase in prosecutions and also in convictions for theft from persons occurred in the first half of the nineteenth century. Paradoxically, it may have resulted from progressive reform of the 'Bloody Code', emboldening authorities to prosecute and juries to convict for offences in cases where previously they would have adjudged the punishment too harsh.[*][78] The process was gradual, with the value at which a theft qualified as 'grand' larceny (subject to capital punishment) being progressively raised from the old twelve pence. Different figures applied at different times and in different circumstances (whether the larceny was from a ship, shop, house or from the person, for instance), but the process of amelioration was continuous. In 1816 there were still over 200 capital crimes on the statute book; by 1861 only four remained: high treason, murder, piracy with violence, and destruction of public arsenals and dockyards.[†][79]

The gentler, more humane values championed by the evangelicals joined forces with the political radicalism of those who blamed bad social conditions for the upsurge in crime to push through penal reform. But it was in the teeth of opposition; attempts prior to 1810 being defeated. Property was everywhere at risk, none more so than that of the poor who struggled to remain honest in spite of appalling suffering and great temptation. Mechanics 'could hold in safety no personal property of any sort', a later report was to write of the period that culminated in the establishment of the Metropolitan Police.[80]

Public opinion in England was very slow to accept the necessity of a police force, seeing it as a Continental instrument of political repression. The parish watch was the accepted defence against criminality. The City

---

[*] Even where the penalty of death was pronounced, it was seldom enacted. Of 8,483 criminals sentenced to death in the years 1828–34, only 355, or less than 5 per cent, were actually executed (Tobias, p.233).

[†] Not until 1957 was there any change. In practice, except for treason in time of war, no execution was carried out after 1838 except for murder (Gowers, p.26).

of London was well patrolled by a well-administered watch, but beyond and between the old centres of population in the City and Westminster lay 90 parishes scattered across Kent, Surrey and Middlesex, with malefactors nipping across parish boundaries and disappearing into the courtyards and alleyways of the rapidly expanding 'rookeries'. Fielding's Runners, operating from his own home in Bow Street (Westminster), was a pioneer institution.[*] Attempts by the Solicitor-General in the aftermath of the Gordon Riots to establish a metropolitan police authority met with opposition, but in 1792 the Home Office funded the appointment of salaried constables in each of seven offices, two in Westminster, four in Middlesex and one in Surrey. Then in 1798 the merchants trading with the West Indies established their own river police to cope with depredations on their cargoes. In 1800 the state took over responsibility for the Thames River Police. Finally, in 1829, Sir Robert Peel succeeded in persuading Parliament of the necessity for a unified police force, and the 'Peelers' or 'Bobbies' appeared on the streets of London – apart from the City, which continued with its old watch until 1838–9, when it established its own force.[81]

Even in London, however, the level of violence associated with crime seems to have been low, and to have diminished as the century wore on. By 1805 the Bow Street Horse Patrol had cleared the highwaymen from Hounslow Heath,[82] by 1815 mounted robbers (as distinct from footpads) had disappeared from around London, and by 1839 they were everywhere extinct.[83] 'It is acknowledged on every side,' said a report of 1829, 'that crimes attended with acts of violence have diminished.' An 1839 report by a royal commission on 'a Constabulary Force' wrote that 'street "depredations"' were 'rarely accompanied by violence'. There was an alarming outbreak of garrotting in Manchester in 1850, swiftly emulated in London, but even these unpleasant attacks on the throat from the rear were intended only to render the victim temporarily helpless, not permanently injured or killed. There was a period of alarm, but the perpetrators were arrested, and public anxieties allayed.[†] Indeed, by

---

[*] Two hundred and thirty years later, on 5 October 1992, Bow Street Police Station, built in 1881 on the site of Fielding's headquarters, closed down, its duties transferred to a new station at Charing Cross (*The Times*, 6 October 1992).

[†] After 1861 judicial corporal punishment was restricted to a very limited range of crimes, but the Garrotters Act of 1863 reintroduced corporal punishment for attempting to choke or strangle to facilitate the commission of an indictable offence, and for robbery with violence. The Cadogan Committee which in 1937 (unsuccessfully) recommended the complete abolition of judicial corporal punishment did not accept that the passing of the Act had been instrumental in the rapid demise of garrotting (*Corporal Punishment*, Report of the Advisory Council on the Treatment of

1862 'great amelioration in resort to violence in the last 15 or 20 years' was being reported.[84]

In 1888 in Whitechapel began the series (there were to be nine in all) of murders and mutilations of young women ascribed to the unidentified Jack the Ripper. *Punch* magazine, which for almost thirty years had been campaigning against 'this poisonous exotic, Sensation', queried in September, after the fourth such victim, whether the widespread advertisements for various dramas, depicting sensational scenes of murder, might not have acted on 'the morbid imagination of an unbalanced mind' to precipitate the Ripper's actions. Public opinion was sufficiently receptive to this view for the management at the Lyceum abruptly to terminate the successful run of *Dr Jekyll and Mr Hyde*.[85]

Horrifying though these incidents were, they hardly threatened society at large. In the 1890s Charles Booth found that violence was regarded by criminals and police alike as a breach of the 'rules of the game'.[86]

The prevailing ethos in England was still basically Christian. It is true that by 1830 the Church of England had experienced a century of decline. There were only six communicants at St Paul's Cathedral on Easter Sunday 1800,[87] at which time the number of Easter communicants as a percentage of the population aged fifteen and over in the country at large stood at 9.2. A nadir of 7.2 was reached in 1820. At the same time the various Methodist sects were growing rapidly, as were the numbers of Baptists and Congregationalists.

'I believe there is no more exact criterion of the moral advancement of a people, than the sanctity which they accord to the Christian Sabbath.' So reflected William Gladstone in 1830.[88] In this respect, too, nineteenth-century England was to manifest an increasing preoccupation with traditional Christian standards.

Sabbath-keeping had become less and less strict during the eighteenth century. After the rigours of the Puritan Commonwealth the alliance between Sabbatarianism and the legislature had substantially weakened, though a general preference for a quiet Sunday had led, in 1677, to a Sunday Observance Act which prohibited worldly labour, retail trade, and unrestricted travel. The Societies for Reformation of Manners, in their heyday in the early eighteenth century, had obtained more convictions for Sunday trading than for any other single offence. But throughout the century a series of Acts had been passed exempting, for one good reason or another, specific trades from strict observance of the

Offenders, November 1960, Cmnd 1213, HMSO, London, pp.2–3).

1677 Act.* An Act of 1780 provided for a £200 fine for organizers of Sunday amusements for which a charge was made, but when in 1795 an attempt was made to tighten the provisions on Sunday trading, the Bill was rejected by the House, aware that the labouring poor had no other option but to shop on a Sunday. Sunday observance, especially in London, grew even more slack.[89]

By the 1820s most religious denominations other than the Roman Catholics were becoming concerned. In 1827 Anglicans founded the Lord's Day Society; by 1830 the Congregationalists had a Sunday Trading Suppression Society, and the Nonconformists were seeking, through their Sabbath Protection Society, to persuade shopkeepers not to trade. The Lord's Day Observance Society dates from 1831. For the remainder of the century (and beyond) Sunday observance remained a lively political issue, crisscrossed by compromising considerations such as whether, if places of sober amusement such as museums and parks were opened, there might be less drunkenness; whether the interests of the working class (mostly without votes) were best served by compulsory Sunday leisure or by the opportunity to earn at overtime rates; and by shifting alliances made up of those who preferred only to countenance legislation which acknowledged the divine origin of the commandment to keep holy the Sabbath, those who kept strict Sabbaths themselves but deeply distrusted state interference in matters of conscience, those whose primary concerns were with social welfare, and those anxious to ensure that whatever else happened, their own travel and comfort should not be disrupted by obligatory cessation of labour on the part of their servants. Consciences were searched as to whether purchases could be made on a Sunday from unattended (i.e. labour-free) vending machines, whether shareholders in railways allowed to carry Sunday excursions should donate a proportion of their dividends to charity, whether letter-writing was a permissible Sunday pursuit, whether the Salvation Army was desecrating the Sabbath with its band music. A constant series of Bills was introduced, occasional Acts passed or repealed, sometimes to liberalize, sometimes to place further constraints on, Sunday activities relating to such matters as pub opening hours, bands in parks, museum opening or the conveyance of the Royal Mail. Petitions were circulated. There were riots.[90]

On the whole, concludes Wigley in *The Rise and Fall of the Victorian*

* For instance, an Act of 1698 allowed forty watermen to ply for hire on the Thames; a 1762 Act permitted fish carts to travel on Sundays. It may be observed that the heroine of Jane Austen's *Persuasion*, suffering doubts as to the worthiness of her suitor Mr Elliot (later unmasked as a rogue), 'saw that there had been bad habits; that Sunday-travelling had been a common thing . . .'

Sunday, by mid-century Sabbatarian sentiment was in the ascendant, and continued to be so throughout Victoria's reign.[91]

The evangelical strand which contributed so markedly to the religious revival of the late eighteenth and early nineteenth centuries was joined in the mid-nineteenth by a fervour of a different kind, one which was to transform both the Anglican and Roman Catholic churches in England.

The pre-eminence of the Church of England was under threat. The repeal of the Corporation and Test Acts in 1828–9 had relieved Nonconformists and Roman Catholics of most of their civil disabilities. In the centuries when Parliament consisted solely of Anglicans it was not of much moment that the Convocation of the Archdiocese of York had not met since 1698, that of Canterbury since 1717, but churchmen were enraged in 1832 by the Church Temporalities Act which reorganized the finances and administration of the Anglican Church in Ireland over the heads of the Church authorities. In an Oxford still restricted to those who accepted the 39 Articles of the Anglican Church, where at least half the undergraduates were destined to fulfil clerical callings, John Keble, in July 1833, preached at the University Church of St Mary on the subject of 'National Apostasy'.[92]

Among his hearers was the young John Henry Newman. Inspired by what he felt as a call to revitalize the Church in the life of the nation, Newman published, in September, the first of the *Tracts for the Times*, goads which were to result in the formation of the Tractarian, or Oxford, Movement. Its origins lay in the tensions between Church and State, but in moving to examine the whole question of the source of authority, the Tractarians re-emphasized a theology of otherworldliness that had all but vanished from practical Anglicanism. Preaching had been the strength of the churches of the Reformation, philanthropy based on Christian love the main motivation of the evangelicals. An advertisement for the first volume of *Tracts for the Times* summed up the stance of the Tractarians: 'The sacraments, and not preaching, are the sources of divine grace.' 'Over against the aridities of empiricist philosophy and utilitarian ethics, the Tractarians sought a renewed awareness of transcendent mystery and a renewed sense of human life as guided by a transcendent power to a transcendent goal', as E.R. Fairweather puts it in the editorial introduction to his 1964 reprint of the *Tracts*.[93]

The Tractarians were united in distrusting a rationalism which, rejecting all appeal to tradition, set greater store by man's mental prowess than by God's powers to change man's nature. In elevating the Church as 'the tangible, historical link between the historical Incarnation and believers in each and every age', the Tractarians stressed the apostolic succession in the consecration of bishops, and sought in doctrine and practice to recapture the simplicities of the early Church, free of the (in their eyes) later excrescences of Romanism. Newman introduced weekly communion at the University Church – in most parishes communion services were not more frequent than quarterly.[94] The practice of fasting before communion was enjoined, Lent was observed, religious communities began to be founded, and church rituals and ceremonies were introduced that appealed to aesthetic and emotional sensibilities.[95]

An unfriendly critic of the movement, Thomas Arnold, noted:

God's grace, and our salvation, come to us principally through the virtue of the sacraments; the virtue of the sacraments depends on the apostolic succession of those who administer them . . . What wonder if to a body endowed with so transcendent a gift, there should be given also the spirit of wisdom to discern all truth; so that the solemn voice of the Church in its creeds, and in the decrees of its general councils, must be received as the voice of God himself.[96]

To the Tractarians, this was no *reductio ad absurdum*. As Newman pondered the heresies that plagued the early Church he became agonizingly convinced that Anglicanism was itself a heresy. In 1845 he joined the Roman Catholic Church, to be followed by many of his fellow Anglicans. In 1850 a papal brief recreated the Roman Catholic hierarchy in England.[97]

In the long term, the Tractarians made a greater and more long-lasting impact on the discipline and devotional practices of the Church of England than they did upon its doctrine. Towards the end of the century, however, there arose in America a new religious otherworldliness which was to deny all validity to the material world.

Bishop Berkeley, early in the eighteenth century, had come to the conclusion, which he elaborated in his *Principles of Human Knowledge*, published in 1710, that our perceptions are unable to assure us of the objective existence of matter. The whole concept of 'material substance' he rejected, and although in this he was at odds with Locke, who had required 'material substance' if only as the content of scientific investigation, Locke too had realized that 'material substance' was in fact an empty phrase, indicating something unknowable which gave rise to perceptions. 'Science', on this assumption, amasses general rules, identifies regularities, but does not *explain* anything.

An assertion that something exists is, in this philosophy, an assertion that it is *perceived* to exist. Such perception is no more than the recognition of a mental event, an impression on the mind, that does not entitle us to assume some kind of corresponding external reality. Boswell describes how Dr Johnson dealt with this proposition:

> After we came out of the church, we stood talking for some time together of Bishop Berkeley's ingenious sophistry to prove the non-existence of matter, and that everything in the universe is merely ideal. I observed that though we are satisfied his doctrine is not true, it is impossible to refute it. I never shall forget the alacrity with which Johnson answered, striking his foot with mighty force against a large stone, till he rebounded from it, 'I refute it *thus*'.[98]

Johnson, however, had done nothing of the kind. The Bishop never denied that we have sensations of solidity, only that there is an inert, senseless substance in which it supposedly inheres.

There was for Berkeley only one explanation of a world which could be vouched for solely in terms of ideas in the mind. 'There is not any other substance than *spirit*, or that which perceives.' But since conjunctions of apprehensions do not depend on the perceiver's will,[*] there must be a causative agent, and that agent is the infinite, all-pervading spirit, God. Everything exists in the mind of, and by the will of, God – a concept which also offered the reassurance that the continued existence of objects of perception was not dependent on the perceiving presence of a human observer; and that, God being benevolent and trustworthy, the world as perceived by our senses would remain orderly and coherent.[99]

Berkeley had a religious as well as a philosophic mission to fulfil in elaborating his theory of knowledge. Failure to appreciate the active, unceasing daily presence of God would, he feared, result in scepticism, atheism, and vice, the inevitable consequences of according autonomy to materialism.[100] In the next century and a half, as one scientific and technological triumph succeeded another, his theories lapsed into abeyance. Then, in 1866, a New England widow fell heavily on the January ice; and suffered injuries from which she believed herself suddenly and unexpectedly cured as a result of a spiritual revelation as to the true nature of matter.

Mary Baker Eddy's inspiration owed nothing to controversies over

---

[*] Berkeley was well aware of the problem posed by dreams and hallucinations, and took trouble to distinguish them from other apprehensions.

the processes by which knowledge is acquired. Her conviction that the senses are deceitful, that they defraud and lie,[101] came as a consequence of, not as an inducement to, her examination of human understanding of the natural world. She was deeply concerned to account for sickness, pain and suffering in a world supposedly the creation of a benevolent deity, and puzzled at the ease with which Jesus and the early Church, without any intervention from doctors, had worked miracles of healing. In her book *Science and Health* she spelt out the conclusions to which her meditations pointed, conclusions which she felt warranted the status of revelations.

> To . . . consider matter as a power in and of itself, is to leave the creator out of His own universe; while to . . . regard God as the creator of matter, is not only to make Him responsible for all disasters, physical and moral, but to announce Him as their source, thereby making Him guilty of maintaining perpetual misrule in the form and under the name of natural law.[102]

Many had pondered this dilemma. Mrs Eddy went on to draw practical conclusions. In a universe which is the expression of an all-encompassing, wholly spiritual, wholly benign deity, there could be no place for the limitations of matter, nor for evil. Unlike the ancient gnostics, who had accorded reality to matter but had regarded it as the creation of evil genius, Mrs Eddy held that evil arises from mankind's erroneous credence in the reality of matter – errors not just of individual belief, but of a totality of human misconceptions. Right thinking, meditation and prayer, and constant reading of the Scriptures alongside her own exegesis of them in *Science and Health* could liberate mankind from the suffering, including sickness, inseparable from these false notions.

In calling her insights 'Christian Science' Mrs Eddy was not merely claiming an internal logical consistency for her views, she was also averring that they could be empirically demonstrated. She began sharing her conclusions with a solitary student in about 1867. In 1875 she published *Science and Health*, and in 1876 the first Christian Scientist Association was formed, going on to organize the Church (later entitled 'First Church') of Christ, Scientist, in Boston in 1879. By 1891 thousands of students had attended her Metaphysical College in Boston, and over the next decade the movement spread across the North American continent and to Europe, in particular to England and Germany. Adherents readily testified to the huge improvements the faith had brought to their lives, especially to their physical as well as mental health. The highly respected *Christian Science Monitor* was founded in 1908, two years before Mrs Eddy died.[103]

This fundamental challenge to the tenets of materialism is all the more surprising because materialist science was, in the nineteenth century, making huge strides in its investigation, and manipulation, of the natural world, not least in the practice of medicine.[104] The stethoscope, a huge diagnostic advance, had been invented in 1819, the same year which saw the introduction of iodine as a medicine. Quinine followed a year later. The introduction of anaesthetics in 1846 went a long way towards diminishing the dread of operations and refining the expertise of surgeons, though because of infections the death rate remained at about 10 per cent until the discovery of antisepsis in the 1860s. In the 1880s, in swift succession researchers (chiefly in France and Germany) identified the bacilli of typhoid, pneumonia, tuberculosis, rabies, cholera, diphtheria and tetanus, and the search began for vaccines that could do for these diseases what Jenner had done, in 1798, for smallpox. Epidemiological studies had already pinpointed the connection between cholera and infected water supplies, and by the 1840s work was proceeding on sewerage systems for London and Manchester, though as late as the major London renewal scheme of 1866 the untreated effluent was simply moved downriver to the sea.[105]

Life in America and north-west Europe was being transformed. Steam-powered river transport was operating on the Hudson in America by 1807;[106] the first crossing of the Atlantic by steam occurred in 1819. On land, the transport revolution began with the railway; the first, the Stockton and Darlington, started operating in 1825. By 1863 England had its first Underground (steam) trains.[107] Bicycles came in shortly after mid-century; motor cars, initially propelled by steam, by coal gas or by ponderous and short-lived electrical batteries, were by the end of the century being powered by petrol-driven engines, a seemingly inexhaustible supply of this ancient, but hitherto largely unharnessed, fuel having been discovered in Pennsylvania in 1859, during a search for a substitute for the increasingly scarce and expensive whale oil used for lamplighting. Goodyear had, in 1839, patented the vulcanization of rubber, thus preventing it cracking in the cold or melting in the heat. At first it served chiefly for domestic uses such as furniture and shoes (the gum boot, it was claimed, saved thousands from deadly chills induced by cold, wet feet), but ultimately found its form in the pneumatic tyres that eased the passage of cars and rendered obsolete the name of the old boneshaker bicycle.

Coal gas was first used for domestic lighting in 1792 by an

enterprising engineer of Redruth, in Cornwall, then a highly productive mining area. Before the end of the eighteenth century, he had installed modest gas lighting in James Watt's steam engine factory in Birmingham. In 1807 an English factory risked installing 904 burners for coal gas, and found the system much cheaper than tallow candles.[108] By then the proprietor of the Lyceum Theatre (then known as the English Opera House) had switched to gas, and in 1807 it was used for the streetlamps in Pall Mall. By 1813 the Houses of Parliament had gas illumination, and shortly afterwards London became the first city in the world to have gas-lit streets.[*109] Covent Garden theatre proudly announced the installation of gas lighting for the grand hall and staircase at the opening of the 1815–16 season, and by 1817 both Covent Garden and Drury Lane had extended the new system throughout the auditorium, to great critical acclaim.[110] Initially, the whole theatre remained bathed in light, but by 1849 methods had been found of putting the illumination under the control of the prompter, who darkened the auditorium during the performance.[111] A brief foray into the stage use of limelight during Macready's 1837–8 season at the Garden was abandoned because of its high cost, but it returned in the 1850s, to become a metaphor for denoting the centre of attention.[112]

Coal tar, a by-product of coal gas production, proved a fertile source of new products. From it chemists produced new dyes, artificial flavourings and perfumes, and products as diverse as mothballs and saccharine.[113] From the chemical industry, too, came methods of treating wood pulp that developed the artificial silks which were to liberate women of only moderate means from the tyranny of dowdy textiles; and, producing paper far more cheaply than did the old rag methods (at a cost to local waterways that only later generations were to appreciate), launched the newspaper industry on its heady path to wealth and influence, a path bestrewn with innovations such as the application, in 1814, of steam to the presses of the London *Times*, and new inventions such as the linotype method of setting whole lines of type at a time, first used in 1886 by the New York *Tribune*.[114]

Not until 1833, with the invention of the first 'friction' matches, did the old tinderbox become obsolete; the 'safety' match followed in 1855. Another commonplace of twentieth-century life, margarine, dates from 1860. It was the chemists, too, who, by the development first of photography and then of malleable celluloid in place of glass plates for

---

[*] As late as the 1950s the peregrinating figure of the lamplighter was still to be seen in London's more archaic districts, holding his long, flame-tipped wand to the gas mantles.

negatives, made possible the evolution of a wholly new and utterly absorbing popular entertainment – the cinema.

The consummation of this art form required a parallel development in electronics. As early as 1808 Humphrey Davy had demonstrated the use of electricity for arc lighting, but not until 1858 was it successfully in practical use – in the South Foreland lighthouse. The light was considered too harsh and flickering for domestic or theatrical use, and although the more satisfactory alternative, the incandescent electric lamp, had been invented by 1840, it was not until late in the century that legal and practical problems had been overcome to the point where it could pass into general use. By 1900 electricity was well established in urban, though not in rural, areas, and its application was in the process of transforming domestic life.

Most of the ingenious tools of the nineteenth century – such as typewriters and sewing machines – had to wait until the twentieth century for their adaptation from manual to electric operation, but already before the century's end Americans had access to electric kettles and irons, and refrigeration plants were offering blocks of ice for use in domestic 'ice boxes'.* The vacuum cleaner was invented in London in 1901.[115]

Hugely though these innovations affected daily life, especially that of women, none were as influential in revolutionizing society as the long-distance transmission of messages: the telegraph and the telephone. Morse had, in 1832, devised the code which (later much amended) came to bear his name, and on 24 May 1844 the first message was tapped out in electric impulses along the wires from Washington to Baltimore. The transmission of speech was first demonstrated by Alexander Graham Bell in 1876; within three years Britain had its first telephone exchange. Two years later Edison patented his method for capturing and reproducing evanescent sounds on the gramophone. By the last decade of the century the transmission of messages without the aid of electric cables – the 'wireless' – had been demonstrated at the level of Morse impulses – the transmission of speech had to wait for technical advances which did not occur until the early twentieth century.

The inventions, innovations and discoveries of the nineteenth century were welcomed with uninhibited and almost universal delight. A few did, indeed, grieve over polluted waters and dark satanic mills, Matthew Arnold reputedly questioned the use of the newly opened railway line

---

* British kitchens had long been supplied by an enterprising company which owned a spring-fed lake in Norway subject to natural freezing (*The Times*, 11 September 1868).

between Islington and Camberwell if all it did was permit travellers to pass from one dismal and illiberal place to another, and Emerson gloomily acknowledged the news that Maine could now speak to Florida with the well-known response: 'Yes, but has Maine anything to say to Florida?';[116] but when, in the 1860s, barbed wire began to snake out across the American prairies to marshal the cattle of the range, none can have foreseen the searing images of the wires of no man's land that were to typify World War I; nor envisioned Jutland when, shortly after mid-century, the French set sail in the first seagoing ironclad, and the British, in 1859, launched H.M.S. *Warrior.** Weaponry shared in the general acceleration of achievement – Dr Gatling's machine gun was an invention of the American Civil War, Maxim improved on it; Colt's pistol, Smith and Wesson's revolver, Mauser's rifle – all owed their origin to nineteenth-century ingenuity.

Technological fervour proceeded alongside a lively appreciation of the wonders of God's world. It is true that some half century after the first use of anaesthesia in obstetrics, the story was promulgated that there had been widespread theological objection to any alleviation of pain in childbirth on the grounds that it was a contravention of Genesis 3:16 ('in sorrow thou shalt bring forth children'), but even at the time no evidence was adduced, and subsequent investigation has rebutted the story.† Attitudes to the miracles of science were summed up rather in the text of that first message that hummed from Washington to Baltimore, inaugurating the age of the telegraph: 'What hath God wrought?' One end-of-century commentator mused of the telephone that

> in its wonderful function of placing one intelligent being in direct vocal and sympathetic communication with another a thousand miles away, its intangible and mysterious mode of action suggests to the imagination that unseen medium of prayer rising from the conscious human heart to its omniscient and responsive God.[117]

* Now in Portsmouth Harbour.

† James Simpson, who introduced anaesthesia in childbirth, himself a practising Christian, expected opposition, and prepared a theological defence of his action which was frequently quoted later as evidence that the Church had attacked him. There was indeed some disquiet, but it was chiefly from fellow doctors on medical and ethical, rather than theological, grounds, though one doctor did voice Biblical objections. When some of Simpson's patients expressed religious anxieties, it was the clergy who came to his support, assuring dubious mothers that God did not vengefully impose pain, and that the word in Genesis usually translated 'sorrow' or 'travail' could equally well be translated 'labour', just as for Adam food would in future be obtained only at the cost of 'sorrow', or 'labour'. So far as Great Britain was concerned, the controversy was over within the year (for a full account, see A.D. Farr, 'Religious opposition to obstetric anaesthesia: a myth?', *Annals of Science*, 40, 1983, pp.159–77).

In the world of commerce, as in the applied sciences, devout men continued under the post-Reformation benediction on the pursuit of a secular calling. Quakers in particular were building steadily on the prosperity already established in the previous century, and their business success was wholly disproportionate to their numbers: Cadbury, Fry and Rowntree in the manufacture of chocolate; Huntley and Palmer, Peak Frean and Carr in the production of biscuits; Cash's silk ribbons (and name-tapes), Bryant and May for matches, and Clark for shoes are among the names which were to remain well known into the twentieth century.[118]

Conscience compelled some disinvestment. Though the Nonconformists of the eighteenth century had abhorred 'spirituous liquors', wine and beer had not been forsworn, and a number of Quakers had been prominent brewers. The nineteenth century saw increasing concern about the connection between alcohol and crime and domestic violence, and in the latter half of the century there developed a movement for total abstinence, which began to make a real impact on society in the last four decades of the century. Temperance joined pacifism as the principal issues for the Quaker conscience, and one by one the Quaker brewers abandoned brewing until by 1850 only one remained. His sons left the Society of Friends.[119]

The progress of medicine posed, as it had done before and has done since, the most serious moral dilemmas. There was, for instance, the shortage of corpses for the practice of dissection. While eighteenth-century surgeons tried to buy from the hangman, relatives and friends of those executed fought, sometimes with actual violence, to preserve the deceased from so ghastly a fate. The prospect of being 'anatomized' was even more dreaded by those condemned to the gallows than was the death sentence itself; the Murder Act of 1752 which permitted judges to order post-hanging dissection was intended as an additional deterrent.[120] Medical students outnumbered capital convictions, encouraging body-snatchers to rob graves, or to obtain the bodies of paupers by falsely claiming to be their next of kin. Surgeons turned a blind eye to what they knew was going on – in one case, a surgeon bribed friends of a noted Irish 'giant' to sell him the corpse, from which he hurriedly boiled off the flesh, the 'giant', fearing such a fate, having left strict instructions that he wished to be buried at sea. The discoloured skeleton is still retained by the Royal College of Surgeons.[121]

Rumours abounded in Ireland in the late 1820s that the body-snatchers were facilitating their task by murdering children. Medical students were at risk of attack from incensed members of the public. Late in 1828 came the dreadful discovery that Burke and Hare were indeed luring victims to their deaths. Body-snatching was only ended when the Anatomy Act of 1832 provided for the unclaimed bodies of paupers, previously buried at public expense, to be made available for dissection. 'It was the fear of dissection, after all,' writes Peter Ackroyd in his review of Ruth Richardson's *Death, Dissection and the Destitute*, 'that rendered the workhouse and hospital such emblems of terror to our grandparents; in these places the state became in a literal sense a vampire, preying on the bodies of the powerless and the dispossessed.'[122] Dying in lonely poverty may have become a fate more dreaded even than execution, but at least an adequate supply of corpses at last became available to trainee surgeons.[123]

Medicine also demanded increasing numbers of animals for purposes of experimentation on the living. The concern for animals that had prompted the closure of the bear-gardens in the previous century brought legislation on to the statute book in 1822 to protect horses, asses and cattle from cruelty. Bulls were not classed as 'cattle', so were not protected, but in 1835 legislation (which proved difficult to enforce) outlawed the baiting of bears, badgers and bulls, and forbade dog- and cock-fighting, though instances of cock-fighting were still being recorded some forty years later.[124] The Society for the Prevention of Cruelty to Animals was founded in 1824, receiving from Queen Victoria in 1840 the accolade 'Royal'.[125] The infliction of suffering on animals in the pursuit of scientific investigation, however, disturbed few consciences. Dr Johnson, in the eighteenth century, had voiced strong disapproval. Commenting on a scene in *Cymbeline* in which the Queen is proposing to try out some 'compounds' on animals, only to be cautioned with the words 'Your Highness shall from this practice but make hard your heart', Johnson remarks that

> the thought would probably have been amplified, had our author lived to be shocked with such experiments as have been published in later times, by a race of men that have practised tortures without pity, and related them without shame, and are yet suffered to erect their heads among human beings.'[126]

It was a minority voice. The painter Joseph Wright's *Experiment on a Bird in the Air Pump* (1768), showing a group in various stages of distress or indifference watching the death of a dove demonstrating the effect of a vacuum, prompts the art critic Richard Dorment to note that 'The central figure of the scientist, obsessed as he is with the pursuit of knowledge, is indifferent to questions of life and death or right and wrong.'[127]

In the mid-nineteenth century, members of France's Académie des Sciences were prominent proselytizers for the importance of vivisection. Claude Bernard, perhaps in overcompensation for the disquiet they knew they were arousing, stressed the importance of delighting in the tasks to be accomplished. Organized anti-vivisection movements (as distinct from isolated protests) were beginning to be founded by the 1860s in Italy, to be followed in England, in 1876, by what came later to be called the National Anti-Vivisection Society, and in France in the 1880s by the Société Française contre la Vivisection, which boasted Victor Hugo as its president.[128]

Their influence was minuscule. By the late 1860s laboratories for vivisection were being established at universities in Russia, Sweden, Germany, Holland, Belgium and Italy. There were new institutes of physiology at St Petersburg, Heidelberg and Leipzig. In England an attempt to introduce legislation ended in 1876 with an Act that did more to protect vivisectors from prosecution than animals from torture.[129]

Anna Kingsford, one of the early British campaigners, was shocked when visiting Rome in the late 1880s at the treatment of animals in general. She concluded that all that the Church (she was herself a Roman Catholic) could now 'see and teach was a selfish form of humanism – what man, here and hereafter and at whatever cost to the rest of life, might obtain for himself alone'.[130]

There was, indeed, a new form of humanism, one that found it could dispense entirely with the idea of transcendent realities or obligations; but it was in England rather than Rome that it had originated.

Chapter 18

Secular Certainties: the Early Twentieth Century

Hobbes in the early seventeenth century had constructed his political theory on the basis that 'good' meant pleasurable, 'bad' meant painful. Locke's later proposals on civil government were designed to prevent oppressors from destroying what he held to be man's fundamental good – the prospect of happiness. In the eighteenth century David Hume elaborated the moral implications of defining virtue in terms of human psychological responses.

Hume's *Treatise on Human Nature* accepts the pursuit of happiness as the primary human motivation and criterion of moral action. He contends that 'right' and 'wrong' are not properties of deeds, of activities, but are labels designating our reactions of approval or disapproval. However, these are not simple responses of pleasure or pain, they include a disinterested element based on concern for others. This sympathy, benevolence or fellow-feeling Hume recognizes to be somewhat frail, at its strongest where bonds of blood or friendship exist; nevertheless, he holds that its existence is vouched for in general introspective experience. 'We shall not doubt,' he concludes, 'that sympathy is the chief source of moral distinctions'; and on this essentially optimistic appraisal of human psychology he rests his case.[1] God was superfluous to Hume's thesis; indeed, Hume was suspected of harbouring atheistic tendencies. His *Dialogues concerning Natural Religion*, published posthumously, employ the time-honoured device of a supposed discussion between friends as a means for advancing unacceptable propositions without committing the author to sharing them. 'Epicurus's old questions are yet unanswered', says Philo, one of his protagonists. 'Is [God] willing to prevent evil, but not able? then is he impotent. Is he able but not willing? then is he malevolent. Is he both able and willing? whence then is evil?'[2] In the course of refuting all the standard arguments for the existence of God, the same speaker avers, 'It is certain, from experience, that the smallest grain of natural honesty and

363

benevolence has more effect on men's conduct, than the most pompous views suggested by theological theories and systems.' Philo defends the deist conception of a first cause, but rejects all mystical or transcendental claims to know anything about it, or its relationship to human beings; it is a purely philosophical concept. There seems little doubt that Philo reflects Hume's own opinion, though he judiciously ended the *Dialogues* by siding with one of the other disputants.[3]

Jeremy Bentham in the late eighteenth century accepted Hume's thesis that the basis of moral conduct is to be deduced from the experience of human psychology; but he was not content with Hume's static analysis. He wanted to promote change, to improve society. How could the benevolent impulse be harnessed to that end?

In 1768 Bentham had come across the phrase 'the greatest happiness of the greatest number', and though not the originator of the expression, he devoted his life to its application. No more than Hume did Bentham require a religious framework for his ethical theories, indeed Bentham considered the conflicting behests of different religious authorities simply confusing.[4] The test of the validity of moral action lay in its usefulness – or utility – in achieving the goal of the greatest happiness of the greatest number; hence the name of these moral philosophers: Utilitarians.

While Bentham welcomed the implied egalitarianism of the 'greatest happiness' principle, and sought to make no cultural distinction between one person's sources of gratification and another's, he recognized the difficulty of deciding, in particular instances, just how the greatest happiness of the greatest number was to be identified. For many years he struggled unsuccessfully with the impossible task of elucidating a quantitative theory of happiness which could serve as a sort of ready-reckoner for moral action. As time went by, he was to turn his attention to radical politics, advocating (among other things) annual parliaments, a secret ballot, female as well as male suffrage, and the abolition of the monarchy and the House of Lords, all in the interests of maximizing personal autonomy and thus control for the individual over his own destiny.[5]

There remained the problem of the strength and wisdom of the individual impulse to benevolence on which this moral philosophy relied. Education was clearly crucial, if choices at the level of both personal conduct and (in view of the proposed institutional reforms) political action were to be enlightened and effective. Bentham elaborated a theory of punishment and reward by which governments could promote the general happiness principle. With his close colleague James

Mill he advocated a wholly secular educational curriculum, in the moral aspects of which lavish resort to praise and blame would condition the child out of primitive selfish hedonism and into a recognition of the pleasure to be associated with the practice of altruism.[6]

James's son John Stuart Mill endeavoured to refine Utilitarianism by introducing qualitative distinctions between different sorts of pleasures and pains. He was not departing from the empirical justification for Utilitarianism, but claiming that experience confirmed the existence of different levels of pleasure. Altruism afforded pleasure of a 'higher' quality than selfishness, man having a social as well as an individual nature.[7]

For John Stuart Mill, 'In the golden rule of Jesus of Nazareth we read the complete spirit of the ethics of utility: To do as one would be done by, and to love one's neighbour as oneself constitute the ideal perfection of utilitarian morality.'[8] This conformity of Christian ethics with Utilitarian moral principles is not intended to imply that Christianity is in any way essential to Utilitarianism – on the contrary, it is Christianity which is the optional extra. But the full implications of this order of priorities were slow to emerge; for the moment, Utilitarianism joined forces with evangelical Christianity in a programme of humanitarian social reform.

On the Continent, a far more aggressive attack on religion in general and Christianity in particular was about to emerge – from the work, though he did not intend it, of a pious Lutheran, Friedrich Hegel. His philosophy was to be the launching-pad for the most influential atheist of all time: Karl Marx.

Hegel had died in 1831, before Marx joined the circle of Hegelian students in Berlin. Hegel's search for truth had been inspired by the contradictions inherent in man's isolation as an autonomous, essentially rational being (the human being of the Enlightenment), coupled with his intense psychological longing to escape from alienation, from a sense of futility and meaninglessness, and feel himself at one with his fellows and all creation. Christians interpreted the sense of alienation as man's separateness from God ('For Thou has created us for Thyself,' said St Augustine, 'and our heart cannot be quieted till it may find repose in Thee').[9] The Romantic movement of the late eighteenth and early nineteenth centuries had turned to art and intuition to effect the reconciliation (and most, says Charles Taylor in his authoritative study *Hegel*, ended up as Christians), but Hegel was not satisfied to abandon man's distinctive, essential rationality.[10]

The rationality of the Utilitarians Hegel found vapid, omitting, as it did, any conception of purposes at work in the universe other than the satisfaction of human desires. The Romantics had struggled towards, but, as Charles Taylor puts it, it was Hegel who finally hammered out, the only theory which reconciles human moral autonomy with harmony with cosmic spirituality: 'the power underlying nature, as spirit, reaches its fullest expression in self-awareness ... spirit reaches this self-awareness in man'.[11] Through the practice of rationality, man comes to understand his oneness with all creation, his egoism and selfishness melt away in the consciousness of his true destiny and identity as a vehicle for the fulfilment of Being.* The conflict between finite, limited Self and the infinite Other vanishes.† Ultimately, spirit is evolving, by a long historical process – social, moral and intellectual – individuals who consciously and conscientiously desire what the community requires of them.[12] The spiritual and material worlds are wholly reconciled, and equally important.

To Hegel, the Trinity symbolized the essence of his thesis: God the Father, the inchoate creative urge; Jesus, its incarnation as Man; and the Holy Spirit, the fully self-conscious consummation of the Will to Be. Pentecost, on this reading, is of far more significance than Christmas or Easter.[13] Hegel's spirit – *geist* – was far from the Christian conception of God, and orthodox Christians were soon to object to his delineation of a form of deity which was by inner necessity dependent on human beings for its realization, was loveless and graceless and devoid of any capacity to respond to prayer; nor was there any place for the immortality of the human soul.[14] For Hegel, however, religion, though helpful in articulating through art and myth the truths which he was endeavouring to expound, nevertheless was a second best, the recourse of the 'unhappy consciousness' not yet able to reach full enlightenment.[15] Pride of place went to philosophy, to a logical process through which, he believed, he

---

* Hegel's theory required this consciousness to be general throughout the community, a *volksgeist*, for no one individual could be an adequate vehicle of the *geist*; and he even elaborated in detail the sort of civil society in which the *geist* could best find expression. Surprisingly, in view of the universality of the fulfilled *geist*, he did not stipulate a world community, but accepted the state as the proper level of organization for the ideal society. He considered that the Germanic civilizations that had developed in most of the Western Roman Empire (including Frankish France, Visigothic Spain and Gothic/Lombard Italy) were furthest advanced among the myriad of world civilizations, but that the Protestant nations of north Europe were the most fully evolved because, in rejecting Roman Catholicism, they had accepted a greater exercise of that autonomous rationality which lay at the very heart of Hegelianism. The combination of the superiority of the collective over the individual, and of the 'pure' nordic Germans over any others, was enthusiastically adopted by twentieth-century National Socialists, blackening Hegel's name by association (Plamenatz (1963), p.208; Taylor, Charles, pp.377ff. and Chapter XVI).
† An echo of the paradox embodied in the Second Collect said at Matins in the Anglican Church, addressed to the God 'whose service is perfect freedom'.

had rendered his metaphysical beliefs absolutely incontrovertible.[16] More than that even, he believed he had demonstrated that his logical concepts were not mere instruments for thought, but were themselves transcendent realities, of which the material world was an embodiment.[17]

Hegel's logical process was the dialectic, the conjunction of opposites from which a synthesis emerges that is then itself subjected to a repeat of the dialectic, so that, step by step, logical certainties are established. Hegel began with the idea of Being (the thesis). Until some content is added to the concept of being, however, it is meaningless, it is nothing, it is Non-Being (the antithesis). The two are reconciled in the concept of Becoming (the synthesis).[18] This is not a process of reaching a compromise, but of finding a deeper level of understanding in which seeming contradictions are resolved. Hegel's *Science of Logic* and his *Encyclopaedia*, expounding these ideas, were published over the period 1812 to 1817. To his followers in Berlin, Hegel had achieved the philosophers' stone, the tool of ultimate understanding. All that remained was to apply it.[19]

By 1835, when Karl Marx joined the Hegelian circle in Berlin, Hegel's legacy had undergone a fundamental change. A substantial group of his admirers had come to question his belief in spiritual reality. Feuerbach was later to dismiss Hegel's philosophy as 'rational mysticism'; Hegel's former colleague Bruno Bauer put it about that Hegel himself had not believed the spiritual substratum of his theory – what was really being analysed and identified was human self-consciousness. In Feuerbach's words: 'The essence of God is nothing but the consciousness of the human species.' In his doctoral thesis, completed in April 1841, Marx, who swiftly abandoned the Lutheran faith to which his Jewish family had converted, was to maintain that philosophy is against 'all gods in heaven and earth that do not recognize human self-consciousness as the highest godhead.* There shall be no other beside it.'[20]

Hegel's careful intellectual constructions were treated as no more substantial than a house of cards. To the Young Hegelians he had been trapped in 'a circle of pure ideas'. Thought, said Feuerbach, arises from being, being does not arise from thought. The essence of being is to be found in Nature; physical, material Nature, including human beings.[21]

Feuerbach returns to the tenet that the western world had cherished since the Renaissance – that the senses are the gateway to the apprehension of reality. 'Sense experience must be the basis of all

---

* Or 'highest divinity' in some translations.

science – including the science of man.'[22] Though Hegel's affirmation of concepts as the ultimate reality was abandoned, the dialectic in which he had believed his conclusions inextricably embedded was not. It was Marx's friend and colleague Engels who, gratefully acknowledging that Feuerbach had destroyed 'the dialect of concepts', did most to propagate the revised 'materialist dialectics'.[23] This was to become the philosophic cornerstone of Marxism, the guarantor of the absolute truth *and necessity* of the Marxist analysis of history, the inspiration of a substantial proportion of intellectuals in both science and the humanities, and the begetter to the present day of libraries of works on the application of dialectical materialism to every sphere of human activity.

Marx and Engels were insistent that in the 'new religion of humanity' it was not enough to have analysed historic processes – the dialectic must be applied to the manipulation of the future, to social change, to politics. Here, however, there was a revision of the Hegelian dialectic that was to have devastating consequences. Where Hegel had required that thesis and antithesis be both subsumed into the final synthesis, the Young Hegelians rapidly came to the view that the antithesis constituted not a vital component to be embraced, but an opposition that must be destroyed.* Hence Bakunin's 'the joy of destruction is also a creative joy'.[24]

With humankind established as, in Marx's phrase, the 'highest godhead', the 'whole' from which the individual suffers the pangs of alienation was now reinterpreted as the whole human species.† It is *secular* relationships that hold the key, and secular relationships are, in the Marxist view, fundamentally a reflection of relative standing in the processes by which wealth is generated. So long as the distribution of property is unequal, so long as one man can be the wage-slave of another, deprived of a personal interest in the means of production, so long must alienation persist. From these premises, widely held among the Young Hegelians, was developed the insistence on state ownership of the means of production, distribution and exchange, on the prohibition on the employment of man by man, and on the inevitability of violent revolution and the vanguard role of the proletariat, since the possessing classes would obviously not voluntarily surrender their property.[25] Class conflict was both the explanation of all past history and the cherished key

---

* A principle in pursuit of which millions were to die, as did, for instance, the Ukrainian peasants in 1932–3.
† Neither Marx nor his successors ever took proper cognisance of the existence among human beings of any more limited 'sense of belonging' in the flight from alienation, hence their inability to understand nationalism or accommodate the idea of ethnic loyalties (Lukes, pp.75–6).

to all future development – the ultimate dialectic on which progress must be built.

Once the longed-for revolutionary consummation was achieved, human beings would be in full realization of their mutual fellowship and brotherhood. Crime, for which Marx and his associates recognized only property motives, would cease to exist, law and the police would become redundant, and there would be no further need for the instruments of the State, which would wither away.[26] The English, American and French developments for protecting the individual through the definition of 'rights' was anathema – smacking, as it did, of egoism, of the vaunting of the individual in contradistinction to the community, and, all too often, of the protection of private property.[27]

There was an important corollary. The Marxist Utopia required not only that economic inegalities be obliterated, but scarcity, too, must be eliminated. Nature must be mastered through the wonders of science, and production harnessed in the interests of an abundant prosperity – indeed, it is part of Marxist historical chronology that the achievement of a certain level of productive capacity was a necessary concomitant to the revolution of the proletariat, which would have been premature without it. Nature was a challenge, there to be conquered. In attitudes to the exploitation of the natural world, there was in practice nothing to choose between the developing free-enterprise capitalist, and the as-yet-embryonic communist, approach.*

Marx was the polemicist who focused and publicized the thinking of these revolutionary socialists. His passionate concern for the oppressed and the exploited, the seeming incontrovertibility of his historical analysis, his insights into the mechanisms of capitalist economics, the common-sense materialism with its evident validation in the advances made by science, all served to win dedicated adherents to his views.

Some found Marxist moral precepts more difficult to accept. Marx's atheistic analysis of society categorized all moral values as no more than the expression of class interests, religion a mere instrument by which the rich kept the poor in subjection while doping them with the illusory comforts of some other world to which docile conduct might equip them to aspire.[28] Marx's thesis illuminated, and still does, all subsequent discussion of social problems, but it offered no guidance whatever on

---

* The extent of the contrast between the modern attitude (capitalist or communist) to the natural world and that of a society permeated by 'primitive' respect is illustrated by Heinrich Harrar, describing the building of a dam in Tibet in the spring of 1948. 'There were many interruptions and pauses. There was an outcry if anyone discovered a worm on a spade. The earth was thrown aside and the creature put in a safe place' (Harrar, p.211).

personal conduct. The only imperative was to do whatever could hasten the (in any case inevitable) proletarian revolution, an imperative which his followers accepted as an absolute moral end, justifying any means to its accomplishment. This is not consistent with Marx's own theory that all values are merely the expression of class interests, but in Marxist theology the achievement of the classless society is an exception, the consummation to which all creation is moving, as willed by the only source of purposefulness – human consciousness.

Change, not a static condition but a dynamic process of 'becoming', is at the heart of the Marxist explanation of human history. In England Charles Darwin was contemplating the effect of change over time in an entirely different sphere – biology. In 1859 he published *The Origin of Species*, to be followed twelve years later by *The Descent of Man*.

Darwin's grandfather Erasmus, noted member of Birmingham's scientific club the Lunar Society, had been a free thinker. Perhaps he enjoyed teasing the conventional, certainly he shocked one acquaintance, who reported that he often used to say:

> Man is an eating animal, a drinking animal, and a sleeping animal, and one placed in a material world, which alone furnishes all the human animal can desire. He is gifted besides with knowing faculties, practically to explore and to apply the resources of this world to his use. These are realities. All else is nothing; conscience and sentiment are mere figments of the imagination. Man has but five gates of knowledge, the five senses; he can know nothing but through them; all else is a vain fancy, and as for the being of a God, the existence of a soul, or a world to come, who can know anything about them? Depend upon it, my dear Madam, these are only the bugbears by which men of sense govern fools; nothing is real that is not an object of sense.[29]

As a young man, Charles Darwin did not share his grandfather's dismissal of religion. After a failed start as a medical student (both his father and his grandfather were physicians), he had intended to enter the Church, but the fascination of science preoccupied him, and his clerical ambitions evaporated. The emerging contradiction between the Book of Genesis and his growing conviction in the truth of his theory of evolution through natural selection was a source of distress to him. He did not share Marx's aggressive detestation of religion, but intellectual integrity forced him, by the end of his life, into agnosticism.

Some sort of theory of evolution was being widely advanced among near-contemporary geologists, biologists and palaeontologists, but in introducing the suggested mechanism, natural selection, Darwin made a revolutionary contribution which posed especial problems for religious people.

Many Christians found themselves able to accommodate the idea of evolution fairly comfortably. They simply accepted that creation had taken rather longer than the Biblical seven days. But if Genesis was not literally true, how much else of the Bible was merely allegorical, and not to be taken literally? This was a more bitter pill for the Protestants, the People of the Book, than for Catholics, for whom the Church's traditional wisdom permitted another source of authority; and initially Catholics were less disturbed by *The Origin of Species* than were Protestants. After *The Descent of Man*, which sought to account for all human attributes with no more recourse to spiritual hypothesis than was required for other animals, Catholics too reacted with condemnation.[30]

The serious challenge of *The Descent of Man* to religious faith was the implication that the necessity for a creator was now redundant. Darwinism dispensed with purpose; blind chance could, over the aeons of time, account for everything in the observable world. The argument from design that had bolstered the deists in their loyalty to a first cause was now destroyed, undermining the place of rationality in the defence of religious ideas. Christians clung to the notion of a *purposeful* evolution – in which God was working his purpose out, as year succeeds to year. Towards the end of the century, ecclesiastics suggested that God intervened to promote the variations on which differentiation could develop, and Frederick Temple, later Archbishop of Canterbury, offered the proposition that God had, so to speak, 'seeded' creation with the necessary variable ingredients.[31] Mendelian genetics and the much later theory of random mutations were to render these interpolations, too, superfluous.

Others, no longer confident of the existence of a benevolent providence, found in evolutionary theory not only a scientifically attractive explanation for natural phenomena, but also an opportunity to recapture purpose and meaning for human beings. In 1872 Winwood Reade published *The Martyrdom of Man*, the 'substitute Bible' for secularists, as it was described, or 'the gospel for heretics', as Michael Foot, later to be leader of the Labour Party, called it in his introduction to the 32nd English reprint in 1968.[*]

---

[*] It was reprinted again in America in 1981.

Dismissing all conventional religious notions as bogus and destructive, and holding out no hopes of personal immortality, Reade nevertheless harboured an almost mystical concept of mankind, a whole of which individuals are no more than cells, moving through the centuries towards some ultimate perfection. 'Finally, men will master the forces of Nature',* he says. 'They will become themselves architects of systems, manufacturers of worlds. Man then will be perfect; he will then be a creator; he will therefore be what the vulgar worship as a god.' He goes on to add that 'even then, he will in reality be no nearer than he is at present to the First Cause, the Inscrutable Mystery, the God', but as he maintains there is no relationship whatever between the first cause and human beings, this is of no significance.[32]

> Not only will Man subdue the forces of evil that are without; he will also subdue those that are within. He will repress† the base instincts and propensities which he has inherited from the animals below; he will obey the laws that are written on his heart; he will worship the divinity within him.[33]

> Our religion therefore is Virtue, our Hope is placed in the happiness of our posterity; our Faith is the Perfectibility of Man.‡ [34]

Most of the quality press refused even to review Reade's book, though the *Saturday Review* deigned to mention it: 'wild, mischievous . . . and blasphemous'; and the *Athenaeum* dismissed it as 'a thoroughly worthless book, needlessly profane and indecent into the bargain'.[35] But at the grass roots, secularist humanism was developing quasi-religious

---

* Steps along the way, which would promote universal prosperity, Reade identified as (1) the discovery of an energy source to replace steam; (2) the invention of some method of 'aerial locomotion'; and (3) the manufacture of flesh and flour in laboratories: 'posterity will look back upon us who eat oxen and sheep just as we look back upon cannibals' (p.422).

† Freud's influence was not yet current.

‡ Winston Churchill, then a young subaltern serving in India, read Reade's book in 1897, and in a letter home to his mother commented that it was 'the crystallization of much that I have for sometime reluctantly believed'. But he went on cautiously, 'He may succeed in proving Christianity false. He completely fails to show that it is wise or expedient to say so. "Toute verité n'est pas bonne a dire" . . . One of these days – perhaps – the cool bright light of science and reason will shine through the cathedral windows and we shall go out into the fields to seek God for ourselves. The great laws of Nature will be understood – our destiny and our past will be clear. We shall then be able to dispense with the religious toys that have agreeably fostered the development of mankind. Till then – anyone who deprives us of our illusions – our pleasant hopeful illusions – is a wicked man and should – (I quote my Plato) – "be refused a chorus" . . .' (Randolph S. Churchill, *Winston S. Churchill*, Heinemann, London, 1966, Vol.I, p.319).

institutions of its own. From early in the nineteenth century, chiefly in the industrialized areas of England, groups, largely motivated by enthusiasm for the radical politics of Tom Paine and the Utopian socialism of Robert Owen, began to form; and in 1852 held their first national conference in Manchester. Charles Bradlaugh soon emerged as the principal leader, and in 1867 founded the National Secular Society, with the primary objective of campaigning for free, secular and compulsory education. The Society was not avowedly atheistic, only agnostic, but it went further than a pro-pluralist opposition to doctrinal schooling in that it favoured religious scepticism and firmly championed civil liberties in the untrammelled search for truth. Under its auspices secular halls were built in a number of major cities, where non-religious Sunday schools and services were conducted and a social programme to rival the churches was instituted, including outings and youth clubs (Leicester's was called The Young Person's Ethical Guild). Religious services provided the pattern: there were secular hymnbooks, readings from free-thinking classics and a lecture in place of a sermon, while 'mankind's own, innate religious impulse' was nourished with quasi-mystical celebrations of human achievement.[36]

There was considerable overlap with the Unitarians. Unitarian congregations, heirs to the deist traditions of the Enlightenment, were ceasing, as Hume had done and Reade was to do, to feel that the first cause had any immediate relevance. The promotion of virtue without religion was seriously exercising the minds of atheists and agnostics, actively seeking a basis for ethical conduct, personal and political. During the 1860s, for example, a Unitarian chapel established in 1824 in London's South Place gradually abandoned belief in a deity, and in 1888 became an ethical society. In 1897 it ceased to appoint a minister, replacing pastoral care with a panel of lecturers, and such relics of its religious past as prayers and hymns, including even those seeking to express 'modern thought', were allowed to lapse.

Charles Bradlaugh had, in 1860, provided the movement with a mouthpiece, the *National Reformer*. A Propaganda Press Committee was set up which, in 1899, became the Rationalist Press Association, later taking over, among much else, responsibility for further imprints of Reade's book. Although at the end of the century, under the influence of William Morris's somewhat romantic socialism, the tyranny of industrial capitalism came to be seen as the main threat to a dignified and creative life, in the earlier decades secularists tended towards robust liberal individualism, concerned with personal liberty in face of the oppression imposed by traditional religious morality. A National

Sunday League was formed to campaign against the Sabbatarians and assert the proposition that Sunday was no different from any other day (attempts by Leicester's secularists to stage Sunday cricket matches in 1885 were abandoned after over a thousand Sabbatarians chased them from the field). In 1884 an Association for the Repeal of the Blasphemy Laws was formed in the interests of freedom of speech, and though this campaign was unsuccessful, Bradlaugh did succeed, in 1888, in changing the law to permit affirmations in place of religious oaths in all cases when required.[37]

Bradlaugh was briefly imprisoned in 1880 for his refusal, when elected to Parliament, to take the oath. Three years previously he and Annie Besant had received sentences of six months (later quashed on a technicality) for publishing a pamphlet on birth control – a document held to deprave, though the defendants were cleared of the *intention* to produce any such effect.[38] Bradlaugh had founded the so-called 'Malthusian League'[*] in 1861. Other sexually liberating proposals included easier divorce (with marriage 'de-sacramentalized' and treated as a civil contract; and grounds for divorce extended beyond adultery) and the legitimization of children born out of wedlock. This last went too far for Leicester secularists, who refused to accept a speaker on the topic. They continued to live on the moral capital of their Christian inheritance, greatly disliking the crudity of 'neo-Malthusianism' and dealing severely with any evidence of sexual impropriety in their midst. In Leeds the local secularists felt personally sullied when they discovered that their hall had been hired by a group selling beer illegally, and indulging in semi-nude dancing and transvestism.[39]

By the start of the twentieth century the currents of free thought were moving swiftly through the intelligentsia, and tension between playwrights and censors was rising as the former sought increasingly frank and naturalistic treatment of social issues, especially those with a sexual component. The introduction, during the 1890s, of supposedly private 'theatre clubs' went some way towards meeting the interests of the avant-garde, for although all productions were legally subject to the Lord Chamberlain, in practice his office treated leniently productions arranged by groups whose finance came from subscriptions rather than

---

[*] Malthus himself, a devout clergyman, had not advocated birth control, but he was persuaded that the human reproduction rate would inevitably outrun the rate at which resources for their sustenance could be generated, with progressive pauperization inevitable unless sexual restraint could be inculcated. The opening up of the American prairies to agriculture in the second half of the nineteenth century proved him temporarily wrong. Whether, in the long run, his thesis will prove correct remains a moot point.

ticket sales, and where the cast received little but an honorarium for their performance.[40] From 1891 (in which year Ibsen's execrated *Ghosts*, about the effect on a family of the husband's syphilis, was presented for a one-night performance) to 1897, the Independent Theatre Society functioned, and after they folded the Stage Society was formed, in 1899, to mount plays unlikely – or unable – to find a place in the commercial theatre. The Stage Society, whose players and directors were professionals, lasted until 1940, hiring a regular theatre and putting on single or, occasionally, repeat performances slotted in at times such as Sundays that did not disrupt the normal business of the theatre. Ibsen, Shaw and Maeterlinck were staples of the repertoire (a Maeterlinck play *Monna Vanna* had failed to get a licence for public performance in 1902 – because, according to Findlater, of a reference to the heroine 'being naked beneath her mantle').[41] But these private performances did little to put an income into playwrights' pockets.

Meanwhile the discipline of censorship for the public stage continued. In France Brieux was writing of the menace of venereal disease, in Sweden Strindberg (who said he had searched for God and found the devil) was exploring relationships touched with psychosis, Wedekind was concentrating his moral but morbid attention on sex problems.[42] In England 1907 was a climactic year. Plays dealing with abortion, unmarried pregnancy and political skulduggery were banned, including Granville Barker's *Waste* and Edward Garnett's *The Breaking Point*. During the year seventy-one authors, including such luminaries as Barrie, Conrad, Galsworthy, Gilbert, Hardy, Housman, Henry James, Masefield, Shaw, Swinburne, Synge and Yeats, petitioned the House of Commons for the abolition of the Lord Chamberlain's office ('instituted for political, and not for the so-called moral ends to which it is perverted').[43] Another committee of inquiry sat in 1909, and was the recipient of a submission from Shaw, found so unacceptable that the committee refused to take formal cognisance of it.

With his usual mischievous logic, Shaw argued that it was not morality that needed defending, but immorality. Valuable as it was in imposing 'conventional conduct on the great mass of persons who are incapable of original ethical judgment', morality was already buttressed by the full pressure of public opinion and the law. It was immorality that needed protection – for 'every advance in thought and conduct is by definition immoral until it has converted the majority'. 'Immorality' is the enlightened challenge to the dead weight of tradition, toleration the only escape from stagnation, even if, in times of dire emergency, temporary suspension of toleration might be necessary. Leave control of the theatre, said Shaw, to the local licensing authorities, whose remit would be concerned not with the content of the plays staged, but with the conduct of the management – and Shaw goes on to paint a picture of provincial theatres that would not have surprised Ovid or the Puritan moralists, of stages cluttered with 'young women who are not in any serious technical sense of the word actresses at all', free tickets issued to male punters, and a general ambience a cross between a brothel and (thanks to the bar) an after-hours drinking den. That, said Shaw, is where the clean-up is needed.[44] His was a voice crying in the wilderness – neither actors nor managers really wanted to be left to the tender mercies of local prosecutions, and audience opinion was still in favour of censorship. The inquiry resulted in no material change.[45]

Shaw himself had suffered at the hands of the censor.[*] Only three of his fifty-three plays were actually denied a licence, one of them being *Mrs Warren's Profession*, written in 1894, the eponymous lady being the madam of a brothel. It was over thirty years before a public performance was given. Even a 'club' performance proved difficult to arrange, the Independent Theatre Society refusing to stage it; but in 1902 the Stage Society gave a single private performance. Shaw permitted a performance of a licensed bowdlerized version staged for copyright reasons, an expedient which became unnecessary once international agreement on copyright law had been achieved.[46]

In the preface to his *Three Plays for Puritans* (1900) Shaw railed at the 'nauseous compliances of the theatre with conventional virtue'. So-called problem plays 'invariably depended for their dramatic interest on foregone conclusions of the most heart-wearying conventionality concerning sexual morality.'[47] It was not the peccadilloes of sexual conduct that were preoccupying Shaw – he was wrestling with the significance of the sex drive as a manifestation of the life force itself, and how mankind could harness this elementary creative urge in the interests of evolution. In the settings-to-partners in *Man and Superman* (1901) he tried to indicate the ideas which he made explicit in the article 'The Revolutionist's Handbook and Pocket Companion', printed with the published text. There was, said Shaw, no evidence whatever of any

[*] He also refrained from tackling subjects he knew would be rejected – he confessed that he would like to have written on the life of Mahomet, but knew it would be suppressed. Henry Irving reported in 1892 that he had himself started on such a project, which came to the ears of the Lord Chamberlain's office, as a result of which he was required to desist, because 'protest had been made by a large number of our Mahometan fellow subjects' at any proposal to represent the prophet on stage. Findlater is very contemptuous of this political pusillanimity – but he was writing in 1967, long before the Salmon Rushdie affair (Shaw (1927), p.332; Findlater, pp.88–9).

moral evolution of humanity – we were distinguished from our primitive ancestors merely by the possession of more gadgets. All reforms were those of money (the barefoot have boots; schooling is extended) rather than of character. Civilization after civilization would founder unless we could begin to produce a type of human being (a superman) greatly superior to the existing model, for which purpose the State should establish a Department of Evolution. 'The only fundamental and possible Socialism is the socialization of the selective breeding of Man.'[48]

Harley Granville Barker played the lead in *Man and Superman*, a play rather less heavily weighed down by Nietzsche, Reade and Francis Galton than the 'Handbook' would suggest. Barker was at the same time studying *The Bacchae*, and was himself brooding on the significance of the life force, on the mystery of the conjunction within it of creative and destructive impulses. In 1907 he wrote *Waste*. The story concerns a dedicated and high-minded politician who, succumbing to a brief and casual liaison, is ruined when the lady involved dies as a result of a botched (and of course illegal) abortion. He shoots himself. His suicide, however, is not the result of disgrace, nor of any grief for the dead woman, in whom he clearly has no particular interest. He ends his life because he connects the destruction of his unborn child (he has refused to help fund an abortion) with the destruction of his life's work, now vitiated by his exclusion from the Cabinet. He has been destroyed by 'a misdirected sexual urge', yet an urge 'which is basic to the nature of man'.[49]

Waste was refused a licence unless all reference to the abortion was removed, which would have rendered the play meaningless. It was not licensed until 1920, and not actually performed (in a version revised not for censorship reasons but because the author was not satisfied with the original) until 1936. Barker's biographer Eric Salmon considers it 'a deeply religious play', presenting 'the crude and often destructive power of physical passion and the intricate and mysterious relationship between this and other human creative impulses', to the point at which the protagonist 'has achieved that moment of quiet understanding and acceptance which is the mark of and the reward of the truly tragic figure'.[50]

Shaw, too, was cogitating on religious issues – not those of conventional Christianity, but on the challenge of meaning and purpose in human life. He had had a stab at explaining his ideas in *Man and Superman*, but was dissatisfied with the result. 'Ever since Shakespear [*sic*],' he wrote in the Preface to *Back to Methuselah* (published 1921), playwrights have been struggling with the same lack of religion; and many of them forced to become mere panders and sensation-mongers because, though they had higher ambitions, they could find no better subject matter. From Congreve to Sheridan they were . . . sterile in spite of their wit . . . and they were all (not without reason) ashamed of their profession, and preferred to be regarded as mere men of fashion with a rakish hobby.

After castigating an assortment of subsequent dramatists (fashionable theatre has only one 'serious subject: clandestine adultery'), and apologizing for his own peregrination over numerous social issues which 'though it occupied me and established me professionally, did not constitute me an iconographer of the religion of my time and thus fulfil my natural function as an artist', Shaw put his cards on the table.

Civilization needs a religion as a matter of life or death; and as the conception of Creative Evolution developed I saw that we were at last within reach of a faith which complied with the first condition of all the religions that have ever taken hold of humanity: namely that it must be, first and fundamentally, a science of metabiology.[51]

Back to Methuselah ranges ambitiously from Adam and Eve to AD 31,920. Many topics are explored with the usual Shavian wit and paradox, but the underlying theme is the activity through the aeons of time of the primordial life force, an activity which can be shaped and directed by the human will. In *Man and Superman*, Shaw had, in the words of his Don Juan, categorized the life force as blind and stupid, devoid of moral imperatives, but its aim is 'to build up that raw force into higher and higher individuals, the ideal individual being omnipotent, omniscient, infallible and withal completely, unilludedly self-con-scious; in short, a god'. These suppositions, uttered during a dream sequence, are overshadowed in *Man and Superman* by the pressing need of social democracy 'to eliminate the Yahoo, or his vote will wreck the Commonwealth', but in *Back to Methuselah* the metaphysical (or 'metabiological'?) theme comes to the fore. Act V comes to a near-Hegelian conclusion. 'The day will come when there will be no people, only thought – and that will be life eternal.' 'I am Lilith', says the first woman (who according to the Talmud precedes even Eve). 'I brought life into the whirlpool of force, and compelled my enemy, Matter, to obey a living soul.' Now that the distant seed is aware of its task to

378

transcend matter, the created race is to be permitted to continue until it has learnt how to become one with its origin.

With this Hegelian resolution, Shaw had come to an accommodation with the absence of traditional belief that left him possessed of a measure of meaning and purpose. Others found no such resolution. As Bertrand Russell said: 'Only on the firm foundation of unyielding despair can the soul's habitation henceforth be safely built.'[52] On the Continent, dramatists devoid of any shred of religious consolation looked out at the stark awfulness, injustice, suffering and horror of the material world – and raged. With the experience of World War I adding to the sense of nightmare, Continental drama in the second and third decades of the twentieth century became more anguished and more angry. In Germany audiences were invited to traverse a urinal in order to be confronted with 'a young girl, dressed as if attending her first communion, reciting obscene poetry in the centre of [a] glass cage'.[53] 'German Expressionist drama,' says Berthold,

> responded to the crisis of self destruction with a scream. Night-mares and Utopias, the determinism behind the individual's decisions, the socialist vision of the future, the conflict between uninhibited instinct and emasculated vestiges of religion – all these added up to a load so heavy that it disrupted coherent language. Ecstasy, confession, protest, exploded in tattered phrases, in a frenzied condensation of language, in strident dynamics of sound – in the scream. Such plays as August Stramm's so-called *Schrei-Dramen* ('Scream Dramas') and Reinhard Goering's *Seeschlacht* ('Sea Battle') which begins with a scream – all seem to groan with the agony of being lost.[54]

The Expressionist rejection of the naturalistic, representational drama of the late nineteenth century symbolized the disillusionment with the prevailing norms of sensate society, but it had nothing positive to say. Antonin Artaud was born in 1896. Beyond the chaos and nihilism of Expressionism he was hammering out a positive theory of dramatic art – terrible, but at least coherent. 'There is somewhere a disordering which we cannot master whatever name we choose to call it by', he wrote in 1933 (had he been a Christian he might have called it original sin, and gone on to speak, as St Paul did, of the whole creation groaning and travailing in pain together).[55] 'All sorts of inexplicable crimes inside the self, gratuitous crimes, are part of this disordering. So are the far too frequent occurrences of earthquakes, volcanic eruptions, marine torna-does, and railway accidents.'[56] This apprehension of reality had to be communicated in dramatic form. He produced a First Manifesto in October 1932, following it with a Second Manifesto in 1933, and these, together with pertinent letters developing his ideas, were published in 1938 as *Le Théâtre et son Double* ('the Bible of sick theatre', as Laurence Kitchin, drama critic of *The Times*, was to call it).[57] Much in this work was concerned with problems of form, of staging, lighting, costume, of the significance of masks and of music. The core of his creed, however, lies in his assertion that the theatre will never find itself again – that is constitute a means of true illusion – except by furnishing the spectator with the truthful precipitates of dreams,

> in which his taste for crime, his erotic obsessions, his savagery, his chimeras, his utopian sense of life and matter, even his cannibal-ism, pour out, on a level not counterfeit and illusory, but interior. In other terms, the theatre must pursue by all its means a reassertion not only of all the aspects of the objective and descriptive external world, but of the internal world, that is of man considered metaphysically.[58]

The ultimate metaphysical truth, for Artaud, was a quality he called cruelty. Cruelty is

> appetite for life, cosmic strictness, and implacable necessity, in the gnostic sense of the whirlwind of life that eats up darkness, in the sense of that pain which is ineluctably necessary to the continuation of life. Good is willed – the result of an action; evil is continuous. When he creates, the hidden god conforms to the cruel necessity of creation, which is imposed on him, and he is not free not to create. So he cannot exclude from the centre of the willed whirlwind of good a nucleus of evil which is increasingly reduced, increasingly consumed.[59]

The title 'Theatre of Cruelty', Artaud explained, he had chosen in preference to the more accurate but less explicable 'alchemical or metaphysical theatre', signifying 'a kind of cosmic cruelty, a near relation of the destruction without which nothing can be created . . .'[60] In 1935 he founded the Institute for a Theatre of Cruelty in Paris.[61]

Artaud concedes the difficulty of finding suitable plays to illustrate his theme. In practice, in this idolization of 'cruelty', Shelley's *The Cenci* had an immediate appeal, as did Jacobean shockers like *The Duchess of Malfi* and *The White Devil*, work by de Sade, *The Revenger's Tragedy*, and the story of Bluebeard, incorporating 'new ideas about eroticism and cruelty'.[62] Artaud considered that 'one cannot find a better *written* example of what is meant by cruelty in the theatre than all the tragedies of Seneca, but above all *Atreus and Thyestes*',[63] but text, language and poetry were of little significance to his concept of theatre. Action and spectacle were what mattered ('without an element of cruelty at the root of every spectacle, the theatre is not possible'),[64] and Artaud confesses that his interest in Elizabethan theatre is in the characters, the 'climate of the time', and the action, not the words.[65] 'We shall renounce the theatrical superstition of the text and the dictatorship of the writer . . . we rejoin the ancient popular drama, sensed and experienced directly by the mind without the deformation of language and the barrier of speech.'[66] He thus repudiates the one element which others see as redeeming much of Elizabethan tragedy from Grand Guignol.

However sophisticated his apologia, Artaud resonates with the sadism of the overripe sensate society, to which his enthusiasm for *The Fall of Jerusalem* ('with the blood-red colour that trickles from it'), the late medieval epic that provided the fourteenth century with such lavish buckets of blood, bears witness; as does his obsession with Heliogabolus, about whom he wrote a play in 1933, in which, *inter alia*, he sought to justify the Emperor's frequent resort to castration of his opponents. Another echo occurs in the thrill, which excited audiences both of late Rome and of the later Middle Ages, of subjecting performers to the real danger of mutilation or death. In his production of *The Cenci* in 1935 Artaud proposed that Iya Abdy, playing Beatrice, should hang by her hair from the torturer's wheel.

> A convenient footstool under her feet, camouflaged, would prevent her from hanging in reality. Rightly or wrongly, Mme Abdy suspects Artaud of wanting to overturn the little stool on the night of the première to make her reaction more truthful, more striking . . . Stool or no stool she does not want to be hanged . . . There will be no wheel and no hanging.[67]

In 1937 Artaud, already a drug addict, succumbed to mental illness which kept him in asylums intermittently until two years before his death in 1948.[68] By then his Theatre of Cruelty was sharing the limelight with a less coherent cry of despair – the Theatre of the Absurd.

British playwrights, says Frederick Lumley in *New Trends in*

Twentieth Century Drama, 'preserved an atmosphere of jocular irrelevance right up to 1956 and Suez. Long before then the European theatre had surrendered to profound pessimism; the dramatist had become a kind of lay analyst with the theatre in a state of nervous depression.'[69] Of Pirandello he says, 'In *Enrico IV* we have Pirandello's most complete achievement, where man is alone in his solitude, where the life force continues to reproduce humanity, but where age overtakes the individual and only illusions remain.'[70] Authors from Roman Catholic backgrounds – Lorca in Spain, O'Neill in America – desert their heritage, says Lumley, while Cocteau uses it for dramatic impact, but without profound attachment. Salacrou understands 'the necessity of God without being able to believe in God', Anouilh subsides into 'the Romanticism of despair'.[71]

'On humanist assumptions,' says H.J. Blackham in his *Objections to Humanism* 'life leads to nothing, and every pretence that it does not is a deceit . . . Human life may be absurd from this point of view, but it is absurd to look at it from any other point of view.'[72] 'The decline of religious faith was masked until the end of the Second World War,' says Martin Esslin in his *The Theatre of the Absurd*, 'by the substitute religions of faith in progress, nationalism and various totalitarian fallacies. All this was shattered by the war. By 1942 Albert Camus was calmly putting the question why, since life had lost all meaning, man should not seek escape in suicide.' Everything is futile, meaningless. 'When man is cut loose from his religious, metaphysical and transcendental roots, he is lost, everything he does becomes senseless, absurd, useless, is nipped in the bud', said Eugène Ionesco. This theme, says Esslin, permeates the work of Giraudoux, Anouilh, Salacrou, Sartre and Camus – but in the drama of the playwrights of the Theatre of the Absurd, of Ionesco himself, of Samuel Beckett, Arthur Adamov and Jean Genet, irrationality permeates not just the content but also the form of the play. Logical dialogue cannot transmit the nightmare. The Theatre of the Absurd does not *discuss* absurdity; it *presents* it, as an experience.[73] If this was to be the theatre of the future, it would be, feared Kenneth Tynan, a 'bleak new world from which the humanist heresies of faith in logic and belief in man will forever be banished'.[74]

Though the dramatists of the Theatre of the Absurd do not have Artaud's ideological commitment to cruelty as the ultimate metaphysical and aesthetic truth, they nevertheless see mankind's experience of living as one of pointless brutality and suffering. 'The most absurd thing is to be conscious of the fact that human existence is unbearable, that the human condition is unbearable, and nevertheless cling to it', said

Ionesco.[75] In addition to inconsequential dialogue and incomprehensible situations, the plays are full of rape, mutilation, suicide and murder – the lofty vision of mankind held by the humanists of the Renaissance is replaced by a preoccupation with the inadequate, the morally and physically deformed, the psychopath. This has gone far beyond the typical sensationalism of an increasingly sensate society into inchoate rage at life's futility and meaninglessness. Becket himself had suffered pointless brutality – his lung had been punctured in Paris in a completely unprovoked attack, and when he later confronted his assailant in prison to ask why, he received the answer '*Je ne sais pas, monsieur.*' Ionesco wrote a play, *Tueur Sans Gages*, 'The Motiveless Killer', in which the killer proved to be death himself, rendering everything futile.[76] Genet, never able, apparently, to overcome his rage at being abandoned as a child by his mother, lived in a nightmare world in, or on the fringes of, prison, determined to invert conventional morality, and extolling his trinity of virtues: theft, treachery and homosexuality.[77]

We are isolated and alone. There will be no *deus ex machina*. The tramps in *Waiting for Godot* (which came to London in 1955) evade the issue; they discuss suicide in a desultory way, but decide instead to go on waiting – for nothing. 'The "Absurd" play,' said the dramatist Wolfgang Hildesheimer, 'becomes a parable of life precisely through the intentional omission of any statement. For life, too, makes no statement.'[78]

But absurdity is not merely pathetic – it is also amusing. The Theatre of the Absurd cocks a snook at the grim futility of life. It is funny. It invites the audience to laugh. According to Ionesco:

> Humour is the only possibility we possess of detaching ourselves – yet only after we have surmounted, assimilated, taken cognizance of it – from our tragicomic human condition, the malaise of being. 'To become conscious of what is horrifying and to laugh at it is to become master of that which is horrifying . . . the comic alone is capable of giving us the strength to bear the tragedy of existence.[79]

To restore our apprehension of life's mystery, explains Esslin, we must 'learn to see the most commonplace in its full horror'.[80] The Theatre of the Absurd is

> . . . an effort . . . to sing, to laugh, to weep – and to growl . . . in search of a dimension of the Ineffable; an effort to make man aware of the ultimate realities of his condition, to instil in him again the

lost sense of cosmic wonder and primeval anguish, to shock him out of an existence that has become trite, mechanical, complacent, and deprived of the dignity that comes of awareness. For God is dead, above all, to the masses who live from day to day and have lost all contact with the basic facts – and mysteries – of the human condition with which, in former times, they were kept in touch through the living ritual of their religion, which made them parts of a real community and not just atoms in an atomized society . . . The dignity of man lies in his ability to face reality in all its senselessness; to accept it freely, without fear, without illusions – and to laugh at it.[81]

This has a Stoic ring to it, but Esslin goes further. He wishes to equate the insights of Absurdity with an altogether different spiritual tradition.

To confront the limits of the human condition is . . . a profound mystical experience. It is precisely this experience of the ineffability, the emptiness, the nothingness at the basis of the universe that forms the content of Eastern as well as Christian mystical experience.

He cites St John of the Cross, and Meister Eckhart's 'The Godhead is as void as though it were not'.[82]

It is a weight of meaning that the Theatre of the Absurd cannot sustain. The mystics' experience of absorption into the infinite nothing is an experience of bliss, not of horror. There is no evidence that the practitioners of the Absurd won through to such a consummation. 'What is there?' asks Adamov.

I know first of all that I am. But who am I? All I know of myself is that I suffer. And if I suffer it is because at the origin of myself there is mutilation, separation. I am separated. What I am separated from – I cannot name it. But I am separated.

And in a footnote he adds, 'Formerly it was called God. Today it no longer has any name.'[83]

Adamov took the route out of his dilemma that had already appealed to many of the Expressionists – he made a deliberate decision to espouse Marxism, and in 1957 began to tailor his dramatic output to that end. His reasons were paradoxical:

When the material obstacles are overcome, when man will no longer be able to deceive himself as to the nature of his unhappiness, then there will arise an anxiety all the more powerful, all the more fruitful for being stripped of anything that might have hindered its realization.[84]

Perhaps it was not surprising that in 1970 despair overcame him, and he committed suicide.

Attacks on the middle class, on bourgeois respectability, had been inherent in Absurdist theatre from the start. The dramatists could not vent their spleen on a God in whom they did not believe; in the complacency of the comfortable middle classes, with their shallow religious consolations and hypocritical conventional morality, their relatively less vulnerable prosperity, the playwrights found a suitable substitute. As long ago as 1896 Alfred Jarry's *Ubu Roi*, with its notorious opening line the obscene expletive '*Merdre!*', had fired the first shot in a campaign to shock and disgust that has not yet run its course.[*] The play portrays a stupid, selfish bourgeoisie, a 'terrifying image of the animal nature of man, his cruelty and ruthlessness'.[† 85] Genet, ardently siding with black protest against white exploitation in his play *Les Negres* (1959), Artaud, romanticizing indigenous Mexican society in comparison with the brutality of the conquistadors in his (never-produced) *The Conquest of Mexico* symbolize the trend.[86]

Those who sought, in overt political commitment, to escape from the corner in which they were boxed did so in thoroughly worldly terms. Wretchedness, suffering and isolation are not to be seen as metaphysical inevitabilities, part of the very structure of Being. They result from the social system. Inequality and exploitation become the paramount injustice, the fount of all misery. In the campaign against the exploiter, purpose, meaning and hope are resurrected.[87]

Czeslaw Milosz, who defected to the West while serving at the Polish Embassy in Paris, has explained, in *The Captive Mind*, how firmly the

---

[*] The expletive is repeated 33 times in the course of the play, and is actually a deformation, though of course immediately recognizable, of the French expletive '*merde*'. The original word had to be retained in the Royal Court performance of 1966, the Lord Chamberlain refusing to permit translation (Beaumont, pp.47–50, 69–70).

[†] Beaumont maintains that the politicization of the play which made it so popular with left-wing theatre groups from the 1960s on missed the point that Jarry's attack was not on the bourgeoisie but on humanity as a whole, on Everyman. He contends that *Ubu Roi* is Absurd only in the incoherence of its form rather than in its content. But the relentless comedy and the assessment that Jarry 'implicitly subverts all humanistic belief in the inherent goodness and rationality of man' (Beaumont, p.57) seems to justify the play's place as a precursor of Absurdism.

writers in the countries of eastern Europe which became Marxist only after World War II were condemned for 'the slightest signs of a metaphysical tendency'.

> For instance, a play that introduces 'strangeness', revealing the author's interest in the tragedy of life, has no chance of being produced, because the tragedy of human fate leads to thoughts about the mystery of human destiny. One forgives certain writers like Shakespeare these predispositions, but there is no question of permitting any contemporary author to harbour them. It is for this reason that Greek tragedies are not deemed suitable for theatre repertoires.[88]

Explicitly Marxist theatre had enjoyed a lively existence, pre-dating Artaud, chronologically parallel with the Absurdists. Its matrix, of course, was the USSR, and its guiding principle: to replace the theatre of individual protagonists with the recognition that what matters is classes.[89] In pursuit of this ideal, Bertolt Brecht, the foremost exponent of Marxist drama in the West, endeavoured to prevent his audiences from being emotionally sucked into the life of the characters portrayed on stage; nor, he required, should the actor 'at any moment ... allow himself to be completely absorbed by the character'. What matters is that the spectator's critical faculty should be engaged, that he should *understand* the hidden connection between the social system and his own problems and dissatisfactions.[90] As Peter Weiss was to say, half a century after the Bolshevik revolution, in his *Notes on Documentary Theatre*, 'It is not individual conflicts that are portrayed, but human behaviour conditioned by socio-economic factors.'[91] It is the psycho-pathology of society, not of individuals, that is to be explored.[92]

George Steiner has pointed out that there is, in this reading of society, no place for tragedy, indeed, 'in a communist state, tragedy is not only bad art; it is treason'; the inexorable dynamics of dialectical materialism have already ordained the triumph of the working class. As Trotsky had said, 'A society without social contradictions will naturally be a society without lies and violence.'[93] Tragedy, as a concept, is replaced by waste. Brecht's *Mother Courage*, says Steiner, is an allegory of pure waste. Not only are all her children killed in war, but she herself learns nothing from this, and continues to vend supplies to the warriors.[*94]

---

[*] *Mother Courage* illustrates the difficulty Brecht had in 'alienating' his spectators' emotions. His protagonist's dogged defiance of fate tends to win audience sympathy instead of repelling them with contempt for her purblind refusal to recognize the true causes of the disasters that engulf her.

Brecht saw in the theatre a means not merely to interpret but also to change the world.[95] He had dabbled in early Absurdity before deciding that it was only the capitalist world that needed to be represented as 'negative, despairing and absurd'. In form, his Marxist polemic retained the clowning and knockabout humour of early Absurd drama.[96] In content, he did not shrink from teaching the harsh lessons of Marxist ethics. 'Who aims at the end cannot reject the means', Trotsky had said; it would be up to the Party to dictate the precise tactics.[97] In *The Measures Taken* Brecht explored the implications. 'He who fights for Communism has of all virtues only one: that he fights for Communism', intone the chorus in this play. So when a comrade threatens, by his impetuosity in seeking to relieve immediate distress at the expense of the long-term success of the revolution, to betray the mission on which he is embarked, he is killed by his colleagues. The play was performed late in 1930 in Berlin, and caused great controversy among the comrades, who felt that expulsion from the Party should have been punishment enough. Brecht rewrote the drama, making the guilty comrade recognize the necessity for, and accede to, his own death – indeed, he seeks the help of his colleagues in shooting him, and burning his body in a lime pit. It was a chilling prescience of actual show trials yet to come in the Communist world.

Jean-Paul Sartre, the pre-eminent French Marxist dramatist, was equally willing to confront the dilemmas of Marxist ethics. Sartre came to Marxism by way of his own philosophy of existentialism. There is no God; we are totally, terrifyingly free – free to recognize the existential pointlessness of our existence. Man has no option but to choose, he must take full responsibility for himself.[98] As worked out in the bulk of Sartre's plays, the result is a living hell, but Sartre, too, found an escape in Marxism, for we could elect to make choices that benefit humanity as a whole. In *Les Mains Sales* Sartre explored Marxist ethics in relation to the choices available in achieving the revolution.

The play is set in a central European country (Hungary?) after World War II, when the Party leader is compromising the purity of the Party's ideals by entering into a coalition with peasant and Social Democrat parties as a tactic in the pursuit of supreme power (the tactic which was, in actuality, followed throughout eastern and central Europe in the period 1945–50). A comrade is dispatched to assassinate the offending leader, but grows attached to him and fails to carry out his mission until suddenly motivated by the belief that the leader is having an affair with his wife. This was staged in England in 1948 under the title *Crime Passionnel*, which focuses the whole attention on the assassin's sexual jealousy. But it is the leader who, in the original French, refers to soiled hands. *'Comme tu a peur de te salir les mains'*, he says to the – as yet reluctant – assassin, who has upbraided him for considering collaborating with other political parties. 'My hands are filthy. I've dipped them up to the elbows in blood and filth. So what? Do you think you can govern and keep your spirit white?'[99]

Throughout the interwar period, the English mainline theatre remained immune to the Continental maelstrom of Marxism. Beneath the surface, however, a vigorous fringe workers' theatre movement was developing. Committed socialists, usually of the urban/industrial/class-confrontational complexion rather than the rural/romantic/William Morris brand, gathered together groups of the unemployed and the politically dedicated who, with indefatigable zeal, performed on street corners and at factory gates, sometimes from the backs of lorries, always keeping one step ahead of the police with their uncensored agitprop material designed to 'raise consciousness' and preach the gospel of revolution. Props and staging were kept to a minimum – 'a propertyless theatre for the propertyless working class'. The groups kept in touch with, and learnt from, Continental Marxist theatre, and at a national conference in 1932 (attended by 22 groups; a further 10 could not afford to come) promulgated their faith in a theatre revolutionary in form, setting and content, punching their message across in song, dance and revue, ensuring that themes concentrated on class types, and did not permit the worm of inappropriate sympathy to creep in through rounded characterizations of the class enemy.[*][100]

Ewen MacColl has described how he (then known by his real name of Jimmy Miller) and his wife Joan Littlewood, both Party members, built up the Theatre of Action in Manchester, only to have the group substantially destroyed by the local Party hierarchy.[101] Serious disagreements arose as to whether naturalistic drama, in the bourgeois tradition, could be used to further the cause, or whether only revolutionary methods of presentation, as advocated by MacColl and Littlewood, should be allowed – a dispute which ended in their expulsion from the Party.[102] Equally divisive difficulties lay ahead. The workers' theatre groups had been as steadfastly anti-Labour as they had been anti-Tory, but in the mid-1930s, faced with the rising threat of Fascism, the Party line promulgated by Moscow changed, and the Popular Front demanded

---

[*] 'A worker asked the speaker if a dramatist put a bourgeois happy family upon the stage, would not the dramatist be portraying the truth? To this we reply that it is only a half truth. To give the whole truth it would be necessary to place opposite the joyous bourgeois family the misery of the working class family which is the reason for the bourgeois joy' (Samuel, et al., p.195).

co-operation with non-revolutionary left-wing political parties. Revolution and the class war were removed to the back burner, concerned members of the middle class were accepted, 'no longer to be seen as the infected bearers of bourgeois poison'.[103] In London the Unity Theatre was founded, largely out of a workers' theatre group in Hackney. To the profound displeasure of some of the old troupers, left-wing theatre reverted to conventional productions in conventional structures. Nevertheless, it swept away much traditional paraphernalia – such as evening dress, the star system, and footlights fencing the actors from their audience.[104]

Unity was an amateur initiative.* It was not financially supported by the Party, but received strong backing from Party members, and participants were subjected to extensive educational programmes on the tenets of Marxism-Leninism.[105] There was no shortage of left-wing plays, and Unity (and its sister Unity theatres in other parts of the country) embarked on ambitious programmes of American and Continental, mostly Soviet, drama,† in addition to the diet of satirical song and dance in revue format traditional to the peripatetic groups.

Home-produced drama tended to be thematically crude. The sort of ethical dilemmas which Sartre and Brecht had scrutinized were evaded;‡ for instance, in a play about the Rosenbergs, executed in America for passing secrets on the atomic bomb to the Russians, the author wanted to debate the nobility of their action, but the management insisted, backed by the Party, that the play must assume their total innocence of the charge.[106]

Many ideological crises, political and aesthetic, punctuated Unity's history, but problems were invariably overcome under the umbrella of a somewhat smug Stalinism, ugly rumours about the price the Soviet people were being asked to pay being either discounted or excused. But in 1956 Khrushchev's revelations of the horrors of Stalinism shook the Party's confidence, and the Soviet invasion of Hungary in the autumn of the same year damaged Party solidarity irreparably. Chambers considers it the effective end, but the movement soldiered on, focusing now on peace, anti-militarism and anti-Americanism, and making its building

---

* A professional left theatre company presenting Sunday evening West End performances, like the Stage Society, had been founded in 1934, but had failed for financial reasons (Chambers (1989), pp.33–4).
† Favourite authors were the Americans Clifford Odets and Irwin Shaw, Jack Lindsay and Stephen Spender provided material, Nikolai Pogodin's *Aristocrats* was the principal Soviet play performed, and Brecht supplied one drama about the Spanish Civil War.
‡ Indeed, Brecht was not staged at all in the period 1938–56 (Chambers (1989), p.354).

available to left-wing touring groups. The end finally came in 1988, when the site was sold.[107]

War conditions, the call-up, the lack of transport had disrupted the old companies of poverty-stricken but dedicated touring players. Remnants of the Littlewood/MacColl group reassembled in Manchester after the war, and for seven years, living communally, touring, playing to tiny audiences in schools and hired halls, they eked out a meagre and intermittent living before, in 1952, finding a permanent home for their theatre workshop at Stratford, east London. Financially, their survival remained precarious, local audiences minuscule. By 1957 they were in receipt of subsidy from the local authority, but it was never adequate to bridge the gap. Transfers into the West End proved their financial salvation; no fewer than five productions made the transition in the two years from February 1959 to March 1961.[108] Inevitably, the nucleus of players was broken up, and much of the original ethos lost. MacColl had left the company, fearing just the developments that subsequently occurred, at the time of the move to Stratford. Littlewood left in 1976.

Other groups were forming. Stalinism had long been dead, the Soviet Union exposed as state capitalist, but the martyred Trotsky beckoned from his grave. International Socialists, the Workers' Revolutionary Party, the Revolutionary Socialist League (later the Militant Tendency), these were the new class warriors.

CAST (the Cartoon Archetypical Slogan Theatre) was founded in 1965 by a group at the Unity Theatre who were finding the established old Party theatre too staid. They were, says Catherine Itzin in *Stages in the Revolution*, 'the first avowedly socialist theatre company of the sixties'. Others followed – Red Ladder, Welfare State, 7.84, Belt and Braces, General Will, Northern Spanner, Gay Sweatshop, Joint Stock, Monstrous Regiment[109] – for whom the Unity Theatre provided a London venue.[110] 'The establishment is the enemy', explains Itzin.

> It was this attitude which characterized many of the writers and theatre workers who made an impact in the British theatre in the ten year period from 1968 to 1978. They were not, for the most part, just socially committed, but committed to a socialist society. They were the writers of agitational propaganda and social realism . . .[111]

There was a significant difference between the penniless troupes of the twenties and thirties and the ambitious propagandists who multiplied in every sphere of theatre activity after the traumatic year of 1968, when the Paris students came near to toppling the French State, and America was trammelled in the hapless toils of the Vietnam War. During World War II there had developed in Britain, for the first time, regular state support for the arts. This had been the *sine qua non* of Brecht's pre-Nazi German Marxist theatre, where, until the severe cuts instituted in and after 1928, 'most of the theatrical institutions relied on state subsidies for their existence'. Back in post-war East Berlin after his long sojourn abroad in flight from the Nazis, Brecht's Berliner Ensemble again was in receipt of huge state subsidies.[112]

The new fringe groups would be content with nothing less. A Local Government Act of 1948 had permitted local authorities to support music and drama with money from the rates. In 1946, as a successor to the wartime Council for the Encouragement of Music and the Arts which had been partially funded from charitable sources, the Arts Council was established, funded wholly by the Treasury (in other words, the taxpayer), with a brief that included grants to theatres and assistance for various aspects of theatrical training, and specifically excluded any influence on policy.[113] Unity Theatre itself failed to attract Arts Council money,[114] but a number of fringe groups were more successful, though not at levels that enabled them to turn full-time professional. In 1973 forty groups formed the Association of Community Theatres to provide an umbrella organization for socialist theatre groups, and to campaign for higher subsidies, membership of Equity (the actors' union), and entitlement to Equity rates of pay. Equity agreed to back the claim that grants should be calculated on the basis of Equity minimum pay rates.[115]

In 1974 the Independent Theatre Council was formed to campaign for increases in, and wider distribution of, subsidies. It took a highly confrontational stance in its relationship with the Arts Council, and by the end of the 1970s had manoeuvred itself into the position of receiving its own Arts Council grant, and was seeking to form a theatre workers' union that might replace the very unrevolutionary Equity.[116] The right to Equity membership cards was conceded, and political activism at Equity meetings embarked upon. John McGrath, founder of the left-wing 7.84 group, acknowledged, during his lectures at Cambridge in 1979, that alternative theatre, building on the old workers' theatre movement, Unity and rising class solidarity, developed rapidly in the period 1968 to 1975 thanks to Arts Council funding.[117] By 1978 there were at least eighteen full-time subsidized socialist theatre groups (one of them being CAST, which had been enabled to go full-time in 1976), in addition to many unsubsidized.[118]

Alternative theatre – and particularly political theatre – could not have developed on the scale it did in the seventies without subsidy. This was, from the beginning, one of the fundamental ironies – that theatre companies whose stated aim and *raison d'être* was to do away with the capitalist state and its institutions (including the Arts Council of Great Britain) and replace it with a socialist society could only work to achieve those ends with financial assistance from the hated state.[119]

It was indeed an irony from which the state-financed theatres of Greece and Rome had not suffered, but it was inherent in the political creed of the modern British State, where the Arts Council, when challenged by right-wing objectors, could not but rally to its own principles that politics were irrelevant to grant decisions.[120]

Wafted on wings of subsidy, socialist drama prepared to assault the bastions of main-line theatre.

Chapter 19

Secular Triumphs: the Late Twentieth Century

Religious themes – and the exalted language in which they had traditionally been explored – enjoyed a brief post-World War II twilight. In France the plays of the strongly orthodox Paul Claudel, intelligently probing the disciplines and symbolism of Catholicism, dated from the early decades of the century, but the Paris of the 1950s staged them with interest. In England the 1930s had witnessed T.S. Eliot's *The Rock* and *Murder in the Cathedral*, embodying, in Lumley's words, 'the same liturgical echoes of ritual and the same search for a poetical language' as had been engaging Claudel.[1] The original staging of the latter, in the Chapter House of Canterbury Cathedral, could be expected to attract an audience self-selected to approve; but its subsequent success up and down the country demonstrated the breadth of its appeal.

The Religious Drama Society endeavoured, through festivals at Canterbury and Chichester, to animate credal Christianity, and at the Mercury Theatre between 1945 and 1948 E. Martin Browne, who had directed *Murder in the Cathedral* at Canterbury in 1935, made a determined effort to recapture the theatre for poetry and spiritual issues. Ronald Duncan, Christopher Hassall, Dorothy Sayers, Christopher Fry (several of whose plays, as well as having religious themes, were written for performance in churches) and Eliot himself were among those whose work was staged.[2]

In August 1949 Eliot's *The Cocktail Party* was produced for the Edinburgh Festival. 'London can scarcely afford to ignore entertainment of so much distinction', declared *The Times* (24 August 1949), but London had to wait for a suitable theatre vacancy until May 1950, by which time the Edinburgh production had moved to New York, where it was pronounced 'a masterpiece' (*The Times*, 24 January 1950). The theme concerns a foundering marriage which is re-established on the basis of a recognition of mutual inadequacy following the departure of the husband's mistress in pursuit of a depth of fulfilment not to be found in mundane relationships. She becomes a medical missionary, and is later reported very nastily martyred.

The fulfilment that is only to be found by traversing the Valley of the Shadow, of death to self, is a commonplace of religious belief. Renunciation as a gateway to serenity enjoys a currency far wider than Christianity. In 1950 such a proposition could still move and disturb an audience.

> The scene where three wretchedly unhappy people – husband, wife and husband's mistress – come to seek advice and receive it, making each his or her decision according to his or her need and capacity to love, is one of the finest things the theatre has given us ... disturbing, even deeply moving as such drama of the mind and the soul seldom is

said Philip Hope-Wallace in *Time and Tide* (13 May 1950). 'First nighters were dazzled and enthusiastic', reported Cecil Wilson for the *Daily Mail* (4 May 1950). 'A fine, thought-compelling piece of work', commented *Everybody's*, while Harold Hobson, who initially reviewed it as 'a great play' in the *Sunday Times* (7 May 1950), was still, nearly forty years later, recalling the incandescence of Irene Worth's performance as the mistress when in 1987 he wrote:

> The consciousness of all the sins of the world was in her, and she was ready to expiate them, without protest, without reluctance, without regret. At the heart of the Greek tragedy there is the realization that a power exists greater than the power of men and women, but also that men and women can prove their superiority to it by the meekness and the serenity with which they accept the punishment exacted from them ... in Irene Worth's Celia Coplestone, [the peace and reconciliation which is the hallmark of tragedy] brought into the theatre a holiness that those who experienced it can never forget.[3]

There were a few contrary views; Beverley Baxter and J.C. Trewin (for the *Evening Standard* and the *Sketch* respectively) did not enjoy the evening, but the critic who spoke for future values and attitudes was Ivor Brown, drama correspondent of the *Observer* and author, in 1939, of *Life within Reason*, a plea, in a world menaced by dictatorships, for the politics of personal liberty, rationality and balance. 'His counsel,' he writes of the psychiatrist who is the pivot in whom the characters confide,

> has sent a young woman who might have been, with good advice, happy and useful at home to waste her life on savages who crucify her over an ant-heap. Is he horrified at this revolting result of his busy-body stupidity? . . . He is not disgusted in the least. Apparently that is all for the best in the best of Christian worlds, a strange conclusion and one which I cannot share with Mr Eliot.[4]

Nor, by the time the play was revived in 1986, could anyone else. The *Tablet* (9 August 1986) managed a grudging 'Eliot has said there is no one meaning to this play, and that we should all take our own meanings from it. In this production, that possibility is largely given to us', but most reviewers were scathing. 'It is a preposterous and, as we can now see, a vulgar play', said the *Observer* (3 August 1986); 'Dead duck' (*Punch*, 6 August 1986); 'dreadfully glib' (*Jewish Chronicle*, 8 August 1986); 'A long unpalatable evening' (*City Limits*, 7 August 1986); ' "I want to apologise for this evening" says [a character], one of the few sensible comments heard all night' (*Today*, 4 August 1986); 'T.S. Eliot wrote two fine, if flawed plays. Unfortunately *The Cocktail Party* is not one of them' (*Sunday Telegraph*, 3 August 1986); 'High-flown Anglican poppy-cock' (*Financial Times*, 29 July 1986); 'Its central character . . . is an appalling Moonie-like manipulator of lives, though the lives he influences hardly seem worth the effort' (*Sunday Express*, 3 August 1986); 'the Christian symbolism, intruding like a vegetarian at a barbecue, casts a lugubrious damper over the affair' (*London Standard*, 29 July 1986); and finally 'Even more offputting to me,' said Michael Billington in the *Guardian* (30 July 1986), 'is the artistic temperament behind the play that suggests that marriage, childbirth, human relationships are a compromising second best to the consolations of pain, martyrdom and sacrifice'; while *The Times*'s main response (30 July 1986) was plain incredulity. An ethic that rejected the pursuit of immediate worldly self-fulfilment for the sake of a transcendental goal had by the late twentieth century become simply incomprehensible.

In this as in other respects there was no audience resonance to which the religious playwrights could appeal, no shared credal assumptions or even vocabulary. Both George Steiner in *The Death of Tragedy*[5] and Moelwyn Merchant in *Creed and Drama*[6] draw attention to the religious substratum of Eliot's *The Family Reunion* (revived in 1946, its original run having been interrupted by the war), but for Steiner the play fails because the echoes of the Eumenides which gripped Aeschylus's audience are lost on secular twentieth-century man; while for Merchant the absence of any common ground is symbolized by the fact that though the play explores guilt and expiation from a Christian viewpoint, it tactfully does so without explicit Christian references.

Graham Greene, first in *The Living Room* (1954), which concluded with a suicide, then in *The Potting Shed* (1958), an arid examination of religious versus atheistic belief, failed to translate the moral vision of his novels into satisfactory dramatic form. Christopher Fry's scintillating use of language brought him some success, and for over a decade his plays enlivened the West End, but critics unsympathetic to his exploration of issues of life and death ('confused and boring')[7] tended to find little meat or dramatic development behind the jewelled text, and he had suffered decades of obscurity by the time his *Venus Observed*, first performed in 1950, was revived for the 1992 Chichester Festival.*

Pseudo-religious themes continued to surface, but they were really exercises in political polemic (like Arthur Miller's *The Crucible*) or psychological biography (John Osborne's *Luther*), with Robert Bolt's *A Man for All Seasons* perhaps having a foot in both camps. The Royal Shakespeare Company in 1972 revived Eliot's *Murder in the Cathedral*, but the 'living core' of the play, as detected by Martin Esslin for *Plays and Players*, was political: 'the determination of an individual who refuses to submit to the power of the State . . .'[8] Ronald Millar's *Abelard and Heloise* achieved a mention in the *Annual Register* for 1970, chiefly for the 'conspicuous lack of costume at one amorous moment' (but this is to anticipate the effects of the demise of the Lord Chamberlain's powers in 1968). A different *Heloise and Abelard*, played at the Lyric Studio in 1991, might have been expected to retrace the great choice that was central to *The Cocktail Party*, but the author avoided the issue: 'on the real enigma – Abelard's banishment of her to the convent – he offers no comment'.[9]

Christians had on the whole not realized the extent to which their viewpoint was evaporating. Complacency had been induced by the apparent upsurge in church, and especially Sunday school, attendance in the late nineteenth century. A mid-nineteenth century religious census had caused shock by revealing that only some 40 per cent of the population attended a place of worship on Sunday, a revelation which, notwithstanding the Darwinian doubts that were troubling intellectuals,

---

* Both *Venus Observed* and *The Cocktail Party* were lampooned by Unity Theatre in the early 1950s (Chambers (1989), p.317).

induced a fervour of missionary zeal. Edwin Orr, in *The Second Evangelical Awakening in Britain*, calculates that between 1859 and 1865 denominational records suggest there were a million accessions to the evangelical churches throughout the British Isles.[10] In Leicester no fewer than ten new churches were built between 1860 and 1884.[11] Satisfaction was voiced that in both church and chapel attendance was rising, and that there were more children under Christian instruction in 1890 than had been the case in 1850, even if various Acts of Parliament between 1854 and 1899 did progressively deprive the universities of Oxford, Cambridge and Durham, and King's College, London, of their Anglican identity. Few noticed that the proportional increase nowhere near matched that of the population in general, and though evangelical and Anglo-Catholic enthusiasm sustained Anglican numbers tolerably well until 1914, Methodist, Baptist and Congregational numbers were in decline after 1880; after 1914 all Protestant denominations were declining, the Roman Catholics for the moment sustaining their numbers largely as a result of Irish immigration.[12]

Looking back, some commentators consider that the decline had less to do with ideological challenges than with the social disruption to a nation becoming, by 1900, predominantly urban, in which urban clergy lacked the influence of their rural counterparts; many alternative avenues to status and distinction were opening up for the laity; and many non-religious sources of information and education becoming available.[13] Subsequent developments suggest that there may have been a considerable element of civic respectability involved in Victorian religious adherence, reminiscent of the strenuous efforts made by Augustus to restore conformity with traditional religion to the increasingly secularist Rome of the early Empire. Nonetheless, the ethos of the nation remained Christian, the socialism of the new Labour Party was predominantly Methodist rather than Marxist; temperance, Sunday observance and Gladstonian rectitude ('the Nonconformist conscience') dominated public morality. Moreover, not only was crime insignificant compared with the latter twentieth century (crimes against the person, for instance, totalled 2,258 in 1857, 2,546 in 1906, and 190,300 in 1991), but 'offences of violence' actually declined in absolute numbers, from 1,737 in mid-century to 1,443 in 1906.[14]

In the twentieth century the assault on traditional beliefs intensified, and now a new strand developed – Christian theologians themselves joined the debate on the side of scepticism. In 1863 a Frenchman, Ernest Rénan, had published a widely read life of Jesus which, like Euhemerus's demolition of the Greek deities at the start of the third century BC, denied that Jesus had supra-human attributes; he was a human, not a divine, being; and though he himself, being no charlatan, believed in his supposed but in fact imaginary miracles,* they 'were a violence done to him by his age, a concession forced from him by a passing necessity'.[15]

The invincible supremacy of natural science was inhibiting belief in the possibility of miracles, not only those which Jesus had reputedly performed, but also the two great claims central to his supranatural status: the Virgin Birth and the Resurrection. German Biblical criticism had during the nineteenth century made strenuous efforts to throw out the bathwater of supranaturalism without at the same time disposing of the baby of Christ's unique significance, but in Britain their cogitations had had little influence outside theological circles. During the interwar years, however, an Anglican cleric, E.W. Barnes, a former mathematics fellow of Trinity College, Cambridge, who in 1924 was consecrated Bishop of Birmingham, raised aloft the standard of liberal modernism in the English Church. In a sermon preached to the British Association for the Advancement of Science in August 1920, and a subsequent elaboration of his theme in Westminster Abbey a week later, he embraced the theological implications of Darwinian evolution to the point that, with the loss of Adam and Eve and the Garden of Eden, he denied the doctrine of the Fall and its consequence, the inherent sinfulness of humanity; and hence the need for Christ's atoning sacrifice – with all that such a denial implied for the whole doctrine of the Eucharist. The brutal reality of sin he did not deny, but its origin was less important than the long, slow struggle to conquer it through the evolution of civilized rationality.[16] In 1947, in his book *The Rise of Christianity*, he followed Rénan in submitting the New Testament to textual analysis, and concluding that no credence could be given to any miraculous element, either in the birth and death or in the reported actions of Jesus, though he did not dispute his significance as a supreme teacher.[17]

In Church circles, the proposal to prosecute the Bishop for heresy was debated but rejected. The Archbishop of Canterbury, speaking to the Convocation of Canterbury later in the year, said of the Bishop: 'If his views were mine, I should not feel that I could still hold episcopal office in the Church', but he left it to Barnes's own conscience how to respond.[18] Barnes was fortified by enormous public interest and support.

---

* Rénan simply dismissed most accounts as being the work of credulous spectators, considered that the degree of derangement manifested by various exorcised lunatics was slight, and cited Jesus's frequent appeals for secrecy as evidence that he had no desire to place emphasis on these manifestations of his powers.

Over 18,000 copies of his book were sold within sixteen months, more were demanded but postwar paper shortages limited the publisher's response. The *Sunday Pictorial* serialized it.[19] The Church settled for the proposition that Anglicanism had a great breadth of tolerance.

In Germany during the second quarter of the century the Lutheran theologian Rudolf Bultmann was working out his own version of 'de-mythologized' Christianity. In his *New Testament and Mythology*, published in Germany in 1941, he wrote: 'Experience and control of the world have developed to such an extent through science and technology that no-one can or does seriously maintain the New Testament world picture.'[20] Along with spatial concepts of Heaven and Hell, out went miracles, spiritual entities (especially the demonic ones supposedly associated with illness), the sacraments, and the existence of a sort of hybrid God-man in whose survival beyond the grave we all mysteriously partake. He retained the notion that something happened to the disciples at Easter (perhaps as a result of a vision), and that the essence of Christianity is that this something should happen to the contemporary seeker, too. His attempt to jettison the supernatural while retaining significance for the person of Jesus Christ centred on the existential philosophy of Heidegger – he sought to encapsulate the uniqueness of the Christian revelation in the individual experience (induced by the preaching of the Gospel) of the saving grace of God in Christ; an experience which replaced the nebulous doubts and anxieties of the isolated and despairing human being with the certainty and personal authenticity of the child of God.[21]

There still remained, for Bultmann though not for all his fellow radical theologians, a historical Jesus, the account of whom preserved by the Church could transform contemporary awareness of what it is to be a human being. The de-mythologizing of his person did not imply that the God he was reputed to serve did not exist, nor that he himself had not some deep significance, rooted in historical fact, in the individual's quest for salvation. The religious authenticity, however, lay, and could only lie, in the experience of the human psyche.

Bultmann's book was published in English translation in 1954,[22] and deeply influenced, among others, two prominent English-speaking Christians, Paul Van Buren, an American theologian, and John Robinson, Anglican Bishop of Woolwich. In 1963 both published books further demolishing traditional Christian doctrine. Van Buren, in *The Secular Meaning of Christianity*, defined modern man as totally and correctly committed to the view that certainty resides solely in empirical observation, and he addressed himself to the task of refashioning

Christianity accordingly, not so much to ease obstacles to evangelism as to allay the 'spiritual schizophrenia' of sincere but troubled contemporary Christians. For this to be effected, *all* transcendental hypotheses had to go, not just crudities like a spatially determined Heaven and Hell, but even the very concept of transcendentalism, including the idea of God, from which all possibility of empirical verification was absent; anyone who claimed some sort of non-material God-encompassing experience was only talking about their own sentiments, not about an entity by definition unavailable to sense-observation. Jesus himself understood this, says Van Buren, and it is what is meant by his phrase 'He that hath seen me hath seen the Father'. To search beyond the empirical here and now is an unprofitable endeavour.[23]

So what was the meaning of Christianity today? It was more than just learning about an exceptionally fearless and unselfish man who had lived, died and been buried two thousand years ago – there had been other such characters in history. What had happened at the first Easter was that Jesus's fugitive disciples were jointly grasped by a new and dazzling discernment that his total surrender to the needs of others was the pattern of true humanity; a discernment in the light of which they could not but commit themselves, too, to a life dedicated to loving relationships with their fellow human beings, no matter how vicious or hostile they might be. It was their discernment experience that was historically significant, not some hypothetical resuscitation of a dead body. That moment of discernment was as open to the twentieth century as to the first, and could be experienced by a process of 'contagion' from those already enlightened. The principal meaning of the 'real presence' in the Lord's Supper was that it provided one such opportunity. Such discernment and commitment are observable and empirically verifiable facts. The Church is nothing to do with buildings or institutions, but consists of those who share the insight and its consequences.

Van Buren accepted readily that on this analysis, theology was 'reduced' to ethics. He made no apology for that, any more than there should be apology for 'reducing' astrology to astronomy, or alchemy to chemistry; it was a logical consequence of scientific advance.[24] The two New Testament commandments, to love God and to love our neighbour, were, he admitted, tautologies on his interpretation, but 'if man is slowly learning to stand on his own feet, and to help his neighbour without reference to the ''God hypothesis'', the Christian should rejoice'; and understand that prayer 'means reflecting on the situation and then doing something about it, if there's anything he can do'.[25] Social and political activism is, on this reading, the very essence of Christianity, a stance that was to find an increasing resonance among sections of the Roman Catholic Church under the soubriquet 'Liberation Theology'.

Van Buren's mentor is not Heidegger and existentialism but Wittgenstein and linguistic analysis, and a large part of his thesis consists of a linguistically creative reinterpretation of the New Testament and of theological disputes from the early Fathers on, in order to demonstrate that his logically unassailable, empirically based theology for twentieth-century man can be made consonant with orthodoxy.* His work was far too abstruse to appeal to a mass readership. John Robinson's *Honest to God*, however, had enormous popular appeal.

Like Barnes, Bultmann, Van Buren (and others), Robinson (who shared Barnes's background as a Cambridge don) rejected all miraculous claims, and like them, though he accords a special place to Easter, it is to the experience undergone by the disciples and not to the event, whatever it was (some sort of apparition?), that prompted the experience. He too found he had no awareness of a God 'out there'. But he was much less ruthless than Van Buren in discarding the transcendental, stressing God as 'the creative ground and meaning of all our existence' – an interpretation made familiar by the German-American theologian Paul Tillich, and specifically rejected by Van Buren as meaningless. 'The final definition of this reality from which "nothing can separate us" since it is the very ground of our being,' continues Robinson, 'is "the love of God in Christ Jesus our Lord"'.[26] The 'deep things of God', he says, are not attainable in isolation, but only in human relationships, and like Van Buren he sees the essence of Christianity in social concern. 'The Christian community exists . . . to be the embodiment of . . . love.'[27]

Robinson goes further than Van Buren, however, in elucidating the implications of these conclusions for ethics. 'The New Morality' is the subject of the last third of his book. Robinson sees the surrounding apostasy from traditional Christianity as terminal for the old morality – 'the fathers rejected the doctrine, the children have abandoned the morals'.[28] Fortunately, this is not too serious, for the old morality was no more true Christian morals than was the doctrine eternal Christian doctrine. With the abandonment of outworn formulations based on notions of revelation and externally imposed authority, including absolute moral commands (such as the Ten Commandments, 'the morality of Sinai'), human beings, now 'come of age', can be trusted to formulate their own moral response to the imperative of love of others.

---

* For instance, he interprets the Church's rejection of the Arian insistence that Jesus was a man owing allegiance to a God as meaning that the Church, in refusing to separate Jesus and God, was in fact endorsing the statement that the historical Jesus is the totality of godliness.

'There can for the Christian be no "packaged" moral judgements – for persons are more important even than "standards".' 'Utilitarianism, evolutionary naturalism, existentialism – These systems . . .' he writes, 'have this in common: they have taken their stand, quite correctly, against any subordination of the concrete needs of the individual situation to an alien universal norm.' But to leave the matter there is to be bogged in a morass of subjectivism and relativism. The solution lay in seeking, in the ground of our being, 'the Christ who is love of others'. Love can be trusted to meet 'every situation on its own merits, with no prescriptive laws'.* [29] As long ago as the 1928 revision of the Book of Common Prayer, Church of England clergy had been offered the option of reading out the two 'love' commandments of the New Testament at the service of Holy Communion in place of the austere severity of the Ten Old Testament Commands, and increasingly it was the new formulation that was used. Soon, few Anglicans could, if challenged, have specified what it was that the Ten Commandments enjoined.

The next prominent challenger in the lists was the Anglican priest Don Cupitt, again from the Cambridge stable, well known in theological circles for his book *Taking Leave of God* long before his TV series, *The Sea of Faith*, achieved a cult following in the autumn of 1984, followed by publication under the same title in 1986. Essentially this repeated the 'de-mythologizing' themes elucidated above, but this time for a TV audience. Again, however, the logic is pushed a little further along the empirical path. Whatever it is that we are categorizing as 'religious', it can only be a reflection of something already present in the human psyche – it is, in essence, a human construct. The supreme human response to life is a noble, rational stoicism, described by the author as 'Christian Buddhism'. It struck a chord. In 1989 a network of sympathizers set up the Sea of Faith movement (known by its detractors as Faith at Sea), which by 1993 numbered about 500 in Britain and 250 overseas, a third of them priests or ministers from the Roman Catholic, Anglican and Nonconformist churches, the remainder drawn both from

---

* The Bishop illustrated his theme with an example which, a generation later, reads somewhat quaintly. Faced with the temptation to seduce a girl, the young man should ask himself how genuinely he loves her. If not very much, then to sleep with her would be wrong. If he sincerely loves her, 'then he will respect her far too much to use her or take liberties with her' (Robinson, John, p.119). This was not, however, the message which reached the general public, who were more influenced by the Bishop's testimony as a defence witness at the trial for obscenity of *Lady Chatterley's Lover*. It was not so much his belief that D.H. Lawrence was trying to portray the sex relationship as something sacred, 'as an act of Holy Communion' that proved morally liberating, but the fact that this interpretation was offered in the context of an adulterous relationship (*The Times*, 3 November 1960).

the laity and from those outside formal religion who were interested in 'exploring and promoting religious faith as a human creation'. As the chairman of its steering committee pointed out, 'we very much hope this effort will include people from religious traditions other than the Christian one'.[30] On Easter Day 1993 the BBC made their regular Sunday night *Heart of the Matter* programme over to those Anglican parish clergy who wished publicly to deny the truth of the risen Christ, the real import of which, as one of them explained, 'is about the sun rising in the morning. It is about spring after winter.' Where all this differed from secular humanism, apart from the fact that a number of the participants were holding down benefices, was not clear to all observers.

The paramount effect of the new doctrine was to concentrate on the individual as the fount of moral authority, and to diminish to vanishing point the place of ancestral wisdom or the claims of absolute values. 'With the widespread belief that religion derives from the emotional sensations of individuals rather than from the objective teaching of the scripture,' points out Edward Norman (chaplain of Christ Church College, Canterbury, formerly Dean of Peterhouse, Cambridge), 'the arts become the accepted repository of truth, and truth is relative to individual sensation.'[31] One after another, churches and cathedrals began to stage secular artistic events, attracting audiences rather than congregations.

Any hope that this incorporation into theology of the perplexities of the man/woman in the pew would cement his loyalty to religious institutions was destined to be confounded. By the third quarter of the twentieth century, the apathy of the bulk of the population towards their religious heritage could no longer be denied. The 40 per cent Sunday attendance which had so shocked the early Victorians had declined to 10 to 15 per cent by the 1960s. Church of England Sunday school attendance more than halved (allowing for demographic change) between 1895 and 1960; the number of Sunday school teachers fell from 196,000 to 85,000.[32] An accurate statistical picture over time is impossible to compile, for the various denominations use many different bases of compilation (baptisms, confirmations, family membership, Easter attendance, etc.), some without religious significance (for instance, parish electoral rolls); and sources such as the *UK Christian Handbook* and *Social Trends* vary over time as to which denominations are amalgamated in the published figures. Whatever measure is used, however, the picture for all Trinitarian churches, including by now the Roman Catholic, is one of unremitting overall decline. By 1989 a census by Marc Europe, a Christian research organization, estimated that not more than one in ten of the adult population of England attended a place of traditional Christian worship – in the major cities the figure fell to between one and two per hundred of the adult population. Christian Research, which conducted a census in October 1994, found that church attendance in Scotland was declining even more rapidly than in England, a trend that, if it continued, would leave the traditional churches empty by the year 2044.[33]

A Gallup survey carried out in 1992 found that 50 per cent of students and professional people (mostly graduates) surveyed, all born in Britain and none claiming adherence to any non-Christian faith, were unable to quote a single verse from the Bible (apart from the Lord's Prayer) and, offered a selection of eleven prominent religious writers such as Bunyan, Milton and T.S. Eliot, a quarter were unable to name a single work.[*][34] It was significant of the nation's scale of priorities that in the summer of 1989, on the five hundredth anniversary of the birth of Thomas Cranmer, author of the once treasured Book of Common Prayer, the only special commemorative stamps issued by the Post Office were of achievements, such as Ironbridge, Shropshire, of the Industrial Revolution. Early in 1987 it was revealed that in nine prisons the chapel was being used for the screening of films, and in response to Parliamentary protests, the prisons concerned were instructed by the Home Secretary to cease including violent and pornographic films in the selection shown.[35] In both the United States (1985) and Britain (1991) the Scout and Guide movements were challenged by youngsters refusing to assent to an oath that required them to say they believed in God. In both countries compromises were found that reinterpreted 'God' as whatever the youngster chose to mean by the phrase.[†][36] Also in 1991 the British Red Cross Society decided that 'no official Red Cross services or events should be organized which might lead to a public perception that the Red Cross was anything other than an organization without religious affiliation of any kind', a 'denial of its history' in the view of one churchman, and a move at which the Archbishop of York voiced his concern.[37] Justice, a legal pressure group, campaigned from 1973 on for the religious oath in court to be replaced by a simple undertaking to tell the truth.[38]

It was the historian D.W. Brogan who once wrote: 'The Church of England may only be the Church that the majority of English people stay

---

[*] Among the younger group, the students, the percentages rise to 73 per cent and 45 per cent.
[†] In Britain the Guides amended the old phrase 'I promise to do my duty to God . . .' with the phrase 'I promise that I will do my best to love my God'. The Scouts set up a working party with the intention of finding some similar compromise (*The Times*, 12 and 14 June 1995).

away from. But they want it to be there to stay away from . . .'[39] Perhaps. But whatever residual loyalty remained was ceasing to influence public observance, which increasingly ignored Christian sensitivities. Though the Lord Chamberlain had not since 1861 sought to regulate the opening of theatres in the week before Easter,[40] the custom of closing during Holy Week persisted (perhaps because audiences were sparse) until well after World War I. In 1923, for instance, ten London theatres closed either for the whole week, or for Maundy Thursday, Good Friday and Easter Saturday. In 1938, at least two (the Duke of York's and the Globe) closed, and the Duchess, Lyric, Playhouse and Wintergarden all advertised closure in Holy Week 1939. By 1946 only one theatre, the Vaudeville (which was staging a straight play, not music hall) closed, after which the custom seems to have lapsed entirely. Ascension Day had been a holiday in many schools in the 1930s; the Whit weekend was still a public holiday in 1964, when Edward Heath, at the Board of Trade, announced the Government's intention to transfer the Whit Monday holiday to the last Monday of May in order to extend the summer season for the benefit of the summer tourist trade. The churches accepted the change without demur. Good Friday, the most solemn day in the Christian year, succumbed more slowly to secular trends, but by 1987 most shops, large and small, were trading, though not till 1992 did Harrods open for the first time ('in response to public demand').[41] Bad weather in 1993, encouraging shoppers to seek shelter from the rain, gave the store a 28 per cent increase in sales over the previous year.[42] Christmas has become, for the bulk of the population, predominantly a costly spending spree, a reversion to the mid-winter Roman Saturnalia which early Christianity had attempted to sanctify. Where once the nation began its Christmas preparations only with Advent (other, that is, than the pudding preliminaries of Stir-up Sunday),* commerce now dictates that Christmas lights and decorations should appear in the streets not later than mid-October, Santa be in his grotto in time for the school half-term holiday. Carols, once restricted to little more than the twelve days of Christmas, regale shoppers on every high street, promiscuously interspersed with 'Jingle Bells' and 'Rudolf the Red-nosed Reindeer'. The hot cross buns of Good Friday and the chocolate eggs of Easter, once available only during Holy Week, are on sale soon after the post-Christmas sales are over, and television trills 'Don't forget the pancakes on Jif Lemon Day – February 16th!'[43] to a populace that has

---

* The last Sunday before Advent, when the collect for the day began, 'Stir up, we beseech thee, O Lord, the will of thy faithful people.'

long forgotten the name of Shrove Tuesday, let alone knows what 'shrove' means. In 1986 a firm called Luncheon Vouchers Ltd took a whole page of *The Times* to proclaim that 'Man cannot live by bread alone', but the missing ingredient turned out to be not the word of God, but all the other things, like tagliatelle vongole, that the luncheon voucher could buy. The Halifax Building Society welcomed Christmas 1993 with 'Glad Tidings of Comfort and Joy'. They were making new, lower mortgage rates available.*

The notion dinned into schoolchildren of the 1920s and 30s that it is inappropriate to clap performances of sacred music, since these are for the glory of God not the delectation of the audience, had long since gone; and the Salvation Army had to delete 'Abide with Me' from its Cup Final repertoire, so bawdy were the versions being purveyed. Sacred music found a new use as a stirring accompaniment to TV advertisements. Lloyds' black horse performed his leisurely gallop to the solemn strains of Bach's 'Wachet Auf'; the music to which an earlier generation had sung, 'I vow to thee, my country', poignant for its associations with the mass slaughter of World War I, swelled to accompany advertisements for National Power electricity generation, found a new niche throughout the summer of 1991 advertising Dulux paints, and was syncopated and sentimentalized for Kiri Te Kanawa's 'The World in Union', theme song of the Rugby World Cup in 1991. Wagner's majestic Pilgrim's Chorus from *Tannhäuser* spent 1989 rewritten on behalf of Harpic lavatory freshener. Sorokin was remarkably prescient when in 1941 he wrote of the advanced sensate society:

> Even the greatest cultural values of the past will be degraded. Beethovens and Bachs will become an appendix to the eloquent rhapsodies of advertised laxatives, gums, cereals, beers and other solid enjoyments. Michelangelos and Rembrandts will be decorating soap and razor blades, washing machines and whiskey bottles.[44]

Secularism, as a professed allegiance, meanwhile marched from strength to strength, basing its appeal on such cardinal tenets as: that man is an evolutionary product of nature; that the highest ethical goal is

---

* The contrast with Islam is inescapable. When the Chanel fashion house inadvertently embroidered in Arabic a phrase from the Koran on the low-cut bodice of a dress shown at a Paris fashion show in January 1994, protests were lodged at government level, and the Indonesian Muslim Scholars' Council, swiftly emulated by Egypt's parliamentary religious affairs committee, called on Muslims to boycott Chanel products, and to prevent them from entering the country. Chanel apologized, and withdrew the dress from sale (*The Times*, 21 and 25 January 1994).

happiness, freedom and progress; and that the widest use should be made of the scientific method as a means of solving problems, with full freedom of expression.[45] The First Humanist Manifesto, consisting of fifteen clauses, had been published in *The New Humanist* in the early summer of 1933. It denied the separate existence of a 'sacred' domain; rejected the existence of uniquely religious emotions and attitudes of the kind hitherto associated with belief in the supernatural; asserted that man was 'at last becoming aware that he alone is responsible for the realization of the world of his dreams, that he has within himself the power for its achievement'; declared that religious humanists aim to foster the creative in man and to encourage achievements that add to the satisfactions of life; and called for the establishment of a social and co-operative economic order that would result in the equitable distribution of the means of life.[46] An international congress of the World Union of Freethinkers had assembled in London in September 1938, its organizers including the Rationalist Press Association, the South Place Ethical Society, the Ethical Union and the National Secular Society. Participants included the president of the French Chamber of Deputies and an ex-premier of the French Republic, with an intellectually distinguished panel of professors forming the Committee of Honour. Horrified traditionalists, including Cardinal Hinsley and a number of Conservative MPs, endeavoured to get the congress banned, and when that failed, to have the intending foreign visitors excluded from Britain – but the Home Secretary was deaf to their pleas.[47]

The horrors of World War II, like its 1914–18 predecessor, had further undermined faith in a beneficent, omnipotent deity. In 1963 the British Humanist Association was founded, at the instigation of the Ethical Union and the Rationalist Press Association, 'to offer a fresh challenge to the Christian churches'. As president Sir Julian Huxley explained, 'we want to consolidate and expand the upsurge of humanism that has taken place recently'. Peter Ustinov and E.M. Forster were among the luminaries serving on the advisory council, as were ten fellows of the Royal Society, including Professor G.M. Carstairs, the then current Reith lecturer.[*][48] In the following year the National Secular Society promoted Secular Education Month, campaigning for the elimination of

---

[*] By 1989 the Association was commenting that the demand for humanist funeral services was so great that with only 87 'officiants', they needed 8,700 (*The Independent*, 21 November 1989). So many people are now leaving instructions that their ashes should be scattered at the goal mouth of their favourite football club that the turf is being seriously damaged, and by 1993 Liverpool, Everton, Spurs and Arsenal were all having to limit unrestricted ash-scattering (*The Times*, 24 November 1993).

collective worship from morning assembly in county schools, the removal from their curricula of the promotion of the Christian religion and its link to ethics (which should instead be 'socially based'), the abolition of compulsory chapel from the public schools, and of all grants to denominational schools. Michael Foot, Harold Pinter and Ted Willis were among the promotors of this programme.[49] Hopes rose for its implementation when, in the following month, no fewer than five members of the newly elected Labour Government refused to swear their oath of office, but chose the alternative of affirmation achieved under the 1888 Oaths Act, almost the only tangible legislative victory yet achieved by the National Secular Society.[50]

Their hopes were to some extent fulfilled. The 1944 Education Act had required religious instruction in schools, and a collective act of worship (from which parents could, if they wished, withdraw their children), but had not specified which religion, it being universally assumed at the time that the religion referred to was Christianity. As time went by, and the number of humanist teachers in the schools increased, the Act fell into effective abeyance, a process accelerated by the increasing numbers of immigrant children in the schools who were not of Christian allegiance or cultural heritage. Faced with the facts of multiculturalism, the synod of the Church of England in 1977 debated whether it could any longer expect the state schools to inculcate Christianity, or whether the Church should itself prepare to step into the breach.[51] In the schools, so-called religious education, once intended as a period of committed scriptural instruction, became either a general canter through comparative religious history; or a branch of current affairs in which emphasis on the social activism now regarded as the embodiment of Christian religious sentiment vied with a social criticism which provided a convenient entry point for Marxism and for the denigration of Western culture calculated to enhance the self-esteem of the newcomers.

By 1988 it was reported that most secondary schools no longer held a daily assembly.[52] When the Education Reform Bill* came to Parliament that year, a rearguard action of Christian peers, not strongly supported by the Anglican bishops whose main anxiety was to avoid antagonizing adherents of other faiths, initiated amendments, later accepted in the Commons, which in effect required schools to reflect in their worship

---

* Chiefly concerned with the opportunity for schools to opt out of local authority control, and with the establishment of a compulsory 'core' curriculum.

and education the pre-eminence of the Christian religion, though schools with a predominantly non-Christian attendance were entitled to draw on their own traditions, and parents would have the right not only to withdraw their children, but to require alternative provision; an arrangement which the National Union of Teachers abhorred as potentially divisive. The Professional Association of Teachers, themselves deeply divided on the issue, were told by their founder-president at their annual conference in 1989 that teachers should not be seen to side with one religion.[53]

The legislative latitude permitted the authority responsible for Ealing to produce a religious education syllabus which managed to exclude all mention of the Bible, Jesus or God,[54] while in Croydon in 1993 the local authority RE advisor returned to a local church a series of donated religious books, explaining that the 1988 Act did not permit state schools to 'evangelise'.[55] The decade closed with the Act still largely unimplemented. Attempts by the Education Secretary in the 1990s to encourage observance of the 1944 Education Act's provision for collective worship met with studied resistance from the teaching profession, and by the summer of 1994 head teachers were demanding that a government circular on the subject be rescinded, a survey having shown that in some three-quarters of secular secondary schools nearly half the staff and a third of heads were prepared to exercise their option not to lead or attend collective worship.[56] Notwithstanding the provisions of the Education Act, the School Curriculum and Assessment Authority in the summer of 1994 dropped from its recommendations the suggestion that 50 per cent of time in religious education classes be devoted to the study of Christianity.[57] By the summer of 1995 the chief executive of the School Curriculum and Assessment Authority announced that in a recent survey almost half the 16- to 24-year-olds questioned did not know what Good Friday commemorated, and seven out of ten did not know what happened on Palm Sunday. Quite apart from religious allegiance, such monumental ignorance guaranteed, as commentators were not slow to point out, an 'artificial isolation from 80 per cent of Western art, literature and music', and deprived them of the essential key to understanding the past of which we are the inheritors.[58]

In other respects the long-term secularist programme achieved, though not without opposition, Parliamentary approval. The battle for a secular Sunday continued. The 1780 Act remained the dominant influence on Sunday entertainment, but came under increasing pressure. A rally in Maidstone in 1927 to defend traditional observance against encroachment, particularly from sport and the theatre, received messages of support from the Archbishop of Canterbury, Ramsey MacDonald and Harry Lauder, all bewailing the threatened loss of 'the quietude and recuperative restfulness of Sunday'.[59] In 1932, however, the Sunday Entertainments Act clarified uncertainties by stating that no offence was committed under the Act by the opening of a museum, picture gallery, zoo or aquarium, or by the holding of a lecture or debate. The Act further allowed concerts to be held (provided there was no music-hall patter) and permitted cinemas to open at the local authority's discretion, a contingency that led to many years of local dissension until in 1972 the local option to prevent opening was removed. In 1972 the Sunday Theatres Act permitted some restricted theatre opening, but trade union objections to Sunday working nullified the Act until, in February 1992, a musical, *Return to the Forbidden Planet*, took the gamble, to be followed in the autumn of the same year by another musical, a touring production of *Annie Get Your Gun*; but by the end of 1994 the example had been little emulated. However, negotiations with Equity and the backstage unions revealed a flexible approach, and in May 1995 *A Passionate Woman* played at the Comedy Theatre on a Sunday, the producer having secured his position by obtaining from '39 vicars, one canon and a deaconess', out of a total of 200 to whom he had sent free tickets, an assurance that they would not only be among the audience, they would wear their dog-collars.[60]

Wimbledon finals, Test matches and FA Cup semi-finals were already being played on Sundays; Monaco-style motor racing came to Birmingham in 1986, disrupting church services which had to be cancelled or rescheduled;[61] and on 26 July 1992 the Jockey Club embarked (at Doncaster) on Sunday horse-racing, to gratifying public support, notwithstanding the fact that the Betting, Gaming and Lotteries Act (1963)* limited Sunday betting to telephone bids, a restriction the abolition of which, those involved in the sport insisted, was essential to the economic health of the industry.[62] Parliament acceded to their pleas, and in May 1994 agreed to permit seven-day race betting.[63] An attempt by a Government-owned ferry company in 1990 to run Sunday ferry services to various ports in the Western Isles, following their successful outfacing of local opposition in Skye some twenty years earlier, was defeated by the strength and obstinacy of local public opinion.[64] However, in 1995, when an expensive new ferry, the *Isle of Lewis*, was launched and, bowing to continuing Sabbatarian feeling, did not run on

---

* Which incorporated provisions first enacted in 1934.

Sundays, the managing director promised that 'We are not sailing on Sunday in the first year, but we will be doing so in future. You don't build an asset of this worth and have it lying idle one day a week.'[65]

Yet again, it was Sunday trading that was to prove the crunch issue. The latest legislation was the 1950 Shops Act, which had endeavoured to combine Sunday observance with permission for the sale of emergency goods such as motor car spares and pharmaceutical supplies (to help consumers) and perishables such as specified foods and newspapers (to help purveyors of goods), the list becoming, over time, hopelessly anachronistic and ludicrously illogical. Widespread disregard of the specified commodities was alleged, and even sharp practice, such as charging exorbitant prices for some item of food while offering a free gift of hardware. Numerous attempts at amendment by private members' bills had been unsuccessful for a variety of reasons, and in 1985 the Government introduced a Bill providing for total deregulation. It was opposed by the Lord's Day Observance Society, still actively campaigning along Sabbatarian lines, as it had done since its foundation in 1831. It was now joined by a new organization, the Keep Sunday Special campaign, Christian in origin but putting its main emphasis on the practical social and economic consequences of Sunday trading, such as the disturbance to shop workers' family life, the effect on the elderly and immobile of the likely closure of small local shops and the questionable desirability of a probable increase in part-time rather than full-time jobs. Against all expectations, and after a hectic campaign in which specifically Christian objections were allied with the shopworkers' union and a number of major retail traders unwilling to be coerced, by competitive pressure, into Sunday opening, the Bill was defeated. The Government having refused to contemplate any alternative but total deregulation, the position perforce remained that of the universally derided 1950 Act.[66]

A number of large retailers then changed their tactics. Citing as their reason their desperation at the effects of the recession, in defiance of the law they opened their premises for trade on Sundays in the run-up to Christmas 1990, one of them claiming that any enforced closure by the local authorities would be in breach of the free trade provisions of the Treaty of Rome. A prolonged legal battle ensued, involving local authorities, the English courts, the European Court, all in effect passing the final decision to someone else. DIYs proceeded to open on Sundays throughout 1991, and by the Christmas season it was obvious that the trickle was about to become a flood, spearheaded by Sainsbury's, Tesco, Asda and Safeway. The John Lewis partnership made clear their opposition to Sunday trading (a stand that by the end of 1992 was reckoned to be losing their Waitrose supermarkets some £1 million a week),[67] Marks and Spencer informed their shareholders that although in principle they favoured trading on the four Sundays preceding Christmas, they were not going to condone law-breaking, and C & A took out large advertisements in the press to make the same point.

The Lord's Day Observance Society continued to campaign, but was virtually ignored by the media. However, in late November 1991 the Archbishop of Canterbury, the Roman Catholic Cardinal Archbishop, the Chief Rabbi and the Moderator of the Free Church Federal Council jointly protested to the Prime Minister at the 'widespread and deliberate flouting' of the law. Sporadic protests by churchgoers in the aisles of the houses of Mammon rather than of God were easily contained by the police. By mid-December Sainsbury's, Asda and Tesco had announced that they would continue to open on Sunday in the New Year as well as in the run-up to Christmas, and though the Bishop of Oxford called for a boycott of the offending shops, and their chairmen received stiff protests from a Church Estates commissioner, Sunday trading continued – indeed, the New Year honours list contained a knighthood for one of the offending chairmen.

As more and more Sunday shoppers thronged the open stores, the case for deregulation seemed 'democratically' unanswerable, and the Government made clear its intention to bring forward legislation to that effect after the general election. Another impassioned campaign ensued, in which the four religious leaders of the Christian and Jewish faiths again took a joint stand, and in which the Keep Sunday Special group, anxious not to divide the opposition, accepted, in their preferred option, progressively more generous definitions of the size of 'small' shop (initially 500 square feet; finally 3,000 square feet) that should be permitted to open for trade on a Sunday; but they had lost the support of the Shopworkers' Union which, scenting premium wages on Sunday, switched sides. All strands of opinion now conceded that commercial considerations must take precedence during the four Sundays of Advent. In December 1993, on a free vote, the Keep Sunday Special option was defeated, and an option adopted which allowed all shops to open on any Sunday. The largest stores were limited to six hours, but supporters interviewed by the BBC were confident that this would soon be extended, and that the example would soon spread to banks and building societies – a prophecy fulfilled within the year, when in December 1994 the NatWest opened 23 of its branches on Sundays in the run-up to Christmas.[68] A year later, in the teeth of fierce opposition from the

Banking, Insurance and Finance Union, NatWest revealed plans to open 78 branches on the Sundays leading up to Christmas, and celebrated the first with a balloon send-off.[69] Whether this was a good or a bad thing, in one respect all commentators agreed: 'Sunday will never be the same.' In May 1994, in the words of *The Times*, 'the Archbishop of Canterbury effectively conceded defeat in the battle to keep Sunday sacred . . . and urged churches to welcome congregations to worship throughout the week'.[70]

Sunday 28 August 1994 marked the start of the new dispensation, even Marks and Spencer reluctantly opening some of its stores (and reporting customers knocking on the doors an hour before the permitted opening time); and John Lewis opening some of its Waitrose food outlets, though holding firm on its main shops. Customers crowded into the shopping centres, cars queueing for up to fifteen minutes to enter a Bristol hypermarket car park, while at the Gateshead MetroCentre, leased from the Church Commissioners, the throng was estimated to number some 90,000.[71] By the beginning of 1995 a survey found that Sunday had become the busiest shopping day, with profits increasing for shops that opened at the expense of those which did not. There was no evidence of extra total spending.[72]

The long campaign to remove from the State any authority over the right of the individual to autonomy in sexual matters made strides in a number of respects during the 1960s. Easier divorce, access to contraception, the legitimization of children born out of wedlock had been on the agenda of the nineteenth-century secularists. Following the foundation of the British Humanist Association in 1963, removal of legal impediments to abortion and to sexual relationships outside marriage, including homosexual relationships, was added to the list of avowed objectives. As the Second Humanist Manifesto of 1976 was to put it (sixth clause), 'short of harming others or compelling them to do likewise, individuals should be permitted to express their sexual proclivities and pursue their life-styles as they desire'.[73]

Secular divorce, permissible only since the Matrimonial Causes Act of 1857 had made adultery grounds for the termination of a marriage, had been extended in 1937 to encompass cruelty and desertion. In 1969 (effective 1971), in addition to these matrimonial offences, 'no blame' marital breakdown became grounds for divorce, provided the couple had lived apart for two years in the case of an uncontested, or five in the case of a contested, divorce. For the first time, a marriage in which no offence was alleged could be terminated contrary to the wishes of one of the spouses.

413

The synod of the Anglican Church, whose assumption of the indissolubility of marriage provided even less flexibility than did the Roman Catholic, decided in the summer of 1981 to permit second marriages in church of those with divorced spouses still living. Traditionalists balked at the implied recourse to the secular philosophy that the path to happiness lay in the removal of impediments to the satisfaction of wants, but the move was popular. 'A lot of the things that Jesus taught are ideals, not moral absolutes' was the new watchword. By 1987 some 4 per cent of marriages in Anglican churches involved a divorced person with living spouse, the number of such ceremonies increasing tenfold between 1976 and 1987.[74] Uncertainties remained, however, and when the Princess Royal contracted a second marriage in 1992 the ceremony was conducted by the Church of Scotland, which had since 1959 permitted the remarriage of divorced people with living former partners. In the USA a divorced woman was, in a very jolly ceremony on 11 February 1989, consecrated suffragan bishop of Massachusetts, but in Britain opposition faced the proposal for legislation to permit even the ordination of men divorced or married to divorcees, and the measure was rejected after an all-night sitting of Parliament in July 1989.[75] At parish level, however, personal inclination prevailed. Outrage was noisily expressed when the Bishop of Norwich, in the autumn of 1994, required the resignation of a parish priest with two former living wives who was openly resident with his intended third, and in Yorkshire a newly ordained female curate, preparing to marry her divorced organist in the local register office, protested that when 'it is the real thing', there seemed no reason to exclude the divorced from remarriage in church.[76] In recognition of the insecurity of tenure resulting from bishops' powers of discipline over their clergy, the Manufacturing, Scientific and Finance Union opened, in the autumn of 1994, a clergy section to help priests unite to protect their interests.[77] By May 1995 the MSF national officer responsible for the clergy section was demanding national negotiating rights for clergy in return for a no-strike deal, and triple stipends as compensation for the loss of job security.[78]

Marital status was in any case losing its significance. A series of judicial decisions in the early 1970s blurred the distinction between the married and the unmarried state, giving cohabitees various tenancy rights. In 1969 the Family Law Reform Act gave to illegitimate children or their issue property rights closely similar to those of legitimate children. In 1975 the Inheritance (Provision for Family and Dependants) Act gave cohabitees inheritance rights and equated the rights of illegitimate children with those of legitimate in cases of intestacy. The phrase 'single mother' was deliberately introduced in place of the former 'unmarried mother', thus blurring any distinction between those whose lone responsibilities resulted from widowhood or divorce, and those who had never burdened themselves with formal matrimonial commitments. In 1981 both Debrett's and the British Rail concessionary staff ticket system acknowledged the existence of 'stable cohabiting couples'.[79] It was not long before the description 'partner' replaced 'husband' and 'wife', and any inference as to the degree of commitment involved in the relationship was studiously avoided. Where hotels had once co-operated in enforcing traditional moral standards by requiring occupants of double rooms at least to pretend they were married, by the 1990s a conference centre inviting participants to 'bring your partner' felt no compunction about changing the wording of its brochures to the less prescriptive 'bring *a* partner'. These developments in the advanced sensate society were predicted with perfect accuracy by Sorokin in 1941: 'The family as a sacred union of husband and wife, of parents and children will continue to disintegrate. Divorces and separations will increase until any profound difference between socially sanctioned marriages and illicit sex-relationships disappears.'* [80]

Church opinion on the subject became increasingly marginalized. Desperate not to lose touch entirely with young people, and burdened perhaps by a sense of guilt for having at times soiled sexuality through the prominence accorded to neurotically misogynist churchmen, pastors began to weaken in their defence of chastity. Insisting that such a state was impossible, pressure built on the Pope to rescind the vow of celibacy for the Roman Catholic clergy, pressure to which he did not accede.[81] In New Jersey Bishop Spong in 1989 published *Living in Sin*, claiming (among much else) that sexually active single people should be welcomed into the church, that medieval moral standards should not be applied to young people for whom puberty had 'run back one year in each century for the last 400 years'. A Westminster Abbey canon called, in 1993, for a revision of the Church's attitude to premarital sex, at least for engaged couples.[82] On the whole the clergy stuck to traditional prescriptions, but a survey in 1991 revealed that almost a third of members of church youth groups thought sex before marriage morally

---

* One result of multiple divorces and remarriages is the increased possibility that blood relatives living in separate establishments and meeting only as adults may, untrammelled by the traditional incest taboo within families, fall in love and produce children. A BBC 2 *Public Eye* investigation on 27 May 1994 raised the question whether the current law prohibiting incest should be ameliorated to allow for changing social circumstances.

acceptable, and a BBC survey the same year found that one in twenty fifteen- to seventeen-year-old girls thought it reasonable for a man to expect sex on the first date.[83] In a Brunel University survey the following year, fewer than one in ten of those under twenty-one thought it important to remain a virgin until marriage.[84] In June 1995, a Church of England working party, bowing to the inevitable ('wrestling with the realities of contemporary society', as one member put it), concluded that 'living in sin' should no longer be condemned, the phrase should be dropped, and government policy favouring one family form over another deemed unacceptable. Both the Anglican Archbishop of Canterbury and the Roman Catholic Cardinal Archbishop of Westminster distanced themselves from these conclusions.[85]

Much of this change in sexual morality stemmed from improvements in contraceptive methods. Birth control had been an important issue for the Victorian secularists, with the founding, in 1861, of the Malthusian League, which evolved into the Family Planning Association.[86] The FPA was accorded fairly general approbation, subject to the proviso that techniques of birth control should not fall into the hands of the unwed. Religious opinion, initially greatly shocked, had, apart from the Roman Catholic Church, come to accept family limitation for the married, while entirely eschewing any suggestion that it should be used to free men and women from all propensity to procreate. The (Anglican) Lambeth Conference of Bishops had in 1908 unequivocally denounced the 'growing practice of the artificial restriction of the family', and had called upon all Christian people to condemn 'the use of all artificial means of restriction . . .' In 1916 they accepted family limitation in principle, by approving the use of the 'safe period' in certain circumstances (chiefly the wife's physical unfitness for child-bearing). In 1930 the grounds for contraception were widened, with a recognition of the symbolism of sexual intercourse within marriage – that it had a 'relational', not merely 'generational' significance.[87] 'Within marriage', however, was the cardinal qualification. The Vatican never accepted artificial methods of birth control, and the objections were reiterated in the papal encyclicals *Humanae Vitae* in 1968 and again in *Veritatis Splendor* in 1993, a stance to which increasing objection was taken, by both disaffected laity and recalcitrant priests.

Birth control was not, in itself, illegal, but there was consternation in Parliament in 1949 when it was reported that in Brighton, and in certain areas of Kent, Surrey and Greater London, contraceptive vending machines were being installed outside cinemas. The Home Secretary, having come to the conclusion that 'the social mischiefs involved were so serious as to require immediate action', undertook at once to draft a model by-law for local authorities to implement to bring the practice to an end.[88]

The problem, as the Roman Catholic theologians had appreciated, was that once it was accepted that sexual intercourse had other purposes and benefits than the potential procreation of children in circumstances in which the parents would share joint responsibility for their subsequent rearing, it was difficult (in the Roman view impossible) to draw a hard and fast line. Over the next decades the mission to ease the lot of mothers hopelessly overburdened by child-bearing evolved into a demand for 'sexual liberation' in general. This was greatly facilitated by the arrival in Britain, in 1960, of pharmaceutical methods of birth control, 'the Pill'. By 1964 the Brook Clinic, another distant descendant of the Malthusian League, had opened to prescribe the Pill to single women, though not until 1974 did it become available from the National Health Service.

Very strict conditions had hedged the practice of abortion, only permissible to save a mother's life. In 1967 the Abortion Act widened the grounds, legalizing abortion provided two medical practitioners certified either that the prospective child was seriously abnormal, or that the mother's circumstances were such as to render either her physical or mental health at risk, a restriction which was to prove not over-onerous.[*] The time limit of 28 weeks was intended to reflect the earliest age at which a foetus could be viable outside its mother, which in effect made the morality of the operation dependent not on any absolute sanctity with respect to a potential human life, but on current medical techniques. Following medical advances in keeping premature babies alive, the time limit was, in the face of considerable opposition, reduced to 24 weeks in 1990, but at the same time a loophole was introduced for terminations without any time limit in cases of abnormality. A further liberalization was achieved in 1991, when the Department of Health licensed for use a drug whose sole purpose is to induce miscarriages.[89]

---

[*] Dostoevsky regarded this development as inevitable in a society that abandoned Christian absolute moral standards. In *Notebooks for the Possessed* (p.241) he envisaged a time when Europe was short of food and fuel and 'the instinct of self-preservation being first and foremost, it follows that babes must be burned . . . Malthus isn't so very wrong at all, for there hasn't been enough time to prove his theories . . . The burning of babes will become habitual, for all moral principles in man are only relative, *if he must rely on nothing but his own strength.*' He had envisaged this, however, as the response of a society *in extremis*. Hospital incinerators kept legally busy disposing of foetuses that were socially or economically inconvenient (thus endangering maternal mental health) were beyond even his angry mid-nineteenth century imagining. (They are not invariably incinerated; press reports in 1991 referred to an alternative method of disposal, maceration and flushing down drains: *The Times*, 31 October 1991.)

Humanists remained dissatisfied with this situation, since the power to offer or withhold abortion still lay, at least nominally, with the medical profession, and crucial to the humanist demand was the underlying ethic that a woman should have the right to determine what happens to her own body, a view in direct opposition to the traditional Christian precept that we do not 'own' our bodies, which are first and foremost temples of God.* By the late twentieth century the 'woman's right' contention had at least reached the stage of excluding the putative father from any say in determining the future of his unborn child.

Science had achieved, in the abortion debate, a dominant influence in determining what morality the law should embrace. In the next advance towards more 'permissive' attitudes, it was to play an even greater role. In America in 1948 Dr (not of medicine but of biological sciences) Alfred Kinsey published his *Sexual Behavior in the Human Male*, to be followed five years later by the companion volume *Sexual Behavior in the Human Female*. These works claimed to be scientific studies of the actual facts of human sexuality, based on interviews and questionnaires with several thousand men and women, the results of which were projected as percentages applicable to the American population as a whole. Their validity as science was, over time, subjected to severe criticism, not least because the use of volunteers in a subject as delicate as sexual conduct almost certainly leads to a bias in favour of exhibitionists and of those with most activity to report and least reticence in reporting it.† Worse still from the point of view of a representative sample, present and former prison inmates constituted up to 25 per cent of the group used to assess 'normal' male sexuality, a statistic that might be expected to yield somewhat questionable results when, for instance, levels of male homosexuality were being assessed.[90] At the time of publication, however, and for long afterwards, Kinsey's statistics on the prevalence of conduct traditionally regarded as aberrant were accepted as true.

The crucial change in public attitudes, however, lay in the growing acceptance of Kinsey's contention that conduct shown (supposedly) to

---

* 'Know ye not that your body is the temple of the Holy Ghost which is in you, which ye have of God, and ye are not your own', I Corinthians 6:19.
† A particularly damning analysis of Kinsey's claims to be 'scientific' is Reisman and Eichel, *Kinsey, Sex and Fraud – The Indoctrination of a People*. Among the points overlooked at the time of the original publication of Kinsey's work was the observation that his statistics on infant sexuality can have been obtained only through extensive child sexual abuse on the part of the researchers.

be commonplace was, for that very reason, to be judged 'normal' and therefore not open to censure. Kinsey himself

> frequently concluded that outlawed sexual practices were entirely natural because they conformed to 'basic mammalian patterns' . . . [and] even sought to invest [sexual relations between humans and animals] with a certain dignity by suggesting they could achieve a psychological intensity comparable to that in exclusively human sexual relations.[91]

Kinsey's success in establishing that 'what is' is to be equated with 'what should be' was not what Bishop Barnes had in mind when he wholeheartedly accepted man's mammalian descent and with it the human task of evolving out of brute savagery, but it spawned a generous progeny of imitators keen to research mammalian sexuality in order to prove or disprove this or that sexual indulgence as 'natural'. The idea that fidelity in marriage was either possible or desirable was an early casualty. By the late 1980s the former United States Ambassador to Moscow was remarking on the impossibility of finding non-seducible US marines – married no less than single – to maintain the security of the Moscow embassy.[92] As the 'it's only natural' thesis filtered to progressively less sophisticated social classes, the predictable reactions were registered. Following a vicious gang rape of two teenage girls in Texas (whom the rapists subsequently killed), a schoolboy contemporary explained, 'It's nature. Look at the female dog and the male dog. You see 20 dogs on a female dog. It's the male nature in a way'[93] – an interesting reiteration of the posture that earned the Cynics their name in ancient Greece.[*] Thuggery, on football terraces or in street demonstrations, is justified on the same grounds.

Mammalian evolutionary example proved, on investigation, less liberating than the human imagination. Kinsey and his fellow researchers, while posing as scientists detached from any particular moral stance, in fact assumed a value system in which all forms of achieving orgasm were equally beneficial and acceptable. Sexual liberation from the restrictions imposed by religious moral codes and in particular from their embodiment in law was now followed by a crusade for genital liberation, for the pursuit of sexual gratification free from any considerations of commitment or even of transitory affection for another person. Masturbation, a hitherto furtive activity even if no longer

[*] See p.52.

419

incurring nineteenth-century comminations of hell-fire or at least incurable insanity, became respectable, and in 1961 was, for the first time, explained in Webster's dictionary. Sex shops multiplied, mail order catalogues primarily devoted to cosmetics and other beauty aids openly advertised electrically vibrated dildos (batteries not supplied), assuring women that 'to seek sexual fulfilment' is 'something every woman should be immensely proud of – regardless of whether it occurs within the intimacy of a loving relationship, or on her own'.[94] It took only fifteen minutes for a jury at Preston Crown Court in January 1994 to conclude that there was nothing indecent about selling to children such fun toys as a clockwork penis and glow-in-the-dark vibrators.[95] Activities hitherto regarded as perverted, such as anal and oral sex, mentioned prior to the 1980s neither in public nor, for large sections of the population, in private, became the common currency of commerce and comedy, with flavoured condoms replacing flavoured lipsticks as the target of adventurous consumerism. 'Agony aunts', nestling between the recipes and knitting patterns in women's magazines, elaborated on the hygienic implications of swallowing semen, and reassured women worried by their partners' predilection for copulating in the posture of bitches and dogs.

In association with widespread misunderstanding of Freud's condemnation of repression (by which he meant deep-seated self-deception rather than self-aware restraint), the climate of opinion was ripe for untrammelled promiscuity. Erstwhile pejorative terms such as 'lecher' and 'trollop' ceased to carry judgemental overtones, nymphomania and satyriasis emerged from medical textbooks and became simply alternative lifestyles.

For the increasing numbers of ill-informed youngsters liberated for active sexuality in the 1960s, pregnancy and venereal disease threatened. Alongside liberation, therefore, came urgent campaigns to extend their knowledge through more sex education in schools. Only in the late 1950s had schools begun to teach children about human sexuality. The 1963 Newsom Report on secondary education, *Half our Future*, had said that sex education should be given on the basis of 'chastity before marriage and fidelity within it'.[*][96] In the succeeding years, however,

---

[*] In August of the same year the Principal Medical Officer at the Ministry of Education had said, at a Central Council for Health Education conference for teachers, that he did not consider it immoral, though it might be unwise, for engaged couples forced by, for instance, economic reasons to postpone marriage, to sleep together. So far did this depart from current standards that a motion in Parliament called on the Minister of Education to repudiate these views. Sir Edward Boyle in reply drew a distinction between promiscuity in general, and premarital relations between engaged

teaching material began to concentrate increasingly on the explicit mechanisms of sex, with illustrations (not merely diagrams, but also photographs) not only of genitalia and the process of giving birth, but of human beings engaged in intercourse and masturbation. The transmission of one such film, Dr (not of medicine but of plant genetics) Martin Cole's *Growing Up*, on the BBC schools' programme was prevented by public opposition,[*] but this was a very temporary setback to the campaign to concentrate on biology and hygiene, and free sexuality from the deleterious 'social conditioning' of emotional or ethical overtones – 'body plumbing with a bit of . . . "Malthusian Drill" thrown in', as a later commentator was to call it.[97]

Teenage mothers, who numbered fewer than 29,000 in 1941 (some 4.3 per cent of the total), by 1971 totalled over 92,000 (10.6 per cent of the total).[†] By 1979 contraception and abortion were reducing these totals, but there were still, in that year, nearly 75,000 teenage pregnancies outside marriage, around 10,000 of the girls being under sixteen, the nominal 'age of consent' for sexual intercourse. Some 33,000 of these pregnancies were aborted, and the number of abortions was increasing, a development which a professor of obstetrics and gynaecology welcomed as a sign of increasing responsibility on the part of the young.[98] Given that pubescent youngsters, too, were sexually 'active', the Department of Health in 1974 sanctioned the prescription by general practitioners of the contraceptive pill to under-age girls. The fringe Women's Theatre Group (sustained by an Arts Council grant) spent 1974 and 1975 touring youth clubs and schools with *My Mother Says I Never Should*, enjoining fifteen-year-olds to go on the Pill in order to feel free to enjoy casual sexual intercourse.[99] A dilemma arose over those girls who did not wish their parents to know of their sexual activity, and there were some contradictory responses from the Ministry, which finally acceded to British Medical Association guidelines, with the General Medical Council threatening disciplinary action against any doctor who failed to respect the schoolgirl's right to confidentiality. This advice was challenged in the courts, the challenge succeeded on appeal in December 1984, but by the end of 1985 the House of Lords had reversed the judgement, thus definitively freeing doctors to prescribe the

---

couples (*The Times*, 2 August 1963).

[*] His efforts were not, however, wasted. The film 'was thought suitable advertising material for a Birmingham strip-tease club' (Longford Report, p.26).

[†] This did not surprise those familiar with surveys showing higher levels of unwanted pregnancy among nurses than among a comparable group of students with much less knowledge of human physiology (Longford Report, p.354).

Pill without parental knowledge to girls for whom sexual intercourse was nominally illegal. The British Medical Association had made clear its intention to press for immediate amendment of the law had doctors been prevented from so doing.

Abortions for unwed teenage expectant mothers continued to increase, however, totalling almost 44,000 by 1986 (nearly 4,000 of them for girls aged under sixteen). 'We are particularly concerned about unplanned pregnancies in the teenager, which point directly to the lack of education in schools on the importance of family planning and related matters', said a 1991 report from the Royal College of Obstetricians and Gynaecologists, calling for confidential family planning services aimed at young people, and for far more effective sex education. 'Twenty per cent of young people are sexually active by the age of 16', pointed out a member of the working party, the chairman of the Birth Control Trust.[100]

By 1991 the total of abortions for unwed teenagers had dropped to just under 32,000, still over seven times the 1969 figure, with the number of under-age abortions down to just over 3,200.[101] This improvement was in all probability the result not of any sort of return to chastity but of more intensive use of contraceptives. In 1989 contraceptive vending machines, the public accessibility of which had so distressed Parliament in 1949, began to be installed in schools. Initially Conservative local councillors objected, but by 1993, with the British teenage pregnancy rate the highest in Europe, a junior health minister was supporting the issue of free condoms to school sixth forms provided the governors and parent-teacher organizations agreed.[102] By 1994, with over 8,000 under-age girls still becoming pregnant annually, the Department of Health proposed the general sale of 'morning-after' abortifacient pills through pharmacies, while the Royal College of Obstetricians and Gynaecologists called a conference on whether the abortifacient pill should be made available in supermarkets, all-night garages and vending machines. The pill 'is only as good as its availability', a spokesman pointed out.[103] In Manchester, in 'an attempt to reduce the number of teenage pregnancies', a young people's centre funded by the local health authority began issuing teenagers (including an eleven-year-old; 'age does not matter. Some children are mature for their age') with flavoured condoms and advice on oral sex.[104]

By 1990 a manual of sex instruction for primary schools, *Knowing Me, Knowing You*, advised teachers on how to instruct five- to eleven-year-olds on contraception, sexual positions during intercourse, masturbation, homosexuality and VD, the authors claiming that there were 'much lower rates of abortion and sexually transmitted diseases among the young in those countries where sex education is properly taught'.[105] Within three years, however, the Family Planning Association, still concerned that inadequate sex education was a significant cause of unplanned pregnancies among teenagers, were calling for sex education to start with the four-year-olds, in a comprehensive curriculum which, for the older primary school children, would include VD and homosexuality, and discussions of what constituted orgasm.* [106]

Teenage same-sex crushes had long been tacitly accepted, particularly in single-sex schools, provided the passions unleashed activated no overt sexual behaviour. Teenage homosexuality was a condition out of which people were expected to mature in good time. Its presentation as an acceptable permanent alternative lifestyle became possible only after adult homosexuality ceased to be a criminal offence.

English law had always been severe in its attitude to homosexuality, with medieval penalties including burial alive and death by burning, though Norman St John Stevas, in his *Law and Morals*, suspects that in the days when it was an offence punishable in the ecclesiastical, rather than the civil, courts, spiritual punishments such as excommunication were more probably imposed. For three hundred years, after Henry VIII transferred jurisdiction to the common law courts, the death penalty was occasionally exacted, until in 1861 a sentence of ten years' penal servitude was substituted. Sharpe's survey of seventeenth-century Essex concluded that 'however common in London and court circles', homosexuality 'was not a widespread phenomenon in rural Essex' – indeed, there was only one indictment in the sixty years 1620–80.[107] McLynn, in his survey of the eighteenth century, notes that homosexuality was a familiar aspect of the London scene, and that indictments, though rare, usually resulted, on conviction, in the death penalty. Unproven suspects were put in the pillory, and McLynn cites a number of incidents in which death was only prevented when local magistrates organized the rescue of the condemned man from mob violence.[108] In 1885 the Criminal Law Amendment Act introduced a maximum sentence of two years, with or without hard labour. In 1954 a committee, under the chairmanship of Sir John Wolfenden, recommended that private homosexual acts between two consenting adults (group orgies

---

* Whatever other effects may have stemmed from this dissemination of facts, it certainly equipped children with a battery of information on which to ground accusations of sexual abuse, and by 1994 the National Association of Schoolmasters/Union of Women Teachers were complaining of the increasing levels of false accusations being directed against teachers towards whom streetwise children harboured a grudge, accusations which, even when unsubstantiated, could result in many months of suspension and anxiety (*The Times*, 13 January 1994).

were not envisaged) no longer be criminal offences. A Bill to this effect was introduced in the House of Commons in 1960, but failed to secure adequate support. However, in 1967 a further legislative attempt (the Sexual Offences Act) was successful, and adult homosexual practices between consenting males* in private were, for the first time in British history, decriminalized.

Kinsey's assertion that 10 per cent of American males were 'more or less' exclusively homosexual and 37 per cent involved in homosexual contacts at some stage between the ages of 16 and 55 was influential in moulding opinion,† again on the precept that what can be shown to be widespread is therefore acceptable. Science, in the guise of statistics, overrode traditional moral precepts, which were held to stem from defective scientific knowledge. Some traditionalists sought a compromise by postulating a psychological distinction between perverts, who chose to be homosexual, and inverts, who couldn't help it, but this line of reasoning had a short currency as the rights of individuals to pursue their perceived sexual orientation, whatever its derivation, came to be accepted. Campaigns then switched to demands for homosexual marriage to be recognized, and, pending such recognition, for overseas partners to be allowed settlement rights in Britain, and for rights of tenancy succession such as were accorded to cohabitees.[109] Other areas of discrimination such as the higher age of consent (21 for homosexual relationships, 16 for heterosexual), restrictions on service in the armed forces and obstacles placed in the way of adoption by homosexual couples remained focal points for resentment and campaigning pressure, which by the 1990s had achieved some partial successes, such as the decriminalization (though not immunity from dismissal) of homosexuals in the armed forces, and a limited acceptance of homosexual adoption. The realization that a section of the community substantially without responsibility for child-rearing had large amounts of disposable income ('the pink pound') encouraged the development of commercial

---

* Female homosexuality had never been a criminal offence, largely because most people did not believe such a condition existed.

† Projected figures for AIDS victims in the USA were predicated on the basis of Kinsey's 10 per cent estimate of homosexuals. When they failed to materialize, credit was given to the success of safe sex propaganda. However, a survey in 1993, 'the most thorough carried out in the United States since the famous Kinsey report of 1948', found that only 1.1 per cent of American males considered themselves exclusively homosexual, and only 2.3 per cent of men aged 20 to 39 admitted to a homosexual experience in the previous ten years (*The Times*, 16 and 17 April 1993). Reisman and Eichel (pp.178ff.) consider that Kinsey's insistence on amalgamating transitory teenage experimentation with mature experience may, together with his use of male prostitutes and prisoners for 25 per cent of his sample, account for the distortions of his results.

enterprises geared to homosexual needs and interests, such as special sections in book shops and targeted holiday and leisure pursuits.* [110] The conjunction of the pink pound and the age-old concentration of homosexuals in the theatre was producing, by 1994, such a large number of plays with homosexual themes and characters that critics began to carp, one even remarking that 'there is a real possibility now that contemporary drama will be perceived as a no-go area for straight people . . . the serious theatre seems perilously close to becoming a ghetto'. [111]

The Roman Catholic hierarchy remained opposed to homosexuality, but the Protestant churches began to waver. In October 1987, following a controversial resolution passed by the General Synod to the effect that homosexual acts fell short of the Christian ideal and demanded repentance, the Anglican Church set up a working party 'to review thinking about the nature and practice of homosexuality and lesbianism . . . [and] . . . to consider the method and content of Christian theology and ethics as they relate to these issues . . .' [112] The resultant report was not published, but a leaked version reputedly advocated greater understanding of sexually active homosexual practice, called for the blessing of homosexual 'marriages', and coyly affirmed its belief in 'the value and the richness of same-sex friendships', calling on the Church to consider ways in which support and structures could be provided to enable 'friendships' to flourish. Where homosexuals were not 'living in committed relationships', it was proposed that 'the experience of gay Christians learning to live their Christian lives in a variety of different ways needs to be heard'. [113]

In America in 1989 the Anglican Bishop Spong ordained a professed homosexual in the 'fervent hope', according to the *Church Times*, 'that his life could offer to the homosexual population of our metropolitan area a model of holiness, fidelity and monogamy with which we could counter promiscuity and other forms of predatory or casual sexual behaviour'. [114] By February 1990, after the new priest had given it as his opinion that 'monogamy was basically a crazy idea . . . just as unnatural as celibacy', and that 'Mother Theresa would be better off if she got laid', his resignation was requested. [115] In Britain, notwithstanding a survey claiming that 15 per cent of those Anglican clergy who responded were 'gay', [116] episcopal opinion, as expressed in 1991 in the Church of

---

* An interesting example of the influence of the homosexual dollar occurred in the United States in 1992, when Levi Strauss, whose jeans were reputedly the preferred wear of three out of four homosexuals, withdrew their subvention to the Boy Scouts of America in protest at their continuing exclusion of homosexuals and atheists from their movement (*The Times*, 10 June 1992).

England's *Issues in Human Sexuality*, though sympathetic, remained unresponsive, and was castigated for not recognizing that once it had been accepted that sexual relations could be 'relational' as well as 'generative', a stance now adopted by all but strict Roman Catholics, there could be no logical objection to active homosexuality.[117] A proposed homosexual liturgy drew from the Archbishop of Canterbury the warning to the publishers, SPCK, that its divergencies from the bishops' report were too numerous and significant for him to continue his patronage of the publishing house if it persisted with its plans, which it did not, leaving the liturgy to be published elsewhere, and drawing down upon itself threats from a number of authors to boycott the company in future.[118] Methodists, confronted by the same dilemma, were deeply divided, but in the summer of 1990 the Methodist Conference concluded that 'no-one should be excluded from ordained ministry simply on the ground of their sexuality', leaving the individual decisions to be taken by 'those appointed to make such a judgement', a conclusion that provoked a dissenting campaign by the start of 1992.[119] Judaism, too, was riven with division on the issue, Reform Judaism in the USA determining, in the summer of 1990, to break with 4,000 years of teaching and accept homosexuals for ordination, while the Orthodox maintained the traditional stance.[120]

The United Church of Canada ordained its first openly homosexual priest in May 1992,[121] and shortly thereafter a female homosexual minister was appointed by the Presbyterian Church in New York State, notwithstanding that the Church's General Assembly had in 1978 declared homosexuality 'incompatible with Christian faith and life'.[122]

American Roman Catholics, despite the unswerving adherence of the Vatican to pre-sensate moral norms, have largely accepted Enlightenment values. Surveys in 1986 showed that more than a third of US Catholics favoured legal abortion, and that a majority believed people should be allowed to divorce and remarry, use contraceptives and engage in pre-marital sexual intercourse. About half were in favour of legalizing homosexual relations.[123] By 1987 the menace of AIDS had persuaded the American bishops to condone the use of condoms, a concession subsequently withdrawn in the face of conservative protests, but it was not thought that many of the flock paid any attention to traditional teaching.[124] By the time the Pope visited the United States in 1993, 'survey after survey suggests a deepening, expanding rift between America's Catholics and the Vatican', including almost 90 per cent of American Roman Catholics reputedly in favour of abortion. Church liberals were insisting that 'although the Pope will find admiring throngs in Denver, his popularity will end when his preachings begin'.[125]

As in previous history, a climate of permissiveness encouraged the spread of sexually transmitted diseases (STDs). At the end of World War II cases of VD had, after a considerable surge in the first two years of the war, declined to a level below that pertaining immediately before the war. In 1949 new notifications of STDs in England and Wales totalled about 111,000, and ten years later, in 1959, had reached only just over 112,000. Ten years after that, at the end of the 1960s, the figure for England alone stood at 221,000. Within this figure, syphilis among teenagers increased from 116 in 1964 to 188 by 1977, gonorrhoea from 4,564 in 1964 to 12,377 by 1977. Since the middle 1980s, total new cases of syphilis and gonorrhoea have declined markedly. Separate figures for teenagers have not been published since 1987, at which time they, too, were declining, though still some 30 per cent above the 1964 level. Other sexually transmitted diseases, however, continue to increase in prevalence. A peak of over 647,000 in 1986 was followed by a brief decline in 1987, only the second year since 1956 when there had been a decrease,* but the improvement was not sustained, and by 1990 the Department of Health was reporting that 'the reassuring downward trend in sexually transmitted diseases in the mid 1980s was . . . not maintained in 1989'.[126] By 1992 the previous peak had been passed, and by 1993 the total had reached 661,261.[127]

As had happened at similar cultural periods in Rome and in the Middle Ages,† a new, deadly and incurable sexually transmitted menace made itself known: in this case AIDS, the auto-immune deficiency syndrome, attitudes to which were to mirror the panic and the assumptions of divine retribution that had accompanied the great syphilis pandemic of the late fifteenth and the sixteenth centuries. There was even a replication, from the World Health Organization, of Tiberius's edict against kissing.[128] First diagnosed among homosexual males in the early 1980s, the disease cut a swathe, particularly through highly articulate and visible media and entertainment circles. Death rates are only a fraction of those suffered, for instance, by women with breast, ovarian and cervical cancer,‡ but

---

* The other year registering a decrease was 1962.
† See Chapters 9 and 13.
‡ The average *annual* number of deaths from breast cancer is approximately 14,000; from ovarian cancer, 4,000; and from cervical cancer, 2,000 (OPCS *Cancer Statistics Registrations*, London, HMSO). The total number of deaths from AIDS in the United Kingdom in the entire period 1982 (or earlier) to the end of June 1995 was some 7,570, with about 3,500 further cases confirmed. At that time there were known to be about 24,500 additional cases of HIV infection (at risk, in current medical belief, of developing AIDS), of whom approximately 15,000 were homosexual or

the fact that the disease poses a challenge to 'the permissive society' at the point of most direct confrontation with previous religious-based moral standards, namely sexual conduct, makes it an emotionally highly charged issue.

Within a quarter-century of World War II, British mores had thus undergone a profound change. The extent to which the change could be mirrored in the theatre was, however, limited. The year 1968 witnessed the culmination of another long-fought battle for free expression. On 26 September 1968 the Theatres Act became law, and the Lord Chamberlain's office was, after over 400 years, deprived of all powers of theatrical censorship.

bisexual men; 4,300 (2,300 of them women) infected by heterosexual intercourse; 2,700 injecting drug users; 1,300 infected by blood products; about 300 by mother-to-infant transmission; and the remainder of unknown exposure (*AIDS/HIV Quarterly Surveillance Tables*, Public Health Laboratory Service AIDS Centre, London).

Chapter 20

Art for Art's Sake

By the 1920s the excessive sensitivity of the Lord Chamberlain's office which had so exasperated the playwrights of the early years of the century had, at least so far as themes were concerned, largely disappeared. One after another, the plays that had caused so much earlier disquiet received licences for performance to the general public. Brieux's 1902 *Damaged Goods* was unbanned in Britain as early as 1914, thanks to wartime anxiety about its subject matter, VD, and Ibsen's *Ghosts* was liberated for similar reasons; Shaw's *Mrs Warren's Profession* in its full, unmutilated version, finally achieved public performance in 1925; *The Cenci* was licensed in 1922, but Oscar Wilde's *Salome*, also touching upon incest (in its wider definition – Herod's interest in his stepdaughter), remained banned until 1929, partly because of its representation of Scriptural characters.[1] Noel Coward's *The Vortex*, dealing with drug-taking, disgusted George V, who nevertheless recognized that it was not possible to prohibit it;[2] and a play about teenage delinquency and syphilis, *Pick-up Girl*, was approved for transfer to the West End in 1946 partly because among those who attended its performances at the New Lindsay Club was the august figure of Queen Mary.[3]

Findlater states that plays were censored for being unfriendly to the Fascist governments of Germany and Italy, overfriendly towards the Soviet Union, but the examples he gives fall mainly under the heading of protecting living or recently dead public figures.[4] Robertson in *Obscenity*, dealing with a later period, also refers to political censorship, remarking that it was of little impediment to the (politically bland) commercial theatre, but the subsidized theatre, specifically the Royal Shakespeare Company, free to transcend the market, chafed under the restrictions on its anti-American stance[5] – though they were still able to stage such virulent criticisms of contemporary American policy as *US*. The old left-wing Unity Theatre had club protection, though this was only provisional in that it was always open to the censor to intervene; but Chambers's 1989 retrospective survey suggests that in the thirties the censor was more anxious to change 'lavatory' to 'bathroom' and 'lavatory paper' to 'shaving paper' than to censor exhortations on behalf of the anarchists, concern himself over rollicking satire of Conservative politicians, or interfere with the consistently anti-American tone of the theatre's postwar productions.[6]

Already after World War I, according to Findlater, 'the censor appeared to recognize the growing force of disillusionment with official Christianity created by the war'; in the 1960s he licensed two virulent attacks on Christianity, both containing crucifixion tableaux, Peter Shaffer's *The Royal Hunt of the Sun* (closely mirroring Artaud's unproduced *The Conquest of Mexico*) and John Osborne's *A Bond Honoured*, a translation of a seventeenth-century Spanish play extolling brother-sister incest.[7] The use of 'Christ!' or 'Jesus!' as expletives remained banned, and stage representations of God, Christ and the Virgin Mary continued to be prohibited, though revivals of miracle plays* (themselves, of course, from a late stage in the culture of medieval Christendom) made the prohibition increasingly difficult to defend.[8]

Foul language, too, followed a course of gradual liberalization. 'Bloody' was not heard on stage from 1912, when its use in *Pygmalion* caused appropriate shock, until 1936 (in *Red Peppers*). By 1956 *Billy Liar* was getting away with 249.[9] It meant, of course, that the word ceased to have any shock effect, and the 1956 musical version of *Pygmalion*, *My Fair Lady*, had some difficulty in producing an equivalent audience response by using the word 'arse'. Such words as shit, turd, fuck, tits and bugger, having in common only that they were not in everyday polite usage, retained their potential to shock thanks to the censor's persistent excisions.

Some sexually troubling themes – impotence was one – failed to gain acceptance, but *Breach of Marriage* in 1949, dealing with artificial insemination, and in 1959 *Aunt Edwina*, about a sex-change, were approved by the censor, though the latter play provoked criticism from the public.[10] Homosexuality, male or female, was not an issue until the 1950s, since such themes were not being submitted (even words such as 'queer', 'camp' and 'fairy' were banned), but in that decade a number of foreign imports, including Lillian Hellman's *Children's Hour*, Sartre's *Vicious Circle*, Arthur Miller's *A View from the Bridge*, Robert

---

* The York Cycle was staged in York in 1951.

Anderson's *Tea and Sympathy* and Tennessee Williams's *Cat on a Hot Tin Roof*, arrived. The New Watergate Theatre Club, already in dormant existence, was re-activated to stage such banned plays, and in October 1956 took over the Comedy Theatre as a 'club' venue for their performance, soon achieving a membership of some 68,000.[11] In 1958 the Lord Chamberlain let it be known that homosexual themes would be considered, provided they were not proselytizing, physically explicit or campaigning for a change in the law (a liberalization for which Findlater gives the Watergate's pioneering much of the credit), and under this new dispensation plays such as *Ross*, *A Taste of Honey* and *The Killing of Sister George* were accepted for public performance.[12] John Osborne's *A Patriot for Me* was considered (in 1965) too explicit to be granted a licence, so the Royal Court Theatre was turned into a private theatre club for its staging. Edward Bond's *Early Morning*, which portrayed Queen Victoria and Florence Nightingale as homosexual lovers and toyed with cannibalism in its denouement, received an outright ban. The Royal Court staged it, but cancelled performances after the first night, which was attended by members of the Vice Squad who made appropriate representations to the management.[*][13] Inventive producers were finding ways of getting round the prohibition on explicit stage homosexuality by imaginative staging of, if not classic plays, at least classic authors. Tyrone Guthrie's Old Vic production of Shakespeare's *Troilus and Cressida* in 1956 introduced an Achilles and Patroclus who hugged and kissed one another.

There still remained bans on sexual innuendo; stage representations of individuals, particularly those in public life, if living or recently dead;[†] attacks on the Crown and royal family; depictions of violent or sexual activities deemed offensive; and nudity, where, under provisions agreed in 1930, static nudes were permitted, but mobility required a minimum of briefs and bra.[14] Sexual offensiveness included references to anal and oral sex; and copulatory or masturbatory gestures, though the uncensored ballet was by now aping its imperial Roman progenitors by miming such activities.[15]

None of this prevented the theatrical 'revolution' initiated by John Osborne's *Look Back in Anger* at the Royal Court in 1956, a play which, by bringing working-class attitudes and values centre-stage, extended the nineteenth-century exploration of naturalism/realism which had, for several decades, been languishing in class-bound triviality. This

---

[*] It was promptly staged, in 1969, after the ending of theatre censorship.

[†] If a member of the family objected, the censor was expected to forbid portrayal of a family member for up to three generations (Findlater, pp.160–1).

exemplified the drive, in sensate society, to pay increasing artistic attention to, in Sorokin's words, 'the poor, the disenfranchised and the unfortunate'. Nor did the Lord Chamberlain's office much impede the further extension of this drive, the 'increasing fashion to choose the hero or the heroine from somewhat abnormal, pathological, and defective types or criminal groups' (a 'gravitation toward the "social sewer" ', Sorokin called it).[16] *The Beggar's Opera* had briefly challenged conventional society in the eighteenth century, but nineteenth-century melodrama had represented its criminal characters as villainous – and doomed. Now they were to figure as sympathetic principals, as in the ex-convict Frank Norman's *Fings Ain't Wot They Used to Be*, with its cast of prostitutes, ponces, small-time thieves, and razor gangs.[17] The show was accused of being sordid, but it was not banished to club status. The hit musical *Oliver!* rewrote Dickens's searing condemnation of prostitution and child abuse as a romp among lovable rogues, falsifying the brutality and sadism of the original, and omitting the desperate nemesis which the book meted out to Fagin and the Artful Dodger.[18]

Texts dating from before the 1843 Theatres Act were not subject to licensing. The Lord Chamberlain's office might still be apprised of offensive staging, but the revival of old plays, even their elevation to 'classic' status, offers an insight into the way theatrical values were evolving. The saucy, cynical, immoral Restoration comedies that had been virtually unperformed for over a century and a half were being resurrected by the end of the 1940s, both Vanbrugh's *The Relapse* and Congreve's *The Way of the World** receiving commercial productions in 1948. Wycherley's *The Country Wife*, of which Findlater perhaps unguardedly wrote in 1967, 'perhaps even now no writer would dare base a comedy on the central situation ... a man who pretends impotence, through syphilis, as a way of bedding other people's wives in perfect security',[19] was revived by the Royal Court's English Stage Society in 1956, and was to receive many subsequent revivals, though by the time it was performed at Chichester in September 1969 Hugh Leonard, reviewing for *Plays and Players*, was to conclude that it 'has at last ceased to shock; its morals are too close to our own'.[20] Its 1993 revival by the RSC earned from the critic of *The Times* the description of 'a dark, even an ugly play', in which 'for the men, the women are mostly sexual pickings, to be treacherously won, quickly enjoyed, then

---

* Nigel Playfair had given this play a rare 'inspired production' at the Lyric, Hammersmith, in 1924 (*Annual Register*, 1948).

callously disposed of. The women are as greedy, though they camou-
flage their promiscuity with cant about "honour" ',[21] an assessment
which may have encouraged the producers of the 1993 musical version,
launched under the somewhat unimaginative title *Lust*. Meanwhile, a
succession of the plays by Vanbrugh, Congreve, Dryden and Wycherley,
so castigated by the moralists of the late seventeenth and early
eighteenth centuries, were staged to plaudits (under such press headings
as 'Casual Depravity') for their coruscating wit and accomplished
playing.[22] The Restoration playwright, George Farquhar, enjoyed a
sudden renewal of fame/notoriety with the revival, in 1963 at the
National Theatre,[*] of *The Recruiting Officer*, whose principal character, Sergeant Kite, was later described by Max Stafford Clark (artistic
director of the Royal Court Theatre, who ranked Farquhar third behind
Shakespeare and Chekhov) as 'a devastatingly accurate picture of a
psychopath brutalized by a life that has left him with little choice but to
join the army'.[23]

The theatrical exploration of violence now adopted the device that
was proving so successful in the sexual sphere – the staging of 'classics'
that public taste had long refused to countenance. In 1955 came Peter
Brook's landmark *Titus Andronicus* at Stratford, with Laurence Olivier
in the title role.

Robert Atkins had in 1923 presented a few performances at the Old
Vic, during celebrations of the three hundredth anniversary of Shakespeare's First Folio. 'They told us that two or three people had been
carried out fainting and I could well believe it', wrote one of that
production's 'walk-on' performers. The Stratford governors contemplated a performance in 1929, but took fright. Critical opinion was still
strongly against the play: 'One of the stupidest and most uninspiring
plays ever written, a play in which it is incredible that Shakespeare had
any hand at all . . .' as T.S. Eliot remarked.[24] In 1953 the play received
two airings, one on the Third Programme, one in an amateur production
by the Cambridge Marlowe Society.

Then came the Stratford production of the play which, as one critic
remarked, 'delighted the Elizabethans and had very understandably been
neglected by their successors'.[25] Nightly people were carried fainting
from the auditorium.[26] But twentieth-century audiences had stronger
stomachs than their Victorian predecessors. 'Curtain fall that August
evening brought the longest, loudest cheer in Stratford memory', wrote

---

[*] A National Theatre Company had been assembled in 1962 using the Old Vic Theatre pending
the construction of its own building on the South Bank.

Trewin. 'One heard people, normally decorous, shouting at the pitch of their voices, hardly knowing that they did so and denying it afterwards; a critic said it could have been the scene at a Cup Final.'[27] Audiences were soon acclimatized to the horrors portrayed. *Titus Andronicus* became a stock production, repeated the following year by the National at the Old Vic, revived by the RSC in 1972 and again in 1981 and 1987, a production which moved to London in 1988 ('one particularly ghoulish moment has blood spurting from slit throats into a bowl held between the stumps of a handless girl').[28] Desensitization had, however, set in; there are no more accounts of audiences fainting. Indeed, 'once Shakespeare's least-loved play, *Titus* has become, in an age inured to horror, something of a cult object: tickets ... are apparently at a premium' was the comment greeting the 1988 production.[29]

Just as the seventeenth century had rewritten Shakespeare to heighten ghoulishness, and the eighteenth for sauciness and sentimentality, so now the twentieth expressed itself by manipulations designed to enhance the sensationalism of cruelty and horror. In 1962, Brook had directed *Lear* at Stratford, describing it as an 'epic unfolding of the nature of the absurdity of the human condition'. In Brook's *Lear*, the lure of Cruelty and the despair of Absurdity were wed. Edgar is hunted like an animal, his almost naked body smeared with mud.[30] Gloucester is not only blinded, but as he tries to stagger away he is buffeted by servants enjoying his plight – Shakespeare's original lines of compassion from the servants being excised.[31] Kitchin has drawn attention to the cutting of texts to heighten callousness, to the introduction, in the RSC's *The Wars of the Roses*, of extra cruelties.[32] The thrust has not diminished over the years. Viewers familiar with the text may have noticed, in Kenneth Branagh's filmed *Henry V*, that the hanging of Bardolph has been brought from its Shakespearian off-stage occurrence into full view of the camera; and when, in 1991, the RSC staged a *Julius Caesar*, one critic noted: 'The attack on Cinna the Poet is a horribly prolonged piece of killer-hooliganism, though it is still rather shorter than the assassination of ... Caesar, who terrifies his murderers by displaying Rasputin-like indestructibility.'[33] Marlowe, too, was to contribute his not inconsiderable mite, with an RSC production of *The Jew of Malta* (a play of 'fast-footed callousness')[34] at the Barbican in 1988, and, in 1993, *Tamburlaine the Great* ('a relish in the violence, an unashamed sensuality in the savagery').[35]

The long-unexplored Jacobean playwrights'[*] penchant for incest

---

[*] 'Heirs,' as one critic called them, 'of Shakespeare's language but not of his humanity' (Michael

and revenge provided another rich furrow to plough. A *Duchess of Malfi* had starred Peggy Ashcroft in 1945. The Duchess was resurrected by the RSC in 1960, again in 1971, in which year the Royal Court also staged it, and further productions have followed. Its author's *The White Devils* resurfaced in the repertory of the National Theatre in 1969, as did, in 1982, Kyd's *The Spanish Tragedy*. 'There is something positively rich in the malignancy of the work,' wrote one reviewer of the former, 'a relish for stage ketchup that is almost seductive.'[36] Directors were even more drawn to Tourneur's *The Revenger's Tragedy*, the play which, with its unmitigated ferocity, had so appealed to Artaud. The RSC staged it in 1966 and 1967 at Stratford before bringing it to London in 1969, and revived it in 1987 (at which time a critic made special reference to the magnificent playing of the lead character as a psychopath).[37] Middleton's pitiless *The Changeling* had a considerable vogue in the eighties and early nineties, playing at the Cambridge Arts Theatre, at the National and at the RSC, as well as receiving an experimental Chinese setting in the commercial theatre. Ford's *'Tis Pity She's a Whore*, a tale of smouldering incestuous passion, was revived in Glasgow in 1988, set a fashion, was staged in Liverpool in 1990 where it provoked the comment, 'a singularly nasty play, both morally and dramatically', and the reflection that 'if this sort of melodrama was drawing the crowds [in 1633 when this work was written], perhaps it was high time the theatres were closed down';[38] and by 1991 had entered the RSC's repertoire, where a year later the critical view was that 'Ford's dark vision can seldom have seemed more contemporary . . . We feel uncomfortably close to a world in which beliefs have evaporated and moral ties loosened . . .'[39]

'Acknowledge what thou art, a wretch, a worm, a nothing', warns an early couplet in *'Tis Pity She's a Whore*. This was the message of the twentieth-century Absurdists. Their violence and sexual convolutions had come to London during the latter 1950s, mostly in club performances, for as modern plays they were often too offensive to receive licences from the Lord Chamberlain, and even club performances were circumspect.* Genet's *The Balcony*, for instance, first performed in London in 1956, was restaged considerably more explicitly in 1971, after the abolition of censorship.[40] In 1958 Artaud's manifesto and expository

Schmidt, *Daily Telegraph*, 10 February 1990).
* In Paris the Théatre du Grand Guignol, which had catered, according to the *Oxford Companion to the Theatre*, for an oversophisticated and decadent taste, specializing in 'short plays of violence, murder, rape, ghostly apparitions and suicide all intended to chill and delight the spectator', closed down in 1964, pre-empted by the competition (Kitchin, p.22).

letters were translated into English.[41] Peter Brook was among those most deeply influenced, both by Artaud and by European developments of his implications, for instance the Polish director Jerzy Grotowski's elaboration of cruelty in *The Constant Prince*, in which a flagellation was enacted with a verisimilitude that enabled the audience to see the victim's 'body bouncing and his back going red'.[42] In 1964 Brook (who was to become a supporter of CAST as it strove to transcend the confines of the Unity Theatre[43]) formed a special company for a 'Theatre of Cruelty' season at the Donmar theatre club in London, which included work by Genet (from *The Screens*), Artaud's *Le Jet de Sang*; and *The Persecution and Assassination of Marat as Performed by the Inmates of the Asylum of Clarenton under the direction of the Marquis de Sade*, or *Marat/Sade* for short, by the Marxist/Jewish writer Peter Weiss, which the Royal Shakespeare Company took to the Aldwych.[*][44]

'Violence is the natural artistic language of the times . . .' Brook had said.[45] By March 1968 he was producing Seneca's *Oedipus*, hitherto thought unactable. New York had pointed the way, inserting some of Seneca's more gruesome passages from his *Medea* into a production of the Euripides version of the same story.[†] Brook used Seneca's text, with Irene Worth miming her own on-stage impaling on a golden spike.[46] The RSC's 1988 production of *Oedipus* also used a translation of Seneca, not of the Greeks.

New writing suffused by violence usually sheltered in club performances, as was the case with Fred Watson's *Infanticide in the House of Fred Ginger*, and David Rudkin's *Afore Night Come*, in which an elderly labourer is done to death with a pitchfork and a bloody cross scored on his chest; a severed head subsequently rolls into sight.[47] Club protection was not absolute. Edward Bond's *Saved* at the Royal Court included a scene in which an illegitimate baby had its face smeared with its own excrement and was then stoned to death by a group of yobbos including the baby's father. The censor demanded cuts to which the author refused to accede. In 1965 the play was performed under club conditions, provoking execration from some critics and admiration from others, who saw in it a parable of modern Britain. 'There comes a point,' wrote the critic of the *Sunday Times*, 'when both life and art are irretrievably

---

[*] Lumley reports that prior to the London performance, Weiss announced that Marat, who symbolizes revolution, must be shown to win the debate with de Sade, who stands for individualism (Lumley, pp.249ff.).

[†] The production was by the Morningside Players of Columbia University, with a Broadway actress playing Medea. It is mentioned in Bieber's 1961 version of *The History of the Greek and Roman Theatre*, p.234, though not in the 1939 edition, but the exact date is not given.

debased, and Edward Bond's play, in this production, is well past that point', but it was Findlater who spoke for the future: 'Far from representing The End, it was just the beginning.'[48] This time the censor, who had received many complaints, refused to wink at club audacity, and a court case in 1966 found the English Stage Society, the theatre licensee and the director guilty. The punishment was minimal – they were all given conditional discharges, and required to pay a total of 50 guineas costs. But the principle involved strengthened the resolve of playwrights intent on abolishing all theatrical censorship.[49]

The Lord Chamberlain's task was indeed becoming increasingly anachronistic. Public opinion was moving rapidly, an evolution which Perrin, in *Dr Bowdler's Legacy*, ascribes largely to the spread of the Freudian idea that bowdlerism was not only ludicrous, it was psychologically damaging. From about the turn of the century, expensive full editions of hitherto expurgated late-eighteenth-century works began to appear (cheaper editions remained purged); in 1950 the United States pioneered a facsimile edition of Rochester's 1680 poems, though the English edition of 1971 still omitted three of them. Smollett's self-censored *Peregrine Pickle* was given a full, though restricted, edition in 1930, a general edition in 1964.[50]

The legal definition of obscenity stemmed from a court case brought in 1868 under the 1857 Obscene Publications Act, which, without defining obscenity, permitted the seizure and destruction of obscene material. The judgement in 1868 referred to obscene material as that which had 'a tendency to deprave and corrupt those whose minds are open to such immoral influences', some confusion prevailing as to whether material found shocking and disgusting was *ipso facto* obscene. A response of shock and disgust implied that the consumer, however sullied he or she might feel, was at any rate *not* being depraved and corrupted; but a delighted response from a targeted readership suggested that the corruption had already occurred, so it was too late to worry about the recipients' state of mind. Neither juries, nor most witnesses, wanted to confess to being depraved or corrupted by the material put in front of them, but so long as juries were drawn from a restricted section of the population, it was always possible to argue that a less privileged section of the populace might be more vulnerable. After the abolition, in 1972, of the property qualification for jurors, this approach lost its cogency.

Nevertheless, unsatisfactory though it is universally recognized to be, the 'deprave and corrupt' formula was given statutory form in the 1959 Obscene Publications Act. Prior to the 1959 Act, much of the material judged obscene had been on homosexual themes, a topic which was now becoming acceptable (Radcliffe Hall's *Well of Loneliness*, for instance, banned in 1928, was a BBC choice for Book at Bedtime by 1974).[*][51] Sexual explicitness and variations thereof were the issues on which most post-1959 trials hinged, with endless confusion as to the distinction and/ or acceptability of soft porn, hard porn, or the merely erotic, and uncertainty as to whether all material that aroused sexual fantasies and led to masturbation was therefore to be condemned. The conclusions reached by different juries at different times and in different parts of the country made it impossible for prosecutions to assume any consistency of outcome. Some guidance did emanate from a jury at Portsmouth Crown Court in September 1975, who concluded, in relation to a selection of magazines and films, that explicit portrayals of sex between men and women, including group sex, and depictions of homosexuality were acceptable, but they drew the line at bestiality, incest, sado-masochism and necrophilia.[52]

The 1959 Act was intended as a liberalizing measure, because it exempted from the provisions of the Act works of scientific, artistic or literary merit, or works serving the public good; a provision logically inconsistent with the Act's supposed intention of protecting the community from harm, since if literature (or any other art) could do harm, the very brilliance of the work might enhance its capacity to deprave. Juries were not expected to identify these categories unaided, and as, in the post-1959 dispensation, trial succeeded trial, a peripatetic posse of experts was assembled by lawyers specializing in defence in obscenity trials.

With the increasing proclivity of sensate culture to evaluate art ('art for art's sake') by the extent of its author's imaginative creativity and ability to communicate emotions, regardless of content,[†] there were no grounds for excluding from the canon of literary excellence exempt from the Act the work of a talented psychopath (such as de Sade).

---

[*] *Book at Bedtime* became something of a litmus paper for the extent to which hitherto banned books were adjudged acceptable. *Lady Chatterley's Lover* ('almost uncut') was the selection that opened 1990, and James Joyce's *Ulysses*, 'complete with the sort of strong sexual expletives condemned by the Broadcasting Standards Council', featured in July 1991 (*The Times*, 9 September 1989 and 18 July 1991). In October 1995 the BBC added a later-night reading of 'a more modern, urban, racy, nervous and ironic voice in fiction', works that might be 'too extreme for the tastes of its traditional listeners', but denied that it was a Dirty Book at Bedtime, only including explicit sex scenes and bad language if they could be justified in the context of the work (*The Times*, 2 August 1995).

[†] An example is the critic David Robinson's comment on Peter Greenaway's work as a film-maker: 'Even when his narratives exploit killing, sexual violence, blood, putrefaction and scatology, they are staged in decors and images of painstakingly calculated beauty' (*The Times*, 24 January 1994).

Scientific expertise once more replaced moral intuition as the criterion on which judgements were to be based. At trial after trial expert witnesses drawn from various specialist disciplines testified that pornography could not be proven to be in any way harmful, either to individuals or to society. Indeed, in 1972 for the first time the argument was advanced that pornography was positively therapeutic and thus for the public good. It might disgust; but aversion therapy was all to the good surely?[*] Its depictions of oral and anal sex as normal would help practitioners to overcome any residual guilty feelings that might be troubling them in this respect; and the liberation of obsessive sexual fantasies and the masturbation induced by the consumption of pornography, far from being a source of depravity and corruption, would, it was argued, purge the consumer and be a substitute for the acting out of such fantasies in real life.[† 53] A similar argument was not advanced with respect to pornography depicting anti-Semitic or racist atrocities, nor for pornography involving child sexual abuse, perhaps because in these cases the educated consensus regarded the material as corrupt in itself, regardless of potential effect – whether cathartic or inflammatory.[‡]

---

[*] In his book *Obscenity* (p.20) Geoffrey Robertson recounts Pepys's aversive encounter with pornography. 'On 13 January 1668 "homeward by coach and stopped at Martin's, my bookseller, where I saw the French book which I did think to have had for my wife to translate, called *l'escholle des filles*, but when I came to look in it, it is the most bawdy lewd book that ever I saw, rather worse than *La Puttana errante*, so that I was ashamed of reading in it". Curiosity soon got the better of indignation, however, and a few weeks later Pepys returned to the bookshop, and after browsing an hour, doubtless to pluck up courage, bought "the idle, rogueish book . . . in plain binding, because I resolve, as soon as I have read it, to burn it, that it may not stand in my list of books, nor among them, to disgrace them if it should be found". The next day he was reading it avidly, excusing himself with the rationalization of many a subsequent researcher into the problem of pornography: "a rightly lewd book, but yet not amiss for a sober man once to read over to inform himself in the villainy of the world." That evening, after partaking of a "mighty good store of wine" the diarist returned [to] the task of educating himself about world villainy, a course of instruction which soon prompted him to masturbate, an activity which he recorded for posterity in guilty shorthand, and "after I had done it, I burned it, that it might not be among my books to my shame".'

[†] In 1972 detailed descriptions of anal intercourse were deemed by the jury not to be obscene after three eminent psychiatrists had 'testified that disseminating information about the practice was for the public good', and in 1976 a jury at the Central Criminal Court acquitted the publishers of *Inside Linda Lovelace*, describing the pleasures of oral sex and advising on techniques, after hearing the book praised by literary experts, doctors, psychologists, women journalists and the Oxford Professor of Jurisprudence (Robertson, pp.284–6, 296). This line of 'public good' defence was ultimately ruled inadmissible, and ceased to be offered (Whitehouse (1977), p.199). Linda Lovelace was the actress in the film *Deep Throat*. In 1983 she testified to the Minneapolis City Council public hearings on pornography and sexual violence that her appearance in the film had been coerced as a terrorized prisoner of the pimp who had kidnapped her, and that her participation in the scenes of oral sex had only been achieved under hypnosis (Minneapolis City Council, pp.24–30).

[‡] In giving evidence to the Longford Committee on Pornography in 1971, Kingsley Amis and

The failure, in 1960, of the trial of Penguin Books for publishing an unexpurgated version of D.H. Lawrence's *Lady Chatterley's Lover* was the watershed that largely freed the written word from the trammels of the Act,[*] at the same time, incidentally, liberating the word 'fuck' into artistic, if not general, usage. Kenneth Tynan, literary manager at the National Theatre, delighted libertarians when on 13 November 1965, in a late-night BBC TV programme, he firmly pronounced 'I doubt if there are very many rational people in this world to whom the word "fuck" is particularly diabolical or revolting or totally forbidden.'[†][54]

Literature was finding little difficulty in evading the intentions of the Obscene Publications Act; the film industry, to which the Act did not apply but which had its own long-standing code operated since 1912 by the British Board of Film Censors, could shelter its more daring products behind the protection of Adult or X classifications; and television (also exempt from the 1959 Act) was subject to the elastic responses of the Independent Broadcasting Authority and the BBC Board of Governors, whose operating charters[‡] supposedly precluded anything offensive to good taste and decency, but both of whom were keen to move with the times – or, in the case of Hugh Greene, the BBC Director-General from 1960 to 1969, to pioneer new frontiers of public acceptability.[§]

Elizabeth Jane Howard took precisely this view with regard to all pornography, going on record as saying that it was not a question of whether pornography corrupts and depraves. 'It *is* corruption and depravity' (Longford Report, p.156).

[*] Insofar as prosecutions subsequently succeeded, they usually referred to imported material, and were initiated under the 1952 Customs and Excise Act, which consolidated previous statutes permitting the seizure of indecent material by Customs (Robertson, p.193). The tactic was far from certain to result in conviction. Magistrates at Great Yarmouth in July 1992, for instance, refused to accept as obscene a song, based on a real incident, including the words 'I slaughtered the whore, skin her alive. I did it for the thrill, I had never dreamed it was nice to kill', which had been played on Radio 1 and had sold some 2,500 records in England. On the contrary, they awarded £7,500 to the defence, a result which was greeted by the band's lead singer as a great victory for free speech (*The Times*, 30 July 1992).

[†] Tynan was wrong. Although the word was to pass into very general usage on stage and screen, it never ceased to offend. In 1991 the Broadcasting Standards Council had found that of 1,056 listeners and viewers surveyed, 87 per cent said that they suffered discomfort on hearing the word used on radio or television (*The Times*, 18 July 1991). It was still, at the start of 1994, causing headline controversies involving the council and the chief executive of Channel 4 (*The Times*, 13 and 26 January 1994).

[‡] Until 1973 the duties imposed by the IBA's 1954 charter and accepted by the BBC in 1964, specifically not to offend against good taste or decency or encourage or incite to crime or lead to public disorder or be offensive to public feeling, stemmed from common-law provisions. In 1974 the provisions were embodied in the Independent Broadcasting Authority Act. No such statutory provision was then extended to the BBC (Robertson, p.270).

[§] A minor indicator of change was the withdrawal, within three years of Greene's tenure of office, of *The Variety Programme's Policy Guide for Writers and Producers*, which had sought to minimize crudity, innuendo, suggestive references, etc. (Munro, pp.162–3). *Doubles entendres,*

Malcolm Muggeridge's broadcasting subcommittee of the Longford Committee on Pornography was to castigate the BBC for the total moral vacuum in which it was operating by the end of the 1960s.[55]

By 1963 public concern was being expressed at the 'stream of suggestive and erotic plays' emanating from the BBC 'which present promiscuity, infidelity and drinking as normal and inevitable'. Mary Whitehouse launched the 'Clean Up TV Campaign' in 1964, with a petition that obtained some half-million signatures in four months. The National Viewers' and Listeners' Association was formed the next year.[56] It received support from some prominent churchmen and women, but on the whole was dismissed, particularly by the articulate young and those in the media, as a risible remnant of outmoded attitudes. In 1960 ITV had refused to transmit a play by an American writer because it included a pregnant girl who declared she would have a child out of wedlock; and in 1964 jibbed at scenes of striptease in Granada's *The Entertainers*. Within a year, the scenes were considered acceptable.[57] In every sphere opinion-formers were moving towards greater permissiveness. The days of theatre censorship were clearly numbered.

The Theatres Act of 1968 terminated the Lord Chamberlain's power of censorship, and with it all protection for the Church and for heads of state (including the monarch and members of the royal family). Certain controls remained, and were applicable to club as well as public performances. There was provision against racial hatred, or action designed to promote breaches of the peace. Obscenity was still prohibited, in terms which mirrored the (virtually inoperable) 1959 Act. 'A performance of a play shall be deemed to be obscene,' said the Act, 'if, taken as a whole, its effect is such as to tend to deprave and corrupt persons who are likely, having regard to all the circumstances, to attend it', but again there was a clause exculpating plays from any charge of obscenity if they were 'in the interests of drama, opera, ballet or any other art, or of literature or learning'.[*] The Act did not, of course,

---

particularly centring on such words as 'cock' and 'balls', enjoyed a heyday, but by the late eighties and the nineties had been supplanted by less subtle hilarities, mostly concerned with anal sex and fantasies about sodomizing the Pope (see, for example, *The Independent*, 14 April 1987; *The Independent Magazine*, 28 October 1989; *The Times*, 19 August 1993; Montreal International Comedy Festival, Channel 4, 28 December 1993).

[*] This provision unleashed a torrent of bad language, defended on the grounds of its artistic authenticity. The persistent campaign waged by the Viewers' and Listeners' Association on this topic owed much to its founder's insistence that once offensive words became commonplace and thereby lost their impact, physical violence would supersede verbal violence in the expression of strong confrontation, a contention which the subsequent development of drama appears to have justified.

exempt the theatre from laws applying generally to all pursuits, such as blasphemy, sedition, conspiracy, corruption of public morals, criminal libel, breach of parliamentary privilege and contempt of court, but any prosecution could proceed only with the consent of the Attorney-General (a provision which did not apply to other aspects of the media subject to the 1959 Act). Vulgarity, bad taste, indecency or causing offence were no longer grounds for objection.* [58]

The Act came into force on 26 September 1968. By the next evening, 27 September, *Hair* had opened at the Shaftesbury Theatre, the cast erupting on to the stage – naked.

Nudity was the most evident and obsessive change initially inaugurated by the Theatres Act. One director, Clifford Williams, had boldly engaged an ex-Bluebell Girl in the non-speaking role of Helen of Troy in his RSC production of Marlowe's *Dr Faustus* in the summer of 1968, when the Theatres Act was still on its passage through Parliament. She had crossed the stage briefly, and one critic had found it rather ridiculous, in the circumstances, for Faustus to be preoccupied with the *face* that launched a thousand ships. [59] There had been no response from the Lord Chamberlain's office.

For climatic if for no other reasons, nudity has not, historically, been particularly 'natural' in northern Europe – indeed, when Shaw's *Back to Methusaleh*, with Adam and Eve somewhat scantily clad, was revived at the Arts Theatre during the fuel shortage of 1947, special permission was given for the heating to be turned on during Act I. [60] But stage nudity has little in common with the 'naturism' of the nudist colony, where the obese and the scrawny, the sagging and the mutilated, are invited to come to terms with, and feel comfortable about, their limitations. As the producer of one nude show was at pains to explain, *Let My People Come* (1974) was not about nudity, it was about sexuality. [61] Only those with sexy bodies could expect to be hired – including, in *Pyjama Tops* (which installed an on-stage swimming-pool; shades of the Roman *maiuma*!), a cast 'mammiferous to a stupefying degree'. [62]

When Shaw had fought his battles with the Lord Chamberlain's office it had not for a moment occurred to him that immodesty would result. Controversial ideas, not human flesh, was what he wanted to see exposed. It was ludicrous to suppose, he wrote, that without censorship,

---

* Nor was the portrayal of living or recently dead persons. Thus, among many other examples, within four years of the murder of an army officer's wife by his mistress, for instance, the families concerned were confronted by a dramatized version of the event, a programme justified by Carlton, the TV company concerned, on the grounds that the story was already 'in the public domain' (*The Times*, 20 February 1995).

actresses would appear nude on stage. 'If an actress could be persuaded to do such a thing (and it would be about as easy to persuade a bishop's wife to appear in church in the same condition) the police would simply arrest her on a charge of indecent exposure.'[63] But as the director Clifford Williams said, when he staged *Back to Methusaleh* at the Old Vic in 1969 with a clothed Adam and Eve (as the early Middle Ages would have done), 'There was a touch of the prude in old Shaw.'[64]

Shakespeare, of course, was soon recruited to the cause. The 'growing toleration of male nudity on stage has enabled the director to cross Shakespeare's homosexual "t's" as surely as he dots the author's heterosexual "i's". The explicitness with which he does this makes one realize why the Victorians never revived the play ...' wrote one reviewer of the RSC's 1968 production of *Troilus and Cressida*, and on its revival the following year it was greeted as a 'dazzling set piece of erotic, torch-lit revelry, with Achilles sporting a blonde Helen of Troy wig and indulging in some overt sexual foolery with Thersites and his phallic codpiece', an appendage which the earlier reviewer had described as 'an ugly dangling penis attached to a sore and diseased body ...'[65] This was followed by an 'Ariel as a naked castrate (except for a generous sprinkling of white powder, a mane of long hair and neat little cache-sexe')[66] at Stratford in 1970. Meanwhile, a Lady Macbeth diaphanously clad in see-through material had featured at the Open Space Theatre in 1969. Then, at the Mermaid Theatre in 1971, the actress playing Desdemona discovered, to her unwelcome surprise, that she was expected to appear naked. She refused, and the part went to another actress, whose more compliant husband was on the dole.[67] Bernard Miles, proprietor of the Mermaid, maintained that there was strong textual evidence for the innovation, and a learned correspondence ensued in the columns of *The Times* on the subject of Tudor fashions in nightwear, not to speak of the complication involved in the Elizabethan theatre's use of boys in women's roles, Miles admitting that the nude scene must, in Shakespeare's time, have been played with Desdemona's back to the audience. Erudite excuses were soon replaced by art for art's sake. By the late 1980s Goethe's *Faust* had included naked orgies (1988 at the Lyric, Hammersmith, where 'it was pleasurably plain why certain members of the cast had been hired, that is for their sensuous bodies');[68] Rosalind had stripped to the waist in *As You Like It* (the Old Vic in 1989); and by 1991 even the eminent theatrical knight Sir John Gielgud had played a (discreet) nude Prospero in Peter Greenaway's film *Prospero's Books*. In Ireland in August 1993 Hamlet was being played as a mud-caked nude, to a drunken, homosexual Polonius.[69]

By the mid-1970s nude scenes or episodes, whether in classics or contemporary drama, were so commonplace as hardly to merit comment, though there were protests – at the nude 'climactic scene' in Shaffer's *Equus* at the National Theatre, for example, a protest countered by the assertion that 'Arts Council support for "men with tumescent penises performing sexual acts on the stage" is certainly no scandal'.[70] The ancient stand-by, *The Judgement of Paris*, of course surfaced again.[71] Critics became jaded. By 1985 Peter Shaffer's *Yonadab* was wearily reviewed as 'but one of innumerable plays which brought gratuitous nudity, male and female, back to the London stage with tedious monotony. Well, there was little enough money for costumes.'[72] The chief problems encountered were with the Indecent Displays Act (1981), primarily intended to sanitize Soho, as a result of which nudes in advertising ran into trouble. Michael Bogdanov of the English Shakespeare Company was much annoyed in 1992 to be required to remove their *Macbeth* poster of three strangely entwined naked crones (a picture dating, not insignificantly, from the sixteenth century); and shortly afterwards the RSC had, for publicity purposes, to clothe their Columbus, though assuring putative playgoers that he would not be wearing anything for the opening of the play *Columbus and the Discovery of Japan*.[73]

Whilst nudity spiced up current productions, it soon ceased to be adequate fare in shows whose purpose was sexual titillation. In New York in 1969 an off-Broadway version of *The Bacchae*, *Dionysus in '69*, involving nude actors and chorus, had departed fairly drastically from its Greek original by inviting the audience to participate in an orgy of sexuality with the cast.[74] Audience participation in live sex shows, as well as demonstrations of bestiality, was available in Denmark* (as Lord Longford was discomfited to discover when his researches took him to Copenhagen), but in England proprietors of live sex shows involving intercourse of any kind (heterosexual, homosexual, bestial, sadistic or necrophilial) could be (and were) arraigned under the Disorderly Houses Act of 1751.[75] It remained to be seen how far simulation could go.

What purported to be a political satire, *Ché*, exhibited copulation (presumably simulated) on the London stage for the first time in 1969, but otherwise appears to have left no trace in the records.[76] Kenneth Tynan, meanwhile, had publicly expressed his view that 'the arousing of

---

* But not for long. Public order offences led to tighter controls, and by 1978 no such shows were publicly available in Copenhagen (Williams, B. (ed.), Paragraph 11.7).

sexual desire is a perfectly legitimate function of art', and his expectation that sexual intercourse on stage would form part of the theatre of the future. He now devised the revue *Oh Calcutta!* as a vehicle 'to use artistic means to achieve erotic stimulation'.[77]

The show opened in New York in 1969, and crept into a disused railway shed, the Roundhouse, in north London in 1970. 'No crap about art or redeeming literary merit: this show will be expressly designed to titillate', Tynan had ordained. It featured scenes of mass masturbation, simulated on-stage copulation, attempted rape, flagellation, and, in the words of one unsympathetic commentator, 'anal ugliness . . . savage humiliation of the audience'.[78] Could it escape the 'deprave and corrupt' provision of the 1968 Theatres Act? The producers waited with some trepidation. It could and did.[*] Two months later, when it was clear that there would be no legal proceedings, the show moved into the West End.

Two nude revues followed, *The Dirtiest Show in Town* in 1971 ('This particular offering may be likened to an old man in a park, who exposes his genitals to anyone who will look . . .'),[79] and *Let My People Come* in late 1974, which had 'a pronounced emphasis on the practices of fellatio and cunnilingus': a typical sketch included 'a class of girls in school being taught fellatio with the help of bananas'.[80]

Critics were not entranced, but the public were. At the start of 1973 *Pyjama Tops*, *Hair*, *The Dirtiest Show in Town* and *Oh Calcutta!* were all running strongly. *Hair* prospered for 1,999 performances until the ceiling of the Shaftesbury Theatre fell in on it in 1973; *Pyjama Tops* clocked up over 3,000 performances. *Oh Calcutta!* ran for nine years in the West End, and was said to have grossed $360 million worldwide by 1987.[† 81]

Voyeuristic episodes infiltrated straight drama. An American import at the Royal Court, *The Beard*, an imaginary dialogue between Jean Harlow and Billy the Kid, portrayed cunnilingus, the actress playing Harlow wearing only an invisible G-string, but as both (real-life)

---

[*] It was this production that led A.P. Herbert to write to *The Times* (26 August 1970) recalling his part in the struggle to end censorship, and bewailing the fact that there was now nothing to prevent public indecency. 'I am sorry to think that our efforts seem to have ended in a right to represent copulation, veraciously, on the public stage.'

[†] The popularity of such shows faded, though whether from boredom or a spreading anxiety about AIDS is not clear. When *Let My People Come* was revived in 1990, the songs were updated 'with small introductory pieces explaining that new health problems have arisen since the 1970s'. One commentator remarked that the 'target audience is the thirty-something theatregoer who has discovered that voyeurism is the safest sex of all' (*Daily Telegraph*, 23 May 1990), but this proved insufficient to provide a new audience. *Hair*, revived at the Old Vic in September 1993, had closed by November, in spite of the cast accepting pay cuts within two weeks of opening (*The Times*, 5 November 1993).

principals were dead they were not in a position to object.[82] By 1989 on-stage cunnilingus had achieved 'artistic' respectability, featuring in the Chichester Festival production of Caryl Churchill's *Cloud Nine*.[83] 'If you shy away from mimed fellatio and the like, stay at home', warned a reviewer of *Unidentified Human Remains* in 1993.[84]

This enthusiasm for nudity and sexual simulation posed problems for members of Equity, the British actors' association. Regulations were agreed in 1969 between Equity and the Theatres National Committee, but by July 1970 reports were current of actors and actresses being required to take part in 'orgiastic and exhibitionist scenes' at auditions.[85] In January 1971, 'to help preserve the dignity of performers', a revised agreement between Equity and the Theatres National Committee was promulgated, covering any requirement for professionals to engage, on stage, in conduct which, if performed in public, would be regarded as indecent.* Among other provisions, 'no sex acts shall be required of any performer at any audition'; an official Equity observer was to be present at auditions requiring nudity, and any contract had to state in writing what precisely was required of the performer.[86]

Given the intense competition for work in the theatrical profession, this provided little protection except against gross abuses at auditions. 'The real victims,' wrote a commentator in 1992 'will be the new generation of actresses, who have to submit to ever more explicit scenes as the frontiers of expectation get pushed further and further.'[87] Harriet Walter was reported to have detested her nude scenes in *The Men's Room*, Imogen Stubbs to have wept and even blacked out over her first naked sex scene, and Diana Rigg to have regarded her nine months of disrobing in *Abelard and Heloise* as pointless. Joanna Lumley, in 1994, remarked:

> I bitterly regret the fact that I, and most actresses of my generation, were made to feel that we weren't proper actresses unless we took our clothes off. We all hated it, but we knew we would lose the job if we didn't take off our pathetic little tops or shorts . . . No-one was spared, and we were all humiliated.

---

* As travellers on long-distance trains and coaches will have observed, intimacies that would have been regarded as shameless half a century ago are now regarded as tolerable. There are, however, still limits. Passengers (who included children) on a busy train on the Margate line in 1992 felt unable to intervene when a couple indulged in full sexual intercourse, but remonstrated when they lit post-coital cigarettes in a non-smoking compartment. They were subsequently charged with both smoking and indecency (*The Times*, 7 August 1992).

Male actors were reported equally mortified by what the coarsening of public taste required of them.[88] The relative helplessness of players without written contracts is illustrated by the fate, in America, of such stars as Whoopi Goldberg, sued for backing out of a film requiring her to play the sexual partner of a dinosaur; and Kim Basinger, ordered to pay £6 million in damages to the producers of *Boxing Helena*, featuring her as a woman kept in a box for sexual purposes after her legs and arms are amputated by a doctor, a role that Basinger abandoned on the grounds that she only considered roles that had 'artistic' rather than 'graphic' nudity. Before the end of the year, she had filed for bankruptcy.[89]

The effect on those involved in nude sex shows appears to have been deadening. One director reported 'one's sexual appetite sharply diminished during the rehearsal period'. He ceased sleeping with his wife: 'I was just off sex.'[90] The male lead in *The Dirtiest Show in Town* explained publicly on television that he was impelled to leave the cast, having found that his participation not only rendered him impotent, but engendered 'huge psychological problems'.[91]

For the keenest exponents of genital liberation however,* the shows were proving too tame. 'Whether from stage fright or the temperature, the male members of the cast were resolutely unaroused – even when it was clearly in the interests of art that they should be', complained a disappointed viewer of *Oh Calcutta!*.[92] 'I'm tired,' said another, 'of seeing a stageful of limp dicks.'[93] But, as director Clifford Williams explained, 'in the three productions I've done, I don't think I've seen an erection more than about three times. Even then it was in rehearsals. During performance, I've never seen anyone remotely disturbed sexually in those productions.'†[94]

Nevertheless, 'what those who have seen *Hair*, *Oh Calcutta!*, *The Dirtiest Show in Town* and the rest will now expect,' wrote a critic in October 1974, 'is some significant move forward . . .'[95] It was a perfect summary of Sorokin's view of the Arts in sensate society. As the administrator of the US film rating system had already noted, sexual explicitness, in the form of nudity or copulation, had become too mechanical a formula for film-makers, and sex-plus-violence was now the form whereby they could 'up the ante' of sensational novelty.[96] In

---

* 'We think it time to liberate your genitalia' was one of the choruses in *Let My People Come* (*Plays and Players*, September 1974, p.21).

† Perhaps this was just as well. The Longford Committee heard eyewitness testimony that simulation had on occasion 'actually become a performance of coition and orgasm', and an unfortunate actor in *The Dirtiest Show in Town* who lost control of himself on stage was accused of rape (Longford Report, p.285; *Evening Standard*, 27 May 1992).

that very October the next move was made – into de Sadean territory. De Sade's *120 Days of Sodom* opened where *Oh Calcutta!* had begun its London run – at the Roundhouse. It disappointed: 'a view of de Sade which does not even hint at the ecstatic or delicious side of sadism'.[97] De Sade remained, however, a fruitful source of drama – *120 Days of Sodom* was revived in 1991 ('each succeeding episode is the same but nastier').[98] In 1993 a Brazilian company brought to London a version of *Juliette* (the book, detailing sexual assaults on 2,500 non-consenting victims, most under the age of sixteen and many under eight, was reissued in paperback by Arrow in the summer of 1991),[99] which included 'explicit scenes of mass masturbation, violent penetration and sexual abuse', and a woman defecating to Bach's Concerto for Two Violins.[100]

In his review of *Troilus and Cressida* in 1968, Peter Roberts had remarked on 'Shakespeare's disgust with the sex act and with the fact that men and women have to give expression to their most tender feelings for one another with organs that are excretory'.[101] The attention that began to be lavished on the excretory organs is an odd element of modern productions. Picasso's play *le Désir Attrapé par la Queue*, written in 1944 but not performed until 1967, in St Tropez, included a woman squatting centre stage in a urinating position while an amplified sound track made appropriate noises.[*] [102] A 1986 production of *Request Programme* followed its female lead into the lavatory and invited its audience to 'note that she tears exactly two sheets from her private roll, folds once, wipes and folds again' ('is this a first for the British theatre?' enquired the reviewer).[103] *Sweet Temptations*, staged in 1992, included, among a variety of masturbatory orgies, a woman pretending to urinate in a pail.[104] Shakespeare was of course called to the new colours: Birmingham Repertory Company's *Twelfth Night* in 1989 included someone urinating in a pool,[105] while the Royal Court's *King Lear* in 1993 saw 'Gloucester and a military Kent swapping pleasantries as they relieve themselves in the palace loo. Later on, Oswald unzips and lets fly at poor Kent as he snoozes in the stocks.'[106] Perhaps the explanation is simply a further extension of the naturalism that had increasingly dominated late-nineteenth-century drama; or it may be no more than the desire to shock the bourgeoisie – the potential for which may be gauged from the fact that when a lavatory was heard flushing off-stage in an innocent 1958 play about modern youth, *No Concern of Mine*, a

---

[*] The play was given a reading in 1944, with a cast that included Simone de Beauvoir and Jean-Paul Sartre (Rookmaaker, p.154).

momentary *frisson* was detectable in the auditorium.[*] More portentiously, however, Picasso's producer had claimed, 'We're not at liberty to emasculate a work of art to pander to bourgeois sentiment.'[107] The culmination (for the moment) of this trend occurred in Milwaukee, USA, in August 1991, when a singer arrested for defecating on stage and then throwing his faeces at the audience pleaded that he was 'exercising artistic freedom'.[108]

In other centuries lascivious and scatological preoccupations in entertainment have manifested themselves, without any cloak of ideological commitment, at a certain stage in the development of what Sorokin called the 'overripe' phase of sensate culture. In the late-twentieth-century manifestation of the same phenomenon, hedonistic sensationalism has been allied with ideological resentment towards traditional family patterns on the part of homosexuals, always influential in theatrical circles;[†] of feminists (male and female), angry at what they see as the patriarchal oppression of the 'nuclear family'; and of Marxists, zealous to challenge and subdue any bastions of the norms heretofore defended by what Shaw had ridiculed as 'middle-class morality'.[‡] A letter published in the *Sunday Times* of 9 August 1970, and reprinted in *Equity* (trade paper of the British Actors' Equity Association) the following March, included quotations from a document reputedly produced under the auspices of the Italian Communist Party encouraging, in the guise of artistic freedom, increasingly daring sex, including pornographic, shows as a device 'to eat away the very roots of bourgeois society'.[§]

The seventies saw the personnel of the left-wing fringe groups of the sixties reaping the rewards of their diligence and enthusiasm. The secretary of the postwar Old Vic company which preceded the National Theatre combined her duties with those of secretary of her local branch of the Communist Party.[109] Activists from the old Unity Theatre movement had obtained senior appointments in drama schools, and other administrative functions in the world of show business. Glasgow

---

[*] The script called for no more than the crashing of a lavatory seat, but no doubt this sound was too ambiguous, and was made more explicit in production. Incidentally, the play as originally written was far from 'innocent' from the viewpoint of the censor, having a homosexual theme, but was rewritten to evade censorship just before the Lord Chamberlain's 1958 change of policy. (Findlater, pp.167–8).

[†] For instance, William Gaskill remarks, of his early years at the Royal Court, that most of the directors were homosexual (Gaskill, p.16).

[‡] Tynan's 'revolutionary hedonistic' Marxism was of a romanticized Cuban variety (see Maurice Cranston, *Encounter*, January 1988, pp.45–7).

[§] Resolute enquiry both in the UK and in Italy has failed to verify the source of this claim.

Unity's general secretary had become general manager and artistic director of the Royal Court, where Unity actors found positions as professionals, and where, so the *Annual Register* had commented as far back as 1958:

> it seemed clear that somebody in that organization had made up his mind firmly in advance that the only young authors worth helping were those in rebellion against orthodox theatrical practice . . . so far did they carry their doctrinaire attitude, that when they invited provincial reps to perform they vetted, and in at least two cases refused to countenance, proffered performances on the ground that it was not the kind of play that they wished to encourage.[110]

' "Fringe" groups such as 7.84 . . . were to provide many of the RSC's best new actors', remarks Colin Chambers, theatre critic of the *Morning Star*.[111] At Stratford, in a move that Catherine Itzin described as a huge boost to political theatre, Buzz Goodbody,* a Party member, developed the secondary theatre, the Other Place, humbly housed (and later supplemented by the acquisition of the Donmar, renamed the Warehouse, near the RSC's London home at the Aldwych Theatre),[112] where the work of new playwrights could be explored, writers such as David Edgar (who had cut his teeth at General Will),† Edward Bond (of Inter-Action and Gay Sweatshop), Howard Brenton (of Portable Theatre), Charles Wood (ex-Unity, and later author of the anti-Falklands War *Tumbledown* on BBC TV),‡ and others of the (by 1978) 250 writers claimed to be working in alternative theatre.[113] The stage was set for, in Chambers's words, 'a theatre in and for an age of reason, science and technology . . .'[114]

With Trevor Griffiths' *Occupation*, discussing two views of revolution, the Bolshevik success and the Fiat workers, post-World War I failure, the RSC in 1971 mounted its first production 'to affirm unambiguously a revolutionary commitment to socialism'.[115] Itzin has charted the growing disillusionment of the socialist writers with their attempt to create a counterculture, their increasing conviction that only violence could usher in the purged culture of their dreams. John Arden, a

---

* Her suicide in 1975, at the age of 28, was regarded by her colleagues as a tragic loss to the theatre.

† 'One of the early, seminal political theatre companies . . . Pre unadulterated Agit-prop' (Itzin (1980), p.140).

‡ Also of the anti-militarist version of *The Charge of the Light Brigade*, made by Woodfall, the film company of the Royal Court's English Stage Society (Chambers (1989), pp.265, 363).

committed pacifist at the time he was penning *Sergeant Musgrave's Dance*; Trevor Griffiths, in whose *The Comedians* 'revolutionary anger and violence', in Itzin's analysis, 'triumph over . . . humanist gradualism'; Howard Brenton, of whom Itzin says, 'despair and disillusionment put the necessity of terrorist violence as a means to change society on to Brenton's political map'; Howard Barker, seeing in crime a natural response to capitalism; Bond, raging inchoately against the society that has created his murderers in *Saved*, realizing by the time he writes *Bundles* that morality lies in society's violent overthrow, and in *The Worlds*, in 1983, showing 'how willing one prominent playwright of the left had become to endorse terrorism as a means of accomplishing social change';[116] these and others were moving to an insistence on the political merit of violence, on exalting hatred of the enemy as a necessary frame of mind.* As in the old Unity days, when sympathetic portrayal of a bourgeois family had been castigated as a betrayal of the cause, John McGrath was deeply critical of Arnold Wesker for his attitude that all humanity was one, his interest in people rather than classes, his ultimate failure to hate.[117]

By 1977–8, of eight new plays at the RSC, five were by socialist revolutionaries.[118] There were some protests – as early as 1964 one of the Stratford governors had accused the RSC of putting on 'dirty plays', and in 1972 a Conservative MP resigned from the board protesting that the company was too left-wing.[†][119] The Institute of Contemporary Arts, venue in the early 1970s for over sixty 'alternative' theatre companies, was closed by its council at the end of 1976, and its far-left management dispossessed before the Institute reopened in 1977. In Manchester a right-wing councillor endeavoured to get the grant to North-West Spanner, a Marxist revolutionary agitprop group, cut or reduced, but the Arts Council stuck to its liberal ideals that politics must not be relevant to grant decisions.[120]

Sacrilege and blasphemy were among the weapons deployed. In 1970

---

* Even the supposed 'love-in' of *Hair* was not immune. Few of those greatly daring middle-aged purchasers of tickets who thought they were about to view pubic hair in public for the first time noticed the *umlaut* over the 'i' in the title. The in-joke was that *haïr* is the French verb for 'to hate' – in this case, fuddy-duddies, militarists and other enemies of the New Age. When the show was revived in 1992 the umlaut had transmogrified into an '8' on its side, but it is clearly evident in the original posters and documents.

† Its left-wing loyalties proved enduring. In 1986 members of the company, by then ensconced at the Barbican Centre in London, were prominent in abusing as 'anti-communist scum' a right-wing speaker, Brian Crozier, who had arrived at the centre to deliver a contribution to a debate on Nicaragua (*The Times*, 8 July 1993).

*Council of Love** was staged in the commercial theatre, portraying God as a dotard, Jesus trundled about in a wheelchair (the aftermath of crucifixion injuries), a Vatican hosting a lubricious party during which 'passions were aroused and sated at such speed that I am sure I missed a perversion or two', the upshot being the infliction of syphilis on the earth by a vindictive deity.[121] Counsel's advice was sought on the show's legality, but the conclusion was that no prosecution under the Theatres Act was likely to succeed. However, the distress caused to Christians by this production was influential in launching in 1971 a Nationwide Festival of Light, estimated to have been supported by 215,000 people up and down the country, with some 35,000 attending the culminating rally held in Trafalgar Square.[122] In the theatrical *avant-garde*, the movement was much ridiculed. Prominent among the counterdemonstrators at Trafalgar Square, Buzz Goodbody of the RSC staged a horrific tableau of family life with a placard saying 'Fuck the F*mily', for which she was arrested and fined.[123]

Howard Barker gave some offence in 1988 at the Royal Court with his *The Last Supper*, in which 'a messianic leader gathers for a final meal with 12 disciples, Christian attitudes receive a battering. Finally, in grisly parody flesh is eaten and blood drunk.'[124] Casual little gestures of blasphemy included, for instance, an RSC *Macbeth* in 1988 in which the witches pop 'bits of bread into a wine goblet rather than the usual grisly ingredients into a cauldron';[125] and the scene of cunnilingus in *The Beard* with which the Royal Court had celebrated the end of censorship had been played to the accompaniment of the Hallelujah Chorus; but on the whole it was left to television, the cinema and the printed word to test the application of the blasphemy law. The theatrical world had more pressing concerns.

High on the list of priorities was the exposure and destruction of contemporary capitalist society. The classics were reinterpreted from that stance, Goodbody subjecting Shakespeare to Marxist class analysis, and her successors finding anti-Thatcherite and anti-militarist parallels in fresh revivals of, for instance, *Timon of Athens* (did Shakespeare write it while undergoing treatment for depression, paranoia and syphilis? enquired one critic)[126] and *Troilus and Cressida*. Even Brook's 1970 'circus' *Midsummer Night's Dream* was seen as indicative of 'the postwar period of capitalist decay'.[127] The long march through late-twentieth-century theatre of the Jacobean melodramas and the Restoration

---

* First staged in 1890 under the title *Heavenly Tragedy*. Its author, Oscar Panizza, received a two-year prison sentence for blasphemy (*The Times*, 15 and 21 August 1970).

comedies was increasingly presented as speaking to modern cynicism, immorality and callousness.[128]

Modern writers vied with the Absurdists of the 1950s in the ferocity and sexual lubricity with which they sought to symbolize contemporary society. Edward Bond chose to present a critique of modern British society in a pastiche of seventeenth-century drama, *Restoration*, staged by the RSC in 1989:

> a sequence of events that carries customary Restoration satirizing of hypocrisy, rapacity and foolishness a stage further – into indictment of an entire social system . . . Regularly, the cast are required to intone sub-brechtian chants about class injustice and the evils of the Establishment.[129]

The violence of Bond's version of *Lear*, with its portrayal of eardrums being punctured, eyeballs popped out (grapes were used), its rape and murder, serves the message that no violence is as bad as capitalism.[130] 'The majority of Warehouse plays,' writes Chambers, 'were rooted in the urban underbelly of a decaying welfare state.'[131] Howard Brenton, Brian Clark, Trevor Griffiths, David Hare, Stephen Poliakoff, Hugh Stoddart and Snoo Wilson collaborated to write *Lay-by*, in which off-stage enforced fellatio and flagellation is followed by a discussion as to whether the victim did or did not swallow semen; by scenes in which the girl, a prostitute, drug-addict and pornographer's model, enacts mimed fellatio but is impeded by the (trouserless) male's inability to produce an erection, then re-enacts, for the police (but with a dildo), the previous sexual coercion, thus demonstrating that it is the female, not the male, who enjoys most power, through her opportunity to bite the proffered penis; and ends, somewhat suddenly, with a hospital scene in which the girl's body (she has died from suppuration following a botched abortion) is the object of some tomfoolery from the hospital porters, before being pulped for jam. As Brenton was to explain:

> When the two hospital attendants are washing the corpses of the three main characters, and pulping their bodies in a huge dustbin into jam, we tried to put every phoney humanist statement that you could hear in the theatre from our elder playwrights into that . . . it was group warfare that created that show.[132]

The Royal Court, who had commissioned this play, at first refused to stage it, though they later relented and presented it as a Sunday evening speciality. Meanwhile, it was presented at the Traverse Theatre, Edinburgh, in 1971, and at the Open Space Theatre. At Edinburgh it began to rival Brook's 1955 *Titus Andronicus* for shock effect. 'People fainted, passed out and dropped over the back of the rostra at the Traverse', reported Snoo Wilson.[133] *Lay-by* went beyond most contemporary writing in its crudity, but callousness and prurience were the emotions projected by much of the new writing. Howard Barker's *That Good Between Us*, an RSC production, included, as described by Bernard Crick, 'remarkable dramatic images: the first naked gang rape on stage (to my knowledge) . . .'[134] The homosexual rape in Brenton's atrocity-ridden *The Romans in Britain* (intended as a parable of the British in Ireland) at the National Theatre in 1980 included, among much other coarseness, references to the disappointment of finding an arsehole full of piles ('like a fistful of marbles'). It led to a private prosecution, not under the impotent obscenity law (in any case requiring the Attorney-General's consent, which he refused to give) but under the Sexual Offences Act (covering public indecency), a prosecution which was aborted short of a judgement; the production was not impeded.

Much of this material failed, at the time, to attract an audience. As William Gaskill at the Royal Court had to admit, Arden, Bond and Barker emptied the house.[135] After *Lay-by* Snoo Wilson gloomily concluded, 'we have alienated permanently a section of the British theatre-going public'.[136] Findlater had noted, before the Theatres Act abolished the censor, 'the most decisive single factor in the defeat or, at least, the retreat of the Lord Chamberlain has been the innovation of State aid for the theatre, and the expansion of the Arts Council budget for the theatre . . .'[137] and Robertson too emphazises the boost which freedom from commercial pressures gave to the RSC when they challenged the censor with their anti-American *US*.[138]

The commercial theatre, meanwhile, had little of depth to offer. Year after year the *Annual Register* finds in the subsidized theatre, including the many provincial houses such as Alan Ayckbourn's in Scarborough, the only springs of originality or theatrical enterprise. In 1972, 'unless a theatre could rely on subsidies, its offerings must be as trivial as possible'. In the following year: 'It has been clear for at least a decade that box office revenue could never cover the costs of producing a new play without stars or a high sexual content.' In 1975, 19 of the 34 West End shows had originated in subsidized houses. The guarantor of commercial success lay in farces and musicals. In 1972 one West End theatre in three was offering musical comedy. The proportions were not much different in 1983: 12 of 40 theatres were housing musicals. By

1986, 'out of 42 commercial theatres in London, 17 house musicals, four are dark, and the rest coddle mostly thrillers or long-running farces'.[139] The pre-eminence of musicals in public taste intensified, attracting almost 50 per cent of West End theatregoers by 1991, compared with 28 per cent in 1983, with 20 per cent of the entire West End box-office takings going to Lloyd Webber musicals.[140] As in the similar phase in the evolution of dramatic entertainment in late Rome or the medieval period, huge investments in technological gimmickry (as in *Starlight Express*, *Phantom of the Opera*, *Miss Saigon*, whose staging was limited to precincts large enough to accommodate a helicopter) sought to astound the customer, raising expectations to a pitch at which, in 1989, the Royal Shakespeare Company declared itself unable to perform *The Plantagenets* at the Barbican unless the whole stage could be rebuilt – at a cost of £50,000.[141]

'The political theatre movement had failed to reach and convert or mobilize the mass of the population', confesses Itzin. Texts made great headway as subjects of study in schools, but remained largely unperformed.[142] However, the exploration of sex and violence by prestige subsidized companies projected an aura of artistic respectability that was to reach well beyond the frontiers of political commitment. John McGrath, in eschewing TV and the cinema as useful media, complained that their dominant ideology accepted the status quo, leaving unexplored the relationship of the human tragedy to social structures.[143] The pace was set by Hollywood, whose products dominated the cinemas and, as ownership of television sets expanded from the 1950s on, the home screen.

Michael Medved's book *Hollywood versus America* surveys how the film industry (largely American, but British directors do not escape his strictures) developed, particularly after 1966, when the industry's Hays Production Code was scrapped. He is guarded in ascribing any precise political agenda to named film producers, but he does explore the relentless hostility to the myths and folk-heroes of white America. He catalogues in considerable detail the unflagging denigration of religion, especially Christianity, and the demeaning of characters portrayed as religious, including the gratuitous imposition of Christian symbols on horrendous characters, even in a remake such as Scorsese's *Cape Fear* about a psychopathic murderer, where the original material had no such associations; the promotion of promiscuity; the belittling of marriage (most principals are portrayed as unmarried, unfaithful or trapped); the acceptability of illegitimacy; the idiocy of parents compared with the sagacity of their offspring; the infatuation with foul language (he alludes to one film, *GoodFellas*, another Scorsese production, which managed to average 'a major obscenity nearly twice every minute' throughout its 146 minutes of running time); the urge to linger on vomit and urine; the developing fascination with incest, cannibalism and bestiality; the automatic use of violence as the 'solution' to all problems; and its escalation into gross and sadistic forms which the audience are invited to find amusing and enjoyable. The key quotation comes from the 'manifestly gifted and serious' film-maker Martin Scorsese, who, describing his remake of *Cape Fear* with its, to quote Medved's summary, 'several vicious beatings, murders, attempted murders, facial mutilations, attempted rapes, drowning, burning, blinding, strangling, sliding in pools of blood, and even the poisoning of a family dog', declared to the *Los Angeles Times*, 'it's a lot of fun'.* [144]

Conflict is the very stuff of drama. In ideational drama the conflict is within the protagonist, between duty and inclination,† but once all inclinations are acceptable, dramatic interest is sustained by physical confrontation. Quality films of the 1930s and 40s sought to hold audience attention (deemed by Hollywood to become jaded within ninety seconds if not arrested by some sort of surprise or confrontation) by rapid changes of camera angle, by repartee and wisecracks, but increasingly with the passage of time producers relied more and more on the progression through verbal confrontation, bad language, smashing up property, and finally interpersonal violence.

In Britain the film industry's Board of Film Censors had, in 1912, notified their intention to forbid (*inter alia*) unnecessary cruelty to man or beast, murder, sudden death and suicide, as well as lampoons, sexual suggestiveness . . . and mixed bathing.‡ [145] The final power of approving

---

* *Cape Fear* was scheduled for transmission by the BBC on 29 March 1996, but in the wake of the Dunblane slaughter on 13 March it was withdrawn (how long was not stated) 'as a mark of respect for the city's people'. (*The Times*, 15 March 1996).

† A late survivor was Noel Coward's *Brief Encounter*, a film tracing the renunciation of an affair between two married people who decide to put the integrity of their marriages above their desire for one another. It moved people in its day (the mid-1940s) but its moral intensity seemed very dated a generation later.

‡ Protection of animals was strengthened in 1937 when the Cinematograph Films (Animals) Act prohibited the exhibition of films which in production involved cruel infliction of pain or terror on animals (Findlater, p.122; Cotterell, p.465) However, in 1974 John Fraser's *Violence in the Arts* (p.169, note 8) was to remark with disquiet on a noticeable increase in the killing of animals in movies – he cites five; and nine years later Members of Parliament exposed to an educative session of video nasties were confronted with one in which 'a monkey [was] killed by having its head smashed open and people eating the warm brains' (*The Times*, 2 November 1983), an experience which may have influenced the introduction of the 1984 Video Recordings Act seeking to control cruelty to animals in the making of videos. Amateur and foreign-made videos continue to circulate; a jury in January 1992 judged 'obscene' a Maltese video 'in which pit bull terriers are seen tearing

films for showing rested with local authorities, who might have their own viewing committees, but generally accepted the guidance of the Board – U films for universal viewing, A for those to which children under sixteen could only be admitted when accompanied by an adult. Some latitude obtained after 1952, when the X certificate (from showings of which children were barred) was introduced, as were private cinema clubs, to which the licensing system did not apply, but which were still covered by the common law on indecency. The number of X certificate films multiplied rapidly, almost doubling (from 110 to 199) in the five years 1966 to 1971.[146] Successive secretaries to the Board endeavoured to move with the times, and the period 1959 to 1975 under John Trevelyan saw liberalization at a speed which upset many viewers, leading the National Viewers' and Listeners' Association to complain of nudity, explicit sex, cruelty, violence, callousness and sadism – in short a catalogue of hate, obscenity and blasphemy.[147] For the Greater London Council, however, where the viewing committee were pressing their council (in the outcome, unsuccessfully) to abandon all censorship of films for over-18s, the Board was still too restrictive, and the GLC gave licences ('X London') to 12 of the 31 films turned down by the Board.[148] There were private prosecutions and campaigns, one of which resulted in the refusal of a licence to Linda Lovelace's *Deep Throat* (with its seven instances of fellatio, four of cunnilingus).[149] In 1977 the Obscene Publications Act was amended to bring the cinema under its provisions, replacing the restrictions previously imposed by the common law on indecency, freeing feature films adjudged 'artistic' from prosecution, and opening up the possibility of a defence on grounds of 'public good', – for example, by being so horrible they would have an 'aversive' effect. At the same time, the right to bring a private prosecution was removed.[150] An immediate effect was the withdrawal of the prosecution then in train of a London cinema club for showing *Salò*, modelled on de Sade's *120 Days of Sodom*, since the charge of indecency was now invalid, and the prosecution would have had to prove the unprovable 'tendency to deprave and corrupt'.[151]

each other's flesh while cheered on by a large crowd' (*Daily Telegraph*, 3 January 1992; *The Times*, 7 January 1992). At the 51st Venice Film Festival, *Before the Rain*, which included a 'particularly nasty sequence involving the protracted shooting of a live cat', won the award for Best Film (*The Times*, 13 and 14 September 1994). The second half of the century saw a resurgence of live entertainment involving animal brutality: cock-fighting, dog-fighting (outlawed in 1835, but a further Act on the subject, increasing the penalties, was passed in 1988) and badger baiting with pit bull terriers, an activity which, according to Scotland Yard, was 'drawing thousands of pounds in bets' as professional criminals staged contests in London high-rise complexes (*The Times*, 18 January 1994).

Much of the output of the film industry was destined for television screens. Made-for-television plays and series had provoked complaints from the National Viewers' and Listeners' Association since the early 1960s, and during the subsequent three decades a substantial monitoring exercise produced statistically tabulated surveys on the extent to which promiscuity and violence were portrayed as the norm, bad language employed, and the police presented as corrupt and aggressive.[*]

Scum, which included homosexual rape and a suicide in a violent and corrupt Borstal, was described in 1978 by the BBC's Director of Programmes as 'the most violent play the BBC has ever made'.[152] He decided not to permit its transmission, but it was shown on Channel 4 in 1984, and by 1991 the BBC, too, decided it was, after all, suitable for screening.[153] Satisfied that their duties to children were adequately discharged by delaying the transmission of 'adult' material until after 9 p.m., television channels embarked on increasingly unrestrained entertainment. The series, *A Bouquet of Barbed Wire*, first broadcast in the 1970s and repeated on Channel 4 in the spring of 1992, was advertised as a 'lurid concoction of incest, infidelity and sado-masochism in the English home counties'.[154] Early in 1993 Channel 4 transmitted *Last Tango in Paris*, a 1973 film of an obsessive sexual relationship, all copies of which were ordered burnt by the Italian government, the Italian director given a (suspended) gaol sentence and deprived of his voting rights, and the star, Marlon Brando, fined. 'I felt violated from the beginning to the end, every day and every moment', said Brando of the making of the film. But by the time Channel 4 showed it, it was commonplace. 'Similar sexual acts have taken place in mainstream Hollywood films such as *Basic Instinct*, *9½ Weeks* or *Bitter Moon*', remarked a critic.[155]

By 1994 Channel 4, in a week dedicated to the artistically highly acclaimed Peter Greenaway, was screening *The Cook, the Thief, his Wife and her Lover* ('a work so intelligent and powerful that it evokes our best emotions' – *New York Times*) which Medved summarizes as follows:

> The opening scene takes place in the parking lot of an imposing restaurant, lit by ghostly neon, where a pack of stray dogs snarl over bloody hunks of rotten meat. Two refrigerator trucks pull up, loaded with dead fish and hanging pig carcasses, respectively.

---

[*] A Home Office research study on screen violence, published in 1977, cited a BBC Audience Research Department analysis of the output of one third of all London television programmes in six months during 1970–1, and found that 54 per cent included violence, many of them being programmes originating in the USA (Brody, pp.102–3).

Attention than focuses on a group of foppishly dressed thugs who tear the clothes off a struggling, terrified victim in order to smear his naked body with excrement. They force filth into his mouth and rub it in his eyes, then pin him to the ground while the leader of the band proceeds to urinate, gleefully, all over him . . . We see sex in a toilet stall, deep kisses and tender embraces administered to a bloody and mutilated cadaver, a woman whose cheek is pierced with a fork, a shrieking and weeping nine-year-old boy whose navel is hideously carved from his body, a restaurant patron whose face is scalded by a tureen of vomit-coloured soup, and an edifying vision of two naked, middle-aged lovers writhing ecstatically in the back of a truck filled with rotting, maggot-infested garbage. The grand finale of the film shows the main character slicing off – and swallowing – a piece of carefully seasoned, elegantly braised human corpse in the most graphic scene of cannibalism ever portrayed in motion pictures. There is, in short, unrelieved ugliness, horror and depravity at every turn.[156]

A former Lord Chamberlain, Lord Scarborough, had in 1966 voiced his apprehensions.

I believe that there is quick money to be made from obscenity, from indecency and from representation of cruelty on the stage, and although I would not for a moment suggest that the theatre, in its fullest sense, would be lured by that, I have little doubt that some persons would be so lured.* [157]

Two years later, at the time of the abolition of the Lord Chamberlain's powers, Lord Cobbold, the then incumbent, confided his regret that no reserve powers existed, for the level of television violence was becoming, in his view, dangerous.[158] Equity, in December 1971, was expressing alarm at the progression to 'realism' reported from the United States, where a film director had

sought and received medical advice about the various parts of the human body into which knives could be plunged with the minimum risk to the victim. He then obtained the agreement of an actress who was prepared to do the stabbing and an actor, who in the interests of

* Tennessee Williams, for one, was on record as admitting, 'I prefer tenderness, but brutality makes better copy' (Lumley, p.194).

'the new realism' and payment of a suitable fee, was prepared to be stabbed.'* [159]

It was the progression towards the frank enjoyment of callousness that had been alarming critics ever since Artaud made cruelty the bedrock of supreme dramatic experience. Kitchin, noting in passing that Artaud's theatrical manifesto was published a matter of months before the first Nazi concentration camp was established, remarks of his subliminal techniques:

> one of the dangers of communicating below the level of conscious-ness is to let loose primitive forces beyond the control of the playwright. It happens every time a film intending to condemn concentration camps gives the audience a sadistic thrill . . . What is there to prevent the result being infective rather than therapeu-tic?† [160]

Fraser, in his *Violence in the Arts*, points out that

> the author or director may begin by postulating a deservedly shockable bourgeois audience, but ends up with an audience that is begging for shocks to be given it, either because it identifies with the artist against 'society' or because it is slumming. And even if escalation is attempted, the new language is rapidly learned, the limits of the expectable expand, the hitherto taboo is commended by society itself in the name of art . . .[161]

Perhaps the Greeks knew what they were doing when they limited violence to narration.

---

* The intensifying relish for genuine injury is equally palpable in sport. Controversy raged over Larwood's 'bodyline' fast bowling in 1932, on the grounds that it was aimed at the batsman and was intended to intimidate, but a few decades later such 'sportsmanship' was common form. June 1978 marked the first appearance of a Test batsman (Sadiq Mohammad of Pakistan) wearing a helmet (though as yet no visor), a development which a *Punch* cartoon of 1854 had foreshadowed, being then considered so delightfully unthinkable as to be good for a laugh. Increasing resort to intentional injury, especially in soccer and rugby, led in 1994 to calls by the Law Commission for tougher laws to penalize violence on the field, and bring perpetrators to court. *Rugby World* advertised its 1994 Review of the Year with the assurance: 'It was a year of VIOLENCE. In 1994 a player was tried for manslaughter after an opponent died, others were punched, bitten and kicked in the head.'

† Did *Natural Born Killers* do 'fifty million dollars' in the USA because audiences perceived it as a trenchant criticism of violence in society in general and the media in particular? Or did its predominantly youthful audience just enjoy mayhem?

When *Saved* was first performed, the drama critic of *The Times* warned that 'the production is as much an invitation to share erotic and sadistic fantasy as to understand it'.[162] The murky nexus in the human psyche where sex and violence meet can be glimpsed in the Roman prostitutes who lingered in the arches round the amphitheatre, in the prevalence of rape in war, in the orgasms of those perpetrating torture to which concentration camp victims testified. It is even more explicit in, for instance, Casanova's memoirs, which include his recollection of a public execution where

> as the screams of the victim filled the air (his flesh was torn with red hot pincers, and boiling oil was inserted into the wounds) Casanova saw Count Tiretta lifting a woman's skirts . . and saw that 'throughout Damien's long dying, Count Tiretta performed sexual gymnastics on the woman'.[163]

The Victorian pornography trader Frederick Hankey, too, 'once took a friend and two women along to a public hanging in order to have sexual intercourse while the hanging took place'.[164] It may be significant that the three productions that have caused most offence as blasphemies – James Kirkup's poem of homosexual desire for which *Gay News* was successfully prosecuted by Mary Whitehouse in 1977; *The Last Temptation of Christ*, the Scorsese film dropped from BBC schedules in November 1991 after protests (but reinstituted, to even more protests, by Channel 4 on 6 June 1995);[*] and *Visions of Ecstasy*, refused a certificate by the British Board of Film Classification[†] in 1989 – all celebrated erotic fantasies centred on, or experienced by, a tortured and bloody victim helplessly undergoing crucifixion.[‡]

---

[*] 'Channel 4 received about 6,000 complaints over the film. The station apologized to Tesco and to the relief agency World Vision after they complained that their advertisements had been screened next to the film.' The Independent Television Commission, however, rejected complaints, maintaining that, though the film might challenge the beliefs of some Christians, it involved neither abusive treatment of those beliefs, nor 'improper exploitation of any susceptibilities of those watching' (*The Times*, 14 August 1995).

[†] The British Board of Film Censors was renamed the British Board of Film Classification in 1985.

[‡] *Visions of Ecstasy* claimed to be inspired by the Bernini sculpture of the mystical experiences of St Teresa of Avila. Her own autobiography relates her 'raptures' to God, 'His Majesty', never to Christ, who is in fact barely mentioned, let alone in the context of the cross. 'When Christ appeared to her it was "always in his glorified flesh", "in his resurrected body" ', quotes Robert T. Petersson in his examination of the Bernini sculpture, *The Art of Ecstasy* (p.39). The well-known erotic symbolism of the flame-tipped spear that pierced her entrails was not related to the person of Christ, but was wielded by a seraph, as indeed the Bernini sculpture portrays (see *The Life of Saint*

The Longford Committee on pornography had noted that by the end of the 1960s pornography was no longer portraying the joys of sex (however depersonalized), it was intent on depicting, in a sexual context, degradation, perversion, mutilation and violent death.[165] The hatred that the political dramatists had regarded as socially wholesome when applied to issues of class now spilled over and saturated all relationships portrayed in entertainment. In March 1993 John Ferman, secretary of the much-tried but still functioning British Board of Film Classification, confessed himself appalled by the hatred for women he found in the cinema, where the Board strove to limit 'scenes contrived to induce the sexual excitation of male viewers through the terrorization, torture or humiliation of naked or semi-naked women'. In his first year as secretary, in 1976, 'we saw 402 films and 58 included rape, and mostly rape as entertainment'. By 1993 the Board's annual report was enumerating the incidence of rape, gang rape, women being bound, hit, whipped, knife threats to bare breasts, strangulation and urination on a murdered woman.[166] Itzin in 1992 was drawing particular attention to the reiterated message of such films: that women enjoy torture and humiliation, 'women are asking for it'.[167]

Writing in the *Guardian* of 30 October 1981, Polly Toynbee referred to 'scenes of castration, cannibalism, flaying, the crushing of breasts in vices, exploding vaginas packed with hand grenades, eyes gouged out, beatings, dismemberings, burnings, multiple rape and every other horror that could befall the human body'.[168] The move from simulation to actuality had occurred in relation to intercourse of all kinds, including bestiality. Pornographic films depicting young girls having intercourse with donkeys and dogs were being made and imported into Britain from Scandinavia by the late 1960s, and Toynbee reported films of women engaged in sexual intercourse with pigs and dogs.* [169] Now came rumours that violence to women was extending to actual murder. In 1975, according to a report in *The Times* in July 1990,

> police in America discovered evidence that prostitutes and immigrants from Mexico were being killed in lurid detail to satisfy the insatiable demands of the multi-million pound pornography industry ... Ten years later a Californian was believed to have

Teresa). It is the imagination of the twentieth century that has chosen to steep the eroticism in blood and suffering.

* Accounts of the making of such films in Mexico were the source material for Mannix's imaginative projection in his book *Those about to Die* of bestiality as a public entertainment in ancient Rome, for which there is no contemporary evidence.

kidnapped and killed 25 women and filmed their torture and death. Video tapes of actual killings became big business for rental firms.[170]

In 1979 a poster for a film called *Snuff* claimed that the final scene showed a woman being killed, and her uterus ripped out.[171]

Initially the general supposition was that much of this must have been trick photography. When the *Sunday Times* in May 1982 discussed the phenomenon of 'video nasties', they noted of 'snuff movies', featuring gory scenes of extreme sadism, including rape, mass murder and mutilation, that the 'killings are believed to be real' but it was uncertain whether this was so.[172] They were, however, banned in the USA, and *Snuff* was suddenly withdrawn from circulation by its British distributors following the *Sunday Times* article.[173] Given that the production of 'snuff movies' involves assault and murder they are obviously illegal, but Catherine Itzin's contributors to *Pornography: Women, Violence and Civil Liberties*[174] and, in particular, Clodagh Corcoran, in *Pornography; the New Terrorism*, provide convincing evidence of their existence.

It is not only women who suffer.

Paedophile rings in Britain and on the Continent appear to have taken snuff films into a new dimension, with children being sexually abused, tortured and killed . . . only recently have police admitted that such films probably do exist and are available commercially as well as for private use.

Scotland Yard admitted, in July 1990, that they were now linking the disappearance of twenty young boys since 1984 with the possible production of 'snuff films'.[175] In a major trial in December 1990, as a result of which fifteen men were convicted of sado-masochistic practices (to the disapproval of libertarians who held that the infliction of pain for sexual purposes was not, if consensual, any concern of the state),[*] detectives were reported 'so alarmed by a violent scene shown on a video film made by some of the men that they suspected it may have been a snuff movie with an actual murder being performed before the camera'; the judge 'went white in the face and asked for an adjournment after

---

[*] Their case was taken up by Liberty, formerly the National Council for Civil Liberties, which, following the failure of an appeal to the House of Lords, in January 1995 obtained the consent of the European Commission of Human Rights in Strasbourg to challenge the verdict of the English courts on the grounds that it breached the European Convention on Human Rights (*The Times*, 18 and 19 January 1995).

watching the most horrifying video'. However, extensive searches failed to unearth any victims, and murder was not among the charges on which the men were convicted.[176]

The public taste for real death on screen is evolving with all the enthusiasm of the amphitheatre. Granada's *World in Action* in November 1987 set a dubious precedent when it screened the contract killing of a Japanese gangster, editing out the actual killing, but 'you saw the knives; you saw the killers breaking in; you heard the muffled sounds of struggle; you saw them emerge, suits literally dripping with blood', this item being broadcast before the children's supposed 9 p.m. deadline.[177] In the United States, strong pressure to permit the televising of executions built up in California during 1990 and 1991. A judge ultimately refused permission, but the issue is expected to resurface in other states.[178] By comparison, British news reporting is restrained, though the frequent repetition of exceptional camera coups, like the shooting of a prisoner in the street in Saigon, the disintegration of the *Challenger* spacecraft or the Bradford football ground fire, betray that the line may be hard to hold. In June 1995 a video, *Executions*, 'including stills of shootings, lethal injections, electrocutions, gassings and beheadings', and ending with 'close-ups of a man being shot repeatedly in the body and head', was found to be on sale in Britain, equipped with a certificate from the British Board of Film Classification which had accepted the makers' contention that the film's purpose was to shock people into opposition to capital punishment. On being made aware of the contents, W.H. Smith withdrew the video from sale, and the John Menzies chain somewhat more cannily vowed they would order no more once existing stocks ran out.[179]

Meanwhile, the public appetite for morbid spectacle is, in the United States, being satisfied by the commercial exploitation of amateur so-called 'I-Witness' videos, sometimes referred to as 'snuff videos', in which amateur photographers, confronted with disasters, reach for their cameras to record such scenes as a policeman being shot, or a pregnant woman diving to her death from a burning building. Some American TV stations are issuing free cameras for the purpose.[180] An incident at Mont-Saint-Michel on 22 August 1994 is illustrative.

> Dozens of tourists . . . watched impassively and even videotaped a young mother drowning while trying to save her child . . . One resident reported hearing a tourist say proudly: 'I got the whole thing on tape' . . . tourists on the ramparts apparently watched without attempting to intervene or summon help. A café owner, his

curiosity aroused by the tourists staying in the same place, realized what was happening and ran to find two firemen. They were able to save the girl, but not the mother.[181]

The successful amateur cameraman subsequently endeavoured to sell his tape to a TV station.[182]

Throughout the last thirty years controversy has raged as to whether dramatic entertainment is simply reflecting life in the late twentieth century; responding to a market in sensational taste; or initiating value changes that are impinging on real life. Is it, in short, a 'mirror held up to Nature'? Or is it a burning glass?

Chapter 21

Where the Rainbow Ends

Pamela Hansford Johnson, listening appalled to the evidence at Chester Assizes where in 1966 Ian Brady and Myra Hindley were on trial for the torture and murder of at least three children, had become convinced that their saturation in pornography, particularly de Sade's *Justine*, had played a powerful role in the development of their obscene enjoyments. In her book *On Iniquity* she commented that it was not the 'lumpen proletariat' but the intelligentsia who set the fashion for works of depravity, and she questioned whether the suppression of pornography really was tantamount to totalitarianism.[1]

Lord Longford's committee on pornography started work some four years later, and its report, published in 1972, made a number of recommendations for changes in the supervision of pornographic productions in all aspects of the media. Central to the committee's viewpoint was its insistence on the need to abandon the 'deprave and corrupt' formula of the 1959 Act, and substitute a new definition along the lines that material is obscene 'if its effect, taken as a whole, is to outrage contemporary standards of decency or humanity accepted by the public at large', outrage being interpreted to mean much more than offending sensibilities. It should apply not merely to sex, but to violence and drugs too, with the inclusion of the word 'contemporary' allowing for evolution of the application of the law in line with changing public perceptions. Proof of harm was, the report conceded, impossible to establish (and was not required in other contexts, for instance, where incitement to racial hatred was concerned), but the committee pointed to the correlation 'dating back to 1955' between the rise in crime and the rise in the ownership of TV sets; and to indicators of desensitization such as disturbing reports from cinema managers of the 'howls of delight' that greeted the rape scene in *Straw Dogs*, and the impassivity with which children watched scenes of sex and violence.[*][2]

---

* James Boswell, who had a penchant for public executions, illustrated the psychological

Stanley Kubrick's filmed version of Anthony Burgess's *A Clockwork Orange* had been released in 1971. Burgess had known violence at close quarters, when in 1944 his wife had been robbed with great brutality in London by four Americans, 'probably GI deserters', and had as a result lost the baby she was carrying. Since the motive was theft, the violence was not as random as the wanton stabbing from which Beckett had suffered; nevertheless, confronted by the teddy boys of the fifties and the mods and rockers who erupted into public consciousness in 1964, Burgess 'saw fairly clearly . . . that the future was going to be plagued by a great deal of youthful energy that . . . had to give itself over to destruction'.[3] This insight, together with the trauma of the attack, combined to produce *A Clockwork Orange*. In interviews given long afterwards, Burgess was to explain, 'If you can objectify a thing in fiction you've got a good chance of forgiving what happened. It wasn't written primarily out of bitterness, but there was that element there.'[4]

The book's four protagonists give themselves over to rape and murder with a gusto that led Burgess to confess 'I was sickened by my own excitement at setting it down.'[5] 'If you set down violence on paper it's bound to exert a kind of pornographic influence on you. You enjoy the violence. And of course this is morally wrong.'[6] He reasoned, though, that these excitements were ancillary, that the purpose of his work was to equate the violence perpetrated by his 'droogs' with the violence of authority which, by subjecting the principal droog to aversion therapy, 'cured' him of his antisocial conduct at the cost of depriving him of his central human characteristic – the capacity for moral choice. 'Without being pretentious, it is what I would call a theological book, in that it posits that you have to have evil if you are going to have good', Burgess was to explain. 'If you only have one, there is no choice.'[7]

Long before the book was filmed, rebellious teenagers had begun to identify with its characters. The manager of the Rolling Stones, recognizing that the work 'embodied the aggressive and anti-social attitude he wanted to foster as an image for his group', toyed with the idea of purchasing the film rights; meanwhile, for the Stones' second album he composed a sleeve note 'urging the penniless record shop browser to find a blind man, "knock him on the head, steal his wallet and

mechanism succinctly: 'I must confess that I myself am never absent from a public execution . . . When I first attended them, I was shocked to the greatest degree. I was in a manner convulsed with pity and terror, and for several days, but especially the night after, I was in a very dismal situation. Still, however, I persisted in attending them, and by degrees my sensibility abated; so that I can now see one with great composure . . .' (Boswell, Vol.ii, p.93).

low [*sic*] and behold you have the loot if you put in the boot, good, another one sold" '. 'This passage,' says Steve Turner, writing on the influence of *A Clockwork Orange* on pop musicians, 'was later removed by the record company after protests from organizations for the blind, and a complaint from a member of the House of Lords to the Director of Public Prosecutions, calling it "a deliberate incitement to criminal action" '.[8]

Teenage audiences of Kubrick's film enjoyed the mayhem and ignored the theological dimension. It was a tremendous success, running in London for 61 weeks when first released. The Longford Committee were sitting at the time, and their report comments:

> Stanley Kubrick, for instance, maintains that social significance justifies the depiction of violence in *A Clockwork Orange*, that blood is used symbolically not realistically, and caricature justifies the claim of fantasy. There is bound to be disagreement on how far such distinctions are understood by audiences.[9]

For the next three years the courts were filled with 'cases of rape, murder and beatings attributed to the film's influence . . . too numerous to be dismissed as tabloid hyperbole. Tramps were killed, girls were assaulted and beatings were dished out as Kubrick's symphony of violence rang in the heads of the perpetrators', who in some cases were dressed in the peculiar cult clothing of the 'droogs'.[10]

Burgess rejected any suggestion that the book or film were triggering these responses. 'Art only imitates life', he said. 'Evil's already there. Original sin . . . Once you start admitting that a work of art can cause people to start committing crimes, then you're lost. Nothing's safe. Not even Shakespeare. Not even the Bible . . .'[11] This was not the view of the archpriest of dramatic violence; in a letter of 30 December 1933 Artaud had written, 'what we do not want to recognize is that an entertainment can be a lightning-conductor, that what is enacted on the stage can go on to be acted out in life'.[12] Kubrick either came to agree with Artaud or perhaps tired of the execrations heaped upon him. In 1974 he banned further screenings of the film in the United Kingdom, and all importation of videoed copies – though its distribution elsewhere remained unaffected.[*]

---

[*] When the Scala Cinema showed it in December 1992 they were immediately and successfully sued for breach of copyright (*The Times*, 24 March 1993). A version freshly scripted by Burgess was performed by the Royal Shakespeare Company in February 1990. Reviews were lukewarm, but one viewer, who had painful personal cause to remember the effect of the film on his youthful

In May 1977 the Home Office published the results of its research study on screen violence and film censorship. It noted that

> currently it is a matter for concern that popular taste seems to require that female characters be represented as objects to be raped, humiliated and subjugated, often, as it turns out, with their compliance. The message, if there is one, is that women not only deserve to be treated in this way, but unconsciously desire it.

However, the report came to the conclusion that the possible development of social values and individual attitudes favourable to a culture in which violence is acceptable and inevitable, natural abhorrence of violent action diminished, and feelings of sympathy replaced by emotional indifference was a topic too complex and 'least amenable to scientific study' to be pursued. It accepted that there were studies showing a correlation between exposure to violent films and the indulgence in aggressive (though not necessarily criminal) behaviour, but held that the relationship might well be that people predisposed to aggression were more likely to enjoy watching violent material. 'It can be stated quite simply that social research has not been able unambiguously to offer any firm assurance that the mass media in general, and films and television in particular, either exercise a socially harmful effect, or that they do not.'[13]

A major enquiry, chaired by the philosopher Bernard Williams, was established in the same year, and published its report, *Obscenity and Film Censorship*, in 1979. The enquiry dismissed anecdotal evidence of imitation, including the arraigning of *A Clockwork Orange*, and, noting that research trials differed in their outcomes, concluded that there was very little evidence from these sources of a connection between scenes of violence, including sexual violence, and any acting out in real life. Evidence of correlation was not only dubious in itself, it was in any case not evidence of causation. Though they acknowledged widespread indulgence in pornographic magazines (with probably some four million male readers a month) they eschewed any connection between rising

contemporaries, noted their middle-aged resurgence for the RSC performance, where they 'found the play's violence highly amusing', appreciative of the gang rape of a schoolgirl, and 'laughing uproariously' at a scene 'in which an old man is humiliated, stripped and beaten' (Andy Bull, *The Independent*, 6 February 1990). The arts editor of *The Times* remarked that the RSC's 'entire motivation for turning Anthony Burgess's *A Clockwork Orange* into a musical . . . appeared to be to cash in on the novel's existing notoriety, partly gained through the weird application of its imagery in the heavy-metal rock world (*The Times*, 25 September 1990).

circulation of pornography and rising statistics for sexual crime on two main grounds – statistics for other forms of crime were increasing even more rapidly than those for sexual crime; and the principal increase in sexual crime was in London, whereas the perusal of pornography was not so geographically limited. 'We unhesitatingly reject,' they stated, 'the suggestion that the available statistical information for England and Wales lends any support at all to the argument that pornography acts as a stimulus to the commission of sexual violence.' Only the already deviant would be tempted into further novelties; children were too robust to be damaged and must, in any case, learn to face facts; marital relations, far from being degraded, were more likely to be enhanced; and as for the suggestion that pornography was degrading to women, this was a political argument from the left who, once the chips were down, would opt for freedom of expression rather than censorship. Performers in pornography presumably earned a living in that way voluntarily[*] (though how the law stood on voluntary submission to serious injury was not clear) and a new law, the Protection of Children Act 1978, forbade the employment of juveniles in such material, though the report recorded its doubt whether such legislation had really been necessary.[†] As for the notorious 'snuff' movies, they were fakes. 'Another film ... which purported to include actual documentary sequences of mutilation and death was subsequently reported to have been, *at least in part* [emphasis added] faked.' 'The role of pornography in influencing the state of society is a minor one.'[14]

The committee recommended that no publication consisting solely of written material should be in any way restricted. Illustrations (including comics) and live performances should not be subject to pre-censorship, but should be liable to prosecution: in the case of illustrated material, for offensive portrayal of violence, cruelty, horror, or sexual, faecal or urinary functions or genital organs; in the case of live entertainment, if it involved offensive sexual activity, including masturbation and genital, anal or oral connection between humans, or humans and animals, or sexual exploitation of under-16s. Simulated activities should not be restricted unless offensive. A formula was required replacing the

---

[*] Evidence to the Minneapolis City Council Government Operations Committee in December 1983 conclusively proved otherwise, detailing the terrorization to which performers in pornographic films were subject (Minneapolis City Council, pp.24ff.).

[†] All such material inevitably involved child sexual abuse. The new legislation eliminated the middle-man rather than the trade, which continued through the formation of paedophile rings, making and exchanging material about their activities (see, for instance, Itzin (ed.) (1992), Chapters 11 and 12).

'deprave and corrupt' provision with a classification of 'offensive to reasonable people'.[15]

About films, the committee were less sanguine. 'It is not simply the extremity of the violence which concerns us', said the report.

> We found it extremely disturbing that highly explicit depictions of mutilation, savagery, menace and humiliation should be presented for the entertainment of an audience in a way that appeared to emphasize the pleasures of sadism. Indeed, some of the film sequences we saw seemed to have no purpose or justification other than to reinforce or sell the idea that it can be highly pleasurable to inflict injury, pain or humiliation (often in a sexual content) on others.

Continued licensing and classification was recommended, with a category introduced of films too extreme to be granted the current X certificate, which would thus (in deference to the committee's profound antipathy to censorship) obtain exhibition, but be restricted to club showing and regarded as wholly inappropriate for television.[16]

Videos were not mentioned. In 1979, when the report was published, video recorders were the toys of a few rich people. The explosion in video ownership that came with the 1980s* (by 1982 there were some six million in British homes, a number which had more than doubled by 1989)[17] brought fresh alarm as Members of Parliament became aware of the material that was flooding into private homes, where any restriction on children's viewing was outside statutory control, and where techniques of 'freeze-frame' could overcome the brevity on the grounds of which some dubious material had in films been given the benefit of the doubt. A major survey of 6,000 children revealed that four out of ten were accustomed to seeing video 'nasties' such as *Killer Driller* and *I Spit on your Grave*, and Coventry teachers were startled, when prompted to discuss the videos with the children, at the 'bloody and horrific scenes' relished by some, the anxiety and fear reported by others. Lord Coggan, a former Archbishop of Canterbury, was echoing what Mrs Whitehouse and the National Viewers' and Listeners' Association had been saying since its foundation in 1964, when he expressed his conviction that the effect of video nasties would be seen in increasing violence in society.[18]

In November 1983 Scotland Yard's Obscene Publications Squad

---

* Not until 1985 did *Social Trends* first begin to include video ownership among the statistics of household durables. An estimated 17 per cent of all households owned videos in 1983; by 1992 the figure was 72 per cent.

screened material for the information of MPs which rapidly overcame most scruples about censorship.[19] The Video Recordings Act of 1984 required the classification by the British Board of Film Censors of all videos, and permitted the banning of the worst, including depictions of human sexual activity or acts of force or constraint associated with it; torture or mutilation of human beings or animals; and human genital organs or human urinary or excretory functions.[20] There were already some 7,000 titles in circulation, which meant a huge backlog for the censors to work through, and during the two years before the Act came into force, proprietors of video libraries began to divest themselves of their more offensive material – one Exeter shop admitted replacing 800 titles between February and July of 1986.[21] Investigators in September 1988, however, found that although some of the most notorious examples, including *Killer Driller* and *I Spit on your Grave*, were unobtainable, a plentiful supply of unlicensed 'nasties' was on (discreet) offer, a problem virtually beyond the powers of the authorities to police.[22]

In 1988 the Criminal Justice Act made the possession of child pornography a criminal offence. In the same year, and to the gratification of the National Viewers' and Listeners' Association, who had long campaigned for such an innovation, a Broadcasting Standards Council was instituted, empowered to receive complaints, but not to censor broadcast material. It received statutory status in the Broadcasting Act of 1990, and the same Act finally extended the Obscene Publications Act to broadcasting. Neither of these moves were to fulfil the Association's hopes. Though increasing numbers of prominent people ventured to associate themselves with Mary Whitehouse's campaign, the broadcasting authorities continued to test with impunity the limits of public tolerance. An adjudication of the Council in February 1994, for instance, refused to accept objections to masturbation, homosexuality and nudity in *The Buddha of Suburbia*, though it did rule that a depiction of group sex was unduly prolonged;* [23] not that the BBC were at all disturbed by

* Complaints about violence and bad language, however, were frequently upheld. In July 1994 the Council's annual report noted a 60 per cent increase in public complaints about swearing and blasphemy and a 25 per cent rise in concerns about violence, with a tripling in the number of complaints about violence which the Council upheld. It is not clear whether the public is becoming more willing to protest, or the broadcasters more cavalier in their attitude to public taste. Dealing with complaints of bad language, the Council's current chairwoman commented on 'the apparent inability of broadcasters to recognize [that] it may cause a level of offence which can be hard to explain or excuse' (*The Times*, 19 and 22 July, 5 August 1994). A year later, in July 1995, the Council recorded a further 30 per cent increase in complaints, noted public alarm at 'the constant erosion of taste boundaries' and warned of the dangers of 'a descent towards the tacky and falsely

the ruling: they proceeded in January 1995 not only to rebroadcast the series in its original form, but to bring its timing forward to 9 p.m., the very brink of the child-protection 'watershed', leading to renewed complaints, and the publication by the BBC of the Broadcasting Standards Council's repeated, if impotent, condemnation of the protraction of the group sex scene, and of the expression 'Jesus fucking Christ'.[24] The Bishop of Peterborough, who served for four years on the Council, confessed in his diocesan letter in the summer of 1993 that 'during my time television got worse in its prurient and sadistic violence, its sex portrayed as if words like "marriage" and "aids" didn't exist and in the language of the barrack room brought more and more into sitting rooms at earlier and earlier hours'.[25]

In the real world, women were having to come to terms with rocketing increases in reported rape. The 240 instances in 1947 had nearly doubled by 1957, passed the 1,000 level by 1974, 2,300 by 1986, then within only seven years had doubled again to 4,600 by 1993; and it is estimated that only about 8 per cent are reported.[26] Even if the figures are distorted by a diminishing reluctance, in more recent years, to report rape, there is no evading the evidence of increasing assaults on women. The rapes were becoming nastier, involving enforced sodomy and fellatio, and defilement of victims.[27] Hitherto sacrosanct women – nuns, uniformed Salvation Army lasses – began to figure among victims, as well as old women in their 70s, 80s – even 90s; schoolgirls of 11 and 12 and, by the mid-90s, little girls as young as five, were being subjected to rape by lustful teenagers.[28] Multiple rape by groups of men and youths began to be reported, and the degree of ferocity escalated, a victim communicating with the police by writing when her jaw was too smashed to permit speech, a 76-year-old dying of internal bleeding after being raped by a 17-year-old. There were reports of women bundled off the pavement into vans, of women drivers flagged down on various pretexts and raped, of cars halted at traffic lights invaded by rapists. A 15-year-old sentenced in February 1993 was thought to be the first instance of a rape carried out at school. Until 1993 no male under the age of 14 could be accused of rape, but the prevalence of rapes by younger males, such as that of a teacher by a 13-year-old (though the prosecution was aborted

sensationalist'. They further noted that 98 per cent of complaints came from people who wrote not more than twice, there was not a small core of professional complainants. Some programme-makers expressed the view that the number of complaints (some 2,200 to the BSC in the twelve months from 1 April 1994) was not worth considering, but the BBC announced its intention to hold a conference on standards of taste and decency in November 1995 (*The Times*, 12 and 28 July 1995).

for inadequate evidence) led to the Sexual Offences Act of 1993, which removed the lower age limit. By February 1994 a 10-year-old and an 11-year-old were charged with raping a five-year-old, though again the prosecution was aborted for inadequate evidence. Adequate evidence existed, however, for the trial to proceed in June 1994 of a 13-year-old accused of raping a 12-year-old, the first prosecution under the new law.[29] Homosexual rapes of young boys and even gang rape of young men began increasingly to be reported. Terror of contracting AIDS added to the horror of the experience for the victims.[30]

Because parks and commons give cover to rapists and muggers, and attacks are reported even on women accompanied by their children, the numbers using parks are declining.* By January 1994 the promoters of the twelve community forests newly planned for various areas of Britain were being warned that a sustained educational campaign, concentrating on the extreme rarity of attacks on women in woodlands, would be necessary if the forests were to become the hoped-for community resource.[31] In April 1994 it was reported that Greenwich was setting up the first council-run uniformed parks police force to patrol the borough's open spaces.[32] Research by the Countryside Commission in 1994 showed that people were 'now scared to walk freely in woods and open fields in case they are attacked, robbed or sexually abused', and strategies were proposed such as encouraging 'small social groups of women to enjoy woodland walks together'.[33]

Fear of being trapped by a broken-down car haunted women after some appalling assaults including murder in 1986 and 1988. Advice on how to cope began to pour out. In 1989 the Automobile Association produced an audio-cassette of advice; makers of mobile phones emphasized their value in breakdown emergencies. The Royal Automobile Club in 1991 stated that 42 per cent of the women they had surveyed hated driving alone at night, though a survey by General Accident the following year found a lower figure: 20 per cent. The Metropolitan Police produced a video and booklet of advice on precautions women drivers should take. Early in 1992 the AA introduced a 'callsafe' mobile phone service for their members, and by the end of 1992 the RAC's similar scheme had received 5,000 enquiries in its first week, though by the time the warm weather of 1995 arrived, drivers were being warned not to open their windows in an attempt to keep cool, so prevalent had become the crime of snatching mobile phones at traffic lights (not to

---

* The demise of American inner-city parks as a result of the fear of crime was one of the topics at the Green Towns and Cities Conference held in Liverpool in 1984.

mention 'carjacking' as a prelude to robbing the occupant at knife-point of his credit cards, and stealing the car).[34] Press reports continued of vicious attacks on women whose cars had broken down. The 1993 Highway Code included advice to women in such a predicament; women's magazines stressed the importance of never running short of petrol, of travelling with locked doors, of sitting in the passenger seat after telephoning for assistance to give the impression a companion is about to arrive. Lone women were advised not to advertise their status by displaying car stickers of women's organizations. By the end of 1993 Ford were publicizing their invention of a dashboard panic-button linked to a satellite system which would enable motorists to signal their position to rescue services without having to leave their vehicle to summon help.[35]

Obviously increasing apprehension serves some financial interests; there is money to be made from selling safety devices and services. But there is also widespread testimony to women forgoing travel after dark whenever possible, even at the cost of some forfeiture of job opportunities. 'As retailers open more late nights and build more stores out of town, they ought to stop and think what this means for their women workers', said a representative of Usdaw, the shopworkers' union, in September 1989.[36] Marks and Spencer in 1988 initiated a training programme to teach their largely female staff how to defend themselves.[37]

Sir John Glubb, in an analysis of *The Fate of Empires*, remarks that in the tenth century Arab Empire women had achieved considerable standing in the professions. 'Many women practised law, while others obtained posts as university professors. There was an agitation for the appointment of female judges, which, however, does not appear to have succeeded.' Soon after this period, however, there was a collapse of public order and 'the resulting increase in confusion and violence made it unsafe for women to move unescorted in the streets, with the result that this feminist movement collapsed'.[38]

Feminism was the new influence in the moves to control the exploitation of women in entertainment. To left-wing feminists, rape was a product of the power relationships inherent in patriarchy, a view firmly eschewing any suggestion that unbridled lust could be a depravity.* But left and right united in condemning rape as intolerable.

---

* That rape could owe more to culture than biology is a thesis developed by a number of contributors to *Rape – An Historical and Cultural Enquiry* (eds. Tomaselli and Porter), which points out that 'whatever the biological basis for sexuality may be . . . the variation in the incidence of rape cross-culturally demonstrates that culture is a powerful force in channelling the human sex

Intellectually, the position was difficult. Left-wing feminists who had happily been marching and demonstrating to 'reclaim the night' for women so long as what was involved was more police and better street-lighting were profoundly averse to aligning themselves with the – in their view – neurotic aversion to sexual pleasure which underpinned Christian opposition to pornography. Proposing any statutory curtail-ment of media freedom immediately opened their cause to the sort of ribaldry and stereotyping they had previously been lavishing on Mary Whitehouse, as Claire Short, MP, found when in 1986 and again in February 1988 she endeavoured to promote awareness of the canker of pornography by her attempt to expunge 'Page 3' through making the display of sexually provocative naked and semi-naked women a statutory offence.*

A solution was found by defining the issue as one not of morality but of civil liberties, and calling for legislation, along the lines of race relations acts, outlawing discrimination against women. In April 1989 a group of writers, artists, lawyers and trade unionists launched the somewhat casuistically named Campaign against Pornography and Censorship. Supporters repeatedly stressed their abhorrence of and distinction from 'right-wing' moralistic stances against pornography, and neither Itzin's catalogue of the chronology of anti-pornography initiatives in the UK nor her list of organizations concerned about, or active against, pornography deigned to mention Mrs Whitehouse or the National Viewers' and Listeners' Association, which well pre-dated those in Itzin's list. Nevertheless, the basic tenet, that pornography was not a displacement activity, that it did degrade, humiliate and harm women not only in the course of its production but also in its effects on viewers, was common to both political left and right. Itzin's contributors to *Pornography: Women, Violence and Civil Liberties* drew on sources identical to Mrs Whitehouse's to support their contention of the link between viewing and acting out, asserting that consumption of existing material encouraged callousness and diminishing caring and trust in sexual relationships, increasing dissatisfaction with existing partners, and a growing inability to assess the harm of child abuse or rape.[39] The

drive' (Peggy Reeves Sanday, p.85) However, 'culture' in this context is not concerned with the artistic environment. 'Gender relations and gender politics differ radically from society to society, being determined less by anatomy or ''the selfish gene'' than by complex configurations of economic, political, domestic and ideological arrangements' (Roy Porter, p.230) There is an admission, however, that the replacement of repressive moral codes with the 'pleasure principle and permissiveness' is accompanied by more, not less rape; but the possible influence of titillating material is not discussed.

* Both her attempts received considerable Parliamentary support, but failed through lack of time.

analogy of the right of the community to curtail liberty where pollution threatened, whether physical or emotional, replicated points made by the Longford Committee twenty years earlier. Both sets of campaigners were deeply disturbed at the mounting trade in paedophilic pornography, one Itzin contributor pointing to the speed with which, in the course of the 1970s and 1980s, mainstream advertising in respectable magazines lent itself to increasingly sexually provocative portrayal of children,* as well as the casual inclusion of the paraphernalia of bondage in association with voluptuous advertising models.

The suggestions made by the Longford Committee in 1972 and the Williams Committee in 1979, grounding the definition of offensiveness in contemporary reasonable public opinion, had to accept that the degradation of public taste was progressive, that yesterday's hard porn was today's soft porn.† The addictive element in pornography, the need constantly to increase the dose and search for novelty, had particularly engaged the attention of Itzin's contributors. Most chose to believe that the same tendency did not apply to erotica – that is, as they defined it, sexually celebratory and titillating material involving willing participants – a conclusion at variance with the dynamic towards increasing sensationalism which Sorokin sees as central to the cultural development of sensate societies. Indeed, one contributor hoped to liberate erotica, to safeguard the showing of 'an erect male penis, sexual penetration, acts of love-making between adults of the same sex and so on . . .' by the introduction of statutory control grounded in discrimination against women as the sole criterion of unacceptable material.[40]

In practice, a political definition based on degradation proves no less subjective a criterion of unacceptability than does an aesthetic definition based on degree of offensiveness. Appendix 3 of Itzin's book cites approvingly the verdict of a Canadian court that so long as various acts are 'consensual' and do not involve children or violence, they are

---

* The fashion designer Calvin Klein's use of sexually provocative under-age (or purporting to be under-age) models, the images being the work of the photographer previously renowned for Madonna's book *Sex*, provoked such outrage in the United States that in the summer of 1995 the clothing company publicly announced its intention to cease such advertising (*The Times*, 29 and 30 August 1995).
† A trivial example of the process at an elevated artistic level is Michael Tippett's highly acclaimed *The Mask of Time*, which required repeated renderings from his choral singers of '*merde!*', so unspeakably offensive in Jarry's Paris. One result of the progressive debasement of public taste was the increasing number of prosecutions for obscenity which failed to obtain conviction, with the result that fewer and fewer prosecutions were mounted. In 1984, for instance, there were 458 prosecutions in magistrates' courts in England and Wales; by 1986, only 113. Prosecutions pursued in crown courts totalled 258 in 1984, only just over 30 by 1988 (Itzin (ed.) (1992), p.406).

adjudged 'not obscene', but goes on to find obscene the squirting of semen in a woman's face because it 'grossly exceeds community standards' – which returns the criterion to exactly those shifting perceptions, liberated from absolute moral insights, on which sensate culture prides itself.

In spite of anxious searching, no new criterion has presented itself consonant with the modern liberal credo, and the 1959 Act remains in force. However, the fact that concern is now being expressed from all shades of the political spectrum about the impact of the arts in creating a value system hostile to women's safety inevitably raises the question of the extent to which other aspects of violence are influenced by the same source.

For the hundred years from the middle of the nineteenth to the middle of the twentieth century, homicide and offences against the person had been declining in England. Ted Robert Gurr's extensive compilation of research[41] reveals that, with occasional irregularities in the figures, murders, manslaughters and assaults in England and Wales declined dramatically from the 1830s to the 1940s, during and after which there occurred an even more spectacular increase.[*] Crimes of violence in England and Wales approximately doubled between 1938 (the last full peacetime year) and 1948, from 2,721 to 5,183. With each succeeding decade they have more than doubled again: 6,516 in 1951, 17,601 in 1961, over 47,000 in 1971, over 100,000 in 1981; and over 190,000 by 1991 – and are still climbing, to 205,110 by 1993. Homicides, 282 in 1960, numbered 726 by 1991, with a subsequent decline to 675 in 1993 – and this in a period when advances in surgery have greatly improved the proportion of the seriously injured saved from death. Robberies (that is, thefts involving violence or threat of violence), only 217 of which were reported in 1930, totalled just over 2,000 in 1960, almost 58,000 by 1993. Firearm use, which figured in only some 2,000 crimes in 1971 had, by 1993, escalated to just under 14,000.[†] [42] By the summer of 1993 it was reckoned that over a million unregistered firearms were in circulation, and in September 1994 the Metropolitan Police Commissioner said that 'on average, every day in London, one or two shots are fired from an illegal handgun';[43] police raids to seek out black-market

---

[*] Because the statistics can be distorted by the extent to which assaults are reported (for which there may be various reasons, such as the contemporary opinion of what is tolerable, prospects of compensation, etc.), Gurr based his primary research on homicide, which seldom goes unreported.
[†] The National Viewers' and Listeners' Association, reporting on a survey of 47 films on four TV channels between January and June 1994, commented that they included 244 incidents in which firearms were used, and accused the TV companies of making the use of firearms appear normal.

weapons in August 1993 uncovered sub-machine-guns as well as revolvers and shotguns,[44] and a BBC Radio 4 report on 17 March 1994 spoke of large caches of high-quality arms (of criminal, not terrorist, provenance) being discovered in Merseyside and Manchester. In the same month came the first trial of armed robbers charged with using a machine-gun against police officers in the course of committing a crime.[45] In Strathclyde, where armed crime is now virtually a daily occurrence, the police in 1992 instituted a policy of buying up weapons to take them 'out of commission', and in a little over three years acquired some 3,400 firearms, including four Kalashnikov assault rifles and a Sten MK2 sub-machine-gun.[46]

From the 1960s screens began to be inserted in banks, building societies and post offices, separating employees from their customers. By 1970 major raids on banks, virtually unknown in the 1950s and increasingly using acid sprays or firearms, were averaging one a week;[47] by 1992 there were three such raids a day, and one bank in 14 was being raided every 24 hours. By 1993, according to the secretary of the Banking Insurance and Finance Union security committee, raids were numbering about seven every working day, and were increasingly violent.[48] The vice-president of the union reported to the Trades Union Congress in 1992 that robbers were using hand grenades, axes, pistols, stun guns and shotguns, acid and ammonia.[49] JCBs are being used to prise cashpoints out of walls.[50] As security measures at banks and building societies tightened, sophisticated criminals began to take hostage the families of those with access to large deposits of money, enforcing the key-holders' co-operation with threats which, in the autumn of 1992, included that of castrating the keyholders' children.[51] Excluding child abductions, there were 545 kidnapping incidents in 1990, 929 by 1992.[52] A whole new industry has developed, of consultancies advising and counselling managers and staff in coping with armed robbery and the emotional effect of the trauma involved.[53]

Until 1988 filling stations were untroubled by premeditated violent crime, but by 1991 Shell was having to introduce protective measures such as cash limits on tills, closed-circuit television, and door locks operated by the cashier on suspicion of a threatening approach;[54] and by 1994 the industry was reporting that one in four stations had been robbed during the year.[55] BP by 1995 had installed in 24 of their garages sprinkler systems which spray burglars with an indelible, invisible substance detectable for six months under ultraviolet light.[56] 'Ram-raiding' of shop fronts with stolen cars, graphically captured on security videos in the summer of 1991, alerted the public to what retailers in north-east England were suffering, but left them unprepared for the first such raid on a private house, which occurred in the south-west in January 1994.[57]

Already in 1960 the Advisory Council on the Treatment of Offenders had received many letters from residents of Liverpool, Birmingham and Manchester saying that 'they were afraid to go out or to open their doors at night because of the risk of being attacked'. The Council's report had referred to

> the apparent increase in offences of violence, and especially in those committed by hooligans with no motive (such as robbery) other than the infliction of pain and suffering on their victims. We were told that the latter type of offence was not much in evidence before 1939 but had become much more common since the end of the war.[58]

By 1992, as canvassers in the general election that year discovered when they found it impossible to persuade householders to open their doors after dark, such insecurity had spread country-wide. Arts Council research has shown a reluctance on the part of older women to go out to the theatre at night, and a Gallup Poll in 1989 found that some 60 per cent of over-60s rarely ventured out at night, with 44 per cent of the women respondents saying they never went out after dark.[59] Women ceased to wear good jewellery outside the home; and many kept their door keys on chains round their necks and carried extra small change in an inner pocket when out, in order to get safely home if their bag was snatched. In a number of areas the time of Evensong in winter has been moved to the afternoon, or transport to church arranged for frightened parishioners like the blind old-age pensioner who, according to the Bishop of Southwark, was 'three times struck on the face and left helpless on the ground' after collecting his meagre pension at the post office, a fate which he shared with a number of the diocesan clergy.[60] 'Mugging', meaning street robbery with violence, entered the language. According to the *Shorter Oxford Dictionary* 1950 edition, 'mugging' meant pulling funny faces or preparing for an exam. The 1989 revision noted a use of the word 'mug', in inverted commas, meaning 'rob with violence', in the *Manchester Guardian* in 1951, but not until the 1970s did the present ugly connotation come into general usage without inverted commas, the *Daily Mail* having launched the trend with its account of muggers 'who clobber you and steal whatever you have of value' in the Clarendon Road area of Notting Hill.

In 1989 the Kennel Club noted a huge increase in the ownership of dogs with a reputation for savagery. In the first six months of 1989 over 6,000 Rottweilers were registered with the Kennel Club, compared with just over 1,000 in the whole of 1979. By 1991 other breeds, specifically bred for aggression and fighting, were being favoured. These were not defensive initiatives on the part of frightened householders; they were, to quote Janet Daley in *The Times* of 24 May 1991, 'part of a panoply of deliberate terror . . . Benign pedestrian life as it was known until the Fifties has virtually disappeared as a part of urban experience', she continued, citing the deserted concrete wastelands peopled by 'roving delinquents . . . A gang of noisily aggressive youths promenading with their consort of dogs is as terrifying a vision as city life has to offer. The prospect of such encounters keeps the residents of many neighbourhoods and estates confined to their barricaded homes.' In 1991 the Government, forewarned by the Dutch Government of the connection between savage dogs and professional, especially drug-related crime, introduced the Dangerous Dogs Act which, ameliorating an initial intention to have certain specified breeds put down, required the formal registration and muzzling of pit bull terriers; and the banning of two breeds of South American fighting dogs which were suddenly enjoying an unprecedented popularity.[61]

It is unnecessary to flesh out the crime statistics with anecdotes, of which the press is daily replete. What is obvious is the extreme callousness of the perpetrators, often quite young teenagers, whose greed and sadism respects neither age nor infirmity.[*] Elderly people in wheelchairs, old people in homes for the aged, women out walking, people too frail to leave their homes, even a centenarian attacked by a ten-year-old, the melancholy catalogue continues of torture and terrorization, of people deliberately run down, sometimes by their own stolen car, of battered nonogenarians left trussed up to die, of young adults knifed in the street for no or trivial reasons, of the blind not only robbed but their white sticks smashed, of victims doused in petrol and then set on fire. Running through this litany of mayhem is a twisted thread of sexual excitement, as assault and degradation are added to battery. As General Sir John Hackett said, lamenting in 1987 the undeniable prevalence of bullying in the army (as in any human group): 'What is relatively new is

---

[*] The RSPCA were reporting record levels of cruelty to animals in the early 1990s, and while this could merely reflect increased vigilance and inspection, the Society singled out 'malicious cruelty' as the most disturbing feature of the figures, adding that 'research in the United States indicated that people who as juveniles were cruel to animals graduated to more serious crimes as adults' (*The Times*, 22 March 1990 and 8 March 1991).

the increase in sexual aspects of physical and mental ill-treatment. This is deeply disturbing though not unexpected in a time of sexual aberration . . .'[62]

In September 1991 a chief constable who had served in London's East End in the 1960s remarked that, in comparison with the contemporary scene, he looked back 'almost fondly' on the decade of the notorious Kray, Richardson and Fraser gangs.[62] The Krays themselves in March 1993 issued from their prison cells a public protest at being equated with modern criminals. 'In our day,' they said, 'no one would dream of mugging and battering old ladies, stealing from their next door neighbours or molesting and killing innocent women and children.'[64] By October more than 18,000 signatures had been collected for a petition, presented to Downing Street by a group of show-biz luminaries, demanding the release of the Krays. 'During their reign there was no mugging', said one of the presenters. 'I can't help feeling that, had they remained free, the London of today would be a safer place.' 'The Krays only hurt their own, other villains', said another.[65]

Attacks on people going about their professional duties began to cause widespread concern in the 1980s. Hard statistics are not available except over limited areas, and are open to question even where they do exist, because of changing perceptions of what constitutes an assault worth reporting. But during the 1980s it was the universal perception of those involved with the public that threats to their security were becoming more prevalent. By 1986 a conference on hospital security learnt that a survey of staff in five health authority districts found that one in twenty had been threatened with a weapon during the previous twelve months, with community nurses visiting people at home suffering such a degree of intimidation and violence that in Liverpool duties were organized to obviate the necessity for nurses to work alone. 'The dilemma we face is how to improve our security without diverting massive resources from patient care and without creating a fortress-like environment in our hospitals', said the director of the National Association of Health Authorities.[66] By the start of 1989 a Health and Safety Executive survey showed that 2,700 nurses and 200 doctors had been assaulted in five health authority areas (Fife, Newcastle upon Tyne, Birmingham, Croydon and Exeter) in the previous twelve months, and by the middle of 1989 the British Medical Association's annual conference was informed that 'some casualty departments had permanent guards, patients frightened out of their wits and staff who were terrified to go to work'.[67] In March 1995 a police station was established inside a Swansea hospital, to combat the rise in violence against staff and the thefts from patients, with a baton-equipped police constable on regular patrol of the wards and corridors.[68]

Following a report that 11 per cent of London GPs had been assaulted during 1987, the BMA launched in 1989 a national survey of violence and vandalism against family doctors.[69] The results of a survey of 2,000 London GPs made public in 1993 showed that 40 per cent had been threatened, with 9 per cent reporting one or more assaults.[70] A Birmingham University survey reported that two-thirds of West Midland general practitioners were suffering aggression.[71] Under new provisions operative from April 1994 doctors are permitted to remove violent and abusive patients from their lists immediately, the previous seven-day waiting period while alternative provision is sought being abolished,[72] but patients who cannot find a practice to take them are allocated, on a rota system, to a GP who must accept them for at least three months, and attacks are being recorded on the luckless conscripted doctor.[73] In September 1995 the BMA issued a 'survival handbook', detailing the punching, head-butting and finger-breaking tactics to which doctors under attack could resort if all else failed.[74]

In April 1994, presenting the results of a survey carried out by the Royal College of Nursing, the General Secretary commented that it was a sad day for nursing when the uniform ceased to provide protection. 'I remember,' she said, 'the day when it was possible for a nurse in uniform to walk safely through the streets of east London at any time.' New guidelines, however, advised community nurses that they should no longer rely on their uniform to protect them. 'The more the Government promotes community care,' commented a Bradford community nurse, 'the more nurses will be put at risk.' Apart from personal threats and assaults, one in five of the nurses surveyed had had their cars or personal belongings vandalized, and the new guidelines recommended that community nurses make their visits by taxi if the risk of vandalism was high.[75]

Social workers suffered four deaths and numerous unrecorded assaults between 1985 and 1988, in which year the British Association of Social Workers devoted much of its annual conference to the problem.[76] Care staff in residential homes were subjected to daily abuse and violence, according to the National and Local Government Officers' Association, whose journal in 1986 included mention of one home where there were 850 incidents of violence in a year, attacks by glue-sniffing or drug-addicted teenagers being a major problem.[77] The fact that health and welfare staff are inevitably exposed to clients who are mentally deranged or drug-addicted obviously puts them at special risk, and the emotional vulnerability of the unemployed may go some way to account for the mounting attacks on local authority staff in job centres, where, according to the Civil and Public Servants' Association, assaults on staff rose between 1989 and 1990 from 155 to 233.[78] At a DHSS office in Bristol, steel-reinforced public and staff doors and shatter-proof film on windows was installed, extra screens inserted in some private interview rooms, and an official car and driver employed to ferry staff in and out of the area.[79] But, as the Trades Union Congress at Blackpool in 1992 heard, 'workers are facing an unprecedented wave of violence throughout industry and the service sector'. Attacks on post office staff had reached 'a record five a week', according to the Union of Communication Workers, and the dangers long faced by counter staff were now spreading to delivery workers on the streets.[80] A spokesman for the Royal Mail admitted, in June 1990, that in view of attacks on postmen it was now necessary, in some parts of London, 'for delivery staff to be accompanied by escorts when delivering the mail'.[81] The first murder of a postman on his rounds occurred not in London, but in Derby in December 1991, when a postman was stabbed to death as he delivered mail.[82] In the autumn of 1993 a Sheffield postman who was emptying a postbox was coshed, then murdered by robbers who crushed him to death by deliberately driving over him in his own van.[83]

In September 1989 the shopworkers' union, Usdaw, reported a survey claiming that one in five shop staff were threatened at work, one in seven sexually assaulted and one in twelve physically attacked,[84] figures which in the light of the British Retail Consortium's crime survey in 1994 seem very inflated, unless there was a substantial improvement in public conduct in subsequent years. Even so, the BRC survey recorded 14,000 staff subjected to actual physical violence in the year under review, 106,000 to threats of violence, and stated that 'the risk of actual physical violence is 8 attacks per 1,000 staff', commenting that many incidents were going unrecorded. 'There is widespread concern within retailing about this issue and a perception that physical attacks are increasing in frequency.'[85] Two young shop assistants were stabbed to death in trivial robberies in November 1994. In 1990 a public library at Highfields, High Wycombe, known as the fortress because of its wire-mesh-protected windows, was closed down after attacks by youths 'made it untenable for the library to be staffed'.[86]

Growing numbers of drunken and unruly passengers led to discussions, in the summer of 1989, between some airlines and Broadmoor Hospital with a view to helping train airline staff. A Dan Air representative commented, 'This is a problem which is increasing and we will happily investigate anything which can be shown to help.'[87] By 1995 a spokesman for the International Air Transport Association in Geneva was commenting, 'The growing number of incidents raises serious concerns about the safety of aircraft.'[88] Assaults on London bus conductors and drivers peaked at 1,358 in 1985, after which there was an improvement (the 1992 figure was 1,035) thanks to the installation of such measures as driver protection screens, two-way radio, video equipment (now fitted in all buses), personal assault alarms incorporated in conductors' 'Clipper' ticket machines, and a policy of encouraging the presence of police officers by offering them free travel, on or off duty. Even so, an internal report on the 1992 figures noted 'a worrying increase in assaults which are no more than gratuitous violence against our staff'. A policy was instituted of helping staff take out private prosecutions for 'common assaults', that is, those not handled by the Crown Prosecution Service.[89]

Serious assaults (those occasioning bodily harm) on London Underground staff mounted from 218 in 1987 to 335 by 1989; on the railways the same category of offence increased from 413 to 562. Both organizations had begun to look more closely at the reasons for injuries to staff reporting sick, and defensive measures were instituted, including, in the case of London Underground, a policy of prosecuting for 'common assault', of which in 1992 600 were reported, though by then the total of serious (criminal) assaults was diminishing – in 1993 to 339 in British Rail, and 110 on the underground.[90] Psychologists were employed to coach staff in techniques of extracting fares from recalcitrant youths – Scotrail spent some £20,000 on training their guards on one particular line, where gangs of youths regularly threatened staff and smashed windows and seats.[91] The diminution in violent assault was accompanied, however, by increasing levels of vandalism, in which children 'as young as five' were reported to be endangering the lives of passengers.[92]

British Rail had realized, towards the end of the 1980s, that while trespass had always caused anxiety to the railways, vandalism (and graffiti) had begun to increase during the 1970s and 1980s to a point that had reached threatening proportions. When magistrates in Basingstoke, Hampshire, wrote to the head teachers of all the schools in the town asking them to warn pupils that they 'risked loss of liberty' if they placed obstructions on the line, the move was described by *The Times* as 'unprecedented'.[93] Statistical records began to be collated. In the course of 1991 vandals cut signalling and power cables on the railways, and left almost 3,000 objects on the lines, including a motorcycle, a supermarket trolley, dustbins, rail sleepers and, in 1992, waiting room benches. Fifty people were arrested for vandalism in two weeks of December 1991 alone.[94] In June 1994 the inevitable happened; the driver and a passenger were killed by a derailment near Glasgow, but far from shocking perpetrators into desisting, two further incidents occurred within the next three days.[95] Children who used to wave at train drivers were by the end of the 1980s more likely to heave bricks at them,[96] a phenomenon also remarked upon by school bus drivers, who had bricks and bats thrown through their windows even when under police escort.[97] British Rail embarked upon a programme of propaganda in schools, involving 150 train drivers and 39 police officers.[98]

Children followed the pattern of their elders, with the same surge in violence being reported by the mid-1980s. Research published in 1986 covering 85 primary schools in 40 local education authorities painted a picture of 'unprecedented disruption and disobedience among primary school children'.[99] 'Attacks on teachers and on other children, violent temper tantrums in which children throw books and chairs, spitting, stealing, swearing and screaming have all become commonplace in infant and early junior classrooms.' The researchers concluded that 'there is obviously a direct link between violence on television and some behaviour at school', and surmised that showing adults engaged in all kinds of action could be reducing children's respect for their elders.[100] Two years later, at the National Association of Schoolmasters/Union of Women Teachers summer conference, delegates heard that 'children aged four are attacking teachers as the growing wave of classroom violence spreads to nursery schools'; knives and scissors were now featuring in the attacks.[101] A survey that same year by the National Association of Head Teachers 'suggests there are more than 18,000 acts of school violence annually across the whole country, and that nearly 30,000 children a year are suspended for bad behaviour'. It claimed that attacks were occurring on average every four minutes of the school day.[102] By now teachers were frankly maintaining that the 'growing minority of brutalized, selfish, miserably inarticulate children devoid of moral sense, for whom attack is the best form of defence', were not only mirroring social and moral standards which television had served to cheapen, but owed much of their fighting techniques to what they had witnessed on television.[103]

A government enquiry chaired by Lord Elton disputed these claims, but in the interval before the Elton Committee reported, surveys and conference speeches continued to dwell on a catalogue of indiscipline, insubordination and violence. When, early in 1989, the Elton Committee's findings were published, teachers disputed its claim that only '0.5 per cent of teachers [were] subjected to assaults, and 1.7 per cent [were] victims of some form of aggression'. Even on the basis of the Elton figures, however, it was pointed out that they implied that 2,000 teachers were victims of violence in any one week, 76,000 teachers hit or physically assaulted in the course of one academic year. A South Wales teacher described

> letters from parents which contain threats. Parents standing outside the gates, intimidating and jeering at teachers. Parents coming into school to abuse and threaten teachers. Infant and junior pupils regularly kicking and swearing. Every day teachers are verbally abused. Teenage thugs hitting teachers in the face for no reason. Two 17-year-olds hitting teachers at lunch time. Taking a child home and being assaulted by the child with the parents assisting. Concrete blocks being thrown at teachers. Being thumped by someone with a knife because you moved him in the dinner queue.[104]

By June 1993 panic buttons providing for direct communication between school heads and the police were being installed in schools in Newcastle upon Tyne,[105] and at the 1994 Easter conference of the National Association of Schoolmasters/Union of Women Teachers, after a recital of what was perceived as increasing violence over the previous two years, there were calls for the universal installation of panic buttons.[106] After the knife murder, by an intruder, of a twelve-year-old pupil at a Middlesbrough school, publicity began to appear in the press of the extent to which closed-circuit television and personal alarms were already in common use in schools, with one school isolated behind a perimeter fence, entry restricted to those with identity cards.[107] In January 1995 came the first report of an event, commonplace in America, of a pupil taking a loaded gun into school.[108]

Early in 1995 the Government ordered an enquiry into the big increase in the number of disruptive children being expelled from state schools. A survey by school inspectors of a sample of 428 secondary schools suggested that over the system as a whole more than 8,000 children were being excluded for varying periods, with dubious prospects of continuing education for those permanently expelled.[109] The General Secretary of the National Association of Head Teachers reported to the annual conference in May 1995 that permanent expulsions had trebled in three years, and would exceed 10,000 in the current year.[110]

Coping with disruptive, uncontrollably violent children is not, of course, the only source of stress for teachers, but, as delegates to the conferences of the various teaching unions in the last six or eight years have made clear in referring to the rising numbers seeking to take early retirement for stress-related illnesses, it is a major aspect of it, exacerbated in recent years by malicious false accusations of sexual abuse fabricated by overknowing young people against teachers whose attempts at discipline they resented.[111] By 1993–4 over 5,500 teachers were leaving on health grounds, compared with less than half that number ten years previously and a third as many fifteen years previously;[112] about a third of head teachers leaving the profession are estimated to be retiring because of stress-related illness.[113]

The police themselves are in the front line in controlling escalating crime and social disorder. No official record of the killing and wounding of police in the course of their duties exists, but research published in the *Police Review* shows an increase in the murder of policemen outside Northern Ireland in each decade since the end of World War II, from 11 in 1951–60 to 25 in 1981–90 (nine of whom were killed by gunmen), and this at a time when medical advances are improving prospects of survival for the injured.[114] Injury statistics, too, have not been centrally kept, nor indeed by all forces, nor has there been any agreed criteria of what constitutes an injury worthy of record. What can be said is that by 1985, at which time injuries serious enough to require sickness leave were running at over 10,500 annually, the existing facilities for the treatment and rehabilitation of injured officers were found to be quite inadequate for the number and severity of the injuries being sustained, and a convalescent home with wheelchair and hydrotherapy facilities was established.[115] Over the years 1983–5 the number of officers whose injuries forced them into early retirement doubled, and in November 1991 it was reported by the Metropolitan Police that the rate of enforced retirement would have to be increased, as it was no longer possible to find enough desk jobs for injured officers unfit to return to full duties.[116] By April 1988 the *Police Review* was claiming 17,000 assaults on police outside Northern Ireland, and in July the Home Office finally required the Chief Inspector of Constabulary to collect and publish information on police casualties. Injuries in England and Wales alone were running at over 19,000 by 1991. By 1993 the total was back to about 18,000, but concealed within that total is a marked increase in assaults in Northumbria and Merseyside, as well as in relatively rural areas such as

North Wales and Wiltshire, the main improvement being in London, but even there a diminishing overall total concealed a sinister increase, from six in 1992 to 41 in 1993, in the number of incidents in which London police were confronted with firearms.[117] The public who witness attacks on isolated and unarmed police officers may not be unconcerned, but they are too intimidated to intervene, and press reports of officers kicked to a pulp in front of inactive groups of bystanders are occurring.[118] In April 1994 a woman police constable escaped unhurt when her car was wrecked by children in a Yorkshire village where she was arresting a shoplifter.[119]

Until fairly recently it has been culturally unacceptable for policemen to admit to suffering from (as distinct to being exposed to) stress, which must always have been present for a profession constantly confronting the pain of accidents, disasters and distraught relatives. Rising levels of violent crime and social tension have added a new dimension, not only for those, for instance, confronting firearms, but for those required to use them as well. A Home Office study published in 1988 graphically reported officers unable to sleep, suffering nightmares and sweating, weeping, inability to eat, anxiety, depression and withdrawal from social involvement.[120] A special unit staffed by psychologists was in that year set up at the Home Office.[121] With widening recognition that PTSD, post-traumatic stress disorder, could assail even the bravest and most self-disciplined men and women, some 3,000 Metropolitan officers, over 10 per cent of the force, were in 1992 being treated for stress-related conditions, as were about 40 per cent of those admitted to the Police Convalescent Home, usually for conditions which initially masked the extent to which stress was responsible.[122] Early retirement on grounds of ill-health rose fourfold in the ten years to 1991, in which year it accounted for 56 per cent of those retiring.[123]

In the mid-twentieth century, social commentators like Geoffrey Gorer and George Orwell were remarking on the reputation for gentleness of the English people, of the rarity of pub fights or of crowd disorder.[124] By the end of the 1950s drunken hooliganism was becoming commonplace. Increasing disposable income permitted attendance at away football matches; and wrecked trains, to be followed by wrecked ferries once affluence allowed for foreign travel, soon bore witness to the overexuberance of travellers. In 1969 British Rail marooned a trainload of unruly fans at a wayside station in Bedfordshire, where they proceeded to wreak havoc on an unprepared residential area. The 1966–7 league programme saw the start of organized 'hooligan gangs' inside and outside the stadia, with street fighting, and casualties taken to hospital. Clubs began to segregate fans in separate enclosures. Meanwhile, increasingly serious invasions of the pitch led to the installation of steel bars in front of some of the terraces, an innovation that was to prove lethal at Hillsborough in 1989, when there was no escape route from overcrowding, and nearly a hundred people were crushed to death against the bars.[125]

Football matches were the occasion for a change in policing practice small in itself but of symbolic significance in inculcating an 'us versus them' mentality between police and public. Until the late 1960s, police on duty at public sporting and ceremonial occasions had habitually stood with their backs to the crowd, facing the event, an almost token police presence. Political demonstrations at the South African rugby tour in 1969 ensured that the police watched the spectators, not the game, and by the early 1970s, perhaps in response to IRA terrorism, police officers on duty at ceremonial occasions such as the State Opening of Parliament, royal weddings or Remembrance Sunday began to stand surveying the crowd. Earlier customs, like pushing small children to the front, where small mittened fists would stretch up to grasp large blue-gloved ones, came to an end. The public were no longer to be trusted.*

'Teddy boy' violence had shocked the 1950s, bank holiday rampages by mods and rockers in seaside towns, starting with Brighton in 1964, had punctuated the 1960s. After the mid-1970s street rioting by black youths came annually to be associated with the Notting Hill Carnival; by the 1980s widespread weekend mayhem was disfiguring rural market towns as drunken young people with money to burn taunted authority and smashed up property for the fun of it. 'Police faced more than 250 outbreaks of serious public disorder in Britain's once tranquil villages and country towns last year', reported *The Times* on 10 June 1988. 'The most seriously affected areas were also the most prosperous.' Quoting from a report by the Association of Chief Police Officers, *The Times* went on, 'From Petersfield to Penrith, from Barnstaple to Bridlington come reports of unprovoked attacks on property, public and police.' Huge gatherings of young people roaming the countryside in search of 'rave' parties frightened older residents. And the developing potential for nastiness was revealed when a man was shot at a Bristol reggae concert in the spring of 1993.[126]

The appetite for violence for its own sake infected occasions which had always trembled on the brink of disorder – political demonstrations

---

* The insecurity is spreading. Following the stabbing of the tennis player Monica Seles at the Hamburg Open tennis tournament in 1993, bodyguards were stationed on court with their backs to the game, watching the spectators, at the 1994 tournament (*The Times*, 26 April 1994).

and the expression of grievances. In the first half of the nineteenth century Luddism, the protest against labour-saving machinery in both industry and agriculture, and Chartism, the demand for universal suffrage, were the principal engines of protest. Once again, as in eighteenth-century civic disorder, historians detect in the Luddites 'an abiding impression of moderation, loyalty and self-discipline', in which, despite serious destruction in local areas, Luddite objectives were limited and targeted (for instance, no one was killed or injured during the 'Captain Swing' campaign of barn-firing and threshing-machine destruction). T.A. Critchley, in *The Conquest of Violence*, remarks on the deeply responsible conduct of the Chartists, and on the fact that demonstrations in London very seldom deteriorated to the point requiring police to draw their truncheons (though Bristol, which in the early 1830s had as yet no police force, suffered three days of pillage when magistrates and the local army commander hesitated to order the use of force). The second half of the nineteenth century saw a number of demonstrations which degenerated into mob disorder, in 1855 over Sunday trading, in 1866 over the right to use Hyde Park for rallies, in 1887 over similar rights to the use of Trafalgar Square, demonstrations in which injuries were incurred, the police occasionally overwhelmed and the army called in. The first twenty years of the twentieth century, which included disturbances instigated by the Suffragette movement, saw troops deployed on several occasions in the course of industrial unrest, especially in mining areas, and during rioting by returning soldiers in Liverpool. After 1919, however, the 'hooligan element' largely evaporated, and there occurred what Critchley called the 'transition from a turbulent society to a peaceable one'. Despite the General Strike in 1926, the hunger marches and the Fascist rallies of the 1930s, the intense emotions of the Suez and CND protests and the anti-Vietnam demonstrations of the 1960s, Critchley was able to claim that by the late twentieth century we had become 'a non-violent relatively gentle society'. Some 600 years after the first legislation on 'tumultous assembly' was enacted,[*] in 1967 the Riot Act was repealed. On 27 October 1968, at a time when foreign police forces were already equipped in paramilitary guise, unarmed London police in ordinary uniforms and helmets faced some 30,000 anti-Vietnam War demonstrators for a rowdy afternoon that ended with the singing of 'Auld Lang Syne'; a swan song, as it turned out, for the gentle society.

Mary Macarthy, reporting for the *Sunday Times*, described what

---

[*] In 1381, in the twilight decades of medieval Christendom (Critchley, p.42).

happened as 'a unique, improbable, event, something to cherish in our memory book, for short of Utopia, we shall not see it again'.[127]

The pursuit of Irish nationalist political objectives by violence was reactivated at the end of the 1960s, but in Britain too a new ruthlessness became evident. Within four years of the Vietnam demonstration, the spectacle of the police overwhelmed by striking miners at Saltley coke depot in 1972 presaged a new era of industrial confrontation, but even more sinister, because the event was supposed to be a happy one, was the aftermath of the 1976 Notting Hill Carnival, when police were seen on television grabbing dustbin lids to protect themselves from a rain of bricks and stones. The first riot shields were issued the following year. At the beginning of the 1980s riots erupted with unprecedented ferocity in other predominantly immigrant areas, with extensive arson, looting and petrol bombing (the riot shields proved flammable, and had to be changed); and, in 1985, the machete-beheading of a police constable, the first to be killed by mob violence since a constable was kicked to death in Liverpool in 1911. This riot, on the Broadwater Farm Estate in Tottenham, marked the first occasion on which firearms were used by demonstrators, with seven police officers suffering gunshot wounds.

By the 1990s outbreaks of arson and looting, usually sparked off by police initiatives in attempting to make an arrest,[*] were extending to run-down areas well beyond the purview of immigrant discontent. The conduct of participants at political demonstrations such as those against the poll tax in April 1990, when looted shops and burnt-out cars marked the passage of the protesters, showed that the 'hooligan tendency' was achieving an ascendancy it had not enjoyed since the end of World War I. Chief police officers began to report the deliberate use of hoax calls, luring their officers into ambushes where they could be attacked; both policemen and policewomen were beaten unconscious and deliberately run down by cars; they were forced from their homes by death threats and intimidation of their families.[† 128] A general attitude of loathing for all in authority began to extend to ambulance services and fire crews. Firefighters reported to the TUC Congress in 1992 that they were being shot at and stoned; and dangers to ambulancemen escalated to the point

---

[*] The Bristol riots of 1980 occurred when the police attempted to clamp down on drug trafficking. Brixton erupted in 1981 as a result of a concentrated police effort to control street crime. At that time, one fifth of the entire country's street crime was occurring in the Brixton area (BBC 2, *Who Killed Dixon?*, 23 May 1993). The 1991 Northumbria riots resulted from an attempt by the police to 'get tough' on ram-raiders.

[†] In March 1994 the widow of a murdered officer who had called for better protection for the police was hounded by obscene phone calls and her eight-year old daughter harassed (*The Times*, 24 March 1994).

that in February 1994 Manchester's ambulance crews were issued with bullet-proof vests. By then Manchester police had for some years been patrolling in body armour.[129]

The police response was not at first evident to the general public, as the uniform was subtly modified to give more protection, with shin pads, 'cricket box' and specially strengthened helmet; and sartorially defensive redesign, such as a clip-on tie* and Manchester's removal of belts and full epaulettes.[130] From the early 1980s, however, the ethos of policing changed – a 'fashion parade' pictured in *The Times* on 4 June 1980 portrayed the at that time unbelievable 'paramilitary uniform of the late 1980s'. Crash helmets, visors and fireproof overalls, and paramilitary tactics and training became routine parts of every policeman's lot, while behind the scenes forces were acquiring armoured vehicles, plastic bullets and CS gas, the latter being used in Liverpool in 1981, and threatened, though not used, in London in 1985. The year-long battle of the 1984–5 miners' strike, in which nearly 3,000 police north and south of the border and unknown numbers of miners were injured, introduced men from hitherto untroubled areas to the hard realities of modern unrest, and returned them to their county forces battle-hardened and culturally changed.

Scotland Yard had begun testing a new body armour resistant to bullets and stabbing early in 1992;[131] by 1993 hundreds of police officers were paying up to £500 to provide themselves with lightweight body armour.[132] After a particularly heinous murder by stabbing, Northumbria in January 1994 became the first force to give its officers bullet- and knife-proof vests as part of their regular equipment. In March 1994 they were distributed to selected London police.[133] By January 1995 shields incorporating electric shocks were being acquired, though a Home Office minister denied that they would be used in confrontation with demonstrators.[134]

By late 1988 chief constables were being pressed by their officers to follow the example of three forces which had established special armed response units, on 24-hour patrol, albeit under very restricted liberty of action, special authority being needed to access the locked arms repository.[135] By the summer of 1991, when London's first five armed response cars went on the streets, fourteen other forces had established them.[136] Liverpool's Chief Constable stated in March 1994 that all forces had by then got armed response vehicles on patrol.[137] Meanwhile, tests

---

* One of the anxieties expressed when, shortly after World War II, police uniform first replaced the high-fronted tunic with collars and ties was that it would make it easier for criminals to throttle officers.

began on American-style batons, longer than the British truncheon, doubt centring on the desirability of weapons which would, because of their length, destroy the traditional police image by having to be openly visible.[138]

In mid-1994 the Home Secretary, acceding to requests from chief constables, authorized the raising of London's armed response cars from five to twelve, permitted their occupants standing authority to wear and use hand guns (the first British mainland policemen to do so apart from the anti-terrorist patrols at Heathrow Airport and the members of the anti-terrorist Diplomatic Patrol Group), and the replacement of the truncheon with the baton, agreed that bullet- and knife-proof vests were to be standard issue to officers on the beat, and authorized trials of pepper gas sprays, which cause brief but total disorientation.[*][139] By the summer of 1994 both the armed response units and the Diplomatic Patrol Group were being permitted to display their weapons openly, instead of, as heretofore, concealed under their clothes.[140] The demand for all police to be armed is gaining ground, the proud and almost unique boast that Britain has for nearly 170 years been policed by an unarmed force seemingly nearing its end.[141] It is a development in line, correctly or incorrectly, with the expectations of those who opposed the abolition of capital punishment for the killing of police officers. There are, however, marked differences between areas in the response of the officers themselves to the suggestion that all police be routinely armed, with a majority over the nation as a whole revealed, in a poll in the spring of 1995, to be still firmly opposed to an armed police force.[142]

Insecurity of property adds to public despair at crime. Burglaries, running at some 93,000 in 1950, had escalated to nearly 1.4 million by 1993, and other thefts over the same period from a third of a million to almost 2.8 million, contributing to a grand total of 5.5 million indictable crimes in 1993, compared with less than half a million in 1950.[†][143]

In July 1991 a representative of English Heritage, discussing 'a growing wave' of thefts from the grounds of schools, country houses and stately homes, commented that it was not only statuary that was at risk. Thefts of architectural fittings generally had 'mushroomed over the past 10 to 15 years', including chimney pieces, panelling, stained-glass, fireplaces, door cases, ironwork and plasterwork; 'the thefts have now reached epidemic proportions'.[144] Across the country, from Cumberland

---

[*] On 1 March 1996 CS gas was issued to 16 police forces and used on the beat for the first time on 3 March to subdue a man resisting arrest (*The Times*, 4 March 1996).

[†] When the figures are adjusted to allow for the rise in population there is still a tenfold increase, from 1,094 indictable crimes per 100,000 population in 1950 to 10,369 in 1993.

to Kent, quality tiles are being stripped from the roofs of barns and farmhouses, sometimes while the owners are absent merely on holiday.[145] Professional thieves comb public buildings and stately homes, removing their treasures (the National Trust responded in 1992 by, among other measures, forbidding indoor photography). Until about 1981, according to a Trust spokesman, the problem of thefts 'barely existed', but during the 1980s gates, garden statues and urns, even rare plants, water lilies and fish, began to disappear during the night.[146] Two six-ton statues were removed under cover of darkness by a crane from a Merseyside building, and though recovered, will not for security reasons be returned to their niches. A thirty-foot stained-glass window was removed from its site in Liverpool, bronze reliefs crow-barred off the base of a statue.[147] By the summer of 1995, the value of works of art stolen in Britain was estimated by Scotland Yard to be running at about £300 million annually.[148]

These attacks on unguarded cultural treasures are being paralleled by escalating depredations on churches, prompting comparison with the final phase of Greek civilization, when looting of temples ceased to be taboo. Modern crime respects neither people, nor culture, nor faith. In July 1991 the Ecclesiastical Insurance Group stated that one place of worship in four was suffering arson, theft or vandalism in 1989 – by 1995 it was one in three. 'It's a very sad reflection on the state of society that churches are not regarded as sacrosanct as they used to be', commented the Archbishop of York.[149] Marble headstones, chalices, candlesticks, crucifixes, gold and silver plate, paintings, altars, fonts, monumental brasses, statues, tapestries, chandeliers, all have been taken, sets of stained-glass windows removed, and carvings prised off pulpits.[150] 'Thieves are sacking churches in one of the greatest rapes of Britain's heritage since the Reformation', a seminar on church security was informed at the start of 1992.[151] By the autumn of 1992 every Anglican church in the Lichfield diocese, where the 19 incidents recorded in 1980 had increased to 300 by 1992, had been vandalized or burgled.[152] By November 1995 the Ecclesiastical Insurance Group reported that criminal damage had now reached 'unprecedented levels', with 17 Anglican churches being attacked *each day*.[153] Increasing numbers of clergy began regretfully to lock up their churches, spurred on by their insurers, who in 1992 received 9,500 claims.[154]

At least the treasures are being stolen for enjoyment elsewhere, unlike the targets of vandalism. In Leicestershire one night in August 1990 a 2,000-year-old Roman mosaic was hacked to pieces,[155] in Brighton a £28,000 stained-glass window, newly installed to replace one damaged in a hurricane, was smashed within two days of its installation.[156] Accounts in November 1993 of the beheading of public statues in Halifax and Liverpool throw a new light on the numbers of classical statues which have come down to us minus limbs.[157] In Scotland in March 1995 a Henry Moore bronze which had stood in an open-air art gallery for thirty years was decapitated, followed a few days later, also in Scotland, by the mutilation of a fifteen-foot statue, formerly decorating the old Euston station, on display at Leith Docks. *The Times*, harking back to the superstitious terror that seized Athens in 415 BC when it was discovered that the sacred statues, the Hermae, had been impiously mutilated, commented, 'Despair is too strong a word for the emotions stirred by the sight of a desecrated Moore sculpture on a Scottish hillside. But we should not be surprised that a frisson of unease seizes the modern soul when it is confronted by such acts of destruction.'[158]

Concern about vandalism had, by the late 1970s, led to serious study in the Home Office of suggestions for labour camps, corporal punishment and imprisonment for the young males whose assertion of their masculinity was, among other activities, substituting the spray-can for the more basic mammalian methods of claiming territorial supremacy. But lack of parental support (in one case parents had even tried to sue a local authority when their child injured himself in the course of heaving a brick through a sports pavilion window) meant that action was limited to exhortation.[159] Schools, public lavatories, gardens and other municipal responsibilities suffered a mounting intensity of systematic vandalization.[160] Householders in quiet residential areas far from inner-city turmoils faced outbursts of graffiti, orgies of slashed tyres (the Automobile Association reported that 2.6 million cars were reported vandalized in 1993; 300 cars suffered in one night in a Hampshire village in March 1992),[161] smashed bird baths, broken ornamental trees and beds of decapitated flowers. More serious was the development, in the northeast, of stealing cars and then propelling them, unoccupied, downhill to smash into whatever stood in their way, an activity which demolished greenhouses and put lives at risk when private gardens and the walls of houses were breached.[162]

Increasingly businesses and private citizens began to turn to security firms to supplement the help they could look for from the overstretched police. Securicor, founded in 1935, and with a uniformed staff of only two in 1945, was by 1978 employing 23,000.[163] Securicor guards with their Alsatian dogs were patrolling large farms by the early 1970s to deter cattle rustlers,[164] and as poaching metamorphosed from the traditional rural sideline to a major enterprise by well-organized crime syndicates with export outlets and uninhibited intimidation of game-keepers, bailiffs and their families, some of the larger estates began to employ former members of the army SAS.[165] Less wealthy farmers organized 'Farm-watch' schemes among neighbours, while owners of horses and ponies set up Horsewatches in an attempt to avert thefts and retrieve stolen animals. In eighteen months during 1992–3 some 85 Horsewatches were established, though the police warned that 'We're talking shotguns and kneecapping and really nasty sorts of criminal behaviour . . . we always warn Horsewatch members of the risks . . .'[166] In 1989 *Police Review* estimated that more than 1,000 professional patrols were in operation on private housing estates.[167] By 1994 it was thought that private security firms were, by then, employing a quarter of a million people, almost twice the number of police in England and Wales.[168] Neighbourhood Watches, closely supervised by the local police force and strongly discouraged from doing more than reporting suspicious activities to the local station, received official blessing and mushroomed across the country, numbering over 130,000 and covering some five million households by the summer of 1994;[169] a parallel development, Marinewatch, co-ordinated by harbourmasters, was insti-tuted by Devon and Cornwall Police in the spring of 1994 to cope with the massive theft of and from boats along their extensive coastline, while Dorset established Shore Watch in an attempt to improve marina security, some £2 million of equipment such as VHF radios, satellite and land-based positioning systems, radar sets and echo sounders, having been stolen during 1994.[170] Insurers calculate that nationwide in 1992 one in three powerboat owners, four in ten cabin cruiser owners, and five in ten fishing boats were victims of crime.[171] In some areas irate citizens went further and took the law into their own hands, threatening and humiliating known troublemakers, and in some cases making it impossible for criminal families to remain in the community. The Home Secretary inveighed against vigilantes – but opinion surveys found increasing support for them, and a government-commissioned report early in 1990 considered that their continued growth was inevitable unless something was done to increase police presence; the grim result, in the view of *The Times*, 'of declining faith in the State's capacity to keep the peace'.[172] The spectre loomed of a solution already visible in the United States and South Africa, where fortified residential areas repel the unwelcome with privatized security services, and the police endeavour to maintain some sort of order among a sullen rabble of society's rejects.

Much of Britain had by the late 1980s succumbed to a massive breakdown in shared trust and conviviality, with widespread installation, much of it at the insistence of insurance companies, of burglar alarms, locking systems on all windows and doors, and security lights. Aluminium shutters for doors and windows were being advertised. Tragic cases were reported from different inner London housing estates of people dying in fires, the fire brigade unable to break down their personal barricades and grille-protected windows sufficiently quickly to save them.[173] At a more trivial level, London theatres ceased to provide coin-in-the-slot opera glasses, so many were purloined,[174] Durham Council sprayed its evergreens with sewage to deter Christmas thieves,[175] and participants in BBC Radio 4's *Gardeners' Question Time* began seeking advice on what plants to cultivate to deter persistent thefts from their gardens (answer: thorny ones). But reports from Gloucestershire in the summer of 1994 showed that the problem was by no means a joke; with over 100 gardens ransacked of expensive equipment as well as of rare plants, police reported their conviction that 'we are dealing with a very organized crime ring'.[176] The Metropolitan Police, remarking that about one garden in seven was suffering depredation every two years, compared with one in twenty some five years earlier, in 1995 took a stand at the Chelsea Flower Show to alert visitors to the sort of measures, such as bolting window boxes to the wall, and setting containers in concrete, that might help combat garden crime, which by then included rolling up and removing whole lawns of turf.[177]

By 1994 massive thefts of golf equipment and fishing tackle, with individual losses running into thousands of pounds, were being reported (Scotland Yard launched a Golf Club Watch).[178] The food store Asda in Swansea learnt the measure of public honesty when a fuse in their tills blew, they asked customers to add up their own bills – and had been mulct of £7,000 within two hours.[179] Theft put an end to Cambridge's imaginative attempt to solve city transport problems by instituting, in October 1993, a series of special cycle parks equipped with bikes to be borrowed and returned. They were borrowed indeed – but not returned. After most of the 350 community bikes had disappeared, the scheme was terminated in April 1994.* [180] St Andrews in Scotland made over 100 bicycles available between 1992 and 1994, but was forced to abandon the scheme when all had been stolen or vandalized.[181] Bernard Levin tells the story of the solitary policeman in Bath – not a conspicuously degraded area – who, courageously endeavouring to arrest one of a group

---

* It proved very successful in reducing other cycle thefts, and there are plans to reinstitute it in an amended, more controlled, form.

of ram-raiders making their getaway from their foray through the window of the city's principal department store, found himself surrounded by a crowd jeering him, cheering the robbers, and bustling through the gaping window to pillage what they could.[182]

In April 1985 parents of a Scout troop in Reading, Berkshire, had cancelled their children's traditional Scout Job Week because of their fears of muggings and sex attacks against the scouts and cub scouts while they were out on their rounds. In April 1993 'bob-a-job' week, launched in 1914, came to an end in its traditional form, when scouts nationwide were instructed not to knock on the doors of strangers. 'The tradition has been destroyed by the world we have created in the past few years', commented the Bishop of Peterborough. But he regarded the change as right. 'It is a great loss, but nowadays parents cannot trust their children to others.'[183] In 1991, after some sensational child murders, *The Times* argued that the numbers of those killed by random strangers were so small that it was absurd for parents to overprotect their children,[184] but public alarm was not allayed, and a series of murders of boys and girls in the summer of 1995 accelerated the trend towards preventing children from wandering about alone. Young readers of children's literature, such as Richmal Crompton's 'William' series, or Arthur Ransome's *Swallows and Amazons*, could only wonder at the now unthinkable degree of freedom accorded to children in the 1920s and 30s.[185]

The callousness of blackmailers (some with political, some with personal greed as their motives) in contaminating food, including the insertion of glass and portions of razor blades in baby food, has led to the innovation of sealed containers bearing the warning 'Do not accept jar if seal is broken'.

The emotional damage done to victims is incalculable, a state of affairs which the establishment of victim support groups attempts to ameliorate; but as the writer A.S. Byatt, herself a victim of street mugging, recounted, some sufferers are destroyed by the destruction of their trust in their fellow human beings. She cited a woman aged 86 who, though unhurt when her handbag containing only £4 was snatched, 'never smiled again, and she stopped putting her hair in curlers . . . and in a month she was dead'.[186] The elderly who remember a very different social atmosphere are perhaps most affected. The philosopher Leopold Kohr died in February 1994 a broken-hearted man. 'They have finally murdered my career', he said, faced with a fourteenth burglary at his Gloucestershire home that left all his papers ransacked. 'I do not think I can begin writing again.'[187]

To some observers it is fear of crime, not crime itself, that is the real enemy. *The Times*, in particular, never ceases to point out, in leaders regularly printed each time the Home Office releases the latest crime figures, that conditions are far worse in many other countries; that the apparent increase in crime reflects unreliable statistics rather than real increases; and that in any case the statistical likelihood of being a victim of violence remains very low. Whilst it is true that Home Office surveys have revealed a huge discrepancy between crime and reported crime (not, in itself, a particularly consoling discovery),* leaving open the possibility that apparent increases may be due largely to more reporting and recording, anecdote and personal experience convince most people that they are in greater peril than they used to be. A low statistical risk influences perception less than the extreme nastiness of the incidents that do occur. Householders faced with minor vandalism in their localities hesitate to protest, remembering the couple on a south London housing estate who in 1989 perished in the flames when their flat was set on fire following their complaint about their neighbours' loud music.[188] A train passenger who in September 1992 had the gall to remonstrate with fellow passengers for putting their feet on the seat upholstery was stabbed through the heart.[189] A father of three who challenged twenty young vandals on a Cardiff estate in June 1993 was kicked to death.[190] In Christchurch, Dorset, a month later, a 56-year-old man who asked a group of teenagers to quieten down had his teeth knocked out after being kicked to the ground.[191] A man trying to stop a burglary at a neighbour's home near Portsmouth had his leg broken in six places, his assailants including a 13-year-old girl.[192]

Three appalling crimes publicized during 1993 confirmed, in many people's estimation, the connection between the collapse of civilized standards and the influence of popular entertainment. The abduction, slow sexual torture and murder of two-year-old James Bulger by two ten-year-olds held up to the British public a stark and brutal reflection of what sort of conduct the nation was now breeding.† Both perpetrators

---

* The British Crime Survey, based on interviews with a sample of the general public, concluded that in 1991 'the amount of crime actually committed is perhaps three times the number of crimes recorded by the police', the ratio varying with the type of crime and the worthwhileness of reporting it. In the case of robberies and thefts from the person, estimated actual crime was eight times higher. BCS showed an estimated increase in actual crime of 49 per cent between 1981 and 1991, compared with a recorded increase of 96 per cent (*Criminal Statistics*, 1991). The upward trend is not, however, disputed.

† Simon Jenkins in *The Times* (24 February 1993) referred to this as an 'exceptional' incident, condemning those who 'extrapolated and projected [it] onto a vast ethical screen before which public figures can prance and vie with each other in damnatory language'. However, five years previously, though without making the same impact on the media, and hence the public, another two-year-old had been snatched, abused, killed and dumped by a railway line by a twelve-year-old

were video addicts whose first port of call after the murder was a video shop. A number of details in the case reflected incidents in a video 'nasty', *Child's Play 3*,[*] which was known to have been seen by the father of one of the murderers, though it was denied that the child had seen it. Shortly after their conviction there occurred the trial of six adults accused of the torture, sexual and otherwise, of a sixteen-year-old girl whom they finally disposed of by setting on fire, though unexpectedly she lived long enough to give police details of her tormentors. *Child's Play 3* featured overtly in the torture.[193] In neither case did the police impugn the video, though others did. Police did, however, link the kicking to death of the man in Cardiff who remonstrated with the gang for vandalism with the American film *Juice*, which the youths had been watching.[† 194] Commentators tend to describe such violence as 'mindless', but it is no more 'mindless' than enjoying a pint of beer. Destruction and the infliction of suffering is pleasurable. It was, as Martin Scorsese had said of *Cape Fear*, a lot of fun.

In the spring of 1994 the debate on the influence of sadistic material broke out with renewed fervour. The Home Secretary, anxious to defend liberty in general and the livelihoods of an estimated 40,000 people

boy (*The Times*, 9 March 1993). Jenkins was not then to know that within four days of the ending of the trial of the Bulger murderers, two boys, one ten, the other eleven, were to be accused of threatening to kill a six-year-old on a railway line – circumstances paralleling the Bulger killing. (*The Times*, 7, 8 and 16 December 1993). At a court hearing in April 1994 the evidence was considered inadequate for conviction (*The Times*, 27 April 1994). The new case included sexual assault, as had the Bulger case, though at that time this had not been divulged, the details being very harrowing and unnecessary to the prosecution of the case (they were disclosed by Gitta Sereny in two articles in *The Independent on Sunday* magazine, 6 and 13 February 1994, and in David James Smith's *The Sleep of Reason*, Century/Random House, London 1994).

[*] *Child's Play 3* concerns a toddler-doll who is possessed, when unobserved except by the camera, by a malign *alter ego* who proceeds to perpetrate a series of unpleasant murders in the course of seeking a human child in which to lodge. The doll appears at an army-style reformatory (boot camp?) where a young teenager is incarcerated for crimes committed under the influence of an identical doll. The film concerns the lad's principled attempts to save his young friend from the doll's evil influence. Both boys belong to a squad which has been issued with cartridges of blue paint for 'war games' (the doll substitutes real bullets) and the climax comes when the boys succeed in destroying the toddler-doll by smashing it to pieces beside the railway of a ghost train at a local funfair. Blue paint and a railway line featured in the murder of the toddler Jamie Bulger.

[†] *Juice* concerns four Harlem blacks out to prove that they have got 'juice', or 'bottle', as English slang would have it, i.e. that they have courage and bravado. They are presented as truants in ceaseless confrontation with the police, passing their time in shoplifting, DJ contests, squaring up to Puerto Ricans, watching violent TV programmes (though with little concentration), casual copulation and playing arcade machines. The drama arises when one of the four turns killer during a robbery on a shop, threatens the remaining three (who disapprove of the killing, fearing serious police entanglement), kills one, wounds another, and is finally done to death himself by the third. Though the protagonists are motivated chiefly by fear for their own lives, and the film is devoid of any moral sense, there is no direct parallel with the Cardiff incident.

involved in the video distribution industry, was prevailed upon by pressure from some 220 MPs, who had called for a ban on all videos* unsuitable for children, to urge greater stringency on the censor in operating the 1984 Act (a move which was, to the distress of the Directors' Guild of Great Britain, followed by the incorporation into the current Criminal Justice Bill of 'tough new rules'); and to make much harsher the penalties for supplying unclassified films, or for permitting children to acquire unauthorized categories.[195] The video rental industry in May 1994 introduced a system of supplementary labelling to give additional information, primarily for parents' benefit, on the content of videos, and in June the director of the British Board of Film Classification called for the introduction of compulsory identity cards for children, as a step towards the control of all age-barred goods.[196] By June 1994 the BBC was introducing 'tough new guidelines' to prevent the glamorization of violent crime in its news and current affairs programmes.[197]

In his *Hollywood versus America* Medved argues that the sort of rancid films which had, since the abolition of the Hays Code in 1966, come to dominate the industry, and for which the Academy of Motion Picture Arts and Sciences has been incestuously awarding itself Oscars, were unpopular at the box office and would be economically cata-strophic were it not for the receipts from distribution abroad. He provides facts and figures to show that the decline in American cinema audiences preceded, by over a decade, the coming of cable television and home videos; that it equated chronologically with the anti-religious, anti-family, anti-American values and the increasingly explicit, fre-quently psychopathic, lewdness and violence of post-1960s 'artistically liberated' productions.[198] His book is intended as a clarion call to public and patrons to pressurize producers into giving the American public what it wants.

It is not clear to what extent the American public supports the contemporary film industry by home viewing of modern films – Medved gives it the benefit of the doubt by surmising that it may be preferring to rent wholesome entertainment. In Britain taste has, for a substantial number of people, coarsened. Bond and Barker may have failed at the Royal Court in the 1960s, but over the next decades the appetite for violent films and 'video nasties' has grown by what it fed on.† As *New*

---

* The film versions would have remained available for viewing, with appropriate classifications, in clubs and cinemas.
† Gaskill himself sensed what was happening. 'There is ... a strange ambiguity in the presentation of violence that I mistrust in myself as well as in the work of others', he wrote in *A*

Society reported in February 1988, '*Straw Dogs, A Clockwork Orange, The Exorcist* and *Last Tango in Paris* . . . were box office hits. People actually like violence . . . they pay to go and see it.'[199] A seminar on Violence and the Media organized by the BBC in December 1987 (at which time it was remarked that 'in the last few years there has been a marked increase in the incidence and realism of violence in American films and television series')[200] heard from the head of the BBC's Broadcasting Research Department that 'programmes in peak-time involving acts of violence – 8+ per hour . . . – usually attract large audiences, nearly 25% bigger than the average peak-time audience. And they are liked. They achieve an average AI [audience appreciation rating] of 74.'[201] When, in response to some expressions of public concern, a 'red triangle' warning was transmitted indicating strong material in the following film, viewing figures more than doubled; from 800,000 to nearly two million in the case of one series.[202]

Opera North's 1990 production of *The Threepenny Opera* introduced scenes of violence that were not in Brecht's original* because 'it has encouraged people to come in'.[203] That *The Silence of the Lambs*, with its tale of two serial killers, one a cannibal, the other given to skinning his victims,† swept the board at the Oscar ceremony in 1992 may corroborate Medved's view; but it also broke the British box-office record over the weekend following its release at the end of May 1991.[204] When *Basic Instinct* was released in 1992, a British critic commented that, as with *The Silence of the Lambs*, the production team 'squander their skills on nasty material that bludgeons and soils our hearts and minds', but went on to remark that 'box-office takings have justified the controversy and the expense'.[205] *Basic Instinct* and *Cape Fear* were among the top favourites among rented videos in the spring of 1993.[206] *Lay-by* may, as Snoo Wilson feared, have alienated playgoers of the early 1970s, but a similar 'shocker', *Blasted*, which lurched from masturbation to oral sex, to homosexual rape and back via eye-gouging and cannibalism, was being accorded respectful performance at the Royal Court by 1995, with full houses confidently predicted.[207] The Cannes Film Festival of 1995 (in addition to playing host to the

---

Sense of Direction (p.114). Of directing Bond's *Lear* he remarks, 'When you catch yourself saying "When you push the needles in his ears, could you just be a little more ironical . . ." you realize you're in danger of joining the band of sadists yourself' (p.121).

* A scene at the start in which a gang break into a woman's home and tie her up; and another at the end, in which her throat is slit.

† There were protests at the Oscar ceremony – from homosexuals, who objected to the portrayal of one of the killers as a transvestite.

indefatigable Ken Russell's even-more-explicit-than-before *Lady Chatterley's Lover*) featured more than twenty films on serial killers, with 'dozens more available through production companies'.[208]

Pamela Hansford Johnson observed that when the Moors murderers' taste in literature was made known, sales of de Sade's *Justine* rocketed. A similar phenomenon was apparent when the possible connection of *Child's Play 3* with the Bulger murder was mentioned; the film became 'a smash hit in video shops in Liverpool'.[209]

Analysts of the media scene detect a widening gap in taste between the middle-aged and the young. 'What the successes of *Pulp Fiction* and the forthcoming *Natural Born Killers* prove is that the young demand graphic representation of physical pain', wrote Brenda Maddox in *The Times* of 15 February 1995. Symptomatic of the direction in which taste continues to move is the periodic downward revision, by the British Board of Film Classification, of contemporary material. *Reservoir Dogs*, for instance ('in which Michael Madsen steals the show as the soft-spoken psychopath, dancing to a radio DJ while torturing his hostage cop'), was ruled too violent for home viewing in 1993, but passed for video release only two years later.[*][210]

The argument about whether saturation in a depraved culture produces criminals (adult or juvenile), lances criminal propensities, or is a symptom of wider influences which are manifesting themselves in both culture and conduct continues unabated. If the cultural celebration of criminality is primarily a symptom, it does not follow that it should not be subjected to controls, just as medical symptoms are. But it does mean that unless the underlying dynamics of the disease are confronted, the controls will be no more than plasters on a sick organism. Violence and pornography are beamed from satellites, filter by phone line along computer networks[†] (in April 1994 thousands of files of hard

[*] 'The slow, teasing torture, to the accompaniment of rock music, of a bound and gagged policeman by cutting his ear off is one of the nastiest things I have ever seen on the screen', wrote Brenda Maddox. 'I would not show *Reservoir Dogs* on TV uncut on any channel; I would have censored it for the cinema . . .' She reports, however, that the three male TV executives on a panel at the Edinburgh Festival in August 1995 discussing the boundaries of public taste all considered cuts insupportable, either out of respect for the film's artistic integrity or in deference to the supposed maturity of adult audiences (*The Times*, 30 August 1995). Following the Dunblane slaughter Warner Home Video postponed indefinitely the release to shops of *Natural Born Killers* which the BBFC had approved for release, uncut, with an '18' classification (*The Times*, 14 March 1996).

[†] Research presented to the British Association for the Advancement of Science at its meeting in September 1995 showed that 'search words' in pursuit of pornography occupied the first eight places for frequency of use on the Internet. 'You can find any perversion whatsoever and get full details. There are even instructions for paedophiles on the best way to entrap children and kill them.

pornography, allegedly including children as young as two, were seized in a raid on Birmingham University, where a male research associate had established himself as 'librarian' of a pornographic network),[211] seep through computer games sold to children.* The Government bans the sale of decoders for Red Hot Dutch (the most notorious of the satellite pornography channels),[† 212] moves to bring computer pornography under the Obscene Publications Act,[213] the industry proposes film-style ratings for computer games.[214] Meanwhile raids by police and trading standards officers in May 1992 resulted in the seizure of video duplicating equipment and up to 3,000 uncertified videos depicting torture and mutilation, including what the dealers described as 'snuff' movies, though the police were unable to confirm whether they were genuine or not, as 'the simulations are so good'.[215] A further haul in June 1993 yielded thousands of (mostly foreign-produced) examples of lurid scenes of murder and mutilation, such as *Cannibal Holocaust*.[216]

This is very nasty material and it is more prevalent and much easier to find than most people imagine', reported Professor Thimbleby of Middlesex University (*The Times*, 13 September 1995). In July 1995 nine men were arrested in Britain, and 31 in other countries, after an international investigation into paedophiliac material distributed on the Internet (*The Times*, 27 July 1995).

* By January 1993 the British Computer Society had set up an investigation into the availability of computer pornography. In Greater Manchester police had uncovered over 8,000 programs featuring bestiality, homosexual sex, child abuse, rape and images of people suffering violent deaths. Some programs are 'interactive', and some are deviously framed to deceive parents by, for instance, quickly switching to an innocent content. Similar floppy disks have been found in the north west, Swindon, Wiltshire and Guildford, Surrey. They were reputedly available 'in the playground' for as little as 89p. In September 1993 police seized more than 750 disks from children at high schools in Bedfordshire. 'The disks feature explicit sex acts, sometimes involving children or animals, and were changing hands for £10. It came to light when one teenager was caught playing the disks on a computer in his bedroom.' A survey carried out by the University of Central Lancashire and published in June 1994 found that 2 per cent of primary schools and 30 per cent of boys' secondary schools (though, significantly, only 1 per cent of girls' schools) reported the availability of computer pornography on the premises. In March 1994 the defence counsel for a thirteen-year-old boy charged in North Wales with the attempted rape of a six-year-old girl pleaded that the boy had been affected by watching computer pornography at school. Since the programs can, for the cost of an international phone call, be downloaded through international computer bulletin boards bypassing any form of customs inspection, the problems of control are formidable; though it must be remarked that in 41 per cent of the cases investigated by the survey, the source of the material was the children's fathers, brothers or friends. In March 1994 the Home Secretary announced that he was closing a loophole in the Obscene Publications Act by redefining 'publication' to include the electronic transmission of obscene material between computers (*The Times*, 13 January, 23 September 1993, 3 March, 16 June 1994).

† Saudi Arabia in July 1994 decided to route all incoming satellite broadcasts through the Information Ministry, retransmitting (by cable) only those programmes in step with the Kingdom's social and religious values. Owners of satellite dishes were given one month to dispose of them, on pain of heavy fines (*The Times*, 1 July 1994) Similar restrictions were introduced in Iran in February 1995 (*The Times*, 17 February 1995).

None of this would have surprised Sorokin. It fulfils his expectations, based on his analysis of the experience of other sensate societies, of a culture which has run its course, which is morally, aesthetically and spiritually bankrupt. Our woes are the direct and logical result of the belief that the physical universe is the only reality that does or can exist; and that truth resides solely in the analysis and understanding of that 'reality'.

Chapter 22

Cause and Effect

The evangelicals of the Clapham Sect raised children who abandoned their parents' faith but retained their moral standards, striving to ground ethics in reason rather than revelation, and find in scientific evolutionary theory a basis for altruism. Their children moved to Bloomsbury, abandoned both the faith and the moral standards of their grandparents, and found the meaning of life in a worship of art for art's sake, its purpose in the pursuit of sensual satisfaction, material and, especially, sexual; though for many decades their more esoteric *amours*, the 'higher sodomy', to use their own expression, were discreetly concealed from public awareness.

In her book *Marriage and Morals Among the Victorians*,[*] Gertrude Himmelfarb comments:

> There is a discernible affinity between the Bloomsbury ethos, which put a premium on immediate and present satisfactions, and Keynesian economics, which is based entirely on the short run and precludes any long-term judgements. (Keynes's famous remark, 'In the long run we're all dead,' also has an obvious connection with his homosexuality – what Schumpeter delicately referred to as his 'childless vision'.)

She quotes Keynes's denigration, in his 1920 *The Economic Consequences of the Peace*, of thrift and saving, repudiated as an age-old Puritan fallacy designed to hoodwink working people into forgoing consumption; a thesis which, in *The General Theory of Employment, Interest and Money*, published in 1936, was to be elevated into an immensely influential doctrine for the solution of capitalism's crisis of economic

---

[*] Chapter 2 of which, 'A Genealogy of Morals', traces the evolution of values from – quite literally – Clapham Sect parent to Bloomsbury Set grandchild.

depression.[1] So acceptable was the message that half a century later the retail trade were defending the decision to put tinsel, cards and other Christmas displays on sale in September on the grounds that 'people like to spread the cost'; being by then incapable, apparently, of saving up for Christmas.

Not until after World War II did Keynesian economics, deliberate deficit financing, begin to find a place in Treasury strategy. The idea that earning and saving were not the only ways of acquiring the means of consumption received a further official boost when Harold Macmillan, then Chancellor of the Exchequer, launched the first premium bonds. Of course gambling had always had a following in Britain, but on the whole Protestant opinion, certainly traditional Puritan opinion, had disapproved, and the Chancellor was a little wary of how the archbishops would react to State involvement, preparing his defence along the lines that (a) the stake money would not be at hazard, and (b) the Church Commissioners were not doing too badly with their investments on the Stock Exchange. Furthermore, though 'lotteries had been long abandoned as one of the more disreputable features of eighteenth-century finance ... the reverend and learned gentlemen who frequented the galleries and Reading Room had no doubt long forgotten' that 'we owed the foundation of the British Museum to a lottery'. The Leader of the Opposition attacked the scheme in the House of Commons, complaining that 'Britain's strength, freedom and solvency apparently depend on the proceeds of a squalid raffle', but premium bonds were duly launched, though not without qualms on the part of those still loyal to the old Puritan ethic that it is not quite moral to get something for nothing. Initially the highest prizes were worth £1,000. 'Reluctantly' Mr Macmillan permitted an increase to £5,000, swiftly followed by a further increase to £25,000 after the 1964 change of government, by which time the erstwhile Opposition had managed to quieten its collective conscience about the 'squalid raffle'.[2] By 1994, via a series of increases far in excess of inflation, the top prize had burgeoned to the magic figure of £1 million; and in the same year the last bastion of Puritan ethics crumbled (though not without reminders of the Victorian view that gambling was 'a vast engine of demoralization'),[3] and administrators were sought for the management of a National Lottery. Huge accretions of sudden wealth were to be as much part of contemporary Britain as they had been for the spectators who awaited the Emperor's largesse at the Arena.* In the contemporary climate of greed and callousness, big

* See p.139.

winners are advised to maintain secrecy in order to protect themselves and their families from the threat of kidnap. Specialist 'K and R', kidnap and ransom, insurance policies now exist, though are immediately invalidated if any holder betrays that he or she has one, since such admission would obviously invite criminal attention.

Material values came to dominate every aspect of life. The monarchy was routinely evaluated – even by Conservative politicians[4] – in terms of how much it contributed to the tourist trade. An MP who queried the wholesomeness of the Inner London Education Authority's inclusion in its schools' reading list of *Jenny Lives with Eric and Martin*, a tale intended to accommodate children to the idea of homosexuality as a normal alternative lifestyle, was assured by the Authority's leader that what concerned parents was roofs, computers and resources, not 'Victorian values'.[5] With no deity to be blamed for 'Acts of God', someone in the here and now has to be identified as responsible when suffering or loss occurs – and made to pay. Every form of distress, not merely physical pain and mutilation, but grief at bereavement, and shock at being confronted with the trauma of others, came to be seen as worthy of recompense, haggling proceeding in the courts and the columns of the media as to the precise financial costing to be put on the loss of a child. Unexpected side-effects include (in America) a paucity of obstetricians, doctors being unwilling to risk being sued for the hazards of childbirth, while those remaining in the profession opt for performing Caesarean sections where the risks are considered lower.

If this is the only life we can ever enjoy, there is a certain urgency about partaking in its riches. *'When do we want it? Now!'* is a phrase that figures increasingly in political and industrial discourse. Barclays Bank introduced the first credit card in 1966. When Lloyds launched the Access card in October 1972 it was accompanied by the slogan 'Access takes the waiting out of wanting', a disquieting sentiment for those who had been led to believe that an inability to postpone gratification was one of the hallmarks of a psychopath.

The spread of television encouraged people to feel victimized and resentful if they did not possess what television depicted as normal. Advertising (appealing forcefully to a roll-call of the Seven Deadly Sins, especially gluttony, envy, lust and idleness) was not the principal goad. Except in dramas dedicated to making a sociological or political point about poverty, ordinary families were portrayed equipped with the latest in household goods and gadgetry; by the early 1990s, for instance, not merely push-button but even mobile telephones were standard equipment in TV drama. Nor, even in 'sociological' dramas, was there much suggestion that restraint in consumption might be prudent. Huge publicity attended the screening, in 1966, of *Cathy Come Home*, a touching portrayal of a young family destroyed by debt when the wife's childbearing and the husband's accident at work diminish their income, causing them to fall behind with their rent and ultimately to lose their home. Sympathy and outrage centred on the play's message that in these circumstances public policy required the break-up of the family, there being no provision for a father to remain with his wife and children once the social services became responsible for their accommodation.[*] Neither playwright nor most commentators suggested that the young couple had been foolhardy in starting married life with fitted carpets, central heating and smart modern furniture and equipment, the hire-purchase of which, together with their rent, cost (as the author carefully informs us) £20 of their joint peak earnings of £31.

The incentive to the have-nots to steal what they cannot immediately afford is obvious; but theft is not the prerogative of an 'underclass'. The headmaster of Westminster School raised at the Headmasters' Conference in 1980 the concealed but indubitable increase in thieving among children at public schools, and went on to link it to 'the whole thrust of our materialist society . . . in favour of gratifying a desire as soon as it is identified . . . When "I see it, I want it, I'll have it" is the prevailing logic, it is a short step from credit to theft.'[6]

The belief that happiness resides in satisfying, as quickly as possible, our material wants is of a piece with the sensate conviction that our ultimate, essential identity is physically determined – a conviction that has yielded evident results in conventional medicine, where personality problems have been tackled by the use of electrotherapy and surgery such as leucotomy, and where the use of drugs not only to control physical symptoms such as pain and infection, but also to manipulate feelings and conduct has become routine. Laudanum, a tincture of opium, was produced by Paracelsus in the sixteenth century, and came to be widely used in medicine, the stronger morphine and even stronger heroin being isolated during the nineteenth century. As recognition of

---

[*] The play was influential in moving local authorities all over the country to cease separating husbands and wives who had become homeless. Jeremy Sandford, the author, witnessed husbands returning to their families 'in a great gushing stream. It was intensely moving. I was lucky enough to be present on this jubilant occasion, and that moment, if no other, justified in my opinion not only my writing of *Cathy* but also my own existence' (Sandford, in the introduction to *Cathy Come Home*, Marion Boyars, London, 1976). Twenty-five years later the women and children attracting most media and social service attention may have a home; the current source of concern is that there is much less likelihood of there being any husband or father returning to it.

their addictive properties dawned, however, moral opprobrium supervened, certainly where recreational use was concerned, and during and after World War I legislative controls were introduced both on opiates and on cocaine, which had, in the late nineteenth century, been a common ingredient in drinks. A restricted usage among prostitutes and (the subject of Coward's *The Vortex*) some of the 'smart' set in the 1920s, at which time there were about 200 cocaine and opium addicts,[7] had evaporated by the 1930s.[8] A British report to the League of Nations in 1936 could identify a total of only 616 people addicted to narcotic drugs, the use of which, said the report, was 'not prevalent' in the United Kingdom, nor was there evidence of any organized illicit trafficking.[9] By the end of the 1940s the number of known addicts still totalled under 1,000.[10] Drug dependency in Britain until the 1960s was limited to a few hundred doctors and paramedics, and those combating severe pain.

Jazz musicians from America reintroduced cocaine to a rather select spectrum of users in the London of the 1950s; meanwhile, British doctors began to rely more and more heavily on amphetamines (first synthesized in 1887) to pep up tired patients, barbiturates (synthesized in 1864) to help them to sleep, and, the wonder drugs of the 1960s, benzodiazepines, tranquillizers such as Librium and Valium, to help them cope with stress and anxiety. Their place (and that of many newer 'designer drugs') in the list of legally controlled drugs, and the extent of control (whether available by prescription only, whether from all or only specially designated medical practitioners, whether possession was classified as a crime, etc.) varies over time in accordance with what the medical profession currently believes about their properties[*] – virtually all were initially hailed as the answer to various medical problems. By 1971 English doctors were estimated to be writing some 12.9 million prescriptions annually for barbiturates, not then thought to induce dependency, and indeed not included in the Misuse of Drugs legislation until 1985. However, realization of their dangers led to a swift diminution in their medical use, doctors switching to prescribing the allegedly less dangerous tranquillizers, on which by the mid-1980s anything from one to two and a half million people in the United Kingdom were estimated to be chemically and emotionally dependent.[11]

[*] And also on the ingenuity with which addicts abuse their use. Temazepam, for instance, introduced into Britain in 1977, was considered a safe and reliable sleeping pill, but addicts who melted the capsules and injected the drug into their veins suffered horrendous vascular damage for which the only treatment was amputation. In September 1995 possession of the drug without a prescription was made a criminal offence (*The Times*, 9 and 13 September 1995), and in October all marketing of the drug in capsule form was banned (*The Times*, 18 October 1995).

At the start of 1994 an annual total of 12.5 million prescriptions for sleeping pills were still being issued.[12] Aldous Huxley, in *Brave New World*, published in 1932, postulated a society in which daily consumption of 'soma' kept everyone happy, and his fantasy world was being put into practice by 1994, in Wenatchee, Washington State, where the local psychologist prescribes Prozac for all his patients, on the grounds that all humanity has a chemical deficiency leaving it mildly or seriously depressed, consumption of Prozac being as sensible as using glasses if one is short-sighted.[13]

It is assumed, perhaps overconfidently, that patients consuming prescribed drugs remain effective and rational members of society – though doubts have been raised as to the extent to which the confused elderly owe their condition to excessive consumption of prescribed drugs; and anxieties have been expressed as to the driving competence of some of those on medication, and their ability to perform with mental acuity – as jurors or witnesses, for example.[14] Concern about the recreational use – or misuse – of the same substances centres on the personality changes and loss of control over their own lives and conduct displayed by addicts, as well as the appalling health hazards of injecting substances never intended for that purpose, and of contracting AIDS from shared syringes. In the 1960s the young began to experiment with mixtures of amphetamines and barbiturates, 'speed' and 'purple hearts', a taste which late in the decade yielded pride of place to cannabis, then to the hallucinogenic drugs such as LSD. Meanwhile the price of cocaine was dropping, its use increasing, and in 1967 the first special clinics for addicts were opened, the Home Office instituting an addicts' index in 1968.

The 1973 Misuse of Drugs Act made treatment notifiable. Narcotics addicts, as notified at treatment centres, numbered 1,426 in 1970, and climbed almost without respite from then on, totalling nearly 25,000 by 1994 (with newly notified addicts increasing from about 800 in 1973 to nearly 10,000 in 1992).[15] But such figures merely indicate a trend; the great majority of drug users do not seek treatment; one estimate puts the true figures for cocaine- and opium-derived addiction at ten times the notified rate.[16] Nor do the statistics for cautions and convictions present a reliable gauge, but again they do indicate a trend. In 1936 a total of 60 people were charged under the Dangerous Drugs Act; in 1945 fewer than 300 drug offences were recorded; by 1991 some 47,616 people were found guilty or cautioned for drug offences. The 1936 figure for drug seizures was 9 kilos of opium, raw and prepared, and 1 kilo of Indian hemp. Comparable figures for 1991 were 494 kilos of opium-derived drugs and 41,097 kilos of cannabis leaves, plants or resin; in addition, nearly 1,078 kilos of cocaine were seized (seizures of cocaine and heroin, at 1,213 kilos, passed the 1-ton mark for the first time in 1990).[17] By 1994 the figures had escalated still further, cocaine seizures totalling 2,205 kilos, heroin 620 kilos ('equivalent to 280 million medical doses'), and cannabis 47,000 kilos.[18] Given the high cost of illegal heroin, estimates publicized by the Shadow Home Secretary in the spring of 1994 claimed that drug-related thieving to finance a 'habit' was depriving rightful owners of some £2 billion per annum in cash and property.

The acceptability within medicine of drug-induced mood changes as the antidote to feelings of boredom, anxiety and inadequacy fuelled a search for new synthetic substances which the ingenuity of chemists, licit and illicit, has encouraged in generous measure. The Association of Head Teachers' conference in June 1994 was informed that in East Yorkshire a study had discovered that children were even experimenting with drugs produced for animals, including one intended to sedate bovine victims of 'mad cow disease'.[19] The continued control of their use has led to frequent clashes between the police and young people, notoriously so in the summer and autumn of 1989, following the percolation of MDMA, used in psychiatry, on to the UK recreational market in 1986 under the name XTC or Ecstasy.[20] Hordes of young ravers in search of acid house parties clogged the motorways, and police officers attempting to control them and arrest dealers faced onslaughts from CS gas and Rottweiler dogs.[21]

The most widely used controlled drug is undoubtedly cannabis, a favourite recreational drug in the culture of the West Indies. Its prevalence among black immigrants of West Indian origin led to so many clashes between police and immigrants* that already by the end of the 1960s a solicitor handling the cases of black defendants was appealing for cannabis to be legalized, as a contribution to better race relations. By the 1990s the situation was being repeated with cocaine and its highly addictive derivative 'crack', a trade originating largely in Latin America and the Caribbean, the dealers being predominantly Afro-Caribbeans organized into lethally competitive gangs. The murderous proclivities of these gangs, both towards one another and to the police, and their apparently easy access to firearms,† coupled with the often

---

* Both the Bristol and Brixton riots of 1981 were precipitated by police attempts to arrest drug dealers.
† In July 1994 Scotland Yard reported that during 1993 10 murders and 20 attempted murders were linked to the trade in 'crack', with 3 murders and 12 attempted murders in the first five months

violent theft and robbery perpetrated by the addicts in search of ready money, caused so much alarm that by 1994 the proposal to legalize all drugs, and thus draw the teeth of the drug barons and cut costs to the addicts, was being canvassed well beyond the hitherto narrow circles which, out of an exaggerated respect for personal autonomy or a conviction that controls could never be effective, had long pressed for such a measure. The British Medical Association decided, in July 1994, to set up an inquiry into the likely effects of decriminalizing drugs.[22] Majority opinion remained, in 1994, unconvinced by the arguments and firmly opposed to the suggestion. Instead, the Government in October 1994 publicized an intention to abandon the unsuccessful campaign of attempting to shock young people out of the use of drugs, and instead to broaden factual education on the dangers of drugs, including dispensing information to the five- to ten-year-old age group.[23]

Large-scale immigration and the tensions resulting from it are another concomitant of sensate culture. Ever higher living standards, an objective of perpetual growth in the economy, could in theory be pursued solely by increases in productivity resulting from the application of unremitting technological ingenuity and innovation. In practice growth has in the past required an increase in the labour force in excess of what the indigenous population could supply, particularly to do the low-paid and unpopular jobs from which expansion of the economy has liberated the existing workforce – jobs of a status for which the Greeks and Romans imported slaves. As an OECD report in 1978 pointed out, 'the higher the GNP per capita of the country of employment, the more of its workers tend to be foreign',[24] and certainly until the oil crisis and resulting recession of the mid-seventies, the conventional wisdom was that

In the absence of changes in either the growth rate of the indigenous labour force or the rate of capital accumulation or the level of technology, the steady state long-run growth rate of domestic output will be determined by the growth rate of the immigrant labour force . . . labour immigration at an increasing rate will raise the growth rate continuously.[25]

In Britain, where labour shortages were compounded by active emigration of indigenous Britons to the palmier shores of North America

of 1994. Several hundred crack dealers were believed to have access to weapons, and drug dealers battling for profit were believed to be contributing a high proportion of the two criminal incidents per day in London featuring the use of firearms (*The Times*, 1 July 1994).

and the Antipodes, recruits from Pakistan were actively sought for the textile industry, and from the West Indies for the public transport and hospital services. Once settled, they provided a focal point for the arrival of thousands of others, attracted by the higher living standards. Britain's (in the outcome, unachievable) National Plan of 1965, postulating a 25 per cent growth in national output between 1964 and 1970, relied on continuing immigration to fulfil its manpower targets. When successive British governments, in the interests of 'good race relations', introduced measures to limit the influx of foreigners, the director of the Runnymede Trust's industrial unit pointed out that growth prospects were being hindered and economic plans hampered by the refusal to allow more workers into Britain.[26] Despite the serious racial tensions increasingly manifesting themselves across Europe, and the success of anti-immigrant political parties, leaders in both France and Germany in the 1990s stressed the importance of immigrant labour for continued prosperity. 'Zero immigrants,' said France's (right-wing) interior minister in 1993, 'clearly is impossible because our economy may need at one time or other this or that category of foreigners.'[27]

One reason for the projected continuing need for immigrants is the declining birth rate among the indigenous European population. The early 1930s had seen reproduction rates fall below replacement level (to the accompaniment of fears of 'race suicide'), but from then until the mid-1970s the birth rate remained approximately at (in Britain in 1961 to 1965 well above) replacement level. 'The babies cancelled or postponed by mothers in the 1930s were to some extent replaced in the work force by West Indian and Asian immigrants in the 1950s, and even more, by married women', comments *British Social Trends since 1900*. By 1991 no western European country other than Ireland was reproducing its indigenous population at replacement level – a 'reduction in fertility – reached by most industrial countries at about the same time – [which] has no historical precedent'.[28] In Japan, where the reduction is even more pronounced, the finance minister in the summer of 1990 raised the spectre of 'the last days of ancient Rome', saying that the decrease in the number of children is a sign of declining civilization', and besought Japan's educationally ambitious women to 'give birth and multiply'.[29] The International Labour Organization predicted in 1991 that Japan would by the year 2000 be facing a shortage of some 2.7 million workers, a deficiency which might be expected to strain immigration policies that have given Japan the lowest proportion of legal foreign nationals in its workforce.[30]

Contemporary Greek and Roman classical commentators had castigated their fellow countrymen for deliberately limiting their families,
and accused them of doing so out of material greed, an accusation which
has not been absent from modern comments, especially in Germany,
where 25 per cent of couples are childless.[31] Modern historians have
questioned how far despair at the state of their world discouraged the
citizens of late Greece and, half a millennium later, of Rome from
seeking to raise families, and apprehension – of nuclear war, of
environmental catastrophe – is thought to have had some influence on
modern young potential parents. Moreover there was in Britain in the
late 1960s great concern about world overpopulation, which moved at
least some serious-minded citizens to restrict their families out of
concern for the biosphere, though as far as Britain itself was concerned
the unborn indigenous were rapidly replaced by those in flight from less
agreeable areas of the world.

Birth control and the Pill notwithstanding, the number of abortions
has increased steadily – from 54,000 in England and Wales in 1969, the
first full year after legalization, to 186,000 by 1990 (estimates for illegal
abortions in earlier years are variously put at from 30,000 to 100,000).[32]
Between legalization in 1968 and the end of 1974 more babies had been
aborted (776,231) in England and Wales than servicemen had been
killed in World War I (702,410); and by the end of 1976 abortions
(1,044,656) exceeded the total United Kingdom deaths on active service
in both world wars (966,853).[33]

There remains the question of involuntary sterility. With thousands of
anguished would-be parents applying for infertility treatment, much
media attention has been devoted to the subject. Again, the sensate
satisfactions of sexual liberation have played a part. Between 1970 and
1980 *On the State of the Public Health* reported mounting suspicion that
a form of chlamydia was becoming widespread, accounting for at least
half of non-specific genital infections, and dangerous because it could
result in infertility in females,[*] or the birth of babies with damaged
eyes. Diagnostic facilities were sparse, and diagnosis difficult, as the
infection was often symptom-free and could lie dormant for years, but by
1982 concern was being expressed about the costs likely to accrue to the
National Health Service for treatment of infertility and of chronic pelvic

[*] Chlamydia can damage fallopian tubes and can prevent, or result in an ectopic, pregnancy.
According to the *British Medical Journal* (Vol.301, 10 November 1990, p.1057), ectopic
pregnancy has become more common in Western countries since 1970. A survey in Scotland
showed a 50 per cent increase between 1970 and 1985 (up to 200 per cent in some areas), with
76–78 per cent showing antibodies to chlamydia trachomatis.

inflammatory disease. In 1988 statistics for chlamydia began to be published separately from those for non-specific genital infections, revealing about 20,000 female and 16,000 male cases diagnosed annually in the late 1980s and early 90s;[34] but the majority of cases probably remain undiagnosed.

More intractable is the mounting evidence of male infertility. In 1992 reports began to be published that male sperm counts had almost halved since 1940. The Medical Research Council's reproductive biology unit in Edinburgh reported in September 1994 that 'sperm counts in European men were falling by 2 per cent a year', and suggested that 'couples in developed countries would find it increasingly difficult to conceive in 11 years' time'.[35] Together with evidence of a rising trend in testicular cancers and abnormalities in the male reproductive system, the finger of suspicion points at environmental pollution. Is our apparent success at manipulating the natural world, whether with industrial chemicals or with supplementary hormones that percolate through the water supply, and are a component of some food sprays, paralleling affluent Rome's unhappy experience with lead poisoning? By 1994 there was evidence that traces of dioxins used to treat cotton goods were transferring to their wearers, and to other garments when washed. Chemicals in washing powder, cosmetics and detergents are equally suspect. In October 1994 it was reported that the Ministry of Agriculture was embarking on investigations into the process by which even chocolate and crisps could be impregnated with phthalates leaking from the ink printed on wrappers, part of 'a range of modern industrial chemicals [which] are acting together to feminize the unborn male, damaging his sperm count later in life',[36] and by the summer of 1995 even tinned vegetables had joined the list of suspects.[37] Urgent research proceeds, scientists citing some 60,000 chemicals that could be having a feminizing effect on the male foetus.* [38] An unexpected clue surfaced in the spring of 1994 when Danish organic farmers, who eschewed the use of most agricultural chemicals, were found to have sperm counts double those of their colleagues who farmed conventionally.[39]

To all our varied discontents, conventional wisdom has a stock reply: more growth in the economy. Once the prospects of redistributing consumption from rich individuals to the poor or to state-funded enterprises like health and education reached the stage where politically significant numbers of taxpayers were affected (a contingency which

---

* The principal toxicologist at the Water Research Centre, Oxfordshire, stated that 'quite infinitesimally small amounts' of dioxins caused damage to the reproductive system of guinea pigs (*The Times*, 7 September 1994).

even Labour Chancellors of the Exchequer like Denis Healey and Roy Jenkins were by the 1970s openly admitting),[40] democratic politicians, after a few unhappy experiments with running huge deficits in public finance and watching inflation spiral out of control, had no option but to seek to avert the pain of high taxation by the pursuit of economic growth, enabling taxpayers to be better off at the same time as increasing the 'resources' available to the state sector.* Healey, in 1972, was calling for 'a steady increase in the nation's wealth far beyond anything achieved since the war'.[41] In every democratic nation, economic growth is the panacea offered by all political parties other than the Greens (though its feasibility, so far as western Europe and North America is concerned, is questioned by commentators impressed by the speed at which their economic pre-eminence is being challenged by Asia). For those who see poverty and unemployment as the root cause of crime, the expansion of the economy to mop up unemployment is axiomatic, technological change and the widespread entry of women into the workforce (by 1994, four and a half million more even than at peak wartime mobilization)[42] only adding to the urgency; meanwhile more 'resources' must be devoted to additional police and prisons,† to education, especially about drugs and the health dangers of promiscuity, to social work and 'pastoral care', to the housing of women and children

---

* 'Resources' has replaced the word 'money' since inflation taught people that what matters is not hard cash but the extent of the goods and services the money can buy.

† Between 1979 and 1994, police forces were expanded by over 17,000 uniformed officers, and 16,000 civilians (the Home Secretary, speaking on BBC Radio 4, *Today*, 9 September 1994). A growing expense is the protection of jurors and witnesses from intimidation, even to the point of providing some witnesses with new homes and identities. According to a BBC *Panorama* programme, broadcast on 23 March 1994, in the late 1980s the Metropolitan Police in London, and later the Greater Manchester area, set up special witness protection schemes, but intimidation is not limited to those areas. Overall statistics of the number of trials abandoned because witnesses are too scared to speak do not exist, but the programme referred to the collapse, since the start of 1992, of 9 major trials in Manchester, including two within one week for murder or attempted murder, of 17 trials for serious violence, and to 300 investigations abandoned because witnesses were too scared to speak. Three witnesses were sent to prison in Liverpool for refusing to testify; in London witnesses were allowed to testify anonymously from behind screens, a development with obvious dangers for the course of justice. By October 1994 Northumbria had set up a special unit to protect witnesses and where necessary provide them with 'new identities'. More than twenty Northumbria people had been moved from their homes as a result of being threatened by those charged with offences (*The Times*, 29 October 1994). At the Annual Conference of the Police Superintendents' Association calls were made for a national witness protection scheme to be instituted (*The Times*, 5 October 1994). Similar difficulties have impeded attempts to evict anti-social tenants terrorizing their neighbours on council estates. A number of local authorities have resorted to the use of paid, professional witnesses where local residents have been too intimidated to give personal testimony (*The Times*, 6 and 7 March 1995).

whom violence and sexual abuse have forced from their homes.* By the financial year 1992–3, with 21 per cent of families 'single parent', 9 per cent of the entire British budget, a total of £6.6 billion, was being devoted to social security spending on lone parents.[43] Report after report, whether on transport breakdowns, child abuse, prison disturbances or the aberrant behaviour of schizophrenics comes to the same conclusion: the recommendations will require 'a considerable injection of funds', 'an urgent need for more resources'. More resources are needed to treat the infertile, apply novel but expensive techniques like transplant surgery, clean up pollution, eliminate the perceived sources of intercommunal strife.†

Is it all an attempt to run up the down escalator? Crime and vandalism, for a start, are themselves destroying putative wealth, or by fraudulently diverting it, undermining the springs of its creation. A report on crime by the Confederation of British Industry in 1990 estimated the loss to British businesses at more than £5 billion a year.[44] As *The Times* put it in December 1992, 'Much of the statistical rises in national income go on security devices, higher insurance premiums and other mundane spending, which are needed to combat the fear of crime but add nothing to the standard of living.'[45] By September 1994 *Counting the Cost*, a report published by Crime Concern, the national crime prevention organization, put the costs of crime in Britain at more than £24.5 billion, pointing out that 'crime is a major drain on individual, public and corporate resources', with the Government's law-and-order budget running at more than £11 billion, and public authorities, companies and private individuals spending £1.6 billion per year on private security. 'Eventually losses are transferred to society as a whole through higher prices or taxation.'[46]

Business fraud is on a scale probably not seen since 1720, when the South Sea Bubble exploded, ruining thousands of families; Robert Maxwell having the dubious honour of perpetrating the largest fraud in British history. In November 1995 it was reported that large-scale fraud had been increasing throughout the previous eight years, and that fraud

---

* Zero Tolerance, a pressure group under the auspices of the Association of London Authorities, stated in January 1994 that 40 per cent of homeless women were in that situation because of domestic violence.
† In 1988, for instance, when Welsh nationalists were torching English-owned properties in Wales, a cleric suggested on the *Sunday* programme (BBC Radio 4, 15 May 1988) that the solution lay in a Welsh economy strong enough to allow the local Welsh to buy whatever properties came on to the market. It is a rare academic or politician who, as an Oxford politics lecturer did in discussing worldwide ethnic animosities, will voice the opinion that 'economic prosperity and cultural autonomy do not necessarily weaken nationalist demands' (*The Times*, 12 April 1989).

cases handled by the Serious Fraud Office and the Crown Prosecution Service during 1994 involved £10 billion. Furthermore, it was suspected that many firms were, out of embarrassment, concealing their predicament rather than admitting losses to shareholders.[47] A survey ('one of the most substantial surveys of fraud in recent years') published in *Security Gazette* revealed that more than two-thirds of British companies admitted that they had suffered from fraud, most of it perpetrated by management.[48] Trials, however, are expensive: the Blue Arrow trial cost the taxpayer between £35 and £40 million; the Guinness cases more than £25 million.[49] Not even the Government's own Court Funds Office, which holds funds in trust for depositors such as minors and the mentally ill, is immune, the National Audit Office in 1993 unearthing a series of frauds of which £90,000 had not been recovered.[50] Revelations of fraud in the Foreign Office led in 1995 to the suicide of 'a senior British diplomat', and the enforced early retirement of two ambassadors.[51] Early in 1993 12 of London's 32 boroughs were 'calling on the Metropolitan Police to help establish a special unit to investigate local authority fraud'.[52] In Lambeth alone, in 1995, 100 staff were dismissed and three of the borough's seven directorate heads, those in charge of finance, legal services and housing, were either suspended or on extended sick leave.[53] 'Public standards of probity and integrity have fallen to their lowest level since the creation of the modern Civil Service in the 19th century', according to the chairman of the House of Commons public accounts committee, outlining, in early 1994, a catalogue of 'mismanagement, inefficiency and outright fraud'.[54]

General practitioners and pharmacists were found by the Audit Commission in a report published in December 1994 to have defrauded the National Health Service of 'a national figure of tens of millions of pounds' by such devices as a GP's list that included '45 people living in a three-bedroomed house that turned out to be occupied by six', while 'more than half the prescriptions dispensed are worth less to the pharmacist than the £4.75 paid by the patient and some pharmacists destroy the prescription and keep the fee'.[55] Fraudulent solicitors are causing increasing expense and anxiety to the Law Society, which instituted 'Operation Crackdown' to investigate suspected firms, 400 of which were, by May 1994, scheduled for special investigation; in 1994 solicitors were required to contribute a total of at least £31 million (the 1991 figure had been £11.7 million) to compensate victims of dishonest practitioners. In addition, some 100 firms were under investigation for Legal Aid frauds amounting to £8 million.[56] By April 1995 it was announced that over 100 solicitors' firms had been closed down by the Solicitors' Complaints Bureau, or had been taken over.[57]

Loss adjusters estimate that up to 20 per cent of claims made on holiday insurance are bogus, at a cost (on honest travellers' premiums) of some £50 million a year.[58] Computer fraud trebled between 1990 and 1993, affecting 'one in ten organizations', according to an Audit Commission report.[59] Millions of pounds are lost to the taxpayer in fraudulent applications for student loans, the extent of false application being on so extensive a scale that the Metropolitan Police has a team of officers working solely on student awards.[60] Fraud inspectors recouped £92 million in 1994–5 from dole cheats (the Employment Minister stated that about 10 per cent of benefit claims were fraudulent).[61] Britain's contribution to Europe, meanwhile, is being swollen by the 10 per cent of the annual EC budget suspected of being corruptly disbursed.* [62]

Theft and vandalism diminish the worth of state funding in the public sector, burden the voluntary sector and threaten the viability of private enterprise. By the end of 1990 vandalism of schools, public lavatories, gardens and other municipal responsibilities were estimated in a survey by Wolverhampton Polytechnic to be costing some £1.5 billion a year, adding 'an average of £40 to poll tax bills'.[63] By 1994 the Government was budgeting £20 million a year for school security.[64] Goods to the value of over £1 million, including antique furniture and refrigerators as well as office equipment, disappeared from government departments in the year 1994–5, including 129 computers from Customs and Excise, and, at the Department of Employment, the entire switchboard.[65] Pilfering from the NHS was estimated at some £180 million in 1993, theft and mutilation of library books at £200 million annually,[66] and (a small sum, but sociologically revealing) in 1993 for the first time the sums awarded in compensation to teachers injured or falsely accused of improper conduct passed the £1 million mark.[67] The National Trust in 1990 spent some £2 million on measures to protect its – often elderly – volunteer guides from assault.[68] By the end of 1994, the cost to petrol filling stations of measures to deter thieves and vandals had mounted to £50 million a year.[69]

The cost to London Buses of repairing bus seats and cleaning graffiti was running, in 1993, at about £2 million annually, enough to have bought an additional 20 buses.[70] Cleaning up spray-can graffiti was

* 'We are talking not millions but billions of pounds', said the chairman of the House of Lords committee which reported in July 1994 (*Financial Control and Fraud in the Community* (HMSO, London, 1994); and see *The Times*, 29 July 1994).

costing London Underground £5 million a year by 1991.[71] Vandalism on the railways has led to huge repair bills, as well as large sums in compensation to delayed travellers and to injured passengers and drivers. 'External factors' were in 1993 estimated to be costing British Rail some £40–£45 million in damage and compensation (excluding delays caused by terrorist threats), quite apart from the costs incurred to outside agencies, such as the NHS, for treatment of injuries.[72] British Telecom, which saw attacks on its phone boxes rise from about 1,000 a month in September 1991 to about 6,500 a month by January 1993, was forced to invest some £10 million in attempting to secure its cash containers.[73]

These sums are trivial compared with overall losses in the retail trade. A survey by the British Retail Consortium published in 1994 and covering outlets with a combined turnover amounting to almost half of all retail sales in Great Britain found that crime (about a quarter of it by staff) cost retailers £2 billion in 1992–3, nearly a fifth of which went on crime prevention. The annual loss to the retail trade nationally, said Marks and Spencer's publicity manager in June 1993, was equivalent to a Brink's Mat bullion robbery every four days.[*][74] The brewery industry used the same benchmark, reporting in October 1993 that thefts of beer kegs stolen annually, easily melted down for resale as aluminium ingots at £500 a ton, equated to an annual Brink's Mat robbery.[75] Thefts in the haulage business, including that of some 4,000 lorries, was estimated by the RAC in March 1995 to be running at £1.6 billion a year.[76]

Terrorism adds its quotient to commercial and industrial losses. Harrods, in making 15 per cent of its workforce redundant in the spring of 1991, cited, without endeavouring to account for, the fact that 'customers outside the capital are no longer travelling to London to shop'.[77] Liberty's was among those publicly to admit, in the autumn of 1993, that 'increased terrorist activities in central London marred our efforts to achieve an acceptable increase in sales volume'.[78]

Insurance cannot compensate for hypothetical losses, but is expected to make good much of the other loss suffered in all sectors, public and private. At the end of 1991 several insurance companies were reporting large losses, including Municipal Mutual Insurance (MMI), Britain's ninth largest insurance company, which had been trading since 1903,

---

[*] On 26 November 1983, in a haul whose total value exceeded £26 million, at that time the biggest robbery ever carried out in Britain, the Brink's Mat security warehouse at Heathrow Airport was robbed of three tons of gold bullion, 1,000 carats in diamonds, platinum and travellers' cheques (*The Times*, 12 April 1995).

specializing in local authority business, with more than 500 local councils among its clientele.[79] By the spring of 1992 victims of the Hillsborough football ground disaster learnt that MMI, the company involved in their claim, was in financial difficulties. In October it halted all claim payments.[80] Local authorities up and down the country closed down sports halls and took emergency vehicles off the streets while they sought alternative insurers.[81] Premiums quoted at five times the previous rate, surcharges for terrorist insurance (Surrey County Council's bill, for instance, went from £1.6 million to £5 million in the course of three years)[82] could only mean, as the undersecretary of finance at the Association of Metropolitan Authorities pointed out, that 'any extra money required for insurance will reduce the amount of money they have available for other services'.[83] It was estimated that new policies to replace the MMI cover would cost approximately £3 billion instead of the £917 million for which MMI had tried to provide cover.[84]

Prominent among the pressures that destroyed MMI was 'massive theft claims from schools, which, with their videos, computers and televisions, made a tempting and soft target for burglars'.[85] School arson was a second influential factor. By the end of December 1992, it was reckoned to be costing £75 million annually, and by 1994 Home Office figures showed that every year one school in eight was a target for arsonists.[86] A single night's spree by four youths in Stockport in April 1994 caused damage estimated at £1 million. Prior to the 1960s arson had been of minor significance, but by 1969 it was qualifying for publication in the Home Office *Criminal Statistics*. From 2,300 incidents in 1969 numbers escalated to over 19,000 by 1986, and by 1991 arson was reckoned to be costing insurance companies £500 million, half the total bill for loss by fire.[87] Parish churches, suffering fires 'a distressingly high percentage [of which] have been the result of arson', according to a report by English Heritage and the Royal Institution of Chartered Surveyors, found themselves financially unable to insure at a level that covered their potential loss.[88] Claims on the Ecclesiastical Insurance Group in 1994 amounted to a record £7 million, 40 per cent of which arose from arson though it accounted for only 1 per cent of total criminal attacks on churches.[89]

Swiftly rising premiums are part of the price paid for widespread crime. Office insurance premiums for Britain's smallest businesses 'more than doubled over the past few years and are set to rise still further ... because offices have become the latest ''soft target'' for thieves', said a report in August 1994.[90] By the mid-nineties many householders and retailers found themselves, because of the areas in which they were situated, virtually uninsurable.* Shopkeepers in areas affected by the riots of 1981 and 1985 were among the worst affected, either failing to obtain insurance, or having to pay up to four times their previous level of premium.[91] Householders in inner-city areas were rated at five times the premiums of rural areas,[92] until thieves, attracted by good roads and less well-guarded pickings, moved into the country districts and premiums there, too, began to soar.[93] By the autumn of 1992 it was reported that a quarter of people had not taken out insurance cover for their possessions,[94] with 'up to 40 per cent of households in high risk areas' having no insurance; indeed, some notorious 'red line' postal districts of London, Birmingham, Bradford, Bristol, Cardiff, Liverpool and Manchester were, according to a report by the Association of London Authorities, the accuracy of which the insurance companies questioned, ineligible for insurance at any price.[95]

Even the business and domestic losses began to pale into insignificance after 1991, when Lloyd's of London unveiled what were then described as heavy losses of over £500 million for 1988. The 'names', the backers of last resort, were assured that better times were on the way, but in fact losses continued to mount. The 1989 figure was £1.75 billion, later years were worse, with further losses for the four years 1990–3 totalling £7.4 billion.[96] Losses of £11 billion by the spring of 1996 were forecast in November 1995.[97] For individuals, the calls for cash were catastrophic, one country house after another being put on the market, including Pitchford Hall in Shropshire, a magnificent timbered sixteenth-century building on a site which had been occupied by the same family for 500 years, containing family possessions dating back many generations. The contents were dispersed at sales, and the house passed to 'an overseas buyer', English Heritage having declined to intervene.[98] In the autumn of 1993 the director of the National Heritage Memorial Fund was commenting on the inadequacy of government funds to assist the purchase of art treasures likely to go abroad as Lloyd's losses precipitated the break-up and sale of country house collections.[99]

Crime could not be held primarily responsible for the Lloyd's *débacle*,† though the law courts had to decide how far criminal

---

* The Sock Shop was ruined by extending its activities into areas of New York where the hire of security guards to protect shoppers from muggers more than absorbed its profits (*The Times*, 10 February 1990).

† It may be significant, however, that the chairman of one of the most heavily committed Lloyd's syndicates commented that 'a sea-change in the general morality at Lloyd's occurred during the 1980s, so that the 300-year-old principle of utmost good faith started to be replaced by the principle of *caveat emptor* as if you were buying a used car from Arthur Daley' (*The Times*, 26 February 1992).

negligence (another facet of callousness) had contributed to the long catalogue of disasters that swelled insurance claims from the mid-1980s: the Bradford football ground fire which killed 56 people in 1985 and the King's Cross underground fire in 1987, both with uncleared litter in vulnerable locations; the Clapham Junction train crash in 1988 with its dangling signalling wires; the sinking of the Townsend Thorensen ferry at Zeebrugge in 1987 when the doors were left open; and the Piper Alpha rig explosion in the North Sea in the summer of 1988. Nor could human agency be credited with the severe San Francisco earthquake of 1989. But the expectation of huge claims for pollution of the environment, claims that are projected to ruin the entire American insurance industry before Lloyd's, in its turn, is consigned to final bankruptcy, was being widely canvassed by 1994. Earlier generations of those who had been sacrificed on the altar of increasing wealth, whether the slaves of the classical world or of the colonial plantations, the TB-ridden workers of the early Industrial Revolution or the lung-destroyed toilers in the mines and cotton mills, had, on the whole, lived and died uncompensated. By the mid-twentieth century the bills were being presented. Asbestosis claims from the United States amounting to hundreds of millions of pounds are flooding in, and damages running into as yet unassessable millions for other industrial injury and for polluted land are expected to follow.

Even these costs directly attributable to the pursuit of industrial goals are, however, dwarfed by the scale of costs associated with climatic change. Whether this is a result of human industrial activity is still a moot point. We may simply be living through a period of unusual but not unprecedented global climatic instability. Environmentalists, however, are convinced that it is the industrial world's unremitting pursuit of growth, with its inevitable concomitant increase in the use of energy, that is at the root of the global warming.

'Violent weather could destroy the reinsurance market and leave the public uninsured against natural catastrophes', stated *The Times* in April 1993, quoting a Lloyd's underwriter's opinion that 'We are living in a much more dangerous climate. There is no doubt that global warming is taking place, causing much stronger and much more frequent hurricanes', a view seconded by the scientific director of Greenpeace, who predicted 'a globally warmer atmosphere [heralding] stronger and more frequent windstorms, storm surges, rising seas, floods, droughts, increased subsidence following soil shrinkage on clay substrates, and many more unpleasant impacts'. Between 1966 and 1987, no catastrophe cost losses in excess of £700 million. Of fifteen catastrophes that cost from £700 million to £1.4 billion between 1987 and 1993, ten were windstorms, including the October 1987 hurricane in southern England and assorted hurricanes along the Atlantic coast of America, Hurricane Andrew and Cyclone Iniki between them bankrupting nine insurance companies and leaving the state of Florida to pick up the bill.[100] The extensive floods across north Europe in the winters of 1993–4 and 1994–5 led to conjecture that 'one way or another . . . global warming is destined to move swiftly up the European agenda'.[101]

The consequences for insurance companies of our pursuit of increased consumption are not, however, the environmentalists' main concern. The Intergovernmental Panel on Climate Change was by the autumn of 1995 for the first time admitting that industrial activity was at least in part to blame for global climate change, a change expected to precipitate 100 years of drought in Africa, with all its accompanying risk of famine, and equally drastic implications for western Europe if the Gulf Stream altered its course.

Less dramatic but equally threatening predictions had long preoccupied what came to be called the Green movement. In 1962 a book, Rachel Carson's *Silent Spring*, was published in the United States declaring that the industrialized world's lavish release of pesticides into the environment had unleashed a chain of progressive destruction into the biosphere, the life-support system of the entire natural world of which man was not a detached observer but a component part. In 1966 her fellow-countryman Barry Commoner, in *Science and Survival* and later in *The Closing Circle*, emphasized that the casual release of toxic chemicals into the environment as a by-product of industrial activity posed even greater hazards than the targeted war on Nature being waged in agriculture. Unfortunately, Commoner chose to assert that the villain of the piece was the profit motive, that the solution lay in public ownership. The claim was soon challenged by rumours that Lake Baikal in Russia was as polluted as Lake Erie, and the appalling toxic devastation throughout eastern Europe which was confirmed after the fall of the Soviet Empire finally disposed of such an analysis.

The conventional wisdom even in the late 1960s accepted the need for chemical industries to be sited near rivers or the sea in order to facilitate the disposal of their waste products. Pollution was not mentioned. In 1969, millions of fish died when the Rhine throughout Germany and Holland was poisoned. The ground swell of concern was growing. Magazines on the subject of the environment began to appear;* the *New*

* For instance, in America, *Environmental Science and Technology*, January 1967; in Britain, the

York Times appointed, at the end of the 1960s, the first 'environmental correspondent', his brief: to report on 'conservation, pollution, the air, the sea and other factors that affect the environment'.[102] Friends of the Earth was founded in the USA in 1969 and came to Britain in 1970. Manchester University in 1970 set up a Pollution Research Unit, and the same year saw the establishment in Whitehall of a Department of the Environment, though its activities did not quite accord with what some campaigners had expected. In 1972 there was held, at the House of Lords, the inaugural meeting of an Institution of Environmental Sciences to establish professional standards and co-ordinate scientific information.

Early optimism that it was just a matter of finding out what scientific standards should be applied, and then enforcing them, soon evaporated. When the distinguished ecologist Frank Fraser Darling gave the 1969 Reith Lectures, taking as his title 'Wilderness and Plenty', which he interpreted as covering 'population, pollution and the planet's generosity', he stressed the role of wilderness, of Nature in all its unprocessed elemental essence, as an 'active agent in maintaining a habitable world'.[103] Human beings, whether through the pressure of increasing numbers or of unbridled material demands, threaten the system on which their own survival depends. In January 1972 *Ecologist* magazine produced a 'Blueprint for Survival', the central message of which was: 'If current trends are allowed to persist, the breakdown of society and the irreversible disruption of the life-support systems on this planet, possible by the end of this century, certainly within the lifetime of our children, are inevitable.' The normal print run of the magazine was about 8,000, but demand for this edition took extra printings to nearly 100,000. Some 187 British scientists, including nine fellows of the Royal Society and twenty professors, who had declined to sign the blueprint on the grounds that some of its facts were questionable and its proposals debatable, nevertheless wrote to *The Times* welcoming its publication, affirming 'the gravity of this growing crisis' and declaring that 'there is now no escape from the necessity for a fundamental rethinking of all our working assumptions about human development in relation to the world we live in'.[104]

Paul Ehrlich, Professor of Biology at Stanford University, California, in 1968 published *The Population Bomb*, which did for the population issue what *Silent Spring* had done for pollution with its assertion that 'sometime around 1958 the Stork passed the Plough'.[105] He followed it in

International Journal of Environmental Studies, 1970; the *Ecologist*, 1970

1970 with *Population, Resources, Environment*, a detailed analysis of the interaction between people and the planet in terms of food, pollution and resource exhaustion. A team at Massachusetts Institute of Technology, under the auspices of 'the Club of Rome' (a group of industrialists, economists, civil servants and others from a number of different countries who shared a belief that a major part of the challenge was the inter-relatedness of all problems, so that solutions in one domain only made others more intractable), fed various prognostications into the newly developing computer technology, and, in *The Limits to Growth*, came up with the conclusion that growth, whether of population or of the economy, should cease virtually forthwith; 'Computer gives Mankind 100 years' was the *Guardian*'s summary.[106] Sceptics noted that all the sophisticated machinery in the world would produce ridiculous conclusions if fed ridiculous assumptions (GIGO = Garbage In, Garbage Out), but the prestige of both the sponsors and the Institute assured the report a wide influence.

The United Nations summoned a Conference on the Environment in Stockholm in 1972, where well-publicized feuds between capitalists and socialists as to where responsibility for the crisis lay were dwarfed by the extent of conflict between the rich industrial nations, urging population restraint on the Third World, and countercharges to the effect that the populations of the industrialized countries, though smaller and less expansive, were nevertheless by their high and wasteful living standards putting infinitely more strain than were the poor countries both on world resources and on the regenerative capacities of the biosphere; there were explicit accusations of racism. Similar tensions dogged the World Population Conference in Bucharest in August 1974, and the World Food Conference in Rome the following November.

The excitement died down. The more dire prophecies went unfulfilled (India, according to Ehrlich, faced food shortages destined to be so intractable by 1975 that the meagre world surpluses should be directed elsewhere, where they could produce worthwhile results),[107] birth control policies were instituted, pollution controls stringently tightened, recycling to conserve resources became a universally accepted civic duty. Famines, indeed, swept Africa, but war, transport and distribution problems and social disruption were responsible rather than any absolute shortage of food, of which the developed world achieved large surpluses, even if some agronomists continued to doubt the long-term viability of food production so dependent on fossil-fuel fertilizers which are not only based on a non-renewable resource, but also fail to nourish soil structure, opening the way to the soil erosion that has destroyed so many previous civilizations.

Scattered evidence of ecological stress occurred: forests withering, perhaps from acid in the atmosphere; fish and birds poisoned; occasional clusters of malformed children; species dying out (as they always had, pointed out the complacent).* Sad though these instances were, all seemed amenable to remedial action. Even the steady increase in asthmatic children and allergy-oppressed adults as a result of atmospheric pollution was seen as a challenge comparable to the London 'pea-soup' fogs that had dispersed once the 1956 Clean Air Act had been implemented; though projections for increased car-ownership, additional road-building and pleas for government aid to promote the car industry continued in disregard of the probability that traffic fumes were the most likely source of the bad air. Western industrial nations learnt a sharp lesson about the fragility of their economic power when, in 1973, the Organization of Petroleum Exporting Countries began to double, treble and then quadruple the price of oil – but it was a portent less of resource exhaustion than of shifting power structures, having as a principal effect an intensification of western nations' enthusiasm for the development of nuclear power. Then at the end of April 1986 came Chernobyl, the explosion of a Ukrainian nuclear reactor which proceeded to spew radioactivity in a widening arc down into the Balkans, then across Europe to Scandinavia and the British Isles, where the movement of radioactive lambs was to be banned for years to come. Frightening though this incident was, optimists could point to the fact that it was, though the most severe, not the first nuclear accident. It could be blamed on human incompetence; it was not a necessary or inescapable consequence of the pursuit of higher material living standards. Similar considerations applied to the revelation, in 1990, that one in three babies born near the Kazakhstan nuclear testing ground is stillborn or grossly deformed.[108]

The same confidence that salvation lies in more competently managed scientific application, in the 'technological fix', greeted a development that scientists had foreseen but had been unable to persuade people to take seriously – the destruction of the ozone layer, the reality of which was first reported by British scientists in Antarctica. In 1979 they noted changes in the layer, which protects the planet from the sun's (cancer-inducing) ultraviolet rays; in 1985 they reported that the layer had

* 'How many people lose sleep at night because they can no longer see a live dinosaur?' asked Wilfred Beckerman, an economist and doughty opponent of eco-hysteria (*The Times*, 30 January 1991).

partially disappeared. By 1987 their findings had been widely confirmed, and an international conference in Montreal urged nations, though with only partial success, to undertake to phase out the chlorofluorocarbons, discovered in 1930 and extensively used in industry,* which were believed to be the culprits. Much damage has, however, already been done. In succeeding years the thinning of this layer across various parts of the world has been anxiously reported in the press, with weather forecasts now including surprisingly brief recommended maximum minutes of exposure to the sun.

That industrial society's unprecedented release of substances into the atmosphere might induce climate change was a scientific speculation going back into the nineteenth century. In the 1960s assessments anticipating global warming were published, though paradoxically the fear in the 1970s was of a new ice age, caused by the melting of the ice caps and the cumulatively chilling effect of a wider circulation of polar water. By the late 1980s climatologists, insofar as they accepted the global warming thesis – and most did – expected it to take the form of higher temperatures, altered patterns of wind and rain which could be expected totally to disrupt existing agricultural practices, and rising sea levels that could permanently inundate many highly populated areas. CFCs are again part of the problem, but while their phasing out poses a not insuperable challenge, can reductions in the production of the other main components of the so-called 'greenhouse gases', carbon dioxide, released from the burning of fossil fuels, and methane, produced in quantity in agriculture, be reconciled with continued economic growth?

A new phrase came into fashion: 'sustainable development'. It was the basis for a major international conference, the Earth Summit, held in Brazil in June 1992, and attended by leaders and representatives from over 150 states, both 'developed' and 'developing'. The meaning of the phrase is unclear; as John Major said, introducing the UK's *Sustainable Development: The UK Strategy*: 'Sustainable development is difficult to define.' The general objective, however, is, in the words of Britain's Secretary of State for the Environment, 'that our economy can grow in a way which does not cheat on our children', an objective which 'means a change of attitudes throughout the nation'.[109] How far British attitudes had accommodated the discussion was demonstrated shortly thereafter, when public outcry greeted the proposal to make energy more expensive by putting a tax on it.

---

* CFCs have been used in manufacturing since the 1930s. Aerosol propellants were introduced during the 1940s, and in the 1950s the bubble techniques that utilized CFCs in foam plastics for furnishings and insulation were developed.

The dilemma of who should make sacrifices, if indeed they had to be made, echoed the tax dilemma which had so motivated democratic politicians to go for the growth option in the first place. In 1972 the *Observer* congratulated former Labour Chancellor of the Exchequer Roy Jenkins on being 'the first politician in this country' to recognize the political implications of 'the world-wide ecological dangers that will confront mankind if we do not put limits on our use of natural resources'.[110] By then in opposition, Jenkins was spelling out the necessity for greater sharing in the interests of equality, both nationally and internationally, a call which attracted sincere endorsement, but only from small minorities, who began forming Third World support groups under such rubrics as 'Live Simply – that others may Simply Live'.

Others were approaching the quandary from a rather different angle: a reinterpretation of the whole economic definition of wealth. Academic economists began to question their profession's reliance on quantitative data as indicators of wealth when no allowance was made for the quality of what was being measured; so that rising expenditure on ill-health, crime-control or the repair of toxic devastation all contributed to the Gross National Product, and no overall audit of environmental or social degradation was possible. The New Economic Foundation which in 1984 summoned the first TOES, The Other Economic Summit, was among those trying to devise reliable alternative indicators of 'true' wealth, a challenging task, and one in which a number of concerned economists interested themselves. Two American professors, Herman Daly and John Cobb, for instance, had by 1994 devised an Index of Sustainable Economic Welfare (ISEW), adjusting estimates of the Gross National Product to allow for a number of contingencies including spending to offset social and environmental costs of production; the longer-term costs of environmental damage and the depreciation of natural capital; and some weighting of incomes on the assumption that additional income is worth more to the poor than to the rich. Applying these methods to Britain, the Foundation asserted that in the years 1975–90 'GNP has increased by a third while sustainable welfare has actually fallen by around a half.'[111]

Animals are in the front line of the human determination to maximize utilization of the natural world. The drive for increasing quantities of cheap food brought huge changes in the treatment of agricultural livestock. By 1990 80–90 per cent of British eggs came from poultry kept four or five to a wire cage 50 by 45 cm in extent, with a sloping wire floor and no possibility for the hen to perch, scratch the ground or take exercise.[112] Poultry intended for the table and fed growth-promoting drugs put on weight at double the untreated rate, and reach slaughter weight in 49 days. But their bones do not develop in proportion, and the birds suffer fractures and heart attacks. The result is a relatively high mortality, but as there is no way of clearing the resultant corpses they are trodden into the litter, and later scooped up for cattle feed. Turkeys now have such gigantic breasts that they are unable to mate. Ninety per cent of sows were, in the early 1990s, spending four months at a time, until they farrowed, in iron cages barely larger than themselves, in which their only options are to stand or lie down, though the percentage so confined has since declined, according to Sir Richard Body, to about 65 per cent as a result of changes in financial incentives.[113] The rearing of calves in small darkened crates on a restricted diet that kept their flesh pallid was banned in the United Kingdom from 1 January 1990,* and as a result 300,000 calves were, in succeeding years, being annually exported to the Continent where the practice continues. The pursuit of cheap productivity in the beef and dairy industries has led to the use of cows as incubators for multiple embryos, sometimes of breeds too large for the dam to give birth except by Caesarean section; to milk production of a weight that splits the cows' hooves; and to the use of unsuitable feedstuffs, including diseased offal, which is suspected of being the source of the fatal cattle brain disease, bovine spongiform encephalopathy, first diagnosed in 1986. The damage to British exports of meat and of live animals may yet prove ruinous.

Agriculture is now an industry in which animals are regarded not as sentient beings, but as machines, to be run at maximum efficiency. In medicine it is precisely the living qualities they share with human beings that make them valuable research tools. Vivisection[†] is carried out under licence and is subject to a plethora of legislative controls, there being approximately 370 vivisection laboratories in Britain, though since 1981 precise details of individual laboratories have not been published by the Home Office. There is no public access to the laboratories; indeed, Sir Richard Body remarks in *Our Food, Our Land* that even members of the House of Commons Select Committee on Agriculture were not permitted to witness 'grotesque experiments' on pigs at one location.[114]

* The Welfare of Calves Regulations, 1987.
† Defined as 'experimental or other scientific procedures which "may have the effect of causing pain, suffering, distress or lasting harm" performed on "any living vertebrate other than man", including foetal, larval and embryonic forms from the halfway point in gestation or incubation period *re* mammals, birds, reptiles; and when capable of independent feeding *re* fish and amphibians' (Kew, p.115).

In 1990 over three million animals were used, half of them mice, but including more than 4,000 cats, 11,400 dogs and over 5,000 primates. The principal area of medical research is new drugs and agrochemicals, where dosage levels are tested for toxicity and side effects such as deformed offspring, nerve damage and propensity to cause cancer. Other areas of interest are warfare and space exploration, experimental psychology, breeding innovations in farm livestock (including, after the development of genetic manipulation which had followed the discovery of DNA by Crick and Watson, publicized in 1953, 'transgenic' organisms incorporating genes from different species) and the development of new surgical techniques. Over half a million experiments in 1990 were performed not in the interests of health and safety legislation, but to extend the frontiers of knowledge. The processes involved require animals to be 'burnt; scalded; poisoned; shot; inflicted with diseases like cancer, diabetes, syphilis, herpes, arthritis, influenza; have eyes removed; eyelids sewn up; nerves crushed, severed; bones broken . . .'[115] The possible benefits to human beings include, for instance, such hitherto impossible feats as the cure of paraplegia. Scientists in Japan were reported, in January 1994, to have cut the spinal cords of newborn rats, grafted on spinal nerve tissue from rat foetuses, and achieved a regrowth of spinal cord.[116]

In 1980 the US Supreme Court ruled that 'man-made' micro-organisms could be patented, a judgement which in 1987 was elaborated by the US Patent Office with the announcement that all forms of life, including animals, could be patentable provided they had been genetically engineered. Proposals for similar legislation in Europe occupied the EC Commission in 1988.[117] In April 1988 the first patent for a living mammal was granted in the United States to Harvard University for a strain of mice genetically manipulated to develop cancer within 90 days and die soon afterwards.[118] In May 1991 the European Patent Office granted the patent in Europe. In 1992 a mouse genetically programmed to develop cystic fibrosis was achieved, and a group programmed to develop spongiform encephalopathy failed to do so, thus furthering the relevant research.[119] By now genetic engineering was being extensively used to create new strains of crops and animals for a myriad of different uses, and, as the Professor of Animal Husbandry at Bristol University said, 'What we have now to decide is not what we can do, but what we should do.'[120]

The belief that the principal criterion of consumption should be its contribution to the universal right of human beings to 'life, liberty and the pursuit of happiness' was by now, thanks to medical advances, pursuing directions which earlier generations would have rejected as wholly impious.

The use of the bodies of the dead for research purposes had long ceased to disturb most people, even if they were slow to volunteer their own corpse.* The irrational identification with one's own body, even after death, remains a powerful sentiment; Bernard Levin recounts a conversation he had with Field Marshal Montgomery, in which, in response to Levin's query as to how he could bring himself to issue an order that must inevitably result in the death of some of his men, the old soldier replied, 'Provided they know that if they are killed, their bodies will be carefully collected and reverently buried, they will accept casualties, even very heavy casualties.'[121] As the twentieth century wore on, this attitude came to be regarded as atavistic, even selfish, though paradoxically in the same period the respect in which distant tribes held the remains of their ancestors came to be accorded recognition; on receipt of a petition from Australia, for instance, seven Aboriginal warrior skulls were, in 1990, rounded up from various British repositories and returned for ritual burial.[122]

Success in transplanting into the sick items from the bodies of the dead offered a huge new field both of medical expertise and of potential uses for cadavers. Corneal grafts were being pioneered in Paris as early as 1912, but not until after World War II did the transplant of organs become feasible. The first kidney transplant took place in Chicago in 1950, though it was not until 1963 that the feat was replicated in the United Kingdom. Almost five years later, at the end of 1967, Dr Barnard in South Africa carried out the first heart transplant operation, Britain attempting a similar operation less than six months later, though unsuccessfully; the patient died, as did the first British attempt at a lung transplant the same year (1968). Skill and knowledge improved, and in 1972 a kidney donor scheme was instituted in London.[123] Twenty years later medical progress had been so spectacular that the possibility of transplanting limbs and even whole faces (for those suffering bad burns, for example) was being seriously canvassed.[124]

By 1993 some 2,500 transplant operations were annually being performed in Britain.[125] A further 5,500 patients were awaiting treatment. Already in the early 1980s the success of the transplant scheme and the number of potential beneficiaries far exceeded the available organs – a contingency exacerbated by the statutory imposition of

---

* Little publicity was afforded to such – undoubtedly revealing – research projects as the use of bodies to explore the effect of new varieties of ammunition, or the consequences of road accidents (*The Times*, 26 and 30 November 1993).

helmets on motorcyclists, which meant that large numbers of healthy young men who would previously have died were surviving their motorcycle accidents, albeit all too often as paraplegics. In February 1984 Bishop Trevor Huddleston wrote to *The Times* saying that since donor cards had failed to produce an adequate supply of organs, the time had surely come to give doctors the automatic right to remove organs from the dead unless the person concerned had specifically 'opted out'.* Death through the non-availability of spare kidneys was, he said, 'a deprivation of the right to live for hundreds, if not thousands, of kidney patients in this country. And I believe it should be a matter of conscience to promote life rather than to safeguard the dignity – if such it is – of a corpse.'[126]

An objector drew a seemingly fanciful picture of the near-dead kept artificially alive while arrangements were made to harvest their body-parts to the most advantageous uses,[127] a scenario that seemed the stuff of science fiction, and indeed provided the theme for a 1977 thriller called *Coma*, starring Michael Douglas, in which a surgeon, by administering faulty anaesthetics, induced irreversible comas in selected patients who were then arranged in attractive flower-filled rooms when relatives called, but otherwise were retained in hammocks in a medical warehouse pending profitable marketing of their organs. By the spring of 1987 surgeons were expressing concern that lack of intensive care units for use while administrative procedures were completed was resulting in waste of organs by the untimely death of doomed potential donors.[128] In the summer of 1990 it became known that the Royal Devon and Exeter Hospital had devised a scheme for detecting and transferring to intensive care patients without hope of recovery but suitable for transplants, and retaining them on ventilators while permission to use organs was obtained from relatives. Of 11 groups of relatives approached, only two refused, and some 19 extra organs thus became available. The hospital admitted that shortage of equipment and skilled nurses in intensive care units was a limiting factor, and there was general recognition that a point of principle was involved in keeping a patient alive who had no hope of benefiting, and who was thus being used purely as a means to someone else's ends. The underlying assumption, of course, was that the patient

---

* The suggestion frequently recurred. Following the relative failure of a government publicity drive to encourage more people to carry donor cards, a report to the Department of Health in May 1993 proposed that all those applying for driving licences be asked to register as organ donors (*The Times*, 13 May 1993). The Advisory Council on Science and Technology in the same year recommended that 'opting out' be the rule, rather than 'opting in', but the ethics committee of the British Medical Association did not concur (*The Times*, 28 January 1994).

was beyond consciousness or suffering, and this distinguishes the practice from that for which Iran had earned universal odium in 1983, when it became known that prisoners condemned to death had had the blood drained from their bodies prior to execution for use in the treatment of wounded soldiers, a practice which Iranians in exile denounced as contrary to the spirit of Islam.[129] Exeter's solution was discussed in a BBC 2 *Public Eye* programme on 10 June 1994, in which it emerged that there was doubt as to the legality of the practice, which was suspended pending clarification. By then it was common knowledge that the slang for a dying patient among embarrassed doctors was 'GOP': Good Only for Parts. In October 1994 the Department of Health pronounced that keeping patients alive in order to harvest their organs was illegal, a ruling which is expected to lead to the transplant patients' organizations, such as the National Kidney Federation, seeking to initiate changes in the law.[130]

Organ shortage prompted experimentation with parts derived from animals, a prospect which led to vigorous debate during the summer of 1988. The problem of tissue rejection seemed insuperable, though some liver sufferers were helped by having their blood filtered through pig livers external to their body, an expensive expedient as the pig livers had to be renewed daily.[131] Transgenic work was opening up the possibility of animals specially bred to produce organs incorporating human genes which would overcome the problems of tissue rejection and generate a huge new source of transplant spares. The pig was the likeliest contender, and by the end of 1989 the prospect of lungs transplanted from pigs was 'a real possibility', according to a consultant chest physician at Papworth Hospital, Cambridge, the only possible limitations being not skill or money, but ethical hesitations. If these could be satisfied, clinical trials could be expected by 1996, and if successful, hospitals could begin running their own herds of transgenic animals, for use as required.[132]

As in the comparable shortage of corpses for dissection in the early nineteenth century, dubious merchants appeared on the scene. Communist East Germany was reportedly selling parts for hard currency in 1990, and in 1994 it was admitted that German autopsy workers at a hospital in North-Rhine Westphalia were disposing of parts for a financial consideration without the knowledge of relatives. In Bangladesh, activities more akin to Burke and Hare were being extensively investigated in 1988; in April of that year it was reported that 'a further 100 kidnapped Bangladeshis, mostly women and children, have been rescued near the south-western border with India. Last week border guards said 2,667 hostages "destined for sale abroad as prostitutes or for organ transplants" had been saved in the past six months."[133]. Among a number of incidents under investigation in Argentina in 1992 was that of the director of a mental home where over the course of ten years 1,400 patients disappeared; he was accused of selling corneas and kidneys and storing blood.[134] At the end of 1993 reports were widespread of children in both Russia and Latin America being kidnapped for use as organ repositories, of mutilations carried out even on victims who lived to tell the tale, and of a huge, possibly internationally organized, trade in body parts originating in Russia where many Russians, too poor to bury their dead, were providing a wealth of body parts for (illegal) transplant traffickers.[135] Closer to home, in February 1994 a Rome hospital was found to have been skilfully replacing the eyes of the dead with glass, in order to harvest corneas.[136] While philosophers debated to what extent persons owned their body parts exclusively, and thus were entitled to dispose of them as they wished, including by sale, accounts were emerging of Third World citizens being persuaded to part with one of their kidneys, and a British surgeon in a private hospital, though protesting his ignorance that any money had changed hands, admitted accepting kidneys from Turkish peasants who claimed to have been paid £2,000. Investigations revealed a widespread and openly advertised market in kidneys from live donors in Turkey.[137] By 1994 it was reported that in Indonesia early release was being offered to prisoners willing to donate organs.[138] According to Human Rights Watch,

> up to 3,000 organs, mostly kidneys and corneas, from executed prisoners are used every year in transplants in China . . . the consent of prisoners is rarely sought, some executions have been deliberately bungled so that convicts are alive when their organs are removed . . . in some cases, kidneys have been removed from prisoners on the night before their executions . . .'* [139]

In India a widespread traffic in illegal transplant organs was revealed early in 1995, when it was disclosed that over 1,000 unsuspecting donors had been lured into privately run hospitals and deprived of one of their kidneys on the pretext that they were being paid to be blood donors.[140]

The legality of abortion had made available a further category of useful material in aborted foetuses. In 1988 the prospect of injecting

---

* Detailed accounts of these practices published in *The Times* on 26 October 1994 and recounted on BBC 2 *Newsnight* on 27 October 1994 were subsequently denied by Peking (*The Times*, 24 November 1994).

foetal brain cells into sufferers from Parkinson's disease became known, and the British Medical Association was riven by controversy as to the morality involved – including whether it was necessary for the mother to be informed of the use to which the foetal material was being put. Particular unease was expressed at the probability that, in view of the speed with which the cells would deteriorate once deprived of oxygen, the material would have to be extracted before the donor was 'brain dead'.[141] The debate ended predictably – by mid-1989 more than a dozen transplants of foetal brain tissue into the brains of sufferers from Parkinson's disease had been carried out.[142] A dilemma arose over the use of organs from anacephalic babies (those without brains who were doomed to certain early death), since there were advantages to be gained from their being carried to full term, and not aborted. The prospect of making good use of their hearts for babies whose own hearts were defective was particularly stressed in a television programme in mid-1989 by a surgeon who, in 1984 in California, had attempted unsuccessfully to transplant a baboon's heart into a baby.[143] A strict new code of practice was introduced by the Government in the summer of 1989, setting up, *inter alia*, an agency to handle foetal tissue, forbidding financial inducements for its provision, and seeking to prevent pressure on women to become pregnant in order to provide material for a particular purpose, or to time their abortions to suit the convenience of recipients.[144] By mid-1993 medical techniques had reached the stage at which it seemed feasible to 'harvest' and store limbs and organs from aborted foetuses for use in repairing damaged babies. The British Medical Association's head of ethics said that there appeared to be no moral objection provided the decision on abortion was unrelated to the use of the organs. Many advances, she pointed out, including heart transplants, had been regarded as controversial when first proposed.[145] Serious public dissension arose in the autumn of 1994, however, when it was discovered that the measles/rubella vaccination being routinely recommended for all schoolchildren was derived from foetal material. Several Roman Catholic schools refused to use it, a stance adopted also by Moslem leaders. The Chief Medical Officer subsequently approached pharmaceutical companies with a request that they explore other means of creating the vaccine.[146]

The steady acclimatization of public opinion to ever more radical departures from traditional ethical ideas about the 'sanctity' (a meaningless word in secular parlance) of human bodies was the subject of a number of press articles by Bernard Levin on 'The Fallacy of the Altered

Standpoint'.[147] Its progression was particularly evident in the development of 'test-tube' babies and, later, genetic engineering. The first successful fertilization of a human egg in a test tube (IVF, *in vitro* fertilization) had taken place in 1969, in Cambridge. Nine years later, the first baby to be conceived outside the mother's body was born. And with her were born a plethora of ethical dilemmas that have reverberated ever since, going well beyond the question posed for orthodox religion ever since the introduction of artificial insemination by donor (AID) as distinct from artificial insemination by husband (AIH) as to whether AID constituted adultery. It had now become possible to implant a donated egg in a surrogate mother's womb, including 'mothers' well past reproductive age; to fulfil homosexual women's desire for children without sexual congress; or for women of one racial group to give birth to a child with the physical characteristics of a different racial group.

Once more the limitation of inadequate voluntarily surrendered raw material from living donors posed problems (by May 1994 some 2,000 women were awaiting donated eggs),[148] and the prospect of using ovarian material from cadavers was being canvassed. A generous source of human eggs was available, it was pointed out, in the ovaries of aborted girl babies, and, as Manchester's Professor of Philosophy put it in a debate on Radio 4's *Sunday* programme on 29 April 1994, it would be a tragedy to let such a useful source of material go to waste. A doctor at the forefront of the research commented that 'if we believe abortion is permissible in certain circumstances, there is surely a case for using the material to benefit others'.[149] The matter was hotly debated, proponents pointing out that almost every innovation, such as semen donation, had initially provoked revulsion, what they called the 'yuk factor', but familiarity with the idea had overcome objections, as it surely would in the case of foetus eggs (an illustration, perhaps, of Levin's 'Fallacy of the Altered Standpoint'). Emotions, it was pointed out, were an improper guide to ethics, which should be concentrating on the happiness to be enjoyed by the infertile thus made pregnant. Indeed, insofar as their childlessness distressed them to the point that they became mentally ill, they were suffering a sickness that gave them a *right* to treatment on the National Health Service.[150] However, the proposal went beyond what public opinion was (yet?) prepared to accept. A clause was introduced into the Criminal Justice and Public Order Bill making its way through Parliament during the summer of 1994 banning the use of aborted foetus eggs in infertility treatment;[151] but long before it had completed its passage the Human Fertilization and Embryology Authority had interceded to pronounce that, while research on foetal and cadaver ovaries was acceptable,* their use for the generation of new human beings was not approved, in view of the complex issues involved, though the Authority stated that it had no objection in principle.[152] The controversy moved the Anglican John Habgood, Archbishop of York, to write to *The Times* stating that

> From the start the churches have been suspicious of artificial insemination by donor. They have drawn a clear moral distinction between the use of donors, whether of sperm or ova, and 'assisted reproduction' . . . whereby a couple are enabled to have a child which is genetically and in every other way their own.

The use of donors, he said, may satisfy individual wants, but 'the price of meeting a few unfortunate people's desire for children is morally too high'.[153] This opinion was not universal among Anglicans. In 1987 an unmarried American Episcopalian female priest was reported embarking on the process of conceiving a second child by AI.[154]

Genetic engineering research also demanded material. Opportunities were opening up of identifying defects and thus enabling targeted abortions to eliminate the unfit – a prospect greeted with some dismay by physically handicapped contributors to a Channel 4 discussion programme, who feared that future eugenics would deny them the right to exist, or castigate mothers who failed to abort them.[155] The capacity to fertilize human eggs in test tubes usually resulted in some spare embryos from the parents under treatment. Though these embryos were not available for implantation into other women, scientists were initially free to experiment on them, occasioning some moral disquiet. In Britain the Warnock Committee, instituted in the early 1980s, proposed, in a recommendation subsequently accepted by Parliament,† a ban on embryo experimentation after fourteen days, at which time the embryo should be destroyed. Cardinal Hume, on behalf of Roman Catholicism, totally opposed the development, arguing that the conjunction of sperm and egg gave rise to a living organism that could not be other than human.[156] The Methodist Conference accepted a study redefining the result of the sperm-egg conjunction as a 'pre-embryo' and, recognizing that it is surplus to requirements and therefore has no prospect of individual survival, agreed that 'this otherwise wasted life is given purpose if used for experiments which might benefit humanity'.[157] A

---

* Of 10,000 responses to the Authority's consultation paper on the subject, only 7 per cent had supported research, a view which the Authority rejected (*The Times*, 20 July 1994).
† In 1990, by 364 votes to 193, the dissenters wanting a total ban (*The Times*, 24 April 1990).

survey conducted among Anglican bishops found ten opposed to all research and seven, including both archbishops, in favour of controlled experimentation.[158]

By the following year, at a Royal Society meeting, Edinburgh University's Professor of Reproductive Endocrinology was arguing the case for research, subject to the mother's consent, on foetuses scheduled for abortion, on the grounds that such research could provide the clue to preventing the deaths of premature babies, a plea backed by Oxford University's Professor of Clinical Medicine, who said that a majority of British scientists would support the establishment of an ethics committee to investigate the dilemmas posed by such issues.[159] That such dilemmas abound was made evident by American experience, where experiments on condemned foetuses (which, it was held, were incapable of pain or suffering) frequently resulted in the death of the foetus before it was aborted. Without these experiments, however, the world would not have had available the techniques of amniocentesis that enable congenital anomalies to be identified in the womb.[160] There was, nevertheless, disquiet when in June 1994 it was revealed that in the 1940s and 1950s pregnant women scheduled for 'therapeutic abortions' in America had been injected with radioactive substances (whether with or without their consent was, by 1994, in dispute) and the foetuses examined to determine the effect of radiation on the unborn.[161]

With the increasing tendency to treat human body tissue as a consumer good, it was not perhaps surprising that attitudes to cannibalism began to change. This originated with anthropologists and sociologists, anxious to remove from the study of alien cultures any implications of cultural inferiority, and by the 1960s articles were appearing in the press treating the cannibalism of Papua New Guinea, for instance, with studied avoidance of the judgementalism to which cannibalism had traditionally been subjected in the West.[*] That cases of cannibalism have occurred in the history of the West in spite of the strong taboo against it is of course admitted, but known instances have been very rare, the circumstances extreme, the public response one of almost speechless horror. When, in 1854, an expedition sent to the Canadian Arctic to research the disappearance of Franklin's crew some ten years earlier returned with the suggestion that their corpses showed evidence of cannibalism, Charles Dickens was among the many protesting that British people simply wouldn't stoop to eating each other.[162]

[*] The connection between Papuan cannibalism and the brain disease kuru had not then been identified.

George Steiner tells of the impact on a group of travellers, of whom he was one, as they passed a ruined Polish monastery, and learnt that it was the site of the incarceration of a group of Russian officers, abandoned when their guards fled west, two of whom survived by killing and eating the others. When liberated by the Soviet Army, the survivors were given a good meal – and then shot, 'lest the soldiers see to what abjection their former officers had been reduced.'[163] In 1975 Peter Hall staged a monologue, *Judgement*, based on the incident, which imaginatively postulated the circumstances in which an initial agreement to draw lots as to who should be sacrificed to save the others degenerated into murder and suicide, one survivor mad, the other on trial.

This imagined scenario had been acted out in America in the 1840s, when a wagon train of pioneers was trapped in the mountains by the onset of winter, and the travellers finally drew lots as to who should sacrifice himself for the sake of the others. In the event, the lot was ignored, and the alternative was pursued of murdering and eating the two non-consenting Indian guides, a demonstration of how readily, once survival becomes the overriding goal, other moral absolutes are abandoned.[164] *Judgement* had shown the proponent of the original, lot-drawing plan as the exponent of rational good sense, pleading the sanity of his views at his court martial and only regretting that they had not, in the end, prevailed; and the reviewer of a 1987 revival of the play commented on the extent to which this seeming rationality discounted 'whole regions of human feeling – fear, greed, self-disgust'.[165]

Provided murder was not deliberately perpetrated, however, public opinion was coming to rational terms with cannibalism. A German pilot whose plane came down in the Canadian northland in November 1972 was not greatly castigated for eating the British nurse who had failed to survive the crash – though (in a reversal of conventional assumptions about Eskimo willingness to practise cannibalism in extreme circumstances) the Inuit boy who was the only other survivor starved to death after 22 days. Jurors at the inquest, which the pilot did not attend, were troubled by the case, but the Canadian Justice Department decided to file no charges.[166]

In 1973 the extraordinary story emerged of the rescue, after 72 days in the snows of the Andes, of 16 survivors from a crashed plane. They had survived by feeding on the bodies of their dead companions. The story is told with sensitivity and a total absence of sensationalism by Piers Paul Read in *Alive*. Their bishop and their local priest took the view that what they did was not only permissible, it was their duty to sustain their own lives, and the analogy between transplants and cannibalism was made by the bishop, who said that

> eating someone who has died in order to survive is incorporating their substance, and it is quite possible to compare this with a graft. Flesh survives when assimilated by someone in extreme need, just as it does when an eye or heart of a dead man is grafted on to a living man . . .

Read quotes Gino Concetti, theologian of *L'Osservatore Romano*, as saying that 'he who has received from the community has also the duty to give to the community or its individual members when they are in extreme need of help to survive'.[167] In 1993 a Hollywood film was made of the incident, which prompted the BBC 1 *Everyman* programme to interview many of the survivors, by then twenty years older. None, the viewers were assured, felt any guilt, though some spoke with an unease which suggested an element of unresolved disquiet.[168]

Advocacy of cannibalism as a logical extension of transplant surgery began to feature in discussion programmes. Consumerism has, it seems, conquered the last taboo. Had Captain Scott, Dr Wilson and Lieutenant Bowers eaten Captain Oates instead of allowing him to walk out into the blizzard on that last grim march from the South Pole, perhaps they, too, would have returned alive. Whether anything of immeasurable value to human dignity and respect would thereby have been lost is among the questions facing late sensate society.

As the twentieth century comes to an end, a sense of revulsion has begun to challenge the easy certainties of consumerism. Two tenets more typical of ideational than of sensate societies are attracting adherents: that human beings are not to be regarded as the culmination of the creative (or evolutionary) process, to whose welfare all else can and should be subordinated; and that the pursuit, as well as the application, of scientific knowledge is neither value-free nor unimpeachable. The legions who, with varying degrees of fanaticism, march for the new credo have inscribed upon their banners the words 'Animal Liberation'.

Chapter 23

Straws in the Wind

Darwin had set the ball rolling: human beings are a species of animal. Small wonder then that, with our inheritance across millions of evolutionary years of a reptilean cortex, the basic survival mechanisms of reproduction and aggression are deeply embedded in our psyche, surfacing especially readily when alcohol inhibits the later-developed mechanisms of the brain and propels us back up the evolutionary tree. It is a potent dynamic from which contemporary entertainment is happy to profit, its animal origins manifested only too clearly in Bob Geldof's recollections of the smell of urine at his first pop concert,[1] or in the hosing down of the stalls which cinema managers found necessary after Bill Haley and his Comets had enthralled teenage audiences. The devastating force of these primordial impulses, and the folly of trying to ignore their existence, is the focus of Euripides's *The Bacchae*.

By the mid-twentieth century book after book had stressed not only our kinship with animals but the additional message that we are 'nothing but' the product of our animal inheritance. Desmond Morris, with *The Naked Ape* (1967), his thesis of human behaviour, found allies among the clever, competent and articulate scientists who seized on the unravelling of the genetic code to point the same message. The zoologist Richard Dawkins's *The Selfish Gene* demolished even the suggestion that the organism had its own integrity, reducing evolutionary theory to the survival of the genes, and animals (human or not) to machines for their preservation; and went on (in *The Blind Watchmaker*) to account for the entire diversity and complexity of Nature on the assumption, demonstrable in computer programs, of serendipitous creativity – anything can happen by chance, no purposeful mind need be posited. Steve Jones, geneticist, the 1991 Reith lecturer (on 'The Language of Genes'), proselytized the same message, while Francis Crick, one of the discoverers of DNA, published in 1994 *The Astonishing Hypothesis* in which he claimed that analysis of neural realities was well on the way to

544

disposing of the illusion of the existence of the soul. All received generous opportunities on radio and television to disseminate their views.

The 'nothing but' approach had swiftly validated embryo experimentation ('nothing but' insignificant cells were being squashed between the glass slides in the laboratory). It had, to the horror of the outside world once the facts became known, validated experiments on living human beings in Nazi concentration camps, where initially, as had been rumoured but barely believed in Greek Alexandria at the peak of its scientific success two thousand years earlier, imprisoned criminals had been the involuntary guinea pigs for vivisection and experimentation, before a wider spectrum of humanity came to be regarded as expendable. When twenty-two men and one woman, all but three of them with medical degrees and numbering among them eminent academics, went on trial in Nuremberg in December 1946, it was noted that

> the experiments made on prisoners were many and diverse, but they had one thing in common: all were in continuation of, or complementary to, experiments on animals. In every instance, this antecedent scientific literature is mentioned in the evidence; and at Buchenwald and Auschwitz concentration camps, human and animal experiments were carried out simultaneously as parts of a single programme.[2]

Seven of the accused were hanged, nine were sentenced to long terms of imprisonment.[3] Years after the war, facts began to emerge of the use the Japanese had made of prisoners of war in biological warfare and other experiments, and the assertion was advanced that the perpetrators escaped trial in return for turning the valuable results of their investigations over to the Allies.[4] Whether to use the information gleaned from Nazi and Japanese experiments posed a moral dilemma for the Allies, soon resolved in favour of not letting the suffering that had already occurred go to waste.[5]

Secular society, having lost the consensus on what constitutes decent conduct that religion enshrined, seeks to protect human beings from exploitation by their fellows not by the fiats of religious revelation, but by the application of reason, made explicit in the doctrine of human rights.[*] Eighteenth-century Enlightenment tenets had spelt out various

---

[*] In arguing the case for a bill of rights to replace Britain's unwritten constitution, proponents emphasize that 'Secularism has broken down the deposit of common moral assumptions founded on Christianity . . . an unwritten constitution can only work if there is a moral basis to society so

political, legal and property rights. After World War II the newly created United Nations promulgated, in 1948, a Universal Declaration of Human Rights extending the concept into the social and economic sphere with particular emphasis on the protection of minorities; and the nations of the newly formed Council of Europe instituted, in 1950, the Convention of Human Rights with an associated court to which appeal could be made. Rights to be guaranteed included 'security of life and limb' and a long list of political and social freedoms to be enjoyed without distinction of religion, race, national origin or political or other adherence.* The process of unravelling the implications of the doctrine of rights, as first women, then oppressed races and peoples began to stake their claims to political, social and economic liberation, proved a potent force for change in the latter twentieth century.

Why, in the absence of some sort of religious doctrine of human worth, the human animal should enjoy such respect was regarded as self-evident in the countries which accepted the doctrine of rights (and was equally blandly ignored in those countries which did not).† In 1975 the philosopher Peter Singer published *Animal Liberation*, a work which he described as 'about the tyranny of human over nonhuman animals'. There was, he maintained, no rational argument for the equality of human beings with one another that did not apply with equal force to animals – 'equality' being in both cases a moral idea, not a statement of fact. Attempts to define the 'right' to enjoy 'rights' in terms of selected attributes which only human beings enjoyed (for instance, an under-standing of justice)‡ all failed because inevitably there would be found human beings who lacked the chosen attribute, but were not the less human for that. 'Rights' were a human construct which could apply only

deeply rooted and universally shared that there is no need to state it' (Clifford Longley, *The Times*, 15 June 1987).

* The Convention defined essential personal liberties which all participating states would guarantee in addition to any other rights existing under present law as: security of life and limb; freedom from arbitrary arrest, detention and exile; freedom from slavery and servitude and from compulsory labour of a discriminatory kind; freedom of speech and of expression of opinion generally; freedom of religious belief, practice and teaching; freedom of association and assembly; the natural rights deriving from marriage and paternity and those pertaining to the family; the sanctity of the home; equality before the law; freedom from discrimination on account of religion, race, national origin, or political or other opinion; and freedom from arbitrary deprivation of property (*The Times*, 4 August 1949).

† Monsignor Nichols, General Secretary of the Bishop's Conference of England and Wales, recounts the story that one of the members of the commission drafting the UN Declaration of Human Rights reportedly said, 'We are unanimous about these rights on condition that no-one asks why' (*The Times*, 24 June 1991).

‡ The Universal Declaration of Human Rights states in Article I: 'All human beings are born free and equal in dignity and rights. They are endowed with reason and conscience . . .'

to organisms capable of having 'interests', the defining prerequisite of which (and here Singer followed Jeremy Bentham)* was the capacity to suffer. The existence of that capacity was to be determined on neurological grounds: 'somewhere between a shrimp and an oyster seems as good a place to draw the line as any'.[6] 'Speciesism' must join racism and sexism among the ideologies to be rejected by all with any claim to moral understanding.

Singer is uncompromising in his opposition to laboratory experiments on animals, only conceding that the use of an animal would be admissible in circumstances where a brain-damaged human being could, with equal justification, be used.[7] His strictures are very much more severe on American scientific research than on British, where legislative controls are more effective, but when it comes to the treatment of animals in agriculture, he records a litany of abuse so horrific, and so rampant after years of unimplemented recommendations by government committees, that he sees no alternative to unremitting vegetarianism. He is of course opposed to the exploitation of animal products for purposes of human clothing or adornment, and to the use of animals as sources of human entertainment, especially in hunting.

For Singer, Judaeo-Christian justifications for human dominion over the animal kingdom, reaching right back to Genesis, are the source of animal ill-treatment by human beings, and he is scathing in his condemnation of the theologians of the Roman Catholic Church, not least Thomas Aquinas, for the sophistry with which they justify the exploitation of animals for man's convenience, where the only moral worth of kindness to animals is seen as the engendering of a disposition benign towards human beings as well as towards animals. Not even Francis of Assisi escapes his strictures, for while his benevolence encompassed the whole natural world, it never questioned a hierarchical attitude to animals.[8] In this Singer is less than fair to Christian apologists; not only did the Calvinist Stubbes† plead the cause of animals, but in the eighteenth century the Anglican Reverend Humphrey Primatt, in his *The Duty of Mercy and the Sin of Cruelty to Brute Animals* (published in 1776, some thirteen years before Bentham's plea), had upbraided humankind for considering 'brutes', among whom he included beasts, birds, fishes, insects and worms, as unworthy either of any attention, or

---

* Bentham, in his *Introduction to the Principles of Morals and Legislation* (1789), Chapter 17 (footnote), had questioned why an animal should suffer 'the caprice of a tormentor' any more than should a slave – or a speechless, as yet irrational, baby. 'The question is not, Can they *reason*? nor Can they *talk*? but, Can they *suffer*?'
† See Chapter 15.

of attention only insofar as 'we can apply them to our use'.[9] No doctrine of rights intrudes – Primatt's views stem directly from religious revelation (he devotes many pages to quotations of the appropriate passages in Scripture):

> the love and mercy of God are over all his works, from the highest rational to the lowest sensitive, our love and mercy are not to be confined within the circle of our own friends, acquaintance and neighbours; nor limited to . . . creatures of our own rank, shape and capacity; but are to be extended to every object of the love and mercy of God, the universal parent . . . Mercy to brutes is as much a doctrine of divine revelation as it is in itself reasonable, amiable, useful and just.[10]

'Love is the great hinge on which universal nature turns', says Primatt. To suffer pain is to suffer evil, and

> If I know that a man is cruel to his beast, I ask no more questions about him. He may be a noble man, or a rich man, or a polite man, or a sensible man, or a learned man, or an orthodox man, or a church man, or a puritan, or any thing else, it matters not; this I know . . . that being cruel to his beast, he is a *wicked* man.[11]

Primatt opposed hunting and sports such as cock-throwing, but was prepared to allow meat in the diet provided the animals lived happy lives and met their end with minimum suffering. His total silence on the subject of the use of animals in medical experimentation leads to the supposition that in his rural parishes he knew nothing of it – unlike the metropolitan Dr Johnson. His work was influential – it was the inspiration of those who fought in the early nineteenth century for legislation to protect domestic, especially working, animals; and directly inspired a fellow cleric, the Reverend Arthur Broome, to found in 1824 a society which developed into the Royal Society for the Prevention of Cruelty to Animals.

By the secular late twentieth century, however, Scriptural precepts had ceased to be persuasive. Singer's was not an isolated voice. Theologians and academic philosophers began to take seriously the challenge of animal, especially great ape, rights. Increasing numbers of people began to abandon some or all use of animals for food, clothing, adornment or any other human purpose, refusing to accord to humanity the lofty pre-eminence that had so dominated attitudes since the

Renaissance; and confronting the untrammelled pursuit of scientific knowledge with a challenge such as had not been mounted since the end of the Middle Ages. Pressure groups such as the Farm and Food Society and Compassion in World Farming organized demonstrations that by the 1990s were attracting thousands of supporters of every age and class in sustained campaigns against cruelty to farm animals, culminating, by the spring of 1995, in the closure of several ports trafficking in the transport of animals to Europe.

Singer himself had firmly deprecated violence in pursuit of his objectives (though not disapproving of non-violent illegal acts, some of which had been responsible for obtaining invaluable evidence of secret laboratory processes), and most animal liberationists pursued their objectives through persuasion and political campaigns. Following a 1984 recommendation by a working party of the Association of Science Education and the Institute of Biology, dissection progressively ceased to be compulsory in practical biology examinations, while videos and interactive computer programs replaced practical demonstrations.[12] A Fund for the Replacement of Animals in Medical Experiments (FRAME) was instituted in 1969, supported financially by a wide spectrum of British companies.

In congruity with the taste for violence that had invaded so many other aspects of modern life, however, impatient animal rights activists embarked on campaigns of direct action. At first activists were content with such initiatives as laying false scent trails to distract foxhounds. In 1972 members of the Hunt Saboteurs Association began a campaign of arson attacks on animal breeding establishments and laboratories. In 1976 the Animal Liberation Front was formed, under a leader who declared that 'true animal liberation will not come merely through the destruction of the Dachaus and Buchenwalds, but demands nothing more than the driving back of the human species to pre-invasion boundaries'. The panoply of the terrorist, balaclava helmets and manuals for the home-made manufacture of explosives, began to feature in campaigns. ALF activists infiltrated non-violent traditional bodies like the RSPCA and the National Anti-Vivisection Society and as the established groups took steps to distance themselves from the anarchism of the radicals, the activists regrouped under a variety of titles, including the Animal Rights Militia, and stepped up their attacks on all institutions they suspected of exploiting animals. Campaigns have escalated to the bombing of research stations and university laboratories, meat factories, abattoirs, butchers' shops (most of which are now protected at night with shutters) and meat delivery lorries, stores selling furs and even leather goods and woollens, as well as incendiary attacks on Cancer Research charity shops – because cancer research involves vivisection;[13] and to 'consumer terrorism' such as claims to have poisoned Mars bars (in protest at tooth-decay experiments on monkeys).[14] Between 1990 and 1992 Scotland Yard recorded 3,073 crimes, ranging from hunt sabotage to attacks on butchers' shops, with damage in 1991 totalling some £12 million, at which stage animal liberation was causing far more economic damage than was the IRA, though that no doubt changed after the IRA bombs in the City of London in 1994. Even so, £2 million worth of damage was inflicted on Isle of Wight sports and pharmaceutical shops in a single night in August 1994,[15] and Boots the Chemist, which has not tested cosmetics on animals for twenty years, and whose use of animals in pharmaceutical testing is legally mandatory, have had their shops attacked from end to end of the country, with over 100 firefighters called to blazes in York and Harrogate in mid-September 1994.[16]

Fears that there would be casualties fell on deaf ears. 'There will be injuries and possibly deaths on both sides . . . This is sad but certain', predicted the founder of the ALF.[17] Scientists learnt to inspect their vehicles for bombs with all the vigilance of security forces in Northern Ireland, but still had to run the gauntlet of abusive phone calls and graffiti. By the middle of 1994 injuries from parcel bombs had been suffered by furriers, farmers, breeders of laboratory animals, and office workers in laboratories, food companies and even a ferry company involved in animal transport to Europe.[18]

The attacks, both physical and moral, on animal experimentation, profoundly alarmed scientists and their sponsors. At its meeting at Swansea in August 1990 the British Association for the Advancement of Science issued a declaration, supported by the Medical Research Council, the royal colleges, the Imperial Cancer Research Fund and other scientific organizations, as well as a number of eminent individual scientists (including ten Nobel Prize winners) asserting that 'experiments on animals have made an important contribution to advances in medicine and surgery', and that 'continued research is essential for the conquest of many unsolved medical problems, including cancer and Aids, and genetic, developmental, neurological and psychiatric conditions'. The director of the Imperial Cancer Research Fund took the opportunity to assert that ten times as many cats and dogs were destroyed by the RSPCA after being abandoned as were used in animal experiments in Britain.[19] In the course of the following year, 1,000 leading scientists, including 31 Nobel Prize winners, added their signatures to the declaration.[20]

550

Eight medical charities, the Imperial Cancer Research Fund, the British Heart Foundation, the Wellcome Trust, the Cancer Research Campaign, the Multiple Sclerosis Society, Action Research, the Cystic Fibrosis Research Trust and the Muscular Dystrophy Group, united to 'restore public support for controlled animal experiments'.[21] Hopes of ending the personal intimidation of scientists are slender. Utilitarian arguments are faced with a resurgence of moral absolutism. Animal rights may claim to be as rationally argued as the case for human rights, but the fact is that militant adherents to the cause have made of it a substitute religion, to be pursued with all the single-minded fanaticism that Sorokin identified with the early stages of an ideational society.

Legalistic concepts of rights/justice have proved no more successful than adherence to the language of sins/obligations in resolving conflicts. Which right is to predominate – that of parents to go their separate ways if inclination so dictates, or of children to enjoy the support of both their parents? Of an author to total freedom of speech, or of a religious group to protection from blasphemy? Of a woman to incubate a baby in her seventh decade, or of a child to be born to a mother of normal childbearing age? Of a foetus to life, or of a woman to choose?[*]

These issues are being fought out, in some cases literally to the death. The threats to Salman Rushdie, and the fate of some of those associated with his *The Satanic Verses*, are well known. In the United States in 1993 and again in 1994 abortionists were shot by people convinced they were responding to a superior moral imperative. Firebombing of abortion clinics has begun, and the US Senate has called on the Government to institute measures to protect patients and staff at those of the nation's 3,000 clinics deemed most at risk.[22] Even discussions about (not yet the practice of) euthanasia – the supposed right to die – are provoking violence or threats of violence. As the editor of the *Bulletin of Medical Ethics* explained in a letter to *The Times* on 5 August 1991, groups, including disabled people, 'who believe that if one is capable of discussing a subject like euthanasia, one makes it more likely to happen' have, by threats of disruption, forced proposed conferences in Austria and Germany (there being an understandable sensitivity on the subject in former Nazi nations) to be resited in the Netherlands and Switzerland, where even so speakers have not been immune to assault. A conference on Wittgenstein to be held in Salzburg in the summer of 1991 was

---

[*] One illustration of the attempt to recruit 'reason' in the resolution of the conflict of interest between a woman's right to choose and a foetus's right to life is the denial that the foetus is a human being, or (on the Benthamite principle) that it is capable of suffering, at least up to a scientifically determinable stage of neurological development.

cancelled because of threats over one of the intended participants, an advocate of euthanasia.[23]

The cult of the individual, the reverse side of the coin of human rights in the modern pursuit of happiness, is proving equally unpropitious. For decades education has fostered individualism, children being encouraged to explore their own potential rather than accept a cultural corpus handed down from previous generations. Frank Sinatra's 'My Way' has been accorded the reverence of a hymn, has been sung at funerals, performed on television by the choir of St Paul's Cathedral. Novel names with no family or community associations have become popular, and children lumbered with conventional names have sought, in their anxiety for uniqueness, to invent bizarre spellings – the credits on our television screens vibrate with such variations as 'Lezli-An'. Professions that foster personal flamboyance, such as the law and the theatre, attract huge numbers of applicants; Equity, for instance, the actors' union, whose membership of 9,000 to 10,000 barely changed between 1950 and 1960, stood at almost 45,000 by 1994[*] (most of them unemployed most of the time, a fate which the more militant consider should be alleviated by the establishment, at taxpayers' expense, of a nationwide network of municipal theatres).

Individual autonomy has not brought fulfilment. 'The bleakness of the emancipated self is one of the talking points, one of the clichés even, of modern cultural angst', wrote Michael Ignatieff in the spring of 1986, introducing a television series that brought together seven pairs of novelists, poets, philosophers and social scientists 'to tease out this paradox of modernity's disenchantment with itself'. We have, he noted, broken free 'of the attachments, to family, to party, to neighbourhood, to class, which gave individuality its meaning'.[24] The utter alienation, awareness of which had so obsessed Hegel and Marx in the nineteenth century, had become a commonly acknowledged experience.

The 'cultural angst' has a physical concomitant. Calculations as to the number of days lost through hypertensive and neurotic illness published by the Health and Safety Commission for 1991 showed a rising trend,[25] with about 40 per cent of absenteeism attributable to stress-related psychological illnesses (divorce being a leading cause, costing companies about £200 million a year in lost days).[26] A CBI report in the summer of 1994 claimed that 80 million working days are lost annually as a result of stress-related illness,[27] the loss to industry running at some £5 billion,

---

[*] Attributable partly to the amalgamation with the Variety Artistes' Federation, which added 1,600 members by 1967–8, and partly to the drive to achieve a 'closed shop'.

figures which by the autumn of the same year had been inflated to 90 million days at a cost of £7 billion.[28] Far higher costs are to be expected following a High Court judgement in November of 1994 that a social worker reduced to a nervous breakdown by stress at work was entitled to damages from his employer – a ruling that prompted employers to envisage the likelihood of job losses.[29] Nor is stress an exclusively urban problem. Among farmers the suicide level is twice as high as among the general population. Isolation, social rather than geographical, and easy access to firearms no doubt play a part, but criminal depredations on farms, with barn roofs, machinery and stock disappearing, were among the causes of distress identified in 1993 by the National Farmers' Union.[*] [30]

In a survey published by the British Medical Association in May 1994, 'a bleak picture of a stress-ridden Britain' was painted, over four-fifths of the doctors interviewed reporting that over the past fifteen years the number of patients seeking help for stress-related conditions 'had increased significantly', nearly half saying that they were making more psychiatric referrals than they were in 1979, and commenting on the increasing extent to which patients were taking refuge in drink and drugs.[31] A study commissioned by the Department of Health, the Scottish Home and Health Office and the Welsh Office concluded in December 1994 that 'one adult in seven' suffers from depression, anxiety or some other psychological disorder.[32] At the British Medical Association annual conference in July 1995 it was claimed that one in twelve doctors is addicted to drink or drugs, with many suicidally depressed;[33] meanwhile, a report, *Psychosocial Disorders in Young People*, painted a forlorn picture of drug and alcohol dependency, crime, suicide and psychosocial disorder among young people born in and after the 1950s, a report which remarked that the main rise in psychosocial disorder occurred during the economically prosperous period, 1950 to 1973.[34]

Increasingly the collapse of the traditional two-parent family, so welcomed by radicals of the 1960s to whom the family was the acme of patriarchal tyranny,[†] is being identified on both left and right of the political spectrum as a root cause of much of the contemporary social

[*] 'We are seeing a serious erosion of the quality of rural life', said a NFU spokesman in July 1995, while the farm insurers, NFU Mutual, commenting on a 250 per cent increase in claims over the previous six years, advised, among many other recommendations, that stock should no longer be grazed in fields close to roads, so serious had the problem of cattle rustling become (*The Times*, 4 July 1995).
[†] A view eloquently elaborated by Edmund Leach in the 1967 Reith Lectures.

malaise. With a rise in the number of divorces in Great Britain from 4,228 in 1931 to 173,000 by 1992;* with single-parent families increasing inexorably from about 8 per cent in 1971 to 21 per cent by the start of 1994,[35] encompassing over 2 million children;[36] with nearly a third of children born outside marriage[37] (and where registered by a cohabiting couple, such liaisons even less likely to persist than marriages); and with only a quarter of all households with children containing both natural parents,[38] social commentators are forecasting that by the year 2000 only about half the children in Britain will be living in families of the traditional pattern.[39] Teachers in Basildon in 1984 were already experiencing a situation in which,

> in some of the new town's secondary schools, as many as 60 per cent of children come from single parent families, and in one exceptional case, 28 of 30 children in a class were from homes broken at some stage by divorce ... family breakdown meant children were less able to benefit from schooling. Some become attention seekers, causing a discipline problem. Others become withdrawn and more difficult to teach.[40]

From about the mid-1980s, research in both the United States and Britain was corroborating anecdotal evidence suggesting that the children of lone mothers and broken homes are more prone to bad health, accidents, poor performance at school, personal instability and propensity to delinquency than are children from traditional backgrounds; that divorce is more disturbing to children than the loss of a parent through death; that children living in stepfamilies are more likely to be sexually abused,[†] and to be among the homeless runaways in the cities.[41]

The stress suffered by children of divorcing parents was described by a representative of Relate, the former Marriage Guidance Council, in 1989 as all too often resulting in 'under-fives [who] regress to thumb-sucking, bed-wetting and clinging to mother', while children over twelve could feel suicidal, powerless and angry, with some degenerating into vandalism, shoplifting, drink and drugs.[42] Research emerging in

* The estimated proportion of marriages ending in divorce in 1911 was 0.2 per cent (Digby Anderson, *The Times*, 9 December 1986). By March 1990 it was reckoned that 40 per cent of marriages (the highest percentage in western Europe) were ending in divorce (*The Times*, 16 March 1990).
† A survey published in 1988 concluded that girls with resident but unwed 'father-substitutes' (i.e., mothers' boyfriends) were most at risk. Stepfathers ('non-natal fathers') were also 'substantially over-represented' in the sample (*Journal of Marriage, and the Family*, 1988, Vol.50, pp.99–106; see also Patricia Morgan, 'Fidelity in the Family', in Anderson (ed.), p.100.

October 1993 from the London School of Economics Department of Population Studies found that children of broken homes did less well both at and after school than others, including those who had lost a parent by death, but postulated that domestic conflict might be as much to blame as divorce.[43] Further work published in February 1994 from a special study by Exeter University funded by the Joseph Rowntree Foundation concluded unequivocally that 'although severe marital conflict and financial hardship were associated with poor outcomes for children, family reorganization(s) appeared to be the main adverse factor in children's lives', children of 're-ordered' families being 'more likely than children from intact families to have encountered health problems (especially psychosomatic disorders), to have needed extra help at school, to have experienced friendship difficulties and to suffer from low self-esteem'.[44] One of the authors remarked later that he 'was surprised and shaken by the extent of the children's unhappiness'.[45]

Sad though this picture is, it is surpassed in terms of damage to society, as well as to the children themselves, by the deleterious effects of single parenthood. Norman Dennis and George Erdos, the principal contributors to a seminar covering the topic in the summer of 1991, later published their reflections in *Families without Fatherhood*, which concluded, in Professor Halsey's introductory words, that children in single-parent families

> on the evidence available ... tend to die earlier, to have more illness, to do less well at school, to exist at a lower level of nutrition, comfort and conviviality, to suffer more unemployment, to be more prone to deviance and crime, and finally, to repeat the cycle of unstable parenting from which they themselves have suffered.[46]

The absence of fathers as role models for young males is critically important, argued the authors, in the genesis of delinquency. Charles Murray, who had already in the United States in 1984 published work (*Losing Ground*) on the rising tide of welfare-dependent young criminals, was at pains to point out, in *The Emerging British Underclass*, that 'single parent' was an unhelpful phrase that concealed the real focus of the problem: never-married young mothers with no intention of setting up home with the fathers of their offspring.[47] Researchers at Essex University reported that never-married mothers headed 19 per cent of one-parent families in 1981, a third by 1992. By 1995, 60 per cent of unmarried mothers had never lived with the fathers of their children.[48] Recently the focus of interest has begun to switch from the children to the never-married fathers, content to loaf through life leaving it to the State to rear the progeny of their transient liaisons, and to the contribution to crime of a 'warrior class' of males who, though enjoying an 'active sex life', have never been 'socialized' by the responsibilities of equally active parenthood.[*]

By the 1980s philosophers on both sides of the Atlantic were addressing the failure of the doctrine of rights to produce a society that engaged either the respect or the affection of its citizens; a society, on the contrary, cacophonous with egotistical self-assertion. In his *After Virtue*, the moral philosopher Alasdair Macintyre, analysing the history of his craft as it had developed within the tenets of the Enlightenment, came to the conclusion that the doctrine of rights, far from providing an objective criterion, simply generated political friction and confusion, indignation elevated to moral heights whose sole resolution lay in power; ultimately, in Nietzschean Will.[49] Addressing more pragmatic concerns, in America the Responsible Community was founded, an organization 'whose aim is to remind the American public that it's no good claiming rights if you won't meet your share of the corresponding duties'.[50] James Q. Wilson, in *The Moral Sense*, drew attention to the dissatisfaction of citizens confronted with 'a government concerned solely with rights and redistribution . . . a government indifferent to excesses of personal self-indulgence that seem so threatening on the streets of big cities'.[51] In Britain in 1994 considerable publicity was accorded by the broadsheet press to political philosopher David Selbourne's *The Principle of Duty*, which asserted that it was duties, not rights, that constituted the bonds of civic society. He propounded a society in which citizenship was not the unassailable prerogative of birth but had to be earned by good conduct, its benefits and privileges (such as possession of a passport, or of benefit entitlements) open to abrogation if a court of obligation so decreed; in which education stressed the cardinal importance of stable relationships for the safeguarding of society's own future, the rearing of the next generation, and the law co-operated by impeding divorce and penalizing immature and irresponsible, especially unmarried, parenthood, male as well as female.

Selbourne's emphasis on the place of sanctions appeals to traditionalists who have been maintaining all along that society's woes are due to a failure adequately to punish wrongdoing. The huge upsurge of violence,

---

[*] Patricia Morgan's *Farewell to the Family?* contains a powerful chapter exploring this theme, which is also examined, in the context of the churches' bland failure to defend the institution of marriage, by Jon Davis, George Erdos and Norman Dennis in the *Salisbury Review* for June 1995.

firearms use and vandalism, they maintain, has coincided with the abolition of capital punishment, flogging, 'hard labour' and the maxim that punishment precedes rehabilitation in the treatment of the criminal. American public opinion refused to condemn the caning of an American youth for vandalism in Singapore in the spring of 1994.[52] By the late twentieth century the 'barbaric' provisions of the Islamic penal code, including the amputation of the fingers or hands of thieves, was attracting a certain jocular approbation. The novelty of courts of obligation, which would operate through penalties that largely avoided the necessity to lock miscreants up in (expensive and overcrowded) prisons, widens the appeal of sanctions as an instrument of social control – but leaves unresolved the contemporary dissension as to where guilt really lies, with an influential body of professional opinion regarding perpetrators of crimes as just as much victims of circumstances, social or economic, as are their prey. The suggestion, by a Lord Justice, in October 1993,[53] that property owners who fail to protect their property from theft should be fined (as are those who fail to protect themselves when driving by wearing seatbelts) illustrates the fissures among those whose hopes of social redemption rest primarily on sanctions.

As with all rational prescriptions, from classical stoicism to modern humanism, Selbourne's solution invests its hopes in a level of educational achievement which history suggests is utopian – and which Selbourne himself seems to consider unlikely, given his reported view, 'I consider the National Union of Teachers to be enemies of civic order.'* [54] His analysis suffers from the defect that afflicts all rational prescriptions for a better society: it lacks a personal moral imperative, an 'obedience to the unenforceable',† other than the prudential 'do as you would be done by' which, particularly when satisfactions are immediate and consequences distant, regularly proves inadequate to restrain humanity's more destructive impulses.

In 1949 Sorokin, in an attempt to come to terms with this problem, had founded at Harvard a Research Center in Creative Altruism, devoted to the study of the saints of the past, of educational theories for moral

---

* Certainly an invitation to teachers by the general secretary of the Professional Association of Teachers at its annual conference in 1991 reportedly provoked only 'angry silence' and at least one walk-out when it was suggested that, with schools being used as first-aid posts for children who were crippled emotionally by home circumstances, teachers should reassert their moral authority and speak out about the disadvantages of one-parent families (*The Times*, 2 August 1991).
† This phrase is attributed to Lord Moulton, judge, parliamentarian and administrator, who used it in a speech delivered in 1924 on the attributes of civilized society (*The Times*, 15 July 1978).

transformation, and of ego-transcending techniques. True to his conviction that individual consciousness and example are the factors determining society's values, and must be the trail-blazers and pathfinders in the escape from the perils of a disintegrating sensate civilization, he concentrated on the personality of the individual, concluding that there were four levels of consciousness in the human personality, the unconscious (the basic drive), the bioconscious (hunger, sex, etc.), the socioconscious (interaction) and the supraconscious, in which lay the source of altruism. The first three he considered should be amenable to human control, but the last eludes us. Funds for the Center ran out with the mystery unsolved: what is that something that lies beyond biology and human reason?[55]

That only a renewed 'sense of community' can restore meaning and moral imperatives to individual lives is a panacea widely advanced; and pleasantly acceptable provided the notion of 'community' remains vague. More closely defined, it proves to have hazards. Technology, the trump card of a sensate society, has in itself progressively disrupted the old community of shared tasks. Piped water eliminated the gossip at the village pump, combine harvesters terminated the stooking and threshing parties that preceded harvest home; solitary drivers in cars to a great extent replaced the camaraderie of the shared railway carriage; radio and television which once brought families together dispersed them as affluence provided for a set in each person's private domain; and now computer technology and home networking threaten to destroy even the community of the shared workplace.

If 'community' is to imply a group or institution with an identity of its own, demanding loyalty to its standards and administering sanctions for transgressions, it could pose to the Enlightenment cult of the individual a challenge as great as do animal rights to the humanist belief that the human species is a uniquely superior and privileged product of evolution. Substantial strands of libertarian thought would castigate such a 'community' as 'Fascist'.[*] Dr Runcie, then Archbishop of Canterbury, addressed the problem directly in his American series of lectures in 1988, when he spoke of the impossibility, in a world that had

---

[*] Students, for instance, punished in the courts for drug offences, resent any disciplinary measures imposed by their university on the grounds that they are being 'punished twice' for the same offence, rejecting the notion that in transgressing against the codes of two distinct entities they have doubly offended. Thus retribution, the exacting of a debt incurred to society, has become conflated with revenge, the infliction of personal vengeance, and the validity of the first dissipated in the moral obloquy attendant on the second.

experienced 'Hitler's Fascism', of inculcating obedience to authority except 'under an oppressive and totalitarian regime'.[56]

The sensate solution is to regard 'community' as the product of a satisfactorily functioning economy, its morality rooted in communal responsibility for the economic wellbeing of the group rather than in any challenge to personal conduct.[57] In 1988 Clifford Longley identified the Church of England's 'proprietorial interest in the welfare state as one of the ways in which England could justify its claim to be a Christian country'.[58] As Edward Norman has been pointing out over a number of years, leaders in both Church and State 'have interpreted ''moral'' issues to be mainly concerned with the material structure and well-being of society. They are preoccupied with the ethics of wealth creation and distribution.' 'The clergy,' he remarks,

> are more comfortable in the guise of welfare officers than they are as teachers of doctrinal truth and intermediaries of sacramental mysteries ... almost the whole fabric of the much-vaunted contemporary moral sense depends upon the provision of welfare ... the benign paraphernalia of an alternative secular religion.[59]

His point seemed borne out by the Church of England's *Faith in the City*, the Report of the Archbishop of Canterbury's Commission on Urban Priority Areas, whose proponents concentrated on the 'bankrupt social vision which has guided our economic and social policy over the past decade'.[60] 'The religious establishment,' noted Rabbi Ephraim Gatwirth in 1988, 'is too busy with its social welfare programme to have much time to change man for the better ... It is easier to do good than to be good.'[61] Much of the thrust of the church ecumenical movement is seen as joint work to relieve poverty. In this interpretation, the principal threat to 'community' comes from economic liberalism, as exemplified in recent years by the 'New Right'.[62]

In their work on fatherless families, Dennis and Erdos avoid polarizing the discussion in terms of political left and right, identifying instead egotistical socialists and egotistical capitalists who selfishly demand that society grant them *carte blanche* to do exactly as they like, the casualties of their egotism to be picked up by anyone other than themselves; and ethical socialists and ethical capitalists, who expect to pursue their preferred political and personal goals within the discipline of a value system which, for Dennis and Erdos, goes beyond economics.

Politicians disillusioned after half a century of believing that environmental improvement would reform conduct, doubting even whether environmental improvement was achievable at all in the absence of a reformation in conduct, began to vaunt the necessity of a return to religion. Sir David Livingstone had said, back in the 1940s,

> We are left with traditions and habits of conduct inherited from [the Victorians], as the earth may for a time still receive light from an extinct star. But that light will not continue to shine, nor can these habits and traditions long survive the beliefs from which they grew.[63]

Bishop Tom Butler took up the same idea when he remarked that morals in the absence of faith are like the smile on the face of the Cheshire cat: the last thing to fade, but fade they do.[64] Dostoevsky's central theme in *The Brothers Karamazov*, the words of the murderer to the sophist who had instructed him, are quoted more and more frequently: 'All things are lawful. That was quite right what you taught me . . . For if there's no everlasting God, there's no such thing as virtue . . .'

President Clinton was reported, late in 1993, to be summoning groups of religious leaders to private prayer breakfasts, 'convinced that America needs not just new programmes but a spiritual renewal'.[65] Early in 1992, John Patten, then Education Secretary, publicly acknowledged his belief that young people embark on criminal activity because they no longer believe in an afterlife in which they will have to answer for their sins.[66]

Well before the collapse of the Soviet empire revealed the bankruptcy, material and moral, of Marxism, the rulers of the Soviet Union had come to the conclusion that society required an input beyond what rationalism and materialism could provide. Professor Igor Bestuzhev-Lada, a leading Moscow sociologist, was permitted, at a press conference organized in 1986 by the Soviet Foreign Ministry, to cite, without blaming the West, a catalogue of family breakdown, alcoholism and drug-taking, and to refer to the 'increasing, although still statistically small, number of young people in the atheistic state . . . turning to religion'.[67] In 1988 Gorbachev promised a new law on freedom of conscience, a law which reached the statute book in October 1990.[68] Early in 1989 the Russian Orthodox Church received permission openly to preach in Moscow. 'When evil becomes so obvious,' said a preacher to a gathering of some 2,000 in a Moscow sports arena, 'people return to the church. Our problem is not social, economic or political, but religious.'[69]

Five months later, the World Council of Churches, meeting for the first time in Moscow, was welcomed by Prime Minister Ryzhkov, whose speech referred to *perestroika*

> opening up favourable opportunities for the Church to increase its contribution to the establishment of humanity's moral norms of behaviour, of civil responsibility and of the Soviet patriotism. We hope that the Church and the believers will get even more actively involved in the struggle against anti-social phenomena, such as drunkenness and alcoholism, hooliganism and crime . . .[70]

At the turn of the year, in an unprecedented development, Moscow Radio permitted the Orthodox Patriarch to send Christmas greetings to the Soviet people, and TV broadcast a Christmas service.[71] On Christmas Eve 1991 (Epiphany 1992 by the Western calendar) *all* TV channels available to Muscovites were carrying religious broadcasts.[72] By 1994 'hundreds of thousands', young and old, were packing glitteringly restored churches, and Christmas had, for the first time since the Bolshevik Revolution, been restored as a public holiday.[73]

In the United States, Protestant fundamentalism has shown a marked rise over recent years. By 1981 in no fewer than fifteen states serious attempts were being made to require the education system to give to the Biblical account of creation a prominence equal to that accorded to evolutionary theory, and in Arkansas a Bill to that effect was passed, though it was later struck down by the US Supreme Court on the grounds that its religious undertones violated the constitutional separation of Church and State.[74] The Moral Majority, virulently opposed to abortion, homosexuality, drugs and promiscuity, was founded in 1979, and had by the 1980s become a political force to be reckoned with, credited with considerable influence in the election of President Reagan. Southern Baptist by origin, it attracted support across a wide spectrum of religious allegiance, including Roman Catholic, and although the formal nomen-clature was dropped in 1986,[75] the 'religious right' is now accepted as a long-term influence in the American political scene, a probable contributor to the accession to power, for the first time in half a century, of Republicans in both the Senate and the House of Representatives in the 1994 elections. By 1993 the 1962 Supreme Court ruling that barred compulsory prayers in state schools, on the principle of the separation of Church and State, was being challenged, schoolchildren demonstrating to demand school prayers, a restoration which the incoming Republican Party favoured.[76]

In England evangelical Christianity, again with a strongly Baptist input, was making an impact by the late 1980s. The Easter Spring Harvest Bible-teaching convention, attended by 2,000 participants at its start in 1979, attracted over 60,000 ten years later. Though anxious to avoid party political alignments, their hostility to abortion, homosexuality and embryo experimentation inevitably marshals them against liberal permissiveness.[77] By the summer of 1990 some quarter of a million 'Marchers for Jesus' were demonstrating their Christian credentials, though hesitant Anglican clergy remained aloof because they were unhappy about the organizers' avowed belief in demons.[78] The Archbishop of Canterbury claimed that 'in 1991 we opened more churches than we closed'.[79] But it cannot be said that the Anglican Establishment is tending towards fundamentalism – indeed, conspicuous churchmen like the former Bishop of Durham are following in the footsteps of Barnes and Robinson, noising abroad their doubts about most tenets in the traditional creeds, such as the virgin birth and the resurrection.

In India the rise of the Hindu revivalist Bharatiya Janata Party is bringing into question the future of India as a secular state. Ultra-Orthodox (Hassidic) Judaism is consolidating both within and beyond Israel; the Egyptian Coptic church reports 'desert monasteries . . . swamped by applications from educated Copts wishing to take up a monastic life'.[80] Fundamentalist Islam, specifically the ambition to transform the State by uniting the political and religious spheres in one law, the Shari'a, is triumphant in Iran, resurgent throughout north Africa and the Middle East, including Turkey, resolutely secular for almost three-quarters of a century following Kemal Atatürk's revolutionary measures in the 1920s and 1930s, and a force to be reckoned with throughout the rest of the Moslem world, including the Indian subcontinent, south-east Asia and the Islamic republics of the old Soviet Union.

The assumption, widely shared by inheritors of the Enlightenment, that liberal democracy – toleration its byword, consumption its goal – marks the final consummation of human aspiration is being severely challenged as societies all over the world strengthen their allegiance to ancestral creeds. 'According to the secular rationalist,' say Martin Marty and R. Scott Appleby in *The Glory and the Power*, a survey of three representative fundamentalist groups, one Christian, one Jewish and one Islamic,

knowledge comes from the faculty of human reason drawing conclusions on the basis of empirical evidence – that is, on the basis of observable phenomena in time and space – rather than from truths revealed to a select few by a God beyond time and space . . . Ever since the Enlightenment, therefore, most members of the educated classes worldwide have tended to picture a future that would allow little room for religion . . . The smug assumption of the Enlightenment regarding religion's fate has been manifestly proven wrong by the twentieth-century dynamism of fundamentalisms.[81]

That dynamism, however, owes much to the close alignment of religion with ethnic identity. For Marty and Appleby, indeed, extreme fundamentalism is at bottom primarily a defence mechanism against the pressure of alien influences. Even a religion as universal in its claims as Roman Catholicism is conspicuously more dynamic in areas such as Quebec, Poland, Ireland and Croatia, where it serves to distinguish an insecure group from its more numerous or powerful neighbours; and the whole Bosnian conflict is clearly intensified by the rival confessions of its participants. Nor can anyone who experienced it deny the force of the emotions liberated in Britain in 1940, for instance, as the defeated British Expeditionary Force fell back on Dunkirk and a National Day of Prayer was called for Sunday 26 May, the start of the week that was to see the little ships set sail to rescue numbers 'far in excess of expectations', and the first patrols of what was to become the Home Guard move to the southern shoreline of Britain. In modern secular Britain, Remembrance Sunday is more likely than any other to entice the unchurched into a pew.

In *After Virtue* Macintyre sees the success of pre-Enlightenment societies in inculcating into their young a communal respect for the good, for virtue (though the definition of what constitutes virtue varies with time and place), as being achieved through the medium of a shared mythology and inheritance. 'The possession of an historical identity and the possession of a social identity coincide.'[82] Religion, on this analysis, is inextricably part of the culture which expresses it.

David Martin, writing in 1978, claimed that:

A positive overlap with the national myth is a necessary condition for a lively and widespread attachment to religion; the majority of people cannot bear too sharp a contradiction between their universalist faith and their group identity . . . if national myth and religious faith are contradictory the social power of religion is restricted. The religious faith which survives such contradiction is likely to be composed of refugees from the national myth looking for a sectarian haven capable of creating an alternative society.[83]

Brian Wilson, writing in 1966 before the current upsurge of fundamentalism, sees traditional American religion as just such a congeries of sects, their vibrancy drawn from their function as definers of identity, studiously avoiding serious social disruption by a vacuous and universal acquiescence in the overriding materialist goals of the American dream.[84]

In Britain the Christian heritage, even when riven by dissent, has shared more than it disputed, and has been interwoven with an awareness of shared destiny, of belonging, fostered by kinship, with a common language and culture, with shared sacrifices to which the village war memorials of Britain bear witness, with common allegiance to a monarch whose status reaches back a millennium, all of which has provided the emotional security of a sense of identity, and has set standards of conduct. The rise of Celtic nationalism in recent decades has sought to emphasize the extent to which such a summary is idealized, but centuries of mobility and intermarriage within the British Isles have resulted in a populace which to a great extent feels comfortable with the many strands in its mixed inheritance. The resulting nation has, like others built on similar foundations, been exclusive, and at times predatory, but it enjoyed a considerable degree of internal stability and cohesion.

Postwar immigration, introducing new racial stock, often with historical experiences antagonistic to that of the indigenous people, and with alien language, religious and cultural groupings, has terminated, probably permanently, a religious hegemony along traditional lines. Feeble though the influence of Christian morality may have become by the late twentieth century, vestiges of the nation's Christian heritage remained, and now come under assault as inimical to multiculturalism. The Magistrates' Association in 1987 petitioned for the abandonment of the oath in court ('no longer suited to a multiracial society'), the Inner London Education Authority abandoned Christmas nativity plays, Birmingham expunged Christian references from its festive mid-winter decorations, Dr Barnardo's in 1991 dropped the Christian image within which it had operated for 125 years.[85] Even the saying of grace before formal meals has become an embarrassment. The Archbishop of Canterbury ruminated on the need to change the Coronation Oath, currently limited to the upholding of Protestant Christianity, but was overtaken by the heir to the throne's speculation that perhaps he could become Defender of Faith in general rather than of *the* Faith.[86] Both were outflanked by a flood of proposals, including some from the Primate's own bishops, advocating the disestablishment of the Church of

England,[*] whose status as standard-bearer of the idea of a set of public moral standards, historically Christian and white, had come to be seen as condemning the other components of a multicultural populace to second-class citizenhood. 'Only in a society in which all faiths (and atheism) have equal legal status can everyone be fully accepted as a citizen', wrote Clifford Longley in *The Times*.[87]

In these circumstances the notion of 'community' as a source of social cohesion and shared values becomes dubious.[†] In modern Britain 'community' has connotations not of communality but of separation;[‡] indeed, such phrases as 'the black community' (or Jewish, or Asian, or whatever) are normally used in contexts where the main attribute of the so-called 'community' is its antagonism or grievance against some other 'community'. With the entrenchment of minority rights, the social and legal incompatibilities to be reconciled are of an order that lead some to question whether 'multicultural society' is not a contradiction in terms.[§] As the United States moved from the 'melting pot' analogy of its first three centuries (when immigrants were expected to assimilate to a predominantly Anglo-Saxon culture), to a congeries of peoples celebrating their distinctiveness, Allan Bloom's *The Closing of the American Mind* warned of the cultural relativism pervading American education, which justified the dismissal as irrelevant, for those not of European descent, of all products of 'DWEMs' (dead white European males) such as Bach or Shakespeare. John Kennedy's special adviser Arthur Schlesinger, in *The Disuniting of America*, queried the fragmentation likely to assail the United States as a result of an increasing emphasis on ethnicity. Britons have barely dared to voice their anxieties, an exception being *Integration or Disintegration* by Ray Honeyford, whose experience as a head teacher in a predominantly Moslem school

[*] In the United States, the rising tide of fervour on the religious right clashed with political correctness, when in 1994 the American postal service decided that no Christmas stamps would be issued, nor would festival displays include religious symbols stemming from Christian or Jewish traditions. Displays celebrating Kwanza, 'the African-American festival', are exempt from the ban (*The Times*, 22 November 1994).

[†] Indicative is the refusal of a Church of England primary school in Southampton to celebrate the 50th anniversary of VE Day, on the grounds that one third of the pupils were from ethnic minorities (*The Times*, 27 April 1995).

[‡] Its use is frequently redundant. There seems to be no difference between 'the farming community' and 'farmers', 'the ballooning community' and 'balloonists'; or even (as in a recent *Today* interview) 'the defence community' and 'defence lawyers', they, and not the armed forces, being somewhat unexpectedly the topic under discussion.

[§] For instance, there was outrage in Britain when no prosecutions were pursued against Moslems in Britain calling for the assassination of Salman Rushdie for blasphemy against Islam, calls which indubitably offended against British law on incitement to violence.

in Bradford had given him first-hand experience of the pressures from which most Britons studiously avert their gaze.

In the absence of any 'myth' held in common, any shared sense of cultural identity, political philosophers vaunt toleration as the one supreme virtue on which the security of civil life must be based.[*] Sanguine in its disregard for the conflict of perceived rights inherent in multiculturalism, this also leaves empty the vacuum at the heart of contemporary morality, offering as it does no guidance on when toleration shades into the very moral anarchy now discredited by those seeking reformation of conduct.

Inter-faith groups gather to seek a core common code that can underpin moral education in the schools. Suggestions that it should be perfectly possible to agree a basic morality are confronted by the objection that the result would carry no authority. Indeed, the more each creed accords recognition to others, the less can any claim authority for itself. As the Bishop of Birkenhead remarked in a 'state of the nation' television debate broadcast on 26 March 1993, children know 'right' from 'wrong' perfectly well; they just don't intend to let it matter.

The 1988 Education Act had left schools with a re-emphasized obligation to hold religious assemblies, except those with a high proportion of Moslem, Sikh or Hindu pupils (an obligation neglected, according to school inspectors, by 85 per cent of local authority schools, most of whose head teachers wanted the requirement rescinded);[88] and the duty to devote the main emphasis of religious education to Christianity, a duty clarified in October 1993 by the proposal that at least half of the time devoted to religious education be concerned with Christianity.[89] In spite of eighteen months of consultation among the six principal faiths represented in British schools,[90] dissension ensued, from secularists anxious to abolish all but the most detached consideration of comparative religions, from Christians disappointed that the nation's historic – and still majority – faith should be so poorly served, and from a pressure group of Hindu, Jewish, Moslem and Sikh representatives complaining of under-representation.[91] In July 1994, much to the regret of Christian campaigners, it was announced that the School Curriculum and Assessment Authority were dropping the requirement for 50 per cent of religious education to be Christian, but it remained as a voluntary recommendation in the model syllabuses later devised.[92] Moslems, meanwhile, demand the same right to state-funded denominational

[*] See, for instance, the 'Faith and Reason' series of articles in *The Independent* in April 1989, under such headings as 'Pluralism requires a secular public ethic', 'Medical ethics as a moral lingua franca'.

schools as already exist for Jews and Christians. Whether what its opponents called a multicultural mish-mash will have any impact on moral conduct remains to be seen. To many teachers and parents, example is the most persuasive avenue to the transmission of good conduct, a task in which they feel hampered by the ubiquity of television celebrations of violence, uncouth conduct and language, and casual sexual relations.[93]

Beyond the school gates, a novel approach presents itself in the endeavour to unite all faiths in pursuit of environmental awareness and responsibility, a crusade to save Planet Earth from the depredations of humankind. As long ago as 1971 Hugh Montefiore, then Bishop of Kingston, delivering that year's Rutherford Lecture, had taken the ecological threat as his text. He reinterpreted the ten Commandments with appropriate relevance. The fifth became: 'You shall not murder future generations by your present greed'; the tenth: 'You shall not covet an ever increasing standard of living'. We needed, he said in a subsequent expansion of his theme, a

> colossal reorientation of social attitudes ... we must look for happiness not from things but from people. The only possibility of these huge changes taking place is under the compulsion of strong religious conviction (using religious in its proper sense of sacredly binding) ... Religion, far from being outmoded, is literally the only hope of man's survival.[94]

The childless, and those muttering 'What has posterity ever done for me?', could afford to ignore such pleas, but the trend of the times was with the Bishop. In succeeding years the Christian churches have been paying increasing heed to the ecological issue. Then in 1986, under the auspices of the World Wildlife Fund (as it was then called), an inter-faith colloquy was summoned to meet at Assisi, a location chosen in recognition of St Francis's approach to the natural world. Representatives attended from the Christian, Hindu, Buddhist, Sikh, Jewish and Moslem faiths, and a 'religious and conservation network' was established which is bearing fruit in a variety of localized multi-faith ecological initiatives. The impetus was continued with a Creation Harvest service in Winchester Cathedral in October 1987, and a newly created Harvest Festival liturgy at Coventry Cathedral a year later, followed in September 1989 by a Festival of Faith and the Environment at Canterbury Cathedral 'to celebrate through pilgrimage, services, workshops, exhibitions, performances and many other events, the

coming together of the great faiths and the conservation movement'.[95]
Evangelical Christians mounted protests at the extent to which Christ's
unique claims were being jeopardized by such multi-faith celebrations,* the Archbishop of York, writing in *WWF News* in July 1989,
noted that there were irreconcilable differences in Christian and
Buddhist understandings of Nature, and *The Times*'s religious editor,
cautioning against the New Age 'tendency . . . to treat all religions as
equivalently true, even as needing to be synthesized into a new whole',
pointed out that 'the stress on salvation by organic food rather than by
faith worries Evangelicals'.[96] However, the Archbishop of Canterbury
included in his Festival sermon the significant words:

> The conviction that nature does not exist simply and solely for the
> benefit of human kind . . . is becoming increasingly widespread and
> articulate. Because it finds its true source at such deep levels of the
> human spirit, it must, I think, be called a religious conviction. But it
> is not a conviction unique to any one religion in particular, and it is
> shared by some who would profess no religion at all.[97]

Early in 1989, both at the Ozone Conference of that year and in his
Dimbleby Lecture, the Duke of Edinburgh had emphasized the same
point: 'We thought the world belonged to us. Now we are beginning to
realize that we belong to the world.' These avowals of the breadth of the
recognition that humanity is not the be-all and end-all of creation but
rather a species subject to external disciplines which we flout at our peril
– an essentially ideational tenet – herald the twilight of humanism, at
least in its Renaissance and its Enlightenment guise.

The same inexorability had been propagated by James Lovelock, a
respected and experienced scientist (indeed, he had been the first
accurately to measure CFCs in the atmosphere, and to suggest they
might be harmful),[98] when from 1972 on he began publishing articles,
and later books, on what he called the Gaia hypothesis.[99] The thesis that
biological systems modify their environment and are modified by it
through a feedback mechanism that operates to produce stable survival
was not new. Lovelock proposed that the whole planet constituted one
such system, modifying its constituent parts in the interests of the

---

* They have a point. In September 1992, when a Christian priest launched what was described as
Britain's first 'festival of green spirituality' from the Centre for Creation Spirituality of St James's
Church, Piccadilly, it was made clear that 'unlike fundamentalism, which views Jesus as unique,
green Christianity offers a view of the divinity within nature which can be shared with other faiths'
(*The Independent*, 11 September 1992).

survival of the whole, in pursuit of which humankind, if its influence continued to prove destructive, would be eliminated and its place taken by less pernicious organisms long before any question could arise of our 'destroying our planet'. In his initial exegesis, Lovelock was misunderstood to have implied that there was a purposeful consciousness at work, a misunderstanding to which his choice of the name 'Gaia' (the Greek Earth Goddess) to identify the organism contributed. He was strongly criticized by the arch-defender of materialist science, Richard Dawkins, for having introduced 'teleology' (externally imposed purposefulness), but in fact Lovelock regarded his theory as simply a further example of evolutionary dynamics.[100]

'Gaia', however, proved to have a dynamic of her own. The late twentieth century, like the first two centuries AD and the fourteenth and fifteenth centuries, both periods when the emptiness of established religions had left numbers of people lost for meaning in their lives and unable to find heart's-ease in secularism, is providing fertile soil for exploration of new religious initiatives. An appalled contributor to *New Scientist* had seen it coming, deploring the prospect of 'hordes of militant Gaiaist activists . . . crying "There is no God but Gaia and Lovelock is her prophet" '. 'Who,' he asked, 'a few decades ago, would have expected the surge of astrology, fringe medicine, faith healing, nutritional eccentricities, religious mysticism and a thousand other fads and cults which now plague developed societies?'[101]

The phrase 'New Age' derives from astrology: the Age of Aquarius, the period during which the sun, as observed from earth, appears to rise at the spring equinox against the background of the constellation of Aquarius, a transition due to begin approximately in the year AD 2000, superseding the Age of Pisces.

Since World War II, stated *The Times* religious affairs reporter in October 1990, an estimated 800 new cults have established themselves in Britain, attracting large numbers of young former Anglicans and Roman Catholics.[102] Two and a half years later the estimated number of new religious movements known to a government-sponsored monitoring agency had reached 1,400,[103] clear evidence of widespread dissatisfaction with secularism.

There is renewed interest in the attempt, familiar in late Roman times and at the end of medieval Christendom (to the horror, in both periods, of orthodox Christians), to manipulate occult forces in the interest of worldly objectives, a development rife not only with the superstition that a scientific age thought long gone, but with the sort of accusations of

Satanic rituals, child murder and sexual abuse that had sent Joan of Arc's companion Gilles de Rais to his execution in 1440.

'It is sometimes asked whether witchcraft will revive', wrote Pennethorne Hughes in *Witchcraft*, his 1952 examination of the subject. '... the answer is that it will not ... In Europe the Church, and the Rationalist, have won.'* [104] In fact a feminist cult known as Wicca claims to be a revival of ancient fertility cults and of white witchcraft (about which little hard information exists); the councillors of Milton Keynes in 1994 gave formal permission for the Wicca movement to celebrate Hallowe'en in a local park,[105] while determinedly ecumenical Anglican and Roman Catholic priests prepared to attend pagan Hallowe'en celebrations at Avebury, 'the pagan equivalent of a cathedral'.[106] In December 1994, at the invitation of the Leeds University Occult Society, a 'white witch' chaplain was appointed, who explained that 'witchcraft does put a big emphasis on controlling your future by magic. It channels your will – for example "I want to pass my exams" – and one big ritual using magic will help the students by focussing this will.'[107]

As in late Roman times, Eastern meditative techniques are being explored, vegetarianism is flourishing, and pagan Nature-reverence being reborn (as at the site of the proposed new Bath bypass, where the designated meadows were adorned with a cairn raised in honour of the threatened *genius loci*).[108] Like other contemporary enthusiasms, eco-fanaticism has moved in frustration from persuasion to militancy, particularly since the importation from America, in the spring of 1992, of members of Earth First, a group which in its homeland has attracted prison sentences for sabotage, and which rapidly gained British adherents after its intervention in the Twyford Down road extension protest. 'Environmental policies are not being carried out fast enough in Britain. Things have to be speeded up and the only way to do this is through confrontation' is their stated attitude. Their approach, if not their members, was in evidence at the Solsbury Hill bypass near Bath in the summer of 1994, when man-traps containing metal spikes were detected on the proposed route. Violence has bred counterviolence; persons unknown hired a gang, two of whose members were sent to prison in September in 1994 for an arson attack on campaigners roosting in a chestnut tree in protest against the extension of the M11.[109]

'New Age' spans a multitude of components, all ostensibly 'Green',

---

* In Britain the 1735 Witchcraft Act was repealed as recently as 1951, it being presumed that no one any longer believed in the existence of occult forces.

though the New Age travellers who spurn capitalist materialism as they trek from Glastonbury to Stonehenge and back are on the whole content to accept the health and educational provision, and the cash 'income support' that only a materially prosperous society can afford. Nevertheless, these travellers are, said Bryan Appleyard in 1992, 'the shabby, unrespectable tip of a very large iceberg. For New Ageism ... is probably now the fastest growing faith in the West . . . The New Age [is] the belief that the scientific-materialistic-mechanistic era is coming to an end.'[110]

'Ironically,' to borrow the words of the Anglican Shirley Lancaster writing in *The Times* in June 1988, 'as radical theologians are stripping Christianity of supernaturalism, interest in paranormal and psychic experience is growing.'[111] New Agers offer a profusion of as yet not fully integrated insights, prominent among which is the veneration of the 'feminine principle' in creativity, and the conviction that somehow quantitative judgements, for all their vaunted objectivity, must no longer be allowed to ride roughshod over qualitative judgements, subjective though they may be.* Central is the insistence that there *is* a spiritual reality, that it is to be apprehended within the individual, and that only the reintegration of the spiritual and the material can heal not only personal disharmony but the destruction that scientific consumerism is perceived as wreaking on the entire biosphere. While orthodox religions distrust the cul-de-sac of narcissism into which this attitude can too easily degenerate, it is proving fertile in the generation of new thinking and new values. Since 1977 it has been annually celebrated at London's Festival for Mind, Body and Spirit, a cluster of exhibitors with the common conviction that 'what the world lives by at the moment just will not do . . . The crowds pouring through the turnstiles at Olympia,' wrote Bernard Levin of the 1978 Festival, 'are only the first drops in the wave that must soon crash over the ideologues and the politicians, and drown their empty claims fathoms deep in a self-confidence born of a true understanding of their own nature and that universal nature which is so much more than the sum of all its parts.'[112]

Meanwhile, among scientists the old secular certainties are crumbling in the face of the inability of science to assign any place to the one experience of which every human being is personally convinced – consciousness of self.

Scientists with impeccable orthodox credentials to their name have

---

* Robert Pirsig's *Zen and the Art of Motor Cycle Maintenance*, the multilayered cult success of 1974, brilliantly explores how, from the Greek philosophers on, Western thinking has lost confidence in this possibility.

incurred the wrath of their peers by exploring unconvential avenues of cogitation, introducing immaterial impulses into their calculations. The physicist Fritjof Capra, in *The Tao of Physics*, explored the parallels between atomic and subatomic physics and Eastern mysticism. Danah Zohar, author of *The Quantum Self*, commenting on 'the inability of classical physics to account for consciousness, or to assign it any meaningful role', speculated that in the quantum vacuum might lurk 'God as the underlying reality of all that is, a God embodied within and who uses the basic laws of physics, a God identified with the basic sense of direction of the unfolding universe – even perhaps with an evolving consciousness within the universe'.[113] The biologist Rupert Sheldrake rejects the biological determinism of gene-dominated evolutionary theory, and opts instead for 'morphic resonance', an alternative survival mechanism that moulds succeeding generations, physically and mentally, by a sort of telepathic transmission, within a species, of useful adaptations. Orthodox scientists who traduced his ideas as 'dangerous' at least were paying tribute to the hunger for a 'something beyond' which the aridity of conventional science could do nothing to satisfy.

When Arthur Koestler died in 1983, he left a bequest for the establishment at a university of a professorship in parapsychology. After the first shock had abated, several universities plucked up their courage and applied for the bequest, the award going, in 1984, to Edinburgh University.[114] Another manifestation of changed attitudes is the growing distrust of traditional medicine. 'Fringe' diagnostic and curative techniques claiming to address not the symptom but the whole person ('holistic') such as homeopathy, acupuncture, reflexology, and iridology, have acquired multitudinous adherents and in some areas achieved at least ancillary clinical status. *Perestroika* immediately unleashed in the Soviet Union a plethora of alternative-medicine practitioners, of whom *The Independent*'s Moscow correspondent wrote, as he attended their presentations staged at the Foreign Ministry press centre, 'Faith-healing, sorcery, plain old quackery – call it what you will – . . . para-medicine's modern relevance is growing.'[115] A survey in the United States showed that in 1990 there were 425 million visits to providers of unorthodox therapies, compared with 388 million visits to primary care doctors.[116] 'Healers' are working alongside surgeons, pharmacists and general practitioners in the British National Health Service, and by 1994 it was reported that one in four Britons had visited an 'alternative' practitioner in the course of the previous year, 'three-quarters of general practitioners had referred a patient to an alternative therapist at some time', and private medical insurance companies were beginning to accept claims for alternative treatment, provided it had been recommended by the patient's GP.[117]

Exeter University was the first to institute, in 1987, a Centre for Complementary Health Studies, using rigorous traditional scientific criteria, but applying them to topics, such as herbalism and Chinese medicine, previously considered beyond the scientific pale. It is not only daringly new hypotheses, however, that are now attracting serious study. Philosophers are again turning their attention not merely to the processes by which we test knowledge, the validation of our perceptions; but also to how we acquire the hypotheses in the first place. Are there avenues to truth, to 'reality', other than the empiricism of the senses? What part does consciousness play?

This is the context in which has occurred the explosive increase in the use of mind-expanding drugs. People who considered themselves responsible members of society repudiated recreational narcotic drugs, but accepted a cult of hallucinatory drugs, in the belief that they opened new windows on eternal verities. Aldous Huxley made the acquaintance of mescalin (initially derived from Mexican cactus) in 1953. His *The Doors of Perception*, published in 1954, claimed that under its influence he experienced pure transcendent Being, the ultimate is-ness of creation, a state of timeless bliss in which the individual self, intrusive and unwanted, re-obtrudes only as a refuge to which to flee when the brightness of pure Being becomes intolerable; then the filter of the individual mind cuts the infinity of our consciousness down to a level of enlightenment compatible with our animal survival needs. He admits that there seems no place in this vision of ultimate reality for human relationships, and that those dipping into such contemplative states tend not to busy themselves as activists in worldly concerns; but neither are they aggressive or violent.

In 1960, while Huxley was lecturing on his experiences at the Massachusetts Institute of Technology, Dr (not of medicine but of psychology) Tim Leary at nearby Harvard University was experimenting with an ergot-derived drug with properties very similar to those of mescalin: lysergic acid diethylamide, or LSD. Excited by its properties, Leary founded the League for Spiritual Discovery and (unlike Huxley, who considered that mind-expanding drugs should be administered with caution) advocated incorporating LSD into the water supply.[*118] The

---

* In 1970 Leary was arrested for possession of marijuana and sentenced to ten years in prison. He escaped, fled abroad, but later served a further period in gaol, being released on parole in 1976. In 1994 he was again arrested for – in the changed climate of the 1990s – smoking an ordinary cigarette in a non-smoking area (Tyler, p.191; *The Times*, 21 April 1976 and 13 May 1994).

optimism with which Huxley and Leary viewed the hallucinatory drugs was severely shaken by such occurrences as the murders perpetrated by Charles Manson and his acolytes while under the influence of LSD.[119] Some well-publicized (if possibly unintentional) suicides, and evidence of violence such as that accompanying acid-house raves brought the drug under strict legal control in both the United States and the United Kingdom. Books continue to be published, however, trumpeting the religious profundity of the drug-founded experience, and pleading for its deregulation.[*]

Leary himself recanted, saying, 'we failed to understand the enormous variation in human neurology'.[120] The drug's effects, in short, were not superhighways to transcendent truths, but were dependent on the bio-electrochemical composition of the individual. Huxley had accepted this from the start, but had thought that what a later generation was to call a 'bad trip' was a rarity with mescalin: 'the drug brings hell and purgatory only to those who have had a recent case of jaundice, or who suffer from periodical depressions or a chronic anxiety', he had written in *The Doors of Perception*. Two years later in *Heaven and Hell* (1956), largely an examination of the congruencies between drug-induced visions and the work of various artists, he enlarged on the physical and emotional states that could 'plunge the mescalin taker into hell'. 'Negative emotions – the fear which is the absence of confidence, the hatred anger or malice which exclude love – are the guarantee that visionary experience, if and when it comes, shall be appalling.'[121] Visionary experience, he concluded, is not the same as mystical experience. Drugs (though he persisted in believing they could afford 'gratuitous grace') were not the short cut to spirituality he had envisioned.

Society's experience over the forty years since Huxley first wrote *The Doors of Perception* has amply confirmed that psychedelic hallucinations do not appear capable of refining spiritual awareness or leading to any reformation of individual personality except in a deleterious direction. They are, rather, bizarre extensions of sensate material consumerism. As Rookmaaker says,

> drugs are made in a factory, or even when they are natural plants or growths, they belong to the material world. The drug experience does not really transcend physical reality. We have expanded minds and have new experiences, see new things, or rather see

well-known things in a new light – and yet we are still within the framework of the Enlightenment, for we start from our senses, from our human experience ... Drugs ... belong wholly to the framework of the world of scientism and technology.[122]

The quest, of which the use of mind-altering drugs is a symptom, is being pursued in other directions, whose common factor is the desire for knowledge of a 'beyond' validated by personal intuitive experience rather than by the tests of logic or of laboratory reproductability. The search for mystic experience that distinguished third- and fourth-century Christianity, and gave birth in Egypt to the monastic movements that shaped western Europe; that reappeared in the late Middle Ages and burgeoned in the spiritual ferment of the Reformation and Counter-Reformation, proceeded not by the ingestion of extra substances, but by asceticism and self-denial. Huxley indeed contended that the fasting and self-chastisement of the early Christian mystics of the desert had been pursued precisely because they resulted in biochemical changes comparable to drug ingestion, and were productive of similar visions of Heaven and Hell.

Charismatic Christianity has reappeared, at first among gatherings of Christians in small house church groups, but by the 1990s both Anglican and Roman Catholic congregations were experiencing charismatic phenomena, with reports of spontaneous healing, and 'speaking in tongues'.[123] In 1994 the movement intensified with the importation from Canada of a phenomenon referred to as the 'Toronto Blessing', in which whole congregations were 'slain by the spirit' and fell to the floor in varying stages of profound, but fundamentally ecstatic, emotion, some claiming to have had heavenly visions. Comparable phenomena have occurred before – they distinguished, for instance, the Wesleyan mission to England in the eighteenth century – and then as now were distrusted by those not given to 'enthusiasm' as principally demonstrations of mass hysteria.[*] Indubitably, however, the Wesleyan mission precipitated a renewal and extension of religious commitment that profoundly affected society. Time will tell whether a comparable resurgence is afoot.

Other mystical traditions, however, including some of those imported into Britain from the East, regard the whole panoply of visions, pleasant or unpleasant, as superficial; and seek, by meditative techniques which

---

[*] A diagnosis not impeded by the revelations, in the summer of 1995, of the excesses to which devotees had exposed themselves in pursuit of 'the Nine O'clock Service', a charismatic movement in Sheffield which ended with the priest in charge undergoing psychiatric treatment, and arraigned on charges of sexual misconduct.

in Eastern practice involve the use of mantra or mandela to empty the mind of all input from the senses or from the intellect, absorption into an infinite, a ground of Being, a stillness, an emptiness. While the attitude may be one of pure undemanding passivity/receptivity, proponents claim that they emerge from the quietness with distress calmed, resolve strengthened amd serenity enhanced. Such techniques, practised through the ages in the Orthodox Church though long lost in the West, are now spreading, encouraged by the meditative chants emanating from the Christian ecumenical centre at Taizé in France.* Meditative retreats are attracting increasing numbers of participants; indeed, a National Retreat Association has been instituted. Buddhist monasteries are being established that appeal to Western as well as Asian devotees, and, to quote a *Times* report on 'the pleasures of solitary confinement', 'as the New Age movement has gathered pace, retreat communities have sprung up which have no particular allegiance, other than a commitment to spiritual self-discovery and peaceful living'.[124] Such experiences may be no more than personal therapies, generating no cult, code or credal commitments. It is in the return to the mystical roots of religion, however, that some see the best hope of social and personal renewal, and of reconciliation and understanding between the different faiths now planted on British soil.†

'The history of man's ideas concerning his relation to matter will, I am confident, appear to the historian of the future as a significant factor determining the history of the last five hundred years', wrote F. Sherwood Taylor in *The Alchemists*.[125] The abandonment of that quest in modern science profoundly impoverished human beings. 'The present antagonism between science, religion, philosophy, ethics and art is unnecessary, not to mention disastrous', wrote Sorokin:

> In the light of an adequate theory of true reality and value, they all are one and all serve one purpose; the unfolding of the Absolute in the relative empirical world, to the greater nobility of Man and to

---

* The unexpected rise of Spanish Gregorian chant, recorded at the Benedictine monastery of Santo Domingo de Silos in the summer of 1993, to a position in the American top twenty for no fewer than 21 weeks during 1994 may be symptomatic. By November 1995 EMI had sold some half-million records and cassettes of *Canto Gregoriano* in the United Kingdom.

† Even silence, however, is not without its polemics. In Georgia, USA, a silence (lasting only one minute) was instituted at the start of the school day, 'as a way of helping to reduce violence among teenagers by forcing them to reflect in silence'. A teacher deliberately broke the silence, insisting that it was a form of subtly infiltrating into the school day the 'religion' from which the constitution guaranteed freedom (*The Times*, 27 August 1994).

the greater glory of God. As such they should and can co-operate in the fulfillment of this great task.[126]

Such weighty matters do not bear heavily on today's average citizen. Some, perhaps many, feel that we live in the twilight of a dying civilization, and estate agents in such remote but repopulated locations as the Western Isles, reporting that 'all the inquiries for empty houses seem to be from people who want to escape the violence of the cities in the South',[127] bear witness to the recurrence of a phenomenon familiar in the late Roman Empire, de-urbanization. But old-timers nostalgic for the days when neighbours trusted one another, left their doors unlocked and counted on one another for help, comradeship and solace are far outnumbered by those who remember only the anxiety of poverty, and prefer without question the cars, supermarkets, foreign holidays and medical attention of today. The citizens of the Roman Empire withdrew their allegiance partly because of the crushing taxation to which they were subjected, and the anxiety of governments throughout the western industrialized world as to how they are to meet inexorably rising welfare costs may be symptomatic of the approach of a similar crisis. But so long as the economy can be teased into improving on – or at least sustaining – modern living standards (a process watched with obsessional anxiety by daily news bulletins measuring the fraction of a cent or pfennig by which the pound's value has altered on the international exchanges), most people will not deeply question its direction, and will adjust, albeit with some regret, to the surveillance cameras checking their every downtown move,* the probable introduction of identity cards, the aluminium screens and the grilles and locks with which their houses are festooned, the security lighting that permanently blots out the stars, the intermittent theft and vandalism of their cars and other property, the lurking fears that render park and woodland walks unattractive, the intense anxiety for any of their family who are old and vulnerable, young and inexperienced, or

---

* Following the success of closed-circuit television in major cities, the Government in October 1994 made £2 million available for the installation of CCTV in 'small towns and housing estates with widespread crime' (*The Times*, 19 October 1994). By March 1995 grants of £5 million had been allocated to extend the scheme to 'car parks, railway stations and community centres around the country' (*The Times*, 28 March 1995). At the end of August 1995, following strong public demand and spectacular declines in crime in pilot areas, 'surveillance cameras began operating in two English inner-city housing estates for the first time' (*The Times*, 30 August 1995). Towards the end of 1995, when it was reported that the installation of cameras in Newcastle upon Tyne had led to 800 arrests over four years, all but six of the accused pleading guilty and all being convicted, the Government, notwithstanding the anxieties of civil liberties campaigners, made £15 million available for further extensions of the schemes (*The Times*, 23 November 1995).

whose job requires them to confront the public at night. They will accept that in a sex-obsessed culture, close friendships will always be presumed to include physical intimacies, and will feel cheated if the arts omit to explore the sexual potential of encounters. Though more and more of their children may be asthmatic or assailed by skin cancers, suffering will be seen as unacceptable, and monetary compensation sought for its endurance, physical or emotional; but the infliction of suffering will, for increasing numbers of calloused people, be greeted with the indifference, even sadism, that so horrified Colin Turnbull in his survey (*The Mountain People*)* of the desensitized Ik tribe in Africa, which Peter Brook, a weathervane of social dynamics, was in 1976 to dramatize for Western audiences.

If Sorokin's analysis of the past is any guide to the future, such a society is ultimately transformed, either by internal reform in response to increasing levels of disgust and despair; or, more radically, by external conquest and compulsion. Sensate society's superior technology has not, in past experience, necessarily prevailed; it did not enable Greece to withstand Rome, nor Rome to withstand the Nordic tribes. We have caught glimpses of contemporary parallels in the American defeats in Vietnam and Somalia, the Russian failure in Afghanistan. There were disquieting dispatches from correspondents in the Gulf in 1990 and from Cambodia in 1992 about the level of American morale once habitual creature comforts were unavailable.[128] 'It is quite rare for barbarians to possess more advanced technology than the societies they attack . . .' wrote Anthony Hartley. 'Incipient disintegration in the society under attack has played a great part in the barbarians' success.'[129] The British army shows little sign of the decadence that afflicted the legions,† or of

---

* Turnbull spent a number of years living among the Ik people in a drought-stricken mountain region on the Uganda/Sudan border. He was horrified at the extent to which, under the pressure of the extreme struggle for survival, any vestige of kindness or compassion, even in the care of children, of the elderly or the dying, had vanished. Theft and deceit were the norm in human relationships, mutual trust entirely absent, and the only delight left in life, apart from that afforded by brief respites from the prevailing hunger, was enjoyment at the misfortunes of others, enlivened by the deliberate infliction of cruelty. He advanced the thesis that any human society was capable of being reduced to such egocentric individualism, and detected symptoms, such as family breakdown, in Western society, even though it lacked the harsh external circumstances to which he attributed Ik behaviour. He confessed to finding the callousness and sadism of the Ik so incorrigible and so repulsive that, in the conclusion of his work, he could only hope that they would die out – a fate towards which they appeared to be heading (*The Mountain People*).

† But it was disquieting to learn, in March 1995, that over 40 per cent of applicants to the British army were failing the fitness and medical tests, not, as in the early decades of the twentieth century, because of poor health linked to poverty, but because they were too fat to run a mile and a half; too unfit to carry heavy packs (shades of the legions' refusal to wear heavy armour!); lacked the mental robustness to sleep out in a wood or in a hole in the ground on night exercises; or suffered from the

the collapse into drug dependency of which America's army stood accused in Asia; and despite the denigration to which it has for over twenty years been subjected by such anti-Establishment playwrights as Charles Wood,* it is among the few long-standing institutions still widely respected in Britain. But Britain is no longer a great power, and the front line for the defence forces is now on the Treasury's doorstep, facing the constant clamour to transfer resources to other claimants.

With the collapse of Soviet Communism, the main contender as maker and shaper of the culture of the future is Islam. The contest does not, however, have to take military form. 'Western civilization is the sick man of the modern world. It is destined for oblivion and will eventually take its place in the same dustbin of history that has already swallowed up Marxism. Islam alone is the antidote to a morally bankrupt and sick world.' So said Dr Kalim Siddiqui at the opening of his British Moslem Parliament. His words are not without an echo in Western hearts. By late 1993 articles in *The Times* were drawing attention to the '10,000 to 20,000' converts to Islam in Britain, many of them former Christians disillusioned by the ambiguity and compromises of the Christian churches. 'The rate of conversions,' it was claimed, 'has prompted predictions that Islam will rapidly become an important religious force in this country', the number of indigenous converts expected, within twenty years, to rival or surpass that of Moslem immigrants and their descendants.[130] In the United States it is estimated that some 25,000 convert annually to Islam (though the four out of five who are black may be at least partially motivated by the desire for an identity that distinguishes them from mainstream white America).[131]

'The liberal West is constructed on a spiritual vacuum and this may well turn out to be a real political failing. The lesson of Islam may, in the long run, prove to be that a society must believe in something if it is to be a society at all', wrote Bryan Appleyard, in an article tersely entitled 'We ignore march of Islam only at our peril'.[132]

'We are waiting,' wrote Macintyre, in the final lines of his book, 'not for a Godot, but for another – doubtless very different – St Benedict.' He is not referring to some charismatic political leader, of whom the

---

rising scourge of the British population: asthma (*The Times*, 25 March 1995). In October 1995 came the news that Gurkhas might be invited to make up the shortfall in British army recruitment, for which, in the words of an army source, 'Kids today are too soft' – an exact mirror of statements made about the late phase of Rome and of the Middle Ages; and of the solution, recruitment of foreign troops, to which both turned (*The Times*, 14 October 1995).

* Charles Wood's long history of plays denigratory of the army include *H*, *Tumbledown*, *A Breed of Heroes* and the script of the film *Charge of the Light Brigade*.

tormented twentieth century has seen far too many. His earlier words make clear the relevance of a Benedict. In contemplating the last days of the Roman Empire, Macintyre remarked that

> a crucial turning point in that earlier history occurred when men and women of good will turned aside from the task of shoring up the Roman *imperium* and ceased to identify the continuation of civility and moral community with the maintenance of that *imperium*. What they set themselves to achieve instead – often not recognizing fully what they were doing – was the construction of the new forms of community within which the moral life could be sustained so that both morality and civility might survive the coming age of barbarism and darkness. If my account of our moral condition is correct, we ought also to conclude that for some time now we too have reached that turning point. What matters at this stage is the construction of local forms of community within which civility and the intellectual and moral life can be sustained through the new dark ages which are already upon us. And if the tradition of the virtues was able to survive the horrors of the last dark ages, we are not entirely without grounds for hope.[133]

Jonestown, the Branch Davidian cultists of Waco, and the Church of the Solar Temple, whose members died merciless premature deaths, are reminders of how far community, in itself, is from offering a panacea. Yet in a world politically obsessed with larger and larger power blocs, this call to re-establish the validity of the 'little platoons' clearly attracts, whether in the myriad of (mostly short-lived) communes that tried to opt out of mainstream life in the 1960s and 1970s; perhaps in the experiments now developing among the unwaged, under the auspices of the New Economics Foundation, to develop transactions in local goods and services using novel units of exchange in place of coin of the realm;*[134] or even in the more regimented attempts to emphasize moral commitment, of which the establishment of the first Orthodox Jewish *eruv* in North London may be a symptom.[135]

According to Sorokin:

> If a person has no strong convictions as to what is right and what is wrong, if he does not believe in any God or absolute moral values, if

---

* By the autumn of 1994 it was reported that there are well over 300 LETS (Local Exchange Trading Schemes) in the UK, including 25 in various areas of London. One of their attractions is the retention of purchasing power within the local community.

he no longer respects contractual obligations, and finally, if his hunger for pleasures and sensory values is paramount, what can guide and control his conduct toward other men? Nothing but his desires and lusts. Under these conditions he loses all rational and moral control, even plain common sense. What can deter him from violating the rights, interests, and well-being of other men? Nothing but physical force. How far will he go in his insatiable quest for sensory happiness? He will go as far as brute force, opposed by that of others, permits. His whole problem of behaviour is determined by the ratio between his force and that wielded by others.[136]

This analysis goes far to explain why the early stages of ideational societies are so oppressive; force is combating force. If the next phase of our culture is to be, in Sorokin's terminology, ideational, we are likely to see our liberties curtailed, our freedom to 'do our own thing' transmuted from a virtue into a vice. 'Men are qualified for civil liberty,' wrote Edmund Burke, 'in exact proportion to their disposition to put moral chains upon their own appetites.'[137] If we hope to salvage something of our liberties, perhaps even democracy itself, we need to heed Burke's warning, and for the sake of our planet, our human relationships, and our prospects of tranquillity, personal and social, to recognize that only tangentially are we our own creation, that in the last resort we are creatures under constraint. On our response depends whether those constraints are self-chosen, or pitilessly imposed by potencies that are not ours to command.

Notes

For book and periodical details, see Bibliography

Chapter 1 *(pp.7–19)*

1. Sorokin (1937–41) Vol.I, p.60.
2. Sorokin (1947), p.320.
3. Vogt, p.289.
4. *The Independent*, 31 March 1987.
5. Schaeffer, pp.14–16.
6. Deonna, p.226, quoted by Sorokin (1937–41), Vol.I, p.330.
7. *The Independent*, 14 April 1987.
8. Steinberg, pp.1, 8.
9. Sorokin (1941) p.43.
10. Fowler, H. W. p.616. (1927 The definition does not figure in later editions.)
11. *The Independent*, 10 April 1987.
12. Michael Brenson, 'Monet's Complexity and Grandeur Through his Series Paintings', *Sotheby's Preview*, April/May 1990, p.104.
13. Christopher Lloyd, 'New Approaches to Impressionism', *Sotheby's Preview*, September/October 1989, p.7.
14. Nicholas Wadley, 'Renoir and Impressionism', *Sotheby's Preview*, April/May 1990, p.6.
15. *The Independent*, 22 March 1988.
16. *The Independent*, 8 February 1988.
17. Jessica Gwynne, on the Francis Bacon retrospective at the Tate Gallery, *Salisbury Review*, Vol. 4, No. 2, January 1986.
18. *The Independent*, 24 September 1988.
19. *The Times*, 28 June 1985.
20. Ibid.; *The Independent*, 24 September 1988.
21. Polybius, XXXVIII.5.
22. Sorokin (1941), p. 63.
23. Sorokin (1937–41), Vol.I, pp.263–4.
24. Christopher Booker, *Daily Telegraph*, 24 February 1979.
25. Appian, *Punica*, 132.
26. Clark, p.4.
27. Macmullen (1967), p.161.
28. Sorokin (1937–41), Vol.I, p.226.
29. Cowell (1970), p.22.

Chapter 2 *(pp.20–36)*

1. Berthold, p.20.
2. Ibid., p.3.
3. Herbert Weisinger, 'Ritual Origins of Drama', in Gassner and Quinn (eds.) pp.712ff.
4. Aristotle, *Poetics*, IV.
5. Horace, *The Art of Poetry*, 220ff. and note.
6. Virgil, *Georgics*, II. 380–4.
7. Martial, *Epigrams*, III.24.
8. Mantzius, Vol.I, p.102.
9. Kitto (1957), p.104.
10. Kitto (1961), p.106.
11. Ibid., p.38.
12. Mellersh, p.115.
13. Berthold, p.137.
14. Nietzsche, p.2.
15. Ibid., p.81.
16. Ibid., p.79.
17. Ibid., p.50.
18. Ibid., p.62.
19. Ibid., p.128.
20. Ibid., p.50.
21. Ibid., p.55.
22. Arnott, p.40.

23. Ibid., p.60.
24. Sorokin (1937–41), Vol.I, pp.557ff.
25. Plato, *The Republic*, IX.ii.379.
26. Aristotle, *Poetics*, XIII.
27. Kitto (1961), p.99; and (1964), pp.231–5.
28. Kitto (1961), pp.202–3.
29. Berthold, p.138.
30. Nietzsche, p.133.
31. Arnott, p.60.
32. Kitto (1961) p.333.
33. Ibid., pp.334, 356; Euripides [1], *Electra*, 842–3; [2] *The Phoenician Women*, 1179–81 and note, p.435.
34. Fox, p.113.
35. Kitto (1961), p.315.
36. Mantzius, Vol.I, p.207.
37. Kitto (1961), p.317.
38. Berthold, p.139.
39. Ibid., p.358.
40. Mantzius, Vol.I, p.196.
41. Quintilian, X.1.67.
42. Kitto (1961), pp.185–6.
43. Kitto (1964), pp.239–40.
44. Pliny the Elder, XXXVI.82; Fraser, P.M., p.378.
45. Hodges, pp.157ff.
46. Kitto (1957), p.179.
47. Mellersh, p.137.
48. Plato, *Timaeus*, 27D, 28A, 29C.
49. Bertrand Gille, 'Machines', in Singer, C. et al. (eds), Vol.II, p.632.
50. Plutarch, *Lives*, 'Marcellus', XIV.5,6.
51. Dover (1974), p.104.
52. Hill, p.6.
53. Vince, p.46.
54. Ibid.
55. Vitruvius, Vol.I, Introduction, p.ix.
56. Mantzius, Vol.I, p.130.
57. Arnott, p.13.
58. Ibid., pp.79, 83.
59. Bieber, p.117.
60. Vitruvius, VII, Preface, 11.
61. Ibid., V.vi.8.
62. Ibid., I.i.9 and V.v.
63. Fraser, P.M., p.619, Vol.II p.871, note 3.
64. Arnott, pp.74–5.

Chapter 3 (pp.37–49)

1. Harrer, p.214.
2. Aristotle, *Poetics*, V.

3. Mellersh, p.127; Bieber, p.36; Berthold, p.149.
4. Bieber, Chapter III, offers an excellent survey.
5. Mantzius, Vol.I, p.108.
6. Duckworth, p.21.
7. Dover (1974), p.19.
8. Beare, p.1.
9. Kitto (1957), p.160.
10. Beare, p.40.
11. Arnott, pp.72ff.
12. Vitruvius, VII.v.5.
13. Arnott, p.140.
14. Aristotle, *Poetics*, III.
15. Bieber, p.129.
16. Mellersh, p.149.
17. Chorikios, 'In Defence of the Mime', *Revue de Philologie*, New Series, Vol.1, 1877.
18. Ibid.
19. Frank (1930), pp.79–80.
20. Arnott, p.75.
21. Rostovtzeff (1941), pp.1048, 1085.
22. Ibid., p.418.
23. Kitto (1957), p.203.
24. Ibid., p.234.
25. Rostovtzeff (1941), p.1119.
26. Fraser, P.M., Vol.I, p.618.
27. Ibid., p.622.
28. Ibid., p.310.
29. Nilsson, p.230.
30. Fraser, P.M., Vol.I, pp.598, 619.
31. Ibid., p.598.
32. Grant (1982), p.181.
33. Ibid., pp.312–16.
34. Rostovtzeff (1941), p.417; Robinson, V., p.66.
35. Mellersh, pp.175, 183.
36. Rostovtzeff (1941), p.421.
37. Ibid., p.417; Hill, p.79.
38. Fraser, P.M., Vol.I, p.397.
39. Ibid., p.308.
40. Ibid., pp.413–15.
41. Ibid., p.406.
42. Robinson, V., p.81.
43. Mellersh, p.205.
44. Hill, p.6.
45. Plutarch, *Lives*, 'Marcellus', XIV.9.
46. Fraser, P.M., Vol.I, p.429.
47. Ibid., p.432.
48. Hill, p.230.
49. Ibid.
50. Fraser, P.M., Vol.I, p.358.

51. Hippocrates, Introduction, p.vi.
52. Robinson, V., pp.51, 54.
53. Kitto (1957), p.188.
54. Fraser, P.M., Vol.I, pp.339ff.
55. Ammianus Marcellinus, XXII.16.18.
56. Kitto (1964), pp.148, 149, 176.
57. Fraser, P.M., Vol.I, p.446.
58. Ibid., p.350.
59. Robinson, V., p.71.
60. Fraser, P.M., Vol.I, pp.368–9.
61. Rostovtzeff (1941), pp.94ff., 363ff., 562ff., 1180ff., 1224.
62. Fraser, P.M., Vol.I, p.533.
63. Rostovtzeff (1941), pp.927, 1035ff.
64. Ibid., pp.123–5, 163.
65. Ibid., p.440.
66. Ibid., p.1076.

Chapter 4 (pp.50–66)

1. Sorokin (1937–41), Vol.III, p.539.
2. Kitto (1957), pp.19, 195.
3. Dover (1974), p.247.
4. Kitto (1957), p.165.
5. Dover (1974), pp.111, 163.
6. Kitto (1957), p.133.
7. Dover (1974), pp.205, 208; see also Kenneth Dover, 'Classical Greek Attitudes to Sexual Behaviour', *Arethusa*, Vol.VI, 1973, pp.60ff.
8. Kitto (1957), p.226.
9. Dover (1974), pp.250, 251.
10. Kitto (1957), p.167.
11. Ibid., p.166.
12. Plato, *The Republic*, IX.ii.382.
13. *Oxford Classical Dictionary*, 'Cynics'.
14. Andrew Burnett, 'The Arts of the Ancient World', *Sotheby's Preview*, May/June 1990, p.9.
15. Fraser, P.M., Vol.I pp.202–97.
16. Kitto (1964), p.105.
17. Rostovtzeff (1941), pp.200, 201.
18. Dover (1974), p.135.
19. Ibid., p.262.
20. Ibid., pp.262–5.
21. *Oxford Classical Dictionary*, 'Epicurus'; see also Lucretius, Introduction by M.F. Smith.
22. Lucretius, ibid.
23. Frank (1930), p.77.
24. Kitto (1957), p.251.
25. Dover (1978), pp.7, 196ff.
26. Ibid., p.174.

27. Paul Webb, 'Not one as pretty as he', *Spectator*, 27 February 1988.
28. Kenneth Dover, 'Classical Greek Attitudes to Sexual Behaviour', *Arethusa*, Vol.VI, 1973, p.67.
29. Dover (1978), pp.157–64, 210–11.
30. Ibid., p.201; Kitto (1957), p.136.
31. Dover (1978), p.193.
32. Ibid., p.33.
33. Ibid., pp.13ff.
34. Chorikios, 'In Defence of the Mime', *Revue de Philologie*, New Series, Vol.I, 1877, Chapter X; Dover (1978), p.19.
35. Fraser, P.M., Vol.I, p.790.
36. Plato, *Laws*, 838A–41; see also Fox, p.351.
37. Dover (1978), p.79.
38. Kitto (1957), p.155.
39. Dover (1978), p.148.
40. Dover, Kenneth 'Classical Greek Attitudes to Sexual Behaviour', *Arethusa*, Vol.VI, 1973, p.69.
41. Dover (1978), pp.149, 182.
42. Fraser, P.M., Vol.I, p.791.
43. Dover (1978), p.153.
44. Ibid., p.59.
45. Fraser, P.M., Vol.I, pp.564, 595.
46. Ibid., pp.563–4.
47. Ibid., pp.756, 790.
48. Kitto (1957), p.159.
49. Ibid., p.125.
50. Ibid., p.158.
51. Rostovtzeff (1941), pp.96, 421.
52. Wood, pp.42–80, 137–50.
53. Bertrand Gille, 'Machines', in Singer, C. et al. (eds), Vol.II, p.638.
54. Rostovtzeff (1941), pp.203ff. and p.1357, note 53.
55. Ibid., p.1021.
56. Carter and Dale, pp.88ff.
57. Plato, *Critias*, 111B, C, D.
58. Fustel de Coulanges, p.341.
59. Rostovtzeff (1941), pp.96ff, 619ff.
60. Ibid., p.610.
61. Balsdon (1969), p.82; Rostovtzeff (1941), p.623.
62. Rostovtzeff (1941), p.624.
63. Ibid., p.202; Rickman, pp.50–2
64. Fraser, P.M., Vol.I, p.117.
65. Ibid., pp.60, 79, 86–8.
66. Ibid., pp.194, 300, 301.
67. Rostovtzeff (1941), pp.714ff, 877ff.; see also p.1551, note 190.

68. Ibid., p.896.
69. Fraser, P.M., Vol.I, p.805.

Chapter 5 (pp.67–86)

1. Polybius, VI.56.
2. Duff (1910), p.53.
3. Frank (1930), p.9; see also Tenney Frank, 'The Decline of Roman Tragedy', *Classical Journal*, 1916, Vol.12, p.183.
4. Balsdon (1969), p.244.
5. Fowler, W. Warde, pp.333ff.
6. Ovid, *Fasti*, Appendix, pp.414–15.
7. Oman, p.75.
8. Livy, VII.2.
9. Arnott, pp.93–6.
10. *Oxford Classical Dictionary*, 'Ludi Scaenici'.
11. Frank (1930), p.87.
12. Livy, XXXI.4 and note.
13. Balsdon (1969), p.271.
14. Ibid., p.270.
15. Dill, *Roman Society from Nero to Marcus Aurelius*, p.530; see also Frank (1930), pp.12, 27.
16. Duff (1910), p.155.
17. Alföldy, pp.35ff.
18. Polybius, VI.56.
19. Astin, p.163.
20. For further discussion of this point, see Elizabeth Rawson, 'Speciosa Locis Morataque Recte' in Whitby et al. (eds), pp.79ff.
21. *Oxford Classical Dictionary*, 'Naevius'.
22. Horace, *Epistles*, note to II.i.50.
23. Balsdon (1969), p.270; *Oxford Classical Dictionary*, 'Ennius'.
24. F. Warren Wright, 'Cicero and the Theatre', *Smith College Classical Studies*, No.11, 1931.
25. Duckworth, pp.337ff.
26. Beare, p.77.
27. Duff (1910), pp.190–1.
28. Duckworth, p.279.
29. Ibid., p.281.
30. Ibid., p.282.
31. Ibid., pp.143–7, 158.
32. Duff (1910), p.171.
33. Frank (1930), pp.78, 82.
34. Ibid., p.101.
35. Duckworth, p.293.
36. Cumont, p.51.

37. Livy, XXXIX.8ff.
38. Ramsey Macmullen, 'Roman Attitudes to Greek Love', *Historia*, Vol.31, 1982; Fox, p.342
39. Polybius, XXXI.25.
40. Quintilian, X.1; Balsdon (1969), p.273.
41. Livy, XL.51.
42. Ovid, *Ars Amatoria*, I.89ff; Virgil, *Aeneid*, V.288.
43. Arnott, p.102.
44. Bieber, p.170.
45. Tacitus, *Annals*, XIV.20.
46. Livy, XLVIII.
47. Augustine, *City of God* [I], I.31.
48. Livy, VII.2.
49. Arnott, p.109, referring to *Pseudolus*.
50. Tacitus, *Annals*, XIV.21; Livy, XLVIII; Duff (1910), p.157.
51. Vitruvius, V.8; Tacitus, *Annals*, XIV.21.
52. Macrobius, 3.14.7.
53. Ramsey Macmullen, 'Roman Attitudes to Greek Love', *Historia*, Vol.31, 1982.
54. Mellersh, p.235.
55. Plutarch, *Sulla*, 2, 36.
56. C.J. Grysar, 'Der Römische Mimus', *Sitzungsberichte der Kaiserlichen Akademie Der Wissenschaften, Philosophisch-Historische*, Classe XII, Band 1854, p.306.
57. Ibid., p. 276.
58. Fowler, W. Warde, p.92, quoting Valerius Maximus, II.x.8.
59. C.J. Grysar, 'Der Römische Mimus', *Sitzungsberichte der Kaiserlichen Akademie Der Wissenschaften, Philosophisch-Historische*, Classe XII, Band 1854, pp.239–40, 275; Bieber, p.159.
60. Plutarch, *Sulla*, 2, 36.
61. Livy, VII.2; C.J. Grysar, 'Der Römische Mimus', *Sitzungsberichte der Kaiserlichen Akademie Der Wissenschaften, Philosophisch-Historische*, Classe XII, Band 1854, p.238; F. Warren Wright, 'Cicero and the Theatre', *Smith College Classical Studies*, No.11, 1931; Duff (1910), p.221; Beare, p.10; Berthold, p.199; Balsdon (1969), p.278.
62. Balsdon (1969), pp.281, 283.
63. F. Warren Wright, 'Cicero and the Theatre', *Smith College Classical Studies*, No.11, 1931.

64. Seneca, *Epistles*, VIII.8ff; XCIV.28; CVIII.8; Seneca, *Moral Essays*, 'Ad Marciam De Consolatione', 9; Seneca the Elder, *Controversiae*, VII.3.
65. Macrobius, 2.7.
66. Ibid.
67. Cicero, *De Re Publica*, IV.X.12.
68. Tacitus, *Annals*, IV.14; Horace, *Epistles*, II.i.145.
69. Tenney Frank, 'The Status of Actors at Rome', *Classical Philology*, 1931, Vol.26, pp.11–20.
70. Suetonius, *Tiberius*, 61.
71. Macmullen (1967), p.66.
72. Fox, p.49.
73. Tacitus, *Annals*, I.77.
74. Horace, *Epistles*, II.i.145; Suetonius, *Tiberius*, 37; Suetonius, *Caligula*, 27; Suetonius, *Domitian* 7, 10; Tacitus, *Annals* IV.14; VI.29; XIII.25; Dio Cassius, LVII.21; Pliny the Younger, *Panegyricus*, 46; and see Macmullen (1967), pp.170–1.
75. Apuleius, *The Golden Ass*, p.262.
76. Starr, p.98; Valerius Maximus, II.vi.7.
77. C.J. Grysar, 'Der Römische Mimus', *Sitzungsberichte der Kaiserlichen Akademie Der Wissenschaften*, Philosophisch-Historische, Classe XII, Band 1854, p.253.
78. Horace, *Satires*, I.ii.56, 58.
79. Plutarch, *Antony*, IX.4.
80. Friedländer, Vol.II, p.100.
81. Lucian [1], 'Of Pantomime', 63.
82. Ibid., 37ff., 81.
83. Suetonius, *Caligula*, 55; Suetonius, *Nero*, 54; Tacitus, *Annals*, XI.36; Dio Cassius, LX.22, 28, LXI.31, LXII.18; LXVII.2.
84. C.J. Grysar, 'Über die Pantomimen der Römer', *Rheinisches Museum für Philologie*, 1834, p.60.
85. Carcopino, p.251.
86. Lucian [1], 'Of Pantomime', 76.

Chapter 6 (pp.87–105)

1. F. Warren Wright, 'Cicero and the Theatre', *Smith College Classical Studies*, No.11, 1931, *passim*.
2. Polybius, XXX.22.
3. Balsdon (1969), pp.272–3.
4. Carcopino, p.246.

5. Vitruvius, V.vi.2.
6. F. Warren Wright, 'Cicero and the Theatre', *Smith College Classical Studies*, No.11, 1931, p.29.
7. Aristides Quintilianus, II.70.
8. Sorokin (1937–41), Vol.I, pp.553, 563.
9. Arnott, p.98; F. Warren Wright, 'Cicero and the Theatre', *Smith College Classical Studies*, No.11, 1931.
10. Horace, *The Art of Poetry*, 202ff.
11. Quintilian, I.x.17.
12. Dio Chrysostom, XIX.5.
13. Ibid., XXXII.4, 61, 62.
14. Arnott, p.68.
15. F. Warren Wright, 'Cicero and the Theatre', *Smith College Classical Studies*, No.11, 1931.
16. Horace, *Epistles*, II.I.182ff.
17. Duckworth, pp.290–2.
18. Mantzius, Vol.I, pp.142–3.
19. Walcot, p.32.
20. Ibid., pp.27ff.
21. Plutarch, *Moralia*, 'On the Eating of Flesh II', 998E.
22. Stanford, p.6.
23. Aristotle, *Poetics*, XIV.
24. Horace, *The Art of Poetry*, 1.179–88.
25. Balsdon (1969), p.281; Vince, p.73; Quintilian, X.1.98.
26. Tacitus, *Annals*, XI.13; Carcopino, p.245; Quintilian, X.1.98.
27. Tacitus, *Dialogus de Oratoribus*, 2.
28. Seneca, *Epistles*, LXXX.7ff.
29. Lucian [1], 'Of Pantomime', 27.
30. Suetonius, *Vespasian*, 19; *Scriptores Historiae Augustae*, 'Hadrian', XIX, XXVI.
31. Heurgon, p.212.
32. Livy, XXVIII.20.
33. Ibid., XLI.20 (tr. William A.M'Devitte, Bell, London, 1890).
34. Carcopino, p.229.
35. Friedländer, Vol.II, pp.41ff.
36. Carcopino, p.254.
37. Orosius, IV.1.
38. Friedländer, Vol.IV, p.181; Balsdon (1969), p.302.
39. Friedländer, Vol.II, pp.62ff; Vol.IV, pp.181ff; Jones, H. Stuart, p.368; Balsdon (1969), p.302.
40. Friedländer, Vol.IV, p.181.
41. Pliny the Elder, VIII.64 and note.
42. Seneca, *Moral Essays*, 'Ad Paulinum

De Brevitate Vitae', XIII.6.
43. Cicero, *Ad Familiares*, VII.I.3.
44. Pliny the Elder, VIII.18–22.
45. Seneca, *Moral Essays*, 'Ad Paulinum De Brevitate Vitae', XIII.6, 7.
46. Friedländer, Vol.II, pp.63, 72; Jones, H. Stuart, p.369; Robert, p.320.
47. Dio Cassius, XLIII.22.
48. Friedländer, Vol.II, p.62; Balsdon (1969), p.308; Livy, LI.
49. Carcopino, p.265; Strabo, Introduction, p.xix; 6.273C.
50. Suetonius, *Claudius*, 34.
51. Humphrey, p.126.
52. Carcopino, p.234.
53. Dio Cassius, XLIII.22; Carcopino, p.255.
54. Arnott, p.149.
55. Augustus, IV.22.
56. Carcopino, p.259; Friedländer, Vol.II, pp.62ff.
57. Karl Christ, 'Rome and the Empire', in Norwich (ed.), p.54; Dio Cassius, LXVIII.15.
58. Seneca, *Epistles*, VII; Dio Cassius, LX.13.
59. Tertullian, *Apologeticus*, XV.5.
60. Nilsson, p.180.
61. Robert, pp.33–4; Bieber, pp.214–19.
62. Dio Chrysostom, XXXI.121.
63. Friedländer, Vol.IV, pp.201ff; Balsdon (1969), p.334.
64. Friedländer, Vol.IV, p.200.
65. Beare, p.11.
66. Dio Cassius, LX.30.
67. Seneca, *Epistles*, LXX.20; Dill, *Roman Society in the Last Century of the Western Empire*, p.148.
68. Balsdon (1969), p.289.
69. Friedländer, Vol.II, p.44; Dio Cassius, LIX.10.
70. Friedländer, Vol.II, p.44.
71. Dio Cassius, LIX.10.
72. Tacitus, *Annals*, XV.32; Dio Cassius, LXI.9.
73. Lecky, Vol. 1, p.281, note 6.
74. Tacitus, *Annals*, XV.32.
75. Dio Cassius, LXVI.25.
76. Statius, *Silvae*, I.6, lines 53, 54.
77. Robert, Plate XII.
78. Dio Cassius, LXXVI.16.
79. Strabo, 6.273C.
80. Suetonius, *Nero*, 12.

81. Martial, *Epigrams*, VIII.30; X.25.
82. C.J. Grysar, 'Der Römische Mimus', *Sitzungsberichte der Kaiserlichen Akademie Der Wissenschaften*, Philosophisch-Historische, Classe XII, Band 1854, pp.256, 297, who favours Lentulus; Wiseman, pp.189–98; Duff (1960), p.126; Juvenal, VIII.185–7.
83. C.J. Grysar, 'Der Römische Mimus' *Sitzungsberichte der Kaiserlichen Akademie Der Wissenschaften*, Philosophisch-Historische, Classe XII, Band 1854, p.298.
84. Suetonius, *Caligula*, 57.
85. Martial, *De Spectaculis Liber*, VII, XXI.
86. Tertullian, *Apologeticus*, XV.5.

Chapter 7 *(pp. 106–120)*

1. Tacitus, *Annals*, XIV.21.
2. Duckworth, p.73; Vince, p.73; Tacitus, *Annals*, XI.13.
3. Augustus, IV.21.
4. Harold Baldry, 'Theatre and society in Greek and Roman antiquity', in Redmond (ed.), p.19.
5. Suetonius, *Augustus*, 44.
6. Josephus, XIX.143.
7. Quintilian, III.viii.29.
8. Fowler, W. Warde, pp.341–2.
9. Tom Eden, 'Collecting Greek and Roman Coins', *Sotheby's Preview*, May/June 1990, p.20.
10. Balsdon (1969), p.245; Scullard, pp.167, 196.
11. Suetonius, *Julius*, 64; Dio Cassius, XLIII.49.
12. W.M. Murray and P.M. Petsas, 'The Spoils of Actium', *Archeology*, 1988, Vol.41, No.5, p.35.
13. Propertius [2], iii.13,47–50.
14. Alföldy, pp.61, 92; Sallust, 10.2ff.
15. Polybius, XVIII.34.
16. Mellersh, p.217; Livy, XXXIX.6.
17. Pliny the Elder, XXXIV.34.
18. Ibid., XXXIII.153.
19. Livy, XXXIV.2–4.
20. C.N. Bromehead, 'Quarrying', in Singer, C., et al (eds), Vol.II, p.27.
21. Pliny the Elder, XXXIII.57.
22. Ibid., XXXVI.4–8.
23. Balsdon (1969), p.39; Pliny the Elder, XXXVI.2.

24. Friedländer, Vol.II, p.148.
25. Ibid., pp.147–52; Balsdon (1969), pp.31, 36.
26. Mellersh, p.257.
27. Beare, p.24.
28. Carcopino, pp.108ff.
29. Ibid., p.108.
30. Mellersh, pp.269, 279; Tacitus, *Annals*, III.25.
31. Cicero, *Ad Familiares*, VIII.xii.3, xiv.4; Broughton, Vol.II, p.248.
32. Ramsey Macmullen, 'Roman Attitudes to Greek Love', *Historia*, Vol.31, 1982; F. Warren Wright, 'Cicero and the Theatre', *Smith College Classical Studies*, No.11, 1931, pp.80ff. on Chrysippus.
33. Wiseman, pp.10ff., 122–3; Ramsey Macmullen, 'Roman Attitudes to Greek Love', *Historia*, Vol.31, 1982.
34. Dover (1978), p.174.
35. Balsdon (1969), p.134.
36. Friedländer, Vol.II, p.17; Balsdon (1969), pp.280, 281.
37. Dio Cassius, LV.10.
38. Suetonius, *Tiberius*, 35.
39. Quintilian, III.vi.18.
40. Suetonius, *Augustus*, 64; Balsdon (1969), p.259.
41. Ovid, *Ars Amatoria*, I.89ff; III.633.
42. Ovid, *Tristia*, Introduction, p.xxiv.
43. Duff (1910), p.596.
44. Lucretius, IV.1037–1208; Duff (1910), p.285.
45. Duff (1910), pp.583ff.
46. Ovid, *Tristia*, II.497ff.
47. Mellersh, p.269; Zosimus, Introduction, p.lxix; IV.36.
48. Fowler, W. Warde, p.343.
49. Liebeschuetz, pp.93ff.
50. Propertius [1], IV.
51. Frank (1930), p.124.
52. Livy, XXXIX.18.
53. Fowler, W.Warde, p.70.
54. Cumont, pp.51ff; Dionysius of Halicarnassus, II.xix.3–5.
55. Taylor, Lily Ross, p.106.
56. Cumont, pp.81ff.
57. Rostovtzeff (1957), pp.38–9, 77.
58. Liebeschuetz, p.77.
59. F.Warren Wright, 'Cicero and the Theatre', *Smith College Classical Studies*, No. 11, 1931.
60. Ibid.
61. Dionysius of Halicarnassus, II.xviii.3.
62. Duff (1910), p.600.
63. Macrobius, 1.24.6, 7.
64. Ovid, *Metamorphoses* [1], XV.255–61.
65. Sorokin (1937–41), Vol.I, p.80.
66. Lucretius, V.925–1411.
67. Ibid., II.1144ff; V.330ff, 1412ff.
68. Frank (1930), pp.233.
69. Lucretius, IV.478–84.
70. Sorokin (1937–41), Vol.III, p.247.

Chapter 8 *(pp.121–145)*

1. C.N. Bromehead, 'Quarrying', in Singer, C., et al. (eds.), Vol.II, p.28; R.G. Goodchild, 'Evolution of Roman Roads', in ibid., p.500; Nilsson, p.212; Hill, p.77.
2. C.N. Bromehead, 'Quarrying', in Singer, C., et al. (eds), Vol.II, p.28.
3. R.J. Forbes, 'City Streets and Sanitation', in Singer, C., et al. (eds), Vol.II, p.529; Forbes, Vol.II, p.142.
4. Rostovtzeff (1957), p.157; Klemm, p.48; R.G. Goodchild, 'Evolution of Roman Roads', in Singer, C., et al. (eds), Vol.II, pp.500, 504; R.J. Forbes, 'City Streets and Sanitation', ibid., p.530; Hill, p.80; Vitruvius, X.ix.4.
5. Nilsson, p.210.
6. Morton, p.28.
7. Pliny the Elder, XXXVI.121 and notes; Carcopino, p.277.
8. Carcopino, p.277; Morton, p.29.
9. Jones, A.H.M. p.705.
10. Balsdon (1969), p.27; Pliny the Elder, XXXVI.121–4; Morton, p.45.
11. Hill, pp.29ff, 52ff, 69ff.; R.J. Forbes, 'Hydraulic Engineering and Sanitation', in Singer, C., et al. (eds), Vol.II, pp.665ff.
12. Hill, p.39; R.J. Forbes, 'Hydraulic Engineering and Sanitation' in Singer, C., et al. (eds), Vol.II, pp.665ff.; Forbes, Vol.I, pp.166ff.; Carcopino, p.50; Morton, p.32; Friedländer, Vol.II, p.227.
13. Forbes, Vol.I, p.169; R.J. Forbes, 'Hydraulic Engineering and Sanitation', in Singer, C., et al. (eds), Vol.II, pp.665ff.; C.N. Bromehead, 'Mining', in ibid., p.9; Friedländer, Vol.II, p.224;

Hodges, p.203.
14. Dio Cassius, LIV.25.
15. Carcopino, pp.259, 328; Friedländer, Vol.II, p.72; Suetonius, *Domitian*, 4; Dio Cassius, LXVI.25 note.
16. Friedländer, Vol.II, p.228; Nilsson, p.254; Carcopino, pp.277ff.; *Lives of the Later Caesars*, p.258; Grant, Michael (1968), p.101; Norwich (ed.), plate, p.39.
17. Arnott, p.115; Pliny the Elder, XXXVI.103.
18. Pliny the Elder, XXXVI.5, 114–15.
19. Ibid., XXXVI.6.
20. Vitruvius, V.iii.3.
21. Ibid., V.iii–ix.
22. Ibid., V.v.7.
23. Suetonius, *Augustus*, 43.
24. Dio Cassius, LIII.5.
25. Suetonius, *Augustus*, 29; Dio Cassius, XLIII.49.
26. Augustus, IV.20; Suetonius, *Tiberius*, 45; Suetonius, *Caligula*, 21; Suetonius, *Claudius*, 21; Suetonius, *Vespasian*, 19; Tacitus, *Annals*, III.72, VI.45; Dio Cassius, LX.6; LXII.18; LXVI.24.
27. Dill, *Roman Society from Nero to Marcus Aurelius*, p.220.
28. Dio Cassius, LXIII.6; Arnott, p.120; Ovid, *Ars Amatoria*, III.231.
29. Forbes, Vol.VIII, p.181.
30. Fox, p.56.
31. Vogt, p.79.
32. Martin S. Briggs, 'Building Construction', in Singer, C., et al. (eds), Vol.II, p.406; Balsdon (1969), p.209; Pliny the Elder, XXXVI.52; Friedländer, Vol.II, p.92.
33. C.N. Bromehead, 'Quarrying', in Singer, C., et al. (eds), Vol.II, p.28.
34. Pliny the Elder, XXXV.166; Martin S. Briggs, 'Building Construction', in Singer, C., et al. (eds), Vol.II, p.406.
35. Davey, pp.121–3; Martin S. Briggs, 'Building Construction', in Singer, C., et al. (eds), Vol.II, pp.407ff.
36. Martin S. Briggs, 'Building Construction', in Singer, C., et al. (eds), Vol.II, pp.418, 446; R.J. Forbes, 'City Streets and Sanitation', in ibid., p.530.
37. Forbes, Vol.V, p.181.
38. Seneca, *Epistles*, XC.25.
39. Forbes, Vol.V, p.183; Martin S. Briggs,

'Building Construction', in Singer, C., et al. (eds), Vol.II, pp.415ff.; Carcopino p.46; Davey, p.189; Pliny the Elder, XXXVI.189; Martial, *Epigrams*, VIII.14, 68; Pliny the Younger, *Letters*, II.17.
40. Seneca, *Epistles*, XC.25.
41. Forbes, Vol.VI, pp.40, 48; Davey, p.197; Martin S. Briggs, 'Building Construction', in Singer, C., et al. (eds), Vol.II, p.419; Carcopino, p.48.
42. Pliny the Elder, XXXVI.106; Ovid, *Fasti*, Appendix, p.437; Carcopino, p.51; Friedländer, Vol.IV, p.284; R.J. Forbes, 'City Streets and Sanitation', in Singer, C., et al. (eds), Vol.II, p.530.
43. Jones, A.H.M. p.735.
44. Tacitus, *Annals*, XV.44.
45. Dio Cassius, LVIII.19.
46. Suetonius, *Gaius Caligula*, 18.
47. *Scriptores Historiae Augustae*, 'Severus Alexander', XXIV.
48. Friedländer, Vol.II, p.13; R.J. Forbes, 'City Streets and Sanitation', in Singer, C., et al. (eds), Vol.II, p.531; Beckmann, Vol.II, pp.173ff.
49. Rostovtzeff (1957), p.143.
50. Balsdon (1969), p.225.
51. Rostovtzeff (1941), p.868.
52. Apuleius, *Apologia*, 37; Beckmann, Vol.II, p.186; Pliny the Elder, VII.60.
53. Rostovtzeff (1941), pp.371, 539, 698.
54. Forbes, Vol.V, p.179.
55. Rostovtzeff (1957), p.71.
56. Forbes, Vol.V, pp.147ff.; D.B. Harden, 'Glass', in Singer, C., et al. (eds), Vol.II, pp.322–37; Walbank, p.85; Pliny the Elder, XXXVI.199; *Scriptores Historiae Augustae*, 'Aurelian', XLV.
57. *Scriptores Historiae Augustae*, 'The Two Gallieni', XVII.
58. Marcus Chown, 'Glass in Antiquity', *New Scientist*, 18 February 1988.
59. *Lives of the Later Caesars*, p.174; Dal Maso, p.76.
60. Lucretius, IV.74–9; VI.109; Pliny the Elder, XIX.23.
61. Friedländer, Vol.II, p.8.
62. Martial, *Epigrams*, XIV.29; Propertius [1] III; IV.
63. Pliny the Elder, XIX.23; Dio Cassius, LXIII.6.
64. Ovid, *Metamorphoses* [2], III.iii; Virgil,

Georgics, III.24.

65. Horace, *Satires*, I.ii.101; Seneca, *Moral Essays*, 'Ad Helviam Matrem De Consolatione', XII.6.

66. Rostovtzeff (1941), p.564; R. Patterson, 'Fibres', in Singer, C., et al. (eds), Vol.II, pp.193–9; Forbes, Vol.IV, p.231; Friedländer, Vol.II, pp.173–9.

67. Forbes, Vol.V, p.185; Pliny the Elder, XXXIII.130; XXXVI.193; Beckmann, Vol.II, pp.60ff.

68. Pliny the Elder, XXXIII.53, 152; XXV.158ff.; Carcopino, p.47.

69. R.J. Forbes, 'Food', in Singer, C., et al. (eds), Vol.II, pp.134–6; Forbes, Vol.III, p.100; Vol.VI, pp.110, 111; Balsdon (1969), p.43.

70. Balsdon (1969), pp.39, 51; Livy, XXXIX.6.

71. R.J. Forbes, 'Food', in Singer, C., et al. (eds), Vol.II, p.121; Friedländer, Vol.II, pp.166ff.; Rostovtzeff (1957), p.564, note 23.

72. Pliny the Elder, XVIII.112.

73. R.J. Forbes, 'Food', in Singer, C., et al. (eds), Vol.II, p.121; R.J. Forbes, 'Power', in ibid., p.600.

74. Rostovtzeff (1957), pp.36–74, 169; R.J. Forbes, 'City Streets and Sanitation', in Singer, C., et al. (eds), Vol.II, p.531; Forbes, Vol.VI, pp.130, 154, 166; Pliny the Elder, XXXVII 198–200.

75. R.J. Forbes, 'Power', in Singer, C., et al. (eds), Vol.II, p.591; Carcopino, pp.69ff.; Rostovtzeff (1957), pp.54, 58; Friedländer, Vol.II, p.228.

76. Carcopino, p.86.

77. Dio Cassius, LXI.18; LXVI.25; Friedländer, Vol.II, pp.15ff.; Statius, I.vi, 'The kalends of December', lines 9–27.

78. Bertrand Gille, 'Machines', in Singer, C., et al. (eds), Vol.II, p.636.

79. Ibid., pp.632ff.; A.G. Drachmann, 'Notes on Ancient Cranes', in Singer, C., et al. (eds), p.659; C.N. Bromehead, 'Mining', in ibid., p.7; Derry and Williams, p.22.

80. Pliny the Elder, XXXVI, 117–20.

81. Suetonius, *Nero*, 31; see also J. Ward Perkins, 'Nero's Golden House', *Antiquity*, XXX, 1956.

82. Seneca, *Epistles*, LXXXVIII.21ff.

83. Martial, *De Spectaculis Liber*, XXI.

84. Apuleius, *The Golden Ass*, p.263.

85. *Scriptores Historiae Augustae*, 'Carus, Carinus and Numerian', XIX.

86. *The Greek Anthology*, IX, no.418, Loeb, Vol.3, p.232, 1918.

87. R.J. Forbes, 'Power', in Singer, C., et al. (eds), Vol.II, pp.593ff.; Hill, p.159.

88. R.J. Forbes, 'Power', in Singer, C., et al. (eds), Vol.II, pp.593ff.; Forbes, Vol.II, pp.95ff.; Jones, A.H.M. p.699; *Past Worlds: The Times Atlas of Archaeology*, p.179.

89. Hodges, p.196; Forbes, Vol.II, p.93; Vol.VII, p.176.

90. Forbes, Vol.VIII, p.110.

91. Hodges, p.15.

92. Suetonius, *Vespasian*, 18.

93. Walbank, p.44; R.J. Forbes, 'Power', in Singer, C., et al. (eds), Vol.II, p.591; Rostovtzeff (1957), pp.349ff.; Jones, A.H.M., p.1045; Seneca, *Epistles*, XC.11ff., 24ff.

94. Clark, pp.3–4.

Chapter 9 *(pp.146–162)*

1. Van Berchem, p.15. Van Berchem, together with Rickman, is the source for much of the ensuing information.

2. Carcopino, p.28; Rickman, pp.173–4.

3. Dio Cassius, XLIII.21.

4. Veyne, p.454.

5. Van Berchem, pp.32ff; Rickman, pp.182–4, 192–3.

6. Sandys, p.180.

7. *Scriptores Historiae Augustae*, 'Severus', XXIII.

8. Van Berchem, pp.98, 102, 178; Dill, *Roman Society in the Last Century of the Western Empire*, p.122; Jones, A.H.M., pp.702ff.; *Scriptores Historiae Augustae*, 'Aurelian', XLVIII.

9. Van Berchem, pp.120ff. Pliny the Younger, *Panegyricus*, 25 note.

10. Dio Cassius, LXIX.16.

11. *Lives of the Later Caesars*, p.119.

12. Cameron (1973), p.13, note 71.

13. Grant, Michael (1968), p.52; Van Berchem, p.102; Jones, A.H.M., pp.84, 687; Eusebius, VII.xxi.

14. Rostovtzeff (1957), pp.146–7.

15. Carter and Dale, pp.130ff.; Rickman,

pp.36–7.
16. Carter and Dale, pp.143–4.
17. Lucretius, II.1160ff.; Carter and Dale, pp.130–40; Rostovtzeff (1957), p.359.
18. Derry and Williams, p.19; Rickman, pp.123–4.
19. Van Berchem, p.80.
20. Rickman, p.68.
21. Van Berchem, p.82.
22. Tacitus, *Annals*, I.79.
23. Rostovtzeff (1957), p.125.
24. Jones, A.H.M., p.851.
25. Frank (ed.), Vol.I, p.234, quoting Appian, 'The Civil Wars', I.I.7,8.
26. Nilsson, p.260.
27. Carcopino, p.74.
28. Seneca, *Moral Essays*, 'Ad Helviam Matrem De Consolatione', XVI.4.
29. Balsdon (1969), p.84.
30. Polybius, XXXVI.17.
31. Hopkins, p.96.
32. Rostovtzeff (1957), pp. 111, 182, 359.
33. Luttwak, p.127.
34. Forbes, Vol.IX, p.159.
35. Vitruvius, VIII.vi.10,11; Pliny the Elder, XXXIV.167,176; Forbes, Vol.I p.173.
36. Balsdon (1969), p.83.
37. *British Medical Journal*, Vol.301, 10 November 1990.
38. Mandell/Douglas/Bennett, p.1195.
39. Grmek, p.145.
40. Plutarch, *Sulla*, 36.
41. Suetonius, *Tiberius*, 34.
42. Pliny the Elder, XXVI.2, 3.
43. Martial, *Epigrams*, XI.98.
44. Major, p.15.
45. Hippocrates, 'Aphorisms', III.21.
46. Gordon, pp.528ff.
47. *Oxford Textbook of Medicine*, 5.387; Mandell/Douglas/Bennett, p.1323.
48. *National Geographic Research*, Vol.8, No.4, Autumn 1992, pp.446–59.
49. Ammianus Marcellinus, XIV.6.23.
50. *Oxford Textbook of Medicine*, 5.360, 5.361; see also *The Independent*, 29 May 1990.
51. Tacitus, *Annals*, XII.5.
52. Suetonius, *Claudius*, 26.
53. Seneca, *Moral Essays*, 'Ad Helviam Matrem De Consolatione', XVI.4; 'De Beneficiis', III.16.
54. Tacitus, *Germania*, 19.
55. Nilsson, p.287; Walbank, p.63;

Rostovtzeff (1957), p.375.
56. Nilsson, p.287; Starr, p.113.
57. Balsdon (1979), p.52.
58. Nilsson, p.309.
59. Macmullen (1981), p.114.
60. Rostovtzeff (1957), p.397.
61. Tertullian, *Apologeticus*, V.2; XXI.24.
62. Ibid., XXIV.
63. Pliny the Younger, *Letters*, X.96.
64. Fraser, P.M., Vol.1, p.812.
65. Macmullen (1981), p.67.
66. Grant, Michael (1982), p.215 (Lucan, *Pharsalia: The Civil War*, VII, lines 445–7, tr.Grant).
67. Bieber, p.213; Taylor, Lily Ross, p.241.
68. Grant, Michael (1968), p.163.
69. Macmullen (1981), p.107.
70. Sorokin (1937–41), Vol.II, p.77.
71. Macmullen (1981), p.63.
72. Juvenal, XIII.34ff.
73. Duff (1960), p.484.
74. Mellersh, p.245.
75. Taylor, Lily Ross, p.64.
76. Grant, Michael (1968), p.72.
77. Rostovtzeff (1957), p.149.
78. Dill, *Roman Society from Nero to Marcus Aurelius*, p.220; Fox, pp.54ff.
79. Fox, pp.54, 79.
80. Cameron (1973), p.174.
81. Vogt, p.20.
82. Grant, Michael (1968), p.250.
83. Macmullen (1967), p.193.
84. Grant, Michael (1968), p.62.
85. Mellersh, p.343.
86. Macmullen (1967), pp.195ff.; Rostovtzeff (1957), pp.422ff.
87. Luttwak, pp.128–9.
88. Ibid., p.129.
89. Fox, pp.572–3.
90. Luttwak, p.128.
91. Rostovtzeff (1957), p.533; Nilsson, pp.272–7.
92. Rostovtzeff (1957), p.424.
93. Fox, pp.574, 582.
94. Rostovtzeff (1957), pp.392, 464.
95. Ibid., pp.484, 517, 735; Starr, pp.151, 159.
96. Rostovtzeff (1957), p.498; Vogt, p.26; Walbank, p.75.
97. Rostovtzeff (1957), p.484.
98. Ibid., p.424; Jones, A.H.M., p.1039.
99. Walbank, p.80.
100. Dill, *Roman Society in the Last Century of the Western Empire*, p.233; Jones,

A.H.M., pp.700, 1042.
101. Rostovtzeff (1957), pp.470ff.; Hill, p.80.
102. Balsdon (1969), p.354 note.
103. Vogt, p.77; Rostovtzeff (1957), pp.343, 413, 470.
104. Vogt, p.77.
105. Mellersh, pp.365, 377.

Chapter 10 (pp.163–186)

1. Sorokin (1937–41), Vol.II, pp.77–8, quoting F. Cumont, *After Life in Roman Paganism* (Yale University Press, New Haven, 1922), pp.11–12; see also Jones, A.H.M., pp.957ff.
2. Cumont, p.43.
3. Fox, p.74.
4. Macmullen (1981), p.127.
5. Balsdon (1969), p.144.
6. *Lives of the Later Caesars*, p.134; Dio Cassius, LXXII.32.
7. Finley, 'The Silent Women of Rome', p.134.
8. Apuleius, *The Golden Ass*, pp.284–6.
9. Vogt, p.31; Grant, Michael (1968), pp.139–56; Starr, pp.137–8; Mellersh, pp.349, 357.
10. Macmullen (1967), pp.108ff.
11. Walbank, p.96, quoting E. Kornemann, *Römische Geschichte*.
12. Macmullen (1967), pp.108–18.
13. Ibid., pp.120ff.; Macmullen (1981), pp.70ff.
14. Dill, *Roman Society in the Last Century of the Western Empire*, p.51.
15. Cumont, p.205.
16. Dill, *Roman Society from Nero to Marcus Aurelius*, p.620.
17. Cumont, p.140.
18. Macmullen (1981), p.118.
19. Cumont, p.66.
20. Dill, *Roman Society from Nero to Marcus Aurelius*, pp.585ff.
21. Cumont, p.149.
22. Ibid., p.150.
23. Ibid., pp.157–9.
24. Fox, pp.425ff., 595ff.; Mellersh, pp.357, 361, 371.
25. Fox, p.617.
26. Zosimus, Introduction, p.lxix; IV.36.
27. Bingham, XVI.iv.8.
28. Fox, p.667.
29. Jones, A.H.M., p.78.

30. Dill, *Roman Society in the Last Century of the Western Empire*, p.29; Vogt, p.162.
31. Prudentius, *Contra Orationem Symmachi*, p.78 note; see also Introduction, p.xi.
32. Jones, A.H.M., pp.168, 938–9; Fox, pp.71–2; Vogt, pp.158–64.
33. Jones, A.H.M., p.934.
34. Zosimus, IV.33.
35. Dio Cassius, LXXII.29; *Scriptores Historiae Augustae*, 'Marcus Aurelius', XI, XII.
36. Tatian, 23; Tertullian, *On Idolatry*, XI.
37. Hippolytus, p.25.
38. Bingham, XVI.x.14; Tertullian, *De Spectaculis*, XIX.
39. Cyprian, 'Epistle to Donatus', 7.
40. Chrysostom, *Homilies on Corinthians I*, XII.10.
41. Lactantius, VI.20.
42. Bingham, XVI.x.13.
43. Ibid., XI.v.7; *Oxford Dictionary of the Christian Church*, p.73.
44. Augustine, *Confessions*, VI.viii.
45. G. Ville, 'Les Jeux de Gladiateurs dans l'Empire Chrétien', *Mélanges d'Archéologie et d'Histoire de l'École Française de Rome*, 1960, pp.273–335.
46. Balsdon (1969), p.251.
47. Bingham, XI.v.8.
48. Dill, *Roman Society in the Last Century of the Western Empire*, p.29; *Lives of the Later Caesars*, p.254 note.
49. Augustine, *Confessions*, IV.ii.3.
50. Ammianus Marcellinus, XXIX.2.
51. Vogt, p.128; Mellersh, p.391; Grant, Michael (1968), pp.193ff.
52. Rousselle, p.140.
53. Fox, p.603.
54. Rousselle, pp.193, 195, 198.
55. Ammianus Marcellinus, XVI.viii.13; Augustine, *Epistle 138 to Marcellinus*, quoted in *City of God* [1], Vol.I, Preface, p.lxv.
56. I Corinthians 6:19.
57. Liebeschuetz, p.295; Vogt, p.105.
58. Jones, A.H.M., pp.92, 974–5.
59. Ammianus Marcellinus, XXVIII.1.16.
60. Chorikios, 'In Defence of the Mime', VIII.23, *Revue de Philologie*, New Series, Vol.I, 1877.
61. Jones, A.H.M., p.976.

62. Bingham, XVI.xi.9.
63. Martial, *Epigrams*, IX.6.
64. Seneca, *Epistles*, XLVII.11.
65. Carcopino, p.70; Dio Cassius, LXVIII.2.
66. Vogt, p.201.
67. Jones, A.H.M., p.851; Suetonius, *Domitian*, 7.
68. Quintilian, IV.2.68–9.
69. Suetonius, *Domitian*, 8.
70. Suetonius, *Gaius Caligula*, 36; Suetonius, *Galba*, 22; Suetonius, *Vitellius*, 12; Suetonius, *Titus*, 7; *Lives of the Later Caesars*, pp.145, 163ff., 293; Dio Cassius LXII.13, LXXX.13; Tacitus, *Annals*, XV.37; Ammianus Marcellinus, XXXI.9.5; see also Ramsey Macmullen, 'Roman Attitudes to Greek Love', *Historia*, Vol. 31, 1982, pp.484–501.
71. *Scriptores Historiae Augustae*, 'Clodius', XI; 'Severus Alexander', XXIV; 'Heliogabalus', XXXII.
72. Bingham, XVI.xi.9.
73. Brown, Peter, p.383.
74. Procopius, xi.34ff.
75. Tertullian, *De Spectaculis*, XVII.
76. Tatian, 22; Cyprian (Pseudo-Cyprian), 'On the Public Shows', p.227.
77. Tertullian, *De Spectaculis*, XVII.
78. Among the many sources are: Clement of Alexandria, 'Public Spectacles', III.xi; Tatian, 'Attack on Acting, Dancing and Mime', 22; Tertullian, *De Spectaculis*; Cyprian, 'To Donatus', 'To Euchratius' and (Pseudo-Cyprian) 'On the Public Shows'; Lactantius, VI.xx; Chrysostom, *Homilies on the Gospel of St Matthew*, VI.10; LXVI.3, LXVIII.4; Chrysostom, *Homilies on Thessalonians I*, V.4; Chrysostom, *Homilies on St John*, I,6; XVIII,44; Chrysostom, *To the People of Antioch*, XV.11.
79. Cyprian (Pseudo-Cyprian), 'On the Public Shows', p.229.
80. Bingham, XI.v.9,vii.2; XVI.iv.10; Hodkin, Vol.I, p.930.
81. Hippolytus, p.25.
82. Bingham, XI.v.6.
83. Jones, A.H.M., p.700.
84. Dill, *Roman Society in the Last Century of the Western Empire*, p.57.
85. Dio Cassius, LIX.29; LX.7.
86. Ibid., LVI.17,19; Tacitus, *Annals*,

XIV.20.
87. Tacitus, *Annals*, XIV.9.
88. Juvenal, VIII.193.
89. Lucian [1], 'Of Pantomime', 5.
90. *Scriptores Historiae Augustae, passim.*
91. Pliny the Younger, *Letters*, V.19.
92. Vogt, pp.134, 139; Dill, *Roman Society in the Last Century of the Western Empire*, p.34.
93. Macrobius, 3.14.11.
94. Balsdon (1969), p.251; Jones, A.H.M., p.939.
95. Jones, A.H.M., p.35; Alföldy, p.210.
96. Zosimus, II.vii.2; see also Introduction, pp.xxviiiff.
97. Balsdon (1969), pp.245ff.; Carcopino, pp.226ff.; Friedländer, Vol.II, pp.11ff.
98. Bingham, XVI.iv.17.
99. Ibid.
100. Ibid., XVI.xi.12.
101. Augustine, *Confessions*, IV.i.
102. Salvianus, VI.
103. Augustine, *Seventeen Short Treatises*, 'Of the Catechizing of the Unlearned', paragraph 48.
104. Chrysostom, *Homilies on St John*, XI.i.
105. Salvianus, VI.7.
106. Chrysostom, *Homilies on Acts of the Apostles*, XLIV.
107. Bingham, XXI.i.22.
108. Chrysostom, *Homilies on the Gospel of St Matthew*, I.15; LXVI.3.
109. Prudentius, *Crowns of Martyrdom*, X.220.
110. Augustine, *City of God* [1], XIV.24.
111. C.J. Grysar, 'Der Römische Mimus', *Sitzungsberichte der Kaiserlichen Akademie Der Wissenschaften*, Philosophisch-Historische, Classe XII, Band 1854, pp.318–19.
112. *Scriptores Historiae Augustae*, 'Heliogabalus', XXV.
113. Cyprian (Pseudo-Cyprian), 'On the Public Shows', 6; Lactantius, VI.xx.
114. Augustine, *City of God* [1], II.26; [2] VI.10; VII.21.
115. Chorikios, 'In Defence of the Mime', *Revue de Philologie*, New Series, Vol.I, 1877.
116. Bingham, XVI.xi.9.
117. Mannix, pp.58–9 and Author's Note on

final (unnumbered) page.

118. Lucian [2], Vol.VIII (Pseudo-Lucian), 'Lucius or the Ass'.
119. C.J. Grysar, 'Über die Pantomimen der Römer', *Rheinisches Museum für Philologie*, 1834, p.51.
120. Procopius, ix.20.
121. Macmullen (1981), p.21.
122. Bingham, XVI.xi.12; Jones, A.H.M., pp.561, 977, 1021; Chrysostom, *Homilies on the Gospel of St Matthew*, VII.7.
123. C.J. Grysar, 'Der Römische Mimus', *Sitzungsberichte der Kaiserlichen Akademie Der Wissenschaften*, Philosophisch-Historische, Classe XII, Band 1854, p.253.
124. Bingham, XXI.i.22.
125. Salvianus, VI.7, note 26.
126. Jones, A.H.M., p.977; Cameron (1976), p.226.
127. Chorikios, 'In Defence of the Mime', XIII.5, *Revue de Philologie*, New Series, Vol.1, 1877.
128. Ibid., pp.212ff.
129. Jones, A.H.M., p.270; Balsdon (1969), p.285.
130. Jones, A.H.M., p.539.
131. Ibid., p.285.
132. C.J. Grysar, 'Der Römische Mimus', *Sitzungsberichte der Kaiserlichen Akademie Der Wissenschaften*, Philosophisch-Historische, Classe XII, Band 1854, p.336.
133. Ibid.
134. Dill, *Roman Society in the Last Century of the Western Empire*, p.333.
135. Salvianus, VI.8; see also Jones, A.H.M., p.735.
136. C.J. Grysar, 'Der Römische Mimus', *Sitzungsberichte der Kaiserlichen Akademie Der Wissenschaften*, Philosophisch-Historische, Classe XII, Band 1854, p.332.
137. Hodkin, Vol.IV, p.548.
138. C.J. Grysar, 'Der Römische Mimus', *Sitzungsberichte der Kaiserlichen Akademie Der Wissenschaften*, Philosophisch-Historische, Classe XII, Band 1854, p.336; Friedländer, Vol.II, p.21.

Chapter 11 *(pp.187–204)*

1. Zosimus, V.vii.2.
2. Silius Italicus, XI.410–82.
3. Dill, *Roman Society in the Last Century of the Western Empire*, p.148.
4. Epistle 126 to Marcellinus and Anapsychia: J.P. Migne, *Patrologia Latina*, Vol.22, Col.1085. Translation by McCracken in Introduction to Augustine, *City of God* [1], p.lxxv.
5. Orosius, III.20; V.1,10 (for e.g.).
6. Ibid., II.19; IV.21; VII.39ff.; Dill, *Roman Society in the Last Century of the Western Empire*, p.305.
7. Augustine, *City of God* [1], I.32,33.
8. Salvianus, VI.12.
9. Ibid., VII.20–2; Dill, *Roman Society in the Last Century of the Western Empire*, p.305.
10. Vogt, p.249.
11. Salvianus, VI.8.
12. Ibid., VII.1, note 2.
13. Ibid., VII.11.
14. Sidonius, II, to Agricola.
15. Salvianus, V.5.
16. Aristophanes, *The Clouds*, l.1051–3.
17. Balsdon (1969), p.27.
18. Seneca, *Epistles*, 86.
19. Ferrill, p.129, quoting Vegetius, *De Re Militari*.
20. Ibid.
21. Ibid., pp.153, 168–9.
22. Ibid., p.56.
23. Finley, p.146.
24. Rostovtzeff (1957), p.467.
25. Jones, A.H.M., p.1058; Alföldy, p.217.
26. Nilsson, pp.309ff.
27. Sidonius, V.
28. Orosius, V.2.
29. Nilsson, p.305; Macmullen (1967), p.336, note 1.
30. Dill, *Roman Society in the Last Century of the Western Empire*, p.295; Ferrill, p.59.
31. Ammianus Marcellinus, XXXI.4.
32. Ferrill, p.59; Ammianus Marcellinus, XXXI.4.9 note.
33. Ammianus Marcellinus, XXXI.4–13; Ferrill, pp.59ff.
34. Jones, A.H.M., p.157.
35. Ferrill, p.75; Jones, A.H.M., p.1038.
36. Ferrill, p.144; Jones, A.H.M., p.1038.

37. Ferrill, p.84.
38. Ibid., p.75.
39. Vogt, pp.223–5.
40. Ferrill, p.160.
41. Vogt, p.210.
42. Starr, p.165.
43. Ibid., Jones, A.H.M., p.1043.
44. Dill, *Roman Society in the Last Century of the Western Empire*, p.249.
45. Ibid., p.268.
46. Friedländer, Vol.II, pp.10–11; Dill, *Roman Society in the Last Century of the Western Empire*, pp.249–76.
47. Dill, *Roman Society in the Last Century of the Western Empire*, p.276.
48 Salvianus, V.4, note10; V.5.
49. Vogt, p.231.
50. Ibid., pp.249, 256.
51. Ibid., p.255.
52. Ibid., pp.235, 269.
53. Dill, *Roman Society in the Last Century of the Western Empire*, p.148; R.G. Goodchild, 'Roads and Land Travel', in Singer, C., et al. (eds), Vol.II, p.500.
54. Macmullen (1967), p.200.
55. Dill, *Roman Society in the Last Century of the Western Empire*, p.241; Vogt, p.198.
56. Paulys, *Real-Encyclopädie*, Neue Bearbeitung, 2 Reihe, Bd.4 s. 1362/1363.
57. Dill, *Roman Society in the Last Century of the Western Empire*, p.241.
58. Macmullen (1967), pp.163, 167.
59. Dill, *Roman Society in the Last Century of the Western Empire*, pp.148, 239.
60. Bury, Vol.I, p.256.
61. Jones, A.H.M., p.825; Dill, *Roman Society in the Last Century of the Western Empire*, p.334; Ferrill, p.138.
62. Fox, p.47; Jones, A.H.M., p.1040; Mellersh, p.403.
63. Jones, A.H.M., pp.687, 1045.
64. Sidonius, *Epistles*, I.10 (to Campanianus).
65. Vogt, p.257; *Excerpta Valesiana*, Part 2, 12.67–71.
66. *Excerpta Valesiana*, Part 2, 14.83.
67. Vogt, p.254.
68. Ibid., pp.225–8.
69. Mellersh, p.421; Jones, A.H.M., p.533.
70. Jones, A.H.M., pp.711, 933.
71. Lecky, Vol.II, pp.84–5.
72. Ibid., pp.236–8.
73. Vogt, p.282.
74. Ibid., p.207.
75. Forbes, Vol.II, p.99; see also Lynn White, 'Cultural Climates and Technological Advance in the Middle Ages', *Viator*, 1971, Vol.2, pp.187–8.
76. Fox, p.44.
77. Ambrose, *Hexaemeron*, Lib.IV, Caput IV, 12–19 (*Patrologia Latina*, Migne, Vol.14, Col.206).
78. Pliny the Elder, II.161.
79. Lactantius, III.24.
80. Mellersh, p.451.
81. Ammianus Marcellinus, XXIX.2.4 note.
82. Canfora, p.196.
83. Ibid., p.192.
84. Ibid., p.87.
85. Ibid., pp.35, 83, 98, 99.

Chapter 12 (pp.205–219)

1. Sorokin (1941), p.234.
2. C.N. Bromehead, 'Quarrying', in Singer, C., et al. (eds), Vol.II, pp.28, 32; Martin S. Briggs, 'Building Construction', ibid., p.422; R.J. Forbes, 'City Streets and Sanitation', ibid., p.531; Hill, p.71; Davey, p.202; Forbes, Vol.V, p.181.
3. Friedländer, Vol.II, p.225; *The Independent*, 17 May 1988.
4. R.J. Forbes, 'City Streets and Sanitation', in Singer, C., et al. (eds), Vol.II, p.531; Bryan Ward-Perkins, 'The Medieval Centuries', in Norwich (ed.), p.84.
5. 'Lives of the Holy Abbots', in Bede (1843–4), Vol.IV, p.367; Davey, p.190.
6. Davey, p.202.
7. E.M. Jope, 'Ceramics – Medieval', in Singer, C., et al. (eds), Vol.II, p.284.
8. Bertrand Gille, 'Machines', in Singer, C., et al. (eds), Vol.II, p.641.
9. R.W. Symonds, 'Furniture – Post-Roman', in Singer, C., et al. (eds), Vol. II, pp.240–1.
10. Walbank, p.122.
11. E.M. Jope, 'Agricultural Implements', in Singer, C., et al. (eds), Vol.II, pp.87–8; R.J. Forbes, 'Food and Drink', ibid., pp.127, 136, 141; F. Sherwood Taylor and Charles Singer,

'Prescientific Industrial Chemistry', ibid., p.355; Herbert Maryon, 'Fine Metal Work', ibid., pp.450–1; E.M. Jope, 'Vehicles and Harness', ibid., pp.557, 561.

12. Mellersh, p.433; Gimpel (1988), p.32; Jones, E.L., pp.48–9.
13. Bryan Ward-Perkins, 'The Medieval Centuries', in Norwich (ed.)., p.101.
14. Sorokin (1937–41), Vol.III, p.222.
15. Hill, pp.2, 199.
16. Watt, pp.35–6.
17. See O'Leary, Chapters IV and V.
18. O'Leary, p.19.
19. Martin Plessner, 'The Natural Sciences and Medicine', in Schacht and Bosworth (eds), p.428.
20. Watt, p.36.
21. Ibid.
22. O'Leary, pp.95, 151ff., 176–81.
23. Taylor, F. Sherwood, pp.7–17, 230.
24. Holmyard, pp.15–31; Taylor, F. Sherwood, pp.227–30, 235.
25. Holmyard, pp.88–9.
26. Watt, pp.58–9.
27. Holmyard, p.108; O'Leary, p.166.
28. Mackay, p.81.
29. Watt, p.80.
30. Gimpel (1988), p.174, quoting Haskins, p.258.
31. Georges C. Anawati, 'Philosophy, Theology and Mysticism', in Schacht and Bosworth (eds), pp.384–6.
32. Gimpel (1988), p.182; Georges C. Anawati, 'Philosophy, Theology and Mysticism', in Schacht and Bosworth (eds), p.385.
33. Holmyard, p.107.
34. Watt, p.61.
35. Ibid., pp.64–5.
36. Gimpel (1988), p.183.
37. Holmyard, pp.121–2.
38. Gimpel (1988), p.198.
39. Augustine, *City of God* [1], XXII.24.
40. *Viator*, 1971, Vol.2, pp.189–91, 199.
41. Jones, E.L., p.54; Gimpel (1988), pp.13–14, 66–7; R.J. Forbes, 'Power', in Singer, C., et al. (eds), Vol.II, pp.608ff.
42. Bertrand Gille, 'Machines', in Singer, C., et al. (eds), Vol.II, p.650.
43. Jones, E.L., p.54; Gimpel (1988), pp.17, 25; Hill, p.172; R.J. Forbes, 'Power', in

Singer, C., et al. (eds), Vol.II, p.616ff.; 'Rex Wailes,' A Note on Windmills', ibid., pp.623ff.

44. R.J. Forbes, 'Power', in Singer, C., et al. (eds), Vol.II, p.609.
45. Gimpel (1988), p.81; *The Times*, 21 February 1991.
46. R.J. Forbes, 'Hydraulic Engineering and Sanitation', in Singer, C., et al. (eds), Vol.II, p.691; Gimpel (1988), p.85.
47. Gimpel (1988), pp.82–3.
48. E.M. Jope, 'Ceramics – Medieval', in Singer, C., et al. (eds), Vol.II, p.304.
49. Davey, p.67.
50. Martin S. Briggs, 'Building Construction', in Singer, C., et al. (eds), Vol.II, p.438.
51. Forbes, Vol.V, p.181; R.J. Forbes, 'Food and Drink', in Singer, C., et al. (eds), Vol.II, p.128; D.B. Hardin, 'Glass and Glazes', ibid., p.326; Martin S. Briggs, 'Building Construction', ibid., pp.429, 443; Taylor, F. Sherwood, pp.133–7.
52. Davey, p.202; Jones, E.L., p.55.
53. Gimpel (1988), p.147; Watt, pp.20–5; Jones, E.L., pp.58, 73; R. Patterson, 'Spinning and Weaving', in Singer, C., et al. (eds), Vol.II, p.202; R.J. Forbes, 'Power', ibid., p.610; C. Singer, 'Epilogue', ibid., pp.770–1; McLean, p.2.
54. Tatian, p18.
55. Balsdon (1969), pp.93, 132.
56. Jones, A.H.M., pp.708, 735, 1012.
57. Sumption, p.79.
58. Gregory of Tours, p.3 and *passim*.
59. Sumption, pp.76, 84.
60. Martin Plessner, 'The Natural Sciences and Medicine', in Schacht and Bosworth (eds), p.448.
61. Holmyard, pp.92–6; Watt, pp.38, 66–8.
62. Sumption, pp.76, 80, 112, 126.
63. Ibid., p.80.
64. Ibid., pp.66–9; Augustine, *City of God* [1], XXI.7.
65. Sumption, pp.22–52.
66. Ibid., p.116.
67. C.N. Bromehead, 'Mining and Quarrying', in Singer, C., et al. (eds), Vol.II, p.32.
68. Gimpel (1983), p.97.
69. Hill, p.71; Jusserand, p.49.

70. Jones, E.L., p.54; Martin S. Briggs, 'Building Construction', in Singer, C., et al. (eds), Vol.II, p.426.
71. Gimpel (1988), p.134; Vitruvius, Introduction, pp.xv, xvi.
72. Gimpel (1983), pp.82–3.
73. Gimpel (1988), pp.7, 116.
74. Sumption, pp.92, 135.
75. Mantzius, Vol.II, p.121.

Chapter 13 (pp.220–242)

1. C.J. Grysar, 'Der Römische Mimus', *Sitzungsberichte der Kaiserlichen Akademie Der Wissenschaften*, Philosophisch-Historische, Classe XII, Band 1854, p.333.
2. Prynne, pp.545–97.
3. C.J. Grysar, 'Der Römische Mimus', *Sitzungsberichte der Kaiserlichen Akademie Der Wissenschaften*, Philosophisch-Historische, Classe XII, Band 1854, pp.334–5. Grysar dates the wedding to 1054 and numbers Henry II not III, but this appears to be the nuptials to which he refers.
4. Prynne, p.471.
5. Southworth, pp.12–15.
6. Ibid., p.16, note 8.
7. C.J. Grysar, 'Der Römische Mimus', *Sitzungsberichte der Kaiserlichen Akademie Der Wissenschaften*, Philosophisch-Historische, Classe XII, Band 1854, pp.335–6.
8. Merchant, pp.20–1.
9. Berthold, pp.230–1.
10. Cohen, Gustave, p.28; Axton, p.66.
11. Berthold, pp.291–2.
12. Ibid., pp.236, 250, 299.
13. Ibid., p.276; Mantzius, Vol.II, pp.8–14.
14. Mantzius, Vol.II, p.56.
15. Wickham, pp.42–3.
16. Cohen, Gustave, pp.198–9.
17. Southworth, p.3.
18. Lindsay, p.124.
19. Southworth, p.85.
20. Rutherford, p.218.
21. Chaytor, p.13.
22. Lindsay, pp.127–8; Rutherford, p.212.
23. Rutherford, p.204.
24. Chaytor, p.135.
25. Lindsay, p.272.
26. Ibid., pp.217–18, 272.

27. Rutherford, p.163.
28. Lindsay, p.224.
29. Ibid., p.225.
30. Ibid., p.215; Topsfield, pp.250–1.
31. Cohen, Gustave, p.63.
32. Mantzius, Vol.II, pp.123–4. For a full account of these two plays, see Grace Frank, *Medieval French Drama* (Clarendon Press, Oxford, 1954), Chapter XXII.
33. Sorokin (1937–41), Vol.I, pp.618–27.
34. Berthold, pp.236, 242–4.
35. Jones, E.L., p.49; Mantzius, Vol.II, pp.82–3.
36. Pollard, p.xxv.
37. Gayley, p.96.
38. Macgowan, et al., p.35; Berthold, pp.242–4, 251, 259; Mantzius, Vol.II, pp.81–2, 87–8.
39. Elie Konigson, 'Religious drama and urban society in France at the end of the Middle Ages', in Redmond (ed.), p.25.
40. Berthold, pp.236–9.
41. Ibid., p.264.
42. Bradbrook, p.20; Axton, pp.55ff.
43. Axton, *passim*; see also Wickham, Part II, Chapter 4.
44. Cohen, Gustave, p.273.
45. Mantzius, Vol.II, p.30.
46. Tuchmann, p.312.
47. Gayley, pp.148–9.
48. Cohen, Gustave, pp.211, 226–7.
49. Ibid., pp.206–7; Berthold, p.301.
50. Gayley, pp.284–5; Southworth, pp.68, 81, 146.
51. Mantzius, Vol.II, p.182ff.; Bradbrook, p.97; Southworth, p.148.
52. Southworth, p.153–5.
53. Bradbrook, p.25.
54. Southworth, Chapters 9 and 11.
55. Ibid., pp.118–19.
56. C.J. Grysar, 'Der Römische Mimus', *Sitzungsberichte der Kaiserlichen Akademie Der Wissenschaften*, Philosophisch-Historische, Classe XII, Band 1854, p.334.
57. Southworth, p.146; Friedländer, Vol.II, p.92; Vol.IV, p.536.
58. Mantzius, Vol.II, pp.120ff.; Macgowan, et al., p.39.
59. Mantzius, Vol.II, pp.137–8.
60. Ibid., Vol.II, p.130; Berthold, pp.309ff.
61. Mantzius, pp.178–84.

62. Sorokin (1937–41), Vol.I, p.654.
63. Elie Konigson, 'Religious drama and urban society in France at the end of the Middle Ages', in Redmond (ed.), pp.27–8.
64. Mantzius, Vol.II, p.16.
65. Tuchmann, pp.318–19, 515, 590.
66. See, for instance, Hughes; Murray, Margaret (1921).
67. Sumption, pp.191, 258–67.
68. Gimpel (1983), p.119.
69. Parker, pp.11–13.
70. Tuchmann, p.485.
71. Ibid.
72. William Langland, *Piers Plowman*, Text C, Pass.XI, 11.35–9.
73. Gimpel (1983), p.72.
74. Bergin, p.1.
75. Gimpel (1988), Chapter 7.
76. Mumford, p.14, quoted by Gimpel (1988), p.149.
77. Gimpel (1988), p.169; Lynn White, 'Cultural Climates and Technological Advance in the Middle Ages', *Viator*, 1971, Vol.2, p.198.
78. Lynn White, 'Cultural Climates and Technological Advance in the Middle Ages', *Viator*, 1971, Vol.2, pp.197, 200.
79. Tuchmann, p.234.
80. Sorokin (1937–41), Vol.I, p.593.
81. Lynn White, 'Cultural Climates and Technological Advance in the Middle Ages', *Viator*, 1971, Vol.2, p.197, note 124.
82. Southworth, pp.115–16.
83. Macgowan, et al., p.40.
84. Berthold, p.328.
85. Cohen, Gustave, pp.231–2; Mantzius, Vol.II, pp.9, 102–4.
86. Mantzius, Vol.II, p.14.
87. Tuchmann, pp.312, 588; Cohen, Gustave, p.268.
88. Mantzius, Vol.II, pp.37–8.
89. Cohen, Gustave, p.267.
90. Ibid., pp.149, 239; Mantzius, Vol.II, pp.94–5.
91. Tuchmann, p.312.
92. Cohen, Gustave, p.269.
93. Berthold, p.254.
94. Bergin, p.290.
95. Gimpel (1988), p.91.
96. Batsford and Fry, p.8.
97. Tuchmann, pp.42–3.
98. Gordon, p.538.
99. Ibid., p.578.
100. Tuchmann, p.174.
101. Gordon, pp.531, 536.
102. Major, p.30.
103. Gimpel (1983), pp.72–3.
104. Tuchmann, pp.240, 245, 311, 441.
105. Wickham, p.65.
106. Gimpel (1988), p.205.
107. Tuchmann, pp.119, 163–7, 195–6, 222–5, 285–6.
108. Jusserand, pp.151, 168.
109. Tuchmann, p.441.
110. Ibid., p.508.
111. Bergin, p.2.
112. Jusserand, pp.151–2.
113. Tuchmann, p.286.
114. Ibid., pp.119, 164.
115. Ibid., p.316.
116. Sumption, p.56.
117. Ibid., pp.289–97.
118. Tuchmann, pp.487–8.
119. Artz, p.432.
120. Tuchmann, pp.287–9, 338–9.
121. Sumption, p.267.
122. Tuchmann, pp.288–9; Cowley, pp.191–6.

Chapter 14 (pp.243–273)

1. Sorokin (1937–41), Vol.II, *passim*.
2. Talcott Parsons, 'Christianity and Modern Industrial Society', in Tiryakian (ed.), p.58.
3. Kristeller (1961), pp.9, 120–1.
4. Artz, pp.437–8.
5. Kristeller (1961), p.111.
6. Ibid., pp.110ff., 120–1.
7. Faludy, p.17.
8. Kristeller (1965), pp.6–8.
9. Kristeller (1961), pp.13–17, 80, 95.
10. Makdisi, Part Seven.
11. Kristeller (1961), pp.99–102.
12. Ibid., pp.124–5.
13. McLean, p.29.
14. Kristeller (1961), pp.124–5, 139.
15. Makdisi, p.353.
16. William Shakespeare, *Hamlet*, Act II, Scene ii.
17. Kristeller (1961), p.20; (1965), p.65.
18. Sorokin (1937–41), Vol.II, p.498, note 22; see also Artz, p.438.
19. Artz, p.439.

20. Kristeller (1961), pp.130–3.
21. Faludy, p.205.
22. Kristeller, (1961), pp.78ff.
23. Kristeller (1965), p.62.
24. Weber, pp.80–1.
25. Ibid., pp.172–4.
26. Tawney, pp.50–64, 104.
27. Ibid., p.116.
28. Ibid., p.113.
29. Sorokin (1937–41), Vol.II, pp.499ff.
30. Wolf (1950), pp.2–3.
31. Kristeller (1972), p.137.
32. McLean, pp.114–15.
33. Taylor, F. Sherwood, pp.215–22.
34. McLean, pp.189–92.
35. Wolf (1950), p.326.
36. McLean, pp.107, 116–17, quoting
    Frances A. Yates, *Giordano Bruno and
    the Hermetic Tradition* (Routledge and
    Kegan Paul, London, 1964), p.146.
37. Wolf (1950), pp.4–5.
38. Jones, E.L., p.59.
39. Kristeller (1972), p.138.
40. Wolf (1950), pp.383–5; McLean,
    pp.130–7.
41. Wolf (1950), pp.24–37.
42. McLean, pp.1ff.; Jones, E.L., p.61.
43. McLean, pp.25, 88.
44. Vincent, p.466; Wolf (1950), p.37.
45. Wolf (1950), pp.463–6.
46. Ibid. pp.459–63, 504–5.
47. Ibid., p.451; Singer C., et al. (eds),
    Vol.II, p.774.
48. Berthold, pp.356–7, 367, 607.
49. Mantzius, Vol.II, pp.342–4.
50. Berthold, p.361.
51. Cohen, Gustave, pp.152–4.
52. Holmyard, p.204.
53. Berthold, p.390.
54. Cohen, Gustave, pp.142–3.
55. Mantzius, Vol.II, p.73.
56. Cohen, Gustave, p.275.
57. Mantzius, Vol.II, p.73.
58. Ibid., Vol.II, pp.68–9.
59. Southworth, p.131; Wickham,
    pp.182–9.
60. Gayley, p.93; Mantzius, Vol.II, p.118;
    Pollard, p.lix; Wickham, pp.59, 206–7.
61. Prynne, pp.603–4.
62. Mantzius, Vol.II, pp.115–18.
63. Macgowan, et al., p.142.
64. Mantzius, Vol.II, p.324; Vol.III, p.93.
65. Ibid., Vol.II, pp.326–7; Vol.III, p.89–90.
66. Ibid., Vol.III, pp.49–50, 65, 206–7.
67. Ibid., Vol.II, p.174; see also Pollard,
    p.lx.
68. Pollard, p.lv.
69. Gayley, p.315.
70. Berthold, p.309; Macgowan, et al.,
    p.104; Sorokin (1937–41), p.652.
71. Axton, pp.26–9.
72. Duckworth, p.397; Berthold, p.335,
    gives the date as 1486.
73. Duckworth, pp.401, 408.
74. Ibid., p.401.
75. Southworth, p.149; Pollard, p.lvi.
76. Duckworth, p.408.
77. Berthold, p.361.
78. Tuchmann, p.238.
79. Duff (1960), p.217; Artz, p.435.
80. Berthold, p.335.
81. Duff (1960), pp.217–18.
82. Duckworth, p.71.
83. Gareth Lloyd Evans, 'Shakespeare,
    Seneca and the Kingdom of Violence',
    in Dorey and Dudley (eds), pp.124–5.
84. Mantzius, Vol.II, pp.69, 74–5.
85. Ibid., Vol.III, pp.47ff.
86. Ibid., Vol.III, p.90.
87. Ibid., Vol.III, p.107.
88. Levi, p.45.
89. Macgowan, et al., p.101.
90. Kyd, Introduction, p.xxx.
91. Trewin, p.80.
92. Ibid., p.81.
93. Steane, p.13.
94. Wickham, p.183.
95. Kyd, Act II, Scene i, line 87.
96. Ibid., Act II, Scene v, lines 57–9.
97. Merchant, pp.61, 64.
98. Kyd, Introduction, p.xii.
99. Ibid., Steane, pp.7ff., 19 note, 22.
100. Steane, pp.159–60.
101. Marlowe, Act II, Scene i, line 136.
102. Ibid., Act V, Scene ii, line 150.
103. Steane, p.157.
104. Ibid., p.15.
105. Prynne, p.556.
106. Steiner, pp.193–7, 320.
107. Chiari, pp.196, 200.
108. Kitto (1964), pp.223–9, 275, 330.
109. Lloyd Evans, 'Shakespeare, Seneca and
     the Kingdom of Violence', in Dorey
     and Dudley (eds), pp.150–7.
110. Bernard Crick, 'The political in Britain's
     two national theatres' in Redmond (ed.),

p.188.

111. Dostoevsky (1973–6), Vol.II, p.145.

112. Shaw, *Back to Methuselah*, pp.lxxxii–lxxxiii.

113. William Shakespeare, *King Lear*, Act IV, Scene i; William Shakespeare, *Macbeth*, Act V, Scene v.

114. Tolstoy (1907), p.168.

115. Ibid., p.53.

116. Ibid., *passim*.

117. Ibid., p.124.

118. Prynne, pp.598–9.

119. Ibid., pp.570ff.

120. Bradbrook, p.20.

121. Prynne, p.636.

122. Wickham, pp.204–5.

123. Bradbrook, pp.28–9, 31.

124. 'G.M.G.', pp.5, 10.

125. Ibid., pp.5–33; Berthold, p.391; Macgowan, et al., pp.116–17; Bradbrook, pp.35–6; Mantzius, Vol.III, p.127.

126. Berthold, p.459.

127. Mantzius, Vol.II, pp.228–9, 280.

128. Ibid., Vol.II, pp.117–18 note, quoting Petit de Julleville.

129. Prynne, p.496; Collier, pp.241–2.

130. Mantzius, Vol.III, pp.10, 15, 21, 23.

131. Northbrooke, pp.23–9.

132. Ibid., 'To the Christian and Faithful Reader'.

133. Ibid., p.51.

134. Ibid., pp.67–8.

135. Ibid., pp.59–60.

136. Gosson, pp.11–12, 34–6, 40–1.

137. Ibid., p.40.

138. Munday, *passim*.

139. Stubbes, Introduction, p.50; pp.140–50.

140. Mantzius, Vol.II, p.324; Parker, pp.86, 121–3.

141. Parker, pp.121–38.

142. Mantzius, Vol.III, pp.19–21, 26–7, 69–73.

143. Parker, p.117.

144. Macgowan, et al., p.117; Prynne, p.108.

145. Parker, pp.169–219.

146. Prynne, Preface, p.5; Augustine, *City of God* [2], Appendix C, J.E.C. Welldon, 'The Church and the Stage', pp.666–7.

147. Mantzius, Vol.II, p.280; Prynne, pp.214–16, 414 note h.

148. Bradbrook, p.267.

149. Berthold, p.367.

150. Prynne, Preface, p.6.

151. Parker, p.218.

152. Mantzius, Vol.III, pp.79–80, 239–40.

Chapter 15 *(pp.274–303)*

1. Prynne, pp.580ff.

2. Bradbrook, p.20; Wickham, p.141.

3. Wickham, p.140.

4. Gosson, Introduction, p.9.

5. Stubbes, p.149; Wickham, pp.141–2.

6. Mantzius, Vol.III, p.95.

7. Ibid., Vol.V, pp.317–21; 'G.M.G.', p.55.

8. Mantzius, Vol.III, p.315.

9. For a comprehensive account of this period, see Nicoll, Vol.I, Appendix A; see also Mantzius, Vol.V, pp.316–17, 322, 343–4; and Vincent, 'Drama' and 'Theatres in England'.

10. Mantzius, Vol.II, p.346; Vol.V, p.338; Macgowan, et al., pp.138–9.

11. Berthold, p.420.

12. Mantzius, Vol.IV, pp.230–5.

13. Berthold, pp.463–8.

14. Mantzius, Vol.IV, pp.236–43.

15. Dryden (1903), p.91.

16. Ibid., p.17.

17. Mantzius, Vol.V, p.317; Vincent, p.883.

18. Dryden (1903), p.17.

19. Berthold, p.470.

20. Baker, pp.30–2.

21. Ibid., pp.128, 136.

22. Dryden (1903), pp.104, 107, 113.

23. Findlater, p.30.

24. 'G.M.G.', pp.56–7.

25. Mantzius, Vol.V, p.307.

26. 'G.M.G.', pp.67–8.

27. Mantzius, Vol.V, p.314; *Dictionary of National Biography* Vol.II, p.130, Vol.III p.1331, Vol.XII, p.921.

28. Nicoll, Vol.I, pp.19–24.

29. Arthur Bedford, sermon preached at St Mary-le-Bow on 10 January 1733, published 1734 together with 39th report on progress.

30. Francis Hare, Lord Bishop of St Asaph, preaching to the societies at St Mary-le-Bow on 5 January 1730, published 1731.

31. Annual reports of the London and Westminster Society were issued together with the texts of the sermon

preached to the Society annually in
January. Preachers whose sermons exist
in published form, and year of
publication, include: Peter Newcombe,
1710; Edward Gibson, Lord Bishop of
London, 1723; Edward Chandler, Lord
Bishop of Coventry and Lichfield, 1724;
John Wynne, 1725; Richard Smalbroke,
Lord Bishop of St David's, 1728;
Robert Drew, 1735.

32. Anthony, pp.162–3.
33. Mantzius, Vol.IV, pp.77, 181–92,
    222–5.
34. Anthony, pp.53, note 5, 54, note 7,
    65–7, 157.
35. Ibid., p.157.
36. Collier, Chapter VI.
37. Ibid., p.2; Chapters I, II and III.
38. Ibid., pp. 5–6.
39. Dryden (1882), Vol.V, p.199, dedication
    to *Aurenge Zebe*.
40. Collier, pp.68, 163.
41. *Collier Tracts*, p.2.
42. Bedford, pp.4–5, 36–9; Anthony, p.112;
    Collier Tracts, 'A Letter to Mr
    Congreve', p.36.
43. Covered in detail in Anthony; see also,
    e.g., *Collier Tracts, passim*.
44. Anthony, pp.59, 68–9.
45. *Collier Tracts*, 'A Vindication of the
    Stage', pp.6–7; Anthony, p.231.
46. *Antitheatrical Tracts 1702–1704*, 'A
    Scourge for the Playhouses'.
47. Ibid., pp.8–9.
48. Bedford, p.11.
49. Anthony, pp.212–13.
50. Bedford, Preface, pp.8, 8–13.
51. Ibid., Preface, p.8; p.81.
52. Ibid., pp.199–201.
53. Ibid., p.122.
54. *Dictionary of National Biography*, Vol.
    XX, pp.88–9.
55. Anthony, pp.295–8.
56. Dryden (1962), p.538.
57. Ibid., pp.833–4; Dryden (1882), Vol.I,
    pp.364–5.
58. McLean, pp.165–6.
59. Lyons, pp.41, 329–36.
60. Bacon (1889), p.160; McLean, p.232;
    Wolf (1950), p.640.
61. Kristeller (1965), p.62.
62. Lyons, pp.1–4.
63. Sorokin (1937–41), Vol.II, pp.133–40.

64. Wolf (1950), p.640.
65. Kocher, pp.53–4, quoted in McLean,
    p.229.
66. McLean, p.166; Lyons, p.115.
67. Lyons, pp.58–9, 115; Church of
    England *Yearbook*, Church House
    Publishing, London.
68. Holmyard, p.273.
69. McLean, pp.192–207.
70. Duff (1960), p.96; Fraser, P.M., p.350.
71. Galen, p.xiv.
72. Ibid., p.xxiii.
73. Fraser, P.M., pp.348–52, 364, Vol.II,
    p.539 note 240.
74. Augustine, *City of God* [1], XXII.24.
75. Watt, pp.66–7.
76. Wolf (1950), p.403; O'Malley, p.11.
77. Tuchmann, p.105.
78. O'Malley, p.15.
79. Wolf (1950), p.408.
80. O'Malley, pp.14–15.
81. Wolf (1950), p.408.
82. Galen, p.xiii.
83. Wolf (1950), pp.406, 408–9.
84. Ibid., p.62.
85. Ibid., p.409.
86. O'Malley, pp.170–1.
87. Wolf (1950), p.62.
88. Ibid., p.343.
89. Ibid., p.62.
90. Galen, p.1.
91. Stubbes, p.182.
92. Ibid., pp.177–8.
93. Bacon (1920), p.281.
94. Gibson, pp.205–14.
95. Simon, p.12, quoted in McLean, p.55.
96. Gibson, p.33.
97. Ibid., *passim*, especially Chapter VI.
98. Ibid., p.214.
99. Russell, p.622.
100. Gibson, p.99.
101. Hobbes, Part I, Chapter I.
102. Rookmaaker, pp.43–4.
103. Hobbes, Part I, Chapter 6.
104. Hampton, Chapters 1.5, 3.5.
105. Wolf (1950), pp.656–60.
106. Locke, Paragraph 6.
107. Ibid., p.ix.
108. Foner, pp.75ff.
109. Commager, p.100.
110. Godechot, p.96.
111. Paine (1915), pp.94–7.
112. Godechot, pp.117–20; McManners,

Notes

pp.31–60, 74.

113. Paine (1915), pp.41–4.
114. McManners, pp.13–14.
115. Schama, pp.483–4.
116. McManners, p.14.
117. Ibid., p.99.
118. Ibid., pp.85, 106–8; Schama, p.624.
119. Schama, p.778.
120. McManners, pp.100–1.
121. Paine (1910), p.47.
122. Ibid., p.46.
123. Ibid., (1910) pp.52–7.
124. Ibid., p.83.
125. McManners, pp.133–5.
126. Ibid., pp.135–49.

Chapter 16 (pp.304–333)

1. Mantzius, Vol.VI, pp.15–16.
2. Smith, D.F., Chapter XI; pp.113, note 36, 244.
3. Dryden (1903), p.67; Johnson, S., pp.3, 11.
4. Mantzius, Vol.V, p.355.
5. Ibid., Vol.V, p.363; Vol.VI, pp.14–15.
6. Nicoll, Vol.I, pp.265–6; Vol.II, p.160.
7. Ibid., Vol.II, p.160.
8. Perrin, pp.89–90; see also Odell, Vol.I, pp.31–3.
9. Odell, Vol.II, pp.137–8, 200–1.
10. Nicoll, Vol.II, pp.131ff., 143 note.
11. Odell, Vol.II, pp.203–4.
12. Smith, D.F., p.1.
13. Odell, Vol.I, Chapter III.
14. Smith, D.F., p.43; Nicoll, Vol.I, pp.330–1; Vol.II, p.271; Odell, Vol.I, pp.7ff.
15. Odell, Vol.I, pp.193–4.
16. Nicoll, Vol.II, p.426.
17. Odell, Vol.I, pp.217–18, 312–13, 316.
18. Nicoll, Vol.II, p.427.
19. Odell, Vol.I, p.314.
20. Ibid., Vol.I, p.162.
21. Smith, D.N., p.19.
22. Odell, Vol.I, p.315.
23. Mantzius, Vol.V, p.309; Odell, Vol.I, pp.37, 53.
24. Odell, Vol.I, p.381.
25. Ibid., Vol.II, pp.151, 273.
26. Johnson, S., p.161.
27. Kitto (1964), p.242.
28. Odell, Vol.I, p.419.
29. Ibid., Vol.I, p.422.

30. Ibid., Vol.I, pp.427–8.
31. Ibid., Vol.I, pp.422–3.
32. Ibid., Vol.I, pp.307–8, 425–7, 432–3.
33. Nicoll, Vol.II, p.24.
34. Ibid., Vol.II, p.118.
35. Odell, Vol.I, pp.51–3, 341–7.
36. Ibid., Vol.I, pp.60–1.
37. Ibid., Vol.II, p.74.
38. Nicoll, Vol.II, p.54.
39. Ibid., Vol.I, p.130.
40. Odell, Vol.I, p.46.
41. Johnson, S., p.166.
42. Odell, Vol.I, pp.44–6; Trewin, p.80.
43. Odell, Vol.II, p.151.
44. Dryden (1903), pp.60–1.
45. McLynn, p.4.
46. Smith, D.F., p.90, note 25.
47. Tobias, p.33, quoting C. Hibbert, *The Roots of Evil* (Weidenfeld and Nicolson, London, 1963), p.45.
48. Nicoll, Vol.II, pp.11–12.
49. Odell, Vol.I, pp.285–6, 411–12.
50. Liesenfeld, pp.73–83.
51. McLynn, pp.218–19.
52. Nicoll, Vol.II, pp.21–3.
53. Liesenfeld, pp.3–4, 9–13; see also Nicoll, Vol.II, pp.21–4.
54. Odell, Vol.I, pp.13–14, 21, 217–20; Liesenfeld, pp.33–4.
55. Nicoll, Vol.II, p.429.
56. Ibid., Vol.II, pp.272, 429.
57. Kidson, p.61.
58. Liesenfeld, pp.16–22, 163, 191.
59. Ibid., pp.24–6.
60. Ibid., pp.24–54.
61. Ibid., p.85.
62. Ibid., pp.xi, 91–2.
63. Ibid., pp.60–80.
64. Ibid., p.83.
65. Ibid., pp.86–9, 115–16, 121–2.
66. Ibid., pp.163, 191.
67. Nicoll, Vol.II, p.412; Liesenfeld, pp.92, 129ff.
68. Liesenfeld, pp.92–101.
69. Ibid., pp.138–50.
70. Ibid., pp.189–90.
71. Nicoll, Vol.II, p.272; Odell, Vol.I, pp.220–1.
72. Smith, D.F., p.236; Liesenfeld, p.226 note; 'G.M.G.', pp.90–3.
73. Conolly, p.48.
74. Ibid., p.64.
75. Liesenfeld, p.149.

76. McLynn, pp.244–7.
77. Tobias, pp.26–8.
78. McLynn, pp.5–6, 60–1, 78; Sharpe (1984), p.218, note 64.
79. Low, pp.14–16; Sharpe (1983), pp.179–80; McLynn, pp.12–13; Tobias, p.31.
80. McLynn, pp.172–217; Sharpe (1984), pp.121–31, 140.
81. McLynn, p.1.
82. Sharpe (1983), p.138; (1984), pp.120, 175.
83. McLynn, pp.49, 89.
84. McLynn, pp.5, 89, 105–8, 317; R. Porter, in Tomaselli and Porter (eds), pp.220–2; Sharpe (1983), pp.62–3.
85. McLynn, pp.xi–xii, 257; Musson and Robinson p.438; Blackstone, Vol.IV, p.237.
86. Sharpe (1984), pp.148–9.
87. McLynn, p.xv; Sharpe (1984), pp.91–2.
88. Sharpe (1984), p.182.
89. McLynn, pp.257–8.
90. Sharpe (1984), p.151.
91. Ibid., pp.133–5, 139; McLynn, pp.218–41.
92. Wearmouth, Section I, Chapter 1.
93. Sharpe (1984), p.138.
94. Wearmouth, Section I, Chapter 1; McLynn, p.236.
95. McLynn, pp.232–8.
96. Ibid., pp.307–8; Wearmouth, Section III.
97. Andrews, p.52
98. Tobias, p.44; McLynn, pp.13–14.
99. Wearmouth, pp.257–9.
100. McLynn, p.174.
101. Wearmouth, pp.243–5.
102. Wilberforce, pp.260–1, 270–1.
103. Wesley, Vol.III, p.273.
104. Augustine, *City of God* [2], Appendix C, p.668.
105. Beare, p.164.
106. Weber, p.274, note 68.
107. Ibid., pp.174–6.
108. Tawney, pp.251, 320, note 104.
109. Andrews, pp.56ff.
110. Musson and Robinson, p.90.
111. Ibid., p.45.
112. Wolf (1950), p.452.
113. Musson and Robinson, pp.45–58; Chapter III; p.429; see also P. Mathias, 'Who Unbound Prometheus? Science and Technical Change 1600–1800', in Musson (ed.), Chapter 1; R.E. Schofield, 'The Industrial Orientation of Science in the Lunar Society of Birmingham', ibid., Chapter 5.
114. Wolf (1952), pp.500–1.
115. Ibid., Chapters II and III; Musson and Robinson, p.434.
116. Wolf (1950), pp.544–55; (1952), pp.611ff.
117. Wolf (1952), Chapters VII and VIII; Musson and Robinson, Chapter XII.
118. Musson and Robinson, Chapters XIII and XV.
119. Ibid., pp.60–4; Wolf (1952), p.42.
120. Atkins, pp.2–11.
121. Nicoll, Vol.IV, p.86, note 2.
122. Goethe (1959), p.7.
123. Ibid., pp.9–10.
124. Goethe (1890), pp.279, 614.
125. Goethe (1959), p.270.
126. Goethe (1959), p.288.
127. Miller, pp.132–6.
128. Steiner, p.124.
129. Goethe (1959), p.282.
130. Ibid., p.10; (1949), p.71.
131. Goethe (1949), p.41.
132. Ibid., p.42.
133. Miller, p.95.

Chapter 17 *(pp.334–362)*

1. Steiner, p.112.
2. Nicoll, Vol.IV, pp.52–3; Mantzius, Vol.VI, pp.1–2.
3. Mantzius, Vol.VI p.1
4. Ibid., Vol.V, pp.251–2.
5. Conolly, p.138.
6. Nicoll, Vol.III, p.19.
7. Conolly, p.69.
8. Ibid., pp.74–95.
9. 'G.M.G.', p.104; Conolly, p.43.
10. Brown, Ford, pp.18–19.
11. William Shakespeare, *Hamlet*, Act III, Scene ix.
12. Johnson,S., p.193.
13. 'G.M.G.', p.110.
14. Perrin, pp.5, 17, 21, 35–7, 53, Chapter III, pp.253–4.
15. Conolly, p.138.
16. Nicoll, Vol.III, pp.16, 109, 115; Conolly, pp.137–45; *The Times Saturday Review*, 31 October 1992,

p.16.

17. Nicoll, Vol.IV, p.121.
18. Ibid., Vol.IV, pp.16, 43.
19. Ibid., Vol.IV, p.16.
20. Conolly, p.148.
21. Ibid., p.139; Sharpe (1983), pp.68–9; Findlater, pp.80–1.
22. Nicoll, Vol.IV, p.182.
23. Sharpe (1984), p.163.
24. Odell, Vol.II, p.55.
25. Ibid., Vol.II, p.194.
26. Ibid., Vol.II, p.310; Trewin, p.81.
27. Odell, Vol.II, Chapter XXVIII.
28. Merchant, p.73; Nicoll, Vol.V, p.209.
29. Nicoll, Vol.IV, pp.58–65, Chapters IV and V.
30. Ibid., Vol.IV, pp.60–1, 168; Steiner, pp.128–35.
31. Nicoll, Vol.III, p.229.
32. Ibid., Vol.III, pp.208–10; Vol.IV, p.154.
33. Conolly, p.108; 'G.M.G.', p.116.
34. Nicoll, Vol.IV, p.137ff.
35. Ibid., Vol.IV, pp.81, 100ff.
36. Ibid., Vol.IV, p.105.
37. Ibid., Vol.III, pp.16–17.
38. Ibid., Vol.IV, p.88.
39. Radzinovicz, Vol.3, pp.19–21; Kidson, pp.89, 96–9.
40. Steiner, pp.111–12; Nicoll, Vol.IV, pp.22–3.
41. Mantzius, Vol.VI, pp.74ff.
42. Nicoll, Vol.IV, p.224.
43. Ibid., Vol.IV, p.68.
44. Mantzius, Vol.VI, pp.56–7.
45. Ibid., Vol.VI, p.44.
46. Nicoll, Vol.V, pp.27–9.
47. Odell, Vol.II, pp.239–40.
48. Nicoll, Vol.IV, p.70.
49. Ibid., Vol.V, pp.34ff.
50. Odell, Vol.II, pp.104, 164.
51. Nicoll, Vol.V, p.48.
52. Ibid., Vol.V, pp.38–42.
53. Ibid., Vol.V, pp.37–8.
54. Ibid., Vol.V, pp.55, 122.
55. Michael R. Booth, 'The social value of nineteenth century English drama', in Redmond (ed.), pp.60ff.
56. Nicoll, Vol.V, pp.104–6.
57. Ibid., Vol.V, pp.99–100.
58. 'G.M.G.', pp.114, 120.
59. Nicoll, Vol.V, p.151.
60. Ibid., Vol.V, p.17.
61. Ibid., Vol.V, p.185.

62. Ibid., Vol.V, pp.78–9; Findlater, p.83.
63. Nicoll, Vol.V, pp.19–22; Findlater, p.73.
64. 'G.M.G.', pp.108–9, 118.
65. Michael R. Booth, 'The social value of nineteenth century English drama', in Redmond (ed.), pp.68–9.
66. Nicoll, Vol.V, pp.159–61.
67. Findlater, p.71.
68. Conolly, pp.161ff.; 'G.M.G.', pp.120–1.
69. Nicoll, Vol.V, p.776.
70. Ibid., Vol.V, pp.14–18.
71. Ibid., Vol.V, pp.9–10.
72. Augustine, *City of God* [2], p.669.
73. Tobias, p.147.
74. Ibid., p.100.
75. Ibid., Chapter 4; Low, p.4.
76. Tobias, p.189, quoting Grant, J.D.
77. Ibid., pp.210.ff.; Low, p.47.
78. Tobias, p.232.
79. Sharpe (1984), p.186; Radzinovicz, Vol.1, *passim*, especially pp.498–9, 578, 580, 582, 632–3; Gowers, p.26.
80. Tobias, pp.59ff. 136, 182–3; Low, pp.3, 4, 13.
81. Low, pp.17–32, 61; Tobias, p.148.
82. Low, p.32.
83. Tobias, p.221.
84. Ibid., pp.135–6, 163–4.
85. Christopher Frayling, 'The House that Jack Built', in Tomaselli and Porter (eds), pp.208–13.
86. Tobias, p.136.
87. Wand, p.205.
88. Wigley, p.136.
89. Ibid., pp.24–9.
90. Ibid., *passim*.
91. Ibid., Chapters Seven to Ten.
92. Fairweather (ed.), pp.35ff., 102, note 3.
93. Ibid., pp.5, 201.
94. Ibid., p.5; Jay, pp.9–10, 187.
95. Fairweather (ed.), p.12; Chadwick, pp.46, 50.
96. Fairweather (ed.), p.201.
97. Ibid., p.146; Jay, p.83.
98. Boswell, Vol.i, p.471.
99. Warnock, *passim*.
100. Ibid., p.59.
101. Eddy, pp.395, 489.
102. Ibid., p.119.
103. Nenneman; Smith, C.P.; Hoekema, *passim*.
104. The principal sources for this section are

Chant (ed.), Williams,T., and Byrn.

105. Noel Coley, 'From Sanitary Reform to Social Welfare' in Chant (ed.), pp.272ff. F.J. Brüggemeier, 'Medicine and Science', ibid. pp.294ff.; Byrn, Chapters II and XX.

106. *Sotheby's Preview*, July 1993.

107. Chant (ed.), p.21.

108. Wolf (1952), p.665.

109. Byrn, Chapter XXVI.

110. Odell, Vol.II, pp.157–8.

111. Nicoll, Vol.VI, p.46.

112. Odell, Vol.II, p.233.

113. Byrn, Chapter XVIII.

114. Noel Coley, 'Materials: Products of the Chemical Industries', in Chant (ed.), pp.117ff.; Byrn, Chapter XIII.

115. Williams, T., Chapter 30.

116. Williams, D. (1974), pp.73, 77.

117. Byrn, pp.15, 76.

118. T.A.B. Corley, 'How Quakers coped with business success', in Jeremy (ed.), Chapter 8.

119. Tobias, p.213; T.A.B. Corley, 'How Quakers coped with business success', in Jeremy (ed.), Chapter 8.

120. McLynn, pp.271–3.

121. Low, pp.82ff.

122. *The Times*, 21 January 1988.

123. Low, pp.99–103.

124. Niven, pp.61ff.

125. *The Times*, 5 June 1990.

126. Johnson, S., p.181.

127. *Daily Telegraph*, 6 February 1990.

128. Vyvyan (1969), Chapters II and III.

129. Ibid., Chapters III and IV.

130. Ibid., pp.151–2.

Chapter 18 (pp.363–392)

1. Hume, *Treatise*, Book III, Part III, Sections I, III and VI; Plamenatz (1949), Chapter II.

2. Hume, *Dialogues*, p.440.

3. Ibid., Part XII.

4. Davidson, p.37.

5. Plamenatz (1949), Chapter IV.

6. Ibid., Chapter VI; Davidson, pp.57ff., 85ff.

7. Davidson, pp.121ff.

8. Mill, p.16.

9. Augustine (1912), I.i.

10. Taylor, Charles, p.47.

11. Ibid., p.44.

12. Plamenatz (1963), pp.169–73.

13. Taylor, Charles, pp.209ff., 493ff.

14. Ibid., Part V, Chapter XVIII; McLellan, p.2.

15. Plamenatz (1963), pp.159–61.

16. Taylor, Charles, Chapter XVIII; McLellan, p.2.

17. Taylor, Charles, pp.225–7.

18. Ibid., Part III; Plamenatz (1963), p.134.

19. McLellan, pp.9–10.

20. Ibid., pp.21, 54, 71, 87, 89.

21. Ibid., pp.98ff.

22. Ibid., p.109.

23. Ibid., p.111; Kamenka, p.53.

24. McLellan, pp.18ff., 52, 143–4.

25. Ibid., p.60.

26. Plamenatz (1963), pp.340ff., 376ff.

27. McLellan, p.155; Lukes, pp.27ff., 48–70.

28. Elster, pp.180ff.

29. Jennings, p.90, quoting from Christiana Hankin (ed.), *The Life of Mary Anne Schimmelpenninck*, London, Longman, Brown, Green, Longmans and Roberts, 1859.

30. Oldroyd, Chapter 18.

31. Ibid.

32. Reade, pp.423ff.

33. Ibid., p.422.

34. Ibid., p.442.

35. Ibid., p.xxxvi.

36. Nash, pp.19–21, 53ff., 114–16; See also David Tribe, 'Secular Centenary', *Contemporary Review*, No. 209, October 1966, pp.200ff.

37. Nash, p.100, Chapter 9; David Tribe, 'Secular Centenary', *Contemporary Review*, No. 209, October 1966, pp.200–5.

38. Vincent, pp.645, 668ff., 904ff., 'Oaths', 'Parliament', 'Trials'.

39. Nash, pp.128–9; David Tribe, 'Secular Centenary', *Contemporary Review*, No. 209, October 1966, pp.200–5.

40. *Oxford Companion to the Theatre*, 'Dramatic Censorship'; Findlater, pp.82–3.

41. Salmon, p.60; Findlater, pp.82, 131.

42. Macgowan, et al., pp.187ff.

43. 'G.M.G.', Appendix.

44. Shaw (1927), Preface, pp.319–49.

45. Findlater, pp.104ff.

46. Ibid., pp.80, 91–2.
47. Shaw (1931), pp.xii, xiii.
48. Shaw, *Man and Superman*, p.219.
49. Salmon, pp.142–61.
50. Ibid., pp.142, 159.
51. Shaw, *Back to Methuselah*, pp.lxxxiiiff.
52. Quoted by Blackham (ed.), p.106.
53. Macgowan, et.al., pp.239–41.
54. Berthold, p.597.
55. *Romans* 8:22.
56. Hayman, p.93.
57. Kitchin, p.23.
58. Bentley (ed.), p.57.
59. Hayman, p.88.
60. Chiari, pp.205–6.
61. Macgowan, et al., p.246.
62. Chiari, pp.202, 207.
63. Quoted by Brustein, p.375 note.
64. Bentley (ed.), p.64.
65. Chiari, p.207.
66. Bentley (ed.), p.67.
67. Hayman, p.98.
68. Ibid., p.110; Barnes, P., p.65.
69. Lumley, p.4.
70. Ibid., p.34.
71. Ibid., pp.159–60 and *passim*.
72. Blackham (ed.), p.119.
73. Esslin, pp.23–5.
74. Ibid., pp.125–6.
75. *The Times*, 29 March 1994.
76. Esslin, pp.36, 171–6.
77. Lumley, pp.214–16.
78. Quoted by Esslin, p.258.
79. Ibid., p.187.
80. Ibid., p.141.
81. Ibid., pp.390, 419.
82. Ibid., pp.416–17.
83. Quoted in ibid., p.89.
84. Quoted in ibid., pp.93–4.
85. Ibid., p.347.
86. Hayman, p.92; Bentley (ed.), pp.67ff.
87. Macgowan, et al., p.243.
88. Milosz, p.74.
89. Berthold, p.621.
90. Ibid., p.635.
91. Quoted in Redmond (ed.), p.195.
92. H. Castein, 'German Social Drama in the 1960s', in ibid., p.195.
93. Lukes, p.119.
94. Steiner, p.343; see also Ewen, pp.230ff.
95. Ewen, p.211.
96. Esslin, pp.365–8.
97. Lukes, pp.112–13.

98. Lumley, pp.139–56.
99. Sartre, p.85; French version, Cinquième Tableau, Scène III.
100. Samuel, et al., *passim*, especially pp.93ff.
101. Ibid., pp.251–2; see also Goorney, pp.8–11.
102. Goorney, pp.8–11.
103. Chambers (1989), p.37.
104. Ibid., pp.51ff., 92.
105. Ibid., pp.130ff.
106. Ibid., p.335.
107. Ibid., pp.126, 344ff.
108. Goorney, Chapters 7 and 8.
109. Itzin (1980) p.xiv and *passim*; see also McGrath, Chapter 4.
110. Chambers (1989), pp.384–6.
111. Itzin (1980), pp.ix–x.
112. Ewen, p.460.
113. *Oxford Companion to the Theatre*, p.46.
114. Chambers (1989), p.287.
115. Itzin (1980), pp.176–81.
116. Ibid., pp.211–15.
117. McGrath, pp.102–3.
118. Itzin (1980), pp.13, 18, 150, 216–19.
119. Ibid., p.152.
120. Ibid., pp.295–6.

Chapter 19 (pp.393–428)

1. Lumley, pp.61ff., 126ff.
2. John Allen, 'Subsidy and Western European Theatre in the 1970s', in Redmond (ed.), p.233.
3. *Drama*, 1987, Vol.2, pp.19–20.
4. *Observer*, 7 May 1950.
5. Steiner, p.327.
6. Merchant, p.93.
7. Lumley, pp.283–9.
8. *Plays and Players*, October 1972, p.43.
9. Jeremy Kingston, in *The Times*, 15 January 1991.
10. Orr, p.5.
11. Nash, p.94.
12. Chadwick, pp.201–3; Jeremy (ed.), p.9.
13. Chadwick, pp.204ff.; Wilson, B., Chapter III.
14. *Criminal Statistics* quoted in Dennis and Erdos, pp.85–6.
15. Rénan, p.193.
16. Barnes, J., pp.126–8, 149, 205.
17. Ibid., pp.395ff.
18. Ibid., p.405.

19. Ibid., pp.409–12.
20. Bultmann, p.4.
21. Ibid., *passim*; Mascall, pp.8ff.
22. As a contribution to Bartsch (ed.).
23. Van Buren, Chapter VI.
24. Ibid., pp.197ff.
25. Ibid., pp.182–91.
26. Robinson, John, pp.50ff.
27. Ibid., pp.60, 81.
28. Ibid., p.106.
29. Ibid., Chapter 6.
30. Letter to *The Times*, 22 April 1992.
31. *The Times*, 13 February 1993.
32. Wilson, B., pp.2–9.
33. *The Times*, 28 September 1995.
34. Ibid., 10 August 1992.
35. *The Independent*, 15 and 20 January 1987.
36. *The Times*, 2 November 1985; 26 May 1993.
37. Letters to *The Times*, 26 and 28 April, 5 May 1994.
38. *The Times*, 9 May 1986.
39. Brogan, p.105.
40. Findlater, p.64.
41. *The Times*, 16 April 1992.
42. Ibid., 10 April 1993.
43. Spring 1988.
44. Sorokin (1937–41), Vol.IV, p.777.
45. Oldroyd, pp.253–4.
46. *The New Humanist* (American Humanist Association) May/June 1933, Vol.VI, No.3.
47. Brown, I., pp.33–5.
48. *The Times*, 18 and 20 May 1963; *Sunday Times*, 19 May 1963.
49. *Guardian*, 30 October 1964.
50. *Sunday Times*, 1 November 1964.
51. *The Times*, 17 June 1977.
52. *The Independent*, 24 June 1988.
53. *The Times*, 5 August 1989.
54. Ibid., 6 June 1990.
55. Campaign for Real Education *Newsletter*, Vol.7, No.1, March 1993.
56. *The Times*, 1 June 1994.
57. BBC Radio 4 news, 5 July 1994.
58. *The Times*, 29 and 30 June 1995.
59. Ibid., 22 January 1927.
60. Ibid., 6 May 1995; *Daily Telegraph*, 6 May 1995.
61. *The Times*, 2 August 1986.
62. Ibid., 2 August 1986, 27 July, 6 and 12 August, 16 November 1992.
63. Ibid., 11 May 1994.
64. Ibid., 9 and 27 August, 15 September 1990, 22 February 1991.
65. Ibid., 31 July 1995.
66. For a blow-by-blow account of the campaign, see Schluter and Lee.
67. *The Times*, 15 December 1993.
68. Ibid., 12 December 1994.
69. Ibid., 2 and 6 November 1995.
70. Ibid., 26 May 1994.
71. Ibid., 29 August 1994.
72. Ibid., 27 February 1995.
73. *Humanists and Society*, a general statement of policy by the British Humanist Association, 1976; *The Humanist* (American Humanist Association, Amherst, New York), September/October 1973, Vol.XXXIII, No.5.
74. *The Independent*, 27 July 1989.
75. *The Times*, 19 July 1989.
76. Ibid., 26 November 1994.
77. Ibid., 15 September 1994, 2 January 1995.
78. *Sunday Telegraph*, 30 April 1995; *The Times*, 2 May 1995.
79. *The Times*, 17 June 1992, 'Life and Times', p.5, quoting Cate Haste, *Rules of Desire*, Chatto and Windus, London, 1992.
80. Sorokin (1937–41) Vol.IV, p.776
81. *Pastores dabo vobis*, *The Times*, 8 April 1992.
82. Ibid., 27 August, 6 September 1993, 25 June 1994.
83. Ibid., 17 September 1991.
84. Ibid., 31 March 1992.
85. Ibid., 7, 8 and 26 June 1995.
86. David Tribe, 'Secular Centenary', *Contemporary Review*, No.209, October 1966, pp.200–5.
87. Wilson, B., pp.65–7.
88. *The Times*, 21 October 1949.
89. Ibid., 17 July 1991.
90. Reisman and Eichel, pp.9, 187.
91. Ibid., p.7.
92. BBC Radio 4, *Today*, 4 April 1987.
93. *The Times*, 15 July 1993.
94. As advertised in *Health and Beauty Direct*, mail order catalogue.
95. *The Times*, 21 January 1994.
96. Newsom Report, Paragraph 164.
97. Susan Elkin, *The Times*, 26 April 1993.

98. Ibid., 28 April 1981.
99. Itzin (1980), pp.228ff.
100. *The Times*, 4 September 1991.
101. *Social Trends*, 1993.
102. *The Times*, 9 March 1989 and 25 March 1993.
103. Ibid., 21 February 1994.
104. Ibid., 11 June 1994.
105. Ibid., 31 October 1990.
106. Ibid., 26 October 1993.
107. Sharpe (1983), pp.65–6.
108. McLynn, p.284.
109. *The Times*, 20 June 1987, 14 January 1993.
110. See, for example, *The Times Saturday Review*, 13 June 1992.
111. *The Times*, 'Weekend', 8 October 1994.
112. *The Independent*, 17 January 1990.
113. *Daily Telegraph*, 10 February 1990.
114. *Church Times*, 9 February 1990.
115. Ibid.
116. *The Times*, 23 August 1990.
117. Ibid., 4 April, 7 December 1991.
118. Ibid., 12 March, 2 April 1992.
119. Ibid., 10 May, 29 June 1990, 10 January 1992.
120. Ibid., 27 June 1990.
121. Ibid., 26 May 1992.
122. Ibid., 1 August 1992.
123. Ibid., 12 November 1986.
124. *The Independent*, 30 December 1987.
125. *The Times*, 12 August 1993.
126. *Health and Personal Social Service Statistics*, assorted years; *On the State of the Public Health*, 1989 and 1990.
127. *Health and Personal Social Service Statistics*, 1995.
128. *The Times*, 28 November 1991.

Chapter 20 *(pp.429–465)*

1. Findlater, *passim*.
2. Johnston, p.86.
3. *The Times*, 27 May and 24 July 1946.
4. Findlater, pp.138ff.
5. Robertson, p.249.
6. Chambers (1989), pp.71–3, 176.
7. Findlater, pp.154, 182.
8. Ibid., p.15.
9. Ibid., p.170.
10. *Annual Register*, 1949 and 1959.
11. Johnston, p.211; Findlater, pp.165–8; *Annual Register*, 1956.

12. Findlater, p.168; Robertson, p.248.
13. Lumley, p.230; Itzin (1980), p.77; Johnston, p.107.
14. Findlater, p.132; Robertson, p.248.
15. Findlater, pp.187, 193.
16. Sorokin (1937–41), Vol.I, p.653.
17. Samuel, et al., p.114.
18. See an interesting analysis by Richard Morrison in *The Times*, 29 November 1994, 'Fraud, glorious fraud'.
19. Findlater, p.31.
20. *Plays and Players*, September 1969, p.18.
21. *The Times*, 12 August 1993.
22. For example, *Spectator*, 5 July 1986, on Vanbrugh's *The Relapse* at the Chichester Festival.
23. *The Independent Magazine*, 9 December 1989.
24. Trewin, p.81.
25. W.A. Darlington, *Annual Register*, 1955.
26. Trewin, p.88.
27. Ibid., p.82.
28. *The Independent*, 6 July 1988.
29. Michael Billington, *Guardian*, 1 July 1988.
30. Chambers (1980), p.62.
31. Kitchin, p.22; Hayman, p.147.
32. Kitchin, p.152.
33. *The Times*, 1 November 1991.
34. *The Independent*, 25 March 1988.
35. *The Times*, 18 October 1993.
36. *Plays and Players*, January 1970, p.38.
37. *The Independent*, 12 September 1987.
38. Michael Schmidt, *Weekend Telegraph*, p.xv.
39. Harry Eyres, *The Times*, 9 May 1992.
40. *Annual Register*, 1971.
41. Kitchin, p.23.
42. Hayman, p.151.
43. Itzin (1980), p.23.
44. Macgowan, et al., p.246; Trewin, pp.141ff.; Chambers (1980), p.50.
45. Trewin, p.148.
46. Ibid., p.164.
47. Chambers (1980), p.21; Lumley, pp.313–14; Kitchin, p.21.
48. Findlater, p.168.
49. Gaskill, pp.66ff.; Johnston, p.215.
50. Perrin, pp.245ff.
51. Robertson, pp.14, 35.
52. Whitehouse (1977), p.149.

53. Robertson, pp.39, 145, 284ff., 296.
54. *The Observer*, 29 November 1964; Tynan, Chapter 24.
55. Longford Report, Chapter 17.
56. Munro, p.132; Whitehouse (1982), pp.14ff.
57. Munro, pp.141, 156.
58. Robertson, pp.167, 250; Cotterell, pp.449, 459–60.
59. *The Times*, 15 July 1968.
60. *Annual Register*, 1947.
61. *Daily Telegraph*, 23 May 1990.
62. *Plays and Players*, November 1969, p.34.
63. Shaw (1927), p.356.
64. *Plays and Players*, August 1969, p.56.
65. Peter Roberts, ibid., October 1968; Frank Cox, ibid., August 1969.
66. Helen Dawson, ibid., December 1970, p.38.
67. *Daily Mirror*, 6 September 1971.
68. Giles Gordon, *Plays and Players*, June 1988.
69. *Daily Telegraph*, 21 August 1993.
70. Letter to *The Times*, 6 May 1977.
71. *The Independent*, 2 January 1987.
72. *Annual Register*, 1985.
73. *The Times*, 3 March, 16 July 1992.
74. Tynan, p.266; Stanford, p.13.
75. Longford Report, p.122; Robertson, p.228; Williams, B. (ed.), Paragraph 11.3.
76. *Annual Register*, 1969.
77. *Observer*, 29 November 1964; Tynan, pp.276–7; Findlater, p.221.
78. David Holbrook, in Longford Report, p.172.
79. Hugh Leonard, *Plays and Players*, July 1971, p.36.
80. Michael Coveney, ibid., September 1974, pp.21–3; Alan Brien, ibid., October 1974, p.38.
81. Ibid., January 1973, p.36; Tynan, p.285; *Daily Telegraph*, 23 May 1990; *The Times*, 6 September 1993.
82. *Annual Register*, 1968; Gaskill, p.116.
83. *The Independent*, 31 July 1989.
84. *The Times*, 17 March 1993.
85. Longford Report, p.22.
86. *Equity*, March 1971; Cotterell, pp.59–60.
87. Clare Steel, *Evening Standard*, 27 May 1992.
88. Emma Robertshaw, ibid., 26 May 1991; *The Times Magazine*, 22 January 1994.
89. *The Times*, 27 March, 23 June, 9 October 1993.
90. David Nathan, *Observer Magazine*, 29 July 1990.
91. Longford Report, p.285.
92. Helen Dawson, *Plays and Players*, September 1970, p.43.
93. David Nathan, *Observer Magazine*, 29 July 1990.
94. *Plays and Players*, May 1973, p.35.
95. Ibid., October 1974, p.38.
96. Longford Report, p.266.
97. David Zane Mairowitz, *Plays and Players*, November 1974, p.28.
98. *The Times*, 19 November 1991.
99. See articles and letters, ibid., 16 August to 2 September 1991.
100. Ibid., 23 September 1993.
101. Peter Roberts, *Plays and Players*, October 1968.
102. Rookmaaker, pp.154, 161.
103. *The Independent*, 21 October 1986.
104. *The Times*, 5 August 1992.
105. Ibid., 22 November 1989.
106. Ibid., 25 January 1993.
107. Williams, D. (1971), p.18.
108. Medved, p.175.
109. *The Times*, obituary of Sofka Skipwith, 8 March 1994.
110. Chambers (1989), pp.211, 265, 350; Gaskill, p.10; *Annual Register*, 1958.
111. Chambers (1980), p.35.
112. Ibid., Chapter 4; p.50; Itzin (1980), p.184.
113. Chambers (1980), pp.11–12, 77; and see 'List of Productions'; Itzin (1980), pp.110, 136–8, 187ff.
114. Chambers (1980), p.81.
115. Ibid., pp.30–1.
116. *Annual Register*, 1981.
117. Itzin (1980), pp.24, 28, 79–81, 103, 165ff., 187ff., 249ff.
118. Ibid., p.150.
119. Chambers (1980), pp.17–18.
120. Itzin (1980), pp.264–7, 293–6.
121. *The Times*, 15 and 21 August 1970; Hugh Leonard, *Plays and Players*, October 1970, p.28.
122. Longford Report, p.27.
123. Chambers (1980), p.11.
124. Peter Kemp, *The Independent*, 11 March

1988.
125. Peter Kemp, ibid., 9 May 1988.
126. Benedict Nightingale, *The Times*, 8 March 1991.
127. Chambers (1980), p.29.
128. See, for instance, James Wood, *Guardian*, 28 April 1989.
129. Peter Kemp, *The Independent*, 31 March 1989.
130. Itzin (1980), p.76.
131. Chambers (1980), p.78.
132. Itzin (1980), pp.189–90.
133. *Plays and Players*, November 1971, p.20.
134. Bernard Crick, 'The political in Britain's two national theatres', in Redmond (ed.), p.193.
135. Gaskill, p.129.
136. *Plays and Players*, November 1971, p.20.
137. Findlater, p.150.
138. Robertson, p.249.
139. *Annual Register*, 1972, 1973, 1975, 1978, 1983; *The Times*, 8 August 1986.
140. *The Times*, 2 March 1993, and *The Times Magazine*, 19 June 1993, quoting *Cultural Trends* (Policy Studies Institute).
141. *The Independent*, 20 March 1989.
142. Itzin (1980), pp.338, 350.
143. McGrath, Chapter 6.
144. Medved, p.191.
145. Findlater, pp.122–3.
146. Longford Report, p.268; Appendix VI, p.508.
147. Whitehouse (1977), pp.105ff.
148. Robertson, pp.258ff.; Longford Report, p.268.
149. Whitehouse (1977), pp.110–11.
150. Robertson, pp.265–6.
151. Williams, B. (ed.), Paragraphs 8.16 and 8.17.
152. Munro, p.157.
153. Whitehouse (1993), pp.122–3.
154. *The Times*, 11 April 1992.
155. Ibid., 11 February 1993.
156. Medved, p.19.
157. Findlater, p.210.
158. Johnston, p.235.
159. *Equity*, December 1971.
160. Kitchin, pp.25, 32.
161. Fraser, J., p.43.
162. *The Times*, 15 November 1965.
163. Longford Report, p.456.
164. *Listener*, 13 December 1990.
165. Longford Report, p.157.
166. *The Times*, 19 March 1993.
167. Itzin (ed.) (1992), pp.42ff.
168. Quoted in ibid., p.1.
169. Longford Report, p.38; Itzin (ed.), (1992), p.1.
170. Mark Souster, *The Times*, 28 July 1990.
171. Itzin (ed.) (1992), p.34.
172. *Sunday Times*, 23 May 1982.
173. Ibid., 30 May 1982.
174. Itzin (ed.) (1992), pp.49–50, 495, note 46, 569.
175. *The Times*, 28 July 1990.
176. Ibid., 20 December 1990.
177. Andrew Graham-Dixon, *The Independent*, 24 November 1987.
178. *The Times*, 25 May 1990, 5 June, 6 December 1991.
179. Ibid., 20 June 1995.
180. BBC Radio 4, *Today*, 10 August 1992; Channel 4, 17 April 1993, 11.35 p.m.
181. *The Times*, 29 August 1994.
182. Ibid., 30 August 1994.

Chapter 21 *(pp.446–506)*

1. Johnson, P.H., pp.11, 43, 122.
2. Longford Report, pp.51–2, 274, 370–3.
3. *The Times*, 19 January 1990.
4. *Telegraph Weekend Magazine*, 3 February 1990, p.23.
5. *The Times Saturday Review*, 30 January 1993, p.5.
6. *Telegraph Weekend Magazine*, 3 February 1990, p.23.
7. *The Times*, 19 January 1990.
8. Ibid.
9. Longford Report, pp.273–4.
10. Tony Parsons, *The Times Saturday Review*, 30 January 1990, p.5.
11. *Telegraph Weekend Magazine*, 3 February 1990, p.19.
12. Hayman, p.93.
13. Brody, pp.24, 88, 125–6, 136.
14. Williams, B. (ed.), Paragraphs 2.28, 4.26, 6.3ff., 10.6.
15. Ibid., Paragraphs 7.22, 9.29ff., 11.10ff.
16. Ibid., Paragraphs 12.10, 12.11, 12.36ff.
17. *The Times*, 24 November 1983, 14 April 1989.
18. Ibid., 24 November 1983.

19. Ibid., 2 November 1983.
20. Itzin (ed.) (1992), p.428.
21. *Exeter Leader*, 24 July 1986.
22. *The Independent*, 21 September 1988.
23. *The Times*, 25 February 1994.
24. Ibid., 'Vision' supplement, 14–20 January 1995; ibid., 28 June 1995.
25. *Cross Keys*, Peterborough Diocesan News, July 1993.
26. *Criminal Statistics*, assorted years; Jennifer Temkin, in Tomaselli and Porter (eds), p.22.
27. *The Times*, 28 November 1985.
28. See, e.g., ibid., 9 September 1995.
29. Ibid., 23 June 1994.
30. Incidents cited have all featured in *The Times* of various dates.
31. Ibid., 4 September 1993, 7 January 1994.
32. Ibid., 29 April 1994.
33. Ibid., 8 August 1994.
34. Ibid., 20 May 1995.
35. Ibid., 26 November 1993.
36. *The Independent*, 9 September 1989.
37. *The Times*, 11 October 1988.
38. Glubb, p.17.
39. James Weaver, in Itzin (ed.) (1992), Chapter 16.
40. Itzin (ed.) (1992), p.539.
41. T.R. Gurr, 'Historical Trends in Violent Crime', *Crime and Justice*, Vol.3, 1981, pp.295–353.
42. *Criminal Statistics*, assorted years.
43. *The Times*, 21 June 1993, 1 September 1994.
44. Ibid., 19 August 1993.
45. Ibid., 19 March 1994.
46. Ibid., 17 March 1995.
47. *Bankers' Magazine*, 1970, Vol.210, p.22.
48. BBC 2, *Public Eye*, 15 May 1993; *The Times*, 28 April 1993.
49. *The Independent*, 11 September 1992.
50. *The Times*, 21 April 1992.
51. Ibid., 6 October 1992.
52. BBC 2, *Public Eye*, 15 May 1993.
53. *The Times*, 25 January 1995.
54. Ibid., 13 June 1991.
55. Ibid., 29 December 1994.
56. Ibid., 31 August 1995.
57. Ibid., 1 January 1994.
58. *Corporal Punishment*, Report of the Advisory Council on the Treatment of Offenders, November 1960, Cmnd 1213, p.14.
59. *The Independent*, 17 January 1989; *The Times*, 27 October 1989.
60. *The Times*, 14 July 1978, 11 August 1992.
61. Ibid., 20 May, 12 and 26 July 1991.
62. Ibid., 7 November 1987.
63. Ibid., 29 September 1991.
64. Ibid., 1 March 1993.
65. Ibid., 9 October 1993.
66. *The Independent*, 14 November 1986.
67. Ibid., 6 July 1989.
68. *The Times*, 24 March 1995.
69. *The Independent*, 13 January 1989.
70. *The Times*, 4 June 1993.
71. BBC Radio 4, *File on Four*, 17 May 1994.
72. *The Times*, 20 October 1993, 1 April 1994.
73. Ibid., 25 November 1994.
74. Ibid., 28 September 1995.
75. Ibid., 26 April 1994.
76. David Dale, *The Independent*, 8 March 1988.
77. Ibid., 20 October 1986.
78. *The Times*, 13 March 1992.
79. *The Independent*, 25 April 1988.
80. Ibid., 11 September 1992.
81. Letter to *The Times*, 23 June 1990.
82. Ibid., 9 December 1991.
83. Ibid., 18 November 1993.
84. *The Independent*, 9 September 1989.
85. British Retail Cosortium, *Retail Crime Costs*, 1992–3 Survey, 1994.
86. *Daily Telegraph*, 13 September 1990.
87. *The Times*, 10 July 1989.
88. Ibid., 29 September 1995.
89. London Buses Ltd. Network and Safety Services, personal communication.
90. British Transport Police, personal communication; *The Times*, 9 March 1993.
91. BBC Radio 4, *File on Four*, 17 May 1994.
92. *The Times*, 17 May 1994.
93. Ibid., 5 December 1989.
94. Ibid., 21 December 1991, 7 September 1992.
95. Ibid., 28 June 1994.
96. BBC 2, *Open Space: The Face in the Window*, 22 April 1991.
97. BBC Radio 4, *Today*, 19 March 1994.

98. British Rail, personal communication.
99. *The Times*, 21 October 1986.
100. *The Independent*, 20 October 1986.
101. *The Times*, 9 April 1988.
102. Ibid., 17 June 1988.
103. Ibid.
104. *The Independent*, 31 March 1989.
105. *The Times*, 12 June 1993.
106. Ibid., 6 April 1994.
107. Ibid., 30 March 1994.
108. Ibid., 27 January 1995.
109. Ibid., 19 January 1995.
110. Ibid., 31 May 1995.
111. See, e.g., ibid., 2 August 1989; BBC Radio 4, *Today*, 17 December 1993.
112. *The Times*, 27 June, 1 September 1994.
113. Ibid., 16 November 1990.
114. *Police Review*, 6 October and 10 November 1989.
115. Police Convalescence and Rehabilitation Trust, personal communication.
116. *The Times*, 8 November 1991.
117. HM Inspectorate of Constabulary, Home Office, personal communication; *The Times*, 2 August 1994.
118. *The Times*, 26 April 1994.
119. Ibid., 23 April 1994.
120. *Study of Post Shooting Experiences in Firearms Officers*, Home Office, 1988.
121. *The Times*, 1 November 1988.
122. Ibid., 26 December 1992.
123. Ibid., 1 June 1993.
124. Christie Davies, in Anderson (ed.), Chapter 1.
125. See Dunning, et.al., *passim.*
126. *The Times*, 12 April 1993.
127. Critchley, p.212.
128. *The Times*, 20 April 1994.
129. Ibid., 9 and 22 May 1991.
130. Northam, pp.33–4; *The Times*, 17 December 1986.
131. *The Times*, 25 February 1992.
132. Ibid., 23 October 1993.
133. Ibid., 11 March 1994.
134. Ibid., 20 January 1995.
135. *The Independent*, 22 September 1988.
136. *The Times*, 10 May 1991.
137. BBC Radio 4, *Today*, 19 March 1994.
138. *The Times*, 16 and 17 June, 24 November 1993.
139. Ibid., 15 April, 17 and 19 May, 21 June, 24 November 1994.
140. Ibid., 9 August 1994.
141. Ibid., 15 January 1994.
142. Ibid., 16 May 1995.
143. *Criminal Statistics*, assorted years.
144. *The Times*, 8 July 1991.
145. Ibid., 6 July 1994.
146. Ibid., 27 July 1991.
147. Ibid., 27 October 1990.
148. Ibid., 4 July 1995.
149. Ibid., 18 July 1991; 21 November 1995.
150. BBC Radio 4, *Sunday*, 18 August 1991; *The Times*, 10 February 1992, 14 February 1993.
151. *The Times*, 15 January 1992.
152. Ibid., 12 February 1993.
153. Ibid., 21 November 1995.
154. Ibid., 4 February 1993.
155. Ibid., 3 August 1990.
156. Ibid., 26 August 1988.
157. Ibid., 1 November 1993.
158. Ibid., 23 March 1995.
159. Ibid., 12 May 1978.
160. Ibid., 3 November 1990.
161. *AA Magazine*, Issue 8, Summer 1994; *The Times*, 9 March 1992.
162. *The Times*, 23 June 1994.
163. Ibid., 5 July 1978.
164. Ibid., 21 February 1973.
165. *The Independent*, 28 March 1988; BBC Radio 4, *Face the Facts*, 24 January 1990.
166. *The Times*, 18 March 1991, 9 April 1993.
167. *The Independent*, 13 January 1989.
168. *The Times*, 15 March 1994.
169. The Home Secretary, BBC Radio 4, *Today*, 9 September 1994.
170. *The Times*, 1 May 1995.
171. Ibid., 4 May 1994.
172. Ibid., 12 March 1990, 31 August 1993, 15 March 1994.
173. Ibid., 28 January 1989; *The Independent*, 30 January 1989.
174. *Daily Telegraph*, 29 June 1994.
175. *The Times*, 22 December 1994.
176. Ibid., 6 June 1994.
177. Ibid., 22 May 1995.
178. Ibid., 7 December 1994.
179. Ibid., 5 November 1993.
180. Cambridge Green Network, personal communication.
181. *The Times*, 28 October 1994.
182. Ibid., 23 April 1993.
183. Ibid., 11 April 1985, 12 April 1993.

184. Ibid., 17 August 1991.
185. See, e.g., ibid., 1 and 5 August 1995.
186. Ibid., 26 June 1992.
187. Ibid., 2 March 1994.
188. Ibid., 28 January, 24 November 1989.
189. Ibid., 25 September 1992.
190. Ibid., 14 June 1993.
191. Ibid., 19 July 1993.
192. Ibid., 21 April 1994.
193. Ibid., 18 December 1993.
194. Ibid., 22 and 23 March 1994.
195. Ibid. and *Daily Telegraph*, 1 and 2 April 1994; *The Times*, 27 and 28 May, 3 and 8 June 1994.
196. *The Times*, 17 May and 23 June 1994.
197. Ibid., 2 June 1994.
198. Medved, Part VI.
199. *New Society*, 19 February 1988.
200. BBC, p.6.
201. Ibid., p.19.
202. According to Channel 4, *Signals*, 2 November 1988.
203. *The Times*, 6 October 1990.
204. Ibid., 18 June 1991.
205. Ibid., 'Life and Times', 7 May 1992.
206. Ibid., 19 March 1993.
207. Ibid., 20 and 21 January 1995; *Daily Telegraph*, 20 January 1995.
208. *The Times*, 20 and 23 May 1995.
209. BBC Radio 4 news, 26 December 1993.
210. *The Times*, 14 April 1995.
211. Ibid., 15 April 1994.
212. Ibid., 20, 24, 25 March, 3, 29 April 1993.
213. Ibid., 24 November 1993.
214. Ibid., 7 January 1994.
215. Ibid., 8 May 1992; BBC Radio 4, news, 7 May 1992.
216. *The Times*, 25 June 1993.

Chapter 22 (pp.507–543)

1. Himmelfarb, p.37. The Schumpeter quotation is from R. Skidelsky, *John Maynard Keynes* (Macmillan, London, 1983), p.xviii.
2. Harold Macmillan, *Riding the Storm* (Macmillan, London, 1971), pp.33ff.
3. *The Times*, 13 March 1992.
4. E.g., Baroness Trumpington, on BBC Radio 4, *Any Questions*, 28 January 1988.
5. Neil Fletcher, BBC Radio 4, *Today*, 8 December 1987.
6. John Rae, *The Times*, 17 October 1980.
7. Home Office, personal communication.
8. The information on drugs and drug usage is derived, except where otherwise stated, from Andrew Tyler's authoritative survey *Street Drugs*.
9. *The Times*, 24 September 1993, 'On This Day' for 1937.
10. Home Office, personal communication.
11. Tyler, *passim*.
12. *The Times*, 24 March 1994.
13. BBC 1, *Everyman*, 14 August 1994.
14. *The Times*, 5 July 1994.
15. *Social Trends*, various years; Martin Plant, 'The Epidemiology of Illicit drug use and misuse in Britain', in Macgregor (ed.), pp.56–7; *The Times*, 12 February 1994.
16. Tyler, p.355.
17. *The Times*, 24 September 1993, 'On This Day' for 1937; Macgregor (ed.), p.56; *Statistics of drug seizures and offenders dealt with, United Kingdom 1990*, Home Office Statistical Bulletin, Issue 19/91; Issue 25/92, supplementary tables.
18. *The Times*, 20 January 1995.
19. Ibid., 4 June 1994.
20. Tyler, p.180.
21. BBC Radio 4, *Today*, 4 November 1988; *The Independent*, 3 July 1989; *The Times*, 2, 3, 16 October 1989.
22. *The Times*, 8 July 1994.
23. Ibid., 20 October 1994.
24. OECD, p.13.
25. Malcolm Macmillen, 'The Economic Effect of International Migration', *Journal of Common Market Studies*, March 1982, Vol. XX, No.3, pp.248–9.
26. *The Times*, 27 March 1973.
27. Ibid., 2 June 1993.
28. D.A. Coleman, 'Population', in Halsey (ed.), p.125; *Social Trends*, 1993, Table 2.19.
29. *The Times*, 13 June 1990.
30. Ibid., 21 February 1991.
31. Ibid., 22 September 1989.
32. D.A. Coleman, 'Population', in Halsey (ed.), p.57.
33. Abortion statistics from *Social Trends*. Casualty figures supplied by Imperial War Museum.

34. *On the State of the Public Health*, assorted years.
35. *The Times*, 9 September 1994.
36. Ibid., 25 October 1994.
37. Ibid., 9 August 1995.
38. Ibid., 26 July 1995.
39. *New Farmer and Grower*, Spring 1994, p.6.
40. See, e.g., *Observer*, 12 March 1972; *The Times*, 24 January 1976; Denis Healey, *The Time of my Life* (Penguin, Harmondsworth, 1989), p.402.
41. *The Times*, 15 March 1972.
42. Ibid., 5 July 1994.
43. Ibid., 2 September 1993.
44. Ibid., 22 May 1990.
45. Ibid., 22 December 1992.
46. Ibid., 5 September 1994.
47. Ibid., 3 November 1995.
48. Ibid., 5 June 1995.
49. Ibid., 1 February 1994.
50. Ibid., 30 July 1993.
51. Ibid., 28 July 1995.
52. Ibid., 22 February 1993.
53. Ibid., 29 July 1995.
54. Ibid., 28 January 1994.
55. Ibid., 1 December 1994, commenting on *Protecting the Public Purse 2: Ensuring Probity in the NHS*, HMSO, 1994.
56. *The Times*, 6 February 1992, 19 April, 28 May, 12, 13 and 18 October 1994.
57. Ibid., 25 April 1995.
58. Ibid., 21 September 1994.
59. Audit Commission, *Opportunity Makes a Thief* (HMSO, London, 1994).
60. *The Times*, 18 January 1995.
61. Ibid., 31 August 1995.
62. Ibid., 27 September 1993; *E.C. Initiative* (Norton Rose M5 Group, London), July/August 1993; *The Times*, 16 November 1994.
63. *The Times*, 3 November 1990.
64. BBC Radio 4 news, 28 March 1994.
65. *The Times*, 27 April 1995.
66. Burrows and Cooper, p.52.
67. BBC Radio 4 news, 28 December 1993.
68. *The Times*, 1 May 1991.
69. Ibid., 29 December 1994.
70. London Buses Ltd. Network and Safety Services, personal communication.
71. *The Times*, 24 August 1991.
72. British Rail, personal communication.
73. BT Report to Shareholders, September 1993.
74. *The Times*, 30 June 1993.
75. BBC Radio 4, *Today*, 22 October 1993.
76. *The Times*, 21 March 1995, *CAR 95*, 25 March 1995.
77. *The Times*, 20 February 1991.
78. Liberty Annual Report and Accounts, 1993.
79. *The Times*, 18 May 1992.
80. Ibid., 18 May, 1 October 1992.
81. Ibid., 2 October 1992.
82. Ibid., 15 April 1993.
83. Ibid., 2 October 1992, 3 February 1993.
84. Ibid., 2 October 1992.
85. Ibid.
86. Ibid., 4 December 1992, 25 April, 16 June 1994.
87. Ibid., 18 February 1991.
88. Ibid., 3 November 1994.
89. Ibid., 21 November 1995.
90. Ibid., 30 August 1994.
91. *The Independent*, 30 June, 25 August 1988.
92. *The Times*, 14 August 1989.
93. Ibid., 7 April 1993.
94. Ibid., 5 September 1992.
95. Ibid., 7 April, 25 March 1994.
96. Ibid., 24 June 1994, 18 May 1992, 18 May 1994.
97. Ibid., 22 November 1995.
98. Ibid., 2 March, 4 July, 7 October 1992.
99. Ibid., 19 October 1993.
100. Ibid., 15 March, 5 April 1993.
101. Ibid., 6 February 1995.
102. *SPAN*, Journal of the Soil Association, New Bells Press, Haughley, Suffolk, No.24, February 1969.
103. Frank Fraser Darling, *Wilderness and Plenty* (BBC, London, 1970), pp.7, 57.
104. *The Times*, 25 and 27 January 1972.
105. Ehrlich, p.16, quoting W. and P. Paddock, *Famine 1975* (Weidenfeld and Nicolson, London, 1968).
106. Meadows, Donella and Dennis, Randers, J., Behrens, W., *The Limits to Growth* (Earth Island Ltd, London, 1972). *Guardian*, 6 March 1972.
107. Ehrlich, pp.16–18, 99–101.
108. *The Times*, 11 October 1990.
109. *Sustainable Development: The UK Strategy* (HMSO, London, 1994), pp.3, 5.
110. *Observer*, 12 March 1972.

111. Report by Ed Mayo on work by Tim Jackson and Nic Marks, *New Economics*, Issue 29, Spring 1994, pp.6–7.

112. Kew, p.61.

113. Body, pp.51–2, 54, 73–4; BBC 2, *Horizon*, 18 May 1992.

114. Body, p.190.

115. Kew, Chapter 7.

116. *The Times*, 13 January 1994.

117. *The Independent*, 18 July 1988.

118. Ibid., 17 November 1988; *Animals International*, World Society for the Protection of Animals, London, Spring 1992, p.8.

119. *The Times*, 26 August, 17 September 1992, 28 July 1994.

120. *The Independent*, 18 February 1989.

121. *The Times*, 13 February 1989.

122. Ibid., 18 June 1990.

123. Dates are derived from Mercer (ed.).

124. *The Times*, 15 July 1993.

125. Ibid., 28 January 1994.

126. Ibid., 22 February 1984.

127. Ibid., 25 February 1984.

128. *The Independent*, 13 April 1987.

129. *The Times*, 20 May 1990, 1 June 1993, 3 October 1983.

130. Ibid., 10 October 1994.

131. Ibid., 29 September 1993.

132. *The Independent*, 18 December 1989; *The Times*, 5 August 1992, 24 June 1993, 13 September 1995.

133. *The Independent*, 27 February 1988; *The Times*, 22 April 1988.

134. *The Times*, 7 March 1990, 24 June 1992, 21 May 1994.

135. Ibid., 18 November 1993.

136. Ibid., 23 February 1994.

137. Ibid., 23, 24, 25, 26, 27, 28, 30 January, 11 February 1989.

138. Ibid., 28 July 1994.

139. Ibid., 29 August 1994.

140. Ibid., 16 February 1995.

141. Ibid., 18 and 20 April 1988; *British Medical Journal*, Volume 296, 30 April 1988.

142. *The Independent*, 26 July 1989.

143. Mercer (ed.), under October and November 1984; ITV, *This Week*, 6 July 1989; *The Times*, 14 December 1987, 18 April 1988.

144. *The Independent*, 26 July 1989.

145. *The Times*, 31 August 1993.

146. Ibid., 20, 26, 27, 28, 29, 31 October, 2 November 1994.

147. See, e.g., ibid., 11 August 1988, 19 April 1990, 18 February 1991.

148. Channel 4, *Brave New World*, 23 May 1994.

149. *The Times*, 3 January 1994.

150. Channel 4, *Brave New World*, 23 and 30 May 1994.

151. *The Times*, 14 April 1994.

152. Ibid., 20 July 1994.

153. Ibid., 5 and 24 January 1994.

154. Ibid., 8 December 1987.

155. Channel 4, *Brave New World*, 30 May 1994.

156. *The Times*, 16 March 1990.

157. Ibid., 26 June 1990.

158. Ibid., 26 April 1990.

159. Ibid., 20 February 1991.

160. See the abbreviated version of the speech by Suzanne Rini, author of *Beyond Abortion: A Chronology of Foetal Experimentation*, to the International Family Congress, published in *Freedom Today*, December 1990.

161. *Daily Telegraph*, 28 June 1994.

162. *The Times*, 13 May 1995.

163. Steiner, pp.351–3.

164. The story was told in *Death of a Wagon Train*, Channel 4, 20 May 1993.

165. *The Independent*, 24 August 1987.

166. *The Times*, 2 March 1973; (Plymouth) *Herald*, 5 May 1973; *Western Morning News*, 14 July 1973.

167. Read, p.299.

168. BBC 1, *Everyman*, 18 April 1993.

Chapter 23 (pp.544–581)

1. BBC Radio 4, *Desert Island Discs*, 26 March 1993.

2. Vyvyan (1971), p.159. Vyvyan's sources are *Trials of War Criminals before the Nuremberg Military Tribunals under Control Law No.10*, Vols.I and II, 'The Medical Case' (US Government Printing Office 1946–49); and A. Mitscherligh and E. Mielke, *The Death Doctors*, tr. James Cleugh (Elek, London, 1962).

3. Vyvyan (1971), p.158.

4. *The Independent*, 20 January 1989, discussing Peter Williams and David Wallace, *Unit 731* (Hodder and Stoughton, London, 1989).
5. Vyvyan (1971), p.161.
6. Singer, Peter, p.174.
7. Ibid., p.85.
8. Ibid., Chapter 5.
9. Primatt, p.15.
10. Ibid., pp.16, 17.
11. Ibid., p.87.
12. *The Independent*, 27 February 1989.
13. BBC 2, 22 November 1991; *The Times*, 11 August 1994.
14. *The Times Saturday Review*, 7 November 1992.
15. BBC 2, 22 November 1991; *The Times*, 30 December 1993, 25 August 1994.
16. *The Times*, 17 September 1994.
17. *The Times Saturday Review*, 7 November 1992.
18. *The Times*, 4 June 1994.
19. Ibid., 25 August 1990.
20. Ibid., 21 August 1991.
21. Ibid., 21 August, 12 November 1991.
22. Ibid., 7 March, 30 July, 2 and 6 August 1994.
23. Ibid., 29 July, 5 August 1991.
24. *Guardian*, 12 March 1986.
25. *The Times*, 5 February 1991.
26. Ibid., 12 June 1991.
27. Ibid., 8 June 1994.
28. Ibid., 11 February, 8 June, 17 November 1994.
29. Ibid., 18 November 1994.
30. Ibid., 8 June 1993.
31. Ibid., 30 May 1994.
32. Ibid., 15 December 1994.
33. Ibid., 5 July 1995.
34. Rutter and Smith.
35. *The Times*, 27 September 1991, 26 January 1994.
36. Ibid., 1 June 1993.
37. Ibid., 23 June 1994.
38. Ibid., 29 April 1993.
39. Ibid., 25 June 1990.
40. Ibid., 18 May 1984.
41. Ibid., 18 May 1984, 9 December 1986, 29 September 1989, 10 May 1990; *Family Portraits* (Social Affairs Unit, London, 1986); *The Independent*, 28 July 1988; *British Medical Journal*, 27 January 1990, p.236; Dennis and Erdos.
42. *The Times*, 29 September 1989.
43. Ibid., 9 October 1993.
44. *Children living in re-ordered families* (Joseph Rowntree Foundation, York, 1994).
45. *The Times*, 9 February 1994.
46. Dennis and Erdos, p.xii.
47. Murray, Charles.
48. *The Times*, 12 July 1995.
49. Macintyre, pp.67ff., 103ff.
50. Alan Ryan, Professor of Politics at Princeton University, *The Times*, 18 May 1994.
51. Ibid., 5 September 1994.
52. Ibid., 20 April 1994.
53. Ibid., 13 October 1993.
54. Ibid., 24 May 1994.
55. Cowell (1970), pp. 310ff., 407.
56. *The Independent*, 17 January 1988.
57. See, for instance, Professor Plant's 'Communities v. consumers', *The Times*, 28 August 1990.
58. Ibid., 11 April 1988.
59. *The Independent*, 27 May 1988; *The Times*, 'Life and Times', p.5, 20 February 1992; ibid., 26 December 1993.
60. *Faith in the City*, (Church House Publishing, London, 1985), *The Times*, 31 March 1992.
61. Ibid., 13 August 1988.
62. See, for instance, Clifford Longley, 'Spectre of the New Right', ibid., 9 September 1989.
63. Quoted by Clifford Longley, ibid., 15 February 1988.
64. BBC Radio 4, *Thought for the Day*, 28 July 1993.
65. *The Times*, 7 December 1993.
66. Ibid., 17 April 1992.
67. Ibid., 10 December 1986.
68. Ibid., 30 August 1991.
69. *The Independent*, 18 February 1989.
70. TASS report, Translation by *Pravda*, published 22 July 1989, World Council of Churches Central Committee obtained courtesy Church of England Board for Social Responsibility.
71. *The Times*, 8 January 1990.
72. Ibid., 8 January 1992.
73. Ibid., 7 January 1994.
74. Ibid., 7 December 1981, 19 December 1994.

75. Ibid., 6 January 1986.
76. Ibid., 15 December 1993, 16 November 1994.
77. *The Independent*, 20 April 1988.
78. *The Times*, 30 August 1990.
79. Ibid., 19 May 1993.
80. *The Independent*, 28 September 1987, 17 July 1989.
81. Marty and Appleby, pp.11–12.
82. Macintyre, p.205.
83. Martin, p.101.
84. Wilson, B., Part II.
85. *The Times*, 16 December 1987; *The Independent*, 30 December 1987; *The Times*, 26 September 1991, 8 December 1993.
86. *The Times*, 1 February 1993, 28 June 1994.
87. Ibid., 8 June 1991.
88. Ibid., 12 October 1993, 28 May 1994.
89. Ibid., 12 October 1993.
90. Ibid., 10 August 1993.
91. Ibid., 19 October, 9 November 1993, 25, 26 January 1994.
92. BBC Radio 4 news, 5 July 1994.
93. *The Times*, 2 August 1989.
94. Ibid., 20 November 1971; *Observer*, 19 December 1971.
95. *WWF News*, July 1988; *WWF Review*, 1989.
96. *WWF News*, July 1989; *The Times*, 15 September, 25 November 1989.
97. *The Independent*, 18 September 1989.
98. Ibid., 23 September 1989.
99. James Lovelock, 'Gaia as seen through the Atmosphere', *Atmospheric Environment*, Vol.6, 579, 1972; 'Atmospheric Homoeostasis by and for the biosphere: The Gaia Hypothesis', *Tellus*, 26, Vol.2, 1973; 'The Quest for Gaia', *New Scientist*, 6 February 1975; *Gaia – A New Look at Life on Earth*.
100. *Daily Telegraph*, 30 December 1991.
101. John Postgate, *New Scientist*, 7 April 1988.
102. *The Times*, 26 October 1990.
103. Ibid., 21 April 1993.
104. Hughes, p.204.
105. *The Times*, 12 September 1994.
106. Ibid., 24 September 1994.
107. Ibid., 12 December 1994.
108. BBC Radio 4, *Going Places*, 15 April 1994.
109. *The Times*, 28 February 1992, 23 June, 6 September 1994.
110. Ibid., 17 June 1992.
111. Ibid., 18 June 1988.
112. Ibid., 3 May 1978.
113. Ibid., 14 May 1990.
114. Ibid., 14 March, 25 November, 2 December 1983, 23 February 1984, 20 September 1985.
115. *The Independent*, 5 May 1989.
116. University of Exeter Annual Report, 1992–3, p.4.
117. *The Times*, 5 July 1995.
118. Tyler, p.133; BBC2, *Bookmark Special: Aldous Huxley: Darkness and Light*, 23 July 1994.
119. Tyler, p.181.
120. Ibid., p.190.
121. Huxley (1959) p. 110.
122. Rookmaaker, pp.205–7.
123. *The Times*, 4 March and 7 August 1991.
124. Ibid., 'Weekend Times', 11 January 1992.
125. Taylor, F. Sherwood, p.x.
126. Sorokin (1941), p.317.
127. *The Times*, 20 September 1994.
128. *The Times*, 27 August, 23 November 1990, 26 November 1992, 8 July 1993 (reviewing *Afghan Stories*, by Oleg Yermakov).
129. *Encounter*, May 1980, p.22.
130. *The Times*, 9, 10 and 18 November 1993.
131. BBC Radio 4, *Sunday*, 30 January 1994.
132. *Sunday Times*, 12 January 1992.
133. Macintyre, p.244.
134. *New Economics*, Issue 31, Autumn 1994, pp.10–11; *The Times*, 17 October 1994.
135. *The Times*, 22 September 1994.
136. Sorokin (1941), p.205.
137. Burke, p.319, 'A Letter to a Member of the National Assembly' (1791).

Bibliography

Alföldy, G., *The Social History of Rome*, tr. D. Braund and F. Pollock (Routledge, London, 1988)

Ammianus Marcellinus, *History*, tr. John C. Rolfe (Loeb, Heinemann, London, 1950–2)

Anderson, Digby (ed.), *The Loss of Virtue* (Social Affairs Unit, London, 1992)

Andrews, Stuart, *Methodism and Society* (Longman, London, 1970)

Anthony, Sister Rose, *The Jeremy Collier Stage Controversy*, 1937, (reissued Blom, New York, 1966)

Antitheatrical Tracts 1702–1704, ed. A. Freeman (Garland Publishing Inc., New York, 1974)

Appian, *Roman History*, tr. Horace White (Loeb, Heinemann, London, 1912–13)

Apuleius, *Apologia*, tr. H.E. Butler (Clarendon Press, Oxford, 1909)

Apuleius, *The Golden Ass*, tr. Robert Graves (Penguin, Harmondsworth, 1950)

Aristides Quintilianus, *De Musica*, ed. R.P. Winnington Ingram (Lipsiae [Leipzig] Teubner, 1963)

Aristotle, *Poetics*, tr. W. Hamilton Fyfe (Loeb, Heinemann, London, 1946)

Arnott, Peter D., *The Ancient Greek and Roman Theatre* (Random House, New York, 1971)

Artz, Frederick B., *The Mind of the Middle Ages* (Knopf, New York, 1953)

Astin, Alan E., *Cato the Censor* (Clarendon Press, Oxford, 1978)

Atkins, S., *Goethe's Faust* (Harvard University Press, Cambridge, Mass., 1958)

Augustan History (*See Scriptores Historiae Augustae*)

Augustine, *City of God* [1]: Books 1–3 tr. George E. McCracken, 1957; Books 4–8 tr. W.M. Green, 1965; Books 8–11 tr. David Wiesen, 1968; Books 12–15 tr. P. Levine, 1966; Books 16–18 tr. E.M. Sanford and W.M. Green, 1965; Books 18–20 tr. W.C. Greene, 1960; Books 21–22 tr. W.M. Green 1972 (Loeb, Heinemann, London)

Augustine, *City of God* [2], tr. J.E.C. Welldon (SPCK, London, 1924)

Augustine, *City of God* [3], abridged and tr. J.W.C. Wand (Oxford University Press, London, 1963)

Augustine, *Confessions*, tr. W. Watts, 1631 (reissued Loeb, Heinemann, London, 1912)

Augustine, *Seventeen Short Treatises*, tr. C.L. Cornish (Parker, Oxford, 1847)

Augustus, *The Acts of Augustus*, tr. F.W. Shipley (Loeb, Heinemann, London, 1924)

Axton, Richard, *European Drama of the Early Middle Ages* (Hutchinson, London, 1974)

Bacon, Francis, *The Advancement of Learning*, 1605 (Macmillan & Co., London, 1920)

Bacon, Francis, *New Atlantis*, 1629 (reprinted Cassell, London, 1889)

Baker, Richard, *Theatrum Redivivum, or The Theatre Vindicated*, 1662, ed. A. Freeman, (Garland Publishing Inc., New York, 1973)

Balsdon, J.P.V.D., *Life and Leisure in Ancient Rome* (Bodley Head, London, 1969)

Balsdon, J.P.V.D., *Romans and Aliens* (Duckworth, London, 1979)

Barnes, John, *Ahead of his Age* (Collins, London, 1979)

Barnes, Philip, *Companion to Post-War British Theatre* (Croom Helm, London, 1986)

Bartsch H.W. (ed.), *Kerygma and Myth*, tr. R.H. Fuller (SPCK, London, 1953)

Batsford, H., and Fry, C., *The Greater English Church* (B.T. Batsford, London, 1943–4)

BBC, *Violence and the Media* (BBC, London, 1988)

Beare, W., *The Roman Stage* (Methuen, London, 1950)

Beaumont, Keith, *Jarry: Ubu Roi* (Grant & Cutler, London, 1987)

Becker, Carl, *The Declaration of Independence* (Vintage Books, New York, 1942)

Beckmann, John, *A History of Inventions, Discoveries and Origins*, tr. W. Johnston (Bohn, London, 1846)

Bede, *The Complete Works of Venerable Bede*, tr. J.A. Giles (Whittaker and Co., London, 1843–4)

Bede, *A History of the English Church and People*, tr. Leo Sherley-Price (Penguin, Harmondsworth, 1968)

Bedford, Arthur, *The Evil and Danger of Stage-Plays*, 1706, ed. A. Freeman (Garland Publishing Inc., New York, 1974)

Bentley, Eric (ed.), *Theory of the Modern Stage* (Penguin, Harmondsworth, 1968)

Bergin, Thomas G., *Boccaccio* (Viking Press, New York, 1981)

Berthold, Margot, *A History of World Theatre*, tr. Edith Simmons (Ungar, New York, 1972)

Bieber, M., *The History of the Greek and Roman Theatre* (Princeton University Press, Princeton, NJ, 2nd edn.,1961)

Bingham, Joseph, *Christian Antiquities*, 1708 (reissued Straker, London, 1834)

Blackham, H.J. (ed.), *Objections to Humanism* (Constable, London, 1963)

Blackstone, Sir W., *Commentaries*, 1783 (reprinted Garland Publishing Inc., New York and London, 1978)

Bloch, Raymond, *The Etruscans*, tr. Stuart Hood (Thames and Hudson, London, 1958)

Bloom, Allan, *The Closing of the American Mind* (Simon & Schuster, New York, 1987)

Body, Richard, *Our Food, Our Land* (Rider, London, 1991)

Boswell, James, *Life of Johnson*, 1791 (eds G.B. Hill and L.F. Powell, Clarendon Press, Oxford, 1934)

Bradbrook, M.C., *The Rise of the Common Player* (Chatto & Windus, London, 1962)

Brecht, Bertolt, *The Measures Taken*, tr. Carl R. Mueller (Eyre Methuen, London, 1977)

Brody, S., *Screen Violence and Film Censorship* (Home Office Research Study No. 40, HMSO, London, 1977)

Brogan, D.W., *The English People* (Hamish Hamilton, London, 1943)

Broughton, T.R.S., *The Magistrates of the Roman Republic* (American Philological Association, New York, 1952)

Brown, Ford K., *Fathers of the Victorians* (Cambridge University Press, Cambridge, 1961)

Brown, Ivor, *Life within Reason* (Nicholson and Watson, London, 1939)

Bibliography

Brown, Peter, *The Body and Society: Men, Women and Sexual Renunciation in Early Christianity* (Faber & Faber, London, 1989)

Brustein, R., *The Theatre of Revolt* (Methuen, London, 1965)

Bultmann, Rudolf, *New Testament and Mythology*, tr. Schubert M. Ogden (SCM Press, London, 1985 edn.)

Burke, E., *Works* (World Classics, Oxford University Press, London, 1907)

Burrows, John, and Cooper, Diane, *Theft and Loss from UK Libraries: A National Survey* (Home Office Police Department, London, 1992)

Burstall, A.F., *History of Mechanical Engineering* (Faber, London, 1963)

Bury, J.B., *History of the Later Roman Empire* (Macmillan, London, 1923)

Byrn, Edward W., *The Progress of Invention in the Nineteenth Century*, 1900 (Russell, New York, 1970)

Cameron, Alan, *Bread and Circuses* (King's College, London, 1973)

Cameron, Alan, *Circus Factions* (Clarendon Press, Oxford, 1976)

Canfora, Luciano, *The Vanished Library*, tr. Martin Ryle (Hutchinson Radius, London, 1989)

Capra, Fritjof, *The Tao of Physics* (Wildwood House, London, 1975)

Carcopino, J., *Daily Life in Ancient Rome*, tr. E.O. Lorimer (Routledge & Kegan Paul, London, 1941)

Carson, Rachel, *Silent Spring* (Fawcett Crest, New York, 1962)

Carter, Vernon Gill, and Dale, Tom, *Topsoil and Civilization* (Oklahoma University Press, Norman, Oklahoma, revised edn., 1974)

Chadwick, Owen *The Spirit of the Oxford Movement* (Cambridge University Press, Cambridge, 1990)

Chambers, Colin, *Other Spaces, New Theatre and the RSC* (Eyre Methuen, London, 1980)

Chambers, Colin, *The Story of Unity Theatre* (Laurence & Wishart, London, 1989)

Chant, Colin (ed.), *Science Technology and Everyday Life, 1870–1950* (Routledge, London, and the Open University, 1989)

Chaytor, H.J., *The Troubadours* (Cambridge University Press, Cambridge, 1912)

Chiari, J., *Landmarks of Contemporary Drama* (Herbert Jenkins, London, 1965)

Chrysostom, John, *Homilies on Acts of the Apostles*, tr. H. Browne (Library of the Fathers, Parker, Oxford, 1851)

Chrysostom, John, *Homilies on Corinthians I*, tr. H.K. Cornish and J. Medley (Library of the Fathers, Parker, Oxford, 1839)

Chrysostom, John, *Homilies on the Gospel of St Matthew*, tr. G. Prevost (Library of the Fathers, Parker, Oxford, 1843)

Chrysostom, John, *Homilies on St John*, tr. G.T. Stupart (Library of the Fathers, Parker, Oxford, 1848)

Chrysostom, John, *Homilies on Thessalonians I*, tr. James Tweed (Library of the Fathers, Parker, Oxford, 1843)

Chrysostom, John, *To the People of Antioch*, tr. E. Budge (Library of the Fathers, Parker, Oxford, 1862)

Cicero, *Ad Familiares*, tr. W. Glynn Williams (Loeb, Heinemann, London, 1927–9)

Cicero, *De Re Publica*, tr. Clinton Walker Keyes (Loeb, Heinemann, London, 1928)

Clark, Kenneth, *Civilisation* (BBC and Murray, London, 1969)

Clement of Alexandria, *The Writings of Clement of Alexandria*, tr. William Wilson (T. & T. Clarke, Edinburgh, 1867)

Cohen, Gustave, *Histoire de la Mise en Scène dans le Théatre Religieux Français du Moyen Age* (Champion, Paris, 1926)

Cohen, Morris, and Drabkin, I.E. (eds), *A Source Book in Greek Science* (Harvard University Press, Cambridge, Mass., 1958)

Collier, Jeremy, *A Short View of the Immorality and Profaneness of the English Stage*, 1698, ed. A. Freeman (Garland Publishing Inc., New York, 1972)

Collier Tracts, Six Short Contributions, 1698, ed. A. Freeman (Garland Publishing Inc., New York, 1974)

Commager, H.S., *Documents of American History* (F.S. Crofts, New York, 3rd edn., 1944)

Commoner, Barry, *The Closing Circle* (Knopf, New York, 1971)

Commoner, Barry, *Science and Survival* (Viking, New York, 1966)

Conolly, L.W., *The Censorship of English Drama 1737–1824* (Huntingdon Library, San Marino, California, 1976)

Corcoran, Clodagh, *Pornography: The New Terrorism* (Attic Press, Dublin, 1989)

Cotterell, Leslie E., *Performance* (Offord, Eastbourne, 2nd edn., 1984)

Cowell, F.R., *History, Civilisation and Culture* (Thames & Hudson, London, 1952)

Cowell, F.R., *Values in Human Society* (Porter Sargent, Boston, 1970)

Cowley, Patrick, *Franciscan Rise and Fall* (Dent, London, 1933)

Crick, Francis, *The Astonishing Hypothesis* (Scribner, New York, 1994)

Critchley, T.A., *The Conquest of Violence* (Constable, London, 1970)

Cumont, Franz, *Oriental Religions in Roman Paganism* (Open Court Publishing Company, Chicago, 1911)

Cyprian, *The Writings of Cyprian*, tr. R.E. Wallis (T. & T. Clarke, Edinburgh, 1868–9)

Dal Maso, L.B., *Rome of the Caesars*, tr. Michael Hollingworth (Bonechi Edizioni, Florence, 1974)

Davey, Norman, *A History of Building Materials* (Phoenix House, London, 1961)

Davidson, William L., *Political Thought in England: The Utilitarians from Bentham to Mill*, 1915 (Oxford University Press, London, 1950 edn.)

Dawkins, Richard, *The Blind Watchmaker* (Longman Scientific and Technical, Harlow, 1986)

Dawkins, Richard, *The Selfish Gene* (Oxford University Press, Oxford, 1976)

Dennis, N., and Erdos G., *Families without Fatherhood* (Institute of Economic Affairs, London, 1992)

Deonna, W., *L'Archéologie, sa valeur, ses méthodes* (H. Laurens, Paris, 1912)

Derry, T.K., and Williams, T.I., *A Short History of Technology Past and Present* (Clarendon Press, Oxford, 1960)

Dictionary of National Biography (Oxford University Press, Oxford, 1963–5 edition)

Dill, Samuel, *Roman Society from Nero to Marcus Aurelius*, 1905 (Macmillan, London, 1925)

Dill, Samuel, *Roman Society in the Last Century of the Western Empire* (Macmillan, London, 1925)

Dio Cassius, *Roman History*, tr. Earnest Cary and H.B. Foster (Loeb, Heinemann, London, 1914–27)

Dio Chrysostom, *Discourses*, tr. J.W. Cahoon and H. Lamar Crosby (Loeb, Heinemann, London, 1932–51)

Dionysius of Halicarnassus, *The Roman Antiquities*, tr. Earnest Cary and Edward Spelman (Heinemann, London, 1937)

Dorey, T.A., and Dudley, D.R. (eds), *Roman Drama* (Routledge & Kegan Paul, London, 1965)

Dostoevsky, F., *Notebooks for the Possessed*, ed. Edward Wasiolek, tr. Victor Terras (University of Chicago Press, Chicago, 1968)

Dostoevsky, F., *The Unpublished Dostoevsky: Diaries and Notebooks (1860–81)*, Vols.I–III, tr. Arline Boyer and Carl R. Proffer (Ardis, Ann Arbor, 1973–6)

Dover, Kenneth, *Greek Homosexuality* (Duckworth, London, 1978)

Dover, Kenneth, *Greek Popular Morality* (Blackwell, Oxford, 1974)

Dryden, John, *The Dramatic Works of John Dryden*, ed. George Saintsbury (William Paterson, Edinburgh, 1882)

Dryden, John, *An Essay of Dramatic Poesy*, 1668, ed. Thomas Arnold (Clarendon Press, Oxford, 3rd edn., 1903)

Dryden, John, *The Poems and Fables of John Dryden*, ed. James Kinsley (Oxford University Press, London, 1962)

Duckworth, George E., *The Nature of Roman Comedy* (Princeton University Press, Princeton, NJ, 1952)

Duff, J. Wight, *Literary History of Rome from the Origins to the Close of the Golden Age*, 1900 (T. Fisher Unwin, London, 1910)

Duff, J. Wight, *Literary History of Rome in the Silver Age from Tiberius to Hadrian*, 1927 (Ernest Benn, London, 1960)

Dunning, E., Murphy, P., Williams, J., *The Roots of Football Hooliganism* (Routledge & Kegan Paul, London, 1989)

Eddy, Mary Baker, *Science and Health*, 1875 (Trustees under the will of Mary Baker G. Eddy, Boston, 1934)

Ehrlich, Paul, *The Population Bomb* (Ballantine/Friends of the Earth, London, 1971)

Elster, John, *An Introduction to Karl Marx* (Cambridge University Press, Cambridge, 1986)

Esslin, Martin, *The Theatre of the Absurd* (Penguin, Harmondsworth, 1968)

Euripides [1], *Opera*, tr. Arthur S. Way (Loeb, Heinemann, London, 1912)

Euripides [2], *Orestes and Other Plays*, tr. Philip Vellacott (Penguin, Harmondsworth, 1972)

Eusebius, *The Ecclesiastical History*, tr. Kirsopp Lake and F.E.L. Oulton (Loeb, Heinemann, London, 1926–32)

Ewen, Frederic, *Bertolt Brecht: His life, his art and his times* (Calder & Boyars, London, 1970)

Excerpta Valesiana, tr. John C. Rolfe (Loeb, Heinemann, London, 1952)

Fairweather, E.R. (ed.), *The Oxford Movement* (Oxford University Press, New York, 1964)

Faludy, George, *Erasmus of Rotterdam* (Eyre & Spottiswoode, London, 1970)

Ferrill, Arthur, *The Fall of the Roman Empire: The Military Explanation* (Thames & Hudson, London, 1986)

Findlater, Richard, *Banned* (MacGibbon & Kee, London, 1967)

Finley, M.I., *Aspects of Antiquity* (Penguin, Harmondsworth, 2nd edn., 1977)

Foner, Eric, *Tom Paine and Revolutionary America* (Oxford University Press, New York, 1976)

Forbes, R.J., *Studies in Ancient Technology* (E.J. Brill, Leiden, Vols.I–IX, 1955–64)

Fowler, H.W., *Modern English Usage* (Clarendon Press, Oxford, 1927)

Fowler, W. Warde, *The Roman Festivals of the period of the Republic* (Macmillan, London, 1899)

Fox, Robin Lane, *Pagans and Christians* (Viking, London, 1986)

Frank, Tenney (ed.), *An Economic Survey of Ancient Rome* (Johns Hopkins Press, Baltimore, Vols.I–VI, 1933–40)

Frank, Tenney, *Life and Literature in the Roman Republic* (Cambridge University Press, Cambridge, 1930)

Fraser, John, *Violence in the Arts* (Cambridge University Press, Cambridge, 1974)

Fraser, P.M., *Ptolemaic Alexandria* (Clarendon Press, Oxford, 1972)

Friedländer, Ludwig, *Roman Life and Manners*, tr. J.H. Freese and Leonard Magnus (Routledge, London, Vols.I–IV, 7th edn., 1913)

Fustel de Coulanges, *The Ancient City*, 1864, tr. Willard Small, 1873 (Doubleday, New York, 1955)

Galen, *On Anatomical Procedures*, tr. Charles Singer (Oxford University Press, London, 1956)

Gaskill, W., *A Sense of Direction* (Faber, London, 1988)

Gassner, J., and Quinn, E. (eds), *Readers' Encyclopaedia of World Drama* (Methuen, London, 1970)

Gayley, Charles Mills, *Plays of our Forefathers* (Chatto & Windus, London, 1908)

Gibson, A. Boyce, *The Philosophy of Descartes* (Methuen, London, 1932)

Gimpel, J., *The Cathedral Builders*, tr. Teresa Waugh (Michael Russell, Salisbury, 1983)

Gimpel, J., *The Medieval Machine: The Industrial Revolution of the Middle Ages* (Wildwood House, Aldershot, 2nd edn., 1988)

Glubb, Sir John, *The Fate of Empires* (Blackwood, Edinburgh, 1978)

'G.M.G.', *The Stage Censor – An Historical Sketch 1544–1907* (Sampson Low, London, 1908)

Godechot, Jacques, *France and the Atlantic Revolution of the Eighteenth Century 1770–1799*, tr. Herbert H. Rowen (The Free Press, New York, 1965)

Goethe, J.W., *Faust*, tr. Bayard Taylor (Ward Lock, London, 3rd edn., 1890)

Goethe, J.W., *Faust*, tr. Philip Wayne (Penguin, Harmondsworth: Part I, 1949; Part II, 1959)

Goorney, Howard, *The Theatre Workshop Story* (Eyre Methuen, London, 1981)

Gordon, B.L., *Medieval and Renaissance Medicine* (Peter Owen, London, 1960)

Gosson, Stephen, *The School of Abuse*, 1579, ed. Edward Arber (A. Murray, London, 1868)

Gowers, Sir Ernest, *A Life for a Life* (Chatto & Windus, London, 1956)

Grant, J.D., *The Great Metropolis* (Sanders & Otley, London, 1836)

Grant, Michael, *The Climax of Rome* (Weidenfeld & Nicolson, London, 1968)

Grant, Michael, *From Alexander to Cleopatra* (Weidenfeld & Nicolson, London, 1982)

Greek Anthology, The, tr. W.R. Paton (Loeb, Heinemann, London, 1916–18)

Bibliography

Gregory of Tours, *Glory of the Confessors*, tr. Raymond Van Dam (Liverpool University Press, Liverpool, 1988)

Grimaldi, Joseph, *Memoirs of Joseph Grimaldi* (Routledge, London, 1853)

Grmek, Mirko D., *Diseases in the Ancient Greek World*, tr. M. and L. Muellner (Johns Hopkins University Press, Baltimore, 1989)

Halsey, A.H. (ed.), *British Social Trends since 1900* (Macmillan, Basingstoke, 1988 edn.)

Hampton, Jean, *Hobbes and the Social Contract Tradition* (Cambridge University Press, Cambridge, 1986)

Harrer, Heinrich, *Seven Years in Tibet* (Hart-Davis, London, 1953)

Haskins, C., *The Renaissance of the Twelfth Century* (Harvard University Press, Cambridge, Mass., 1971)

Hayman, Ronald, *Artaud and After* (Oxford University Press, Oxford, 1977)

Herodotus, *Histories*, tr. A.D. Godley (Loeb, Heinemann, London, 1920–57)

Heurgon, Jacques, *Daily Life of the Etruscans*, tr. James Kirkup (Weidenfeld and Nicolson, London, 1964)

Hill, Donald, *A History of Engineering in Classical and Medieval Times* (Croom Helm, London, 1984)

Himmelfarb, Gertrude, *Marriage and Morals Among the Victorians* (Faber, London, 1986)

Hippocrates, *The Genuine Works of Hippocrates*, tr. Francis Adams, 1849, reissued with introduction by Emerson Crosby Kelly (Williams and Wilkins, Baltimore, 1939)

Hippolytus, *The Apostolic Tradition*, tr. and ed. Gregory Dix (SPCK, London, 1937)

Hobbes, Thomas, *Leviathan*, 1651 (Scolar Press, Menston, 1969)

Hodges, Henry, *Technology in the Ancient World* (Allen Lane, London, 1970)

Hodkin, T., *Italy and Her Invaders* (Clarendon Press, Oxford, 1892–1916)

Hoekema, A.A., *The Four Major Cults* (Paternoster Press, Exeter, 1969)

Holmyard, E.J., *Alchemy* (Penguin, Harmondsworth, 1957)

Honeyford, Ray, *Integration or Disintegration* (The Claridge Press, London, 1988)

Hopkins, K., *Death and Renewal* (Cambridge University Press, Cambridge, 1983)

Horace, *The Art of Poetry*, tr. H. Rushton Fairclough (Loeb, Heinemann, London, 1926)

Horace, *Epistles*, tr. H. Rushton Fairclough (Loeb, Heinemann, London, 1926)

Horace, *Satires*, tr. H. Rushton Fairclough (Loeb, Heinemann, London, 1926)

Hughes, Pennethorne, *Witchcraft* (Longman, Green, London, 1952)

Hume, C.W., *The Status of Animals in the Christian Religion* (Universities Federation for Animal Welfare, London, 1957)

Hume, D., *Treatise on Human Nature* and *Dialogues concerning Natural Religion*, ed. T.H. Green and T.H. Grose (Longman, Green, London, 1874)

Humphrey, John H., *Roman Circuses* (B.T. Batsford, London, 1986)

Huxley, Aldous, *The Doors of Perception* (Chatto & Windus, London, 1954)

Huxley, Aldous, *Heaven and Hell*, 1956 (Penguin, Harmondsworth, 1959)

Issues in Human Sexuality (Church House Publishing, London, 1991)

Itzin, Catherine (ed.), *Pornography: Women, Violence and Civil Liberties* (Oxford University Press, Oxford, 1992)

Itzin, Catherine, *Stages in the Revolution* (Eyre Methuen, London, 1980)

Jay, Elisabeth, *The Evangelical and Oxford Movements* (Cambridge University Press, Cambridge, 1983)

Jennings, H., *Pandaemonium 1668–1886*, ed. Mary-Lou Jennings and Charles Madge (Deutsch, London, 1985)

Jeremy D.J. (ed.), *Business and Religion in Britain* (Gower, Aldershot, 1988)

Johnson, P. Hansford, *On Iniquity* (Macmillan, London, 1967)

Johnson, S., *On Shakespeare*, ed. Walter Raleigh (Oxford University Press, London, 1908)

Johnston, John, *The Lord Chamberlain's Blue Pencil* (Hodder & Stoughton, London, 1990)

Jones, A.H.M., *The Later Roman Empire: 284–602* (Blackwell, Oxford, 1964)

Jones, E.L., *The European Miracle* (Cambridge University Press, Cambridge, 1981)

Jones, H. Stuart, *Companion to Roman History* (Clarendon Press, Oxford, 1912)

Josephus, *Jewish Antiquities*, tr. Louis Feldman (Loeb, Heinemann, London, Vol.IX, 1965)

Jusserand, J.J., *English Wayfaring Life in the Middle Ages*, tr. Lucy Toulmin Smith, 1888 (T.F. Unwin, London, 1909)

Juvenal, *Satires*, tr. G.G. Ramsay (Loeb, Heinemann, London, 1918)

Kamenka, E., *Marxism and Ethics* (Macmillan, London, 1969)

Kew, Barry, *The Pocketbook of Animal Facts and Figures* (Merlin Press, London, 1991)

Kidson, Frank, *The Beggar's Opera* (Cambridge University Press, Cambridge, 1922)

Kitchin, Laurence, *Drama in the Sixties* (Faber, London, 1966)

Kitto, H.D.F., *Form and Meaning in Drama* (Methuen, London, 1964)

Kitto, H.D.F., *The Greeks* (Pelican, Harmondsworth and London, 1957)

Kitto, H.D.F., *Greek Tragedy* (Methuen, London, 3rd edn., 1961)

Klemm, F., *A History of Western Technology*, tr. D. Singer (Allen & Unwin, London, 1959)

Kocher, H., *Science and Religion in Elizabethan England* (Huntingdon Library, San Marino, California, 1953)

Kristeller, P.O., *Renaissance Concepts of Man and Other Essays* (Harper & Row, New York, 1972)

Kristeller, P.O., *Renaissance Thought I* (Harper, New York, 1961)

Kristeller, P.O., *Renaissance Thought II* (Harper, New York, 1965)

Kyd, Thomas, *The Spanish Tragedy*, ed. J.R. Mulryne (A. & C. Black, London, 1989)

Lactantius, *The Divine Institutes*, tr. William Fletcher (Clark, Edinburgh, 1871)

Lea, K.M., *Italian Popular Comedy* (Clarendon Press, Oxford, 1934)

Lecky, W.E.H., *History of European Morals from Augustus to Charlemagne* (Watts, London, 1911 edn.)

Levi, Peter, *The Life and Times of William Shakespeare* (Macmillan, London, 1988)

Liebeschuetz, J.H.W.G., *Continuity and Change in Roman Religion* (Clarendon Press, Oxford, 1979)

Liesenfeld, Vincent J., *The Licensing Act of 1737* (University of Wisconsin Press, Madison, 1984)

Lindsay, Jack, *The Troubadours and their World* (Muller, London, 1976)

Lives of the Later Caesars, tr. A. Birley (Penguin, Harmondsworth, 1976) (the first part of *Scriptores Historiae Augustae*)

Livy, *Ab Urbe Condita*: Books 1–22 tr. B.O. Forster, 1919–29; Books 23–30 tr. Frank Gardner Moore, 1940–9; Books 31–39 tr. Evan T. Sage, 1935–6; Books 40–42 tr. Evan T. Sage and Alfred Schlesinger, 1938; Books 43–end tr. Alfred Schlesinger, 1951–9 (Loeb, Heinemann, London)

Locke, John, *Second Treatise of Civil Government*, ed. J.W. Gough (Blackwell, Oxford, 1948)

Longford Report, *Pornography* (Coronet, London, 1972)

Lovelock, J., *Gaia: A New Look at Life on Earth* (Oxford University Press, Oxford, 1979)

Low, Donald A., *Thieves' Kitchen* (Dent, London, 1982)

Lucan, *Pharsalia: The Civil War*, tr. J.D. Duff (Loeb, Heinemann, London, 1928)

Lucian, *The Works of Lucian* [1], tr. H.W. and F.G. Fowler (Clarendon Press, Oxford, 1905)

Lucian, *The Works of Lucian* [2], tr. A.M. Harmon, K. Kilburn and M.D. Macleod (Loeb, Heinemann, London, 1913–67)

Lucretius, *De Rerum Natura*, tr. M.F. Smith (Loeb, Heinemann, London, 1975)

Lukes, Steven, *Marxism and Morality* (Clarendon Press, Oxford, 1985)

Lumley, F., *New Trends in Twentieth Century Drama* (Barry & Rockcliff, London, 1967)

Luttwak, Edward N., *The Grand Strategy of the Roman Empire* (Johns Hopkins University Press, Baltimore, 1976)

Lyons, Sir Henry, *The Royal Society 1660–1940* (Cambridge University Press, Cambridge, 1944)

Macgowan, K., Melnitz, W., and Armstrong, G., *Golden Ages of the Theater* (Prentice-Hall, London, 1979, revised edn.)

McGrath, John, *A Good Night Out* (Eyre Methuen, London, 1981)

Macgregor, S. (ed.), *Drugs and British Society* (Routledge, London, 1989)

Macintyre, A., *After Virtue* (Duckworth, London, 1981)

Mackay, A., *Spain in the Middle Ages* (Macmillan, London, 1977)

McKenna, Terence, *Food of the Gods* (Rider, London, 1992)

McLean, Antonia, *Humanism and the Rise of Science in Tudor England* (Heinemann, London, 1972)

McLellan, David, *The Young Hegelians and Marx* (Macmillan, London, 1969)

McLynn, Frank, *Crime and Punishment in Eighteenth Century England* (Routledge, London, 1989)

McManners, John, *The French Revolution and the Church* (SPCK, London, 1969)

Macmullen, Ramsey, *Enemies of the Roman Order* (Harvard University Press, Cambridge, Mass., 1967)

Macmullen, Ramsey, *Paganism in the Roman Empire* (Yale University Press, New Haven, 1981)

Macrobius, *The Saturnalia*, tr. Percival Vaughan Davies (Columbia University Press, New York, 1969)

Major, Ralph H., *Classic Descriptions of Disease*, 1932 (Charles Thomas, Springfield, Illinois, 3rd edn., 1965)

Makdisi, George, *The Rise of Humanism in Classical Islam and the Christian West* (Edinburgh University Press, Edinburgh, 1990)

Mandell/Douglas/Bennett, *Principles and Practice of Infectious Diseases* (John Wiley and Sons, New York, 1979)

Mannix, Daniel, *Those about to Die*, 1958 (Collins, London, 1986)

Mantzius, K., *A History of Theatrical Art*, Vols.I–VI, tr. Louise Von Cossel 1903–21 (Peter Smith, Gloucester, Mass., 1970)

Marlowe, Christopher, *The Tragical History of Dr Faustus*, ed. F.S. Boas (Methuen, London, 1949)

Martial, *De Spectaculis Liber*, tr. Walter C.A. Ker (Loeb, Heinemann, London, 1925)

Martial, *Epigrams*, tr. Walter C.A.Ker (Loeb, Heinemann, London, 1925)

Martin, D., *A General Theory of Secularization* (Blackwell, Oxford, 1978)

Marty, Martin E., and Appleby, R. Scott, *The Glory and the Power* (Beacon Press, Boston, 1992)

Mascall, E.L., *The Secularization of Christianity* (Darton, Longman & Todd, London, 1965)

Medved, M., *Hollywood versus America* (HarperCollins, London, 1993 edn.)

Mellersh, H.E.L., *Chronology of the Ancient World* (Barrie & Jenkins, London, 1976)

Mercer, Derrik, (ed.) *Chronicle of the Twentieth Century* (Longman, London, 1988)

Merchant, Moelwyn, *Creed and Drama* (SPCK, London, 1965)

Mill, John Stuart, *Utilitarianism*, 1863 (Dent, London, 1972)

Millar, David Fergus, *The Emperor in the Roman World* (Duckworth, London, 1977)

Miller, R.D., *The Meaning of Goethe's Faust* (Heffer, Cambridge, 1939)

Milosz, Czeslaw, *The Captive Mind*, 1953 (Penguin, Harmondsworth, 1980)

Minneapolis City Council, *Pornography and Sexual Violence* (Everywoman, London, 1988)

Morgan, Patricia, *Farewell to the Family?* (Institute of Economic Affairs Health and Welfare Unit, London, 1995)

Morris, Desmond, *The Naked Ape* (Cape, London, 1967)

Morton, H.V., *The Waters of Rome* (Connoisseur, London, 1966)

Mumford, Lewis, *Technics and Civilization* (Harcourt Bruce, New York, 1939)

Munday, A., *A Second and Third Blast of Retreat from Plays and Theatres*, 1580, ed. A. Freeman (Garland Publishing Inc., New York, 1973)

Munro, Colin R., *Television, Censorship and the Law* (Saxon House, Farnborough, 1979)

Murray, Charles, *The Emerging British Underclass* (Institute of Economic Affairs Health and Welfare Unit, London, 1990)

Murray, Margaret, *God of the Witches* (Faber & Faber, London, 1931)

Murray, Margaret, *The Witch Cult in Western Europe* (Oxford University Press, Oxford, 1921)

Musson, A.E. (ed.), *Science, Technology and Economic Growth in the Eighteenth Century* (Methuen, London, 1972)

Musson, A.E., and Robinson, Eric, *Science and Technology in the Industrial Revolution* (Manchester University Press, Manchester, 1969)

Nash, David, *Secularism, Art and Freedom* (Leicester University Press, Leicester, 1992)

Nenneman, Richard A., *The New Birth of Christianity* (Harper, San Francisco, 1992)

Newsom Report, *Half our Future* (HMSO, London, 1963)

Nicoll, Allardyce, *A History of English Drama* (Cambridge University Press, Cambridge, 4th edn., 1955)

Nietzsche, F., *The Birth of Tragedy*, 1872, tr. W. Haussman (Russell & Russell, New York, 1964)

Nilsson, Martin P., *Imperial Rome*, tr. G.C. Richards (Bell, London, 1926)

Niven, Charles D., *History of the Humane Movement* (Johnson Publications, London, 1967)

Northam, Gerry, *Shooting in the Dark* (Faber & Faber, London, 1988)

Northbrooke, John, *A Treatise*, 1577 (Garland Publishing Inc., New York, 1974)

Norwich, J.J. (ed.), *The Italian World* (Thames & Hudson, London, 1983)

Odell, George, *Shakespeare from Betterton to Irving*, 1920 (Constable, London, 1963)

OECD, *The Migratory Chain* (OECD, Paris, 1978)

Oldroyd, D.R., *Darwinian Impacts* (Open University, Milton Keynes, 1980)

O'Leary, De Lacy, *How Greek Science Passed to the Arabs* (Routledge & Kegan Paul, London, 1948)

O'Malley, C.D., *Andreas Vesalius of Brussels* (University of California Press, Berkeley, 1965)

Oman, C.W.C., *The Byzantine Empire*, 1893 (Fisher Unwin, London, 3rd edn., 1902)

Orosius, Paulus, *Seven Books of History Against the Pagans*, tr. Irving Woodworth Raymond (Columbia University Press, New York, 1936)

Orr, Edwin, *The Second Evangelical Awakening in Britain* (Marshall, Morgan & Scott, London, 1949)

Ovid, *Ars Amatoria*, tr. J.H. Mozley (Loeb, Heinemann, London, 1929)

Ovid, *Fasti*, tr. Sir James Frazer (Loeb, Heinemann, London, 1931)

Ovid, *Metamorphoses* [1], tr. Alan Melville (Oxford University Press, Oxford, 1986)

Ovid, *Metamorphoses* [2], tr. Frank J. Miller (Loeb, Heinemann, London, 1916)

Ovid, *Tristia*, tr. A.L. Wheeler (Loeb, Heinemann, London, 1924)

Oxford Classical Dictionary, eds M. Cary et al. (Oxford University Press, London 1949)

Oxford Companion to the Theatre, 3rd edition, ed. Phyllis Hartoll (Oxford University Press, London, 1967)

Oxford Dictionary of the Christian Church, ed. F.L. Cross (Oxford University Press, London, 1974)

Oxford Textbook of Medicine, 2nd edn., eds D.J. Weatherall, J.G.G. Ledingham, D.A. Warrell (Oxford University Press, Oxford, 1987)

Paine, Tom, *The Age of Reason*, 1795, ed. M.D. Conway (Putnam, New York, 1910)

Paine, Tom, *The Rights of Man*: Part 1,1791; Part 2, 1792 (Everyman, Dent, London, 1915)

Parker, Kenneth L., *The English Sabbath* (Cambridge University Press, Cambridge, 1988)

Past Worlds: The Times Atlas of Archaeology, ed. Chris Scarre (Times Books, London, 1988)

Perrin, Noel, *Dr Bowdler's Legacy* (Macmillan, London, 1969)

Petersson, R.T., *The Art of Ecstasy* (Routledge & Kegan Paul, London, 1970)

Petronius, *Satyricon*, tr. E.H. Warminton (Loeb, Heinemann, London, 1969)

Pirsig, Robert, *Zen and the Art of Motor Cycle Maintenance* (Bodley Head, London, 1974)

Plamenatz, John, *The English Utilitarians* (Blackwell, Oxford, 1949)

Plamenatz, John, *Man and Society*, Vol.II (Longman, London, 1963)

Plato, *Laws*, tr. R.G. Bury (Loeb, Heinemann, London, 1926).

Plato, *The Republic*, tr. Francis Macdonald Cornford (Clarendon Press, Oxford, 1941)

Pliny the Elder, *Natural History*, tr. H. Rackham/W.H.S. Jones/D.E. Eichholz (Loeb, Heinemann, London, 1938–63)

Pliny the Younger, *Letters*, tr. Betty Radice (Loeb, Heinemann, London, 1969)

Pliny the Younger, *Panegyricus*, tr. Betty Radice (Loeb, Heinemann, London, 1969)

Plutarch, *Lives*, tr. Bernadotte Perrin (Loeb, Heinemann, London, 1914–26)

Plutarch, *Moralia*, Vol.XII, tr. W.C. Helmbold (Loeb, Heinemann, London, 1957)

Pollard, A.W., *English Miracle Plays, Moralities and Interludes* (Clarendon Press, Oxford, 3rd edn., 1898)

Polybius, *Histories*, tr. W.R. Paton (Loeb, Heinemann, London, 1922)

Prescott, W., *History of the Conquest of Mexico* (Routledge, London, 1874)

Primatt, Humphrey, *The Duty of Mercy and the Sin of Cruelty to Brute Animals*, 1776, ed. Richard D. Ryder (Centaur, Fontwell, 1992)

Procopius, *The Secret History*, tr. H.B. Dewing (Loeb, Heinemann, London, 1954)

Propertius, *Elegiae* [1], tr. M. Hubbard (Duckworth, London, 1974)

Propertius, *Elegiae* [2], tr. H.E. Butler (Loeb, Heinemann, London, 1912)

Prudentius, *Contra Orationem Symmachi*, tr. H.J. Thompson (Loeb, Heinemann, London, 1949)

Prudentius, *Crowns of Martyrdom*, tr. H.J. Thompson (Loeb, Heinemann, London, 1949)

Prynne, William, *Histriomastix, or the Scourge of Players*, 1633, ed. A. Freeman (Garland Publishing Inc., New York, 1974)

Quintilian, *Institutio Oratoria*, tr. H.E. Butler (Loeb, Heinemann, London, 1920)

Radzinovicz, Leon, *A History of English Criminal Law* (Stevens, London, 1948–56)

Read, Piers Paul, *Alive* (Secker & Warburg, London, 1974)

Reade, Winwood, *The Martyrdom of Man*, 1872 (Watts, London, 1925 edn.)

Redmond, James (ed.), *Themes in Drama I: Drama and Society* (Cambridge University Press, Cambridge, 1979)

Reisman, J., and Eichel, E.W., *Kinsey, Sex and Fraud – The Indoctrination of a People*, eds J. Court and J. Gordon Muir (Lochinvar-Huntington House, Lafayette, Louisiana, 1990)

Rénan, Ernest, *Life of Jesus*, 1863 (Kegan Paul, London, 1893)

Renault, Mary, *Mask of Apollo* (Longman, Green, London, 1966)

Rickman, G., *The Corn Supply of Ancient Rome* (Clarendon Press, Oxford, 1980)

Riddle, J., *Contraception and Abortion from the Ancient World to the Renaissance* (Harvard University Press, Cambridge, Mass., 1994)

Robert, Louis, *Les Gladiateurs dans L'Orient Grec* (Champion, Paris, 1940)

Robertson, G., *Obscenity* (Weidenfeld & Nicolson, London, 1979)

Robinson, John, *Honest to God* (SCM, London, 1963)

Robinson, V., *The Story of Medicine* (Tudor Publ., New York, 1931)

Rookmaaker, H.R., *Modern Art and the Death of a Culture* (Intervarsity Press, London, 1970)

Rostovtzeff, M., *The Social and Economic History of the Hellenistic World* (Clarendon Press, Oxford, 1941)

Rostovtzeff, M., *The Social and Economic History of the Roman Empire*, revised P.M. Fraser (Clarendon Press, Oxford, 2nd edn., 1957)

Rousseau, J.J., *Lettre à Mr D'Alembert sur les Spectacles*, 1758 (Droz, Geneva, 1948)

Rousselle, Aline, *Porneia: On Desire and the Body in Antiquity*, tr. Felicia Pheasant (Blackwell, Oxford, 1988)

Russell, Bertrand, *History of Western Philosophy* (Allen & Unwin, London, 1946)

Rutherford, John, *The Troubadours* (Smith Elder & Co., London, 1873)

Rutter, Michael, and Smith, David J., *Psychosocial Disorders in Young People* (John Wiley & Sons, Chichester, 1995)

Saklatvala, A., *Arthur: Roman Britain's Last Champion* (David & Charles, Newton Abbot, 1967)

Sallust, *Works*, tr. J.C. Rolfe (Loeb, Heinemann, London, 1931)

Salmon, Eric, *Granville Barker: A Secret Life* (Heinemann, London, 1983)

Salvianus, *On the Government of God*, tr. Eva M. Sanford, 1931 (Octagon Books, New York, 1966)

Samuel, R., MacColl, E., and Cosgrove, S., *Theatres of the Left 1880–1935* (Routledge & Kegan Paul, London, 1985)

Sandys, Sir John E., *Latin Epigraphy* (Cambridge University Press, Cambridge, 1919)

Sartre, J.-P., *Crime Passionel*, tr. Kitty Blade (Hamilton, London, 1949)

Schacht, J., and Bosworth, C.E. (eds), *The Legacy of Islam* (Oxford University Press, London, 2nd edn., 1974)

Schaeffer, Francis A., *Escape from Reason* (Intervarsity Press, London, 1968)

Schama, S., *Citizens* (Viking, London, 1989)

Schlesinger, Arthur, *The Disuniting of America* (Whittle Direct Books, Knoxville, Tennessee, 1991)

Schluter, M., and Lee, D., *Keeping Sunday Special* (Marshall Pickering, Basingstoke, 1988)

Scriptores Historiae Augustae, tr. David Magie (Loeb, Heinemann, London, 1921–32)

Scullard, H.H., *Festivals and Ceremonies of the Roman Republic* (Thames & Hudson, London, 1981)

Selbourne, David, *The Principle of Duty* (Sinclair-Stevenson, London, 1994)

Seneca, *Epistles*, tr. Richard M. Gummere (Loeb, Heinemann, London, 1917–25)

Seneca, *Moral Essays*, tr. John W. Basore (Loeb, Heinemann, London, 1928–35)

Seneca the Elder, *Controversiae*, tr. M. Winterbottom (Loeb, Heinemann, London, 1974)

Sharpe, J.A., *Crime in Early Modern England 1550–1750* (Longman, London, 1984)

Sharpe, J.A., *Crime in Seventeenth Century England* (Cambridge University Press, Cambridge, 1983)

Shaw, G.B., *Back to Methuselah*, 1921 (Constable, London, 1928)

Shaw, G.B., *Man and Superman*, 1901 (Constable, London, 1928)

Shaw, G.B., *The Shewing up of Blanco Posnet*, 1909 (Constable, London, 1927)

Shaw, G.B., *Three Plays for Puritans* 1900 (Constable, London, 1931)

Sidonius, *Poems and Letters*, tr. W.B. Anderson (Loeb, Heinemann, London, 1936–65)

Silius Italicus, *Punica*, tr. J.D. Duff (Loeb, Heinemann, London, 1927–34)

Simon, J., *Education and Society* (Cambridge University Press, Cambridge, 1966)

Singer, C., Holmyard, E.J., Hall, A.R., and Williams, T.I. (eds), *A History of Technology*, Vols.I–VIII (Clarendon Press, Oxford, 1954–84)

Singer, Peter, *Animal Liberation*, 1975 (Cape, London, 1990)

Smith, Clifford P., *Historical Sketches*, 1941 (Christian Science Publications, Boston, Mass., 1969)

Smith, Dane Farnsworth, *Plays About the Theatre in England 1671–1737* (Oxford University Press, London, 1936)

Smith, David Nichol, *Shakespeare in the 18th Century* (Clarendon Press, Oxford, 1928)

Sorokin, Pitirim A., *The Crisis of Our Age* (Dutton, New York, 1941)

Sorokin, Pitirim A., *Leaves from a Russian Diary; and Thirty Years After* (Beacon Press, Boston, Mass., 1950)

Sorokin, Pitirim A., *Social and Cultural Dynamics* (Allen & Unwin, London, Vols.I–IV, 1937–41)

Sorokin, Pitirim A., *Society Culture and Personality*, 1947 (Cooper Square Pub. Inc., New York, 1969)

Southworth, John, *The English Medieval Minstrel* (Boydell, Woodbridge, 1989)

Spengler, O., *Decline of the West*, tr. C.F. Atkinson (Allen & Unwin, London, 1932)

Stanford, W.B., *Greek Tragedy and the Emotions* (Routledge & Kegan Paul, London, 1983)

Starr, Chester G., *The Roman Empire 27BC–476AD* (Oxford University Press, New York, 1982)

Statius, *Silvae*, tr. J.H. Mozley (Loeb, Heinemann, London, 1928)

Steane, J.B., *Marlowe: A Critical Study* (Cambridge University Press, London, 1964)

Steinberg, Leo, *The Sexuality of Christ in Renaissance Art and in Modern Oblivion* (Faber, London, 1984)

Steiner, George, *The Death of Tragedy* (Faber & Faber, London, 1963)

Stevas, Norman St John, *Law and Morals* (Burns & Oates, London, 1964)

Strabo, *Geography*, tr. H.L. Jones (Loeb, Heinemann, London, 1917–24)

Stubbes, Phillip, *The Anatomy of the Abuses in England*, 1583, ed. Frederick J. Furnivall (Trubner, London, 1877–9)

Suetonius, *De Vita Caesarum*, tr. J.C. Rolfe (Loeb, Heinemann, London, 1913–14)

Sumption, Jonathan, *Pilgrimage: An Image of Mediaeval Religion* (Faber, London, 1975)

Tacitus, *Annals*, tr. John Jackson (Loeb, Heinemann, London, 1931–7)

Tacitus, *Dialogus de Oratoribus*, tr. W. Peterson, revised M. Winterbottom (Loeb, Heinemann, London, 1970)

Tacitus, *Germania*, tr. M. Hutton, revised R.M. Ogilvie (Loeb, Heinemann, London, 1970)

Tacitus, *Histories*, tr. Clifford H. Moore (Loeb, Heinemann, London, 1925)

Tatian, *Oratio ad Graecos*, tr. Molly Whittaker (Clarendon Press, Oxford, 1982)

Tawney, R.H., *Religion and the Rise of Capitalism*, 1925 (Pelican, London, 2nd edn., 1938)

Taylor, Charles, *Hegel* (Cambridge University Press, Cambridge, 1975)

Taylor, F. Sherwood, *The Alchemists* (Heinemann, London, 1951)

Taylor, Lily Ross, *The Divinity of the Roman Emperor* (Porcupine Press, Philadelphia, 1975)

Teresa of Avila, *The Life of St Teresa*, tr. J.M. Cohen (Penguin, London, 1957)

Tertullian, *Apologeticus*, tr. T.R. Glover (Heinemann, London, 1931)

Tertullian, *De Spectaculis*, tr. T.R. Glover (Loeb, Heinemann, London, 1931)

Theophilus, *Treatise to Autolycus*, tr. Marcus Dods (T. & T. Clarke, Edinburgh, 1867)

Tiryakian, E.A. (ed.), *Sociological Theories, Values and Sociocultural Change* (Free Press of Glencoe, London, 1963)

Tobias, J.J., *Crime and Industrial Society in the Nineteenth Century* (Penguin, Harmondsworth, 1972)

Tolstoy, L.N., *Tolstoy On Shakespeare*, tr. V. Tchertikoff and I.F.M. (Funk & Wagnalls, New York, 1907)

Tolstoy, L.N., *What is Art?*, tr. Aylmer Maude (Oxford University Press, London, 1929)

Tomaselli, S., and Porter, R. (eds), *Rape – An Historical and Cultural Enquiry* (Blackwell, Oxford, 1989)

Topsfield, L.T., *Troubadours and Love* (Cambridge University Press, Cambridge, 1975)

Trewin, J.C., *Peter Brook* (Macdonald & Co., London, 1971)

Trollope, Fanny, *Domestic Manners of the Americans* (Allan Sutton, Gloucester, 1832)

Tuchmann, Barbara W., *A Distant Mirror* (Penguin, Harmondsworth, 1979)

Turnbull, Colin, *The Mountain People* (Cape, London, 1973)

Tyler, Andrew, *Street Drugs*, 1986 (Hodder & Stoughton, London, revised edn., 1988)

Tynan, K., *Life of Kenneth Tynan* (Weidenfeld & Nicolson, London, 1987)

Ulansey, David, *The Origins of the Mithraic Mysteries* (Oxford University Press, Oxford, 1989)

Valerius Maximus, *Factorum et Dictorum Memorabilium*, (Berolini, Impensis Georgii Reimeri, 1854)

Van Berchem, Denis, *Les Distributions de Blé et d'Argent à la Plèbe Romaine sous l'Empire* (Georg, Geneva, 1939)

Van Buren, Paul M., *The Secular Meaning of Christianity* (SCM Press, London, 1963)

Velleius Paterculus, *Historia Romana*, tr. Frederick W. Shipley (Loeb, Heinemann, London, 1924)

Veyne, Paul, *Le Pain et le Cirque* (Seuil, Paris, 1976)

Vince, Ronald W., *Ancient and Medieval Theatre* (Greenwood Press, Westport, Conn., 1984)

Vincent, B., *Haydn's Dictionary of Dates* (Ward, Lock & Co, London 19th edn., 1889)

Virgil, *Aeneid*, tr. H. Rushton Fairclough (Loeb, Heinemann, London, 1916)

Virgil, *Georgics*, tr. H. Rushton Fairclough (Loeb, Heinemann, London, 1916)

Vitruvius, *De Architectura*, tr. Frank Granger (Loeb, Heinemann, London, 1931–4)

Vogt, Joseph, *The Decline of Rome*, tr. Janet Sondheimer (Weidenfeld & Nicolson, London, 1967)

Vyvyan, John, *The Dark Face of Science* (Michael Joseph, London, 1971)

Vyvyan, John, *In Pity and In Anger* (Michael Joseph, London, 1969)

Walbank, F.W., *The Awful Revolution: The Decline of the Roman Empire of the West*, 1969 (Liverpool University Press, Liverpool, 1978)

Walcot, Peter, *Greek Drama in its Theatrical and Social Context* (University of Wales Press, Cardiff, 1976)

Wand, J.W.C., *A History of the Modern Church* (Methuen, London, 1952 edn.)

Warnock, G.J., *Berkeley* (Penguin, Harmondsworth, 1953)

Watt, W. Montgomery, *The Influence of Islam on Medieval Europe* (Edinburgh University Press, Edinburgh, 1972)

Wearmouth, R.F., *Methodism and the Common People of the Eighteenth Century* (Epworth Press, London, 1945)

Weber, Max, *The Protestant Ethic and the Spirit of Capitalism*, 1930, tr. Talcott Parsons (Allen & Unwin, London, 1962)

Wesley, John, *The Works of John Wesley* (Abingdon Press, Nashville, Vols. I–IV, 1984–7)

Whitby, Michael, Hardie, P., and Whitby, Mary (eds), *Homo Viator* (Bristol Classical Press, Bristol, 1987)

Whitehouse, Mary, *A Most Dangerous Woman* (Lion, Tring, 1982)

Whitehouse, Mary, *Quite Contrary* (Sidgwick & Jackson, London, 1993)

Whitehouse, Mary, *Whatever Happened to Sex* (Hodder & Stoughton, London, 1977)

Wickham, Glynne, *The Medieval Theatre* (Weidenfeld & Nicolson, London, 1974)

Wigley, John, *The Rise and Fall of the Victorian Sunday* (Manchester University Press, Manchester, 1980)

Wilberforce, William, *A Practical View of the prevailing religious system of Professed Christians in the Higher and Middle Classes in this Country, contrasted with Real Christianity*, 1797 (Cadell, London, 1818)

Williams, Bernard (ed.), *Obscenity and Film Censorship* (Cambridge University Press, Cambridge, 1981 abridged edn.)

Williams, Duncan, *To be or not to be* (Daris-Poynter, London, 1974)

Williams, Duncan, *Trousered Apes* (Churchill Press, Enfield, 1971)

Williams, Trevor, *A Short History of Twentieth Century Technology* (Clarendon Press, Oxford, 1982)

Wilson, Bryan R., *Religion in the Secular Society* (Watts, London, 1966)

Wilson, James Q., *The Moral Sense* (Free Press, New York, 1993)

Wiseman, P., *Catullus and His World* (Cambridge University Press, Cambridge, 1985)

Wolf, A., *A History of Science, Technology and Philosophy in the 18th Century*, revised D. McKie (Allen & Unwin, London, 2nd edn., 1952)

Wolf, A., *A History of Science, Technology, and Philosophy in the 16th and 17th Centuries*, revised D. McKie (Allen & Unwin, London, 2nd edn., 1950)

Wood, Ellen Meiksins, *Peasant-Citizen and Slave* (Verso, London, 1988)

Yates, F.A., *The Art of Memory* (Routledge & Kegan Paul, London, 1966)

Zohar, Danah, *The Quantum Self* (Bloomsbury, London, 1990)

Zosimus, *Histoire Nouvelle*, tr. (into French) F. Paschoud (Belles Lettres, Paris, 1971–9)

Periodicals and Series

AA Magazine, The Automobile Association, Basingstoke

Annals of Science, Taylor and Francis, London

Annual Register, Longman, Harlow

Antiquity, A Periodical Review of Archaeology, Cambridge

Archaeology, Archaeological Institute of America, New York

Arethusa, New York State University, Buffalo

Bibliography

Atmospheric Environment, Pergamon Press, Oxford
Bankers' Magazine, Waterlow and Sons Ltd., London
British Medical Journal, British Medical Association, London
Church of England Yearbook, Church House Publishing, London
Classical Journal, Menassa, Wisconsin
Classical Philology, Chicago University Press, Chicago
Contemporary Review, Contemporary Review Co. Ltd. London
Crime and Justice, An Annual Review of Research, University of Chicago
Criminal Statistics, Home Office, HMSO, London
Drama, British Theatre Association, London
Ecologist, Ecosystems, Wadebridge
Egyptian Archaeology, Egypt Exploration Society, London
Encounter, Encounter Ltd., London
Environmental Science and Technology, American Chemical Society, Washington
Equity, British Actors' Equity Association, London
EU Initiative, Norton Rose, London
Freedom Today, Freedom Association, London
Health and Personal Social Service Statistics, HMSO, London
Historia, Steiner, Wiesbaden
International Journal of Environmental Studies, Gordon and Beach, Science Publishers, London
Journal of Common Market Studies, Basil Blackwell, Oxford
Journal of Marriage and the Family, National Council on Family Relations, Lake Mills
Journal of Roman Studies, Society for the Promotion of Roman Studies, London
Knitting International, International Textiles, Benjamin Dent, London
Listener, Listener Publications Ltd., London
Mélanges d'Archéologie et d'Histoire de l'École Française de Rome, Rome
National Art Collections Fund Review, National Art Collections Fund, London
National Geographic Research, National Geographic Society, Washington
Nature, Macmillan, London
New Economics, New Economics Foundation, London
New Farmer and Grower, British Organic Farmers and the Organic Growers Association, Bristol
New Scientist, IPC Magazines, London
New Society, Statesman and Nation Publishing Co., London
On the State of the Public Health, HMSO, London
Oxford Today, Blackwell Publishers, Oxford
Plays and Players, Brevet, Croydon
Police Review, Police Review Publishing Co. Ltd., London
Revue de Philologie, Klincksleck, Paris
Rheinisches Museum für Philologie, Frankfurt am Main
Salisbury Review, London
Sitzungsberichte der Kaiserlichen Akademie Der Wissenschaften, Vienna
Smith College Classical Studies, Smith College, Northampton, Mass.
Social Trends, HMSO, London
Sotheby's Preview, Sotheby's, London
Spectator, The Spectator (1828) Ltd., London
Tellus, Swedish Geophysical Society, Stockholm

Holding up a Mirror

UK Christian Handbook, Christian Research *et al*, Eltham, London
Viator, University of California Press, Berkeley
WWF News, Gland, Switzerland
WWF Review, Gland, Switzerland

Index

Index

Index

Index

Goodyear, Charles, 356
Gorbachev, Mikhail, 560
Gordon, B. L., *Medieval and Renaissance Medicine*, 237
Gordon Riots, 324, 349
Gorer, Geoffrey, 489
Gosson, Stephen, 268
Goths, 187–8, 189, 191, 193–4, 203
    conquer Dacia (271), 193–4
    expulsion from Italy, 200
    flee from Huns, 194
    Gothic wars, 200
    occupy Rome (410), 170, 187–9, 190
    settlement, 194–200
Graham-Dixon, Andrew, 13–14
Granger, Frank, 218
Grant, Michael, *From Alexander to Cleopatra*, 43
Gratian, 114, 167, 168
Great Yarmouth magistrates' court, 440
Greek civilization: 6th to 4th centuries BC: from metaphysics to physics, 20–36
    drama, 20–36
    music, 25–6
    theatres, 33–6
Greek civilization: 4th to 2nd centuries BC: hellenistic pleasure and prosperity, 27–49
    comedy, 38–40
    drama, 38–43, 47
    mime, 40–1
Greek civilization: 2nd and 1st centuries BC: disintegration, 50–66
    absorbed by Rome, 65–6
    homosexuality, 56–60
    lawlessness and immorality, 63–6
    piracy, 63
    slave labour, 61
    soil erosion, 62
Greek philosophy, 207–11
Greenaway, Peter, 438 fn, 443, 458
Greene, Graham
    The Living Room, 396
    The Potting Shed, 396
Greene, Hugh, 440
Greenwich parks police, 474
Gregory, Bishop of Tours, 215–16
Gresham, Sir Thomas, 286
    Occupation, 450
    The Comedians, 451
Grimaldi, Joe, 84 fn
Grosseteste, Robert (Bishop of Lincoln), 211, 274
Grotowski, Jerzy, 436
Grysar, C. J., 79, 80 fn, 85 fn, 221, 230
Gurr, Ted, 478
Guthrie, Tyrone, 431
Gwynn, Nell, 277, 283
Gwynne, Jessica, 14

Habgood, John, 540
Hackett, General Sir John, 481–2
Hadrian, Emperor, 94–5, 149, 152, 159, 174
Hadrian's Wall, 205
Halifax, crime in, 496
Hall, Sir Peter, 542
Hall, Radcliffe, *Well of Loneliness*, 438
Halle, Adam de la, 226
    Adam's Play, 219, 226
    Robin and Marion, 226
Halsey, Professor, 555
Hankey, Frederick, 461
Hannibal, 187

Hardy, Thomas, 24, 375
Hare, David, 453
Harrer, Heinrich, *Seven Years in Tibet*, 37–8, 369 fn
Harrison, John, 251 fn
Hart, Charles, 275
Hartley, Anthony, 578
Harun ar-Rashid, Caliph, 209
Hassall, Christopher, 393
Hazlitt, William, 275
Healey, Denis, 518
Heath, Sir Edward, 405
Heathrow Airport, Brink's Mat robbery, 522
Hegel, Friedrich, 365–8, 552
    Encyclopaedia, 367
    Science of Logic, 367
Heidegger, Martin, 399, 401
Heliogabalus, Emperor, 165, 175, 182, 381
Hellman, Lillian, *Children's Hour*, 430
Henrietta Maria, Queen, 272
Henry II, 224
Henry III, Emperor, 220
Henry VI, 230
Henry VII, 229
Henry VIII, 229, 252, 266, 423
Henslowe, Philip, 256
Herbert, A. P., 445
Herbert, Sir Henry, 278
Herculaneum, 131
Hero of Alexandria, 140, 144, 249
Herodotus, 122 fn
Herodus Atticus, 127
Herophilus, 46, 47, 48, 289
Hexham riot (1761), 323–4
High Wycombe, crime in, 484
Hildesheimer, Wolfgang, 383
Hill, Donald, *A History of Engineering in Classical and Medieval Times*, 143, 207
Himmelfarb, Gertrude, *Marriage and Morals Among the Victorians*, 507
Hinsley, Cardinal, 407
Hipparchus, 48
Hippo, 188, 189
Hippocrates, 46–7, 152, 153, 216
    On Ancient Medicine, 46, 137–8 fn
    The Sacred Disease, 46
Hobbes, Thomas, 363
    Leviathan, 294–5
Hobsbawm, E. F., 324 fn
Hobson, Harold, 394
Hodges, Henry, *Technology in the Ancient World*, 144
Hollywood, 455–6, 458
Homer, 56
    Iliad, 17
    Odyssey, 54
Honeyford, Ray, *Integration or Disintegration*, 565
Honorius, Emperor, 180, 187, 188
Hooke, Robert, 291
Hope-Wallace, Philip, 394
Horace, 72, 88, 89, 110 fn, 112, 114, 310
    Epistles, 81–2, 89–90
    Satires, 84, 136
    The Art of Poetry, 21, 92
Housman, A. E., 375
Howard, Elizabeth Jane, 440 fn
Huddleston, Bishop Trevor, 535
Hughes, Pennethorne, *Witchcraft*, 570
Hugo, Victor, 362
Hulme, Cardinal Basil, 416, 540
humanism, 362, 418

643

Index

Tynan, Kenneth, 382, 440, 444–5, 449
  Oh Calcutta!, 445

Ulansey, David, *The Origins of Mithraic Mysteries*, 166 fn
Unitarians, 373
United Nations, Universal Declaration of Human Rights (1948), 546
Unity Theatre movement, 389–90, 391, 429–30, 436, 449–50
Ustinov, Sir Peter, 407
Utilitarianism, 364–6

Valens, Emperor, 171, 202
Valentinian, 171
Van Berchem, Denis, 147, 149 fn
Van Buren, Paul, 399–401
  The Secular Meaning of Christianity, 399
Van Eyck, 11
Vanbrugh, John, 283, 284, 308 fn, 314, 338, 433
  The Provok'd Wife, 282, 283, 284
  The Relapse, 282, 432
Vandals, 186, 188, 195, 203
  conquest of Carthage, 189–90, 195, 199
  sacking of Rome, 190, 195, 198
Varius, Rufus L., 93
Varro, 111
Vega, Lope de, 276
Vegetius, *De Re Militari*, 191–2
Velleius Paterculus, 107 fn
Vergilius, 202
Verona, 101, 199
Vesalius, Andreas, 290, 291
  On the Structure of the Human Body, 290, 291
Vespasian, Emperor, 94, 131, 144
Vespucci, Amerigo, 251
Veyne, Paul, 147
Vicenza, 254
Victoria, Queen, 346, 361
video nasties, 463–5, 471–2, 501–2, 503, 504, 505
Video Recordings Act (1984), 456 fn, 472
Vienna, 254
Vietnam War, 391
Ville, G., 170 fn
Vince, Ronald, 93
Virgil
  Aeneid, 76, 118
  Georgics, 21, 136
Vitellius, 110
Vitruvius, 34–6, 40, 46, 122, 126–7, 129, 140 fn, 143, 152, 218, 249, 253
Vitry, Jacques de, 216
Vives, Juan Luis, 292–3
Vogt, Joseph, *The Decline of Rome*, 10, 128, 159, 201
Voltaire, 300, 326 fn
Volterra, de, 12
Vortigern, King, 195 fn

Waco massacre, 580
Wadley, Nicholas, 13
Wagner, Richard, 25, 406
Walbank, F. W., 144, 206
Walpole, Horace, 315, 316, 317–18, 319, 335
  introduces Licensing Bill for theatres, 317–18
Walter, Harriet, 446
Warner, Marina, 10
Warnock Committee, 540
Warrington, 133
Washington, George, 297

Watson, Fred, *Infanticide in the House of Fred Ginger*, 436
Watson, John D., 533
Watt, James, 329, 357
Wayne, Philip, 330, 331 fn
Wearmouth, R. F., 323
Webb, Paul, 57
Webber, Andrew Lloyd, 455
Weber, Max, 2, 248
  The Protestant Ethic and the Spirit of Catholicism, 247, 327
Webster, John
  Duchess of Malfi, 260, 381, 435
  The White Devils, 260, 381, 435
Wedekind, Frank, 375
Wedgwood, Josiah, 328
Weiss, Peter
  Marat/Sade, 436
  Notes on Documentary Theatre, 386
Welldon, J. E. C., 347
Wells Cathedral, 274
Wesker, Arnold, 451
Wesley, John, 324, 325, 327, 337
  Compendium of Natural Philosophy, 327
  Thoughts upon Slavery, 325
Westminster Confession (1647), 297
White, Lynn, 212, 234
Whitehouse, Mary, 441, 461, 471, 472, 476
Wicca movement, 570
Wickham, Glynne, 261
Wigley, John, *The Rise and Fall of the Victorian Sunday*, 351–2
Wilberforce, William, 325, 336
  A Practical View of . . . Christianity, 326
Wilde, Oscar, *Salome*, 429
William of Bavaria, Duke, 221 fn
William of Ockham, 233
William of Orange, 282
Williams, Bernard, 469
Williams, Clifford, 442, 443, 447
Williams, Tennessee, 459
  Cat on a Hot Tin Roof, 431
Williams Committee: *Obscenity and Film Censorship* report (1979), 469–71, 477
Willis, Ted (Lord), 408
Wilson, Brian, 564
Wilson, Cecil, 394
Wilson, Snoo, 453, 454, 503
Winchester, Bishop of, 221, 283
  Cathedral, 234, 567
Winstanley, Henry, 283
Wiseman, P., *Catullus and His World*, 104, 112
Wittenberg, 242
Wittgenstein, Ludwig, 401
Wodde, John A., 257–8
Wolf, A., 249, 250, 253, 287, 291, 328
Wolfenden, Sir John, 423–4
Wood, Charles, 450, 579
Wood, Helen Meiksins, *Peasant-Citizen and Slave*, 61
Worcester, 125
Wordsworth, William, 339
World War I, 359, 379, 516
World War II, 382, 391, 407, 563
Worth, Irene, 394, 436
Wren, Sir Christopher, 306
Wright, F. Warren, 72
Wright, Joseph, *Experiment on a Bird in the Air Pump*, 361–2
Wycherley, William, 338